SACRED HISTORY

Sacred History

*Uses of the Christian Past in the
Renaissance World*

Edited by

KATHERINE VAN LIERE, SIMON DITCHFIELD,
AND HOWARD LOUTHAN

OXFORD
UNIVERSITY PRESS

OXFORD

UNIVERSITY PRESS

Great Clarendon Street, Oxford OX2 6DP,
United Kingdom

Oxford University Press is a department of the University of Oxford.
It furthers the University's objective of excellence in research, scholarship,
and education by publishing worldwide. Oxford is a registered trade mark of
Oxford University press in the UK and in certain other countries

First published in 2012

Impression: 2

British Library Cataloguing in Publication Data

Data available

Library of Congress Cataloging in Publication Data

Data available

ISBN 978-0-19-959479-5

Printed in Great Britain
on acid-free paper by
MPG Books Group, Bodmin and King's Lynn

Preface

For well over a millennium after the appearance of Christianity, the story of the Christian Church occupied a privileged place in western historical thought. The Bible was the most respected historical text in medieval schools and universities, and salvation history was understood to be the central narrative in world history. These assumptions were manifested in a variety of historical writings, from universal chronicles (which began with the creation of the world and ended with the expectation of Christ's return) to the copious lives of saints that constituted one of the most popular genres of medieval writing. Greco-Roman historiographical traditions that antedated Christianity did not die out entirely, but such classical genres as civil and diplomatic history, political biography, and natural history became largely subservient to the larger story of God's providential care for his chosen people. Sacred history, in whatever literary form it appeared, was generally regarded as worthier than its counterpart, profane history.

This privileged status did not endure until modern times. By the eighteenth century profane history had regained centre stage, many traditions of classical historiography had been revived, and history had come to be seen, as it has been generally regarded ever since, as an essentially secular discipline. The most esteemed historical writers now sought human and natural causes and explanations for events. They tried to discern rational patterns that could be attributed not to a divine plan but to human nature, or to natural forces like geography, climate, or economics. When Enlightened philosophers wrote about the usefulness of history for European civilization, they typically high-lighted these natural and secular inquiries and disparaged 'sacred history' as an archaic pursuit belonging to a less advanced stage of civilization. The sceptical *philosophe* Voltaire, for example, wrote an entry on *histoire* for the *Encyclopédie* (1764) that enumerated a wide range of other forms of history and their utility for modern life. He began it by tersely dispensing with 'sacred history' altogether:

> The history of events is divided into sacred and profane. Sacred history is an account of divine and miraculous operations by which God was formerly pleased to guide the Jewish nation and today guides our faith. I shall not pursue this respectable matter.[1]

---

[1] Voltaire, 'Histoire' in *Encyclopédie*, ed. Denis Diderot, 3rd edn (Geneva: J. L. Pellet, 1778–9), translated in Kelley (ed. and tr.), *Versions of History*, p. 442.

Voltaire's anti-Christian bias by no means represents eighteenth-century European thought as a whole, but his attitude towards sacred history does reflect an undeniable trend: in historical thought, as in many other spheres of European intellectual life, the Christian world-view was the dominant paradigm before the Renaissance, and by the Enlightenment its importance had greatly diminished.

As a consequence, the intermediate period—the fifteenth, sixteenth, and seventeenth centuries, or the long Renaissance—has suffered the unenviable fate of many a 'transitional period': it has been recognized as a forerunner of later developments more than appreciated on its own terms. Ever since Jacob Burckhardt's 1860 masterpiece, *The Civilization of the Renaissance in Italy*, it has been a commonplace that the Renaissance ushered in 'modern' culture. In Burckhardt's wake, cultural historians of the fifteenth and sixteenth centuries have often emphasized the secular and sceptical, or at least the pagan and unorthodox, elements of Renaissance thought, singling out writers like Niccolò Machiavelli for their bold reassertion of pre-Christian traditions such as classical republicanism and their denial of orthodox Christian teaching on political and moral subjects.

Burckhardt's thesis, and later variants such as Hans Baron's 'civic humanism' thesis (which identified republican patriotism as the defining innovation of the Italian Renaissance), contain a great deal of truth. Yet in some fields, including the history of Renaissance scholarship, such arguments have often had the effect of diverting attention away from Renaissance writers who continued to practice more 'medieval' forms of historical writing, such as Church history and hagiography (the writing of saints' lives). As Alison Frazier has recently observed in an important study of Renaissance saints' lives, such literature has often been treated with condescension, or simply overlooked altogether.[2] Historical writing that adhered to a Christian world-view and centred on ecclesiastical themes seems difficult to reconcile with the characteristic 'Renaissance' attitudes that Peter Burke summed up in his 1969 classic, *The Renaissance Sense of the Past*: a keen sense of the distance between past and present; a critical approach to sources; a sceptical attitude towards myths; and an appreciation for human and natural (as opposed to supernatural) causation. Indeed, most of these attitudes seemed to point distinctly away from, rather than toward, traditional Christian historiography. Yet 'sacred history' was produced in abundance in the fifteenth, sixteenth, and seventeenth centuries, both in traditional forms and in newer forms that were influenced by Renaissance humanism. The vast majority of European thinkers before the eighteenth century did not share Voltaire's conviction that the supernatural had no

[2] Frazier, *Possible Lives.*

place in historical thought. They would much more readily have agreed with the Englishman Mathias Prideaux, who in the 1640s listed 'Ecclesiasticall History' first among seven branches of history and accorded it 'precedency before other [kinds of history], in regard of its Antiquity, Dignity, and directive Certainty'.[3]

The writing of sacred history in the long Renaissance period has certainly not been overlooked altogether in modern times. Many histories of scholarship, including the above-cited study by Peter Burke, have recognized the formative role that humanist Church historians such as Lorenzo Valla played in early modern scholarship. Modern Church historians of the Reformation era have long acknowledged the central place of ecclesiastical history in the debates of the Reformation and Counter-Reformation. And as the reach of cultural history has expanded over the last three decades, social and cultural historians have paid increasing attention to many aspects of religion and religious thought, including some of its historical dimensions. Yet there still exist few comparative or synthetic studies of early modern sacred historiography. Some of the most important works on this important branch of learning, particularly from the Reformation and Counter-Reformation period, have appeared in relatively specialized contexts that are better known to Catholic or Protestant Church historians than to general historians, let alone the wider reading public. This volume aims to draw attention to recent scholarship in the emerging field of early modern sacred historiography, and to suggest some fruitful directions for comparative thinking within the field, across national and confessional lines as well as across literary genres. While each chapter may be read in its own right as a case study of a particular form, instance, or use of sacred history, each one also engages with two broad comparative themes: the interplay between tradition and innovation in the scholarly methods of sacred historical writing, and the cultural uses of these writings within the various societies that produced them.

These uses were many and varied: some personal, some political, some unifying, and some divisive. Sacred history in the Renaissance was not simply a holdover from an earlier, more religious era. It was a way that Europeans continued to articulate some of their most deeply cherished values and identities. Renaissance Christians turned to the Christian past for spiritual and moral guidance, aid in prayer and pilgrimage, insight into the religious history of newly discovered lands and peoples, and support for various kinds of corporate identity—whether national, provincial, dynastic, or confessional. In the interconfessional conflicts of the Reformation and Counter-Reformation, which grew in part out of conflicting visions of the Christian past, sacred

---

[3] Mathias Prideaux, *An Easy and Compendious Introduction for Reading All Sorts of Histories* (Oxford: Leonard Lichfield, 1648), p. 1.

history became the terrain on which some of the bitterest conflicts about Christian life, doctrine, and liturgy were waged.

In this context, the study of the very early Church had particular significance. Like the Renaissance, the Reformation as an intellectual movement looked back to an exemplary (often idealized) past, and the early Protestant reformers took many of their sharpest critical arguments from Renaissance ecclesiastical history. Catholics countered the Protestant historical critique of the medieval Church with their own competing histories. By the later sixteenth century, this competition between Protestant and Catholic visions of early Christianity became, arguably, the dominant theme in sacred historiography, and debates about the nature of the early Church worked their way into more and more kinds of historical writing. These often polemical writings do not always constitute good history by the standards of modern critical scholarship. But if we judge the value of history by how much it mattered to contemporaries, then sacred history was perhaps never more valuable than in the Reformation and Counter-Reformation.

This volume is divided into three thematic sections. Part I introduces Renaissance sacred history in its most traditional form, as a continuation of the genre of ecclesiastical history established in the fourth century by Eusebius of Caesarea. In Chapter 1, Anthony Grafton discusses the influence of Renaissance humanism on ecclesiastical history from the mid fifteenth to the early seventeenth century. Renaissance Church historians were often self-consciously conservative and adhered closely to precedents established by Eusebius. But Grafton demonstrates that Church historians also introduced creative innovations in methods of research and publication. Humanism posed critical challenges for writers of Christian history. While some embraced the new critical methods and standards of evidence introduced by the humanist movement, the humanist emphasis on critical examination of evidence sometimes did threaten to undermine religious traditions that rested more firmly on communal consensus than on unambiguous textual or physical evidence. Thus religious historians often had to wrestle with inescapable tensions between criticism and piety. Many of the subsequent chapters in the volume offer further examples of the ways that writers in both the Catholic and the Protestant tradition tensions faced these critical challenges.

Perhaps nowhere was the demand for sacred history greater in the fifteenth and sixteenth centuries than in the various movements for religious reform. Although the uses of history by Protestant and Catholic reformers have been treated quite extensively in earlier publications, we include two chapters on core elements of Protestant and Catholic historical scholarship, as an indispensable foundation to the stories told in the rest of this collection. Both the Protestant and Catholic Reformations were profoundly historical movements that aimed to restore earlier, more authentic versions of Christian worship and

Christian society, and both used historical arguments to defend their positions. In Chapter 2, Euan Cameron explains how Protestant understandings and use of history came to differ radically in fundamental respects from Catholic ones. For Protestant reformers, the visible Catholic Church had ceased to be identical with the true Church founded by the Apostles. This posed the historical question of just when and how error and abuse could have entered into a Church that was under God's providential care. Cameron shows that early Swiss and German historians, approaching these questions with a humanist appreciation for human fallibility, were willing to concede that the true Church in the past could sometimes have combined purity with error. As the Reformation progressed, however, and doctrinal positions hardened, humanist arguments allowing for error in the Church's past gave way to more dogmatic approaches which insisted on sharper divisions between the true invisible Church and the false Roman one. By the end of the century the more dogmatic approach, often tinged with apocalypticism, had come to dominate Protestant thinking (in both reformed and Lutheran circles). This can be seen, for example, in the largest and most influential Protestant historical enterprise, the *Magdeburg Centuries*, which was more concerned with true versus false doctrine than with institutional Church history per se. The humanist and dogmatic approaches, however, were never wholly separate and irreconcilable paradigms. They were, rather, tendencies that different thinkers in subsequent decades would combine in varying measures.

Challenged by these Protestant arguments, sixteenth-century Catholic writers reaffirmed the integrity of the visible Church and the historical continuity between the primitive Catholic Church and the modern one. This meant not only defending the medieval Church against Protestant charges of corruption, but also establishing the antiquity of Roman Catholic jurisdictional claims and liturgical practices. Thus in the wake of the Council of Trent (1545–63), historical research into Christian antiquity became an indispensable tool of Catholic apologetics. Here, too, humanist and dogmatic approaches were often consciously in tension. In Chapter 3, Giuseppe Guazzelli examines the first great Catholic historical enterprise of the Counter-Reformation, the *Annales ecclesiastici* composed under papal auspices by Cardinal Cesare Baronio. Guazzelli shows how Baronio combined many of the critical techniques of humanist antiquarianism with an inevitably dogmatic treatment of early Church history, depicting an unchanging Catholic Church, *semper eadem*, always wisely and truly guided by the papacy. Baronio's *Annales* were immensely influential both as a model for later Catholic writers and as a spur to Protestant competitors. Chapters 6, 7, and 9 all deal in part with historical projects that were inspired by Baronio's work.

Anti-Protestant polemic was not, however, the only theme of Catholic historical writing after Trent. As Simon Ditchfield makes clear in Chapter 4,

historical writers in the service of the post-Tridentine Church responded
not only to Protestant challenges but also to a range of internal needs—
jurisdictional, liturgical, and theological—most of which predated the Reformation. For the Roman clergy, *historia sacra* meant a body of literature
documenting the deeds of the Church and the clergy that stretched back
uninterruptedly to New Testament times. Post-Tridentine Catholic scholars
reprinted early medieval works on the history of the Church and its saints in
great number. They also continued the tradition of documenting and recording the Church's deeds by producing new historical works in a variety of
traditional genres. Indeed, with the resurgence of the Counter-Reformation
papacy and the energetic worldwide expansion of Roman Catholicism, new
works of Catholic *historia sacra,* many of them collaborative projects, were
written and published on an unprecedented scale. This Catholic historical
enterprise included both Roman-centred projects, such as the creation of the
Vatican archive, and more provincial (if ultimately global) projects, such as the
massive compendia of saints' lives undertaken in the Low Countries by the
Bollandists.

Although both Catholic and Protestant writers conceived of the Church in
universal terms, most early modern Christians defined themselves largely by
regional identities—whether national, regional, provincial, or local. Part II
considers the complex ways that sacred history intersected with national
history writing, both in traditional chronicles and in other scholarly treatments of particular churches and patron saints. Religious themes were often
central to chronicles and other national histories, since regional identity rested
on shared understandings of a people's Christian origins, patron saints, and
struggles against religious enemies. As David Collins argues in Chapter 5, the
prevalence of religious themes in German national histories of the Renaissance
has been largely obscured by modern historians' anachronistic imposition of
two distinct categories of 'secular' and 'sacred'. Collins examines German
historiography down to the start of the Reformation, focusing on the energetic
group of humanist writers whose collective efforts to elevate German history
writing are known as the *Germania illustrata,* and showing that the 'sacred'
elements of national history were central in their work. In Chapter 6,
I examine the treatment of the early Spanish Church by Spanish chroniclers
in the Renaissance and Counter-Reformation. Particularly after the unification
of Castile and Aragon by the Catholic monarchs, Ferdinand and Isabel, and
the energetic promotion of humanist history writing by them and their
Habsburg successors, national history became a valuable stage on which to
highlight—and indeed to exaggerate—the antiquity of the Spanish Catholic
Church and to stress its links with Rome and the biblical Apostles. This
enterprise, like many of its kind, required writers to wrestle with difficult
critical issues, and during the Counter-Reformation Spanish chroniclers increasingly favored Catholic piety over critical scepticism.

By the second half of the sixteenth century, the writing and reading of national history could not be separated from the international conflict between Catholic and Protestant Churches, and national identity came to be redefined increasingly in confessional terms. Chapters 7, 8, and 9 present three case studies of the uses of sacred history in societies in central Europe and in the British Isles that were bitterly divided between Catholic and Protestant allegiances. In Chapter 7, Howard Louthan shows how scholars in the Catholic principalities of Cologne, Bavaria, and Bohemia sought to reconstruct their regions' earliest Christian past as a way to solidify modern Catholic identity in the politically charged context of the Counter-Reformation. In Chapter 8, Rosamund Oates examines the post-Reformation debates between English Protestants and Catholics over the origins of English Christianity and its relationship to the history of the universal Church. In Chapter 9, Salvador Ryan examines the corresponding debates that emerged in the neighbouring and subject kingdom of Ireland after the mid sixteenth century, when the intrusion of 'new English' Protestant settlers induced Irish Catholics to come to terms with both Protestantism and English political hegemony. Here the intersection between national and religious identity was even more complex, for the 'old English' settlers who were descended from medieval English conquerors shared a Catholic heritage with the indigenous Irish, and the Catholic population was divided over whether to offer political resistance to the Protestant English monarchy. In this context, Irish Catholic intellectuals constructed a historical account of Irish identity that stressed doctrinal orthodoxy and continuity above national origin. In all these scholarly enterprises, humanist historiography influenced the authors' choice of sources and rhetorical strategies, but the critical approaches of humanist scholarship were often (in Rosamund Oates's words) 'subordinated to the larger purpose of illuminating God's will'.

Although Church history and national history constituted the two most influential paradigms for approaching the Christian past, not all historical writing in the early modern period took the universal Church or the nation as its point of departure. Part III offers a series of case studies of other ways in which Catholic writers sought meaning in the early Christian past, both in traditional forms of sacred history that grew directly out of medieval literature, and in more innovative kinds of writing with sacred historical themes. In Chapter 10, Jean-Marie Le Gall examines the broad range of Renaissance literary genres that depicted the lives of the early saints. As a Catholic kingdom with a large Protestant minority where humanism made deep inroads into intellectual life, France offers an excellent opportunity to observe the cultural cross-currents that shaped hagiographic writing in these centuries. Le Gall shows that despite the long hiatus in canonizing new saints (from 1523 to 1588), and despite the critical challenges to the cult of the saints from humanism and Protestantism, hagiography continued to flourish in Renaissance France, and was energetically revived in the late sixteenth and seventeenth centuries, because it served a wide range of cultural needs.

The next two chapters discuss two other areas in which Catholic scholars inspired by Renaissance humanism sought to bring the early Christian past to bear on contemporary religious questions: understanding the history and geography of the Holy Land, and interpreting the earliest vestiges of Christian art. In Chapter 12, surveying the scholarly treatment of the early Christian paintings that were discovered in the Roman catacombs in the late sixteenth century, Irina Oryshkevich explains that the most conventional Catholic response to these discoveries was a dogmatic one; since Protestant polemicists had claimed that the early Church had not engaged in the 'idolatrous' use of religious images, Catholic polemicists responded polemically that these paintings proved the timeless liturgical importance of holy images. But Oryshkevitch highlights one remarkably sensitive Catholic writer, Jean l'Heureux (Macarius), who took a less doctrinaire approach to these paintings and (employing a 'developmental' model reminiscent of the early Protestant humanists described by Euan Cameron), recognized the mixture of truth and error in the early Church. Macarius used the catacomb paintings as the basis for a subtle argument about how the Christian uses of art changed over time. Adam Beaver shows in Chapter 13 that for Christian pilgrims, the critical standards of humanist historiography threatened to undermine the very foundations of pilgrimage itself by calling some of its geographical objects into question. Thus Renaissance writing about the Holy Land remained remarkably faithful to medieval historiographical traditions that grew out of pilgrim literature. By contrast, in the historiography of early Christian art, a much newer scholarly enterprise, Catholic authors exhibited a wide range of attitudes.

Overseas imperial expansion in the sixteenth century gave European Christians new venues and new motives to seek out Christian origins. In Chapter 11, Liam Brockey considers the search by Portuguese chroniclers for the traces of the biblical Apostle Thomas in south-eastern India. Just as legends of apostolic foundations enhanced the status of individual churches in European lands, early Portuguese explorers and missionaries in India were intrigued by tales claiming that the Christians they encountered on India's south-eastern coast were descended from the Apostle's first converts. A series of Portuguese chroniclers scrutinized these legends and tried to reconcile them with the known records of the Apostle's life, martyrdom, and relics. The task proved difficult, however, and in the end Christian missionaries found it easier to validate their own efforts in India by rejecting more of the local legends than they embraced.

The editors and contributors to this volume are aware that it is neither exhaustive nor perfectly balanced in its treatment of early modern sacred historiography. Had space permitted, we would have liked to include more treatment of the projection of Christian origins legends into non-western cultures, as well as more substantial treatment of the influence of Jewish thought on Christian scholarship, and cross-cultural comparisons with Islamic and other traditions of sacred writing. We also recognize that Catholic writers are disproportionately represented here over Protestants. To some degree this is justified, given that Catholics outnumbered Protestants in Europe during this whole period and that Catholic historical writers were more inclined to embrace the notion of *historia sacra* (a term which, indeed, was rarely if ever used by Protestant scholars in the sixteenth century). Furthermore, such Protestant historiographical enterprises as the *Magdeburg Centuries* and John Foxe's *Acts and Monuments* have been quite amply treated in other recent literature. Still, we regret that there was not space to devote greater attention to less well-known Protestant writers. As our primary aim is to provoke interest in this burgeoning field, we hope that some of these inevitable omissions will serve as a stimulus to further research.

This book has been more than two years in the making. It grew out of two colloquia, in October 2008 at Calvin College in Grand Rapids, Michigan, and June 2010 at the Notre Dame Centre in London. Draft versions of the chapters were shared and critiqued at these meetings, and the vision for the volume as a whole was refined. Three valued colleagues—Margaret Meserve, Alison Frazier, and Joanna Weinberg—played an important role in that early development process. Although unfortunately they were not able to contribute to the final volume, their enthusiasm for the project and stimulating interchanges with fellow authors have certainly enriched the final product. We are particularly indebted to Margaret Meserve, who organized and hosted our second colloquium and assisted with procuring reproducible images for the book. We are also grateful to our invited discussants at that second meeting—Matthias Pohlig, Jean-Louis Quantin, and Alexandra Walsham—for helping us all to sharpen our focus and to appreciate the complexity and richness of the many genres that fall under the aegis of *historia sacra*.

The two colloquia were generously funded by the Calvin Center for Christian Scholarship at Calvin College and by the Institute for Scholarship in the Liberal Arts, the Nanovic Institute for European Studies, and the Medieval Institute at the University of Notre Dame. The Calvin Center for Christian Scholarship (CCCS) also funded editing and publishing costs for the volume. I am very grateful to two successive CCCS directors, James D. Bratt and Susan M. Felch, for their consistent enthusiasm and support for this venture; to Donna Romanowski and Dale Williams of CCCS and Harriet Baldwin of Notre Dame's College of Arts and Letters for skilled organizational help with our two colloquia; to José Alvarez, T. J. Anderson, Matt Dorn, Dylan Fay, John Quinn, and Erin Zavitz for their assistance with compiling the Index; to Jennifer Vander Heide for valuable editorial assistance; to Krista Robertson for two excellent maps; and to Frans Van Liere for both scholarly advice on a range of topics and endless patience during the whole editing project. Most of all, I am indebted to Simon Ditchfield and Howard Louthan for their expert collaboration in all the organizing and editing stages of this project, and to all of our contributors for their scholarly expertise, collegiality, and patience throughout the long revision process. It has been a joy to work with and to learn from them, both in person and long-distance, and to experience first-hand the truth of the humanist adage, '*Paritas studiorum conciliat amicitiam.*'

Katherine Elliot Van Liere

Grand Rapids, Michigan

Table of Contents

List of Maps and Figures   xvii
List of Abbreviations   xix
List of Contributors   xxi
Bibliographical Note   xxiii

Part I: Church History in the Renaissance and Reformation

1. Church History in Early Modern Europe: Tradition and Innovation   3
   Anthony Grafton

2. Primitivism, Patristics, and Polemic in Protestant Visions of
   Early Christianity   27
   Euan Cameron

3. Cesare Baronio and the Roman Catholic Vision of the Early Church   52
   Giuseppe Antonio Guazzelli

4. What Was Sacred History? (Mostly Roman) Catholic Uses
   of the Christian Past after Trent   72
   Simon Ditchfield

Part II: National History and Sacred History

5. The *Germania illustrata,* Humanist History, and the
   Christianization of Germany   101
   David J. Collins, S.J.

6. Renaissance Chroniclers and the Apostolic Origins
   of Spanish Christianity   121
   Katherine Elliot Van Liere

7. *Imagining Christian Origins*: Catholic Visions of a Holy
   Past in Central Europe   145
   Howard P. Louthan

8. Elizabethan Histories of English Christian Origins   165
   Rosamund Oates

9. Reconstructing Irish Catholic History after the Reformation   186
   Salvador Ryan

Part III: Uses of Sacred History in the Early Modern Catholic World

10. The Lives of the Saints in the French Renaissance *c.*1500–*c.*1650   209
    Jean-Marie Le Gall

11. Doubting Thomas: The Apostle and the Portuguese Empire
    in Early Modern Asia   231
    Liam Matthew Brockey

12. Cultural History in the Catacombs: Early Christian Art
    and Macarius's *Hagioglypta*   250
    Irina Oryshkevich

13. Scholarly Pilgrims: Antiquarian Visions of the Holy Land   267
    Adam G. Beaver

Bibliography   285
Index   325

List of Maps and Figures

Map 1 Europe in the sixteenth century   2

Map 2 India in the sixteenth century   230

Figure 3.1 *Martyrologium romanum* (Rome: Basa, 1586), p. 149.
           Reproduced from a copy in the author's possession   56

Figure 3.2 Cesare Baronio, *Annales ecclesiastici*, III (Rome:
           Tornieri, 1592), p. 69. Reproduced from a copy in
           a private collection   66

Figure 4.1 Title page of Cesare Baronio, *Annales ecclesiastici*, I (Antwerp:
           Plantin, 1589–1609). Reproduced from the original held
           by the Department of Special Collections of the University
           Libraries of Notre Dame   78

Figure 4.2 Title page of Johannes Bollandus and Godefridus Henschenius,
           Acta sanctorum, I (Antwerp: Johannes Meursius, 1643).
           Reproduced from the original held by the Department of
           Special Collections of the University Libraries of Notre Dame 79

Figure 5.1 Conrad Celtis, *Quatuor libri amorum secundum quatuor
           latera Germanie feliciter incipient* (Nuremberg: Sodalitas Celtica,
           1502), 6^v. Munich, BSB Rar. 446. VD16 C1911. Reproduced
           with permission of the Bayerische Staatsbibliothek, Munich   109

Figure 5.2 Facsimile (1899) of 'Aventins Karte von Bayern', 1523.
           Munich BSB, Mapp. XI, 24 xbb. Reproduced with permission
           of the Bayerische Staatsbibliothek, Munich   116

Figure 6.1 Ambrosio de Morales, *Coronica general de España* (Alcalá
           de Henares: Juan Iñiguez de Lequerica, 1574), fol. 233^r.
           Reproduced with permission of Bryn Mawr College Library,
           Special Collections   141

Figure 7.1 Allegory of History. Frontispiece to Bohuslav Balbín, *Epitome
           historica rerum Bohemicarum* (Prague: Typis Universitatis
           Carolo-Ferdinandeae, 1677). Reproduced with permission
           of the Strahov Monastic Library   159

List of Abbreviations

AEM *Acta ecclesiae mediolanensis*, ed. Achille Ratti [Pius XI], 3 vols. [2–4]. (Milan: Typographia Pontificia Sancti Iosephi, 1890–1900).

BAV Biblioteca Apostolica Vaticana, Rome.

BHL *Bibliotheca hagiographica latina*, 2 vols. and supplement (Brussels: Société des Bollandistes, 1899–1901, 1998).

BVR Biblioteca Vallicelliana, Rome.

Cgm Munich, Bayerische Staatsbibliothek-München: *Codices germanici monacenses.*

Clm Munich, Bayerische Staatsbibliothek-München: *Codex latinus monacensis.*

DBI *Dizionario biografico degli italiani* (Rome: Istituto della Enciclopedia italiana, 1960).

GW *Gesamtkatalog der Wiegendrucke* (Stuttgart: Anton Hiersemann, 1968–).

MGH *Monumenta Germaniae Historica* (1826–) (see <http://www.dmgh. de/>).

ODNB *Oxford Dictionary of National Biography*, 60 vols. (Oxford: Oxford University Press, 2004).

RIS *Rerum Italicarum scriptores*, 25 vols. (Milan: Societatis Palatinae, 1723–51).

VD16 *Verzeichnis der im deutschen Sprachbereich erschienenen Drucke des XVI. Jahrhunderts* (Stuttgart: Heisemann, 1983–95).

List of Contributors

Adam G. Beaver, Assistant Professor of History at Princeton University.

Liam Matthew Brockey, Associate Professor of History at Michigan State University.

Euan Cameron, Henry Luce III Professor of Reformation Church History at Union Theological Seminary in the City of New York and Professor in the Department of Religion at Columbia University.

David J. Collins, S.J. Associate Professor of History at Georgetown University.

Simon Ditchfield, Reader in History at the University of York (UK).

Anthony Grafton, Henry Putnam University Professor of History at Princeton University.

Giuseppe Antonio Guazzelli, doctoral candidate in Religious History at the Sapienza University of Rome.

Jean-Marie Le Gall, Professor of Modern History at the University of Paris 1 Panthéon-Sorbonne.

Howard P. Louthan, Professor of History at the University of Florida.

Rosamund Oates, Senior Lecturer in History at Manchester Metropolitan University (UK).

Irina Oryshkevich, Adjunct Lecturer in Art History and Archaeology at Columbia University (New York).

Salvador Ryan, Professor of Ecclesiastical History at the Pontifical University of St Patrick's College, Maynooth (Ireland).

Katherine Elliot Van Liere, Professor of History at Calvin College (Grand Rapids, Michigan).

Bibliographical Note

At the end of the book, readers will find a composite bibliography that includes the sources cited throughout the volume (including the Preface). To streamline the footnotes, references to works that are included in the bibliography are given in the footnotes in abbreviated form (Author, *Short Title*). More specialized sources that would not be of general interest to students of Renaissance historiography are cited in full in the notes and are not included in the bibliography.

Part I

Church History in the Renaissance
and Reformation

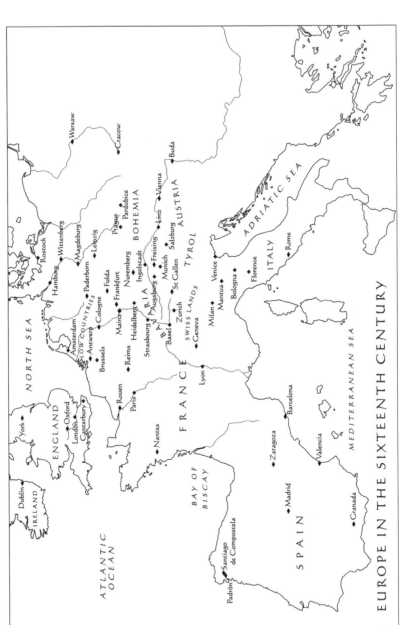

Map 1. Europe in the sixteenth century

1

Church History in Early Modern Europe: Tradition and Innovation

Anthony Grafton

On 6 March 1581, Michel de Montaigne visited the Vatican Library. Though he had now retired from his career as a lawyer, Montaigne (1533–92) was no ordinary tourist. Splendidly educated—as a boy, he had spoken Latin as his first language, so fluently that the teachers at the school he attended in Bordeaux hesitated to converse with him in that tongue—he had just published a book: a collection of short, elegantly meandering pieces on everything from cannibalism to education. His *Essays*, as he called them, found readers and imitators across Europe. While in Rome, Montaigne was elected mayor of Bordeaux—clear evidence of the esteem he enjoyed at home. This influential and articulate Frenchman was also known to be a political and religious moderate. He hated the Wars of Religion that had raged intermittently in his native France since 1562, and believed that Catholics like him, as well as Calvinists, must cease persecuting others for their beliefs.

Unlike less favoured visitors to the library, Montaigne was allowed to wander its 'five or six large rooms' at will. He examined the statues of ancient worthies that adorned the collection, the dozens of books that were chained to its desks, and even the further books kept in cases 'which were all opened to me'. And the authorities showed him a selection of their most precious books. Some of these, notably a 'book from China, in strange characters', seemed to have little to do with the great religious debates of the sixteenth century. But most of the books that Montaigne saw fell into a clear and coherent order. They included the handwritten breviary of Gregory the Great, pope from AD 590 to 604 and one of the creators of the medieval Catholic liturgy; a book by St Thomas Aquinas, the thirteenth-century Dominican theologian who had constructed two of the greatest syntheses of scholastic theology, the *Summa theologica* and the *Summa contra gentiles*, with corrections in his own handwriting; and the Polyglot Bible printed by Christopher Plantin at Antwerp in

1569–72—a magnificent work of Renaissance scholarship and typography in eight immense volumes, which offered the reader texts of the Old Testament in Hebrew, Aramaic, Greek, and Latin, and of the New Testament in Greek, Latin, and Syriac, along with scholarly commentaries on the language and meaning of the biblical texts.[1]

No one as learned as Montaigne could miss the point of this selection of texts. It was a history of the Church, presented in the material form of precious manuscripts: a history designed to show that the Roman papacy had always been the centre of Christianity. As distinguished visitors like Montaigne saw these volumes, they were meant to realize that the Church had fostered every new form of Catholic scholarship in turn, from the reform of the Mass to the study of Oriental languages. In the collections of the Vatican Library, the Church possessed the physical evidence to prove its claims to age and continuity. One of the most important lessons a privileged visitor was meant to take away from Rome, in other words, was historical. The historical record revealed that the Roman Catholic Church had always been the true Church, the one that never abandoned its traditions, and still found new and productive ways to combine learning and devotion.

It is not surprising that history mattered so much to Montaigne's hosts. The great religious debates of the sixteenth and seventeenth centuries turned in substantial part on historical questions: questions about the origins and development of Christianity.[2] Writers in all religious camps—Catholic, Lutheran, Calvinist, Anabaptist, and Anglican—painted portraits of Christian heroes and panoramas of the Christian past and used them as the bases for arguments about the present. Church history (the history of the institutional Church) was not the only kind of sacred history produced in the Renaissance. But it was the most fully developed as a genre, dating back to Eusebius of Caesarea (c.265–339/40), and makes an appropriate starting point for this volume's investigation of Renaissance sacred history. As scholars of many kinds set about making historical arguments for their vision of what Christianity had been and should be, the genre of Church history expanded in multiple ways.

***

Traditionally, modern scholars have drawn few connections between Church history and the new, critical history introduced by Renaissance humanists in the fifteenth century and developed by philologists, jurists, and antiquarians from Guillaume Budé (1467–1540) and Polydore Vergil (1470–1555) to Jacques-Auguste de Thou (1553–1617) and William Camden (1551–1623).

---

[1] Montaigne, *Travel Journal*, pp. 85–7; for the original, see Montaigne, *Journal de voyage*, pp. 111–13. The best study of Montaigne's visit to the library is Boutcher, '"Le Moyen de voir ce Senecque escrit à la main"'. Warm thanks to François Rigolot, who is currently reconstructing the event in still more detail, for information and advice.

[2] See the classic study by Polman, *L'Élément historique*.

Instead they have tended to emphasize the increasingly secular orientation of Renaissance historiography—its privileging of secular over religious subject matter, sources, and explanatory schemes—and to suggest that Church historians ignored or rejected these innovations. In this traditional interpretation, humanists did their best, as the great antiquarian Cyriac of Ancona (1391–1452) had explained to a curious priest, 'to speak with the dead'; they saw themselves as engaged on a literal and metaphorical voyage of discovery into an unknown past.[3] Church historians, on the other hand, set out to find evidence that supported pre-existing theses.[4] Humanist historians like Leonardo Bruni (1370–1444) innovated by attributing events to the decisions of human actors.[5] Church historians, however, stuck to tradition, seeking the hand of providence at work and identifying the miracles that took place when it intervened with special force. Humanists like Lorenzo Valla (1406–57) insisted on the distance that separated the past from the present, and that could be glimpsed in every realm from language itself to customs and beliefs.[6] But Church historians sought continuity. If they were Catholic, they tried to show that the Church had never changed substantially since Jesus founded it; or if they were Protestant, that the alleged heretics whom the medieval Church persecuted had actually preserved true Christianity intact from the corruption of later centuries, believing and acting just like modern Lutherans or Anabaptists.

Modern accounts have also portrayed early modern Church historians as mired in outdated geographical and chronological schemes. The new history of the Renaissance was cosmopolitan, attuned to the information pouring into Europe from Africa, Asia, and the Americas. Church historians continued to use old models. Lutherans, for example, remained loyal for centuries to the historical framework laid down by the biblical book of Daniel, which prophesied that four great empires in succession, Assyrian, Persian, Greek, and Roman, would dominate history from the Flood until the end of the world. As the French historical theorist Jean Bodin (1530–96) complained, they thus blithely ignored the fact that the Turkish sultan ruled over far more territory than the Holy Roman Emperor of the German Nation, which they wrongly saw as the continuation of ancient Rome.[7] The new Renaissance history was

---

[3] See e.g. Ligorio, *Pirro Ligorio's Roman Antiquities*; Weiss, *Renaissance Discovery of Classical Antiquity*; Gaston (ed.), *Pirro Ligorio, Artist and Antiquarian*; Rowland, *The Culture of the High Renaissance* and *The Scarith of Scornello*; Miller, *Peiresc's Europe*; Stenhouse, *Reading Inscriptions and Writing Ancient History*.

[4] For strong presentations of this view, see Cochrane, *Historians and Historiography*; Pohlig, *Zwischen Gelehrsamkeit und konfessioneller Identitätsstiftung*.

[5] Cochrane, *Historians and Historiography*; Hankins, 'Introduction', in Bruni, *History of the Florentine People*, I, pp. ix–xxi.

[6] Levine, 'Reginald Pecock and Lorenzo Valla on the Donation of Constantine', repr. in Levine, *Humanism and History*; Levine, *The Autonomy of History*.

[7] For the full story, see Seifert, *Der Rückzug der biblischen Prophetie*.

critical: humanists prided themselves on demolishing the legendary history by which the nations of Western Europe had traced their origins back to Troy. But Church historians often valued and preserved legends. Matthias Flacius Illyricus (1520–75), the Lutheran scholar from Croatia who organized the first great Protestant history of the Church (the *Ecclesiastica historia . . . secundum singulas centurias* (Basel, 1559–75), known in English as the *Magdeburg Centuries*), agreed with the humanists in principle: Church history must not rest on forged texts like the apocryphal works of Bishop Abdias of Babylon. In practice, though, he never grasped the deeper humanist argument that every text comes from a particular context and can be understood only in its terms, since accepting that would have compromised his effort to trace the continuity of the true Church.[8]

All too often, moreover, Church historians not only refused to use new approaches, but also doctored the existing evidence to make it prove their points. Onofrio Panvinio (1529–68), an Augustinian Hermit, was one of the leading Roman scholars of the mid sixteenth century.[9] An expert on the technical details of early Roman history and a valued employee of the Vatican Library, he was also, unfortunately, unscrupulous when in need of evidence. (He made money by selling Italian aristocrats spurious genealogies that traced their ancestry back to ancient Rome.[10]) In 1562, he published a new edition of the Latin text of the lives of the popes written by the fifteenth-century humanist Bartolomeo Platina, who had served as Vatican librarian. Platina had said of the evangelist Luke that '*Vixit annos octuaginta tres: uxorem habuit in Bithynia*' ('He lived for eighty-three years; he had a wife in Bithynia'). Panvinio could not accept that Luke had been a married man. Accordingly, he arbitrarily changed the sentence in two ways: he made *octoginta tres* (83) into *octoginta quattuor* (84) and he dropped in the word 'non', so that the text read, rather unconvincingly, '*uxorem non habuit in Bithynia*' ('he did not have a wife in Bithynia'). When later scholars noticed this change, they inferred that Panvinio had systematically corrupted Platina's text. In fact, he had not done so, but his one deliberate alteration had ruined his reputation and that of his edition as well.[11]

Examples of such questionable scholarly practices by ecclesiastical historians continue to crop up throughout the early modern period. The Roman Catholic Church historian Cesare Baronio (1538–1607), for example, wanted to show, in his great papal-sponsored history of the Church, the *Annales ecclesiastici*, that the first Christian emperor, Constantine (r. 306–337), had built both the Vatican and Lateran basilicas. To prove this he included an

---

[8]   Lyon, 'Baudouin, Flacius, and the Plan for the Magdeburg Centuries'.
[9]   Ferrary, *Onofrio Panvinio et les antiquités romaines*; Stenhouse, *Reading Inscriptions and Writing Ancient History*.
[10]   See Bizzocchi, *Genealogie incredibili*.
[11]   Bauer, *The Censorship and Fortuna of Platina's Lives*.

image of a brick stamp found when the old St Peter's was torn down to make way for the new one in the Renaissance. In fact, though, a contemporary record shows that these brick stamps actually attributed the building not to Constantine but to his son Constans.[12] It seems that Baronio willfully altered the evidence. Such scholarly offenses were not confined to Catholic historians. In fact, one of the best recent studies of ecclesiastical historiography, Matthias Pohlig's *Zwischen Gelehrsamkeit und konfessioneller Identitätsstiftung* (2007), insists over and over again that Lutheran Church historians were not, in the end, either modern or critical. Their task was not to recreate the past as it really was, but to create a confessional identity, and to carry it out they could not, and did not want to, apply the full range of new scholarly tools that the humanists had forged.

***

Nevertheless, early modern Catholics and Protestants were profoundly interested in history. Irena Backus, a great expert on the ways in which early modern scholars used the Fathers of the Church, has recently argued that 'the sixteenth and early seventeenth centuries were characterized by an interest in history first and foremost', and 'that the very omnipresence of history made it the obvious means whereby theologians of all religious parties could affirm their confessional identity'.[13] The literature of Church history exploded in the Renaissance and Reformation. Ancient, medieval, and modern Church histories, martyrologies, collective biographies, and liturgies went through the press, some of them numerous times. New forms of Church historical literature also took shape. Beginning with Flacius Illyricus, Lutherans, Calvinists, and Catholics drew up guides to the literature of the Church, some of which included extensive bibliographies of published and unpublished sources as well as hermeneutical suggestions about how to read them.[14] A vast range of apocryphal and pseudepigraphical texts—such as those included in the Basel collections *Mikropresbutikon* (1550) and *Monumenta S. patrum orthodoxographa* (1569)—expanded ideas about what the early Church had really been like.[15] The sixteenth century saw the creation of the great rival Church histories—the *Magdeburg Centuries* of Flacius and his collaborators, and the *Annales ecclesiastici* of Cesare Baronio—as well as more tightly focused controversial works by the Protestant scholars John Jewel (1522–71) and Isaac Casaubon (1559–1614) and the Jesuit Jules-César Bulenger (1558–1628). The seventeenth century witnessed the compilation of the massive collections of texts and information on which medievalists and early modernists still

---

[12] Bowersock, 'Peter and Constantine', pp. 5–15.
[13] Backus, *Historical Method and Confessional Identity*, 3.
[14] See e.g. Haye, 'Der Catalogus testium veritatis des Matthias Flacius Illyricus'; Hartmann, *Humanismus und Kirchenkritik*.
[15] *Mikropresbutikon*; Grynaeus (ed.), *Monumenta S. patrum orthodoxographa*.

depend, such as the *Acta sanctorum, Germania sacra, Italia sacra,* and the *Monasticon anglicanum.*[16] In the late seventeenth century, the skeptical age of Baruch Spinoza (1632–77) and Pierre Bayle (1647–1706), great Church histories, highly varied in type, by Jacques Basnage de Beauval (1653–1723), Gottfried Arnold (1666–1714), and many others, continued to take shape. So did whole new disciplines, such as palaeography, the discipline created by Jean Mabillon (1632–1707) and Bernard de Montfaucon (1655–1741) to serve the needs of the Church by authenticating manuscripts, documents, and material remains.[17] A staggering mass of correspondence—often extensive and erudite in character, much of it still unpublished—records the processes and clarifies the human relationships by which these works took shape.[18] Any conclusions about the production of Church history in early modern Europe must rest on direct exploration of this daunting mass of sources. Stefan Benz's excellent survey of Catholic historiography in the Baroque Holy Roman Empire, *Zwischen Tradition und Kritik* (2004), comes to more positive conclusions than Matthias Pohlig's book on the Lutherans, perhaps because Benz lays more weight on efforts to edit and use new sources, while Pohlig emphasizes the polemical shape and tenor of historians' theses and narratives.[19] But whether Benz or Pohlig's assessment is more valid overall, the very length of Benz's informative and judicious book (nearly 800 pages) shows just how immense the field of early modern sacred history is. The beginning of wisdom in such a vast field is to recognize how little we actually know about the precise practices of ecclesiastical scholarship and how they mutated from generation to generation, community to community, and subject to subject.

***

One central point has yet to attract as much attention as it should, especially from students of the Reformation and later periods: serious scholarly interest in the history of the Church was an important part of the scholarly revival known as the Renaissance, one that manifested itself long before the Reformation and Counter-Reformation. Traditionally, historians have treated fifteenth-century humanists like Leonardo Bruni (1370–1444) and Poggio Bracciolini (1380–1459) as men of basically secular interests. These scholars noted and remarked on the corruption of the clerics of their day, from time to time, it was thought, but took no fundamental interest in the history and development of the Church. In fact, however, by the early fifteenth century, humanists were drawing up experimental Church histories of many kinds. In

---

[16] On the *Acta sanctorum,* see now the vastly informative study of Sawilla, *Antiquarianismus, Hagiographie und Historie im 17. Jahrhundert.*

[17] See e.g. Barret-Kriegel, *Jean Mabillon;* Mabillon, *Brèves réflexions sur quelques règles de l'histoire.*

[18] See e.g. Hurel (ed.), *Érudition et commerce épistolaire.*

[19] Benz, *Zwischen Tradition und Kritik.*

1416, for example, Poggio wrote the most eloquent account of a Christian martyrdom to be crafted by a fifteenth-century humanist. His hero, named Jerome, boldly stood up to the authorities who accused him of heresy, showing the combined power of integrity and eloquence:

> It was astonishing to witness with what choice of words, with what closeness of argument, with what confidence of countenance he replied to his adversaries . . . It is incredible with what skill and judgement he put in his answers. He advanced nothing unbecoming a good man; and if his real sentiments agreed with his professions, he was so far from deserving to die that his principles did not even give just ground for the slightest offence.[20]

The prospect of an agonizing death left Jerome unmoved:

> When fire was set to the pile he began to sing a hymn, which was scarcely interrupted by the smoke and flame . . . When the executioner was going to apply the fire behind him, in order that he might not see it, he said, 'Come this way, and kindle it in my sight, for had I been afraid of it I should never have come to this place.'[21]

When Poggio composed this account, and portrayed his protagonist as fearlessly undergoing the most extreme punishment, he drew on rhetorical conventions of ecclesiastical history that had been laid down more than a thousand years before by Eusebius of Caesarea, who had filled his own *History of the Church* with detailed accounts of the sufferings of similarly heroic figures. The second-century martyr Blandina, for example, was as brave as Jerome:

> After the scourging, after the wild beasts, after the roasting seat . . . [she] was finally enclosed in a net, and thrown before a bull. And having been tossed about by the animal, but feeling none of the things which were happening to her, on account of her hope and firm hold upon what had been entrusted to her, and her communion with Christ, she also was sacrificed. And the heathen themselves confessed that never among them had a woman endured so many and such terrible tortures.[22]

Eusebius's work, written in Greek but adapted in Latin soon after his death by the Italian theologian and translator Rufinus, had served as a model for later Church historians from Socrates and Sozomen in the Greek East to Bede in the

---

[20] Poggio Bracciolini, *Letter on the Trial of Jerome of Prague* (Constance, 1416) in Ross and McLaughlin (eds.) *The Portable Renaissance Reader*, pp. 615 and 617; for the original text, see Garin (ed.), *Prosatori latini del Quattrocento*, pp. 230 and 232.

[21] Garin (ed.), *Prosatori latini del Quattrocento*, pp. 623 and 238–40.

[22] Eusebius, *Church History*, 5.1.5. Throughout this chapter Eusebius's work is cited from the translation by McGiffert and Richardson, from Schaff and Wace (eds.), *A Select Library of Nicene and Post-Nicene Fathers of the Christian Church*, available online at <http://www.ccel.org/ccel/schaff/npnf201.toc.html>.

Latin West.[23] In this area, as in his history of Florence, Poggio continued an ancient tradition—as did the dozens of other humanists who continued to write the lives of saints.[24]

Poggio's account of heroic martyrdom struck only one discordant note, but it vibrated loudly. The martyr he chose to praise was Jerome of Prague, a Hussite heretic from Bohemia who was controversially executed in 1416 at the Council of Constance, to which he had come with a safe-conduct. Poggio himself worked as a papal abbreviator—writer of official documents—and secretary. He was a habitué of the Roman Curia, the central papal administration which some called the 'Chamber of Lies', where fellow humanists employed as papal bureaucrats told dirty jokes and argued about whether the ancient Romans had really spoken Latin in the street. Yet Poggio devoted his most earnest and distinctive piece of hagiographical prose to the death of a heretic.[25] In fact, he even voiced his own doubts as to whether so skilled and honourable an orator could really have entertained erroneous beliefs.[26] Poggio's treatment of Church history was perversely unorthodox. Intellectuals who worked for the Church had traditionally written the history of the institution in order to identify the orthodox bishops and theological positions of the past and set them apart from pretenders and heresies. But Poggio's sympathetic treatment of this victim of papal justice showed that this traditional form had unsuspected critical potential.

This critical potential manifested itself even more dramatically in the work of Poggio's fiercest rival and critic in the papal service, the iconoclastic Roman scholar Lorenzo Valla.[27] Before Valla came to work for the Curia, he served one of the fiercer opponents of papal claims to sovereignty in Italy: Alfonso I of Naples (r. 1442–58). In this capacity Valla too devised a radically novel way to write about the history of the Church. Since the eighth century, when the papal chancery first created the documents that claimed that Constantine had given the western Roman Empire to the papacy in return for being cured from leprosy, many critics of the Church had attacked this 'Donation of Constantine' as illegitimate and papal rule as tyrannical. Valla, however, gave the old attack a new point. Partly inspired by the erudite German cardinal Nicholas of

---

[23] See esp. Rosamund McKitterick, *History and Memory in the Carolingian World* (Cambridge: Cambridge University Press, 2004).

[24] Frazier, *Possible Lives*. For historians' recent recovery of interest in hagiography as a form in the Renaissance, and more generally for the lives and deeds of saints, see Sawilla, *Antiquarianismus, Hagiographie und Historie*, pp. 77–8, noting the impact of Sallmann, *Naples et ses saints à l'âge baroque*. Other milestones include Burke, 'How to Become a Counter-Reformation Saint' and Zarri, *Le Sante Vive*.

[25] For the culture of the papal Curia in this period, see Celenza, *Renaissance Humanism and the Papal Curia*; McCahill, 'Humanism in the Theater of Lies'.

[26] Ross and McLaughlin (eds.), *Portable Renaissance Reader*, pp. 615–16; Garin (ed.), *Prosatori latini del Quattrocento*, p. 230.

[27] On Valla and the Church, see above all Camporeale, *Lorenzo Valla*.

Cusa (1401–64), a leader of efforts to reform the Church in the first half of the fifteenth century, Valla argued not that the Donation of Constantine was illegitimate but that the historical events it recorded could never have happened. As Nicholas had pointed out, it was illogical that this purportedly revolutionary event had left no trace in other histories of the West. More original, and even harder to refute, was Valla's argument that the document claiming to be a first-hand record of the fourth-century event was written in patently medieval language.[28] Commenting on the Donation's account of the bejewelled diadem that Constantine had allegedly bestowed on Pope Sylvester, he scoffed:

> This ignorant man was unaware that a diadem was made of cloth, or perhaps of silk . . . And . . . who ever heard of a *Phrygian tiara* in Latin? Although you talk like a barbarian, you apparently want me to think this is the language of Constantine or Lactantius.[29]

Later in the document, Valla expanded his attack to the contemporary Church. While Pope Sylvester would have refused the emperor's misguided gift, he argued, the Church of his own day had heaped its own pilgrimage sites with faked relics, spurious objects recording events that had never happened. Even the most prominent Roman pilgrimage sites were disfigured by ecclesiastical kitsch. 'These stories do more to overturn faith, because they are false, than to strengthen it because they are miraculous. Does the vicar of truth dare to tell lies under the guise of piety?'[30]

At times, Valla drew his tools from medieval intellectual traditions. Indeed, for all his scorn for the medieval papacy, Valla was not averse to invoking papal authority when it served his own scholarly purposes. For example, he considered the correspondence of Christ with King Abgar of Edessa, which Eusebius quoted in his *History of the Church*, a risible fake. But when he condemned it as such, in the course of a bitter argument with Poggio Bracciolini, he drew his critical arguments not from philology or history but from canon law:

> One day when we had begun to argue, he cited Christ's letter to Abgar. I mocked the man, who thought that Abgar was not only a king, but also a real person, and said: 'Do you not know that this letter is placed among the apocryphal ones, and thus the fakes, in the *Decretum*?'[31]

The *Decretum* was the medieval compendium of canon law texts, whose very principles of classification Valla himself, in other moods, would have rejected.

---

[28] See Camporeale, 'Lorenzo Valla's Oratio on the Pseudo-Donation of Constantine'; cf. Fubini, 'Humanism and Truth'.

[29] Valla, *On the Donation of Constantine*, p. 43.

[30] Ibid., p. 72.

[31] Valla, *Antidotum in Poggium, Opera*, p. 356.

The principal methods that Valla applied to rebutting the Donation were the ancient ones of rhetoric, especially the principle of decorum, which held that a given work should be stylistically uniform and appropriate to its purported author.[32] Yet Valla also brought his own iconoclastic approach to the table. Commenting on Quintilian's remark that a good orator may need to show that records of events are flawed and fallible, Valla crisply told his students that a Christian orator might need to do the same to records of a much more sensitive kind, and noted that a wide variety of methods might be applied to these texts:

> This question can also be raised in ecclesiastical matters, as about Susanna, about Tobias, about Judith. Also about more recent histories, like that of Saint George, where we have many arguments to use in refutation.[33]

Here, as in his attack on the Donation, Valla showed that in his view, a true Christian scholar and orator—in short, any well-trained and honourable humanist—was honour-bound to inquire into the traditions of his Church, and reject them when necessary.

***

From the first half of the fifteenth century, then, the most intellectually aggressive humanist scholars were deeply and creatively engaged with the history of the Church. Many of those interested in Church history were antiquarians, who scrutinized Greek and Roman monuments and artefacts as well as texts, and reconstructed institutions, rituals, and practices rather than political affairs. Examining early Christianity, these men wanted to know not only what had happened year by year, but what it had felt like to belong to the Church in earlier periods. To this end, the material record mattered as much as the textual one. The construction and adornment of the Lateran and Vatican basilicas interested Valla nearly as much as the papacy's documentary archive, for they were material markers that identified the beginning of the Church's departure from its original simplicity. Valla's fellow humanist and papal servant Leon Battista Alberti (1404–72) used his expert knowledge to argue the same point even more sharply. An artist and architect as well as a scholar, Alberti spent much of his time in Rome advising on projects for the restoration of the Pantheon and the old basilica of St Peter's.[34] He even wrote a detailed site report on the Vatican obelisk, which Nicholas V (pope 1447–55) wanted to move to a more prominent position, where it would occupy the centre of a huge sculptural complex.[35] Like Valla, Alberti believed that the Church had been at its purest before the great churches of late antiquity were

---

[32] Ginzburg, *History, Rhetoric and Proof.*
[33] Valla, *Postille all''Institutio Oratoria' di Quintiliano*, p. 52.
[34] See in general Grafton, *Leon Battista Alberti.*
[35] Curran and Grafton, 'A Fifteenth-century Site Report'.

erected. He did his best to sketch the sort of church services early Christians would have held in their small, plain churches:

> In ancient times, in the primitive days of our religion, it was the custom for good men to come together and share a common meal. They did not do this to fill their bodies at a feast, but to become humbler through their communication . . . Once the most sparing of portions had been tasted rather than consumed, there would be a lecture and a sermon on divine matters. Everyone would burn with concern for the common salvation and with a love of virtue . . . Later . . . [t]here followed the practice of our own times, which I only wish some man of gravity would think it fit to reform. I say this with all due respect to our bishops, who, to preserve their dignity, allow the people to see them scarcely once in the year of festivals, yet so stuff everything with altars, and even . . . I shall say no more.[36]

Some humanists, like Flavio Biondo (1392–1463), took a more positive view than Valla and Alberti of the Church's development. They agreed that the study of the Church's past went hand in hand with that of its buildings—and their restoration. Biondo, Maffeo Vegio (1407–58) and others made elaborate efforts, using both textual and topographical information to work out exactly where in Trastevere St Peter had been crucified. Biondo's reconstruction won the assent of Pope Eugenius IV (pope 1431–47). Accordingly, it served as the basis for the artist Filarete's portrayal of the event on the great bronze doors that he sculpted for the Basilica of St Peter's in the 1440s—one of many cases in which reconstruction of the ecclesiastical past had a profound contemporary meaning.[37]

Defenders of the established Church also tried to use material artefacts to support their own visions of history, although sometimes with less plausible results. Pope Paul II (pope 1464–71), the believer in papal majesty who succeeded the humanist pope Pius II, replied to Valla's ridicule of Sylvester's papal tiara in a wonderfully vivid way: he commissioned and wore an especially large tiara. Platina described him as looking like 'a Cybele with turrets on her head', and characterized his trappings as 'womanish'.[38] Yet even Paul II was outdone by Julius II (pope 1503–13). He commissioned Giulio Romano to create a series of historical frescos for the Sala di Costantino in the papal palace. Giulio and his colleagues mobilized minutely precise archaeological scholarship with all the dramatic flair of a scene designer recreating a chariot race in Hollywood in 1959. They represented exactly the events that, according to Valla, had never happened, their participants wearing meticulously depicted costumes and armor and playing their roles before architectural settings that reflected the latest archaeological findings.[39]

---

[36] Alberti, *On the Art of Building*, 7.13, p. 229; for the original, see Alberti, *L'Architettura*, II, p. 629.
[37] Huskinson, 'The Crucifixion of St Peter'.
[38] Bauer, *The Censorship and Fortuna of Platina's Lives of the Popes*, p. 156.
[39] See Chastel, *The Sack of Rome, 1527*.

Church historians were not always critical, or self-critical. But their field was always in dialogue with other forms of history, and it provoked and inspired some of the most innovative historical thinkers of the early modern period. The many scholars who between the mid sixteenth and the mid seventeenth century wrote theoretical manuals about how to study history, from Jean Bodin (1530–96) to Degory Wheare (1573–1647), acknowledged that the field of history included that of the Church. François Baudouin (1520–73) consulted on the *Magdeburg Centuries*, drawing up rules for the interpretation of texts for the compilers (although their use of his instructions left him dissatisfied).[40] Jean Bernaerts (1568–1601), whose manual *De utilitate legendae historiae* (*On the Usefulness of Reading History*) appeared in 1593, used the story of Joan, the legendary female pope, to examine the larger question of which sorts of witnesses deserved credence. Should the modern historian trust eyewitnesses only, or also those who offered second-hand testimony of the pope's *sedes stercoraria* (dung chair or pierced chair) and Joan's career as prostitute, savant, and mother?

Many of these scholars taught both forms of history, civil and ecclesiastical. The Lutheran Rostock professor David Chytraeus (1530–1600), whose work on the art of history went through many editions, followed the great theologian and historian Philipp Melanchthon (1497–1560) in connecting ecclesiastical to secular history at every point.[41] So did the Calvinist convert Johann Jakob Grynaeus (1540–1617), who lectured to enthusiastic audiences on both political and ecclesiastical history.

***

No one did more to frame a powerful, polemical vision of the history of the early Church than the Dutch Catholic humanist Desiderius Erasmus (1466–1536). He set out to transform the lives of Christians by making available to them, in eloquent Latin translations and paraphrases, exact and moving versions of the Gospels and the Epistles of Paul.[42] In the *Paraclesis*, one of the introductory texts he wrote for his edition of the New Testament in Greek and Latin, he evoked the more radical reconfiguration of society and culture that he hoped scholarship like his might someday help to bring about. The Gospels, if translated into the vernacular, could seep into and illuminate the language, and then the lives, of ordinary people:

> I would wish that all ordinary little women could read the Gospel and the letters of Paul. And I wish they could be translated into all languages, so that they could

---

[40] Lyon, 'Baudouin, Flacius and the Plan'.

[41] Chytraeus, *De lectione historiarum recte instituenda*. See also Chytraeus's widely read *Chronologia historiae Herodoti et Thucydidis*, and Völkel, 'Theologische Heilanstalt und Erfahrungswissen'.

[42] See Bentley, *Humanists and Holy Writ*; Rummel, *Erasmus' 'Annotations' on the New Testament*; Pabel and Vessey (eds.), *Holy Scripture Speaks*.

be read and known not only by the Scots and Irish, but also by Turks and Saracens. For the first step is to know them, in whatever way that is possible. True, many might laugh: but some would be caught. I wish the farmer sang something from this source at his plow (*ad stivam*), the weaver at his wheel (*ad radios*), that the traveler would use stories like this to while away the boredom of his journey. All the speech of all Christians should be drawn from the source.[43]

Erasmus's image of a Christian 'golden age' appears at first sight to be both poetic and original, but it is actually a strategic allusion to Jerome (*c.*341–420), one of the most important patristic writers.[44] In AD 365 Jerome had written, under the names of his female friends Paula and Eustochium, to another Christian woman, Marcella. He tried to make clear why the eremitical life that Paula and Eustochium led in the Holy Land was more Christian than a pious life in Rome. Rome had unique trophies of the martyrs and Apostles. But life there was all about power and display, visiting and being visited, seeing and being seen. By contrast:

> in the cottage of Christ all is simple and rustic: and except for the chanting of psalms there is complete silence. Wherever one turns, the labourer at his plough (*stivam tenens*) sings alleluia, the toiling mower cheers himself with psalms, and the vinedresser while he prunes his vine sings one of the lays of David. These are the songs of the country; these, in popular phrase, its love ditties: these the shepherd whistles; these the tiller uses to aid his toil.[45]

In echoing Jerome's call that Scripture should be accessible to working men and women, Erasmus was not asking the Church to create a new Christian Utopia, but to restore the linguistic conditions that had existed in what we would now call late Antiquity. In those days, as the words from Jerome that he wove into his own text suggested more elegantly than any formal argument could have, women, as well as men, not only read the Scripture but also lived, spoke, and wrote in ways that reflected immediately how it had transformed their lives. Before the outbreak of the Reformation, Erasmus and his readers could imagine the early Church as a very foreign country that required skilled and courageous exploration.

In the years after 1520, as the Protestant Reformation called into question the origins, and thereby the validity, of all established ecclesiastical institutions, doctrines, and practices, polemical histories like Erasmus's multiplied. The most ambitious Protestant historical enterprise was that of Flacius

---

[43] Erasmus, *Ausgewählte Werke*.

[44] On this point, see the judicious account of Pabel, *Herculean Labours*. On the larger and more complex question of Erasmus's identification with the historic figure of St Jerome, see the pioneering work of Jardine, *Erasmus, Man of Letters* and the important article by Vessey, 'Erasmus' Jerome'.

[45] Jerome, Epistola XLVI, *Patrologia latina*, XXII, pp. 490–1; Paula and Eustochium, *The Letter of Paula and Eustochium to Marcella*.

Illyricus, which began to take shape in the 1550s. Flacius and his colleagues hunted for sources across Europe and catalogued their authors in a massive list of heretics, the *Catalogue of Witnesses to the Truth*, that appeared in 1556.[46] He also printed numerous manuscripts that recorded the ideas and liturgies of so-called heretics. The group he founded to research and write a Protestant history of the Church soon swelled into a hierarchically organized research team, with students panning the sources for information, more advanced MAs writing up their results, and a group of *curatores* overseeing all expenditures and negotiating with their publisher, Johannes Oporinus, in Basel. The very success of the Magdeburg scholars brought them under unfair suspicion. Flacius himself was accused of having cut the documents he wanted out of their original volumes with his *culter flacianus* (Flacian razor), and the Centuriators more generally were accused of wasting their patrons' money.[47]

Yet other Protestant scholars followed Flacius's lead. In 1558, Queen Elizabeth ascended the English throne and restored Protestant worship to the Church of England, ending the five-year Catholic restoration of her half-sister Mary. Elizabeth's first archbishop of Canterbury, the erudite Matthew Parker (served 1559–74), supervised an ambitious historical project to collect documents illustrating the historical continuity of the Protestant Church of England. The immediate inspiration for this document-hunting venture came from the Magdeburg Centuriators, who wrote to Parker in 1560 to ask him to supply them with materials.[48] Parker's efforts resulted in the publication of numerous medieval chronicles, and a historical narrative, the *De antiquitate Britannicae ecclesiae et privilegiis ecclesiae Cantuariensis* (*On the Antiquity of the Church of England and the Privileges of the Church of Canterbury*), published by London printer John Day in 1572. This polemical work traced the Church of England back to Joseph of Arimathea (the biblical figure who prepared Jesus's tomb) and argued that it represented a form of Christianity historically distinct from, and in every way better than that of, the Church of Rome. The death of the Catholic Queen Mary in 1558 was still a recent memory, and many Catholics hoped to see the Elizabethan settlement reversed and Catholicism reestablished as the national Church. Parker's book supported its vision of the English ecclesiastical past with a massive apparatus of learning. Long quotations from primary sources of all kinds interrupt the flow of narrative even as they convey authority, and precise references to the sources from which they come from dot the margins.[49]

---

[46] Flacius Illyricus, *Catalogus*. For more on Flacius's enterprise, see below, Ch. 2.

[47] Grafton, *The Footnote*, p. 162.

[48] Norman Jones, 'Matthew Parker, John Bale, and the Magdeburg Centuriators'.

[49] Parker, *De antiquitate Britannicae ecclesiae*. On Parker's treatment of English Church history, see below, Ch. 8. On his life, see David Crankshaw and Alexandra Gillespie, 'Matthew Parker (1504–1575)', *Oxford Dictionary of National Biography* (Oxford: Oxford University Press,

Archbishop Parker built up a massive library to support his scholarly efforts. He systematically gathered manuscripts (more than 500 of these have been identified) and printed books (numbering several thousand). After 1568 Parker had official support from Queen Elizabeth's Privy Council. He ransacked collections and engaged a staff of book professionals—secretaries like John Joscelyn (1529–1603), scribes, illuminators, and binders—who repaired damaged manuscripts, supplemented partial ones, and brought texts together in new volumes. Careful annotations paginated many of the manuscripts and indicated useful passages.[50]

In the seventeenth century, Protestant scholars and patrons continued to invest in the resources for ecclesiastical history. The extraordinary manuscript collection of the MP and antiquarian Robert Cotton (1571–1631), neatly arranged in presses identified by the busts of Roman emperors, provided ammunition for Anglican Church history. Thomas Bodley's new library in Oxford, first opened in 1602, was designed to serve Anglican controversialists by collecting everything from manuscript evidence to the newest printed tracts.[51] Bodley's innovations delighted Isaac Casaubon, who had seen nothing like them in France, Protestant or Catholic. He especially liked Bodley's absolute prohibition on removing books from the library (the only exception he made was for his friend Henry Savile of Merton College and Eton). This rule meant that all the serious scholars in Oxford spent the six or seven hours a day when the library was open, 'enjoying these feasts', and forming a new kind of research community.[52]

***

Ultimately, all of these institution builders looked back to Eusebius, just as Poggio had, as their methodological model. Eusebius was not only the first historian of the institutional Christian Church; he was also the creator of a method of compilation that would be copied through early modern times. His innovation lay in the systematic use of primary sources. Arnaldo Momigliano (1908–87) long ago identified the formal characteristic that distinguished Eusebius's work from other forms of history written in the ancient world.[53] Instead of offering a coherent narrative and mentioning sources only when they disagreed, the normal technique of ancient historians, Eusebius interspersed

---

2004). For the scholarship practised in his circle, see McKisack, *Medieval History in the Tudor Age*, and Graham and Watson, *The Recovery of the Past in Early Elizabethan England*.

[50] See the website of the Parker Library in Corpus Christi College Cambridge, <http://parkerweb.stanford.edu/parker/actions/page.do?forward=home>; and Summit, *Memory's Library*.

[51] Tite, *The Manuscript Library of Sir Robert Cotton*; Tite, *The Early Records of Sir Robert Cotton's Library*; Nelles, 'The Uses of Orthodoxy and Jacobean Erudition'.

[52] Isaac Casaubon, *Ephemerides*, II, pp. 1228–9.

[53] Momigliano, 'Pagan and Christian Historiography in the Fourth Century A.D.'. Momigliano in turn built on a 1908 essay by Schwartz, 'Über Kirchengeschichte'.

the chapters of his *History* with primary documents: letters, quotations, accounts of the suffering of martyrs like the one quoted above. Church history, as Eusebius framed it, was not a smooth narrative—the normal form of ancient historiography—but a choral work, in which the voices of many witnesses were heard, along with that of the author. From the start of his work, Eusebius made clear to readers that he had had no precedent to follow, but had to assemble the surviving pieces of earlier accounts:

> Since I am the first to enter upon the subject, I am attempting to traverse as it were a lonely and untrodden path. I pray that I may have God as my guide and the power of the Lord as my aid, since I am unable to find even the bare footsteps of those who have traveled the way before me, except in brief fragments . . .[54]

Eusebius also claimed to be pioneering in his choice of subject matter. While other historians dealt with political or military history, he stuck to Christian doctrines and actions:

> Other writers of history record the victories of war and trophies won from enemies, the skill of generals, and the manly bravery of soldiers, defiled with blood and with innumerable slaughters for the sake of children and country and other possessions. But our narrative of the government of God will record in ineffaceable letters the most peaceful wars waged in behalf of the peace of the soul, and will tell of men doing brave deeds for truth rather than country, and for piety rather than dearest friends. It will hand down to imperishable remembrance the discipline and the much-tried fortitude of the athletes of religion, the trophies won from demons, the victories over invisible enemies, and the crowns placed upon all their heads.[55]

Eusebius's inclusion of original sources gave readers a uniquely rich sense of what the martyrs had done and suffered—and, of course, lent credibility to his efforts to define the biblical canon and orthodox doctrine. To acquire these sources, Eusebius worked in Christian archives in Jerusalem and elsewhere, and built up the diocesan collection in Caesarea. This collection grew so copious that he sometimes lost his chronological way as he hacked paths through the documents, martyrdom by martyrdom, and digressed from his main narrative.[56] For all the differences between Eusebius's work and later Church histories—the work of Bede (673–735), for example, or that of William of Malmesbury (*c*.1090–after 1142)—the basic format he established remained standard through the seventeenth century. The reader who opened a Church history, ancient, medieval, or modern, expected to find a work divided into books and chapters, and one in which primary sources regularly interrupted the main text.[57]

---

[54] Eusebius, *Church History*, 1.1.4.   [55] Ibid., 5.1.2–4.

[56] See Grafton and Williams, *Christianity and the Transformation of the Book*.

[57] This point needs emphasis because so many historians of the early modern period ignore it—e.g. Seeberg, who argued, in his otherwise excellent treatment of Gottfried Arnold's

In compiling ecclesiastical histories based on massive collections of primary sources, Flacius and Parker knowingly followed Eusebius's ancient model. What made their efforts different from those that had gone on in Caesarea—or in the monasteries where Eusebius's medieval successors did their work—was less their methods than the scale on which they were now employed. The Vatican Library, though founded as a secular, humanistic collection, was considered a vital resource for arguments about the Church's past by the 1540s, when its librarian, Agostino Steuco, mobilized Greek manuscripts of the Donation of Constantine to refute Lorenzo Valla.[58] Cesare Baronio, in arguing that his *Annales ecclesiastici* rested on a solid source base, stressed that he had laboured for three decades in many 'noble libraries' of Rome, especially the Vatican; he also compared himself to the ancient historian Dionysius of Halicarnassus, who had boasted that living in Rome gave him a uniquely accurate vision of all events.[59] Baronio was hard at work on the *Annales* and several other historical research projects in the early 1580s when Montaigne was given his tour of the library's rich resources for Church history.[60]

Religious subjects generated more collaborative research projects in the sixteenth and seventeenth centuries than any other area of scholarship. Although only one learned academy before the eighteenth century (the short-lived Academia Basiliana founded in Rome to study relations between the Roman and Greek orthodox Churches) took ecclesiastical scholarship as its central aim,[61] some libraries were conceived, at least for a time, as active research centres. Bodley's first librarian in Oxford, Thomas James (*c*.1573–1629), organized a community of full-time researchers tasked to show that Catholic scholars had systematically corrupted the texts of the Fathers of the Church. His enterprise did not last long or produce much, as Bodley, a realist, had predicted.[62] But it was one of many similar efforts. In 1609, only seven years after the Bodleian opened, Federico Borromeo (1564–1631) opened a Catholic study centre in Milan with permanent research posts, the Biblioteca Ambrosiana.[63]

Unpartheiische Kirchen- und Ketzerhistorie, that Arnold innovated when he 'cited his sources' at length, drawing them from '*eine Unmenge von auf Zetteln niedergeschriebenen Exzerpten*' (Seeberg, *Gottfried Arnold*).

[58] Delph, 'Valla Grammaticus, Agostino Steuco, and the Donation of Constantine'.

[59] Baronio, 'Praefatio Baronii in Annales ecclesiasticos ad lectorem' in *Annalium ecclesiasticorum . . . apparatus*, pp. 395–9, esp. p. 396, citing Dionysius of Halicarnassus, *Roman Antiquities*, 1.7.2–3.

[60] On the composition history of the *Annales* and Baronio's other works, see Ch. 3.

[61] Herklotz, *Die Academia Basiliana*.

[62] See Nelles, 'Uses of Orthodoxy'.

[63] Pamela Jones, *Federico Borromeo and the Ambrosiana*.

In the course of the seventeenth century, ecclesiastical scholarship became a collective humanistic venture on a scale never seen before in the West.[64] The Jesuit community established in Antwerp by Héribert Rosweyde (1569–1629) and Jean Bolland (1596–1665) took charge of the refounding of Catholic hagiography.[65] Their *Acta sanctorum*, a massive effort to sort out truth from secondary elaboration in the lives of the saints, began publication in 1643, and their work continues today. In similar fashion, the Benedictines of Saint Maur (est. 1621, more commonly called the Maurists) became an organization of 600 researchers schooled in textual scholarship and linked by pulsing, vibrant correspondence networks. Across the channel, antiquarians collaborated to recreate the history of the Church in medieval England, and Richard Bentley (1662–1742) placed the Cambridge University Press's proposed critical edition of the New Testament into the hands of specially organized teams of expert philologists. Even those who worked alone, or claimed to, often sustained themselves, as scientists did in the same period, with the help of anonymous research assistants and generous correspondents. The scientific societies which sprang up in the seventeenth and early eighteenth centuries were but one instance of a larger phenomenon, a new way of organizing intellectual work, and in the humanities the realm of ecclesiastical scholarship saw the most striking innovations.[66]

In book production, too, the Church historians of the early modern period both followed and transcended the precedents that Eusebius had set. Eusebius the pioneering historian and source collector had also been a brilliant impresario of book design. He and the skilled scribes in his scriptorium crafted Christian books in which form elegantly reinforced function. He drew up the first world chronicle in parallel columns and a geographical work on Palestine equipped with maps. In the New Testament texts prepared in Caesarea, the Gospels were cut into numbered sections, while ten comparative lists, the so-called canon tables, enabled readers to compare parallel passages without rearranging the Gospels themselves.[67]

Eusebius's early modern successors, working in an age of more sophisticated technology, delegated their production work to professionals. When Matthew Parker wanted to bring his work on the antiquity of the British

---

[64] The fullest study of one of these organizations is Sawilla, *Antiquarianismus, Hagiographie und Historie.* Useful case studies appear in Knowles, *Great Historical Enterprises,* and in Schwaiger (ed.), *Historische Kritik in der Theologie.*

[65] For the actual origins of this enterprise, see Sawilla, *Antiquarianismus, Hagiographie und Historie,* pp. 386–471.

[66] Up to now monographs have surveyed only single quadrants of this *mare magnum* of libraries and study centres—e.g. the excellent studies of the British case by McKisack, *Medieval History,* and Summit, *Memory's Library.* Soon, however, Paul Nelles will offer us the first comprehensive, precise map of the bright archipelago of study centres that stretched across the dark night of Europe in the age of religious wars.

[67] Grafton and Williams, *Christianity and the Transformation of the Book.*

Church to the attention of the public, he relied on the skillful and dedicated book producer John Day, a London printer who had suffered under Mary for his Protestant allegiance. As talented an impresario of the book as Eusebius, and one who could deploy the new technology of the press, Day had already printed the first edition of the greatest of all English Protestant histories: John Foxe's *Book of Martyrs*—a vast task that involved setting some 1,800 large-format pages, introducing countless last-minute additions and changes, using typography to clarify the difference between Foxe's text and quoted sources— and commissioning some fifty illustrations.[68] For Parker he produced impressive facsimiles of Anglo-Saxon documents, designed to prove the continuity of the English Church. Not all experiments with local production succeeded; Baronio's *Annales* was first published in Rome, but did not become a bestseller until the Antwerp printer Christopher Plantin (*c*.1520–89) took over. Plantin editions of the *Annales* reached libraries around the world, from Peru and New Spain to India.

***

Early modern Church historians did more than refine and polish the methods of scholarship and publishing they had adapted from Eusebius. They also expanded the agenda and content of their field in ways that represented a clear departure from ancient norms. One particularly significant departure from fourth-century thinking concerned a question that has become central to all contemporary histories of the early Church: the place of Jews in the history of Christianity. The fact, Eusebius acknowledged, that:

> the Hebrew nation is not new, but is universally honoured on account of its antiquity, is known to all. The books and writings of this people contain accounts of ancient men, rare indeed and few in number, but nevertheless distinguished for piety and righteousness and every other virtue.[69]

But Eusebius also insisted that the truly pious Hebrews depicted in the Old Testament 'were Christians in fact if not in name': 'They did not care about circumcision of the body, neither do we. They did not care about observing Sabbaths, nor do we. They did not avoid certain kinds of food.'[70] Eusebius admitted that 'the apostolic men . . . were as it seems of the Hebrew race, and hence observed, after the manner of the Jews, the most of the customs of the ancients'.[71] But he hardly recognized them as participants in a living Jewish culture. Most of the Jews who made appearances in his work were simply being mustered for Christian polemical purposes.[72] And sometimes they failed

---

[68] Evenden, *Patents, Pictures and Patronage*. On Foxe's work, see below, Ch. 8; Evenden and Freeman, *Religion and the Book in Early Modern England*.
[69] Eusebius, *Church History*, 1.4.5.
[70] Ibid., 1.4.8.   [71] Ibid., 2.17.2.
[72] See Jacobs, *Remains of the Jews*.

to make an appearance where one might have expected them. After Eusebius quoted Philo's discussion of the Therapeutae, for example, a group of ascetics in Egypt who devoted themselves to the singing of hymns and the study of Scripture and practiced celibacy, he commented that they must have been 'the first heralds of the Gospel and the customs handed down from the beginning by the apostles'[73]: early Christian monks. Yet Philo, as Eusebius knew, was Jewish, and so were the Therapeutae.[74]

In the fifteenth and sixteenth centuries, however, Christian scholars studied Hebrew, as well as Aramaic and other Semitic languages, and they began to investigate the biblical texts, translations, and commentaries preserved in those languages. Christian Hebraism remained a somewhat specialized pursuit in the sixteenth century, and one that continued to bring suspicions of unorthodoxy on the scholars who practised it—from the German humanist Johannes Reuchlin (1455–1522), whose public defence of Hebrew studies earned him the ire of fellow scholars and denunciation by the University of Paris in 1514 (though a German inquisitorial court exonerated him of heresy), to Benito Arias Montano (1527–98), whose use of Hebrew Scriptures and rabbinical writings for his Polyglot Bible edition led fellow scholars to denounce him to the Spanish Inquisition in 1574 (which likewise absolved him of heresy, although it criticized his work).[75] Nonetheless, interest spread, and a wide range of basic tools for Hebrew studies, from grammars and lexica to scholarly commentaries, gradually became available.[76] The Christian printer Daniel Bomberg produced hundreds of copies of the Hebrew Bible with the most important rabbinical commentaries, and of the great compendium of Jewish ritual and law, the Babylonian Talmud. Theologians and exegetes began to recognize that the sayings of Jesus and others who appeared in the New Testament had parallels in ancient Jewish texts. As early as 1542, the Lutheran Paulus Fagius printed a collection of Hebrew prayers in order, as he explained, to recreate the religious customs of the ancient Jews, which Christ himself had sometimes followed.[77] In the 1550s the Catholic Angelo Canini (1521–57) dedicated a book to explaining the Hebrew and Aramaic words and turns of phrase in the New Testament.[78] On both sides of the confessional divide, scholars realized that early Christianity had come into being in a Jewish world—a fact that an accurate history of the Church must reflect.

---

[73] Eusebius, *Church History*, 2.17.24.
[74] Joseph Scaliger, who made this point with some force, regarded Eusebius's error about the Therapeutae as a sign of basic incompetence in scholarship. See Grafton, *Joseph Scaliger*, II, pp. 299–300.
[75] See Rummel, *The Case against Johannes Reuchlin*; Rekers, *Benito Arias Montano*, pp. 58ff.
[76] For a wide-ranging and splendidly illustrated survey of these new resources, see van der Heide, *Hebraica veritas*.
[77] Fagius, *Precationes hebraicae*; see Friedman, *The Most Ancient Testimony*.
[78] Weinberg, 'A Hebraic Approach to the New Testament'.

Thus in the 1550s, when Flacius Illyricus and his colleagues set out to write their Protestant history of the Church, they adopted an approach that was radically different from that of Eusebius. From the start, they realized that one could not hope to understand the new Church Jesus had created without first surveying the Jewish beliefs and institutions that he had known. François Baudouin, the distinguished lawyer and historian whose advice Flacius and his colleagues asked as they shaped their work, insisted that the history of the 'Jewish church' was directly relevant to Christianity, and must be included.[79] The Centuriators explained with great clarity why this was true:

> Christ arrived at a time when the Jewish religion was still in some sense intact. Therefore he used certain ceremonies, especially those that God established through Moses, and did not use others, such as the traditions of the elders, which had elements of superstition. Accordingly, before we go over the new and splendid rituals that Christ established, we will describe the received and customary ceremonies of the Jewish people.[80]

They followed the Roman Jewish historian Josephus (37–c.100) in treating the division of the Jews into rival groups of Pharisees, Sadducees, and Essenes as the basic fact about Judaism in the last centuries before Christ, and they quoted him—rather than Eusebius—as their prime authority. They also offered substantial accounts of these three great Jewish sects and of Jewish customs and practices, some of which made ingenious historical use of the Gospels.[81]

Not all later Church historians followed the Centuriators' lead. The Lutheran scholar Lucas Osiander (1534–1604), who issued what he described as an epitome of the *Magdeburg Centuries* in 1592–9, suggested that they had wasted too much time on Jewish sects. 'The countenance of God's Church was sorrowful in those days', he explained, and after a very brief account of Pharisees, Sadducees, and Essenes he passed rapidly on to the life of Jesus.[82] But in Rome, Cesare Baronio, committed to refuting the Centuriators text by text and line by line, followed their lead and investigated Jewish life and institutions with considerable care and seriousness. He too examined at length the major sects of the Pharisees, Sadducees, and Essenes—as well as a host of minor ones, including Samaritans, Hemerobaptists, Ossenes, and Herodians. The margins of his book swarm with references to the Code of Maimonides and other Jewish sources, often quoted in the original.[83] True, Baronio's fierce Calvinist critic Isaac Casaubon dismissed the Catholic scholar's efforts as

---

[79] Erbe, *François Bauduin (1520–1573)*, p. 267.

[80] Flacius et al., *Centuriae*, I, col. 237.

[81] Ibid., I, i.5–9, cols. 227–72. For a particularly ingenious piece of argument, note the passage on synagogues, I, cols. 240–1.

[82] Osiander, *Epitomes historiae ecclesiasticae centuria I. II. III. [-XVI.]*, I.i.2.2, I, 2–4.

[83] For a fuller discussion, see Grafton and Weinberg, *'I Have Always Loved the Holy Tongue'*.

pointless: 'Baronio', he wrote, 'has a long discourse about the Jewish sects. In this, I must confess, I have not been able to detect a single gleam of truly solid, subtle learning; for as he recites the errors of others he makes them his own, and accordingly he does not lack errors for which he himself is responsible.'[84] Nonetheless, for all the shortcomings of his understanding of Judaism, Baronio did assign a striking amount of room in his work to Jewish actors and themes.

The history of the early Christian Church would retain a substantial Jewish component for a century and more to come. In 1705–6 the Calvinist Church historian Jacques Basnage de Beauval brought out a massive history of the Jews, which became celebrated for its pity for its human subjects, its contempt for the core texts of later Judaism, from the Talmud to the Kabbalah, and its sharp eye for the problems that the texts then known left unsolved:

> It is a surprising thing that the *Old Testament* should make so little mention of *Synagogues* . . . How were the Sabbaths kept, if there were neither Temples, nor any other Publick Places Consecrated for Devotion? This Objection is puzzling. However, the Scripture is so profoundly silent in this Matter, that we are not able to discover any one of these places.[85]

Like the Magdeburg Centuriators, Basnage put his finger on a puzzling historical question, to which archaeology has provided partial answers in much more recent times. Perhaps the most imaginative follower of their example, though, was not Basnage but Gottfried Arnold, who included in his 1699 *Unpartheiische Kirchen- und Ketzer Historie* (*Impartial History of the Church and of Heresy*) a sympathetic account of Muhammad, treating him not as the Antichrist but as one whose teachings synthesized the best elements of what natural man could think and believe.[86]

Church history, in other words, became far too important in the early modern period to be confined to Christianity alone. This principle was followed with enthusiasm by the Jesuits and others who described the history of Christianity in the New World and in Asia, emulating Bede more than Eusebius as they offered strikingly rich accounts of pagan belief and practice.[87] To watch the Church historians of the sixteenth and seventeenth centuries struggling, however awkwardly, with sources in Hebrew and Aramaic, noting the Jewish elements in Jesus's ceremonies, and comparing the Last Supper to the Passover rituals recorded in the Haggadah, is to feel dissatisfaction less with them than with their successors, who gradually exiled the Jews from their former place in the history of the Church (and, in the case of the Göttingen

---

[84] Casaubon, *De rebus sacris et ecclesiasticis exercitationes XVI*, pp. 53–4.
[85] Basnage, *The History of the Jews*, IV, p. 406. On Basnage, see Elukin, 'Jacques Basnage and the History of the Jews'.
[86] Seeberg, *Gottfried Arnold*.
[87] See Stroumsa, *A New Science: The Discovery of Religion in the Age of Reason*.

scholar Johann David Michaelis, argued that the traditions of Jewish scholarship shed no light even on the Old Testament).[88] By the 1880s, when the Protestant Emil Schürer published his massive and influential *History of the Jewish People in the Age of Jesus Christ*, hardly anyone remembered that the Church historians of the early modern period had already cultivated the same difficult ground.[89]

***

The Eusebian model of Church history proved capable of expansion in many directions. From its inception Church history took as its task a broader scope of human experience than most kinds of traditional history, encompassing what today might be called the 'intellectual' and the 'cultural', as well as the institutional, development of Christianity. Political history, Flacius Ilyricus explained, dealt with relatively simple matters: wars and their outcome. Ecclesiastical history, by contrast, must take on 'the explication of the doctrines and religion which scholars, at different times, either corrupted or defended or obscured or illuminated, with true or false opinions and teachings'—that is, the history of theology, in all its incredibly diverse and contentious proliferation of opinion. Yet even theology did not exhaust the field: the historian of the Church also had to take into account the devotions, the prayers, and even the Church music used in the past. As Flacius told a correspondent, 'We want to show not only what doctrines existed in the church in each century, but also what sort of ceremonies and songs—though briefly, to be sure. For all these things are organically connected to one another.'[90]

Ideally, then, Church history would offer readers a vivid picture of how the Church had functioned, epoch by epoch, as theology, liturgy, and organizational forms interacted. At least one influential early modern reader who interests stretched well beyond ecclesiastical history found this plan immensely challenging and fruitful. The English polymath Francis Bacon (1561–1626), as is well known, called, in the early seventeenth century, for the creation of a new kind of history—a 'just story of learning', in his terms, that would:

> include the nature of regions and peoples, their disposition, whether suited or unsuited to the various disciplines; the accidental qualities of the period which were harmful or favourable to the sciences; rivalries between and minglings of religions; the harmful and the favourable disposition of the laws; and finally the outstanding virtues and ability of certain individuals for promoting letters.[91]

---

[88] See Legaspi, *The Death of Scripture and the Rise of Biblical Studies*.

[89] See Schürer, *The History of the Jewish People in the Age of Jesus Christ*.

[90] Vienna, Österreichische Nationalbibliothek, Ms. 9737b, fols. 14^v–15^r. For an interesting example of the way these principles were put into practice, see Sawilla, *Antiquarianismus, Hagiographie und Historie*, pp. 357–61.

[91] Bacon, *De augmentis scientiarum*, 2.4; in Bacon, *Works*, II, p. 200 (tr. Grafton).

By following this story in detail, Bacon argued, those charged with fostering the growth of philosophy and other fields would learn what had proved productive, and what harmful, in the past. This would serve not just 'curiosity' but a 'more serious and grave purpose':

> it will make learned men wise in the use and administration of learning. For it is not St. Augustine's nor St. Ambrose'[s] works that will make so wise a divine, as ecclesiastical history, thoroughly read and observed; and the same reason is of learning.[92]

When Bacon suggested that such a history be composed by excerpting past writings, 'century by century or for shorter periods', he made clear that his new history of learning was adapted from the existing form of Church history. Over the next century and more, intellectuals of many stripes did their best to provide a history of learning, or '*historia litteraria*', that lived up to Bacon's demands. When they did so—though few of them can have known it—they were paying tribute to the innovative character of ecclesiastical scholarship.[93] Bacon may also have been paying tribute to Flacius and the *Magdeburg Centuries* when he described his ideal institution for the study of nature in the *New Atlantis* (1627) with its hierarchical research teams, staffed by specialists, each assigned to gathering, interpreting, or presenting the data.[94] Like so many other early modern scholars and thinkers, Francis Bacon saw the history of the Church as an innovative and fertile field of scholarship.

[92] Bacon, *Advancement of Learning* (English translation of *De augmentis scientiarum*), 2.4 in *The Advancement of Learning and New Atlantis*, p. 68.

[93] Schmidt-Biggemann, *Topica universalis*.

[94] For the text of the *New Atlantis*, see Bacon, *The Advancement of Learning and New Atlantis*.

2

Primitivism, Patristics, and Polemic in Protestant Visions of Early Christianity

Euan Cameron

The Protestant Reformation of the sixteenth century held at its heart a series of controversial claims and visions of the Christian past. Although the reformers did not immediately turn their dogma or their apologetics into historical narratives, they soon realized how profoundly those arguments depended on a particular understanding of history. That understanding contradicted in fundamental ways the assumptions of the Catholic authors whose writings form the core of most of the chapters of this book, and ultimately led to many of the bitterest debates of the confessional era being waged over the territory of early Church history. The Reformation also engaged with the Northern European Renaissance in a particularly complex fashion. History was a defining discipline for the Renaissance humanists, one in which they displayed their most characteristic approaches and ideals.[1] The reformers were in some senses humanists and in others anti-humanists: the tension between secular, humane, political explanations for the outcomes of human affairs and divine, providential, apocalyptic explanations for those same outcomes played itself out in their writings over the sixteenth century. This chapter will analyse Protestant Church histories in the light of the shifting relationship between humanist and confessional values as seen in texts from both the Lutheran and the Swiss reformed (Zwinglian) traditions. Humanism influenced both Lutheran and reformed traditions in complex ways, and in tracing humanist influence in these different historiographies it is important not to expect clear-cut distinctions. The ideals of the Renaissance remained always one ingredient in a complex mix, always present but rarely discernible in a pure form.[2]

---

[1] See Cochrane, *Historians and Historiography, passim.*
[2] Fueter, *Historiographie*, sometimes presupposes a clearer and more uniform concept of 'humanism' than the sources support.

1. INTRODUCTION

The rhetorical architecture of Renaissance Christian humanism rested on the foundational belief that the oldest and most primitive expression of something represented its essential and perfect form. Humanist rhetoric, therefore, implied a critique of the centuries between biblical and modern times. That critique addressed not just the collapse of the Roman Empire and the breach in cultural continuity with antiquity that ushered in the *medium aevum*. It also challenged the subsequent centuries of accumulated tradition, the organic development of medieval thought between the rise of scholasticism in the twelfth century and the humanist literary movement of the fifteenth century. In classical literature, it meant doing away with the extracts, *florilegia*, and encyclopaedias, and returning to the text in its pristine integrity. In Christianity, it led religious commentators, most famously Erasmus of Rotterdam, to criticize or satirize activities that had grown up over time within the Church. Those activities, humanists argued, led people away from ethical life in community; they encouraged sinful pride in difference and exotic skills, whether the self-conscious distinctiveness of monastic orders or the arcane mysteries of academic theology.

Like the Christian humanists, the leaders of the European Reformation argued that much of medieval Christian practice had little or no justification in Scripture or correct theology. The primitive Church, the *fons et origo* of the Christian life, represented the touchstone by which later developments were to be evaluated and (mostly) found wanting. The oldest and purest form of Christianity was the best.[3] In this sense the Reformation embodied humanist historical sensibilities from its very inception. Yet the relationship between Renaissance critical values and Reformation theology was not merely one of simple analogy or dependence. First, many reformers passed through the two movements of thought within their careers, and it is often difficult to discern where the humanist ended and the religious reformer began.[4] Some Reformation historians have identified a 'humanist Reformation' alongside, and distinct from, the Lutheran one. They note Huldrych Zwingli's taste for humanist literary flourishes, and his commitment to biblical scholarship, and construe the Swiss movement as a 'humanist' version of the Reformation.[5] If this argument implies that Martin Luther lacked humanist culture, it cannot hold; Luther shared with his generation in the humanist culture of the

---

[3] See Melanchthon quoting Tertullian in Carion, *Chronicon Carionis*, p. 3; Bullinger, *De origine erroris* (1539), fols. 3ᵛ–4ᵛ.

[4] See e.g. Bonorand, *Vadians Weg vom Humanismus zur Reformation*.

[5] See e.g. Léonard, *History of Protestantism*, I, pp. 129–82: ch. 4 is entitled 'Lutheranism Checked by the Humanist Reformation'.

Northern Renaissance.[6] As a way of highlighting different theological emphases, however, this argument can be helpful. 'Humanist reformers' such as Zwingli are sometimes plausibly alleged to have different theological priorities from their Lutheran counterparts, more focused on ethics and less on dogma. To explain these differences, some scholars claim that Lutheranism arose as a product of late scholasticism and the Swiss Reformation as an outgrowth of humanism.[7] Others discern a chronological shift in later sixteenth-century Protestant thought, from a Renaissance humanist world-view employing more rhetorical and literary modes of thought, towards a more dogmatic outlook emphasizing particular reformed confessions, supported by a rediscovered scholasticism. Theological precision took over from the rhetoric of exhortation. This was, of course, quite ironic given the initial hostility to scholastic theology shared by humanists and reformers alike.

Protestant history was always 'ecclesiastical history', the history of the *ecclesia*, the congregation, the community living its religious life. One rarely if ever finds the term '*historia sacra*' in the writings of the first generations of reformers. By the time that Friedrich Spanheim the Younger (1632–1701) published his *Introduction to Sacred Chronology and History, Especially Christian* (1683) the term 'ecclesiastical history' had long been standard in the Protestant world, and would remain so.[8] This choice of terms was not accidental. The reformers rejected the notion that anything in human life could be made 'sacred' or imbued with holy properties through association with religion. God consecrated everything in creation, and nothing could be made more holy than it already was.[9] 'Sacred history' carried, for the early reformers, the unacceptable connotation that the things and people located in the world of the clergy were more holy, more worthy of respect, closer to God than the rest. The reformers still had a very high estimation of ecclesiastical history and its place in the scheme of human knowledge, as will be seen. However, it was not 'sacred'.

The core message of the Reformation called for a shift in perceptions of the Christian past. In the reformers' eyes, Catholic theologians had for several centuries been asking the wrong question about human salvation. Medieval thinkers had analysed minutely how God might cleanse and purify a sinful human soul sufficiently to make it fit to be saved. For Martin Luther and those who followed his arguments, the whole point was that God did not purify the soul in order to accept it. God chose out of pure grace and for Christ's sake to

---

[6] Spitz, *Luther and German Humanism*, *passim*; for humanist influences on the younger Luther, see Dost, *Renaissance Humanism in Support of the Gospel*.

[7] McGrath, *Intellectual Origins of the European Reformation*.

[8] Spanheimius, *Introductio ad chronologiam et historiam sacram*. Spanheim's interest lay in biblical history and geography, which could be called '*sacra*' without ambivalence.

[9] Cameron, *Enchanted Europe*, pp. 196–204.

accept the soul in spite of its continuing and fatal impurities.[10] Righteousness before God came through trust in a divine gift of grace, apprehended in knowing, conscious faith. The duty of the Church was, and should always have been, to proclaim grace, not to mediate purification. Insofar as the Church had sought to achieve such purification through 'good works', it had betrayed the Gospel. Its ceremonies, performed mysteriously in an arcane language, had lacked the essential element of teaching informed faith. After the Reformation, the Church was no longer a single organic entity linked mysteriously to the heavenly economy; it needed neither a single centralized organization on earth, nor a separate caste of clergy governed by distinct laws. The individual churches of each political entity were local manifestations of the one universal and invisible Church. Their ministers were specialist servants drawn from the community, not separate from it.[11]

This theological re-envisioning diametrically reversed—and in due course condemned—the definitive achievements of the medieval papacy and Latin Catholicism. To the reformers, the ritual and legal separation of clergy from laity, derived from the eleventh-century Gregorian movement and consolidated in the codification of medieval canon law, had illicitly divided clerics from the community and assigned them a political superiority contrary to the Gospel. Sacramental absolution and penance in the life of the Christian, made definitive by Innocent III (1198–1216), had blasphemed the cross of Christ and corrupted the theology of grace. The claims of the papacy to supranational authority and universal monarchy, vigorously promoted by Boniface VIII (1294–1303), though not original to him, embodied an unchristian misunderstanding of ministry. How had the Church's leadership managed for so long to err so egregiously about the fundamental truths of salvation and the proper means to approach God? What was the relationship between the visible hierarchy, where such error and political pride had reigned, and the eternal, unfailing but also invisible congregation of the faithful? Theological error now was no longer external to the Church; it was the foe that had reigned in the citadel of Christendom for centuries. The true Church had to be sought somewhere other than in the papacy; and the apparently ruinous defection of so much of the Christian polity had to be explained.

In the early sixteenth century it was axiomatic that history should be written in the manner of classicizing Renaissance humanism. History formed a branch of rhetoric, a moral discipline dedicated to humane improvement through exemplary narrative. It drew upon inspirational and canonical classical models. The first generation of Florentine humanist historians, writers such as Leonardo Bruni (1370–1444) and Flavio Biondo (1392–1463), endowed historical writing with certain characteristics that sat particularly *badly* with the

---

[10] See Cameron, *European Reformation*, pp. 121–3 and references.
[11] See ibid., pp. 144–55 and references.

theological dilemmas of the early Reformation. Renaissance history was about human events, political life, and the individual actors who determined its outcomes. It typically adopted a secular rather than providential approach to the unfolding of human affairs. It tended to be monographic rather than universal in its approach, avoiding multi-century or epoch-defining approaches.[12] In some forms it eliminated religious questions and events altogether. In some instances (for instance, if one can admit the *Commentaries* of Pius II as historical writing) Renaissance historiography analysed the Church and its leadership as just another group of political actors engaged in the perennial quest for influence, power, control, and wealth.[13] Humanist historiography supplied no models for a narrative of 'salvation history', or for the explanation of the grand-scale theological defection of the medieval Church. Moreover, the prevailing model for ecclesiastical history, derived from Eusebius of Caesarea (*c.*265–339/40) and his continuators, suited the reformers even less well. It stressed the permanence of the Catholic Church through the succession of its hierarchy: that hierarchy determined the authenticity and continuity of true doctrine. In other words, Christian doctrine was true and orthodox *because* it was conserved by a continuous succession of bishops.

The historians of the Reformation therefore had to reimagine their discipline. This chapter charts the quest of early Protestant historians for adequate approaches to their craft. It has long been recognized that Reformation Church history grew out of the Protestant forms of Renaissance humanism.[14] On the other hand, by the late sixteenth century there emerged a historical literature more driven by doctrine, more theologically focused in its sense of chronology, more concerned to integrate the apocalypse and the ultimate destiny of human events into the cosmic drama of God, the created order, and the end of history. The humanist-inspired and doctrinal-apocalyptic approaches, moreover, did not remain in any sense independent of or isolated from each other.[15] However, slight differences of rhetoric and emphasis may be detected between the most and the least humanist-inspired of these commentators. The earliest historians responded to the elemental issue of the defection of the medieval Church in two different ways. The first approach emphasized human fallibility. It took responsibility for the cumulative process of error and deviation from first principles. It stressed how some modes of the religious life may have begun with good intentions, and then deteriorated over time. It tended to value the ethical over the doctrinal. It appealed to a sympathetic understanding of human nature.

---

[12] Cochrane, *Historians and Historiography*, pp. 3–9.

[13] Pius II, *Commentarii rerum memorabilium*, e.g. pp. 443ff.

[14] Fueter, *Historiographie*; and Scherer, *Geschichte und Kirchengeschichte, passim.*

[15] Despite the sometimes rigid characterizations in Fueter, *Historiographie* of writers as derived from or independent of humanism.

The second approach, which appeared somewhat later than the first, belonged typically to the dogmatic, scholastic mode of Reformation historical thinking. According to this view, so long as the Church maintained purity of belief it remained true to its mission and its heritage. Once the primordial teachings of the Gospels and Epistles were diluted, then error reigned in the Church, and false pastors inspired by wrong teachings misled and misguided their flocks. In works written from this perspective, one typically reads much less about the gradual deterioration of things begun with good intentions, and much more about the fatal effects of Antichristian error. Bearing in mind that the two approaches are ideal types that never existed in pure forms, it is worth considering how each developed in the first decades of the Continental Reformation. To what extent did the 'human fallibility' approach derive from a Renaissance humanist-inspired historiography? Insofar as it did so, was it humanist because it was non-Lutheran, or simply because it appeared earlier? Conversely, did the dogmatic approach to error in the Church derive from one particular confessional perspective? Or did a typically 'Confessional age' approach transcend any one theological perspective? Such questions call for a sensitive response to the nuances of the texts. They also require that one evaluate the histories in the context of their authors' life and work. The rest of this chapter will explore the writings of several generations of Protestant historians, beginning in 1520s Switzerland, where humanist historical thought first emerged in the Continental Reformation.

2. EARLY SWISS CHURCH HISTORIANS

Concerted and comprehensive attempts to rewrite ecclesiastical history in the Reformation first appeared between the 1550s and the 1570s. Earlier essays in reformed historical writing tended to be smaller and monographic in character. One group of such earlier works, written in the late 1520s and 1530s in eastern Switzerland, is especially revealing for the transition from Renaissance to confessional approaches in historical writing. The authors in question were Joachim von Watt (1484–1551), better known as Joachim Vadian of St-Gallen; his younger contemporary Heinrich Bullinger (1504–75) of Zürich; and Vadian's younger protégé Johannes Kessler (c.1502–74). Their works represented the most 'humanistic', but also an early, experimental stage in the writing of Protestant Church historiography, before better-known writers set their stamp on the discipline. Vadian and Bullinger reflected at some length on the comparison between the Church of their day and the early Church. Bullinger sought to defend the extreme liturgical simplicity of the Swiss Reformation by citing the simplicity and purity of apostolic Church worship. Kessler, despite being a devoted friend and follower of Vadian and embracing many of his perspectives on the St-Gallen reformation, exemplified the dogmatic approach to the history of error more fully than his mentor.

Joachim Vadian had a more distinguished profile as a Renaissance humanist writer before his conversion to the Reformation than after it, at least in print.[16] At the University of Vienna he fell under the influence of the German humanist Conrad Celtis (1459–1508). Honoured as a poet laureate by the Habsburg Emperor Maximilian I in 1514, he studied medicine, geography, natural philosophy, and history. Returning home at the end of the 1510s, he was thrown into the controversies provoked by Zwingli's preaching in Zürich, and joined the cause of religious reform.[17] A learned layman and *Bürgermeister* with theological, medical, and literary education, Vadian led the Reformation process in St-Gallen without the help of any colleague of remotely equivalent learning. Johannes Kessler, his devoted follower, lacked his intellectual range. Vadian's political destiny was wrapped up in his home town; so was his scholarly output. He wrote a chronicle of the abbots of the great Benedictine abbey of St-Gallen, the abbey that he attempted without success to secularize. The chronicle presented the abbots as a diverse group of individuals, rather than the embodiment of a mistaken religious principle.[18] Most of Vadian's histories remained in manuscript in his lifetime. He did, however, publish with Johann Stumpf (1500–76) a history of the Swiss Confederation in 1547–8.[19]

Vadian published in 1534 a work of biblical geography, the *Epitome of the Three Parts of the World, Asia, Africa and Europe, Containing Descriptions . . . Especially of those Places which the Evangelists and Apostles Related*.[20] This work's reflections on Christian antiquity locate it delicately poised between Renaissance and Reformation. Vadian warned against claiming too much certainty in matters of Church history and tradition. When (if ever) did Peter and Paul visit Rome? The chronology made it improbable that Peter reached Rome much before Paul, or that they were the particular founders of the Church there.[21] Vadian then added, 'I do not say this with the desire to grudge this glory

---

[16] For Vadian's output in Latin classics, see e.g. *Strabi Fuldensis monachi, poetae . . . Hortulus* (Nuremberg, 1512); *P. Ovidii Nasonis artis amandi libri tres . . .* (Vienna, 1512); *C. Plinii Secundi praefatio in historiam mundi, ad Vespasianum* (Vienna, 1513); *Donati grammatici sive, ut alii volunt, Lactantii argumenta compendiaria in fabulas potiores Ovidianae metamorphosis . . .* (Vienna, 1513).

[17] Gordon, *Swiss Reformation*, pp. 89–92, 326–7; Rupp, *Frontiers of Reformation*, pp. 357–78. See also Bautz, *Biographisch-bibliographisches Kirchenlexikon*, article 'Vadian, Joachim'.

[18] Vadian, *Deutsche historische Schriften*. Vols. I and II comprise *Chronik der Aebte des Klosters St Gallen*, while vol. III contains *Fragment einer Römischen Kaisersgeschichte; Geschichte der fränkischen Könige; Epitome; Diarium*.

[19] Stumpf and Vadian, *Gemeiner loblicher Eydgnoschafft . . . Chronick*. As this work does not address Christian origins, it is not examined here.

[20] Vadian, *Epitome trium terrae partium*.

[21] Ibid., pp. 122–5.

to that city . . . rather I wish to advise the reader that it is quite a different thing to prove something from Scripture, than to confirm it with conjectures.'[22] Like a humanist, Vadian warned against pernicious certainty of one's own orthodoxy. He recalled how the heretical Donatists, whom Augustine (d. 430) had combated in the fourth century, believed that they alone were the true Church and despised all others 'just as the Anabaptists nowadays think that they alone are right'.[23] Augustine had argued that only those who were proved to be in error by Scripture should suffer legal penalties for their dissent; those penalties, moreover, ought to consist of money fines rather than anything worse.[24] Persecution should be moderate, and be ruled by *sola scriptura*. The Nicene Fathers could tolerate some level of error if it was not accompanied by malice, and modern theologians ought to follow the Fathers in this (allegedly) indulgent attitude. Instead 'nowadays distinguished and pious men are accused of heresy because of certain doctrines clearly found in the Scriptures, and by those whose opinions themselves seem nothing other than heresy'.[25] Vadian objected to the schismatic fastidiousness that divided Churches from each other over minor details. It was absurd to call the Armenians heretics because they differed from the Latins by not mixing water with wine in the Eucharist.[26] Catholics regarded the Greek Churches as schismatic at best, because they differed from the Roman Church in using leavened bread in the Eucharist or denying belief in Purgatory, or refused to recognize the pope as the successor to Peter and the Vicar of Christ.[27] Dissent over religious questions was always a bad idea, as the protracted Investiture Contest between eleventh- and twelfth-century popes and emperors had shown.[28] The tone of Vadian's rhetoric—praising flexibility not only in matters of ritual but even in lesser matters of doctrine—partook as much of his Erasmian as of his Reformation heritage.

Vadian, a married layman who served several times as *Bürgermeister* of a town dominated by a large Benedictine abbey, had every reason to take a negative view of monastic life. Yet in his historical writings he adopted a nuanced approach to the monastic vocation. Religious institutions often began with a good intention and then deteriorated. Vadian argued (not quite correctly) that monasteries arose under the sons of Constantine in the mid fourth century, after the deaths of the hermits Paul and Antony. Originally hermits had escaped to the desert to avoid persecution and to devote themselves to the Scriptures; thereafter monasteries were established to provide schools for the training of religious teachers in ascetic discipline and scriptural learning. Monks did not artificially distinguish themselves from other Christians, nor did they make perpetual vows. They could change their way of life as often as reason required: many thus trained became priests and bishops. They had no

[22] Vadian, *Epitome trium terrae partium*, p. 125.
[23] Ibid., p. 145.   [24] Ibid., pp. 145–6.   [25] Ibid., pp. 194–6.
[26] Ibid., p. 417.   [27] Ibid., pp. 422–6.   [28] Ibid., pp. 426–7.

rule of life besides the Scriptures.[29] The life of an anchorite, eremite, or monk, was pragmatic, modest, and not loaded with superfluous rules:

> At that time this novelty seemed tolerable, given that it was allowed for discipline and the preservation of learning, since they did not bind anyone to any of these so-called 'solemn vows' as they have today, they did not feign constant fasting, and took no notice of what clothing they went about in so long as it was decent . . . finally they were not vexatious to the Churches with mendicancy, let alone inflated with arrogance or pomposity.[30]

Basil of Caesarea (d. 379), the brother of Gregory of Nyssa, was celebrated (among other reasons) for the founding of monasteries, 'that is, schools in which, having cast aside the cares of the world, they might devote themselves to learning, good habits, decency and continence, the better to serve God and their neighbour'. Modern-day monks boasted of following Basil, but exhibited almost nothing of the true monastic vocation but the name: they were ignorant of Scripture and obsessed with their vows, habits, and fasts.[31]

Vadian criticized the futility and misdirected enthusiasm that he saw in modern monasticism, its misconceived claims to superiority and its mistaken pursuit of trivial objectives, rather than the theological error in a vow that claimed to place God under an obligation.[32] He drew naturally on the humanist language and values of his earlier years. These small observations typify a larger characteristic of Vadian's work. His history of the abbey and its abbots presented a political history in genuine Renaissance manner. He exemplified a critical and analytical approach to his sources long before such an approach was general. As Eduard Fueter observed, Vadian stands out as the most persuasive example of how an early humanist historian north of the Alps could apply humanist critical principles to religious material.[33]

Heinrich Bullinger's *Origin of Error*, published in 1539 though based on work started years earlier, offers instructive comparisons with Vadian's work. The two reformers were friends; Vadian included a long dedicatory letter to Bullinger in the *Epitome*.[34] Both based their apologetic on historical arguments. Bullinger wrote a tendentious history of the Swiss Reformation, which

---

[29] Ibid., pp. 187–8.

[30] Ibid., p. 189.

[31] Vadian cited Filelfo's translation of Basil's *On the Solitary Life* addressed to Gregory Nazianzen, where Basil explained the true purpose of being a monk. See also Vadian, *Epitome*, pp. 433ff. Compare *Subnotata hic continentur: Magni Athanasij in psalmos opusculum . . .* (Strasbourg: Mathias Schürerius, 1508), pp. 76–84: 'Basilij epistola: de vita solitaria ad Gregorium Nazanzenum [*sic*] per Franciscum Philelphum e Graeco traducta'.

[32] Compare *The Judgement of Martin Luther on Monastic Vows* in Luther, *Luther's Works*, XLIV, pp. 243–400.

[33] Fueter, *Historiographie*, pp. 218–20.

[34] Vadian, *Epitome*, pp. 3–18.

like several of Vadian's works long remained unpublished.[35] However, whereas Vadian wrote as a humanist converted to reformed theology, Bullinger, who
spent his entire adult life in the service of the Zürich reformation, conveys the
impression of a theological reformer who ornamented his work with scholarly
flourishes.[36] *On the Origin of Error* challenged two Catholic customs particularly offensive to the reformers: the cult of saints and the liturgical elaboration
of the Eucharist.[37]

In the history of the early Church, Bullinger was confident, the primitive
form was invariably the best and the ideal. To 'reform' something was to
restore it to its pristine character, before the depravations produced by error
and mischief. Historical Christianity consistently lapsed from the better to the
worse.[38] In remote antiquity people had recognized and worshipped the one
God: over time their primitive monotheism lapsed into polytheism, and from
polytheism idolatry and the cult of images developed.[39] Echoing Vadian,
Bullinger argued that the monastic life began among those escaping persecution in the desert, but gradually degraded: 'religious practice generated wealth,
and the daughter devoured her mother: that is, wealth drove out devotion and
introduced self-indulgence'.[40] This narrative of primitive simplicity and decline also informed Bullinger's account of the cult of saints and the Catholic
Mass. Jesus must have blessed the Last Supper in the simplest possible way.
Subsequently the Apostles gathered together, preached the Gospel, offered
prayers, and broke bread. Cyprian of Carthage (d. 258) and other Fathers
preserved and transmitted a brief, simple Eucharistic prayer, which Bullinger
believed was used up to the time of Augustine.[41] Even Bartolomeo Platina
(1421–81), in the *Lives of the Popes*, admitted that successive popes had added
more and more items to the celebration of the Eucharist, though Bullinger
regarded the attribution of liturgical elements to particular popes as
mythical.[42]

Bullinger deployed a second argument about decline in early Christianity,
one sometimes attributed to the Enlightenment but actually found in the
Reformation.[43] Many customs mistakenly introduced into Christian worship
and belief were meant to make it easier for former pagans to adjust to

---

[35] Bullinger, *Bullingers Reformationsgeschichte*.

[36] On Bullinger, see Gordon, *Swiss Reformation*, esp. discussion of his historical writings on
pp. 322–3. See also Gordon and Emidio Campi (eds.), *Architect of Reformation: An Introduction
to Heinrich Bullinger, 1504–1575*.

[37] Bullinger, *De origine erroris* (1539). See also Bullinger, *De origine erroris in negocio
Eucharistiae ac missae* (1528) and *De origine erroris, in diuorum ac simulachrorum cultu* (1529).

[38] Bullinger, *De origine erroris* (1539), fols. 3^v–4^v.

[39] Ibid., fols. 33^r–45^r.

[40] Ibid., fols. 54^v–56^r.

[41] Ibid., fols. 202^r–205^r.

[42] Ibid., fols. 209^r–215^v.

[43] Brown, *The Cult of the Saints*, discusses this argument.

Christianity after the time of Constantine. The custom of offering prayers for the dead in the Mass derived not from the Apostles but from the Fathers: those Fathers had admitted the practice as a means to drive out the memory of the pagan *parentalia*, 'so as more conveniently with one key to push out another'.[44] The need to accommodate recently converted pagans manifested itself even more clearly in the rise of the cult of saints and their images. Bullinger quoted one of the earliest descriptions of a Christian image, where Eusebius told the story told about two statues which stood in Caesarea, representing respectively the woman cured from hemorrhages and Jesus reassuring her.[45] (Eusebius had actually implied that these statues were thank-offering images made by a 'Gentile', like those made and dedicated to tutelary gods in classical paganism.) Images at that time, Bullinger insisted, were private property and were not placed in Churches, far less were they prayed to. They resembled the 'icons' of the reformers used in Bullinger's own time, memorials kept out of admiration and affection, not cult-objects to worship.[46] Here the leader of the most iconophobic Church in the entire Reformation approved of the portraiture later found in Theodore Beza's *Icones*.[47]

Bullinger, however, distinguished sharply between the memorial or peda-gogical use of images and idolatry. The worship of saints and their images among Christians, he argued, resembled the pagan worship of idols.[48] Like pagan gods, Christian saints cared for particular animals, diseases, arts and crafts, and indeed all different sorts of people. Agatha took care of fire in place of Vesta; Nicholas cared for sailors in place of Castor and Pollux; 'instead of Venus and Flora people turn to Afra and Magdalene, even if they have no thought of changing their lives'.[49] Images, temples, sacrifices, feasts, and offerings found among Christians and pagans bore comparison one with another, as Bullinger demonstrated with an unexpected display of classical erudition.[50]

As Bruce Gordon has observed, Bullinger cited the Fathers of the Church extensively but often selectively.[51] The later the Church Father, the more likely it was that a reformed theologian would find error in his writings. The worst of all the Latin Fathers, on most issues, was Gregory the Great (d. 604). Augus-tine could be cited with approval when he stressed that the commemoration of martyrs was an act of remembrance only, or when he said that 'we do not raise

---

[44] Bullinger, *De origine erroris* (1539), fols. 221^v–223^v.
[45] Eusebius, *History of the Church*, ed. Louth, bk 7.18, pp. 233–4.
[46] Bullinger, *De origine erroris* (1539), fols. 113^v–114^v.
[47] de Bèze, *Icones*.
[48] Bullinger, *De origine erroris* (1539), fols. 160^{v}ff.
[49] Ibid., fols. 164^v–167^r.
[50] Ibid., fols. 167^{v}ff. Erasmus, *Praise of Folly*, sections 40–1; also Luther, *Decem praecepta*, sig. C iv^r, for similar arguments.
[51] Gordon, *Swiss Reformation*, p. 186.

altars to the martyrs, nor do we offer them sacrifices'.[52] When Cyprian described the simplest of Eucharistic rites he was cited with approval as an authority. When Augustine stated that there was no miracle around the consecration of the Eucharist, he became a welcome ally against the doctrine of transubstantiation.[53] However, when Augustine and Jerome argued that the saints in heaven must be expected to hear the prayers of their devotees and respond to them. Bullinger argued them down with scant respect.[54] Here, as throughout his writings in general, Bullinger placed the needs of theological reform and doctrinal purity above the consistent application of humanist scholarly principles.

If Bullinger was somewhat more doctrinaire than Vadian, our third Swiss writer, Johannes Kessler of St-Gallen, was still more so. Kessler rose from a minor player in the Swiss Reformation to become, in the last years of his life, an important pedagogue, preacher and church administrator in his town. Before Vadian diverted him to school teaching, he worked as a saddler and wrote his historical work on days of rest: hence the title of his history of the St-Gallen reformation, *Sabbata*.[55] Because Kessler worked under Vadian's shadow, it is striking to observe differences between the older and the younger writer in their approach to error in the Church. Kessler introduced his history of the St-Gallen reformation with two 'epitomes' (echoing Vadian's use of the term), one on Christ and one on the papacy. By the latter he meant the entire rise of medieval Catholicism, summed up in the impact of papal government on the life of the Church.[56]

Compared to Vadian or even Bullinger, Kessler took a providentialist approach to salvation history. Christianity was (as Eusebius had said) the most ancient monotheism, the faith revealed to the patriarchs and prophets.[57] The Old Testament prophets had foretold the coming of Christ, and the ceremonies of the Mosaic law were provisional until Christ came. The Reformation was also predicted by latter-day prophets. The Bohemian reformer Jan Hus (burned as a heretic in 1415) had foretold the coming of a swan a century after his goose was cooked.[58] Critics of the clergy from within the Church foresaw its downfall.[59] Prophecies from Daniel onwards predicted the rise and downfall of Antichrist, explicitly identified with the papacy in Kessler's rhetoric.[60]

---

[52] Bullinger, *De origine erroris* (1539), fols. 57ᵛ, 61ᵛ.
[53] Ibid., fols. 239ᵛ–40ʳ.
[54] Ibid., fols. 64ᵛ–70ᵛ.
[55] Kessler, *Sabbata*, p. 13.
[56] Ibid., pp. 18–27 and 28–62 respectively.
[57] Ibid., pp. 19ff.
[58] For Hus's prophecy, see Haberkern, "'After Me There Will Come Braver Men'".
[59] Kessler, *Sabbata*, pp. 8–13.
[60] Ibid., pp. 23ff.

Kessler agreed with Vadian and Bullinger about the gradual change and decline of the Church from its primitive purity. The papacy grew progressively in its pretensions to authority over other churches and the grandeur and pomp of its activities. Kessler cited Flavio Biondo to the effect that Boniface III (whose pontificate in 607 lasted less than a year) was the first pope to be called *papa*, or *pater patrum*.[61] The papacy gained political influence by supplanting the Merovingians with the Carolingians.[62] Like Vadian, Kessler argued that monasticism began as an informal means for devout Christians to be educated away from the distractions of everyday life; only over time did it acquire set rules, perpetual vows, distinctive clothing, and the sectarian exceptionalism of each order.[63] With Bullinger, Kessler pointed out that the Mass grew over time as successive popes added prayers and canticles to the original simple rite.[64]

But Kessler adopted a more deeply doctrinal view than Vadian or Bullinger of the origins of abuse and error in the life of the Church. The fundamental problem with the medieval Church was the proliferation of ceremonies; the source of that proliferation lay in the claims of the papacy and hierarchy. Kessler cited Luther's *To the Christian Nobility* for its concept of 'walls' erected around the clergy to protect them from reform.[65] Three fundamental theological errors drove the growth in ceremonies. First, the papacy claimed that the popes, cardinals, and hierarchy constituted the Church, and that they could therefore add new ceremonies as they thought fit (such as the elaboration of the Mass).[66] Secondly, like 'Pharisees and Pelagians', they claimed that people had free will to earn merit before God. From this erroneous premise derived auricular confession, works of satisfaction, and the 'fable' of purgatory, 'the priests' kitchen'.[67] Thirdly, the error arose that people needed mediators and patrons besides Christ: thus grew up not only the cult of saints, but also the idea of specialist saints and travelling preachers offering protection from their saint's specific illness.[68] Kessler ended with a series of complaints against the wickedness of canon law that closely echoed Luther's *To the Christian Nobility*.[69]

Within this compact group of friends, then, one observes distinct, albeit overlapping, approaches to the historical dilemma of a Church fallen away from the intentions of its first Apostles. All three thinkers embodied humanist influence, but in Kessler, the humanist notion that even the best Christians could fall victim to errors over time gave way to a doctrinally driven view in which error inevitably generated wrong religion. In both Lutheran and reformed worlds, the future certainly belonged to Kessler's more dogmatic approach. But one way of thinking did not simply supplant the other

---

[61] Ibid., p. 31.   [62] Ibid., pp. 32–5.   [63] Ibid., pp. 38–42.
[64] Ibid., pp. 43–4.   [65] Ibid., pp. 34–5.   [66] Ibid., pp. 43ff.
[67] Ibid., pp. 47–50.   [68] Ibid., pp. 57ff.   [69] Ibid., pp. 59ff.

inexorably throughout Reformation Europe. That Vadian's supple humanism and Kessler's more dogmatic approach appeared in the works of two Zwinglian Swiss reformers so close together in time, and with even closer personal ties, should call into question any explanation of this ideological difference as a simple matter of Swiss vs. German, or Zwinglian vs. Lutheran, let alone early vs. late Reformation thinking. At this early stage, there may well have been two contemporary and parallel approaches at work, one humanist and one dogmatic. An age gap between older humanists and younger, more theologically absolute writers may also help to explain the differences to some degree. The simplicity and naivety of style seen in Kessler's writings disguise the complex parentage of his ideas. Although he came from the heartland of Zwinglian Switzerland, Kessler had studied at Wittenberg between 1522 and 1523 and was deeply influenced by Luther and his writings. If Kessler's ideas display multiple approaches, one should expect no less diversity and complexity in the Church histories which appeared in the context of German Lutheranism in the years after 1550.

3. CHURCH HISTORIES IN GERMANY IN THE LATER SIXTEENTH CENTURY

By the 1550s Church history emerged as a distinct discipline in the Protestant world. Full-scale world histories integrated the history of the Church with the story of the created order, its social and political systems, and grand-scale movements of empires and kingdoms. These general histories incorporated the emerging Reformation narrative, by which the Church began in simplicity and purity, only to be gradually corrupted by the elaboration of ritual, the overlaying of teaching with error, and the accumulation of political power. The lines between Renaissance-humanist and dogmatic-apocalyptic strains in Reformation historical thought became progressively blurred. However, humanist influences continued to play a critical role in shaping the form and manner of Protestant Church history. Nearly all the major exponents of the genre owed some debt to humanism. One of the first major historical works to emerge from Protestantism, though it did not speak directly to Christian origins, deserves mention. The *Commentaries on the State of Religion and the Commonwealth* of Johann Sleidan (1506–56) first appeared in 1555.[70] Sleidan, to the exasperation of contemporaries, refused to present Reformation history as the history of doctrine, completely ignoring some of Luther's

---

[70] Sleidanus, *Commentarii*.

most important writings.[71] A Strasbourg Protestant pulled between Lutheran Wittenberg and reformed Zürich, he prudently hedged his bets by stressing the underlying agreement between reformers and minimizing the tensions between the different traditions.[72] Even the bitter sacramental strife between Wittenberg and Zürich was played down in his account.[73] Sleidan wrote a political history of religious events: neither the criteria for right action, nor the marks of a genuinely Christian community, were defined in doctrinal terms. Theologians were not the heroes of the story; their disagreements risked disaster. If anything, the marks of a Church were defined by its conformity with the norms of the secular political community. Those reform movements which worked in concord with the magistrates and ensured civic stability earned his approval; those which did not, such as the Zwickau prophets, Müntzer and Pfeiffer, or the Anabaptists, earned little but scorn and hostile tale-telling.[74] Sleidan, in short, approached Reformation affairs as one would expect a civic humanist historian to do.[75]

In the Lutheran movement, Renaissance scholarly impulses manifested themselves especially among Luther's friend Philipp Melanchthon (1497–1560) and his circle. Melanchthon, who exerted influence at Wittenberg as an educator even more than as a theologian and exegete, strenuously resisted the pressure for biblical theology to supplant all other intellectual inquiry at Wittenberg.[76] He rehabilitated and refashioned much of the rest of the curriculum to conform to, or at least not to contradict, the norms of Lutheran theology.[77] However, history consumed most of the energies of Philipp and the Philippists from the 1550s onwards.[78] Scholars taught by Melanchthon produced a series of handbooks, accompanied by essays on the theology of history in general and Church history in particular.[79] They tried to integrate the history of the Christian Church into a larger vision of universal history. The breadth of this vision sacrificed the monographic and politically focused narrative chosen by classical historians, the Italian humanists, and even by Sleidan. In other respects, however, the Philippist vision extended the trends of Renaissance historiography.

---

[71] Vogelstein, *Sleidan's Commentaries*, pp. 64ff, 69ff.

[72] Kess, *Sleidan and the Protestant Vision*, pp. 89–119. For this period in Strasbourg's history see Abray, *People's Reformation*.

[73] Sleidanus, *Commentarii*, preface and fols. 18ʳ, 36ᵛ, 39ʳ, 44ʳ⁻ᵛ; compare Sleidanus, *General History*, pp. 22, 48, 51, 57, 97ff; cf. p. 141 for later coverage of the Eucharistic debate.

[74] Sleidanus, *General History*, pp. 52, 83ff, 110.

[75] Fueter, *Historiographie*, pp. 202–3.

[76] Melanchthon, *Melanchthons Briefwechsel*, nos. 237 (T1, 492), 258 (T2, 57–8), 273 (T2, 63–4); cf. also 330, (T2, 144–5), 342 (T2, 178).

[77] Kusukawa, *Transformation of Natural Philosophy, passim.*

[78] Scherer, *Geschichte und Kirchengeschichte*, pp. 49–51.

[79] See Major, *Vitae patrum* and *De origine et autoritate verbi Dei*; Flinsbachius, *Confirmatio chronologiae*; Chytraeus, *Chronologia historiae*; Pezel, *Mellificium*.

The largest and most complex monument to Philippist world history was the massive Latin translation and rewriting of Johannes Carion's *Chronicle*. This work began as a German chronicle compiled by the astrologer Johannes Carion (1499–1537), a near contemporary and possibly a student of Melanchthon.[80] In the 1550s, Melanchthon began completely to rewrite the work in Latin. Carion's name remained as an act of *pietas*. Melanchthon wrote the preface to the first two parts in 1558 but died before the revision was complete. His son-in-law Caspar Peucer (1525–1602) took up the task and completed the revision of the entire work, extending it to the year 1517, for the edition of 1572.[81]

The *Chronicle* was structured around the four empires of antiquity, as understood according to sixteenth-century readings of the prophecy in Daniel 2.[82] Biblical historians inferred that God ordained the monarchies of antiquity to be the supreme rulers of the known world, then cast them down and replaced them, perhaps within predictable terms of years.[83] Framing world history within the structure of the four great empires allowed historians to integrate the histories of Greek, and later Roman antiquity into the picture while affirming that the Pentateuch was older than either.[84] Archaic Greece appeared briefly under the first monarchy of the Assyrians/Babylonians; classical Greece and early Rome under the second, that of the Persians. With the third monarchy of the Macedonians, Seleucids, and Ptolemies, canonical Hebrew Scripture largely gave out, to be supplemented by Roman history and Josephus's *Antiquities* as sources.[85]

A primary objective for Carion, Peucer, and later Philippist historians was to assign to a single sequence of dates the historical records of the various cultures of known antiquity. The Philippist-trained Rostock professor David Chytraeus (1531–1600), in his *Chronology of the Histories of Herodotus and Thucydides*, would integrate biblical, classical, and modern Church history into a coherent sequence.[86] Consequently, great effort was expended in tracking events against a scale of years since creation, and in due course since the

---

[80] Carion, *Chronica*.

[81] Carion, *Chronicon Carionis*.

[82] Ibid., Melanchthon's preface, p. 2; compare also Sleidanus, *De quatuor summis imperiis*; Chytraeus, *Chronologia historiae*, sig. B 1^{r–v}.

[83] See Caspar Peucer's preface to *Chronicon Carionis* at sig. a iii^{r}.

[84] See *Chronicon Carionis*, pp. 49ff for the Trojan War; Pezel's *Oratio* in *Chronicon Carionis*, sig. B iii^{r–v}; Chytraeus, 'De lectione historiarum recte instituenda', in *Chronologia historiae*, sig. B 6^{r}.

[85] *Chronicon Carionis*, pp. 11–143. This interpretation of the four monarchies (the last is the Roman) is not favoured by modern exegetes. Davies, 'Daniel Chapter Two', argues that the dream depicts Nebuchadnezzar and his successors, and the decline of the Babylonian monarchy.

[86] Chytraeus, *Chronologia historiae*. Chytraeus converted to Gnesio-Lutheran beliefs late in his career. See P. F. Barton in *Theologische Realenzyklopaedie*, VIII (Berlin: de Gruyter, 1981), p. 88.

founding of Rome and the birth of Jesus. There was little agreement over the precise age of the world at the birth of Christ: most claimed that it was something like 3,950–75 years old at the start of the Common Era.[87] Within each era, the Chronicle followed the classical and Eusebian organization by kings and emperors, including (after the fall of the Western Roman Empire) the Frankish kings and later the Holy Roman Emperors. Later on sequential chapters named after Western emperors alternated with grouped sequences of the Byzantine emperors, and with sections entitled 'on the Church'.[88]

On one hand the Philippists sought to integrate biblical and ecclesiastical history into the general history of the known world. Melanchthon and his pupils loved to quote from Thucydides that since human nature is the same, similar things will happen always.[89] Human explanations for cause and effect—the very essence of humanist historiography—always stood in the foreground. On the other hand, the Philippists also had a strong sense of what they called 'ecclesiastical' history, which included Old Testament and salvation history from the creation onwards. Melanchthon presented a functional philosophy of Church history in the 1558 preface that he wrote for Carion's *Chronicle*. History offered a source of reassurance and explanation additional to the Scriptures. Melanchthon found it comforting to read even in the very earliest ante-Nicene Fathers statements about the *logos* that anticipated Nicene orthodoxy. It was even more useful to see how wrong decisions had been made, such as those about papal authority, the 'adoration of dead people', the carrying of the Eucharist in procession, and clerical celibacy. Early Church history as well as Scripture could discredit such things.

Church history also offered global insights that seemed to draw more on humanist observations about human nature than on dogmatic or providentialist thinking. The two 'empires' of the declining age of the world, Islam and the Papal Monarchy, both arose because of disputes and weakness in Christianity. Islam arose when the Eastern Churches were so distracted by disagreements over doctrine that they allowed space for Muhammad's ideas.[90] As Melanchthon pointed out later, Islam enjoyed the advantage of a strong social ethic while it eschewed difficult doctrines of the kind that alienated believers

---

[87] *Chronicon Carionis*, p. 147: note differences with Chytraeus, *Chronologia historiae*, pp. 383ff, and Pantaleon, *Chronographia*, sig. A 2ᵛ, which lists different estimates of the date of Christ's birth in years since creation. For chronological tabulation, compare Chytraeus, *Chronologia historiae*, pp. 215ff, 259ff.

[88] Sections headed '*de Ecclesia*' figure e.g. in *Chronicon Carionis*, pp. 58ff, 187ff, 231ff, 259ff, 502ff, 616ff, 701ff.

[89] *Chronicon Carionis*, p. 187; see also Pezel's *Oratio* in *Chronicon Carionis*, sig. b iiᵛ; Chytraeus, *Chronologia historiae*, sig. B 5ʳ.

[90] *Chronicon Carionis*, preface, pp. 3–4.

from Christianity.[91] The Papal Monarchy arose because the popes exploited the Franks' distrust of the Greeks to persuade them to expel the representatives of the Eastern Empire from Italy in the eighth century. Then the popes established their own power at a time of political weakness and division. Melanchthon explained both the progress and the misfortunes of the Christian Church largely in terms of secular, human explanations.

Within the 1572 edition of the *Chronicle*, however, there also lay a more ideologically driven vision of Church history, one shaped by Philipp's pupils. The newly minted professor Christoph Pezel (1539–1604) contributed to the 1572 edition an *Oration on the Themes of History and the Benefits of Reading It*, originally delivered as a lecture at Wittenberg in 1568.[92] Pezel began with prayer to God to prove the truth of the reformed faith and the falsity of its enemies' accusations. He urged that there were two forms of history—ecclesiastical and secular—and that the former was much the superior. It showed the promises of grace as well as the severities of divine law and judgement. It was the oldest history, and the only one ornamented with miraculous testimonies of divine favour. In more emphatic tones than Melanchthon, Pezel argued that theologians needed to know:

> what errors slipped into the Church and when, and especially when this new form of doctrine was brought in, when these recent superstitions were received and established, that sacrifices should be made for the dead, and profaned against the institution of the sacrament of the Lord's Supper, and that dead people should be prayed to, and that admiration for the monastic order should be increased: from all of these things there grew the power of the Roman Pontiffs, initially increased by the generosity of the German Emperors, then by the Pontiffs' own deceit and violence.[93]

History should be read to sustain, support and defend true doctrine against its adversaries.

The stronger dogmatic bent of the younger Philippists manifested itself decisively in the later sections of the *Chronicle* prepared by Caspar Peucer, who took over for the third part of the *Chronicle*, from around the year 600 onwards. Peucer's preface bemoaned not only the terrible corruptions introduced into doctrine and worship, but also the depravation of the very sources of Church history by 'false, suppositious, tyrannous and impious decrees of recent canons' and the unreliable chronicles prepared by monks and papalists.[94] The papacy committed one cardinal sin from which many

---

[91] Ibid., pp. 275–9.

[92] Ibid., sig. b i[r]–b vi[v] includes Pezel's 'Oratio de argumento historiarum, et fructu petendo ex earum lectione, recitata in Academia VVitebergensi Anno M. D. LXVIII'.

[93] *Chronicon Carionis*, sig. b vi[r]. For praises of Church history, compare Chytraeus, *Chronologia historiae*, sig. B 7[v] [= p.13]ff.

[94] *Chronicon Carionis*, pp. 291–2.

other faults flowed: it set itself up as a political monarchy with legal jurisdiction, something quite alien to the true nature of Christian ministry.[95] Inevitably, that decision put the popes on a collision course with the emperors. Like other Protestant historians, Peucer assumed that the normal relationship between empire and papacy was hostility and rivalry.

Peucer divided the history of the Christian era before the Reformation into three periods of 500 years. In the first period, despite bitter controversies over doctrine, the apostolic legacy was retained and preserved, and the Church flourished even in persecution. The second (medieval) period manifested gradual and progressive deterioration: 'falsehood was mixed in with the truth, superstition with the pure faith, idolatry with the true worship of God . . . until eventually [the bad aspects] became prevalent and overwhelming'. In the remaining 500 years (from the Investiture Contest onwards) 'there matured and grew in the Church idolatry, superstition and ambition, especially that of the popes and bishops'. Doctrine, discipline, and the proper relationship of Church and State were all corrupted.[96] This periodization of the systemic decline and corruption of the Church showed close affinities with similar statements made by the English Protestant historian John Foxe in his 1570 preface to the *Acts and Monuments*.[97] The attempt to discern clear phases in the life of the Church also entailed speculations about prophecy and apocalyptic, and divine intervention in history. Peucer linked the Catholic Mass with the idol Maozim in Daniel 11:39.[98] The prophecies of Gog and Magog in Ezekiel 38–9 referred to the Turks.[99] Twice Peucer described the loss of the Eastern Churches as divine punishment for the idolatry of the Mass.[100]

In these rhetorical apostrophes and broad-brush condemnations Peucer more closely resembled his mortal enemy, the Gnesio-Lutheran Matthias Flacius Illyricus (1520–75), than his humanistic mentors. During the bitter intra-Lutheran strife that followed Luther's death, Flacius and his followers furiously denounced the conciliatory Interim that the Holy Roman Emperor had offered to Protestants at Augsburg in 1548, and any dilution (as they saw it) of the doctrinal claims of the Lutheran Gospel on justification and the Eucharist. Above all they denounced their *bête noire*, Philipp Melanchthon and all he stood for. This ironic resemblance between Peucer and Flacius increased when Peucer pointed out that in this time of degeneracy in the

---

[95] Ibid., pp. 347–51. Compare pp. 419–20.

[96] *Chronicon Carionis*, pp. 351–2. Compare pp. pp. 416–17, 419–20, 421–2, 703 for further references to periods.

[97] John Foxe, *The Acts and Monuments*, I (1570), Preface; see <http://www.johnfoxe.org/index.php?realm=text&edition=1570&gototype=modern>.

[98] *Chronicon Carionis*, e.g. pp. 367, 420.

[99] Ibid., p. 276; also p. 584.

[100] Ibid., pp. 368, 506.

Church, there remained a pious remnant who held on to a better doctrine.[101] People mistakenly imagined that the Church must always have consisted of the pope and the hierarchy. These were rather enemies to the Church: it truly consisted in 'those people who reproved and resisted the errors and abuses of the pontiffs, as did the prophets among the people of God, such as were Tauler, Wessel of Groningen, Jan Hus, Jerome of Prague, Hiltenius of Eisenach'.[102] More realistic than the Gnesio-Lutherans, Peucer did not pretend that all these people held perfectly correct beliefs. They held the truth mixed with varying degrees of error, but at least they resisted the prevailing system.[103]

The earlier humanistic approach of seeing error in the Church as the product of once reasonable decisions gone wrong did not entirely disappear in Peucer's work. Like Vadian, Peucer suggested that the monastic order began with a reasonable desire to move away from persecutions and distractions in order to study in peace; only over time was it corrupted into a system of works-righteousness. When monks abandoned education, the princes had to revive it by founding schools.[104] Like Bullinger, Peucer depicted the transition from the primitive Eucharist to the idolatrous sacrificial Mass as a gradual, piecemeal decline. The use of precious vessels began with Charlemagne; private Masses began under his son Louis the Pious (d. 840); in the twelfth century unleavened bread was specified, and laypeople were denied the wine.[105] However, Peucer's approach to Church history seemed to avoid fine detail. The ruling theological arguments—that papal monarchy traduced the role of ministry in the Church, that the Mass was an idol and an act of blasphemy, that medieval theology obliterated the true doctrine of justification—supplanted detailed narrative and occasionally made Peucer's writing repetitious.[106] Peucer lacked the patience to narrate the political acts of an institution of which he so profoundly disapproved on principle.

While writers like Peucer apparently began from humanist-informed historical premises and moved away from them as doctrinal needs dictated, others apparently approached the past with little or no reference to humanist models; instead they placed doctrinal considerations at the forefront from the very start.[107] Some inspiration for this approach came from Martin Luther

---

[101] Compare the discussion of Flacius's *Catalogue of Witnesses to the Truth* below.

[102] Johann Herwick from Ilten near Hanover, known as Hiltenius (d. *c*.1500) a Franciscan friar (though Kessler reported that he was a Carmelite) reputedly prophesied the Reformation when his own criticisms of the Church were suppressed.

[103] *Chronicon Carionis*, pp. 462-4.

[104] Ibid., pp. 418, 436ff.

[105] Ibid., pp. 367-8.

[106] See e.g. Peucer's condemnation of papal errors, ibid., pp. 508ff, which largely repeats points made earlier.

[107] Fueter, *Historiographie*, pp. 246ff: bk 3 is headed 'Die vom Humanismus unabhängige Geschichtschreibung'.

himself. When Robert Barnes (1495–1540) published his *Lives of the Roman Pontiffs* in 1536, a rather premature attempt to construct a Protestant history of the papacy from medieval sources, Luther contributed a preface.[108] Luther lamented the lack of good sources for Church history, and then reflected that perhaps this was just as well, since it threw the focus back on Christ rather than his followers. However, Satan had stepped in and supplied a host of spurious or imaginary saints. God in his wrath had allowed people to believe in these new doctrines. Finally 'Antichrist appeared in the temple of God with his saints' and taught everyone to worship them. This elevation of the pope into a god on earth and a 'foul analogue of the true Christ' might not have happened if good histories of the Church had been available. Luther was pleased to see that Barnes's new history proved, *a posteriori* as it were, what he had already demonstrated from Scripture.

Despite declaring that he was no historian, Luther in his controversial pamphlet *On Councils and the Churches* (1539) addressed historical issues in provocative ways.[109] He began from the premise, common to virtually all reformed thinkers, that the best and purest form of Christianity was found at the earliest date. But he had little time for the humanist notion that error was the inevitable result of good intentions degenerating gradually over time. Errors, in Luther's view, could and should have been avoided from the start. The sole true role of Church councils was to repress, in the name of unchanging correct doctrine, errors that from time to time arose to trouble the Church over the Trinity or the natures of Christ.[110] Bad practices grew up and flourished because councils failed to perform their task adequately. Church leaders were 'like lazy gardeners who permit the vines to grow so rampant that the old true tree has to suffer or perish'.[111] Luther, who knew monasticism, could not believe that it was *ever* useful for people to live in religious communities outside ordinary society. Under the lazy gardening of Church councils, the weeds grew higher than the plants. After Bernard 'it rained and snowed monks'.[112] For Luther, Christian practices and doctrines were to be judged by the all-important standard of justification by free grace alone, and the rejection of the notion of salvation through good works.

---

[108] Barnes, *Vitae Romanorum pontificum*: Luther's preface appears on sigs. A ii^r–A iiii^v. For detailed and sympathetic recent studies of Barnes's work in polemical religious history, see Korey D. Maas, *The Reformation and Robert Barnes: History, Theology and Polemic in Early Modern England* (Woodbridge, UK; Rochester, NY: Boydell & Brewer, 2010); Korey D. Maas, 'Scripture, History, and Polemic in the Early English Reformation: The Curious Case of Robert Barnes', *Reformation*, XIV (2009) 75–100.

[109] *On Councils and the Churches* is found in Luther, *Luther's Works*, XLI, pp. 5–177.

[110] *Luther's Works*, XLI, pp. 58, 85, 91, 104.

[111] Ibid., p. 126.

[112] Ibid., pp. 126–8.

It was the implacable controversialist Matthias Flacius Ilyricus, the first leader of the Gnesio-Lutheran movement, and also an indefatigable manuscript collector, who provided Lutheran Christianity with its first confessional school of Church history. During the wretched period of intra-Lutheran strife after Luther's death Flacius compiled his massive and compendious *Catalogue of Witnesses to the Truth: Who before Our Time Cried Out against the Pope*, which first appeared in 1556.[113] This work presented not so much a history as a collection of sources for one particular argument—that there had been abundant critics of the papal Church in the Middle Ages. The text was widely quoted and debated, and also appeared in an edition for the reformed ('Calvinist') market near the end of the century.[114]

Flacius Illyricus then embarked on a more ambitious collective project to write the entire history of the Western Church from this dogmatically Lutheran standpoint. Flacius, Johannes Wigand (1523–87), Matthaeus Judex (d. 1564), and others led a team of scholars to produce the work formally entitled *Ecclesiastical History, [which] deals with the whole image of the Church of Christ, as to place, propagation, persecution, tranquillity, doctrine, heresies, ceremonies, governance, schisms, synods, persons, miracles, testimonies, religious lives outside the Church, and the political condition of the Empire...* better known simply as the *Magdeburg Centuries*.[115] This colossal work covered one century per volume of the Christian era, and by the appearance of the last volume in 1574 had reached the thirteenth century. Despite its all-embracing title, the focus of the work was dogmatic and theological. The Philippist aim to integrate Church history into the broader sweep of world history, or to allow human explanations for human events, largely disappeared. The work was designed to show how true Lutheran doctrine emerged gradually from the morass of the medieval Church. However, the Centuriators' dogmatic stance overwhelmed their critical faculties. Spurious evidence was accepted if it portrayed the papacy or the hierarchy in a bad light (e.g. in the story of 'Pope Joan' or Pope Sylvester II's league with the Devil). If a miracle appeared to confirm Catholic claims, that was a 'false sign', bogus or demonic.[116] Inconvenient evidence, suggesting that medieval heretics might have held beliefs either too Catholic or too heretical for Lutheran orthodoxy, was explained away.

Ultimately the *Centuries* provided controversial theologians with quarries for disputation more than providing historians with models to follow. Unlike early humanist historians, the authors of the *Magdeburg Centuries* reduced peoples and movements to disembodied lists of beliefs and disbeliefs, without

---

[113] Flacius Illyricus, *Catalogus* (1556).
[114] Flacius Illyricus, *Catalogus*, ed. Goulart (1597) and later edn (1608).
[115] Flacius Illyricus et al., *Ecclesiastica historia*.
[116] Fueter, *Historiographie*, pp. 251ff.

contexts and often without personalities. Because of its massive size and its incomplete coverage of Church history, the text's usefulness for teaching in the universities proved limited.[117] However, the *Magdeburg Centuries* wielded great influence in other ways. Once again an edition appeared for the reformed ('Calvinist') market in the early seventeenth century.[118] Its influence can be seen in other Church histories of the confessional era, such as the works of Johann Hottinger in Zürich or the later editions of John Foxe's *Acts and Monuments* in England.[119] Perhaps the greatest impact of the *Centuries*, however, lay in the stimulus that this controversial and programmatic work gave to a Roman Catholic rebuttal. The *Annales ecclesiastici* of Cesare Baronio owed much to the ambition to disprove the claims of the Centuriators.[120]

Lutheran Church historians recognized that a more usable and compact history of the Church was required than the massive and incomplete *Centuries*. Johann Pappus, the defender of Lutheran orthodoxy in the Strasbourg *Gymnasium*, published his *Epitome of Church History* in 1584.[121] Pappus's *Epitome* focused on the early Church. Its three major sections dealt in turn with the calling of the peoples to Christianity, the early persecutions and martyrs, and the heresies and councils. Pappus obliquely likened modern heretics to their late-antique antecedents.[122] Fuller coverage of later centuries appeared in the recension of Pappus's work by Eusebius Bohemus (1626) and in Heinrich Kipping's extended edition of 1661–2.[123] Lucas Osiander the Elder (1534–1604) published a work that shared the same title of *Epitome of Church History* used by Pappus, but added the organization by 'centuries' found in the Magdeburg histories. This monumental work appeared in multiple volumes between 1592 and the author's death, and was reprinted immediately after. One volume covered the first three centuries of the Church; the fourth to eighth centuries received a volume each; then a large portmanteau volume addressed the ninth to the fifteenth centuries; a colossal final volume of 1,158 pages (published before the previous one) was devoted to the sixteenth century.[124]

[117] Scherer, *Geschichte und Kirchengeschichte*, pp. 127ff.

[118] Flacius Illyricus et al., *Historiae ecclesiasticae*.

[119] Fueter, *Historiographie*, pp. 253–9.

[120] On Baronio, see *Theologische Realenzyklopaedie*, XVIII (Berlin: de Gruyter, 1989), article 'Kirchengeschichtsschreibung', p. 542; Pullapilly, *Caesar Baronius*, and below, Ch. 3.

[121] Pappus, *Historiae ecclesiasticae...Epitome*; Scherer, *Geschichte und Kirchengeschichte*, pp. 123ff.

[122] Pappus, *Historiae ecclesiasticae...Epitome*, pp. 262f, 303, 349–61, 368–9.

[123] Ibid., p. 370; for later enlarged editions, see Scherer, *Geschichte und Kirchengeschichte*, pp. 123–4: Pappus and Bohemus, *Epitome historiae ecclesiasticae*; Pappus and Kipping, *Epitome historiae ecclesiasticae*.

[124] Osiander, *Epitomes historiae ecclesiasticae*. The total amounted to 3,840 pages in one early edition.

Osiander's history shared Luther's and Flacius's apocalyptic reading of Church history, and narrated the centuries of medieval error in a way that clearly looked forward to the controversies of his own time. In the primitive Church the Apostles and their followers preached the gospel and cared for the Church, but claimed no primacy or superiority; they ran the Church by consent. The early Church knew nothing of the various ranks of clergy, and imposed no confession of individual sins or 'works of satisfaction'. Christians gathered in private houses without consecration of churches or altars. The Lord's Supper was given to everyone in both kinds, without the sacrifice of the Mass or any carrying around the sacrament in procession. The cult of statues and images and invocation of saints was not in use.[125] The primitive Church was defined in terms of the things it did *not* do, but which the present-day Roman Catholics did; most of which the Lutherans had removed. The Church had undergone a gradual degradation in the first few centuries, symbolized by the growing claims of the popes to primacy. Osiander argued, following the *Magdeburg Centuries*, that most of the documents supporting papal claims were forgeries, from the first section of the so-called 'False Decretals' dating from around 850. Osiander dissected each bogus papal letter in turn to show its anachronisms and bad Latinity. Almost gratuitously, he dissected the long-discredited Donation of Constantine made famous by Lorenzo Valla in the fifteenth century.[126]

Between the fourth and sixth centuries Osiander was unsure whether to denounce the records of the Church as forgeries or accept them as historically true but condemn the errors they recounted. Worship became more elaborate: people devised 'superstitious' good works. St Antony, the leader of the desert hermits, lived well, was devout, and doubtless saved. However, his fasts and asceticism exalted human efforts and moral worth instead of relying on the merits of Christ. Osiander wrote sarcastically about Antony's struggles with the assaults of demons in the desert: 'If Antony had not chosen this superstitious way of life, of living in the desert, he would undoubtedly have been free from such vexations of Satan (if indeed they are not feigned). Therefore this ought not to be praised, that he exposed himself to many temptations and dangers by the solitary life.'[127] The rot really set in around the time of Gregory the Great, at the close of the sixth century. Antichrist gained a foothold in the Church, and thereafter became entirely dominant:

> In this century we enter the sea of superstitious cults of divine [things], which partly the Roman bishops, and partly other people invented . . . There are many miracles ascribed to bishops, monks, and hermits . . . which either never happened, but were invented by vain people and then taken up and spread abroad by

---

[125] Ibid., Cent. 1, pp. 155–9.
[126] Ibid., Cent. 3, p. 69; Cent. 4, pp. 21–2, 28, 132–3. On Valla, see above, Ch. 1.
[127] Ibid., Cent. 4, pp. 99–103.

foolish and credulous people as though they were true; or, Satan achieved them with his illusions, to erect and confirm superstitious and idolatrous cults, by which the true worship of God might be largely oppressed. God permitted this, in order that superstitious people, by his just judgement, should be punished by darkness, because they preferred lies rather than heavenly truths handed down in the word of God.[128]

Dealing with the history of the medieval Church, for Osiander, was a case, not of condemning forged claims inserted into the records of the Church, but of denouncing terminal theological and moral decay. 'For if ever there was depicted the Roman Antichrist, and how he conducted himself as though he were God... surely in these intervening centuries his malice and impudence are depicted in living colors.'[129]

4. CONCLUSIONS

While the Lutheran and Reformed Churches generated separate and often mutually hostile historiographies, those historiographies stubbornly refused to remain separate: authors from both camps repeatedly borrowed from each other and translated each other's works, with or without acknowledgement that they were crossing confessional lines by doing so.[130] The Philippist Peucer echoed arguments from the Gnesio-Lutheran Flacius; the Lutheran Osiander, writing about Reformed Church history in the sixteenth century, borrowed from the reformed Philippe de Marnix.[131] Within both traditions a continuum of historical perspectives stretched from a less judgemental humanist approach at one end to a dogmatic-apocalyptic one at the other. By the end of the sixteenth century, humanist and dogmatic-apocalyptic approaches had so far merged and cross-fertilized each other that the strands can no longer be separated. As in other disciplines, the long-term legacy of humanism to ecclesiastical history lay more in the scholarly techniques and awareness of critical method than in larger philosophical approaches to human motivation.[132] However, the lessons of Renaissance scholarship, whether seen in Kessler's use of Flavio Biondo or in Lutheran wistfulness about the pure, simple qualities of the primitive Church, would continue to shape Church history until the Enlightenment.

---

[128] Ibid., Cent. 6, pp. 3–4.

[129] Ibid., Cent. 9–15, sig. 2ʳ–4ʳ.

[130] See Cameron, 'One Reformation or Many', esp. pp. 119–26.

[131] See ibid., pp. 122–4.

[132] See e.g. Grafton, *Defenders of the Text*.

3

Cesare Baronio and the Roman Catholic Vision of the Early Church*

Giuseppe Antonio Guazzelli

1. BARONIO'S SCHOLARSHIP: THE ORATORIAN AND POST-TRIDENTINE CONTEXTS

The ecclesiastical historian Cesare Baronio (1538–1607) was born in Sora—a city in southern Lazio which belonged to the Kingdom of Naples—and arrived in Rome in 1557 to complete his studies in civil and canon law.[1] Here he soon became acquainted with the charismatic preacher and urban missionary Filippo Neri (1515–95) and the Oratorio, the vibrant religious community gathered around Neri. Open to both clergy and laymen, the Oratory (as it is usually called in English) was devoted to penitential and devotional practices. These included afternoon meetings to discuss Holy Scripture and sacred history at San Girolamo della Carità, the Roman church where Neri resided, and where he had begun his ministry as a priest in 1551. The Oratory eventually became a community of secular priests, and was formally recognized in 1575 by Gregory XIII (pope 1572–85) as 'Congregazione dell'Oratorio'.[2]

* I thank Simon Ditchfield for revising with patience and attention my 'inglese italianato' and discussing with me many issues on Baronio and sacred history. I am also grateful to Stefan Bauer for his careful reading of this chapter and for his suggestions.
[1] There exists an extensive bibliography on Baronio. An essential point of departure remains, notwithstanding its hagiographical intent, Calenzio, *La vita e gli scritti*, published in 1907 on the third centenary of Baronio's death. Thereafter, the sole monograph devoted both to the Oratorian's life and work is Pullapilly's insufficiently critical *Caesar Baronius*. More thought-provoking assessments have been offered by Pincherle and Jedin, as noted below.
[2] For essential treatments of Filippo Neri, see Frajese, 'Filippo Neri'; Prodi, 'La spiritualità di San Filippo Neri'. On the development of the Congregation of the Oratory, see Cistellini, *San Filippo Neri*.

Baronio's most celebrated work was the twelve-volume *Annales ecclesiastici* (Rome, 1588–1607). The *Annales*, which gave an account of the Church's history from the birth of Christ down to AD 1198, served as the official Roman Catholic reply to the Protestant *Magdeburg Centuries* (Basel, 1559–74).[3] Filippo Neri and the Oratorian context were important influences, not only on Cesare Baronio's spiritual direction and his ecclesiastical career, but also on his intellectual development and scholarship. It is therefore valuable to begin this examination of Baronio's contribution to 'sacred history' by considering the possible influence that Neri and the Oratory had on the *Annales*. In his depositions at Neri's canonization trial, Baronio affirmed that when he had arrived in Rome in 1557 and started to frequent the 'Oratorio', Neri had pushed him towards Church history by requiring him to give sermons on this subject during the community's afternoon meetings. At this point Neri already envisioned the *Annales* as a polemical response to the Protestants.[4] It was thus Neri's imperative that gave Baronio his first contact with ecclesiastical history.

Neri's influence, however, must not be exaggerated. In a note of acknowledgement (the *Gratiarum actio*) published in 1599 as a preface to the eighth volume of the *Annales* and addressed to Neri, Baronio himself did exaggerate Neri's role in producing the *Annales*, stating unambiguously that he was the work's 'prime author and architect'.[5] This claim cannot be taken at face value. By minimizing his own role and attributing the authorship of his *Annales* to Neri, Baronio was promoting the *fama sanctitatis* of his spiritual father (who was finally canonized in 1622). This image of Neri as the *Annales*'s author, repeated for centuries in Neri's and Baronio's lives and hagiographies, was for a long time a serious obstacle to a deeper understanding of the genesis of *Annales*. In this respect, an important historiographical watershed was provided in 1978 by Hubert Jedin, who showed in his study of Baronio that aside from the *Gratiarum actio* and Baronio's depositions there exists no

---

[3] On the *Magdeburg Centuries*, see above, Ch. 2. From 1588 until his death, Baronio was involved in an ongoing revision of the volumes of *Annales* already published, with the result that we have both some new editions of single volumes (esp. vols. I–IV, which he proposed to replace their previous editions), and a large number of *Addenda* and *Corrigenda*, usually published at the end of each new volume. In other words, the *Annales* was a work in progress, and each volume and edition corresponds to a precise stage of Baronio's scholarly work. In this chapter, generally, I quote from the eighteenth-century Lucca edition (see Bibliography), which follows the last edition of the *Annales* that was published with Baronio's agreement and integrates into the text the *Addenda* and *Corrigenda*. The variegated typefaces and appendices of this edition enable the reader to discern the variations that the Oratorian brought to his text over the years. In this edition some elements indispensable for understanding Baronio's methodology and his vision of history, such as the dedications of the twelve volumes and the *Praefatio* to the *Annales*, were published in a separate volume: see, Baronio, *Annalium ecclesiasticorum...Apparatus*, esp. pp. 393–480.

[4] See Baronio's depositions in Incisa della Rocchetta et al. (eds.), *Il primo processo per San Filippo Neri*, I, pp. 136–7 (1 September 1595) and II, pp. 291–4 (22 May 1607).

[5] See the *Gratiarum actio* in Baronio, *Annalium ecclesiasticorum...Apparatus*, pp. 422–4.

documentary evidence of Neri's authorship of the *Annales*.[6] Nonetheless, Filippo Neri, through his personal charisma, and the Oratory, through the intellectual interests of its members, made an important mark upon Baronio's scholarship. As Jedin pointed out, and as several more recent studies have confirmed, Baronio's work and indeed his whole intellectual biography were profoundly shaped by the Oratory. Inside this religious family, whose cultural agenda he shared, Baronio found his major scholarly collaborators: learned proofreaders, assistants who prepare the indexes of his works, and scholars with whom he could discuss his sources and related historical matters and who sometimes suggested to him changes in content which he then integrated into his writings.[7]

If Neri and the Oratory inspired Baronio's first forays into ecclesiastical history, it was the Roman Curia in the years after the Council of Trent that provided the specific institutional context in which the *Annales* were re-searched, written, and published. The enterprise was one of various initiatives taken by the Roman Curia after the closure of the Council of Trent (1563) to codify the history, doctrine, and image of the Roman Catholic Church, largely in polemical response to the Protestants. As Jedin has shown, from 1577, if not earlier, Baronio was conducting historical research towards the definitive writing of the *Annales* under the direction of senior members of the Roman Curia. From this point on, Baronio's contributions to promoting the cultural agenda of the Roman Curia became increasingly active and influential, thanks mainly to the patronage of the powerful Cardinal Guglielmo Sirleto (1514–85). Sirleto was an eminent Greek scholar who headed many papal commissions during the reign of Pope Gregory XIII. From 1577 he was Baronio's principal contact inside the Curia for the *Annales* project. He contributed to Baronio's work by providing him with documents and books from Vatican Library and from his own.[8]

Sirleto also called upon Baronio to play a major role in the project of liturgical reform that was an important part of the post-Tridentine papal agenda. The decrees of the final session of the Council of Trent had stipulated that revised office books should replace the multitude of liturgical books that

---

[6] Jedin, *Kardinal Caesar Baronius*. It should be noted that as early as 1964 Pincherle's entry on Baronio in the *Dizionario biografico degli Italiani* underlined the necessity of verifying many hagiographical traditions relating to Baronio's life and works.

[7] See the miscellaneous volumes: de Maio et al. (eds.), *Baronio storico*; de Maio et al. (eds.), *Baronio e l'arte*; Gulia (ed.), *Baronio e le sue fonti*; Finocchiaro (ed.), *I libri di Cesare Baronio*; Tosini (ed.), *Arte e committenza*; Guazzelli et al. (eds.), *Cesare Baronio tra santità e scrittura storica*. See also the monographs: Zen, *Baronio storico* (extensively reviewed in R. Fubini, 'Baronio e la tradizione umanistica'); and Finocchiaro, *Cesare Baronio e la tipografia dell'Oratorio*.

[8] Ditchfield stresses Sirleto's important role in Baronio's career as historian in *Liturgy, Sanctity, and History*, pp. 51–2, and in 'Baronio storico nel suo tempo'. The principal general study on Sirleto remains Denzler, *Kardinal Guglielmo Sirleto*.

had hitherto been used. The texts of these older liturgies, some printed and some in manuscript, were not standardized, and many were not recognized by ecclesiastical authorities. The post-Tridentine revision of the liturgy was initiated by Pius V (pope 1566–72) with the publication of the revised texts of the *Breviarium romanum* (Rome, 1568) and the *Missale romanum* (Rome, 1570). His successor Pope Gregory XIII continued the project by ordering the revision of the Roman Martyrology. Gregory entrusted this task to a commission chaired by Cardinal Sirleto.

Baronio's most significant contribution to this liturgical reform effort was his work on the new *Martyrologium romanum*.[9] This book recorded the names of the various martyrs and saints celebrated each day, taking the ninth-century Usuard as its main model. Besides providing the names of the individual saints and the places where they died or were venerated, the *Martyrologium* gave brief accounts of how they died and thus had a significant historical dimension. Baronius's work on the *Martyrologium* is first documented in the final months of 1580, when, charged by Cardinal Sirleto, he and other members of the papal commission chose which saints and martyrs would be celebrated in the newly revised liturgical book and began to compose their eulogies. The resulting text was approved for universal adoption in 1584, but in 1583 Sirleto further charged Baronio with composing an apparatus of notes to document and explain the details in the main text. A revised edition of the *Martyrologium* was published in 1586, accompanied by Baronio's prefatory treatise (*Tractatio de martyrologio romano*) and by his extensive notes (*Notationes*).[10]

Sirleto's choice of Baronio, whom he knew to be already engaged in the *Annales*, demonstrates the cardinal's eagerness to ensure that this liturgical book had solid historical foundations. Baronio's work on the *Martyrologium romanum* overlapped significantly in content with the *Annales* project, and his annotations to the 1586 edition of the *Martyrologium* contained references to the yet unpublished *Annales*. Similarly, many subsequent corrections and additions made to the *Notationes* and to the *Martyrologium* made reference

---

[9] See Guazzelli, 'Cesare Baronio e il *Martyrologium romanum*'; Guazzelli, 'Cesare Baronio attraverso il *Martyrologium romanum*'.

[10] This version of the Roman Martyrology was updated by Baronio and reprinted several times (incl. Antwerp, 1589, and Rome, 1598). A final Vatican edition of 1630 incorporated many corrections and additions made by Baronio between 1598 and 1607. Although published after his death, it may be regarded as the 'last' and, in some respect, 'definitive' Baronian version. In what follows, however, I quote from the edition of 1586. Here the *Tractatio* occupies a specific section of the volume (pp. *I–*XIV), while the *Notationes*, like modern footnotes, follow day by day the eulogies to which they refer (see Fig. 3.1). This page layout was retained in the following editions. Like the *Annales*, Baronio's *Notationes* to the *Martyrologium* was a work in progress, so a comparison between the different editions can reveal interesting changes in his views.

Figure 3.1. *Martyrologium romanum* (Rome: Basa, 1586), p. 149. This was the first edition of the *Martyrology* in which the eulogies celebrating martyrs and saints according to their feast days were directly followed by Baronio's *Notationes*.

to the *Annales*, which by 1588 was starting to be published. Baronio's work on both the *Annales* and the *Martyrologium* thus contributed to the dual process—liturgical and historical—by which the post-Tridentine Roman Catholic Church situated itself in relation to its past and examined its liturgical and hagiographical heritage.[11] The text also had a specifically Oratorian dimension: Baronio paid particular attention to martyrs whose relics were held by the Congregation of the Oratory, and in 1596, a year after Filippo Neri's death, he began to use the *Martyrologium* to promote Neri's own saintly reputation (*fama sanctitatis*).

Baronio's participation on such official papal post-Tridentine projects allowed him privileged access to the documents, both manuscript and printed, of the Vatican Library, and to many volumes which since 1559 had been placed on the *Index of Prohibited Books*, including the *Magdeburg Centuries* itself. This did not mean, of course, that he was free to choose the sources at his own personal discretion. In matters of Church's history, doctrine, liturgy, and saints' cults, Baronio was expected to follow, or at least consider seriously, the template provided by other official codifications of the post-Tridentine Church, such as the *Cathechismus romanus* (Rome, 1566), the editions of the Fathers printed in Rome which were promoted by the Curia itself, and the other official liturgical books, especially the *Breviarium romanum* with its hagiographical lessons (*Officia propria sanctorum*) that were to be read on saints' feast days determined for the universal Catholic liturgy by the Roman calendar of saints (*Kalendarium romanum*).

Still, within these parameters, and despite the manifold influences exerted by Filippo Neri, the Oratory and the Roman Curia, Baronio was able to express his own considerable learning. Baronio's scholarly work, then, must be understood neither as a strictly 'official' nor as a truly individual enterprise, but as the synthetic result of the two. Baronio deployed these elements together to justify not only the Roman Catholic Church's official doctrine and the liturgy, but the whole set of ecclesiastical practices—the *forma ecclesiae*—which, in the late sixteenth century, the Roman Catholic Church upheld as evidence that it alone was the true Church and the only legitimate successor to the early Church of the Apostles. In doing so, he paid careful attention to questions of Christian origins and to the early centuries of Christian history. The remainder of this chapter will examine the treatment of early Christian history in the *opus baronianum*, the *Annales ecclesiastici*, and the *Notationes* in particular.

---

[11] Baronio's participation in interrelated historical projects promoted by the Curia is also revealed by other his writings, although these have received less critical attention. In 1580, for example, while work on the *Annales* was underway, Baronio wrote the *Vita S. Gregorii Nazianzeni* at the behest of Pope Gregory XIII on the occasion of the translation of the relics of the saint from Santa Maria in Campo Marzio to San Pietro in Vaticano. This life was first published in 1680 as part of the dossier devoted to Gregory of Nazianzus by the Bollandists in their *Acta sanctorum*. He later wrote the *Vita Sancti Ambrosii Mediolanensis*, commissioned by Cardinal Felice Peretti, later Pope Sixtus V (1585–90), to accompany Peretti's edition of St Ambrose's works. By contrast, the commentary on *Acts of Apostles*, completed in 1580, seems closer to the Oratorian community. It is worth trying to evaluate how this work (still unpublished in Biblioteca Vallicelliana, Rome, Mss. Q 36–37), with its reflections on ancient Christianity, influenced Baronio's historical thinking.

2. 'SEMPER EADEM'

As has been seen, Baronio's historical writings, particularly the *Annales*, were conceived as a polemical response to the Protestant *Magdeburg Centuries*. Baronio chose the annalistic chronological framework in direct imitation of the methodology of the aptly named Centuriators, who divided their work into one-hundred-year sections and, within each 'century', into many thematic chapters (e.g. the '*status ecclesiae*', heresies, and persecutions). But above all, Baronio responded directly to the Centuriators' main argument that there had been a continuous decline of the papacy, (which became especially marked from the pontificate of Gregory the Great, 590–604). On the contrary, he firmly asserted, the Roman Church had been 'ever the same' (semper eadem) since its apostolic origins.[12]

In particular, Baronio emphasized the fundamental importance of Peter's pre-eminent role amongst the Apostles as the basis for Rome's assertion of primacy. To this end he did not limit himself to discussing the New Testament foundations for Peter's primacy, but drew on other early sources as well as on pure conjecture. Emblematic of his approach here was Peter's alleged founda- tion of the bishopric of Antioch, which Baronio treated both in the *Annales* and in the *Notationes* to the *Martyrologium*.[13] This fact, Baronio reasoned with characteristic caution, even if it was accepted by tradition, needed further explanation from a historical point of view. In order to explain why no reference to it was to be found in the Acts of the Apostles, Baronio speculated that Luke the Evangelist:

> concerned (as we can see) to fix in the memory very distinguished miracles made by Peter, omitted the Apostle's other actions and, among them, the institution of the Church of Antioch.[14]

Baronio only found references in decidedly later sources, such as Eusebius of Caesarea and Jerome, which enabled him to establish the date of the foundation of the see of Antioch to AD 39. By doing so, however, Baronio openly called into question the opinion of his contemporary Onofrio Panvinio (1529–68), whose edition of Bartolomeo Platina's papal biographies (Venice, 1562) gave a later date for the establishment of the see, after Peter's installation as bishop of

---

[12] Baronio's desire to trace the history of a Church *semper eadem* can be clearly seen in the 1588 *Praefatio in Annales ecclesiasticos ad lectorem*, in the first volume of his *Annales* (*Annalium ecclesiasticorum . . . Apparatus*, pp. 395–9). See Ditchfield, *Liturgy*, pp. 283–5. On the methodo- logical choices inspired by the polemic with the Protestants that lay behind the *Annales*, see Mazza, 'La metodologia storica'.

[13] Baronio, *Annales*, AD 39, §§ 8–10 (vol. I, pp. 244–9); *Martyrologium*, 22 February, note *a* (pp. 94–5).

[14] Baronio, *Annales*, AD 39, § 8 (vol. I, p. 245): 'intentus . . . (ut apparet) miracula insigniora a Petro edita memoriae commendare, caeteras eius res gestas . . . obvolutas silentio praetermisit, et inter alia institutionem Ecclesiae Antiochenae'.

Rome.[15] Baronio's dating Peter's appointment as bishop of Antioch to AD 39 was not an isolated historical detail; he was laying careful chronological foundations to support the Apostle's primacy. He speculated that the Apostles, by common agreement, had entrusted the see of Antioch to Peter so that the 'prince of the Apostles' would find himself, as bishop, head of the principal city of the main province (Syria) in the eastern Roman Empire.[16] For the same reason, Baronio argued, the metropolitan see within the ecclesiastical division of Palestine was established not in Jerusalem, but in Caesarea, likewise the centre of Roman power in that region.[17] In other words, according to Baronio, it was the administrative logic of the Roman Empire that underlay the ecclesiastical hierarchy of the early Church, a logic which in AD 39 made it necessary to assign to Peter the bishopric of the most important city evangelized by that date and, Baronio emphasized, higher in rank than Jerusalem itself. Baronio reasserted this correspondence between the hierarchy of cities within the Roman Empire and that of Christian bishoprics at the start of the section dedicated to Peter's preaching in Rome:

> and so the prince of the apostles is sent to the city which ruled the world, and the first of the shepherds is directed towards the capital of the whole earth.[18]

In this way, the conferment of the bishopric of Antioch represented the first affirmation of Petrine primacy, and the Apostle's successive translation to the see of Rome, which Baronio dated to AD 45,[19] represented the full realization of this primacy.

Intimately connected with this affirmation of the primacy of Peter and of Rome was Baronio's delineation of a precise *forma ecclesiae* in the apostolic age. This had clear polemical intent vis-à-vis the much younger Protestant Churches. The Centuriators had not questioned the historical facts of Peter's successive occupation of the sees of Antioch and Rome. But they were drawn to the tradition that considered each Apostle as the evangelizer of a particular people; from this perspective the apostolic origins of the oldest episcopal sees implied not hierarchy but equality. The *Magdeburg Centuries* clearly stated

---

[15] *Martyrologium*, 22 February note *a* (pp. 94–5): 'Miratus sum vehementer R. P. Onufrium Panvinium . . . novam quadam, hactenus inauditam, nec ab aliquo excogitatam opinionem de Cathedra Antiochena astruere conatum esse, dum in suis in Platinam additionibus . . . affirmat Petrum Romae primum, ac demum sedisse Antiochiae' ('I am very surprised that Father Onofrio Panvinio . . . has drawn a position entirely new on Peter's bishopric in Antioch: in his Additions to Platina he affirms that the Apostle was first bishop in Rome and then in Antioch'). For Panvinio's statement, see Platina, *Historia de Vitis Pontificum Romanorum . . .* , fols. 8ᵛ–9ʳ. On Panvinio's edition of Platina's *Vitae pontificum*, see Bauer, *The Censorship and Fortuna of Platina's Lives*, pp. 236–41.

[16] Baronio, *Annales*, AD 39, § 10 (vol. I, p. 245).

[17] Ibid., AD 39, § 11 (vol. I, p. 249). See also *Martyrologium*, 2 February, note *d* (p. 67).

[18] Baronio, *Annales*, AD 39, § 26 (vol. I, p. 296): 'sic igitur ad totius Mundi principem civitatem princeps apostolorum mittitur, et ad primariam urbem orbis primus pastor iure dirigitur'.

[19] Ibid., AD 45, § 1 (vol. I, pp. 317–18).

that there was nothing about Peter's preaching in Rome and his authority as bishop of that city that could be construed as implying that the see enjoyed any superior dignity vis-à-vis the other bishoprics founded by Peter and his fellow Apostles. For his part, Baronio viewed the foundation by the Apostles of the first bishoprics not as evidence for the existence of multiple, autonomous Churches, but as a clear indication that from its origins these sees were part of a single Church, at the head of which there could only sit Peter, 'who was the first among the Apostles'.[20] In clear polemical tones, Baronio presented this conclusion as blatantly self-evident, since it could only be denied by 'those who are rendered blind by their own malice and (as said in the Psalms) have eyes but do not see'.[21]

In a continuation of this polemical line of attack, Baronio offered his definition of the adjective 'Catholicus'. He did so under the year AD 43, in the context of an excursus devoted to how the name '*Christianus*' came to be adopted by the followers of early Church. First seen at Antioch, the label '*Christianus*', Baronio asserted, had soon come to enjoy general use to denote all of Christ's followers, but it had also been improperly adopted by heretical sects.[22] It was in such a context that the adjective '*Catholicus*', which Baronio presented as a *cognomen* to describe the *nomen* '*Christianus*', was coined to distinguish true followers of Christ from these false ones. It was in this sense, he asserted, that the word was adopted by the Apostles in their Creed where the Church of God ('*Ecclesia Dei*') was described as '*Catholica*'.[23] Baronio also explained the significance of this adjective in the context of the institution of the Throne of St Peter in Rome.[24] Drawing upon the authority of Cyprian of Carthage, Baronio argued that the adjective referred only to those who were in communion with Rome, and that those who were not could only be described as heretics.[25] At this point the Oratorian devoted an entire section of his text to claiming that the adjectives '*Catholicus*' and '*Romanus*' were, in fact, synonyms used since antiquity to describe those who loyally adhered to the universal Church led by the pope.[26]

By making such claims, Baronio projected back upon the first century AD the adoption of the adjective '*Romanus*' which, as a synonym for '*Catholicus*', was actually only imposed gradually over the course of the Middle Ages and may be considered normative only after the closure of the Council of Trent.

---

[20] Ibid., AD 45, § 3 (vol. I, p. 318): 'qui inter apostolos primatum gerebat'.

[21] Ibid, AD 45, § 3 (vol. I, p. 318): 'sua ipsorum malitia caecantur et offenduntur, et (quod est in Psalmis) oculos habent et non vident'. In this case Baronio referred to Psalm 113:14 (115:5).

[22] Ibid., AD 43, §§ 11–17 (vol. I, pp. 284–6). See also *Martyrologium*, 22 February, note *b* (p. 95).

[23] Baronio, *Annales*, AD 43, § 17 (vol. I, p. 286).

[24] Ibid., AD 45, §§ 1–11 (vol. I, pp. 317–22).

[25] Ibid., AD 45, § 6 (vol. I, p. 319).

[26] Ibid., AD 45, § 10 (vol. I, p. 321).

The new importance of this term after Trent was potently symbolized by the adoption of the suffix '*Romanus*' to describe the various official books which were issued under the direct authority of the pope for universal adoption, beginning with the Catechism in 1566 and the Breviary in 1568.[27] Here Baronio was clearly forcing the evidence to preserve the essential image of the Church as '*semper eadem*'; according to such a viewpoint the Church in its origins must coincide with that of the present day.

This projection of Tridentine practice back onto the apostolic age under the name 'Roman' is very evident throughout the second half of the first volume of the *Annales*. Having affirmed the primacy of Rome, Baronio went on to deal not only with doctrine but also with liturgy and ritual. Within the annalistic framework of his ecclesiastical history, he inserted extensive parentheses on the details relating to the celebration of Mass and other sacramental practices.[28] These included: the consecration of the Eucharist as well as the administration to the laity of communion *sub una specie* ('in one kind', i.e. bread only); celibacy of the priesthood; and the validity of the cult of images, saints, and relics. In this manner, Baronio sought to justify and validate practices and doctrines which were among the most prominent of those called into question by the Protestants. Reaffirmed at Trent, these traditions were then set down in 1566 in the Roman Catechism, which was designed to be placed in the hands of parish priests the length and breadth of the Roman Catholic world. In the process, Baronio claimed apostolic origins for the greater part of the doctrinal and cultic practices of the post-Tridentine Church.

This symbiotic relationship between Catholic history and Catholic orthodoxy (and its counterpart, heresy) underlies Baronio's entire narrative. From the first volume of the *Annales*, the history of the true Church was presented as a history of true doctrine, defended by the Catholics—that is to say, the Church of Rome under the leadership of the pope—against the heretics. Drawing extensively on the works of polemicists from the first Christian centuries, Baronio used the numerous variants of heterodoxy—such as the Montanists, Donatists, and Arians—as foils to affirm the eternal truth of Rome's Roman Catholic doctrinal identity. He viewed the successive defeat of these various groups of heretics, in providential terms, as further proof that Rome was the one true Church and that, by implication, it would be victorious over and against the latest, Protestant, heresies.[29]

---

[27] Tallon, *Le Concile de Trente*, p. 82, notes how the adjective 'Tridentine' used to describe the measures taken by the Council Fathers should more accurately be replaced with the adjective 'Roman' to reflect more closely the determining interpretation of the decrees carried out by the papacy.

[28] See Baronio, *Annales*, AD 57, §§ 11–211 (vol. I, pp. 423–90).

[29] On Baronio's treatment of heresy, see Ditchfield, 'Baronio storico nel suo tempo'; Benedetti, 'Cesare Baronio e gli eretici'.

Although anti-Protestantism was a dominant theme in Baronio's *Annales*, the work also had non-polemical purposes. As Simon Ditchfield has suggested, Baronio's history writing should be considered as being of a piece with his liturgical interests. For the Oratorian, history was a form of prayer, an occasion for the devout to be reunited with the sources of their faith. This was, after all, the purpose for which Filippo Neri had ordered Baronio to make Church history the subject of the sermons he delivered in the heart of the Oratorian community. Ecclesiastical history also lay at the heart of liturgical practice in the form of the liturgy of the hours, which consisted in large part of the recital of the historico-hagiographical texts found in the Breviary.[30] The hagiographical content of the *Annales* and of Baronio's *Notationes* to the *Martyrologium* were both inextricably linked to the cult of the saints. When assessing the historical testimonies of saints and martyrs and their cults, Baronio sought not only to write the history of the Roman Church as a sacred institution, but also to demonstrate the historical origins of the cult of the saints and to validate and justify, for late-sixteenth-century Church orthopraxis, the cults of the oldest saints and martyrs.

This validation required locating trustworthy documents (and the events they described) both chronologically and topographically. Both the *Annales* and the *Notationes* contain frequent topographical excursuses which aim to identify places directly associated with a martyr's or saint's deeds, martyrdom, burial, and cult or, more generally, with relevant aspects of the Apostolic Church's history and life. Both the *Annales* and the *Notationes* described physical evidence in and around Rome of the faith's earliest years there. This included not only the burial places of the Apostles Peter and Paul, but also the catacombs as well as many churches which Baronio believed had apostolic origins, together with the various monasteries and institutions that provided for the welfare of the earliest Christians (such as *xenodochia* and *diaconiae*).[31]

By constructing such chronological and topographical frames of reference, Baronio sought to demonstrate that from its very origins the Roman Church enjoyed not only a continuous doctrinal identity but also a continuous spatial one, in which the devotional practices and the life of the early Christian community had taken place without interruption. It was a particular concern of Baronio's that, where such sites were to be found in a state of ruin and decay, they should be restored for worship. This strategy had already been followed, for example, in the restoration sponsored by Cardinal Enrico

---

[30] Ditchfield, 'Baronio storico nel suo tempo'.

[31] For a preliminary survey of early Christian architecture and topography, above all of Rome, in Baronio's works, see Guazzelli, *Riferimenti archeologici*; Spera, 'Cesare Baronio, "peritissimus antiquitatis"'; Spera, 'Il recupero dei monumenti'.

Caetani (1550–99) at Santa Pudenziana.[32] But it was Baronio himself, once he became cardinal in 1596, who carried out such work in the most exemplary fashion, restoring his own titular church of Santi Nereo ed Achilleo and the nearby church of San Cesareo de Appia. Santi Nereo ed Achilleo was actually a fourth-century church completely rebuilt in Carolingian times, but Baronio mistakenly believed that it was the original burial place of martyrs Nereus, Achilleus, and Flavia Domitilla. As its cardinal he not only restored ancient structures, but also introduced new liturgical elements that he thought historically authentic. These included the *confessio* (a saint's tomb or where relics were kept), the *fenestella confessionis* (a grating therein through which the faithful could view the relics), the raised presbytery, and the *syntronon* (a semicircular row of benches for the clergy, built into the apse); such elements had not previously existed in these two churches, but Baronio knew through some of the Roman examples presented in his works that they been typical of the more ancient churches. To highlight how these interventions were inspired by early Christian models, Baronio built and decorated them using architectural elements taken from the *spolia* of other buildings, including medieval artefacts such as some cosmatesque marbles. Baronio implemented similar interventions at the monastery of San Gregorio al Celio, where he was appointed commendatory abbot in 1602. Here, from a few existing ruins and *spolia*, he built three oratories. In this case he presented them as the restoration of venerably old structures documented by ancient written sources and, above all, related to the early monastic community established there by Pope Gregory the Great, to whom the monastery was still dedicated.[33]

3. THE CHRISTIANIZATION OF ROMAN HISTORY

Narrating the historical development of the early Church required engagement with the political changes that occurred in the Roman Empire during the same period. Accordingly, Baronio's works devoted considerable discussion not only to the political aspects but also to the administrative, military, and religious features of Roman society. Baronio looked to Roman history to

---

[32] Parlato, 'Enrico Caetani a S. Pudenziana'.

[33] For Baronio's restoration work on his churches as cardinal, see Smith O'Neill, 'The Patronage of Cardinal Cesare Baronio at San Gregorio Magno'; Herz, 'Cardinal Cesare Baronio's Restoration of SS. Nereo ed Achilleo and S. Cesareo de Appia'; Zuccari, 'La politica culturale dell'Oratorio romano'; Zuccari, 'Restauro e filologia baroniani'; Turco, *Il titulus dei Santi Nereo ed Achilleo*. On the more general post-Tridentine treatment of early Christian architecture and the restoration of ancient churches, see Herklotz, 'Basilica e edificio a pianta centrale'; Ostrow, 'The *Confessio* in Post-Tridentine Rome'; Turco, 'Cesare Baronio e i dettami tridentini'.

establish the chronological framework that underpinned his whole work. In the *Annales*, the division by years (*per annos*) followed the reigns of the emperors, the annual succession of consuls, and the succession of popes. Such information was always indicated at the start of the narrative for each year '*post Christum natum*'. In this way, the alternative chronologies made up a kind of table of equivalences. Baronio did not passively adopt the chronological schemes of other scholars, such as Onofrio Panvinio, but drew up his own chronology (albeit often erroneous) with reference not only to written sources but also to epigraphic and numismatic ones. However, Baronio was certainly not exhaustive in his treatment of Roman history. He only made reference to it where it directly served his narrative of early Church history.

For the emperors down to Constantine, whose reign started in AD 306, Baronio naturally emphasized their adherence to paganism. This mode of narrative, which characterized the first two volumes of the *Annales ecclesiastici*, was even more evident in the *Martyrologium romanum*, for which Baronio composed a series of explanatory notes on those Roman emperors who were considered the worst persecutors according to the sources he had consulted.[34] This led Baronio to adopt a tradition, which may be traced back to St Augustine,[35] of numbering the different persecutions of the Christians by the emperors. It also posed the challenge of explaining why some emperors, although their names were not linked to any legislative act against the Christians, had been presented in Christian sources, above all in the acts of martyrs, as persecutors. Indeed, in the case of Alexander Severus (in Baronio's chronology AD 223–37, but in fact AD 222–35),[36] whom some sources described as '*Christianorum studiosissimum*' ('most benevolent towards Christians'), Baronio was forced to explain the high number of martyrdoms recorded for his reign as due to the emperor's failure to abolish the anti-Christian laws enacted by his predecessors.[37]

Of still greater interest is Baronio's treatment of Emperor Trajan (in Baronio's chronology AD 100–19, but actually AD 97–117). Here was a figure who, besides being celebrated both in ancient sources and by humanist writers as a model of rulership, had become protagonist of a hagiographical legend. According to this legend his soul, initially condemned to the flames of Hell, was saved from this eternal fate through the intercessory prayers of Pope Gregory the Great. This story had enjoyed considerable diffusion during the Middle Ages, and its authenticity was still being asserted as late as 1576 in a pamphlet by the Dominican scholar Alfonso Chacón (1540–99), which

---

[34] See e.g. *Martyrologium*, 21 January, note *e* (p. 41) on Aurelian's persecution and 30 January, note *g* (p. 58) on that of Hadrian.

[35] Augustine, *De civitate Dei*, 18, 52.

[36] Until the beginning of the reign of Constantine (AD 306), Baronio proposed a chronology at least two years earlier than that currently accepted today.

[37] *Martyrologium*, 1 January, note *f* (pp. 4–5).

enjoyed wide circulation.[38] Baronio demolished this positive image of Trajan, going so far as to engage in direct polemic with Chacón. In the *Notationes* to the *Martyrologium romanum*, Baronio presented Trajan as a persecutor of Christians. When he treated Trajan's reign in the *Annales*, he depicted the emperor as both a vicious man and a cruel ruler (thereby overturning the tradition that celebrated the emperor's clemency and sense of justice).[39] Furthermore, later in the *Annales*, in a lengthy excursus inserted into his treatment of Gregory the Great, Baronio openly refuted the legend of that pope's intercession on behalf of the emperor's soul.[40]

Baronio's treatment of the Roman emperors was very far from the characteristic Renaissance collections of imperial portraits seen in the antiquarian genre of *illustrium imagines* (portraits of famous men). In the *illustrium imagines*, the Roman emperors were not only the principal narrative subject, but they were also presented in an uninterrupted sequence, thereby emphasizing continuity of power. Through the rhetorical device of a list, the Renaissance authors of the imperial descriptions downplayed the negative judgements of emperors that were often found in the classical sources.[41] Baronio's work, by contrast, presented a gallery of unflattering portraits. The Oratorian emphasized the anti-Christian character of each emperor, and highlighted his cruelties or eccentricities, drawing from ancient sources such as Suetonius' *Lives of the Caesars* and the later *Historia Augusta*.

The difference between the Renaissance-antiquarian vision of the Roman emperors and that of Baronio can be seen quite clearly in the ways that the *Annales* employed numismatic evidence as a historical source.[42] Ancient coins were, from the late Middle Ages to the Renaissance, one of the principal and most fascinating ways of obtaining historical, chronological, and prosopographic information on emperors, and of reconstructing the visual gallery of imperial portraits that was integral to the *illustrium imagines*. Baronio made ample use of numismatic evidence for the early centuries of the Christian epoch, but his principal interest was in chronology, not in imperial portraiture.

Baronio's understanding of coins as historical sources grew more sophisticated over time. In the first edition of the earliest two volumes of the *Annales* (Rome, 1588–90), Baronio limited his use of numismatic evidence to the

---

[38] Chacón, *Historia ceu verissima a calumniis multorum vindicata*. On the *fortuna* of Trajan's legend, see Whatley, 'The Uses of Hagiography'; for some observations on the late sixteenth-century debate, Guazzelli, 'Gregorio Magno nell'erudizione ecclesiastica'.

[39] See *Martyrologium*, 23 January, note *c* (pp. 45–6) and Baronio, *Annales*, AD 100–19 (vol. II, pp. 1–86).

[40] See Baronio, *Annales*, AD 604, §§ 29–49 (vol. XI, pp. 58–64).

[41] See Cunnally, *Images of the Illustrious*; Pelc, *Illustrium imagines*. See also Helmrath, 'Bildfunktionen der antiken Kaisermünze'. On the 'passion for lists' more generally, see Eco, *La vertigine della lista*.

[42] For a wider study on Baronio's use of numismatic evidence, see Guazzelli, 'La documentazione numismatica'.

Figure 3.2. Cesare Baronio, *Annales ecclesiastici*, III (Rome: Tornieri 1592), p. 69. Beginning with the first edition of this volume, Baronio used woodcut images like these, inserted directly in the text, to display the coins that he adduced as documentary evidence.

inscriptions usually displayed around the edge of a coin. He transcribed many such inscriptions directly into his narrative text using capital letters (in the same way he copied epigraphic sources) and recorded the information they provided about emperors' names, triumphs, and official titles, to construct his chronology of imperial succession. Only in the third volume's first edition (Rome: Tornieri, 1592) did Baronio show a more complete understanding of the information that coins could provide, reading their legends in connection with the images struck over them. By this stage, in order to use numismatic evidence in the most effective way, Baronio also introduced in his volumes many woodcuts representing coins (above all Roman) which, consequently, became the *Annales'* main visual source (Figure 3.2).

In order to use them in the most effective way, Baronio also introduced in his volumes many woodcuts representing these coins.[43] He paid particular

---

[43] The importance of coins as visual sources in Baronio's *Annales* was first emphasized in Herklotz, 'Historia sacra und mittelalterliche kunst'. For some samples of woodcuts of ancient coins commissioned by Baronio for the *Annales*, see Fig. 3.2 and Guazzelli, 'La documentazione numismatica', *passim*.

attention to the repertoire of images, or 'types', found on the reverse of the coins, which usually commemorated events from the year the coin was minted: for example, a coin on which Trajan was commemorated in the legend as consul for the fifth time and celebrated as '*Dacicus*' (victor over the Dacians), with the reverse side depicting the bridge constructed by Trajan across the river Danube, gave Baronio further proof that the final victory over Decebalus, the establishment of the Roman province of Dacia, and the construction of the bridge had all occurred in AD 105 (the year of Trajan's fifth consulate, according to the Oratorian's chronology).[44] At the same time, Baronio largely ignored the portraits of emperors on coin obverses, which were usually the main element of interest for the *illustrium imagines* genre as well as for many sixteenth-century printed collections of coins.

The reign of Constantine (AD 306–37), of course, marked a dramatic caesura in Baronio's narration of Roman history.[45] Drawing upon the standard sources, particularly Eusebius, Baronio emphasized the emperor's conversion to Christianity, his extensive support for the new religion within the empire and, above all, his liberality towards the Church and his respect for the pope's authority. Although he accepted the humanist critique of the Donation of Constantine as a later forgery, Baronio made use of other sources, above all the *Liber Pontificalis*, which listed Constantine's numerous acts of patronage and described him as a pious ruler, a defender of Catholic orthodoxy, and free of any taint of Arianism.[46] He also drew on numismatic evidence and literary sources to examine in detail the Christian symbols that Constantine had adopted after his conversion. For example, Baronio took from Eusebius the description of the *labarum*, a military sign which Constantine used first in the Battle of the Milvian Bridge against Maxentius. According to Eusebius, this was a cruciform pole, having on the top, inserted in a laurel crown, a *chrismon*, a sign composed of the Greek letters *X* and *P* linked to express the *nomen Christi* (in Greek Χριστός) and, through the *X*, the *signum crucis*. Eusebius also stated that Constantine was portrayed with his sons in a flag hung on the *labarum*'s crossbar. Some coin types allowed Baronio to affirm that the Christian *labarum* sometimes differed from that described by Eusebius. Baronio displayed, in fact, a coin from the reign of Constantine, where the *chrismon* was represented on the flag instead of the emperor and his sons.[47] Because of his unique role as the first Christian emperor, Constantine was the first emperor for whom Baronius closely examined the portraits found on

---

[44] See Baronio, *Annales*, AD 105, § 1 (vol. II, pp. 33–4).

[45] For Constantine's reign in the Lucca edition of the *Annales*, see vols. III, pp. 413–664 (AD 306–18) and IV, pp. 1–322 (AD 319–37).

[46] For Baronio's position on the *Donatio Constantini*, see Zen, 'Cesare Baronio sulla Donazione di Costantino'; Fubini, 'Baronio e la tradizione umanistica', pp. 149–53.

[47] Baronio, *Annales*, AD 312, §§ 18–27 (vol. III, pp. 505–8). See also Guazzelli, 'La documentazione numismatica', pp. 509–11.

coins. Here, too, the Oratorian aimed to show by visual evidence that Constantine had imbued his official portraits, his clothes, and even his military dress with Christian symbols.[48]

Baronio also advanced some apologetic arguments about Constantine's iconography, sometimes in contradiction to late Roman imperial sources, to show how some of the emperor's choices were coherent with his Christian faith. This happened, for example, with the *diadema*, the crown of gems and gold that Constantine began to use to mark his imperial rank instead of the traditional crown of laurel. According to Emperor Julian the Apostate (AD 361–3), this switch demonstrated Constantine's concern for decorating his hair and thus his effeminate character. On the contrary, Baronio stated that Constantine rejected the crown of laurel as a pagan symbol related to Apollo and adopted the *diadema* for its resemblance to King David's crown, which according to Psalm 20 (which Baronio quoted), was composed of gold and gems.[49] All these elements made Baronio's Constantine the model Christian ruler. Baronio emphasized that Constantine's successors, in the East and the West, had ruled happily and won military victories only when they had revived the Constantinian model, adopted Christian symbols, and (most importantly) respectfully accepted Catholic orthodoxy and papal authority. Baronio repeated this pattern throughout the *Annales,* affirming its validity also for the rulers of his own time. In the prefatory letter to the third volume, for example, the Oratorian advised the Spanish King Philip II (1556–98) to imitate Constantine and to learn from the *Annales*'s full accounts of the latter's conversion and conduct how to preserve, strengthen, and spread the Christian faith among the peoples of his empire.[50]

Baronio did not, however, present the imperial succession from Constantine onwards as an uninterrupted series of good Christian rulers following Constantine's model; the *Annales* also show princes and governors in conflict with the Church, including heretics and even apostates. His ample and detailed portrait of Julian the Apostate is emblematic. Baronio presented this emperor, born Christian but openly converting to paganism after his accession to the throne, as in every way the opposite of Constantine, doing his best to destroy the latter's legacy.[51] Baronio presented Julian's apostasy and the consequent renewed persecution against the Christians and the Church as the cause of his military failures and even of his own premature death.[52] In this way, Baronio's portrait of Julian played a specific role in the overall narrative:

---

[48] See Guazzelli, 'La documentazione numismatica', pp. 511–12.

[49] Baronio, *Annales,* AD 337, §§ 28–31 (vol. IV, pp. 305–6); Guazzelli, 'La documentazione numismatica', pp. 512–14.

[50] See Baronio, *Annalium ecclesiasticorum ... Apparatus,* pp. 411–12.

[51] See Baronio, *Annales,* AD 361–3 (vol. V, pp. 18–188).

[52] Baronio also dealt with the persecution carried out by Julian the Apostate in *Martyrologium,* 22 March, note *f* (p. 135).

reinforced by several cautionary paragraphs on the misfortunes and failures of other emperors and princes who had diverged, even briefly, from the Constantinian pattern, it allowed Baronio to demonstrate how providence had allowed the Church to survive, *semper eadem*, through the centuries.

Baronio also paid attention to the geography and topography of the Roman Empire. In the *Notationes* he used a wide range of sources, above all classical (including Pliny the Elder, Ptolemy, and the *Itinerarium Antonini*) to locate beyond any reasonable doubt a place or a city where, according to the *Martyrologium*'s eulogies, a martyr or a saint had witnessed his Christian faith, or was buried or venerated. So the historical geography of the Roman Empire provided a map of cults and devotions shared by the Church.[53] Baronio gave most attention to the city of Rome, its topography and its buildings, both republican and imperial, but here, too, he treated non-Christian history selectively, dealing with Roman antiquities only as needed to demonstrate the role they had played in, or the evidence they offered for, Christian history.[54] To take just two prominent examples, Baronio's observations on the Mamertine prisons were motivated by his desire to locate with precision where St Peter had been imprisoned.[55] His comments about the Mausoleum of Hadrian were not concerned with the burial place of that emperor, but with the site's transformation into a Christian monument. Baronio recalled the legend according to which, during a penitential procession led by Gregory the Great, an angel was seen atop the Mausoleum placing his sword back in its sheath to signal the end of the plague in Rome. In the early seventh century, he explained, a church dedicated to the Archangel Michael was built there to commemorate this fact.[56]

Baronio's treatment of Roman antiquities was no mere antiquarian exercise. It had direct relevance for the church-building programme of the Counter-Reformation Roman Church, of which he himself was one of the leading protagonists. Baronio emphasized how many pagan temples had been subsequently adapted for Christian worship. An emblematic role in this transformation of the city's landscape was played by the Pantheon, consecrated by Pope Boniface IV (who reigned, according to Baronio's chronology, AD 607–14, but actually AD 608–15). The new church was dedicated to the Virgin Mary and called *Sancta Maria ad Martyres* because of many martyrs' relics translated there from Roman cemeteries.[57] Then Baronio showed that these efforts to Christianize the urban landscape of Rome had been renewed in his own

---

[53] See Guazzelli, 'L'immagine del *Christianus Orbis*'.

[54] On Baronio's treatment of Roman antiquities (including topography), see Jacks, 'Baronius and the Antiquities of Rome'; Spera, 'Il recupero dei monumenti'.

[55] *Martyrologium*, 14 March, note *b* (pp. 122–4).

[56] Ibid., 29 September, note *a* (pp. 442–3); Baronio, *Annales*, AD 590, § 18 (vol. X, pp. 494–5).

[57] *Martyrologium*, 13 May, note *a* (pp. 215–16) and 1 November, note *a* (pp. 493–5); Baronio, *Annales*, AD 607, § 1 (vol. XI, p. 84).

day, making reference to the recent transformation of the central hall of Diocletian's baths in the church of Santa Maria degli Angeli (begun in 1561, this was one of the last building projects on which Michelangelo worked before his death in 1564).[58] Baronio also mentioned the columns celebrating the victories of Trajan over the Dacians and of Marcus Aurelius over the Marcomanni, noting how Pope Sixtus V had ordered bronze statues of St Peter (in 1587) and St Paul (in 1589) placed atop them.[59]

4. CONCLUDING REFLECTIONS

According to Baronio's guiding principle of *semper eadem*, the history of the Church of Rome had not experienced significant discontinuities between the earliest centuries and modern times. Indeed, it was precisely this theme of continuity between the epoch of the primitive Church and that of its post-Tridentine successor which conferred such paradigmatic significance on the former. The doctrine, rites, and physical monuments visible in Baronio's own day bore direct witness to the original *forma ecclesiae* of the early Church.

Baronio's historical work was inextricable from his participation in the papacy's post-Tridentine enterprise to renew the Catholic liturgy and defend Catholic doctrine against modern heretics, and from his personal involvement with the Congregation of the Oratory, where his fellow priests shared many of the same concerns. Baronio did not work alone, nor were his historical ideas unique or original. But he was no mere compiler, who simply repeated in his work positions expressed by other scholars or already affirmed in liturgical books. On the contrary, he interpreted many historical and erudite issues in a highly personal way; he criticized not only the Protestants, but also Catholic scholars. (We have already seen this in his attitude towards Panvinio and Chacón, but we could add Lorenz Sauer and Luigi Lippomano—both editors of huge collections of lives of saints—the liturgist Jacques Joigny de Pamèle, and many others.) Ultimately, the *Notationes* were a critical apparatus through which the Oratorian not only explained the contents of *Martyrologium*'s eulogies, but also expressed doubts and reservations about what was officially stated in that liturgical book.

Baronio's appreciation for the Catholic scholarship of the second half of the sixteenth century, and especially for what was officially codified by the

---

[58] Baronio, *Annales*, AD 298, §§ 10–18 (vol. III, pp. 288–90). See Spera, 'Il recupero dei monumenti', pp. 76–8.
[59] For Trajan's Column, Baronio, *Annales*, AD 106, § 1 (vol. II, pp. 38–9); for that of Marcus Aurelius, AD 176, §§ 24–8 (vol. II, pp. 292–3). See also Jacks, 'Baronius and the Antiquities of Rome', pp. 87–8; Spera, 'Il recupero dei monumenti', pp. 76–7.

post-Tridentine papacy, should discourage us from seeing the Oratorian as a demiurge who was in a position to determine for himself how the history of the Church might be written. It is more appropriate to acknowledge the essentially composite nature of Baronio's works. In this sense, much essential scholarship remains to be done in order to disentangle Baronio's own original positions from those that he adopted from previous traditions or, more importantly, from the demands of the post-Tridentine Church. Such an inquiry will require years of painstaking scholarship, which must include both the careful reading of Baronio's entire erudite production, and the reconstruction of his biography with careful attention to the cultural, political, and religious contexts. To this end a scholarly edition of Baronio's correspondence will be particularly useful. Such difficult but essential work will be the only way to discern which elements of the *Annales*, the *Notationes*, and the Oratorian's other works may truly be called the 'Baronian elements in Baronio'.[60]

[60] I have pointed out the need to study Baronio in these terms in my 'Cesare Baronio e il *Martyrologium romanum*', esp. pp. 71–7. The phrase 'Baronian elements in Baronio' is inspired by the title of Eduard Fraenkel's monograph *Plautinisches im Plautus* (Berlin, 1922). [English translation: *Plautine Elements in Plautus*, (Oxford, 2007)].

4

What Was Sacred History? (Mostly Roman) Catholic Uses of the Christian Past after Trent*

Simon Ditchfield

1. A ROMAN MANIFESTO FOR SACRED HISTORY

Research into the ecclesiastical past of institutions, cults, orders, dioceses, and peoples could serve a variety of purposes beyond simply challenging opposing faiths. This latter function of sacred history was analysed by Pontien Polman in his classic account of 1932, which has now been updated and revised by Irena Backus's more recent work from 2003.[1] Polman believed that neither the reformers nor the Roman Catholics were interested in history for its own sake, but rather regarded it simply as a polemical means to a dogmatic, apologetical end. According to this interpretation, the history of dogma flourished in the early modern period, but ecclesiastical history proper declined, and religious controversy ceased to be a struggle between persons and became a contest between systems. By contrast, Backus argues that history had a much more positive role to play in the formation of and reflection upon confessional identities.

* This chapter has benefited immeasurably from the close reading of Kate Van Liere. I have been privileged to draw freely upon the generosity and wisdom of 'the master of them that know' about early modern Protestant sacred erudition, Tom Freeman, and his counterpart in matters Baronian, Giuseppe Guazzelli. I am very grateful also to Markus Völkel for his careful reading and judicious comments. I would finally like to acknowledge the stimulation to my thinking provided by all my fellow participants at both symposia and by the three invited discussants who lent their considerable expertise to the second symposium held in London: Matthias Pohlig, Jean-Louis Quantin, and Alexandra Walsham; in particular to Jean-Louis for his observations about contemporary understanding of the term '*historia sacra*'. Needless to say, all errors of omission and commission that remain are entirely my responsibility.

[1] Polman, *L'Élément historique*; Backus, *Historical Method*.

According to Backus, both Mattheus Flacius Illyricus (1520–75), for the Protestant reformers, and Cesare Baronio (1538–1607), for the Roman Catholics, made substantive contributions to historical method. The *Magdeburg Centuries* (1559–74) did so through its emphasis on the history of dogma, although as Euan Cameron notes above in Chapter 2 this is not to say that Flacius and his colleagues were in any way innovative in their methodology. The *Annales ecclesiastici* (1588–1607), meanwhile, established new ways to write about institutional history, as seen above in Chapter 3. A central contention of this chapter, however, will be that that the traditional focus of the historiography of sacred erudition on its interconfessional uses has resulted in the underestimation of its role in intraconfessional disputes. In the first place, historians of churches the length and breadth of the Roman Catholic world sought to 'save the phenomena' of particular, local cults and devotions in the face of Rome's attempts to regularize worship, beginning with the introduction of the revised Roman Breviary of 1568. The study of this aspect of sacred historiography has been largely neglected in favour of studies of how history was used to reinforce confessional identities against their opponents. I have devoted an earlier monograph to this topic, which examines a local historian seeking to rescue and refurbish the devotional distinctiveness of his diocese through research into the history of its local saints.[2] The present chapter seeks to explore the theme of 'sacred history' not from a local Catholic perspective, but from that of Catholic scholars (mostly) based in Rome itself, in order better to appreciate the nature and purpose of sacred history as it was understood during the century or so after the closure of the Council of Trent in 1563.

The following unpublished articulation of the importance of sacred history is to be found today in the Vallicelliana library, Rome, which belonged to the Oratorians and where Baronio himself was librarian:

> On the excellence of Ecclesiastical history: [it] always accompanies sacred doctrine, not as a waiting-woman but as an ally and indeed perhaps an elder sister. [It] presents a very broad and rich nourishment for both the faithful and the unfaithful. For it teaches what happens to the wicked, namely that sufferings are inflicted and the rewards handed to the more fortunate. It hands down examples of virtue ... It renews the traditions on which rest the Church's most solid pronouncements. Let antiquity be protected.[3]

---

[2] Ditchfield, *Liturgy, Sanctity, and History.*

[3] 'Historicae ecclesiasticae praestantia: H[a]ec namque sacram doctrinam semper comitatur non pedisequa sed socia sed soror cui fortasse primogenitura debeatur. . . . H[a]ec latissima atque pinguissima cunctis tum fidelibus tum infidelibus exhibet papula. Docet enim peracta malis scilicet inflicta supplicia, bonis reddita praemia. Tradit exempla virtutum. . . . Traditionesque recolit ex quibus prodere firmissima illa ecclesiastica pronunciata: servetur antiquitas.' Biblioteca Vallicelliana, Rome (hereafter BVR), Ms. 146, fol. 2v. The phrase: 'Historicae ecclesiasticae praestantia' may be found in margins of the manuscript where it appears to function as a section header. I am immensely grateful to Paul Gwynne for his expert help at deciphering both Becilli's hand and his grammar, and to Kate and Frans Van Liere for their suggestions.

This quotation may be dated from the early 1630s; its author, Cesare Becilli (1573–1649), was a member of the congregation of the Oratory in Rome, the religious order which (until the appearance of the Benedictine Maurists of the later seventeenth century) was most closely identified with the writing and championing of sacred history. Becilli also served as personal physician to Baronio. Institutional acknowledgement of the merits of his arguments came only in 1742 with Benedict XIV's establishment of the chairs of Liturgy and Ecclesiastical History at the Jesuit-run Roman College. Nonetheless, Becilli's manifesto embodies an important Catholic view of the value of sacred history.

This chapter seeks to put Becilli's plea for the renewal of Catholic sacred history into context by surveying some of the principal ways that Roman Catholic scholars after the mid sixteenth century understood 'historia sacra' and what purposes it served, especially for the papacy. It will begin by identifying the cluster of genres that Catholic scholars used to recover, study, and venerate the Christian past, and the language with which they described them. It will then consider some of the principal uses to which they put sacred history, with particular emphasis on its intraconfessional ends. The extent to which genres of early modern *historia sacra* were inherited from medieval prototypes and, for the most part, the questions and methods of early modern Catholic sacred history continuous with medieval ones will also receive emphasis. Where they did innovate, as, for example, in such works as Ferdinando Ughelli's *Italia sacra* (1644–62) or the Bollandist *Acta sanctorum* (1643–1925), the changes had more to do with the scale and degree of collaboration than with any substantive novelty in content or methodology.

2. LABELLING SACRED HISTORY

The term *historia sacra* was usually employed to refer specifically to biblical history in contrast to profane history. An example of this common usage is the chronicle of the world from creation to Constantine the Great penned by the Church of Scotland minister and sometime principal of Glasgow University, Robert Baillie (1602–62).[4] A similar distinction between sacred and profane history lies behind the title of the widely consulted and often reprinted work by the famous Jesuit Chronographer, Denis Pétau or Petavius (1583–1652): *An Account of Time in two parts, divided into thirteen books. In which all of time, both of sacred and profane history, is comprehensively treated according to chronological proof.*[5] There also existed a myriad studies designed to

---

[4] It was published posthumously in 1663 as *Operis historici et chronologici libri duo.*

[5] *Rationarium temporum in partes duas* (1633 and numerous reprints). This was a summary of perhaps Pétau's most famous work, *De doctrina temporum* (1627).

elucidate the comprehension of biblical narrative at the concrete level of providing what was effectively a glossary to the unfamiliar flora and fauna of the Holy Land together with a moral reading of their meaning.[6]

'Sacred history' could also mean the history of the Church since biblical times. For Protestants, the matter appears to have been straightforward enough. With Eusebius as their prototype, authors such as Flacius Illyricus and John Foxe (1517–87) clearly saw themselves as compilers of 'ecclesiastical history' (*historia ecclesiastica*). Indeed, this was the official title of the collaborative work, arranged thematically by century, which was coordinated by Flacius: the so-called *Magdeburg Centuries*.[7] Although the first edition of Foxe's 'Book of Martyrs' was called *Acts and Monuments*, the second and subsequent ones were called *The Ecclesiastical History, containing the Acts and Monuments*.[8] Moreover, in his dedication of the first (1563) edition to Elizabeth I, Foxe famously compared her to Constantine and himself to Eusebius. But this use of the term 'ecclesiastical history' was not unique to Protestant history writers. In the case of England, the illustrious example of the *Ecclesia historia gentis Anglorum* by Bede of Jarrow (672/3–735) undoubtedly ensured its currency amongst both Catholic and Protestant writers of Church history, since both sides sought to recruit the eighth-century monk to their cause. However, the first English translation of Bede's *History of the Churche of England*, with marginal notes, was published by the Catholic controversialist Thomas Stapleton (1535–98) in 1565. Moreover, Foxe's deadly Catholic adversary, Nicholas Harpsfield (whose devastating critique of Foxe's history, written under the pseudonym of Alan Cope, ensured that the second edition of the *Acts and Monuments* was almost twice as big as the first), called his own account of the English Church *Historia anglicana ecclesiastica*.[9]

In 1570, the anti-Protestant controversialist Girolamo Muzio (1496–1576) published his two-volume attack on the Magdeburg Centuriators, which was entitled simply *Della historia sacra*. Muzio took every opportunity to ridicule his opponents for spectacularly failing to disprove the truth that Roman Catholic doctrine had apostolic origins. Muzio held up for particular derision the Centuriators' failure to get their dates right, which led them also to mistake the identities of such leading protagonists as persecuting emperors. He also singled out for ridicule their factual errors in recording which saints had been martyred and where:

---

[6] See e.g. Wolfgang Franzius, *Animalium historia sacra* and Michael Pexenfelder, *Florus biblicus*.

[7] Flacius Illyricus et al., *Ecclesiastica historia* (1559–74).

[8] *The [first/second volume of the] ecclesisaticall history contayning the acts and monumentes of thynges passed in every kynges tyme in this realme . . .*

[9] This was only published posthumously, with an appendix relating Henry VIII's divorce and break with Rome by Edmund Campion, as *Historia anglicana ecclesiastica*. Harpsfield's forensic exposure of the Foxe's failings as a historian are to be found in the last dialogue of *Dialogi sex*.

In their writing of history, the learned centuriators appear more hysterical than historical, giving their readers a good laugh. They write as if the persecutions carried out in France under Marcus Aurelius Antoninus had been carried out under Antoninus Pius. Moreover, they locate (the passion of) Felicitas and her children in Rome [when they were in fact martyred in N. Africa], and that of Bishop Focinus in France (when there can be no doubt that they were martyred under Marcus Aurelius.) They also state that the virgin Santa Prassede was martyred—an event which I never recall having read about. But what makes one laugh hardest is their claim that Marcus Aurelius was the brother of Antoninus Pius, when the former was clearly the latter's adoptive son. All of this forces me to conclude that they have woven stories rather than histories.[10]

The themes Muzio highlights in *Della sacra historia* serve as a useful window into the way that Catholic writers understood *historia sacra* half a century after the onset of the Reformation. In the first place, his critique makes clear why hagiography continued to occupy such an important place in Catholic sacred erudition; in the face of Protestant doubt and disregard for the cult of the saints, it was more important than ever to record their lives and deaths accurately. Muzio avidly defends the cult and miracles of saints; the full index to volume I contains no fewer than fifty-eight references to sanctity and fifty-four to miracles in the lives of saints. The next most prominent theme in the same volume is, perhaps more predictably, the episcopacy (there are thirty-nine references to bishops), followed by virginity (twenty-three references) as embodied most notably in the celibacy of priests and the vocation of nuns. This theme is no less surprising, since celibacy was such a visible marker of Roman Catholic distinctiveness in a confessional age. In volume II, which covered the period from Sixtus I (*c.*117–*c.*126) to Urban I (d. 230), the most prominent theme itemized in the index is papal authority (with twenty references); followed by the Cross with its implications for eucharistic devotion (with sixteen) and (non-scriptural) traditions (with fifteen).

The term *historia sacra* was also commonly used by the end of the sixteenth century to classify book collections in early modern Catholic libraries. One of the largest such collections belonged to Giovanni Angelo Altemps (1586–1620). Arguably the most important collection of printed books outside the Vatican ever assembled in Rome before the nineteenth century, Altemps's collection listed 338 titles on *historia sacra* in its inventory. Altemps was the

---

[10] 'I dotti Centurioni nello scriver le historie mi paiano più histrioni, che historici, che danno da ridere à chi le legge. Scrivono le persecutioni fatte in Francia sotto Marco Aurelio Antonino, come fatte sotto Antonin Pio e nominano Felicita co' figliuoli a Roma e il Vescovo Phocino in Francia, i quale non è dubbio alcuno che sotto Marco Aurelio furono martirizati. Fanno etiando, che la vergine santa Prassede fosse martire: il che in verun luogo non mi ricorda haver letto. Ma quello, che è piu da ridere, dicono, che Marco Aurelio Vero fu fratello di Antonin Pio: e chiara cosa è, che egli fu figliuolo adottato (come habbiamo detto) da lui. Si che questo mi pare che sia tessere stor[i]e [sic] e non historie'. Muzio, *Della historia sacra*, II, p. 19.

grandson of Pope Pius IV's nephew Marcus Sittich Hohenhems, whose family name had been Italianized by the pope.[11] The inventory dates from 1617–18, after the purchase (for 13,000 écus) of what was undoubtedly the most significant library of ecclesiastical interest remaining in non-papal hands in the early seventeenth century: the collection of books and manuscripts belonging to Cardinal Guglielmo Sirleto (1514–85) from the heirs of Ascanio Colonna, in 1611.

The inventory of works of *historia sacra* in the Altemps library followed convention by starting with the largest (folio) volumes, beginning, appropriately enough, with the first eleven volumes of Baronio's *Annales ecclesiastici* in their first, Roman printings (1588–1605). Baronio's *Annales* were by now available in several editions; the publication of the second edition, beginning in 1589, by the Plantin press in Antwerp, which was one of Europe's pre-eminent Catholic publishing houses, attests to the international reach of Baronio's work (Figure 4.1).[12] Baronio was followed, in Altemps's catalogue, equally predictably, by a 1581 collection of standard accounts of the early Church written by Eusebius and his continuators, including Socrates 'Scholasticus' (*c*.380–450), Theodoret, bishop of Cyrrhus (*c*.393–*c*.460), Sozomen (early 5th century), and Evagrius 'Scholasticus' (*c*.536–600). Turning to smaller volumes, pride of place was given to Francesco Panigarola's compendium of Baronio's *Annales* (1590), followed by a series of standard histories of the popes and of Italy, including a 1485 edition of Platina (Bartolomeo Sacchi)'s *Lives of the Popes* and a 1557 printing of the epitome of the same work by the Augustinian scholar, Onofrio Panvinio (1529–68), as well as a copies of Sulpicius Severus's chronicle from the creation of the world to AD 400 (written after 404), Flavio Biondo's *Italia illustrata* (1474), and Pomponio Leto's *Romanae historiae compendium* (1499). These last two works were less obviously sacred in their focus and closer to the chorographical tradition that ultimately went back to the Greek geographers Strabo (63/64 BC–24 AD) and Ptolemy (90–168). However, all these works listed above conceived of their subject within a sacred

---

[11] The inventory may be found in Biblioteca Casanatense, Rome, Ms. 3218–3222. References to books of *historia sacra* are in Ms. 3218, fols. 187ʳ–196ᵛ, 215ʳ–218ᵛ. For a transcription with commentary of the inventory of 1609 which shows the state of the library at the death of Cardinal Altemps in 1595, see Serrai, *La biblioteca altempsiana*. In the 1609 inventory, books of sacred erudition are dispersed between such specific sections as '*Vitae sanctorum et aliorum*' (pp. 148–50); '*Concilia synodi et Constit[utio]nes*' (pp. 159–60); '*Martyrologi et Calendari*' (pp. 168–9); '*De auctoritate Papae et Concilio*' (pp. 169–70); '*De auctoritate Ecclesiastica et residentia episcopi*' (pp. 210–11). I am most grateful to Giuseppe Finocchiaro for drawing this volume to my attention.

[12] For the significance of Baronio's *Annales* to the turnover of the Plantin/Moretus press, see Jan Machielson, 'How (Not) to Get Published'. Machielson calculates (p. 109) that Baronio's works accounted for as much as 13% of the printing house's revenue. My thanks to Kate Van Liere for this reference.

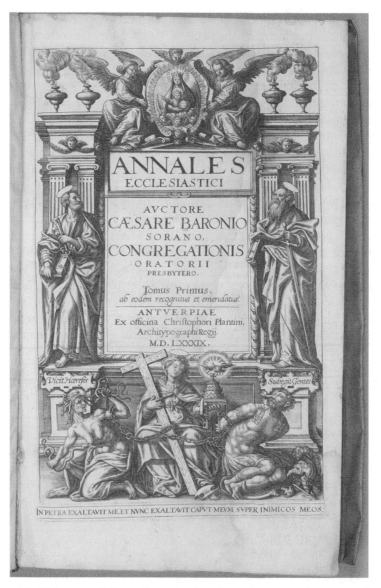

Figure 4.1. Title-page of Cesare Baronio, *Annales ecclesiastici*, I (Antwerp: Plantin, 1589–1609). Striking down heresy; lifting up the faithful. This was the second edition of Baronio's work, following the first edition (Rome, 1588–1607) by only a year. Its publication by the Plantin-Moretus Press, which had become the most important printer of Catholic books for distribution in the New as well as Old World, testifies to the rapid rise of the work to canonical status even before it had been completed.

Figure 4.2. Title-page of Johannes Bollandus and Godefridus Henschenius, *Acta sanctorum*, I (Antwerp: Johannes Meursius, 1643). Erudition at the service of Truth. The *Annales* (Figure 4.1), together with the *Acta sanctorum*, may be considered the twin pillars of early modern Catholic *historia sacra*.

framework and remind us that this was still the default mode for all national history writing of the Renaissance, with very few exceptions.

There were various editions of the Martyrology, the official register of Christian martyrs arranged, month by month, according to their feast days. These included the version by Usuard (d. *c.*875), containing brief details of the saints' lives, which was the most widely circulating martyrology in the Middle Ages. Usuard served as the basis for the various editions of the Roman Martyrology published during the sixteenth century, including those also included in the Altemps collection by Francesco Maurolico, Pietro Gale-sini, and Cesare Baronio himself (whose successive editions became the official Martyrology of the post-Tridentine Church).

The remainder of the section devoted to *historia sacra* was given over almost exclusively to works of hagiography. Amongst these were the standard collections by Petrus de Natalibus (d. between 1400 and 1406), Lorenz Saur (Laurentius Surius, 1522–78) and (in the vernacular) Gabriele Fiamma (1533–85) as well as Robert Parsons's widely diffused 1582 account of the persecution of English Catholics. In addition, there was the Oratorian Antonio Gallonio's excruciatingly erudite and illustrated account of torture instruments mentioned in early Christian accounts of martyrdom, which left very little to the imagination.[13] Contemporary concerns and devotional fashions were also addressed by such titles as Gallonio's life of St Philip Neri (1600) as well as his life of early Christian Roman Virgin martyr-saints (1593), which the author had originally intended to print together with his treatise on torture in order to facilitate his readers' understanding of the ghastly sufferings of the martyrs whose deaths he described. Altemps's books on sacred history also included an account of the first papal canonization since 1523, that of St Didacus (San Diego) of Alcalá in 1588, as well such emblematic Jesuit works as Orazio Torsellino's life of St Francis Xavier (in an edition of Rome, 1596) and Héribert Rosweyde's *Fasti sanctorum* (1607), which became the blueprint for the ultimate collection of saints' lives, the Bollandist *Acta sanctorum*. This work began publication in 1643 with the appearance of two volumes covering saints whose feasts took place in the month of January (Figure 4.2). It came to a halt only in 1925 with a single volume dedicated to just two days: 9–10 November.[14]

The majority of these works in the Altemps library came from Cardinal Sirleto's collection, whose immense value (reflected in its price tag of 20,000 ducats at the cardinal's death, which put off no less a prospective buyer than Philip II of Spain) derived not only from the richness of its Greek and near-

---

[13] Parsons, *De persecutione anglicana*; Gallonio, *Trattato de gli istrumenti di martirio*.

[14] Godding et al., *De Rosweyde aux Acta sanctorum*. (Technically, the *Acta* ceased publication later, with the 1940 publication of the *Propylaeum* to December, but the remaining days in November were never covered.)

eastern manuscripts, many of which passed immediately into the Vatican Library, but also from of its own origins in the library belonging to Cardinal Marcello Cervini (1501–55). Cervini, who reigned briefly as Pope Marcellus II (9 April–1 May 1555),[15] had been the most prominent and active papal legate at the Council of Trent (1545–63) during its opening phase and, as a member of the cardinal's household based in Rome, Sirleto had ensured that his master was supplied with a steady stream of references to and transcriptions of patristic sources to inform the debates on justification and the extra-scriptural sources of tradition which were preoccupying the Council Fathers.[16] Girolamo Seripando (1493–1563), sometime superior general of the Augustinian Order and the only major figure to attend both the opening and closing periods of the Council of Trent, went so far as to assert that Sirleto had done the Council Fathers better service in Rome than if fifty prelates had been sent to Trent.[17]

A similar understanding of *historia ecclesiastica* can be seen in the catalogue of the personal library of over 3,000 books left to the Biblioteca Angelica in Rome by Lukas Holste (1596–1661), the Hamburg-born sacred geographer who converted from Lutheranism to Catholicism in 1625 and served as librarian, successively, to Cardinal Francesco Barberini and Queen Cristina of Sweden before becoming senior custodian (*primo custode*, i.e. deputy to the Cardinal librarian) of the Vatican Library itself (1653–61). Better known under the Latinized form of his name, Lucas Holstenius, he used the heading *Historia ecclesiastica* to list, shortly before his death, no fewer than 303 works in Latin (plus fifty in Greek under the separate list '*Libri ecclesiastici graeci*') which were of a fully representative diversity and range.[18]

---

[15] For a catalogue of Sirleto's library at the time of his death, see Biblioteca Apostolica Vaticana, Rome (hereafter BAV) Vat. lat. 6937, fols. 207ʳ–350ᵛ. The number of books of '*historia prophana*' (165) and the 364 books which were listed under the title of '*historiae diversorum gentium*' in the 1617–18 inventory illustrate the particular range and importance of the library in its incarnation under Giovanni Angelo Altemps. The latter's interest in travel, science and geography is also testified to by the number of titles relating to mathematics, military engineering and architecture (301), natural philosophy (254), and medicine (335 titles). This later inventory of the Altemps library may be found at the Biblioteca Casanatense, Rome, Mss. 3218–3222. Vols. I and II are arranged by subject and location and III–V are in alphabetical order. I am grateful to Giuseppe Finocchiaro and Isabella Ceccopieri for their assistance in my obtaining access to the original manuscript (as opposed to the microfilm: reels 3060–4).

[16] For Cervini's correspondence with Sirleto see BAV, Vat. lat. 6177–6178. Cf. Concilium tridentinum, X, pp. 929–55; Backus and Gain, 'Le cardinale Guglielmo Sirleto (1514–85)'; Piacentini, *La biblioteca di Marcello II Cervini*; and Quaranta, *Marcello II Cervini (1501–55)*, pp. 447–9.

[17] Pastor, *History of the Popes*, XVI, p. 408.

[18] Holstenius had given all his Italian books to his patron Francesco Barberini and so they are not included. The list of the remaining books bequeathed to the Angelica may now be found in the Bibliothèque municipale di Nancy, France (Ms. 1049 (284)). It has been reprinted in Serrai, *La biblioteca di Lucas Holstenius*. The books on ecclesiastical history are listed on pp. 197–201;

What follows is a representative sample rather than an exhaustive list, which nevertheless conveys to the modern reader something of the range and richness of this umbrella category. To begin with, Holstenius owned the most up-to-date edition of the work that stood at the very origins of the genre, the *Chronicon* of Eusebius of Caesarea (*c*.265–339/40) (in Greek but with a Latin translation by Joseph Scaliger in two editions: Leiden, 1606, and Amsterdam, 1648). Next amongst the works from the late antique and early medieval canon of sacred history writing comes the ninth-century collective biography, Anastasius's *Lives of the Popes* (better known today as the *Liber pontificalis*), which was continued in the early modern period by several scholars, including Platina, Onofrio Panvinio, and (with the addition of cardinals) by Alfonso Chacón (Ciacconius). Following the chronological order of their original date of composition, the next items on Holstenius's list of books of *historia ecclesiastica* were two works that came to be identified to a unique degree with the genre they examplified: the Dominican Jacobus de Voragine's thirteenth-century collection of saints' lives, *The Golden Legend* (*Legenda aurea*), and the encyclopedic *Speculum naturale, doctrinale, morale et historiale* of his contemporary and fellow Dominican, Vincent of Beauvais (*c*.1190–1264?).

The last three notable examples of early modern editions of late antique and early medieval texts belonging to Holstenius illustrate the continued value placed on early medieval writings in the seventeenth century. First, there was Héribert Rosweyde's 1628 edition of the lives of the Desert Fathers, the *Vitae patrum*, which date from the fourth and fifth centuries. Next there was John Colgan's *Vitae sanctorum Hiberniae* (1624), a 'Noah's Ark' of Irish saints' lives, which preserved for posterity texts which would otherwise have disappeared, as well as the annotated episcopal calendars organized along national lines. Finally, there was the *Martyrologium romanum*, originally a conflation of several calendars of martyrs' feasts from Roman, African and Syrian churches, here in an edition of 1630 with Cesare Baronio's extensive notes and introduction.

Holstenius's private library also included many works of contemporary erudition. In contrast to the preceding studies, these works represent original contributions to knowledge about sacred history, whether in content—as is the case with Antonio Bosio's extensively illustrated survey of part of the network of Roman palaeo-Christian subterranean burial chambers (known as catacombs), *Roma sotteranea* (1632 [1635])—or in structure, as with Sixtus of Siena's encyclopedic list of approved books for the Roman Catholic reader (a kind of mirror image to the Roman Catholic *Index of Prohibited Books*), the *Biblioteca sacra* (1586). Other examples of studies which added to the content of knowledge about sacred history included Nicholas Harpsfield's account of the English Church and its break with Rome, *Historia anglicana ecclesiastica*

235–68. On Holstenius, see Rietbergen, 'Lucas Holstenius (1596–1661)' and Völkel, *Römische Kardinalshaushalte*, pp. 267–306.

(1622); the first volume of William Dugdale's encyclopedic survey of the monasteries suppressed by King Henry VIII in 1536–9, the *Monasticon anglicanum* (1655); Paolo de Angeli's *Descriptio Vaticanae basilicae* (1646); the German Jesuit Christoph Brower's *Fuldensium antiquitatem libri III* (1612); Leone Allacci's confutation of the myth of Pope Joan, *Confutatio fabulae Joannae Papissae* (1645); Agostino Valier's lives of the bishop saints of his diocese of Verona, SS. *episcoporum Veronensium vitae* (1576); Dionigio Bonfant's extravagantly argued *Triumpho de los santos del reyno de Cerdeña* [*Sardinia*] (1635) together with Holstenius's marginal corrections; Nicolas-Hugues Ménard's *Martyrologium benedictinum* (1626); Martin del Río's defence of the identification of St Denis with Dionysius the Areopagite, *Vindiciae areopagiticae* (1607); Antonio Caracciolo's discussion of the contested tradition whereby St James the Greater was considered as the founder of the Spanish Church, the *Biga illustrium controversiarum: de S. Iacobi Apostoli accessu in Hispaniam* (1618); Eugenio Caracciolo's *Napoli sacra* (1624); Johannes Molanus' pioneering account of regional hagiography, *Natales sanctorum belgii* (1595); Ferdinando Ughelli's *Italia sacra* (1644–); Robert de Sainte-Marthe's *Gallia Christiana* (1626); and, of course, Baronio's own *Annales ecclesiastici*, here bound together with the continuations by both the Dominican Abraham Bzowski and the Oratorian Oderico Rainaldi, and also with the Isaac Casaubon's polemical attack on Baronio, the *De rebus sacris et ecclesiasticis: exercitationes XVI* (1615).

Finally, the list of related Greek material (labelled '*Libri ecclesiastici Graecorum*') included several volumes directly relevant to the ongoing project of a desired union with the Greek Orthodox Church. This may be dated from the foundation of the Greek College in Rome in 1576, but it received renewed impetus with the creation of the albeit short-lived Academia Basiliana (active during the 1630s) under the direct patronage of Francesco Barberini, Holstenius's principal patron.[19] In addition to liturgical works—such as the *Euchologium sive rituale ecclesiae Graecae* (1647), which were central to the liturgical life of the Greek-rite monks settled in Italy, Holstenius owned a series of works which sought to demonstrate the degree of consonance which existed between the Greek- and Roman-rite Churches.[20]

The length and variety of this list of books from the personal library of a major Rome-based scholar of ecclesiastical matters who possessed contacts with the highest level of the Roman Catholic hierarchy is intended to draw attention to the very diversity of material that contemporaries included under

[19] For what follows, see Herklotz, *Die Academia Basiliana, passim*.
[20] These included Petrus Arcudius's *De concordia ecclesiae occidentalis et orientalis* and Leone Allacci's *De ecclesiae occidentalis atque orientalis perpetua consensione, libri tres*. The former author had been an early graduate of the Greek College in Rome and had helped engineer the unification of the Polish-Lithuanian Orthodox Church with Rome in 1596.

the catch-all category of *Historia ecclesiastica*. Another point which becomes clearer the more one examines the range of such works is the degree to which early modern ecclesiastical scholarship was indebted for both form and content to its medieval predecessors. In his nine-volume work, *Italia sacra* (1644–62), the Cistercian scholar Ferdinando Ughelli (1596–1670) had taken the long-established genre that was the list of bishops, known more formally as an episcopal calendar, for each of the Italian peninsula's 320 mainland bishoprics, and grafted onto this chronological framework a brief historical treatment of each diocese, thereby creating the first comprehensive framework of ecclesiastical history that was truly Italian in historical scope. By using the episcopal calendar as its principle of organization, Ughelli was employing a genre that can be traced back at least to Tertullian (*c*.160–*c*.220). In the case of the Bollandist *Acta sanctorum*, the ever increasing scale of erudition brought to bear on ever more detailed philological commentary has undoubtedly led us to exaggerate the scientific nature of the scholarship deployed in the early volumes (and to underrate their polemical purpose).

The sense of *dejà vu* would have been overwhelming to any high medieval Church scholar transported in time to the print shops or libraries of post-Reformation Europe. Collective biographies of saintly bishops and popes abounded, as did individual saints' lives. The passions of early martyrs were of special interest to Holstenius, who transcribed a hitherto neglected manuscript of African origin from the monastery of Montecassino containing the early third-century passion of Saints Perpetua and Felicitas, which was published for the first time in 1663, two years after his death.[21] Finally, in the case of the works of de Angeli and Bosio for Rome and William Dugdale for England, one had extensively illustrated studies that engaged head-on with the challenge of interpreting the material culture of medieval and even palaeo-Christian eras (and in the case of Dugdale from the Protestant perspective). As can also be seen from this list of titles, the cluster of genres that was encompassed by the term '*storia ecclesiastica*' was essentially traditional. That is to say, there was not one member of this family of related representations of sacred history that was fundamentally novel or somehow distinctly 'early modern'.

However, while the form and even content of so many of the works of sacred history compiled during the early modern period exhibited strong continuity with their medieval predecessors, some of the ways they came to be composed did change, as can be seen from the following example. On 5 October 1667, the Augustinian Luigi Torelli, a professor of theology at the University of Bologna, wrote to Ughelli: 'And so it is these days, that whosoever writes sacred histories needs to turn to the famous arsenal of such

---

[21] Holstenius, *Passio sanctarum martyrum Perpetuae et Felicitatis.*

knowledge, built by the most reverend father abbot Ughelli.'[22] As author of both a collective hagiography of members of his order and an eight-volume history of the Augustinians which is usefully consulted by scholars to this day, Torelli certainly knew what he was talking about.[23] The collection of 1,533 letters from 438 correspondents written to Ughelli and now held in the Vatican Library reveals not only the extent to which the Cistercian scholar was dependent on a network of informants to fill the gaps in his local knowledge but also the degree to which he himself was regarded by such local Baronios as a potential source of information relevant to their own churches. His correspondents also show, again and again, the importance that information held in ecclesiastical archives had for the effective governance of their churches. Antonio Severoli, archbishop of Nazareth (a title which since 1330 had been transferred to Barletta in Puglia) told Ughelli that he carried an index to his church's archive with him at all times, 'for the needs that might arise in the service of my church'.[24] The bishop of nearby Giovinazzo, Carlo Maranta, writing in 1665, informed Ughelli that in order to defend his diocese's privileges he had been absent some twelve years doing research in the Vatican archives.[25] For these seventeenth-century churchmen, sacred history had very practical uses.

3. USING SACRED HISTORY

The vast majority of the writers encountered in this book desired to present the past as a model for present behaviour and thus, in one sense, not as really past at all. Indeed, the still-repeated warning of Edmund Burke (1729–97) that 'Those who do not know history are destined to repeat it' would not have made much sense to the scholars surveyed in this book, nor to their readers and listeners. For these writers sought to learn about and present Christian history *in order* to repeat it, 'or at the very least to derive practical guidance or other benefits from its details'.[26] This fact alone, I believe, makes it difficult for us to see the practitioners of sacred history in its many forms as 'historians' in

---

[22] 'é così, chi scrive oggidi di historie sacre bisogna che ricorre al famoso arsenale di quelle, architettato di Reverendissimo Padre Abbot Ughelli'. BAV, *Barb. lat. 3240*, fol. 128ʳ.

[23] Torelli, *Secoli agostiniani* and *Ristretto delle vite de gli uomini e delle donne illustri in santità dell'Ordine Agostiniano*.

[24] 'per li bisogni che mi potrebbero occorrere in servitio della mia Chiesa'. The letter is dated 16 May 1649. BAV, *Barb. lat. 3241*, fol. 267ʳ.

[25] 'sono dodici anni sono assente . . . [per] ritrovare alcuni [next word illegible] nell'Archivio Vaticano'. BAV, *Barb lat. 3242*, fol. 437ʳ. Cf. Ditchfield, *Liturgy, Sanctity, and History*, p. 344.

[26] Adam Silverstein, *Islamic History: A Very Short Introduction* (Oxford: Oxford University Press, 2010), p. 108.

the modern sense of the term. Notwithstanding their historical, philological, numismatic, and archaeological bravura when examining both manuscript and material evidence, their mission was different from that of the modern academic historian who, no matter how engaged with contemporary agendas, claims a degree of sceptical detachment that would have been meaningless to his or her early modern predecessor. Matthias Pohlig, in his comprehensive survey of Lutheran historiography, makes a strong case that early modern ecclesiastical scholarship was essentially at the service of, and shaped by, the building of confessional identity.[27] On the Catholic side, it has even been argued that Cesare Baronio should perhaps not be considered as a historian at all. Rather, his historical research was so completely subservient to his desire to make liturgical practice a path to spiritual intimacy with those holy heroes from the first centuries of the apostolic Church, that one might instead see it as a form of prayer.[28]

In such works as the revised *Martyrologium romanum*, for which, as already noted, Baronio wrote an important historical introduction as well as extensive notes, time became transformed into devotional space, as the Oratorian directly mapped the places of suffering and burial of the martyrs onto Rome's topography, as has been seen in Chapter 3. The provision of historical precedent for the effective exercise and defence of ecclesiastical jurisdiction was to prove an equally powerful spur to research into sacred history as was the correct performance of ritual and worship. Of course, this use of historical precedent in support of present privileges was not new. Long ago, Richard Southern demonstrated just how important was the role played by monastic chronicles in the preservation of property and privilege in the aftermath of Norman Conquest of England in 1066.[29] To invert the famous quip delivered by Tancredi to his admiring if sceptical uncle, Prince Fabrizio, in Giuseppe Tomasi di Lampedusa's historical novel, *The Leopard* (1958): in order to accommodate change, things must appear to have remained the same.[30] However, it must be said that the sheer scale of change brought about by the Reformation and by the consequent attempts of both secular and ecclesiastical governments to extend their jurisdictional authority over the bodies and souls of their subjects, was unprecedented. When one adds to this the advent of printing, with all the scope that this offered for the generation of official decrees and instructions, it is not to be wondered why the preservation of the archival record took on a new urgency in this period.

---

[27] Pohlig, *Zwischen Gelehrsamkeit und konfessioneller Identitätstiftung*.

[28] Ditchfield, 'Baronio storico nel suo tempo'.

[29] Southern, 'Aspects of the European Tradition of Historical Writing', pp. 246–56.

[30] 'Se vogliamo che tutto rimanga com'è, bisogna che tutto cambi' ('If we wish things to remain the same, everything must change'). Tomasi di Lampedusa, *Il Gattopardo* (Feltrinelli: Milan, 1958), p. 21.

Bishops had a distinctive role to play as coordinators of historical research within their own dioceses. Amongst the constitutions approved at the Third Provincial Synod of the archdiocese of Milan in 1573 may be found the following passage:

> The bishop, [as holder of] an office instituted at the very beginning of the history of the Church, should diligently collect together the names, pastoral character and pastoral actions of his predecessors, and he should make certain that all these things are written down, arranged in order and put into a certain book so that the memory be conserved of those things which have been done or instituted by those bishops and so that they [the books] may be of perpetual use and assistance in the good governance of that church.[31]

This was printed as part of what was may justly be considered the most important collection of documents relating to diocesan governance ever published, the *Acta ecclesiae mediolanensis* (AEM). If the canons and decrees of the Council of Trent may be regarded as having provided the 'theory' of a reformed Roman Catholicism, the AEM provided the most comprehensive manual of Tridentine 'best practice'. Owing to its direct association with Carlo Borromeo (1538–84), the model pastor par excellence of reformed Roman Catholicism (who was archbishop of Milan from 1564 until his premature death from overwork and excessive fasting), it enjoyed truly global circulation over the succeeding centuries.[32] This particular passage was sometimes quoted in the front of works of local church history in the same way that Church authorities would require an *imprimatur* to indicate that their printing enjoyed official approval.[33] In this sense, it may rightly be regarded as a manifesto for sacred history and the latter's relevance for ecclesiastical good governance.

---

[31] 'Episcopus, id quod ab initio nascentis ecclesiae institutum fuit, ut rerum episcopali studio curaque gestarum monimenta existerent, conquiri diligentissime curet, tum singulorum episcoporum, qui praecesserunt, nomina, genus et pastorales eorundem actiones. Quae omnia literis consignari, ordineque conscripta, in librum certum referri curet, ut eorum memoria conservetur, et quae ab iisdem, vel acta vel instituta sunt ad aliquam ecclesiasticae disciplinae norman perpetuo usui esse possivit, atque adiumento in illa ecclesiase bene gerenda.' *Acta ecdesiae mediolanensis* (AEM), II, col. 278.

[32] Cf. Cattaneo, 'La singolare fortuna degli "Acta Ecclesiae Mediolanensis"', pp. 291–17. Although there were only two editions of the AEM issued outside the Italian peninsula (Paris, 1643 and Lyon, 1683), there are no fewer than forty copies extant in Polish libraries (of which half had arrived during Borromeo's lifetime). See H. D. Wojtyska, 'L'influsso in Polonia e in Lituania', pp. 527–49 (at 538). Jerzy Radziwill, bishop of Vilnius wrote to Borromeo on 7 January 1581 for a copy of the AEM: 'so that by reading it I can learn about correct ecclesistical governance . . . or at least might try to imitate such a model'. Biblioteca Ambrosiana, Milan, F. 38. *Inf.*, fol. 527ʳ. We also know that Juan de Palafox y Mendoza, bishop of Puebla (1639–49) and for several months in 1642 caretaker viceroy of New Spain had a copy of the AEM and was a champion of episcopal power; see David Brading, *The First America: The Spanish Monarchy, Creole Patriots and the Liberal State, 1492–1867* (Cambridge: Cambridge University Press, 1991), p. 241.

[33] E.g. the 'Lectori optimo' to Rocco Pirri's *Notitiae Siciliensium ecclesiarum* and Sainte-Marthe, *Gallia christiana*, I, preface, note a.

However, they were more than mere exercises in local patriotism and support for devotional distinctiveness, as has been seen from those who corresponded with Ferdinando Ughelli. They were also a way of facilitating the day-to-day governance of the diocese. The passage quoted above from the AEM comes at the end of a section of the synodal constitutions which was dedicated to the exercise of due episcopal jurisdiction ('*De iis quae ad episcopale forum pertinent*'). Near the start of this section, bishops were required to keep their papers in a secure chest to which there were to be two keys: one kept by the bishop himself and the other by his chancellor.[34] Moreover, so as to ensure the functionality (*décor et cultus*) of their churches, parish priests were required to keep written testimony in support of the authenticity of relics and images displayed there (including any information about their previous location).[35] In addition, under the section 'instructions useful for the reform [and exercise] of archiepiscopal jurisdiction', immediately after a passage reiterating the importance of keeping accurate records of relics and related objects, there was a section simply entitled 'organizing archives'.[36] By giving such prominence to the practical utility of records from the past for ecclesiastical governance in the present, Borromeo was simply following up at a diocesan level what he had tried to institute in Rome when he was responsible for the Secretariate of State during the pontificate of his uncle, Pius IV (1559–65). It was at Borromeo's behest that the pope first ordered the formation of the Consistorial Archives and resumed the transfer of the papal archives from Avignon. Moreover, in a brief of 15 June 1565, the pope charged Cardinal Mola with nothing less than the setting up of a central Vatican archive.[37]

This and related initiatives—which included the establishment of the Congregation of the Council charged with preparing a comprehensive edition of the acts and proceedings of the Council of Trent in order to effect its implementation more effectively—turned out to be a short-lived season of papal *perestroika* before the resumption of a deep-freeze on archival access under Pius V (1566–72) and his successors. After the death of Pius IV, the next concerted effort to consolidate the papal archives, which by then were dispersed between the papers kept in the Apostolic Chamber, the Castel S. Angelo, and the Vatican Library, was made under Paul V (1605–21), who

[34] AEM, II, col. 278.

[35] 'Primo, ut scripta, tabulae, literae, certi annalium codices, aliave cuiusvis generis monumenta quae in iis ipsius ecclesiis, earumve atriis, atque aedibus aut aliis loci extant, schedulaeque vasculis, arcusve sacrarum reliquiarum affixae, inclusaeve recognoscantur accurato et diligenter; unde illarum vel traslatio, vel collocatio ibi facta, cognosci, aut alia eiusmodi notitia earundem haberi queat.' AEM, II, col. 300.

[36] 'De archiviis constituendis', AEM, II, col. 1653.

[37] Pastor, *History of the Popes*, XVI, p. 409. Cf. for the broader context: Filippini, *Memoria della Chiesa*, pp. 41–74.

established the Vatican archive in 1612 (which was to be known as the 'private' archive—i.e. *Archivio segreto vaticano*—from the 1640s).[38] However, it was only in 1630, with the transfer from the Vatican Library of the *acta* of the Council of Trent, that the archives became administratively separate from the library. And the former was to remain off limits until Pope Leo XIII opened the Vatican archives to scholars in 1881.[39]

A certain overlap between the roles of librarian and archivist had obtained in this area of papal administration since apostolic times. As the Augustinian scholar Onofrio Panvinio had explained in his brief treatise on the Vatican Library, the two offices had been even less distinct in the library's earliest days:

> Antiently, the president of the library was called librario, then cancellario, whose office was to collect with diligence not only the books but also to copy the Bulls, the Popes' decrees, the acta and constitutions of their synods and to keep everything exactly, because it appeared convenient that the cancellario, or as he is now called the secretary to the pope, should have the managing and preserving of the books, the library being in those days as it were the office of the secretary or Chancery, but in our times the offices of the Chancery and of the Library are divided.[40]

This historical conjunction of roles for the library and its custodian, as both guardian of the Church's institutional memory and its working administrative archive, was indeed central to Panvinio's belief that the papal library had been at the heart of ecclesiastical governance at all points in the Church's history. Paul Nelles argues that Panvinio's treatise was, in fact, written as an integral part of a work on St Peter's and the Papal Palace which remained unpublished in the author's lifetime.[41] This larger work, *De rebus antiquis memorabilibus*, exemplifies the degree to which works of sacred erudition in this period could deploy several genres in the course of a single volume. It began with a biography of St Peter (bk 1), which was followed by an account of the deeds of Emperor Constantine (bk 2). This was succeeded, in turn, by a topographical survey of the Vatican area (bk 3) and then by successive chapters on the prerogatives, dignities, and honours of the basilica (bks 4, 5, and 6). It was in book 7, in the immediate context of a chorographical description of the

---

[38] Filippini, *Memoria della Chiesa*, p. 72, n. 51.

[39] Chadwick, *Catholicism and History*. Notoriously, scholars had to wait until 1901 for the first volume of a scholarly edition of the acts and proceedings of the Council of Trent. Published in 19 volumes by the Görres-Gesellschaft in Fribourg im Breisgau, this edition was only brought to completion in 2001.

[40] This treatise by Panvinio was widely diffused when it was included in Franciscus Schottus's popular guidebook, the *Itinerarium Italiae*, first published for the Jubilee of 1600. The passage above was taken from the translation attributed to Edmund Warcup, entitled *Italy in its Original Glory, Ruine and Revival*, pp. 221–6 (at 224).

[41] Panvinio, *De rebus antiquis memorabilibus*. Cf. Nelles, *The Public Library and Late Humanist Scholarship*, pp. 182–90.

remains of the old basilica and its relation to the new church, that Panvinio integrated his treatise on the Vatican Library.

The first prefect of the separately constituted Vatican archive, appointed in 1630, was Felice Contelori (1588–1652). He had become Vatican librarian in 1626, having previously looked after the Barberini family library, and his several research projects in that role provide eloquent testimony to the utility of historical knowledge for effective papal governance in both the temporal and spiritual spheres.[42] Before his appointment as librarian, Contelori had already compiled a list of the officers responsible for ensuring the grain supply for Rome from the early Middle Ages, which ended with some concrete proposals for this office's reform: *De annona sue de re frumentaria*.[43] Of even more central concern to papal governance was Contelori's major project undertaken in 1627–8: a history of the Apostolic Chamber, containing the texts and summaries of papal bulls and other archival documentation from the period of Urban VI (pope, 1378–89) to that of Clement VII (pope, 1523–34).[44] Contelori's next (and first published) work, *De praefecto urbis liber* (1631), examined the office of Rome's prefect, a topic which had gained pressing relevance in 1624 when the holder of this office, Francesco Maria della Rovere, Duke of Urbino, anticipating his own death, formally agreed to hand over his duchy for annexation to the papal states. Contelori was also a member of the committee set up by Pope Urban VIII to oversee clarification of the legal details attendant on the successful absorption of the duchy into the Papal States after the duke's death in 1631.

Contelori's next project, which bore more directly on the subject of ecclesiastical history, concerned the precise role played by the Republic of Venice in brokering the treaty between Pope Alexander III and the Holy Roman Emperor, Frederick Barbarossa, in 1177. By further research amongst records relating to Alexander's pontificate and in the contemporary chronicle by Romualdo of Salerno (1110/20–82), Contelori reinforced the position already adopted by Cesare Baronio in the *Annales* to the effect that the Venetians had done nothing more than host the negotiations.[45] In 1635, this led Pope Urban VIII to alter the inscription to the fresco commemorating the treaty in the *sala regia* of the Vatican palace so that it no longer attributed any positive role to the Venetians, a move which was to lead to the withdrawal of the republic's ambassador from the papal court.

---

[42] For what follows I have drawn on the article by Petrucci in the *Dizionario biografico degli italiani* (hereafter DBI).

[43] BAV, Vat. lat. 12.247, fols. 10^r–62^r.

[44] *Historia cameralis seu de dominio et iurisdictione sedis apostolicae ecclesiaeque romanae in regna, provincias, civitates, castra, terras et alia loca*. This remains unpublished in five manuscript volumes in BAV, Vat. lat. 2704–2708.

[45] Contelori, *Concordiae inter Alexandrum III S. P. et Fridaricum I imperatorem Venetiis confirmatae narratio*. Cf. the manuscript copy held at BAV, Barb. lat. 2563.

The full extent of Contelori's range can be appreciated if we consider just two further published works. The first, the *Tractatus et praxis de canonizatione sanctorum* (1634), was the fullest treatment yet committed to print of canonization procedure, published in the same year as the papal brief *Coelestis Ierusalem cives*, which became the 'magna carta' for all papal canonization policy down to 1983.[46] Contelori's text provided an exhaustive documentary appendix to facilitate the implementation and operation of the brief's measures. Indeed, until the publication of Prospero Lambertini's landmark treatise, *De servorum Dei beatificatione et beatorum canonizatione* (1734–8), Contelori's *Tractatus* remained the only detailed commentary available. Contelori's annotated list of cardinals made between 1294–1430—*Elenchus em. et rev. S. R. E. cardinalium ab anno 1294 ad annum 1430* e *Martini Quinti vita ex legitimis documentis collecta* (1641)—was intended to correct and supplement Alfonso Chacón's continuation to Platina's *Lives of the Popes*: the *Vita et gesta summorum pontificum a Christo Domino usque ad Clementem VIII* (first edition, 1601). To this day Contelori's *Elenchus* remains the scholar's edition of choice to consult.

It is within such a context of practical relevance for the present governance of the Church of St Peter that we must understand Cesare Becilli's assertion of the importance of *historia sacra*, which was quoted near the beginning of this chapter. Becilli made this clear when he wrote:

> Let the [librarian-archivists] have the task of continuing ecclesiastical history down to our time and into the future; let them restore the ancient lives of the saints to their original simplicity, but elucidate them with notes; let them likewise collect the lives of the Roman popes, also elucidated with notes; let them write the lives of future popes from the annals; let them uphold the tradition of ecclesiastical history and establish a tradition of ecclesiastical geography.[47]

Immediately below, under the list of 'duties to be fulfilled', Becilli specifically indicated that the deeds of popes, as reflected in their bulls and other official edicts, should be ordered chronologically so as to bring Baronio's *Annales* up to date. Here we have sacred history functioning explicitly as an archive of legislative decisions to enable papal governance as well as pastoral tradition to continue, *semper eadem*.[48]

---

[46] Contelori, *Tractatus et praxis de canonizatione sanctorum*.

[47] 'H—m munus sit historiam ecclesiasticam persequi usque ad nostra tempora ac semper in futurum. Antiquas sanctorum vitas in pristinam simplicitatem restituere sed notis illustrare. Vitas Romanorum pontificum colligere notisque itidem illustrare futurorum Pontificum se—um ab annalibus vitas conscribere. Historiam ecclesiasticam tueri. Geographicam ecclesiasticam instruere'. BVR, Ms. 146, fol. 5ᵛ.

[48] Although as Stefan Bauer has shown (*The Censorship and Fortuna of Platina's Lives of the Popes*) after Platina it had become almost impossible to write and publish unvarnished papal vitae.

4. REMEMBERING SACRED HISTORY

Notwithstanding the problematizing of certain genres, in particular lives of the popes, occasioned by confessional strife, the essential continuity between medieval and early modern treatments of sacred history, together with the extent to which 'religious' ways of thinking about the past remained hegemonic during the period covered by this volume, has undoubtedly been obscured by the problem of labels. Here an anachronistic understanding of the distinction between hagiography and historiography has been largely to blame.[49] In Italian, for example, it was not until 1742 that the word '*agiografo*' for the writer of saints' lives entered usage.[50] The giving of a name to the genre itself—'*agiografia*'—had to wait until 1925, when the critic Ugo Ojetti (1871–1946), writing under the pseudonym of 'Tantalo', used it in his appreciation of the recently deceased archaeologist Giacomo Boni (1859–1925) for the Italian daily *Corriere della Sera*.[51] Felice Lifshitz has traced the distinction between hagiography and historiography to the decision of the nineteenth-century editors of the *Monumenta Germaniae Historica* (MGH), founded in 1819, to separate the two genres and privilege the latter.[52] In their tireless efforts to construct the medieval chronicle as an identifiably distinct genre and as the privileged bearer of what they considered the main storyline of the past—chronological narratives of the struggle between and within communities (whether civic or ecclesiastical) and the part this played in the ultimate emergence of a unified political authority and the secular nation state—these editors effectively marginalized hagiography.

The editors of the MGH were not the first to try to excise sacred history from the historical canon. They followed a distinguished Italian precedent. The editor of the twenty-eight volume *Rerum Italicarum scriptores* (RIS) (1723–38), a polycentred narrative account of northern and central Italy during the Middle Ages, Lodovico Antonio Muratori (1672–1750), made extensive use of scissors-and-paste methods to try to render the chronicle genre more coherent. By excising what he considered extraneous matter—such as lists of bishops or of civic officials, as well as eulogies of places or persons which interrupted the annalistic framework of the chronicles proper—he conferred an artificial homogeneity on the civic chronicle as a historiographical genre.[53]

---

[49] For what follows, see Ditchfield, '"Historia magistra sanctitatis"?'

[50] It did so in the *Dialoghi* by the Tuscan scholar Giovanni Lami (1698–1770), where the immediate context was discussion of Baronio: 'Così il Cardinale Baronio all'anno XXXI disse essere stata detta apocrifa la lettera di Cristo ad Abgaro da Gelasio Papa, in quanto non era agiografa [sic], nè faceva parte del sacro canone.' Lami, *Dialoghi di Aniceto Nemesio in risposta e confutazione delle stolte e indigne lettere* ... (Rovereto, 1742), p. xxvii.

[51] The original article appeared on 11 July 1925. I consulted it in Ojetti, *Cose viste*, pp. 650–6 (at 652).

[52] Lifshitz, 'Beyond Positivism and Genre', pp. 95–113.

[53] See e.g. Muratori's rearrangement of the constituent parts of Giovanni Musso's *Chronicon placentinum* in *Rerum Italicarum scriptores* (RIS), XVI (pp. 447–634), when compared to the

A related problem, which has rendered sacred history something of a 'lost continent', has been a teleological approach to the history of hagiography—one that has sought a progression from the absurd, miracle-laden tales in such collections as Jacobus de Voragine's thirteenth-century *Golden Legend*, to the proto-scientific, philological rigour associated, above all, with that greatest of 'great historical enterprises', the Bollandists' sixty-seven volume *Acta sanctorum* (1643–1925).[54] This Whiggish, evolutionary narrative simultaneously underplays the continuing popularity that Voragine's text enjoyed down to the start of the seventeenth century and overplays the 'scientific' nature of the *Acta sanctorum*.[55]

Indeed, the sheer scale and universal scope of this (still unfinished) project to print editions with commentary of the best available lives of the saints following the liturgical calendar may have distracted people from noting its distinctly provincial origins. These lay with Héribert Rosweyde (1569–1629), a Jesuit scholar from Liége, who wished to compile a collection of all the saints' lives that could be found, to begin with, in manuscript in the libraries of the southern Netherlands: the *Fasti sanctorum quorum vitae in belgicis bibliothecis manuscriptae* (1607). That this slight volume of fewer than one hundred pages was to give birth to a monument which finally ran to 60,000 folio-sized pages commands admiration if not downright incredulity to this day.[56] But Rosweyde already had more universal ambitions. Their scale is outlined in the first section of the *Fasti*, in which he sketched a plan for eighteen volumes: three to be dedicated entirely to major feasts relating to Christ and the Virgin, followed by twelve more, one each to be devoted to the feasts of a single month. The next volume (sixteen) was to be devoted entirely to martyrologies, and the one after that (seventeen) to outlining in general terms what was necessary for the better comprehension of such texts. Finally, the eighteenth volume was to contain no fewer than thirteen indices to maximize facility of use. Rosweyde followed this sketch of his intention with a list of over 1,300 saints. In the event, the first two volumes of the *Acta sanctorum*, published finally by Rosweyde's successor, Jean Bolland (1596–1665) with the help of his younger assistant Godfreid Henschen, which covered just the month of January, contained material relating to over 2,000 saints from Europe and beyond. As the title of the first volume of the *Acta* put it:

---

manuscript text which he worked from, Modena, Biblioteca estense, Ms. Lat. XLV. Cf. Ditchfield, 'Erudizione ecclesiastica', pp. 477–8.

[54] David Knowles, *Great Historical Enterprises*, pp. 1–32. Cf. Ditchfield, 'Sanctity in Early Modern History', pp. 98–112.

[55] The year 1613 saw the last edition in any Western European language for the next 230 years, save for a single Latin printing (Madrid, 1688).

[56] Godding, *Bollandistes*, pp. 23–33.

Acts of the saints, who are honoured throughout the world or celebrated by
Catholic writers, collected, ordered and explained by means of notes and based on
ancient documents in Greek, Latin and other languages by Jean Bolland, theologian of the Society of Jesus [who] has sought to preserve the style of the original
texts. He has been assisted by Godfried Henschen theologian from the same
Society.[57] [Figure 4.2]

Despite the universal scale of Rosweyde's ambitions, the actual results were, at
least during his own lifetime, distinctly prosaic and circumscribed.[58] At
Rosweyde's death in 1629, he does not appear to have moved far beyond an
ambition to supplement the work of the most comprehensive collection of
saints' lives then available: the six-volume *De probatis sanctorum historiis*
(1570–5) by the Carthusian from Cologne, Lorenz Sauer (Surius). Rosweyde
worked alone in this enterprise, as did his successor, Jean Bolland, until in
1635 Bolland was joined by Godfried Henschen (1601–81). Together they
produced the first volumes of the *Acta sanctorum* until they were joined
in 1660 by the greatest of all Bollandists, Daniel Papebroch (1628–1714). In
its early decades, this numerically insignificant, informal group of scholars
from a single Jesuit province was less well known to contemporaries than such
scholars as the Irish Franciscans Luke Wadding (1588–1657), author of the
most extensive history of his order ever written, the *Annales minorum* (1625–
54) and John Colgan (*c*.1600–*c*.1657), whose *Acta sanctorum Hiberniae* (1645)
saved so many Irish saints from oblivion. This is unsurprising, especially
when one considers how dependent the Bollandists were—both linguistically
and codicologically—on their Franciscan colleagues for information about
Irish saints.[59] Indeed, the polyglot bravura of the Bollandists of modern
times has perhaps made us overlook the fact that it was only after the
famous pilgrimage to Rome by Henschen and Papebroch for manuscripts in

---

[57] 'Acta sanctorum quotquot toto orbe coluntur, vel a Catholicis Scriptoribus celebrantur,
quae ex Latinis et Graecis, aliarumque gentium antiquis monumentis collegit, digessit, notis
illustravit Ioannes Bollandus Societatis Iesu theologus, servata primigenia scriptorum phrasi.
Operam et studium contulit Godefridus Henschenius eiusdem Societatis theologus.'

[58] E.g. nothing in the inventory (made in *c*.1613) of the more than 500 books that Rosweyde
kept in his rooms indicated the scale the project was later to have. Indeed, the largest proportion
of texts is taken up by '*Historia profana*' (106 titles), which starts by listing geographical works
such as Ortelius's Theatrum urbis (in a 1603 edition) and '*Miscellanea profana*' (102). There
were just forty-four volumes of '*Historici sacra*' [*sic*], which included the 1606 Leiden edition of
Eusebius (with notes by Scaliger), and with a further thirty-one volumes of '*Miscellanea sacra*'
(containing such works as Johannes Molanus's major study of sacred images and Angelo Rocca's
pioneering treatise on canonization of 1601), and sixteen editions of the Martyrology. The
number of titles of '*Historici sacra*' was almost rivalled by the forty-three volumes of poetry.
Rosweyde's personal library also contained an edition of Aesop's fables. I consulted the list in the
Royal Library, Brussels: Ms. 8523 D. For a convenient numerical analysis, see the table in
Godding, *De Rosweyde aux Acta Sanctorum*, p. 196.

[59] See Sawilla, *Antiquarianismus, Hagiographie und Historie*, pp. 343, 529–39, 556–6, 567–76.
Cf. Pádraig Ó Riain, 'Irish Hagiography of the Late Sixteenth- and Early Seventeenth Centuries'.
On Colgan, see below, Ch. 9.

1660–2 that the Bollandists began to include Greek hagiographic material in the original language.[60]

Nevertheless, by the end of the seventeenth century, the Bollandists had established a dense network of correspondents, with Papebroch taking a leading part in turning this small group of scholars based on the geographical margins of Roman Catholicism into a veritable hagiographical research institute.[61] Something of the scale of correspondence may be judged by taking just a single register kept by Jean-Baptiste du Sollier (1669–1740), which listed over 12,000 letters he had sent in the course of fulfilling his duties as a conscientious member of the vibrant pre-Enlightenment Republic of Letters.[62] A catalogue from this period listing all the titles to be found in the *Museum Bollandianum* in Antwerp lists saints' lives according to their city and region ('*Vitae sanctorum singularium urbium et regionum*'); while the numerous martyrologies in the Bollandists' possession were subdivided into categories that included not only the predictable 'by monastic order' ('*martyrologia monastica*') but also 'by nation' ('*martyrologia nationalia*').[63] As the full title of the *Acta sanctorum* reminds us, it is of the very nature of saints to enjoy universal veneration. Although it was a particular preoccupation of the papacy after the Reformation to draw an ever clearer distinction between fully fledged saints and those who were permitted only regional or even merely local cults (the blessed), in reality the distinction was blurred. This was undeniably the case in the countless volumes of sacred erudition—those prayers in prose compiled with love and devotion by local Baronios the length and breadth of the Roman Catholic world—in which one invariably found a prefatory 'declaration by the author' ('*Protestatio auctoris*') which declared how the terms '*sanctus/a*' and '*beatus/a*' were not being used in the canonical sense of the terms but simply as they reflected local tradition and usage. [64]

---

[60] Godding, *Bollandistes*, pp. 61–73.

[61] Du Gaiffier, 'Hagiographie et critique', pp. 291ff.

[62] Pomian, 'De la lettre au périodique', p. 26.

[63] Library of the Société des Bollandistes, Brussels: Ms. 23, fols. 45^r–46^r, 221^r–233^r. My sincere thanks to Robert Godding for drawing my attention to and for allowing me to consult this series of five volumes (Mss. 20–4). The first two are arranged by author; the second two by subject; and the final one is devoted to manuscripts. The catalogue is undated, but the date of publication of the most recent books listed have led Godding to surmise that it was made in the 1740s.

[64] See e.g. that included immediately after the dedication to the Duke of Parma and Piacenza in volume I of Pietro Maria Campi's *Dell'historia ecclesiastica di Piacenza*: 'In the history here before you of the most noble church and city of Piacenza, if by chance one finds the terms Blessed or Saint, it is made clear that such [holy persons] have not been officially recognized as such by the Roman Church [non costi chiaramente che sia stato dianzi [*sic*] dalla Romana Chiesa preconizato, o havuto per tale], the present author declares that he is merely reporting the honour which others have shown to them and written down [protesta qui l'Autore di haver sol trasportato in essa ciò che da altri in onore di quello è stato posto in carta].'

5. CONCLUSION: THINKING WITH SACRED HISTORY

When Catholic writers of the sixteenth and seventeenth centuries sought the historical tools to serve their needs, they had a rich tradition to draw on, because there were already a broad range of medieval genres that dealt with ecclesiastical history. As well as Church histories proper—beginning with that written in the fourth century for a newly respectable faith by Eusebius, whose extensive quotations from original documents provided the model for all his numerous imitators down to Baronio and beyond—there were the more narrowly conceived works which catalogued the sacred patrimony of Rome and its local churches. As has been seen, these included collected lives of popes and cardinals, episcopal calendars, and histories of dioceses and of individual churches within them (often complete with lists of relics they proudly protected). Perhaps most numerous of all, however, were the richly varied accounts of the deeds of the saints. They could be as brief as the bare references made to the place and date of a saint's martyrdom in the Roman Martyrology, as concise as a single liturgical lesson composed as a second nocturn reading for Mattins in the Roman Breviary, or as discursive as the saints' lives compiled for preachers requiring exempla for their sermons by authors of lectionaries such as the thirteenth-century classic *Golden Legend* of Jacobus de Voragine. In addition, there were numerous collective lives of saints arranged by diocese, region, or religious order. Finally, there were individual saints' lives which, increasingly in the post-Reformation period, were presented together with the text of their liturgical office to be recited on their feast day.

This chapter has sought to illustrate, mainly but not exclusively from the perspective of scholars in Rome, the degree to which interest in sacred history was informed by the firm belief that it had practical import for ecclesiastical governance. Demonstration of continuity in legal rights and privileges was not just a strategy to counter Protestant charges of corruption and decline. Nor did it serve only to refurbish and preserve particular, local, or regional religious identities. It was also the *sine qua non* of effective control of priests over their parishes and bishops over their dioceses, as Carlo Borromeo reiterated so influentially in his widely circulated synodal decrees. The same prelate also realized the vital importance of a fully functioning central archive in Rome itself. When his uncle's successor, Pius V, decided, in a more cautious spirit wholly consonant with his previous position as Commissary General of the Roman Inquisition, not to make available the full documentation of the deliberations behind the canons and decrees of the Council of Trent, he was nonetheless displaying an appreciation of the power of the past to disturb the present that was very Borromean in spirit. Moreover, his brief *Inter omnes* (6 June 1566) merely repeated the injunctions concerning the need for ecclesiastical records that Borromeo had already made in his first provincial council.

Pius V's policy left the Roman Church vulnerable to a hostile warts-and-all historical account of the Council, in which the political wheeling and dealing that went on behind the scenes might be brought to the fore. Such a treatment of Trent was in fact carried out barely fifty years after the closure of the Council by the Venetian historian Paolo Sarpi in his polemically brilliant if ultimately two-dimensional *Istoria del concilio tridentino*. Published pseudonymously in London in 1619, having being smuggled out of Venice in a diplomatic pouch, and referred to by contemporaries as 'the Iliad of our times', this gripping if relentlessly materialistic account of the Council of Trent, which gained wide popularity and indeed notoriety, may perhaps help today's readers of works of sacred history to appreciate their enduring capacity to delight as well as instruct.

Part II

National History and Sacred History

5

The *Germania illustrata*, Humanist History, and the Christianization of Germany*

David J. Collins, S.J.

> Celebrated men and well-born youths, wipe away the hackneyed slanders against the Germans by the Greek, Latin, and Hebrew writers who ascribe to us drunkenness, savagery, barbarity, and everything else brutish and deranged. Consider it shameful to be unfamiliar with the histories of the Greeks and Latins. Consider it beyond all shame to be unfamiliar with the antiquities and nations of our own land.
>
> Conrad Celtis, 'Inaugural Lecture at the University in Ingolstadt', 1492.[1]

The inaugural lecture of the humanist Conrad Celtis (1459–1508) at the University of Ingolstadt in 1492 is often taken as having inspired the most important historiographical undertaking in Germany until the founding of the *Monumenta Germaniae Historica* in 1819. Although the origins of a patriotic German historiography and the relative merits of scholarly developments thereafter are surely arguable, it is impossible to overlook that in the fifteenth and sixteenth centuries learned authors across the Holy Roman Empire, Renaissance humanists among them, dedicated themselves with élan to what the poet laureate encouraged in his address, studying and writing about the great personages and events of a newly conceived German past. Celtis's goal was the composition of a *Germania illustrata*, a volume whose title and scope were inspired by the *Italia illustrata* of the Florentine humanist Flavio Biondo (1392–1463). Although Celtis and his contemporaries did not attain the goal in their lifetimes, their abundant efforts and partial achievements have in the

---

* I prepared this chapter whilst at the *Monumenta Germaniae Historica* in Munich as a fellow of the Alexander von Humboldt Foundation and the Gerda Henkel Foundation. I wish to express my thanks to these foundations for their financial support and to the MGH for the working environment and learned collegiality it graciously provided.
[1] Celtis, 'Oratio in Gymnasio in Ingelstadio', in *Panegyris ad duces Bavariae*, pp. 16–40.

meantime collectively become known as the *Germania illustrata* project and are indeed recognized as among the greatest historiographical undertakings of the early modern period.[2]

Even as the pursuit of a *Germania illustrata* has received considerable attention in modern scholarship, the religious dimension of the historiographical developments has been, if not ignored outright, treated with ambivalence.[3] Despite more recently pronounced trends towards recognizing and analysing religion as integral to early modern society in Germany and across Europe,[4] not a little modern German scholarship still maintains, or at least presupposes, that the hallmark of early modern history-writing that best distinguishes it from its medieval antecedents is an orientation towards the secular, both in what was written about and the forms in which it was written.[5] In consequence, modern researchers in search of the historiographically significant have been implicitly guided away from religious content, genres, and arguments in their sources.

The problem with this distinctive privileging of the secular is that it does not account for much of what we find in the patriotic history-writing undertaken by Celtis and his contemporaries. In fact, authors of patriotic histories of Germany and its constitutive regions incorporated abundant religious content (concerning persons, places, and events) into their works; and authors of 'religious' and ecclesiastical documents (such as episcopal chronicles and saints' lives) expounded panegyrically on the beauty of the landscapes, the richness of the natural resources, and the temperaments of local peoples (sometimes virtuous, sometimes wicked) in the regions where

---

[2] Strauss, *Germania Illustrata*, p. vii.

[3] Gerald Strauss's work on early modern patriotic history-writing, however, still merits close attention: Strauss, *Sixteenth-Century Germany*; Strauss, *Historian in an Age of Crisis*. Patriotic history-writing in this period is currently also a popular topic for medievalists and early modernists in German-language scholarship. The scholars most responsible for inspiring this research generally include Johannes Helmrath, Peter Johanek, Dieter Mertens, Ulrich Muhlack, and Hans Patze (dec.).

[4] Dieter Wuttke, an emeritus professor of philology at Bamberg, is representative of the tendency towards attending to the religious dimension of humanist writings. In the introduction to his dissertation on Sebatian Brant's writings on the hermit-saint Onuphrius, Roland Stieglecker, a student of Prof. Wuttke's, offers a critical overview of the historiography: Stieglecker, *Renaissance eines Heiligen*, pp. 19–34.

[5] Ulrich Muhlack, an erstwhile professor of history at Frankfurt, has described the secularity of humanist historiography as *inhaltlich-thematisch* and *formal-methodisch*. Muhlack, 'Die humanistische Historiographie: Umfang, Bedeutung, Probleme', pp. 6–11. Muhlack elsewhere ascribes to humanist historiography secularizing tendencies, described in his words as a movement away from a society defined by the *res publica christiana*: Muhlack, 'Humanistische Historiographie', p. 33. Johannes Helmrath also describes as one of five humanist hallmarks of history-writing the removal of 'divinely directed salvation history': Helmrath, 'Probleme', p. 354. Several recent volumes of collected scholarship on humanism and historiography including its contribution to national, regional, and cultural identity likewise focus on 'profane' history. Helmrath et al. (eds.), *Diffusion*; Patze (ed.), *Geschichtsschreibung*.

their holy protagonists lived and worked.[6] The goal of this chapter is to consider afresh the place of religious history in the construction of patriotic identities in early modern Germany as manifested in the contributions to the early *Germania illustrata* project by Celtis's approximate contemporaries. The Reformation, which introduced new confessionalized interests into history-writing, provides an approximate endpoint.[7]

The authors of the most important and the most typical historical writings in this period used religious materials extensively, blending their telling of sacred and profane history strategically, and scarcely distinguishing them as kinds of history-writing. They contributed to the development of a patriotic history and a sense of political identity not in spite of but *because of* these religious referents. Developing patriotic loyalties in the history-writing become evident even though strong regional loyalties and a weak notion of an overarching *Germania* challenged these writers in their search for a German homeland. In fact, they produced more and better historical literature celebrating regions—e.g., Bavaria, Thuringia, Westphalia—than Germany as a whole. For this reason, the word '*patria*', which does occasionally appear in the writing under investigation, will be used in this chapter to describe the political and cultural communities that, whatever their size, attracted the history writers' attention. Regionalism both shaped and was shaped by the kinds of history-writing falling within the scope of this volume. While the histories of ecclesiastical institutions and saints' lives described localized, particular phenomena, they did so in broadly recognizable forms that might enhance the political, cultural, and religious significance of the region—the *patria*—in question.

What follows aims to elaborate on that development by examining how German history writers between *c.*1450 and 1520 treated the historical process of Christianization, and how they understood its significance. For the sake of clarity, the national and the regional manifestations of this history-writing will be considered in sequence. First the chapter will consider how the overarching

---

[6] E.g. Müller, *Die spätmittelalterliche Bistumsgeschichtsschreibung*; Müller, 'Die humanistische Bistumsgeschichtsschreibung'; Collins, *Reforming Saints*, pp. 75–97. Addressing the religious dimension of medieval regional identities Gabriela Signori has edited several illuminating volumes: e.g., Signori (ed.), *Heiliges Westfalen*; Signori, 'Patriotische heilige?'.

[7] In this regard, the argument has developed in three steps over the last century: first, in *L'Élement historique*, Pontien Polman argued that the history-writing undertaken within during the sixteenth-century Reformation was so polemical as hardly to deserve being called 'history'. His judgement fell equally on Lutheran, reformed, and Catholic writings of the period. Secondly, Donald Kelley has argued since the 1980s that the polemical nature of the sixteenth-century history-writing, and specifically the Protestant revisionist perspective, contributed to the development of modern historical thought. Thirdly, Irena Backus has most recently proposed, against Polman, that new and authentic historical interests affirmed confessional identities. Backus, *Historical Method*; Kelley, 'Johann Sleidan', pp. 573–98; Kelley, *Faces*, pp. 167–74; Polman, *L'Élément historique*.

relationship of Christianity to the lands and peoples of Germany was understood by the three most important authors of patriotic 'German' history in the broadest sense: Aeneas Silvius Piccolomineus, Conrad Celtis, and Beatus Rhenanus. Then, it will examine the three principal authors who described the Christianization of a particular region within Germany, namely Bavaria: Ulrich Füetrer, Veit Arnpeck, and Johannes Aventinus. Each of the latter three authors devoted considerable attention to describing processes of Christianization that were, by his reckoning, essential to Bavaria's identity. For all of them, the process necessarily included the baptism of pagan rulers and peoples, the establishment of ecclesiastical governance and institutions, and an ongoing catechesis through preaching. As we will see, the key figures who brought Christianization about—in the Bavarian histories as elsewhere—are consistently missionary bishops. In examining both the 'German' and 'Bavarian' histories, I will emphasize two crucial questions: which figures and events did these Renaissance historians identify as having carried out the process of Christianization and how did they understand Christianization as a historical process?

The work of these six authors speaks against attempts to draw a sharp frontier between sacred and profane history, either in the *Germania illustrata* in particular or in early humanist history-writing in general. It suggests, rather, a distinction that must accommodate an apparent contradiction: on the one hand, these writers could and did distinguish functionally between sacred and profane history, between ecclesiastical and temporal, and between religious and secular; but on the other, they could and did marshal all such sources in writing the national or provincial histories that were 'patriotic'. How the process of Christianization unfolded, and its relation to the German or Bavarian history that was being told, could and did vary greatly. The authors of patriotic histories nonetheless took it as given that the provinces, peoples, and cultures about which they were writing were 'Christian' and that 'Christianization' was a defining moment in their past.

1. CHRISTIANITY AND *GERMANIA*

a. Aeneas Silvius Piccolomineus

As surprising as it might seem, our consideration of patriotic German history-writing begins with the Sienese humanist Aeneas Silvius Piccolomineus (1405–64). Aeneas Silvius served the Habsburg court in Vienna for most of the period between the Council of Basel (1431–49) and his election as pope in 1458, and enjoyed the confidence of the Holy Roman Emperor Frederick III (r. 1440–93). Christened the 'Apostle of humanism in Germany' in the nineteenth century,[8] Aeneas Silvius warrants our attention because of his historical writings, most especially on Central Europe, and their reception there,[9] and because of his influence on German history writers, especially humanists.[10]

Among Aeneas Silvius's historical works are the *Historia Austrialis* (three editions, 1453–8), the *Historia Bohemica* (1458), *Europa* (1458), and *Asia* (1461). Striking in each of the first three works is the presumption of a definable ethnic, cultural, political sphere—'Austria', 'Bohemia', even 'Europe'—that could be an object of historical reflection without the religious faith of its inhabitants being a focus of attention.[11] Missing, however, is any explicit reference to a *res publica Christiana*, even if the only way for barbarian tribes to enter into 'Europe' was through baptism. By contrast, the religious status of Asia (which denoted first and foremost the Muslim Near and Middle East), presented an overt problem.[12] The Muslim presence in Asia had explicitly disquieted Aeneas as both scholar and churchman since Constantinople's capitulation to the Turks in 1453. The spectre of this Christian defeat can be discerned in addresses calling for a crusade that he delivered at imperial Reichstags in Regensburg in May 1454[13] and in Frankfurt in September of the same year.[14]

Aeneas did not write a comparable history of Germany, but he did have a powerful, if not quite intended, influence on the project of composing one. In 1457 he responded to a complaint received by the Holy See from the chancellor of the archdiocese of Mainz, Martin Mayer, who was also a long-time personal friend of his. The complaint asserted that the papal Curia was driving the German principalities into destitution by its abusive exercise of power, especially in levying taxes. Aeneas's response was made public, printed, widely distributed into the sixteenth century, and eventually became known simply as the *Germania*.[15] Aeneas rejected the assertion of Germany's degradation by affirming Germany's greatness. In the course of his argument he emphasized the common language, laws, and customs of the Germans. In so doing, he asserted the existence of a unified German people, a linguistic and cultural community that existed in historical continuity with the old Germanic

---

[8] Voigt, *Enea Silvio de Piccolomini*, II, pp. xii, 351.

[9] Ibid., pp. xii, 351. See also, Mauro, 'Praeceptor Austriae'. Regarding his influence at the University of Vienna, see Wagendorfer, 'Enea Silvio Piccolomini', pp. 21–52.

[10] E.g. Wagendorfer, 'Enea Silvio Piccolomini', pp. 21–52.

[11] Montecalvo, *Between Empire and Papacy*, pp. 22–92; Montecalvo, 'The New *Landesgeschichte*', pp. 55–86.

[12] Meserve, 'From Samarkand to Scythia', pp. 13–40; Vollmann, 'Aeneas Silvius', pp. 41–54.

[13] Reichstag speech, Regensburg, 16 May 1454, in *Deutsche Reichstagsakten unter Kaiser Friedrich III.*, ed. Weigel and Grüneisen, 5.1, pp. 265–70.

[14] 'Oratio XIII: de Constantinopolitana clade et bello contra Turcos congregando', Frankfurt, 28 September 1454 (?), in Piccolomineus, *Orationes politicae et ecclesiasticae*, I, pp. 263–86.

[15] Piccolomineus, *Germania*, pp. 3–8.

tribes.[16] Amidst the enumeration of Germany's cultural and political accomplishments and topographical highlights, a key point emerges that links Germany's contemporaneous greatness to its Christianity: the Christianization of the barbarians and the concomitant link to Rome and its civilizing influence were, by Aeneas's reckoning, central to Germany's ascent.[17]

b. Conrad Celtis

The implications of Aeneas's reasoning extended beyond the chancellor's concerns, especially once the *Germania* became widely disseminated in print. Its two-pronged presupposition—that there was a single Germany and that its greatness depended on its links to the Church of Rome—gave later learned Germans much to ponder as they evaluated the German past and present.[18] Reactions among Germans were diverse and equivocal. The response of the imperial *poeta laureatus* Conrad Celtis (1459–1508) embodied the deftness with which the best German scholars appropriated Aeneas's German postulations. On the one hand, Celtis accepted the link between the old and the new Germany and the constitutive quality of Christianity for German identity. On the other hand, he rejected the notion that Christianization had converted a barbarous people into a civilized one through the connection to Roman culture. For Celtis, Germans did not need Roman influence to become civilized. Inspired by the *Germania* of first-century Roman historian Tacitus (recently rediscovered in the fifteenth century) which contrasted Germanic virtue to Roman decadence, Celtis and other German scholars resisted the idea of indomitable Italian cultural superiority. Indeed the work's Silver Age authorship gave humanists in particular the warrant they needed to write encomiastically about the ancient, pre-Christian Germans whom Tacitus had ostensibly admired. Celtis was likewise moved by the accumulated experience of German humanists who had been wounded by Italian imperiosity over the contrasting legacies of Roman greatness and German barbarism. This German frustration provided the backdrop to Celtis's address at the University of Ingolstadt in 1492 (quoted at the outset of this

---

[16] Aeneas drew on classical and Christian literature to make his point. Caesar's *Bellum gallicum* and Strabo's *Geographica* provided a rich description of Germanic barbarousness. Although Poggio Bracciolini had discovered Tacitus's *Germania* by 1425, it is unclear whether Aeneas Silvius knew of the work as he wrote his response. The ancient *Germania* was first printed in Germany in 1473/4 (indexed as GW M44720 in the *Gesamtkatalog der Wiegendrucke* (hereafter GW) (Stuttgart: Anton Hiersemann, 1968–)).

[17] Aeneas summarized the long and somewhat convoluted argument, at one point writing, 'Your nation is more magnificent now than ever; it is great, yielding to no tribe; . . . and there is no people as mighty that has gods near to it as the Lord our God is present the German people' (Piccolomineus, *Germania*, II, p. 11).

[18] Krebs, *Negotiatio Germaniae*, pp. 111–56.

chapter), in which he called upon students and colleagues to learn the greatness of the German past, and which inspired the pursuit of a historical
compendium about Germany.[19]

Although a synthesized and exhaustive *Germania illustrata* remained beyond Celtis's own grasp, his pursuit of it was to stir scores of other humanists
to research and write about the German past.[20] He also produced numerous
smaller works that he conceived as pointing in the direction of a complete
Germania illustrata. His *De situ, moribus et institutis Norimbergae libellus*, a
municipal history inspired by Hartmann Schedel's *Liber chronicarum*,[21] is one
such work. Celtis introduced the *De situ* to his patrons, the city council of
Nuremberg, as a prelude to a history of Germany ('*praeludium quoddam
Germaniae illustratae*').[22] Celtis extracted the 'secular history' of the city
from a 'universal history' that by definition included the Creation as its
starting point and the Parousia, or second coming, as its endpoint.[23] He
furthermore placed Nuremberg in the geographic centre first of Germany
and then of Europe as a whole, giving it a topographical dignity traditionally
reserved for Rome or Jerusalem. Such alterations made the work less evidently
soteriological and eschatological than Schedel's *Liber chronicarum*. Still, the
content of the work was no less religious. The work draws on innumerable
religious sources and referents to advance the portrayal of Nuremberg as a
genuinely great city. Celtis included the city's prominent churches and shrines
in its architectural and civic monuments; he recounted the life of the city's
saintly patron, Sebald, at greater length than that of any other individual; and
he enumerated convents and canonries side by side with the imperial free
city's other guilds, sodalities, and other organizations. In short, in this 'secular'
history of Nuremberg, Christian artefacts and monuments were fundamentally constitutive of its past and present greatness.[24]

---

[19] See epigraph at the head of the chapter and note 1; Celtis, 'Oratio in gymnasio in
Ingelstadio' in *Panegyris ad duces Bavariae*, pp. 16–40. In addition to the Ingolstadt address of
1492, the *Panegyris ad ducum Bavariae*, a poem on education that emphasized the kind of
learning that composing such a compendium would require, may be seen as another manifesto:
Celtis, 'Panegyris ad duces Bavariae et Philippum Palatinum rheni', in *Panegyris ad duces
Bavariae*, pp. 4–15. Krebs's analysis highlights the rise of German patriotic feelings in reactions
against Italian critiques of German barbarism especially well. Krebs, *Negotiatio Germaniae*,
pp. 190–225.

[20] Arguably the best of the early attempts was Wimpfeling, *Epithoma Germanorum et suorum
opera contextum*.

[21] Schedel, *Liber chronicarum*.

[22] Celtis, *Norimberga*. See also Werminghoff (ed.), *Conrad Celtis*.

[23] Regarding universal history and its soteriological aspect, see Zedelmaier, *Der Anfang*,
pp. 11–22.

[24] Celtis's *Germania generalis*, a popular teaching poem, reveals a similar strategy of incor-
porating religious elements into a patriotic, historical-topographical poem. Celtis, *Quattuor libri
amorum*.

Other contributions by Celtis to the *Germania illustrata* reinforce, in ways that have been overlooked in modern scholarship, the presupposition that Christianity was essential to German identity. For example, he produced the celebrated *editio princeps* of the tenth-century canoness Hrotsvitha of Gandersheim's oeuvre in 1501.[25] Celtis's interest in Hrotsvitha is generally explained with reference to the classicizing style of her poesy. Yet her appeal to Celtis went beyond her Latinity. His own correspondence reveals that he associated her with a tradition of the *femina docta* and Christian letters that he saw as hallmarks of women's religious life in Germany and that extended, by his reckoning, to his contemporary, the famed abbess Caritas Pirckheimer.[26] Elsewhere, in his *Panegyris ad duces Bavariae*, Celtis proposed a patriotic program of educational reform. Although the novel placement of poetry within his list of eight areas of study has been singled out as evidence of his humanist educational agenda, his insistence on the study of theology in the same list is often overlooked.[27] And among Celtis's historical panegyrics number poems about the saints, including the patron saints of Austria, St Walpurgis (*c.*710–79), and St Sebald (century unknown). An ode to the latter was first published on a broadsheet with a woodcut by Dürer and was later appended to the *Amores*.[28] This work encompassed a collection of topographical descriptions of Germany in the form of love poetry and extended Celtis's argument in favour of a distinctively German contribution to the European tradition of learning (Figure 5.1). In sum, the resentments against Italian superciliosity that Celtis and his German colleagues brought to the *Germania illustrata* had less to do with creating a secularized patriotism and historiography than with putting persons, places, objects, and events, religious and secular, at the service of German patriotism.

c. Beatus Rhenanus

Although the late fifteenth-century wave of research into the German past did not result in Celtis's coveted *Germania illustrata*, it did have significant effects, and among its beneficiaries was the Alsatian humanist Beatus Rhenanus (1485–1547). In contrast to the earlier German humanists, Beatus benefited in his training from a mature humanist programme of education that was

---

[25] Celtis (ed.), *Opera Hrosvite*.

[26] Celtis explicitly associates Christian religion, Germany's praiseworthy history, and Hrotsvitha's deep learning in his dedicatory letter to Frederick, the elector of Saxony. Rupprich (ed.), *Der Briefwechsel des Konrad Celtis*, ep. 267.

[27] Celtis, 'Panegyris', in *Panegyris ad duces Bavariae*, pp. 4–15. His description of theology encompasses Christian morals and soteriology.

[28] Celtis, *Quattuor libri amorum*.

Figure 5.1. Conrad Celtis, *Quatuor libri amorum secundum quatuor latera Germanie feliciter incipient* (Nuremberg: Sodalitas Celtica, 1502), 6ᵛ. Munich, BSB Rar. 446. VD16 C1911. The image *Philosophia regina* illustrates Conrad Celtis's *Amores*. The heading reads: 'The Greeks call me Sophia; the Latins, Sapientia. The Egyptians and Chaldeans discovered me; the Greeks wrote about me; the Latins spread me; the Germans developed me.' Four medallions featuring representative learned figures surround enthroned *Philosophia*: above her, Ptolemy; to her left, Plato; below her, a single profile labelled Cicero and Vergil; and to her right; Albertus Magnus. The importance of Roman antecedents is not denied; rather the substance of a German contribution, epitomized by a thirteenth-century scholastic philosopher, is highlighted. Joseph Meder ascribes this woodcut to Dürer (Meder, *Dürer-Katalog*, p. 245).

confidently patriotic; and by the time he turned to his own history-writing, he had precedents upon which to build. His patriotic sympathies reveal themselves in his 1532 revision of a work that had celebrated the ancient German occupation of Alsace and the German ancestry of Emperor Charlemagne, Jacob Wimpfeling's *Germania* (1501). A period of study in Paris had taught Beatus the paradoxical lesson that had been forced on many a German humanist before him, namely, that although humanism was a genuinely international movement, Germans were commonly regarded as Europe's culturally underprivileged stepchild.[29] Using his edition of Gregory of Nyssa's works as the occasion to express his frustration at this educational chauvinism, Beatus thanked his teacher Jacobus Faber Stapulensis (Jacques Lefèvre d'Étaples) for helping him, a 'mere foreigner', through his studies, and encouraged Faber to teach the great German authors, a list of which he provided, more diligently to his hidebound Parisian students.[30]

Beatus's *Rerum Germanicarum libri tres* (Basel, 1531) is arguably the most successful work in the lineage of Celtis's *Germania illustrata* up to the Reformation. It begins with a description of the ancient German tribes and their relations to the Roman Empire. Its goal, consistent with Aeneas Silvius's assertion in the *Germania*, was to establish the unifying elements—especially in history, religion, and language—of the German tribes. In the second part, Beatus focuses on the Franks and reprises a medieval argument that they were German, thus implicitly justifying the German inheritance of the imperial crown. In the final part, he offers descriptions of contemporary Germany by region and city. Beatus's use of evidence is striking for his integration of religious and ecclesiastical sources into this patriotic historical work along lines set by his humanist predecessors, and for his inclusion of ecclesiastical monuments and religious figures in his topographical descriptions.

The sobriety of Beatus's style is all the more remarkable when contrasted with the triumphalism of similar earlier works and with the confessionalized polemic that shaped German history-writing after him. Indeed, Beatus's work managed to combine reformist and anti-papalist elements with a conventional respect for the Roman Church. On the one hand, he was laudatory of German virtue, and critical of Roman Christianity, papal corruption, and decadent religious life. He also looked with greater favour on theological beliefs and sacramental practices that could be rooted in historical antiquity than on medieval historical developments, which was a hallmark of reformist thought.[31] On the other hand, the *Rerum Germanicarum* fell short of calling Christians to reject outright the criticized ecclesiastical or doctrinal elements of traditional Roman Christianity. The demurral is significant. The *Rerum Germanicarum* reached print more than a decade after the momentous

---

[29] Muhlack, 'Beatus Rhenanus (1485–1547): Von Humanismus zur Philologie', p. 202.
[30] Rhenanus, *Briefwechsel*, p. 41.   [31] See above, Ch. 2.

Leipzig Disputation (1519) and the publication of Martin Luther's three great reform manifestos of 1520. The more radical anti-papal position was being articulated with increasing clarity over that decade and found support in diverse corners of the empire. German princes presented the *Augsburg Confession* at the imperial diet of 1530, a year before the *Rerum Germanicarum*'s publication. In this polemical context, the religious arguments in Beatus's work appeared distinctly muted, and seem to grow out of the older medieval traditions of anti-clericalism and the humanist scepticism of Erasmus rather than out of the more strident reforming theology of Martin Luther (1483– 1546) and Philipp Melanchthon (1497–1560).[32]

2. NATIONAL HISTORY: BAVARIA

Despite the difficulties the German humanists had in producing a satisfactory *Germania illustrata* before the Reformation, the range of scholarship inspired by the project was prodigious. The greater part of what was produced had regional, rather than national, foci. In light of the highly confederated structure of the Holy Roman Empire in its relationship to the German principalities in the early modern period, such a tendency comes as no surprise. While previous generations of scholars lamented the failure of the early modern history writers to produce a national history sooner, more recent scholarship tends to celebrate the vigour and creativity of the regional histories that were produced.[33] Analysis of this regional history-writing brings to light two salient points. First, because regional history-writing was common in the German lands before the advent of humanist learning, humanist history-writing developed organically out of earlier traditions; and secondly, local and regional dimensions of religious culture played a fundamental role in the formation of regional identities in German lands, as throughout Europe. The three historical works analysed next were composed in and for the region of Bavaria. Their authors, Ulrich Füetrer, Veit Arnpeck, and Johannes Aventinus, define that region as a specific political and cultural entity worthy of praise and respect, and put religious content and literary forms to unambiguously patriotic purposes.

---

[32] D'Amico identifies, correctly in my view, explicit Lutheran sympathies in Beatus's other works (e.g. annotations in his editions of Tertullian and Marsilius of Padua) that are not evident in the *Rerum Germanicarum*. D'Amico, 'Ulrich von Hutten', pp. 25–32. D'Amico also provides a thoughtful assessment of Beatus's religious sensibilities in analysis of his relationship with Erasmus. D'Amico, *Theory and Practice*, pp. 187–9.

[33] It is scarcely possible to enumerate fully the literature produced in the last decade on regional history writing in German lands. The newness of the interest may explain why there has yet to appear a synthesizing monograph on regional history writing in general. Brendle et al. (eds.), *Deutsche Landesgeschichtsschreibung*; Fuchs, *Geschichtsbewußtsein*; Werner (ed.), *Spätmittelalterliches Landesbewusstsein*.

a. Ulrich Füetrer

Before he turned to history-writing, Ulrich Füetrer (1430–96), a married layman, was an accomplished painter, sculptor, and author of romances. His most studied work today is the *Buch der Abenteuer* (*Book of Adventures*), a set of thirteenth-century knightly romances compiled and revised for the Duke of Bavaria, Albrecht IV (r. 1465–1508).[34] His *Bavarian Chronicle* (1478–81)[35] relates the history of Bavaria from AD 60 to 1479, with particular attention to the ruling Wittelsbach family, who were his most consistent and generous patrons. Füetrer's work became the touchstone for subsequent Bavarian history writers, including humanists, despite lacking distinctive humanist characteristics itself. Füetrer's chronicle was advantageous for subsequent history writers because of its extensive reliance on and identification of sources. The chronicle was subsequently criticized as a mere compilation, and the great Bavarian humanist and history writer Johannes Aventinus (discussed below) chastised Füetrer for failing to distinguish between myth and history.[36] At the same time, his emphasis on the sources, the Bavarian framework he adopted for his narrative, and his late starting point (which precluded any invented biblical or classical ethnographic origins for the Bavarians) do, in fact, indicate a sense of distinction between myth and history and give Füetrer's work a different character from the medieval chronicles on which he much relied.[37]

Füetrer employed sources of all kinds—religious and secular, ecclesiastical and temporal, sacred and profane—just as did Celtis and Beatus. He cited numerous annals and chronicles of individual monasteries within Bavaria[38] and drew extensively from the *Conversio Bagoariorum et Carantanorum*, a ninth-century polemical work that exalted the Salzburg see and its founder, St Rupert (c.650–718), over proximate, rival foundations of the ninth-century Greek missionaries Saints Cyril and Methodius.[39] Other sources associated with the cult of the saints include the lives of Saints Lawrence (d. 258) and Hippolytus (d. c.236),[40] St Emmeram (d. c.652),[41] and St Kunigunde (d. 1040).[42]

---

[34] Füetrer, *Das Buch der Abenteuer*.

[35] Füetrer, *Bayerische Chronik*.

[36] Aventinus's annotated copy of Füetrer's Chronicle is held in the Bavarian State Library in Munich as *Codices germanici monacenses* (hereafter Cgm) 565.

[37] The principal (late) medieval sources he used were *Ain teutsche Cronick* by Jakob Twinger von Königshofen (1346–1420), the *Chronica pontificum et et imperatorum Romanorum* by Andreas of Regensburg (1380–1438), the *Chronik von den fürsten von Bayern* by Hans Ebran von Wildenberg (1425/35–c.1502).

[38] E.g. *Chronicon Benedictoburanum, De fundatoribus monasterii Diessensis, Historia fundationis monasterii Tegernseensis*.

[39] *Conversio Bagoariorum et Carantanorum*, ed. Losek.

[40] *Bibliotheca hagiographica latina*, 2 vols. and supplement (Brussels: Société des Bollandistes, 1899–1901, 1998) (hereafter BHL), pp. 3960 and 4752.

[41] Ibid., pp. 2538–41.

[42] Ibid., p. 2001.

By Füetrer's reckoning, Bavaria's 'Christian origins' are to be found in St Rupert's eighth-century missionary work, which commenced with an invitation from the ruling prince Theodo (d. *c.*716). Rupert begins by baptizing the prince and his family, and then moving through Theodo's realm, the province of Bavaria, confronting and converting pagans, desecrating their temples, and replacing these with churches. This account of ducal and popular conversions is followed by an outline of the region's ecclesiastical history and topography. Füetrer included description of conflicts between Bavarian bishops and dukes, which resolve generally, if not exclusively, in favour of the former. Careful mention is made of Rupert's establishment of the bishopric in Salzburg under Theodo's patronage;[43] and subsequent chapters outline further ecclesiastical foundations sponsored by Theodo and his ruling descendents. Each generation's loyalty to Bavaria's ecclesiastical institutions is praised, their neglect condemned. Structured according to the ducal succession, Füetrer's history of Bavaria includes as a matter of course religious sources, referents, and arguments. Writing in the service of the Bavarian dukes, Füetrer had no conception of a purely secular history of Bavaria.

b. Veit Arnpeck

Veit Arnpeck (1435/40–95) came to write history by a path quite different to Füetrer's: while Füetrer had no formal humanistic education, Arnpeck trained in the *humaniora* in Bavaria and Austria. In addition to his history of Bavaria, which appeared in Latin[44] and vernacular[45] versions (1490, 1493), Arnpeck composed an Austrian chronicle (1494)[46] and a history of the bishops of Freising (1495).[47] Arnpeck himself was a cleric, and the Freising bishops were his loyal patrons.

Arnpeck drew on sources even more widely and systematically than Füetrer, and he was less likely to quote than to paraphrase them. Like Füetrer's, Arnpeck's sources included ecclesiastical and secular documents. He was more likely than Füetrer to cite both classical and biblical works: Tacitus's *Germania*, at this point fifteen years in print in Germany, and several books of the Bible featured prominently in the chronicle's opening. Arnpeck relied on several older, still widely circulating chronicles—Paul the Deacon's *Historia Langobardorum*, Bernard of Gui's *Chronica imperatorum Romanorum*, Henry

---

[43] Füetrer, *Bayerische Chronik*, p. 60.
[44] Arnpeck, 'Chronica Baioariorum'.
[45] Arnpeck, 'Bayerische Chronik'.
[46] Arnpeck, 'Chronicon austriacum'.
[47] Arnpeck, 'Liber de gestis episcoporum Frisingensium'.

of Herford's *Chronicon*, and others[48]—as well as some of the newest: Aeneas Silvius's *Europa* and *Historia Bohemica*, plus the universal histories by Antoninus of Florence and Hartmann Schedel. He also drew from monastic annals and *foundationes*[49] as well as saints' lives, including the *Legenda aurea*.[50]

One indicator of Arnpeck's humanist perspective on history-writing is his extensive use of sources; another is his exclusion of Creation and Parousia from his narrative, which begins and ends in human time, and so is distinguishable from salvation history.[51] At the same time, Arnpeck did not demur from using religious history to highlight Bavaria's greatness, most notably in two respects: first, in his account of the conversion of the Bavarian dukes and their people and, secondly, in his continuous reference to the network of ecclesiastical institutions that were the counterpart to the military and political control exercised by the Bavarian dukes. Moreover, in the revised version of his Latin history of Bavaria, he added more religious content. Although he addressed the bishop of Freising, Sixtus of Tannberg (r. 1474–95), in the introduction to both versions, he made clear that his subject was the province of Bavaria, and not simply the church or the diocese of Freising.[52] He asserted an analogy between Bavarian and Roman greatness by describing Bavaria's most important Marian pilgrimage site in Altötting and Emperors Octavius and Tiberius as comparable civilizing influences. He credited Christianity with driving the barbarian out of the German and making him the heir of antiquity's greatness.[53] After extensive references to classical, biblical, and medieval works, Arnpeck concluded in his own words: 'Among the Germans the Bavarians spring forth like a brilliant star and a glittering flower.'[54] Then paraphrasing Schedel, he proclaimed:

> How long and broad the province of Bavaria, how pious, how true, how just, how loyal to its promises, how strong and experienced in war, how ornate its churches, how great the glory of its clergy and the magnificence of its princes, oh the splendour of its cities and the firmament of its sky and the fertility of its fields.[55]

One of Arnpeck's aims was to legitimate and augment the authority and prestige of the Freising bishopric. To that end he brought together here

---

[48] These other chronicles included Vincent of Beauvais's *Speculum historiale*, the *Saxische Weltchronik*, Thomas Lirer's *Schwäbische Chronik*, and Johann von Thurocz, *Chronica Hungarorum*.

[49] These included the thirteenth-century chronicle and annals of Scheyern, the 'Regensburg Legend of the Scottish Monks' and foundations and chronicles of the monasteries at Tegernsee, Diessen, Aldersbach, Osterhofen, Bendiktbeuern, Schlehdorf, Wessobrunn, Raitenbuch, Osterhofen, Mallersdorf, Scheyern, Beuerberg, Diessen, Oberaltaich, Ebersberg, Annalen Osterhofen, and Fürstenfeld.

[50] E.g. Maximilian, Florian, Afra, Severin, Rupert, Emmeram, Corbinian, Boniface, Virgilius, Dionysius, Ulrich, Martin, Godehard, Henry and Cunegund, Thiemo, Conrad of Salzburg, Hedwig.

[51] See n. 5.   [52] Arnpeck, 'Chronica Baioariorum', p. 3.
[53] Ibid., p. 4.   [54] Ibid., p. 5.   [55] Ibid.

matters civil and ecclesiastical in the context of a history of 'the province of Bavaria'. Such a history, by his reckoning, encompassed the missionary activities of Corbinian (d. *c.*730), Boniface (675–754), and Rupert (d. 718); the dynastic rivalries of the Wittelsbachs; and the natural disasters that signalled divine judgement and rallied human generosity. Once again we see regional panegyrics utilizing religious materials to make patriotic history.

c. Johannes Aventinus

The third and last regional work we will here examine is the *Annales ducum Boiariae* of Johannes Aventinus (1477–1534).[56] Aventinus was educated by humanists and became a full participant in their republic of letters; he was the student of Celtis in Ingolstadt, of Johannes Cuspinianus (Johan Spießhaymer) and Johannes Stabius (Johann Stab) in Vienna, and of Faber Stapulensis (Jacques Lefèvre d'Étaples) and Jodocus Clichtoveus (Josse Clichtove) in Paris. He pursued further humanist studies in Mantua and Rome and spent time in Cracow to learn mathematics. He was a close friend of Beatus Rhenanus. In 1516, he founded a circle of humanist scholars in Ingolstadt. The Wittelsbachs appointed him their court historiographer the following year, in which capacity he produced the *Annales ducum Boiariae*. Writing it involved two years of travel to nearly a hundred monastic libraries and other archives in Bavaria and Austria and three years in reclusion in his home town of Abensberg.[57] He completed the Latin version of the *Annals* in 1521, and a revised, translated version appeared in 1526 as *Die bayerische Chronik*.[58] Despite the eager anticipation of such humanist colleagues as Beatus Rhenanus, and Aventinus's commissioning of an elegant map for his work (Figure 5.2), neither the *Annales* nor the *Chronik* was printed in its author's lifetime.[59] His Wittelsbach patrons considered the historical narrative too favourable to the empire over against their own princely authority in Bavaria; and religious authorities judged it too anti-papal and anticlerical.[60] Aventinus's other

---

[56] Schmid, 'Die Kleinen Annalen', pp. 69–96; Kraus, 'Bayerns Frühzeit', pp. 435–52; D'Amico, *Theory and Practice*, pp. 181–3; Schmid, 'Die historische Methode', pp. 338–95; Strauss, *Life and Work of Johannes Aventinus*.

[57] The Latin autograph: Munich, Bayerische Staatsbibliothek, *Codex Latinus monacensis* (hereafter Clm) 282–7; Aventinus, *Annales ducum Boiariae*.

[58] *Die Bayerische Chronik*, transcription corrected by Aveninus, Munich, Bayerische Staatsbibliothek, Cgm 1566–8, 1564, 1572; Aventinus, *Bayerische Chronik*.

[59] The *Annales* in 1556 (indexed in the *Verzeichnis der im deutschen Sprachbereich erschienenen Drucke des XVI. Jahrhunderts* (Stuttgart: Heisemann, 1983–95) (hereafter VD16) as T2318), and the *Chronik* in 1566 (VD16 T2320).

[60] Aventinus was confined under suspicion of heresy for eleven days but was released without indictment. Much like Erasmus and Beatus Rhenanus, Aventinus, though sympathetic to aspects

Figure 5.2. Facsimile (1899) of 'Aventins Karte von Bayern', 1523. Munich BSB, Mapp. XI, 24 xbb. Aventinus commissioned a coloured map, titled 'Obern und Nidern Bairn, bey den alten im Latein und Griechischen Vindelicia', in 1523. Two characteristics of this map in particular illuminate the intricacies of Aventinus's patriotic intentions: the emphasis in the title and on the map itself of the pre-Roman region, Vindelicia, then overlaid with Roman and German place names; and the inclusion of temporal and ecclesiastical coats of arms around the border.

historical works included several monastic and local histories,[61] several histories of Germany,[62] and an apocalyptic 'Chronicon quatuor monarchiarum

of the Lutheran criticisms of the Roman Church, did not reject the papacy in favour of the new theologies.

[61] 'Annales Schirenses' (VD16 T2323); 'Narratiuncula de Bathavina urbe' (Bayerische Staatsbibliothek, München, cls 1204), fols 57ʳ–58ᵛ; 'Historia Otingae' (VD16 T2345, T2346); 'Chronicon Ranshofense' (Linz, Landesarchiv, Ms. 138); Descriptio Biburgensis (Clm 28274); and 'Von dem herkommen der statt Regensburg' (c.1528) (Andreas Felix von Oefele (ed.), *Rerum Boicarum scriptores*, 2 vols., II (Augsburg: Adam and Veith, 1763), pp. 740–59).

[62] E.g., 'Chronica von Ursprung, Herkommen und Taten der uralten Teutschen' (VD16 T2324) and 'Indiculus Germaniae illustratae' (VD16 T2347).

emendatum'.[63] In consultation with Beatus Rhenanus, he also began preparations for a *Germania illustrata* that he never completed.[64]

Aventinus's work differs from Arnpeck's in ambivalent ways. Aventinus organized his history into eight books. From the second to the seventh he narrated Bavarian history from the late Roman Republic to his own day. The first book, a prelude, recounts the fanciful origins of the Bavarians from their eleventh king, Alemanus Hercules, to Julius Caesar; and in the last book Aventinus engaged in systematic topographical descriptions of Bavaria. His sources include those used by the previous two authors, and he makes additional reference to the humanist authors Flavio Biondo, Leonardo Bruni, Marco Antonio Sabellico, and Robert Gaguin, among others. The German version incorporates revisions; it draws on more biblical and fewer classical sources and begins with the Creation rather than Alemanus Hercules.[65]

Aventinus distinguished himself from the other two authors in style by more freely interjecting pro-imperial and anti-papal polemic into his history: He introduces Charlemagne as Frankish, thus as German rather than French. He denounces the learned bishop and history writer Otto of Freising (1115–58) for his anti-imperial history-writing. In the preface to book five, which recounts the eleventh-century Investiture Contest, he favours the imperial position. Gainsaying the legitimate election of Gregory VII (pope 1073–85) (already a hoary commonplace of anti-papal polemic in the empire), Aventinus calls the pope by his family name Hildebrandt, and in the German version, with disdain, 'the Norman pope', an epithet imputing perfidy to Gregory for his alliances with the Norman warlords in southern Italy against Emperor Henry IV.[66]

Like Arnpeck, Aventinus wrote a work that celebrates the political and religious history and topography of Bavaria; and he acknowledged his reliance on all kinds of sources and literary forms, secular and sacred, to do so. Both authors incorporated religious monuments into their historical narratives, even though they varied in certain emphases. St Rupert's place in Bavaria's Christianization offers a fruitful point of comparison. While both authors attributed to him a hero's status in Bavarian history for his missionizing

---

[63] Salzburg, Stiftsbibliothek St Peter, cod. b.X.35, pp. 1–14.

[64] Ibid., pp. 15–166.

[65] Such alterations, especially beginning the vernacular version with the Creation, suggest a kind of traditionalism associated with use of the vernacular. In fact, one finds a similar pattern of difference when examining the vitae of holy men and women, e.g. German translations of Latin lives usually include augmented reference to miracles as signs of the subjects holiness. Patrons also sometimes required humanist authors to revise commissioned works in more traditional directions when presented with compositions that deviated too sharply from conventional forms. See Collins, *Reforming Saints*, pp. 29, 58–64.

[66] Cf. Prinz, 'Zeitkritik im Spiegel der Historie', pp. 533–44.

efforts, Arnpeck identified him as one of several founding bishops in Bavaria's ecclesiastical history,[67] while Aventinus gave Rupert clear primacy. This shift is all the more striking when one considers that Aventinus gave less attention overall to the history of ecclesiastical institutions than did Arnpeck, who, it will be recalled, was writing for the bishops of Freising. More striking still is Aventinus's use of Rupert's invitation into Bavaria by the Wittelsbachs as an opportunity to suggest the properly apolitical way for missionary agents to be brought into a region, with the thinly veiled accusation that the Church in this respect was no longer behaving as it should.[68]

A stunning piece of oratory from the mouth of Rupert reveals Aventinus's unvarnished opinion of his own contemporaneous Church, as the ancient bishop sketches a model of pristine Christianity.[69] Aventinus continues with a discourse on the humility and poverty of the bishops and clergy, the sincerity and simplicity of the religious, the authenticity of the liturgies and sacraments, and the generosity and charity of the newly converted people in those days. The commentary concludes with an explanation, in the author's own voice, of the prevailing threat from the Ottoman Empire as punishment for the contemporary failure of Christians to live up to the older standard.[70] Similar ecclesiastical criticisms appear elsewhere in the *Annales*: his history of the Investiture Contest, for example, allowed Aventinus a harangue against scholasticism and dialectic,[71] and then another on greed.[72] Thus as true as it is that Aventinus's *Annales* is more strongly anchored to secular institutional referents—empire and duchy—than Arnpeck's chronicle, Aventinus nonetheless used the *Annales* to make a deeply religious point. He composed a celebratory history of Bavaria, but within it is integrated a stinging critique of contemporaneous Christianity.

3. CONCLUSION

These findings point to two overarching conclusions about patriotic history-writing in late medieval Germany. First, in the century falling within the scope of this chapter, leading humanists and other learned Germans wrote abundant

[67] Corbinian, the founding bishop of Freising, appears much more prominently in Arnpeck's work.

[68] Aventinus, *Annales*, III.2. The passage also includes some typically humanist touches: Rupert is referred to as *divus*, rather than *sanctus*; and his task is that of the 'nuncium et interpraetem sanctissimae philosophiae a Christo servatore nostro'.

[69] Ibid., III.3.

[70] Ibid., III.9.

[71] Ibid., V. *praefatio*.

[72] Ibid., V.13–14.

patriotic histories. The cultural-historical subjects of these histories ranged from all-encompassing notions of Germany to local principalities, even cities. The authors defined their subjects—in the past and in the present—by a range of cultural, political, and topographical characteristics, usually using all of them but exercising a freedom to balance and blend them in a variety of ways. Christian character was taken as a self-evident part of each *patria's* greatness, and every history writer saw the need to incorporate the Christian past into his composition. Authors recognized that the processes of evangelization had occurred in as patchwork a manner as the Holy Roman Empire itself was politically organized. At the same time, the claim that Christianity was a unifying element for all Europe scarcely made an appearance in the German history-writing; humanists in Germany were not writing histories of 'Europe'. Aeneas Silvius addressed Europe's common Christianity, but his appeal to a Christian Europe reached German audiences in the context of his (failed) call for a crusade against the Turks, not in his historical writings. More to the point, Aeneas's assertion of a Christian Germany caused long-lasting consternation among many Germans, who viewed it as an underhand assault on German honour, even as he also asserted an artfully univocal concept of *Germania*. As a result, many later humanist writers pointedly minimized the influence of Rome in the Christianization of the Germans in general or of particular regions. They thereby made two patriotic points at once:[73] that the Germans were not Christianized (at least directly) and thus not 'civilized' through Roman offices, and that contemporary German virtues had strong roots in Germania's past, independent of the arrival of Christianity.

Here emerges the second summary point, regarding distinctions between sacred and secular history in the patriotic history-writing within the *Germania illustrata* project: the writers of patriotic history, including the humanist ones, did not see their literary service to the *patriae* as an effort to secularize their past. They did not privilege one kind of source or literary form, religious or secular, in their research; nor did they privilege one kind of phenomenon in their historical or topographical descriptions. There were at least two reasons for this: first, the medieval authors on whom the history writers examined here relied were inconsistent in making the equivalent distinction in their own history-writing; and secondly, humanists clearly shared the conviction that a given *patria* might be as readily celebrated for its religious monuments, past and present, as for its secular ones, and ought to be celebrated for both in conjunction. Although the history-writing that in retrospect is often recognized as 'the best' seems either to devalue sacred history or sharply distinguish it from secular history, Hartmann Schedel still wrote universal histories with reference to Creation and Final Judgement, Johannes Aventinus still

---

[73] See Stadtwald, 'Conrad Celtis'.

composed an apocalyptically framed history of the empire, and no history writer dismissed or marginalized such genres as illegitimate. Indeed all the authors examined here used religious (or ecclesiastical) history-writing as source material, incorporated it into their patriotic histories, and in other contexts composed it themselves, putting it to patriotic uses. The goal of this review of leading history writers in the German lands at the end of the Middle Ages and before the Reformation is not to deny or even minimize the new ways in which classical sources, styles, and norms of writing history were marshalled to foster new patriotic loyalties; but rather to demonstrate how, even to the humanists, the religious past and present were neither the invisible background too obvious to mention nor the shackles to an ugly barbarism to be discarded in the pursuit of a luminous new age. Rather, the religious past offered materials—inevasible, attractive, and essential—that could inspire and serve their developing notions of *patria*.

6

Renaissance Chroniclers and the Apostolic Origins of Spanish Christianity

Katherine Elliot Van Liere

1. IN SEARCH OF APOSTOLIC ORIGINS

In 1605, Francisco de Padilla, an obscure canon from Malaga, published an *Historia ecclesiastica de España* that he claimed was the first of its kind. Modelled on the *Annales ecclesiastici*, the monumental history of the Roman Catholic Church that Cardinal Cesare Baronio and his colleagues in Rome were still busy writing and revising, Padilla's work dealt specifically with the history of the Catholic Church in Spain. Like Baronio's work, Padilla's began with the birth of Christ and proceeded by chapters labelled 'centuries' through the Roman imperial era and beyond. But unlike Baronio's, its focus was strictly national; it narrated the history of the Spanish Church from the preaching of the Apostle James the Greater (known to Spaniards as Santiago) down to AD 700, the eve of the Muslim conquest, paying particular attention to the question of when and how Christianity originated in the peninsula, who the earliest martyrs were, and how the first bishoprics were established. Padilla invoked Eusebius's *Historia ecclesiastica* (*c.*324) and Bede's *Historia ecclesiastica gentis Anglorum* (*c.*731) as his literary models. As a Church historian Padilla was certainly no match for Eusebius, Bede, or Baronio. By his own admission, his 'genius and erudition' were 'very limited', and he had no time to do original research; virtually all of his narrative was 'taken from other authors'.[1] Modern scholars have found his modesty fully warranted. Yet for all Padilla's shortcomings, his work offers an instructive entry point into the state of Spanish ecclesiastical history at the turn of the seventeenth century.

---

[1] Padilla, *Historia ecclesiastica de España*, I, Prologo, §2ᵛ, §3ʳ.

Padilla was quite right to point out that Spanish ecclesiastical history was under-developed. No collaborative hagiographic enterprise of the scale or quality of Laurentius Surius, Luigi Lippomano, or Cesare Baronio was under-taken in sixteenth-century Spain. The nearest Spanish equivalents, Thomas de Truxillo's *Thesaurus concionatorum* (1585), Alonso de Villegas's *Flos sanctorum* (1590–4), and Pedro de Ribadeneyra's *Flos sanctorum* (1599), were compilations of saints' lives and legends, not synthetic ecclesiastical histories in the tradition of Eusebius or Bede.[2] The same was true even of Juan de Marieta's *Historia ecclesiastica* (1596), whose title, Padilla rightly insisted, was misleading, for it was in fact a catalogue of saints' lives classified thematically rather than chronologically. Padilla criticized these earlier Church histories for failing to pay adequate attention to chronology, 'the principal matter of history'.[3] For a writer like Padilla trying to reconstruct a chronological narrative of Spanish Church history, the most useful and de-tailed accounts were to be found in medieval and Renaissance national chronicles. Those written in the century and a half after 1450 were particularly valuable, and it was in fact from these chronicles that Padilla drew most of his information about the early Church. Just what these Renaissance chronicles had to say about Spanish Christian origins will be the focus of this chapter.

Padilla sorely needed chronologically reliable sources, for he sought not only to emulate and supplement Baronio's work but to challenge some of its claims about Spanish Church history. Despite the tribute he paid to Baronio's *Annales* by imitating its form, Padilla judged Baronio to be gravely mistaken on one crucial point of chronology: the Roman scholar had denied that the Spanish Church was just as ancient as that of Rome. Padilla addressed this problem both in the first *centuria* of the *Historia ecclesiastica* and in its polemical prologue. By criticizing Baronio's treatment of the early Spanish Church, Padilla was joining a scholarly dispute that had erupted in the 1590s, when Baronio and his fellow cardinal Roberto Bellarmino, the two leading ecclesiastical historians in Rome, had publicly cast doubt on the tradition that the Apostle James the Greater had evangelized Spain in the first century.

Like many of the other Spanish authors who entered the scholarly lists to defend the Santiago tradition against foreign sceptics, Padilla believed that the tradition of James's mission to Spain was an immemorial one stretching back to the Apostle's own lifetime, and that one could prove this by uncovering the ancient sources that Baronio had overlooked or misread. But in assembling his case for the first-century origins of the Spanish Church, Padilla rarely appealed directly to ancient or even medieval sources. He relied heavily instead on medieval and Renaissance chronicles, most of them written after 1500.

---

[2] Villegas, *Flos sanctorum* (numerous editions beginning in 1590); Truxillo, *Thesaurus concionatorum*; Ribadeneyra, *Flos Sanctorum* (first edn Madrid, 1599).

[3] Padilla, *Historia ecclesiastica*, Prólogo, §5ʳ.

Particularly valuable were the sixteenth-century chroniclers Lucius Marineus Siculus (*c.*1444–1533), Johannes Vasaeus (*c.*1512–61), Pere Antoni Beuter (*c.*1490–1554), and Ambrosio de Morales (1513–91). Padilla's preference for these Renaissance historians was perfectly logical, for collectively they had articulated a clearer and fuller narrative of the first-century origins of the Spanish Church than any earlier writers.

In a sense, the notion that Spanish Catholicism had been firmly established in first-century Hispania was a Renaissance invention. Around 1500 the claim that the Spanish Church had apostolic roots was absent from most Spanish historical chronicles. In the early sixteenth century, humanist historians in Spain began to take a closer interest in the history of Roman-ruled Hispania, and eventually this interest expanded into a quest for the apostolic origins of the Church. Between the 1530s and the 1570s, chroniclers built up a narrative of first-century Spanish Christian origins that served as a counterpart to the story that Italian scholars like Onofrio Panvinio and Cesare Baronio were elaborating for the early Church of Rome. Many later ecclesiastical historians besides Padilla would turn to these late Renaissance chronicles for guidance. In this sense the chroniclers of Renaissance Spain may be credited with laying the foundations for Spanish ecclesiastical history. These foundations, however, were problematic, for the story they told about the origins of the Spanish Church contained more legend than history. Its protagonists were a combination of first-century figures who (according to modern scholarship) probably never visited Spain; third- and fourth-century martyrs backdated to the first century; and characters who may have been altogether legendary.[4] By the time Padilla published his *Historia ecclesiastica* in 1605, the tradition of Spanish Christianity's apostolic origins was so widely accepted among Spanish Catholics that to doubt it was considered heretical, unpatriotic, or both. Yet those who defended the tradition as vehemently as Padilla did ignored, or chose not to emphasize, its relatively recent appearance, the scholarly difficulties that they behind it, and the considerable leaps of faith that its Renaissance architects had taken in order to construct it. This chapter will examine the process by which Renaissance scholars constructed and defended the narrative of the Spanish Church's apostolic origins in the middle decades of the sixteenth century.

All these writers were trained in the humanist tradition, and they drew on their knowledge of ancient history, classical sources, and source criticism. But when they turned to the question of the Church's apostolic origins, they blunted their sharpest critical instruments, and relied largely on medieval sources that the strictest standards of humanist scholarship would have discredited

---

[4] For a modern perspective on Spain's Christian origins, see José Fernández Ubiña, 'Los orígenes del cristianismo hispánico: algunas claves sociológicas' in Sotomayor, *Historia de la iglesia en España*, I, pp. 120–48.

as untrustworthy. In the absence of more reliable sources, these Renaissance historians used the imperfect ones at their disposal to construct and defend a narrative that Spanish Catholics came to believe was an indispensable foundation for Spanish Catholicism. No single motive drove their cumulative efforts, but a series of cultural and religious interests that changed over time. The first steps in the process were inspired by a humanist passion for Roman antiquity, and by regional and national pride. After the Protestant Reformation and the Council of Trent (1545–63), confessional anxieties about defending Catholic doctrines against Protestant challenges created another compelling reason to defend these newly formulated traditions as if they were truly ancient.

2. MEDIEVAL ELEMENTS OF THE TRADITION

Renaissance chroniclers constructed the narrative of Spain's first-century Christian origins from a bundle of disparate medieval legends. The oldest of these, and the one with the most plausible biblical foundations, was the legend that the Apostle Paul had visited Spain towards the end of his life. This tradition, based on Paul's own declared intention (Romans 15:24–5), was often cited approvingly by medieval Spanish authors, but does not seem to have received widespread attention either in popular devotion or in the historical imagination of medieval scholars. A few medieval churches had patron saints associated with Paul, but before the Renaissance no attempt seems to have been made to construct a narrative of Paul's itinerary or to connect these stray disciples of Paul with one another.[5] By contrast, the other Apostle connected with Spain, James the Greater (James of Zebedee) or Santiago, had inspired considerable interest in the Middle Ages on both popular and scholarly levels, mainly because of the pilgrimage to the site of his relics. But the historical understanding of James's role in Spanish Church history varied considerably over time and place.[6]

Since the ninth century, James's relics were believed to lie in the cathedral church of Santiago de Compostela, Galicia in north-western Spain. For the first few centuries of the cult of these relics, however, their custodians did not claim that the Apostle Santiago had visited Spain during his earthly life; the

---

[5] On the patristic tradition of Paul's mission to Spain, see Sotomayor, *Historia de la iglesia en España*, I, pp. 159ff. Sotomayor notes that the possibility of Paul's mission to Spain 'hardly elicited any interest at the popular level' before modern times (p. 160). More research stands to be done, however, on the medieval origins of the local cults of such saints as Rufus of Tortosa and Peter of Braga, which will be mentioned below.

[6] For a more detailed version of the story told in this section, see Van Liere, 'The Moorslayer and the Missionary'.

local tradition held, rather, that James had lived and preached in Palestine, and that after his beheading in Jerusalem, his body was brought to Spain, where it was buried and forgotten until its miraculous rediscovery by a local hermit in the ninth century. This tradition was disseminated by pilgrims who came to Compostela from across Europe. Santiago was thus widely remembered for his posthumous miracles on behalf of Spanish Christians and other pilgrims, but not for having preached or made converts in Spain while alive. As late as 1130, an influential history of the diocese of Compostela narrated the history of James's life, the translation of his relics, and his subsequent miracles, without making the claim that he had evangelized Spain.[7]

A distinct medieval tradition, however, originating outside of Spain, posited that James had been sent to Spain after the dispersion of the Apostles, just as Thomas had been sent to India and John to Asia. The notion that James had preached in Spain before his martyrdom was appropriated by the anonymous author of the *Codex Calixtinus* (c.1140), a compilation of miracle stories and pilgrim lore that was produced in Santiago de Compostela and falsely attributed to Pope Calixtus II to give it greater authority.[8] The *Codex Calixtinus* embellished the notion of James's visit to Spain into a full-length adventure story, in which James acquired twelve disciples on his missionary journeys, nine of whom were Spanish. Seven of these nine accompanied the Apostle back to Jerusalem, witnessed his martyrdom, and returned to Spain to bury their master's body in the land where he had preached.

Pseudo-Calixtus's story of James and his Spanish apostles was a creative interweaving of three distinct traditions: the biblical story of James's martyrdom (Acts 12:2); the early medieval tradition of James's apostolic mission to Spain; and a completely separate liturgical tradition of 'seven apostles' (*siete varones apostólicos*) which had appeared in several ninth-century French martyrologies.[9] In these liturgical sources, the seven apostles had no connection with James whatever (none of the ninth-century martyrologies mentioned James preaching in Spain). They were seven men of unknown origin, 'ordained in Rome by the holy apostles' (Peter and Paul) and sent to Spain, where they founded seven bishoprics in seven different cities.[10] The twelfth-century author of the *Codex Calixtinus* appropriated these seven confessors for

---

[7] Emma Falque Rey (ed.), *Historia Compostellana*, CCCM 70 (Turnhout: Brepols, 1988), pp. lxvii–lxix; p. 7 (§ I, ll. 1–16); Van Liere, 'The Moorslayer and the Missionary', pp. 525–6.

[8] Klaus Herbers and Manuel Santos Noia (eds.), *Liber Sancti Iacobi/Codex Calixtinus* (Santiago de Compostela: Xunta de Galicia, 1987).

[9] Sotomayor, *Historia de la iglesia en España*, I, p. 159, suggests that the fusing of the two legends may have begun in ninth-century sources, but pseudo-Calixtus's version was certainly the fullest and the most widely circulated medieval account of the combined legend.

[10] The seven apostles were Torquatus (Torquato), Ctesiphon (Tesifonte), Secundus (Segundo), Indaletius (Indalecio), Caecilius (Cecilio), Hesychius (Esiquio), and Euphrasius (Eufrasio). They appear in the breviaries of Florus, 'anonymous of Lyon', Ado, and Usuard under their feast day of 15 May. For the fullest version of the legend, see that of Florus: Jacques Dubois and Geneviève

Spain and turned them into James's first converts, but retained the ninth-century martyrological tradition of their apostolic ordination in Rome, by positing a complex itinerary: bearing the martyred James's body from Jerusalem back to Spain, the seven paid a visit to Rome to be consecrated by Peter and Paul. They were thus fortified by a triple apostolic commission when they founded their respective churches on Spanish soil. Pseudo-Calixtus also adapted and dramatized other elements of the earlier liturgical tradition. The ninth-century martyrologies had named an aristocratic Roman woman as the seven apostles' first convert; pseudo-Calixtus turned her into a hostile adversary who persuaded the 'king' of the (unnamed) region to send a fire-breathing dragon and other fierce beasts on the apostles' trail, until they softened her heart with a series of astounding miracles and she accepted the Christian faith.[11]

Thus in pseudo-Calixtus's hands, the story of the story of James and 'his' seven apostles was not only implausibly dramatized, but denuded of any traces of realistic historical context. This was no obstacle to its wide popular appeal. The story was picked up by two of Europe's most popular thirteenth-century hagiographers, Jacobus de Voragine (d. 1298) and Vincent of Beauvais (d. 1264?), who included it in their widely read compilations of saints' lives, the *Legenda aurea* and the *Speculum historiale*, thus ensuring its wide circulation in and outside of Spain.[12] The story of James and the seven apostles was exactly the kind of fantastic, anachronistic saint's legend that made these collections popular with medieval audiences and later brought them scorn from humanists who loved to point out their absurdities.[13] It was thus ironic that these stories would become the foundation of a lasting national narrative in the hands of Renaissance humanist historians.

Other local medieval traditions connected individual Spanish churches or patron saints with the biblical Apostles, but it is often difficult to ascertain when these originated, for many of them do not appear in writing before the sixteenth century. One saint whose legend can be traced with some certainty is Eugenius of Toledo, who was venerated in Toledo (Spain's archiepiscopal see) as the city's martyred first bishop and a disciple of St Denis of Paris. St Denis himself was identified as Dionysius the Areopagite, a disciple of Paul (Acts 17:34), making Eugenius just two steps removed from an Apostle. His legend was born in 1148, when Archbishop Raimundus of Toledo, travelling home from the Synod of Reims, allegedly saw an inscription in the abbey church of

---

Renaud (eds.), *Edition pratique des Martyrologies de Bède, de l'Anonyme Lyonnais, et de Florus* (Paris: Centre National de la Recherche Scientifique, 1976).

[11] *Liber Sancti Iacobi* (n. 8 above), Lib. III, cap. 1, pp. 186–7.

[12] Voragine, *The Golden Legend*; Beauvais, *Bibliotheca . . .* , IV: *Speculum historiale*.

[13] See e.g. the famous jeer of Juan Luis Vives (1493–1540) that Voragine had 'a mouth of iron and a heart of lead' in *De disciplinis* (1531); cited in editor's introduction to Cano, *L'autorità della storia profana*, p. xlvii.

St Denis in Paris identifying Eugenius as Denis' disciple and Toledo's first bishop.[14] The see of Toledo later arranged for the right arm of this newly discovered saint to be translated (in 1156) from Paris to Toledo, where he was revered thereafter as the first-century founder of the see, despite the awkward fact that Toledo's existing diocesan records identified the first Bishop Eugenius as a seventh-century prelate. While the story of St Eugenius does not seem to have gained much credence outside Toledo before the Renaissance, Toledo's clergy did appeal to it on occasion to justify the supremacy of the see of Toledo.[15]

Although such legends existed locally and some also circulated abroad, they received little attention from most medieval historical writers. As Francisco de Padilla rightly observed, Spanish ecclesiastical history did not exist as a genre before the sixteenth century. Its closest equivalent was the series of national chronicles written by authors such as of Isidore of Seville (d. 636), Lucas of Tuy (fl. 1236), and Rodrigo Jiménez de Rada (d. 1247). These three chroniclers, all bishops, had much to say about the Church in Spain's history, but they gave scant attention to the Roman era. They all understood the Visigothic King Reccared, who had converted from Arianism to Catholicism in the sixth century, to be the real founder of Spanish Catholicism. Lucas of Tuy had prefaced his *Chronicon mundi* with a lengthy tribute to Spain's early martyrs, beginning with the Spanish-born Lawrence (d. 258), but he did not date these early Christians or place them in a historical context. He mentioned the patristic tradition that Paul had visited the peninsula, but reached no firm conclusion about its validity, nor did he mention any converts whom the Apostle Paul might have made.[16] Neither Lucas of Tuy nor Jiménez de Rada mentioned James's first-century mission or the seven apostles, or identified the Church as an institution existing in Roman times. Perhaps most tellingly, Jiménez de Rada, who was himself archbishop of Toledo, failed to mention his supposed first-century predecessor St Eugenius in his *Historia de rebus Hispaniae*.[17] Some sources claim that in 1215 (before he wrote the *Historia*) Jiménez de Rada had made a speech at the Fourth Lateran Council in Rome

---

[14] Raimundus may well have invented this legend, as there was no known tradition of Eugenius in France before 1156. See Rivera Recio, *San Eugenio de Toledo y su culto*; Peter Linehan, *History and the Historians of Medieval Spain* (Oxford: Clarendon Press, 1993), pp. 275ff. On St Denis's legend in France, see below, Ch. 10.

[15] Linehan, *History and the Historians*, p. 278.

[16] José Carlos Martín (ed.), *Isidori Hispalensis Chronica*, CCSL 112 (Turnhout: Brepols, 2003), p. 200 (§ I, l. 408)ff; Emma Falque Rey (ed.), *Lucae Tudensis Chronicon Mundi*, CCCM 74 (Turnhout: Brepols, 2003), Praefatio, pp. 5–10. On the patristic tradition (based on Romans 15:24–5), see Sotomayor, *Historia de la iglesia en España*, I, pp. 159ff.

[17] The earliest Bishop Eugenius mentioned by Jiménez de Rada is Eugenius I (bishop 636–46/7), who presided over the Fifth and Sixth Councils of Toledo in Visigothic times: Juan Fernández Valverde (ed.), *Roderici Ximenii de Rada Historia de Rebus Hispaniae sive Historia Gothica*, CCCM 72 (Turnhout: Brepols, 1987), p. 68 (II.xviiii, 16–18).

rejecting the Santiago legend as pious falsehood, and embracing the tradition of St Eugenius, as proof that Toledo, not Compostela, was Spain's oldest diocese.[18] But if he did make such a speech in order to bolster Toledo's claims to supremacy over Compostela, it did not necessarily reveal his convictions as a scholar, for he chose not to mention either legend in his historical chronicle, written many years later.

A few later medieval historians did find it useful to mention either the James legend, or the legend that the Apostle Paul had preached in Spain, as evidence that the land was and irreversibly Christian before the eighth-century Muslim conquest.[19] But these brief assertions were made without any historical evidence or context, in works that otherwise largely avoided the Roman era. Other late medieval chronicles, such as the *Historia de la Corona de Aragon* (*c*.1370), Pedro de Escavias's *Repertorio de principes de España* (*c*.1470), and Diego de Valera's *Crónica abreviada de España* (1482), compressed the Roman era to a minimum and left out such legends altogether. In fact Valera's best-selling *Crónica* seemed to imply, by a chronological elision of five centuries, that the Goths invaded Spain in the second century BC.[20]

3. HUMANISM AND THE RISE OF ROMAN HISTORY IN SPAIN

The first step towards a new Renaissance interest in the Roman-era Church was the awakening of humanist scholarly interest in the social and political history of Roman Hispania. It took some decades, however, for Spanish humanist Romanophilia to stimulate particular interests in ecclesiastical history, for secular and religious history were quite distinct in the minds of Spain's first humanist historians. The pioneers in Spanish Roman historiography, Antonio de Nebrija (1444–1522) and Joan Margarit i Pau (d. 1484), were both contemporaries of Diego de Valera, but unlike him, both studied at the University of Bologna and were deeply influenced by Italian humanism. Both directed their attention as history writers primarily to Roman topography and chronology, not to ecclesiastical history.[21] Neither Nebrija nor Margarit

---

[18] Antonio García y García, *Iglesia, Sociedad y Derecho*, II (Salamanca: Universidad Pontificia de Salamanca, 1987), pp. 187–208.

[19] E.g. Gil de Zamora, *De preconiis Hispaniae* [1282], ed. Manuel Castro y Castro (Madrid: Universidad de Madrid, 1955), pp. 145–6 (VI.1); Rodrigo Sánchez de Arévalo, *Compendiosa historia hispanica* (Rome: Ulrich Gallus, 1470), fol. 9ᵛ.

[20] *Historia de la Corona de Aragón ... Crónica de San Juan de la Peña*; Escavías, *Repertorio de principes de España*; Valera, *Crónica abreviada de España*. Printed in at least nine editions before 1500 and ten thereafter, Valera's *Crónica* was one of the most widely read histories of this period.

[21] Their works had less immediate impact than Valera's best-selling *Crónica*; Margarit's *Paralipomenon Hispaniae* (*c*.1480) was not printed until 1545, and Nebrija's *Muestra de istoria*

(at least in his surviving works) examined the question of Spanish Christian origins. On the contrary, these early humanist historians were remarkably reserved in their treatment of Spain's early Christian history, probably in large part because they knew that Hispano-Roman sources revealed a thoroughly pagan culture. Margarit's *Paralipomenon* ended (unfinished) around the time of Caesar Augustus, and thus never reached the Christian era. None of Nebrija's extant writings mentions Christian worship or saints in the first three centuries of Roman Spain.[22]

Apparently what was required before Spanish historians began to take the early Roman period seriously as the birth era of the Spanish Church, was a willingness to embrace two scholarly attitudes that often seemed to be in tension: on the one hand, the humanist passion for Roman antiquity that made scholars like Nebrija revere Roman Hispania as the cradle of Hispanic culture, and on the other, a pious credulity that would admit medieval hagiographic accounts as legitimate historical sources. For it was by rediscovering and legitimating local liturgical traditions and questionable sources like the *Codex Calixtinus* that humanist historians finally opened the door to discovering (or inventing) the Spanish Church of the first century. Further research may shed still more light on how, when, and why Spanish humanist chroniclers first decided to embrace these tensions, but one important catalyst was the energetic sponsorship of national history by Queen Isabel of Castile (r. 1474–1504) and her husband Ferdinand of Aragon (r. 1479–1516).[23]

4. RENAISSANCE CHRONICLERS REDISCOVER THE ROMAN CHURCH

Ironically, the first royal chronicler who appears to have given serious attention to the legends of James and the seven apostles was not a native Spaniard but Antonio de Nebrija's Sicilian-born contemporary and bitter rival, Lucius Marineus Siculus (*c.*1444–1533). Siculus had come to Spain in the 1480s as a private Latin tutor and then taken a teaching position at the University of Salamanca. Nebrija, his colleague there, disliked and mistrusted him, and seems to have envied Siculus's appointment by Ferdinand II as royal

---

de las antigüedades de España was printed once (Burgos, 1499) but survives only in fragments. On Margarit, see R. B. Tate, 'Joan Margarit i Pau, Bishop of Gerona', *Speculum* 27 (1952), pp. 28–42. On Nebrija, see R. B. Tate, 'Nebrija the Historian', *Bulletin of Hispanic Studies* 23 (1957), pp. 125–46.

[22] Nebrija did, however, write a learned commentary on Prudentius's *Peristephanon*, a poetic catalogue of fourth-century Spanish martyrs: Nebrija, *Aurelii Prudentii Clementis V.C.*

[23] For the definitive study of Renaissance Spain's royal chroniclers, see Kagan, *Clio and the Crown*.

chronicler for Aragon in 1497.[24] When Nebrija later secured an appointment for himself as royal chronicler for Castile, he warned Ferdinand (in a dedicatory preface) that 'we cannot rely on foreigners to be completely objective about history, least of all Italians, who care mainly about their own reputation. They envy our glory, they resent being governed by us, and . . . they insult us, calling us barbarians and bumpkins.'[25]

Siculus, perhaps eager to prove to the crown and to sceptics like Nebrija that he could be as patriotic as any native Spaniard, wrote two histories, one of Aragon and one of Spain, that gave credence to some of the legends of first-century Christian origins. In the first, the *Crónica de Aragon* (published in Latin in 1509 and in Spanish translation in 1524), Siculus mentioned that King Sancho Ramírez of Aragon (r. 1063–94) had arranged to have the relics of St Indaletius translated from the southern city of Almería to the northern monastery of San Juan de la Peña in 1084, shortly after the Christians reconquered Almería from Muslim rule. Siculus identified Indaletius ('Andalexio') as 'a disciple of Santiago, and one of the first whom Santiago had converted in Spain to the law of Jesus Christ'.[26] This bold claim was apparently not derived from any Aragonese account of Indaletius's cult. Although the monks' own oral tradition at San Juan de la Peña might possibly have associated this early bishop of Almería with the legendary 'seven apostles', no known records before the sixteenth century connect him with the Apostle Santiago. The monastery's own chronicle, the *Crónica de San Juan de la Peña* (1370), simply called Indaletius the first bishop of Urci (Almería) and noted that his disciple and successor was named James.[27] It is tempting to infer that Siculus misread this passage and reversed the roles of teacher and disciple. It seems more likely, however, that he was inspired by the imaginative story of the seven apostles told in the twelfth-century *Codex Calixtinus*, and concluded that the two saints named Indaletius (or Indalecio or Andalexio) must be one and the same.

Whatever Siculus's thought process in composing the *Crónica de Aragon*, the stories in the *Codex Calixtinus* had clearly captured his imagination by the time he wrote his last work, the *De rebus Hispaniae memorabilibus* (1530). Now an old man and retired from the writing of 'official' history, Siculus wrote this survey of Spain to display his classical erudition and his reverence for Spanish culture, dedicating it to Ferdinand's successor Charles V (r. 1516–56). The *De rebus* was not a historical chronicle, but a eulogy of Spain (*laus*

---

[24] On the rivalry, see Rummel, 'Marineo Siculo', pp. 716ff.

[25] Nebrija, Dedicatory Epistle to the *Decades*, in *Obras históricas de Nebrija*, ed. Hinojo Andrés, pp. 127–9.

[26] Marineus Siculus, *Cronica d'Aragon*, fol. 9[r].

[27] See Antonio Durán Gudiol, 'El traslado de las reliquias de San Indalecio a San Juan de la Peña', *Argensola* 109 (1995), pp. 13–24; *Historia de la Corona de Aragón . . . conocida . . . Crónica de San Juan de la Peña*, p. 52.

Hispaniae) in the classical tradition: a catalogue of Spain's merits, organized thematically and geographically. It listed the most 'memorable' features of Spain's geography, climate, great men, and moral and military virtues from ancient to modern times, with a strong emphasis on the Greek and Roman eras. Siculus boasted in the preface that he had travelled nearly the whole length and breadth of Spain examining sources for this work, and these travels must have taken him to Santiago de Compostela, where, if he had not already encountered the twelfth-century *Codex Calixtinus*, the cathedral canons would eagerly have shown the distinguished royal chronicler their prized original copy. Siculus made use of the *Codex Calixtinus* in the chapter on 'Saints and Martyrs', where he described the first-century mission of James and his seven apostles, and told how their preaching converted 'innumerable multitude of Spaniards to the worship of Christ'.[28] He lifted this account almost *verbatim* from the *Codex Calixtinus*, although he left out the more fantastic elements of the story, such as the anachronistic 'king' and the fire-breathing dragon. The well-travelled Siculus also included other first-century legends in his catalogue of memorable saints, most notably Eugenius of Toledo, whom he identified, following Archbishop Raimundus's twelfth-century narrative, as the martyred disciple of Dionysius the Areopagite.[29]

Among the other local legends of first-century Christian origins that Siculus mentioned approvingly but briefly amidst a long catalogue of 'buildings and places in Spain celebrated for religion and miracles' was the tale that the Apostle James had founded the church of La Virgen del Pilar in Zaragoza at the behest of the Virgin herself. Local tradition in Zaragoza held that Mary had appeared upon a pillar (the eponymous pillar on which the church was later built) and commanded the Apostle to build a church in her honour. The 'miracles and great mysteries' that transpired at this church, Siculus reported, again hinting at his own peripatetic scholarly labours, were recorded in 'many writings' now carefully conserved by the church's custodians.[30] As the former royal chronicler for Aragon, Siculus had an obvious motivation to include this story, which made this Aragonese church the very first in Spanish history, although his rather vague reference to these 'great mysteries' and his failure to identify or describe the 'many writings' that substantiated them, may suggest some scepticism about this particular legend. Siculus was, after all, an avowed admirer of the Dutch humanist Erasmus, whose scorn for many aspects of the medieval cult of the saints was well known.[31] Siculus's guarded, almost ironic

---

[28] Marineus Siculus, *De rebus Hispaniae libri XXII*, p. 341. The *De rebus* was translated into Castilian in several editions, beginning in 1533, including *De las cosas memorables de España*.

[29] Marineus Siculus, *De rebus*, p. 340.

[30] Marineus Siculus, *De rebus*, pp. 347–51, at p. 348.

[31] Erasmus, an outspoken critic of both pilgrimage and the cult of the saints in general, had ridiculed the superstitions of pilgrims to Santiago in particular; see Erasmus, 'A Pilgrimage for Religion's Sake', in *Colloquies (Collected Works of Erasmus, vols. 39–40)*, XL, pp. 619–74.

language when describing some of Spain's most famous relic collections in this same chapter did suggest a certain reluctance to accept them all at face value.[32] But this reserve was quite muted, and when the *De rebus Hispaniae* was published in several vernacular editions in 1530s, it is quite likely that the author's own Erasmian reserve was lost on many of its readers.

If Siculus himself hesitated to connect the dots between these hagiographical legends to produce a narrative of first-century Christian origins, later humanist chroniclers were considerably bolder. The Valencian priest Pere Antoni Beuter (*c.*1490–1554) took the legends that Siculus had assembled and incorporated them into a chronicle which emphatically made the Spanish Catholic Church the first in Western Europe. Beuter was not a paid royal chronicler but a civic preacher, humanist scholar, and university professor of theology who wrote, it seems, from a personal passion for sacred history. A keen bibliophile, he also owned of one of Valencia's largest libraries.[33] The title of his *Coronica general de toda España, y especialmente del reyno de Valencia*, first published in 1538 in Valencian dialect (as *Cróniques de València . . .*), revealed his dual loyalties, both to his native *patria* of Valencia, part of the crown of Aragon, and to the more universal 'Spain'.[34] In this dense synthesis of sacred and secular history, Beuter triumphantly demonstrated that the oldest two churches in all of Europe were both found in Spain—one in Aragon and one in Castile.

In a single chapter, Beuter's *Coronica* leapt from Rome to Jerusalem to Hispania and back again, discussing (among other matters) Julius Caesar's civil wars; the reigns of the first six Roman emperors; the persecution of early Christians in the Roman Empire; the personal role of three Apostles—James, Peter, and Paul—in spreading the faith in the Iberian peninsula; James's martyrdom in Jerusalem and his burial in Spain; and the execution of Peter and Paul in Rome in AD 70. He drew on pagan classical sources like Pliny, Livy, and Caesar; early Christian authors such as Tertullian, Eusebius, and Sophronius (d. 639); and later medieval hagiographic collections, including John Beleth (fl. 1182), pseudo-Calixtus, and Vincent of Beauvais. In this account, the story of James's mission to Spain followed logically upon the martyrdom of Stephen in Jerusalem (AD 34) and the conversion of Paul on the road to Damascus (AD 35). James was inspired to go to Spain by a 'divine revelation' from the Virgin herself, who spoke to him in Jerusalem, gave him 'her blessing to sail to Spain', and instructed him to build her a chapel in the place where he managed to make the most converts. After lengthy travels throughout Spain,

---

[32] E.g. see Siculus's respectful but cautious account of the *arca santa* of Oviedo, believed to include the rod that Moses used to part the Red Sea, manna from the time of the Exodus, drops of the Virgin's breast milk, and many other implausible treasures: *De rebus*, p. 348.

[33] Escartí, 'Narrar la historia remota'.

[34] Beuter, *Cróniques de València*. I have consulted the 1604 Castilian edition, *Primera parte de la coronica general de toda España . . .* , which will hereafter be cited as *Coronica*.

James found himself in Zaragoza, where he finally managed to convert eight souls. When he grew discouraged about this meagre harvest, the Virgin reappeared to him in a celestial vision, atop a marble pillar, holding the infant Jesus and surrounded by singing angels, and encouraged him: 'Do not be sad, my son . . . know that the religion of my God will flourish here, through faith and through martyrdom.' She then told him that this was the place to build her a church.[35] The next morning James complied, founding a church on the site of the marble pillar where the Virgin had appeared. He then consecrated his disciple Theodorus as its first bishop and returned to Jerusalem with his seven remaining apostles.[36] Thus the church in Zaragoza was the oldest in Spain. The second-oldest church in Spain was that of Santiago de Compostela, built several years later in Compostela over the tomb of James, where his faithful seven disciples brought and buried him after his martyrdom in Jerusalem. All of this made 'the Spanish people the first Gentiles who received the faith in their lands'.[37] In this way Beuter creatively wove together the oral tradition of la Virgen del Pilar in Zaragoza with the tradition of James and the seven apostles, his own considerable knowledge of Roman history, and his own imagination, to produce the most synthetic (if quite improbable) account of Spain's Christian origins that had been written to date.

Beuter also deemed it important to emphasize the Spanish's Church's direct links with Saints Peter and Paul, the two most important Apostles in the Roman Catholic Church. Thus his *Coronica* highlighted and embellished the medieval tradition of Paul's visit to Spain. Beuter reported confidently that Paul had come to the peninsula in the second year of Nero's reign (AD 58). He also drew assiduously on medieval liturgies to identify early martyrs who were sometimes regarded as disciples of either Peter or Paul. In this way he introduced St Firminius (alias Firmin or Fermin) of Pamplona, sent by Peter from Rome, and Paul's disciples Sergius Paulus (traditionally identified with Paul of Narbonne), and Rufus of Tortosa. He also expanded on Siculus's account of Eugenius of Toledo and his connection to Paul through Dionysius the Areopagite. While Siculus had left the dates of Eugenius's life and death obscure, Beuter reported that both Eugenius and Dionysius were martyred under Emperor Domitian in AD 82, victims of the first serious wave of Christian persecutions in Spain.[38] Since the sources on many of these figures were sparser than those on James and his companions, Beuter offered fewer colourful details, but he dealt with these disciples of Paul and James essentially the same way he had with the earlier figures: he compiled as many sources as he could find and wove them artfully together into a streamlined chronological narrative. He sometimes admitted discrepancies and silences in his sources, noting for example, 'I am greatly

---

[35] Ibid., p. 135. Beuter also claimed here that he had seen documents validating the Jacobean origin of this Zaragozan church in the church of Santa Maria sopra Minerva in Rome.
[36] Ibid., pp. 134–5.   [37] Ibid., p. 136.   [38] Ibid., pp. 137–8.

amazed that the Greeks have not written about the journey of Santiago to Spain.'[39] But he drew no revisionist conclusions from such silences, and rarely if ever rejected any legend wholesale as implausible or incongruous.

By the middle of the sixteenth century, multiple chronicles in several languages were available to give this new Renaissance narrative of Christian origins wide circulation. Beuter's *Crónica* was expanded and translated into Spanish in 1546 and Italian in 1556.[40] In the same decade, the Flemish humanist Johannes Vasaeus (1511–61), a teacher of rhetoric at Salamanca, wrote his own chronicle in Latin, the *Chronici rerum memorabilium Hispaniae* (1552), with the expressed intention of making early Spanish history known to other foreigners.[41] This blended political and ecclesiastical history from the birth of Christ down to the year 1020 in a manner quite similar to Beuter's work, narrating the missionary efforts of James, his seven apostles, and subsequent evangelists sent from Rome to preach the gospel in Spain. Vasaeus freely acknowledged his debts to Nebrija, Margarit, Siculus, and especially Beuter, as well as to more recent humanist scholars such as his Portuguese friend Andrés de Resende (1500–73). He adduced many of the same medieval sources, including pseudo-Calixtus. Vasaeus's style was more scholastic than Beuter's; rather than simply asserting that Paul had preached in Spain, he devoted several pages to weighing the patristic sources and scholarly arguments for and against the tradition. But he reached the same positive conclusion as Beuter. He gratefully acknowledged the assistance of individual colleagues from Salamanca's theology faculty in helping him to build an argument for Paul's mission that would 'bring great honour to Spain'.[42]

Vasaeus also added a new name to the roster of founding bishops compiled by Beuter: St Peter of Braga, martyr and first bishop of Braga in Portugal, whom the liturgies of that church identified as one of James's disciples.[43] Vasaeus had taught at the university in Braga in the 1530s, while serving as tutor to the Cardinal-Prince Henrique (lived 1512–80), who was also archbishop of Braga (1533–40), so he had an insider's knowledge of that diocese's liturgy. The *Chronicon* was dedicated to the prince (who later became King Henrique I of Portugal, 1578–80). In this context it seemed perfectly natural to Vasaeus that 'Hispania' should include the modern kingdom of Portugal and its bishoprics. Once Vasaeus had brought Peter into the received narrative, he would remain firmly lodged there as one of James's many Spanish disciples.

---

[39] Ibid., p. 135.

[40] The second part was initially published in Castilian (1551), not Aragonese; a second (1604) edition, the most widely available, included parts I and II in Castilian. The first Italian edition is Beuter, *Cronica generale d'Hispagna et del regno di Valenza* (Venice, 1556).

[41] Vasaeus, *Chronici . . . tomus prior.* James and subsequent missionaries are discussed at fols. 57^{v}ff. For an assessment of Vasaeus's originality, see Tate, 'The rewriting of the historical past'.

[42] Vasaeus, *Chronici . . . tomus prior*, fols. 60^r–61^r; quote at fol. 60^v.

[43] Ibid., fol. 58^v.

Not all Spanish humanist historians embraced this emerging narrative of the Spanish Church's apostolic origins. At mid century, Spain's most erudite humanist scholars still maintained a circumspect attitude resembling that of Antonio de Nebrija some decades earlier. Antonio Agustín (1517–86), arguably the most learned and critical-minded historical scholar of sixteenth-century Spain, was notably quiet on the subject of first-century Christianity. A skilled canonist and legal historian, Agustín did copious research on the Church history of the Roman and Visigothic period, reading and editing collections of canons from the Councils of Toledo. He knew that the records for Spanish history before the Arab conquest were remarkably sparse, and that most Roman traditions were completely effaced by barbarian and Arab conquests. Thus Agustín limited his own studies to the later, better documented centuries of Christian history.[44] His learned correspondent Jéronimo de Zurita (1512–80) displayed a similar caution. Zurita shared Agustín's passion for Roman antiquity, and the two corresponded at length on matters concerning the history, inscriptions, coinage, and topography of Roman Hispania.[45] Yet when Zurita wrote the *Anales de la corona de Aragón* (1562) as Philip II's royal chronicler for Aragon, he chose to pass over the early centuries of Spain's history altogether, comparing the centuries before the Arab conquest to a 'great desert' with no certain monuments, and beginning his narrative in the early eighth century.[46]

But in the cultural and religious climate of the later sixteenth century, Agustín and Zurita found themselves in a distinct minority, for other Catholic scholars were discovering more reasons than ever to uphold the apostolic origins of the Spanish Church. As the confessional conflict between Catholics and Protestants intensified across Europe, the Catholic Church placed increasing value on the cult of the saints as a hallmark of Catholic identity. The importance of saints ancient and modern was reasserted in the canons of the Council of Trent (1564), and expressed in multiple initiatives enacted by Tridentine reformers across Catholic Europe after the close of the Council. These included a revival of relics translations, the resumption of canonizations after a hiatus of more than six decades, the publication of new saints' lives, and the revision of those saints' lives contained in liturgical books.[47]

There was often a direct link between historiography and popular devotion in these initiatives. Relics translations, for example, were usually accompanied by the publication of books treating the lives of the saints whose relics were being honoured. In Spain, between 1565 and 1594 the Castilian crown sponsored five

---

[44] See M. H. Crawford (ed.), *Antonio Agustín: Between Renaissance and Counter-Reform* (London: Warburg Institute, 1993).

[45] See Van Liere, '"Shared studies foster friendship": Humanism and History in Spain'.

[46] Zurita, *Anales de la Corona de Aragón*, I, p. 11.

[47] See above, Chs. 3 and 4.

major translations of the relics of saints who allegedly dated from before the Muslim conquest, each accompanied by one or more publications that discussed the life of the saint in question. The first saint to be thus honoured was none other than Eugenius of Toledo, whose remaining relics were translated from the Abbey of Saint Denis in Paris to Toledo in 1565, to rejoin the right arm that had made the same journey four centuries earlier.[48] This gift was negotiated as a special concession to Philip II by his brother-in-law, Charles IX of France. The last translation of the century featured St Secundus (San Segundo) of Avila, who by this time was alleged to be one of the seven apostles of James, even though no written narratives from before the sixteenth century had identified him in this way.

Promoting the cult of the saints as a liturgical practice did not *ipso facto* demand of Spanish Catholics the acceptance of a specific set of beliefs about a particular collection of first-century saints. But in the intellectual climate of the Spanish Counter-Reformation, where history was increasingly widely read, and antiquity increasingly prized, and where inspiring stories of first-century missionaries were now readily available in reputable humanist chronicles, it was not surprising that the legends popularized by Siculus, Beuter, and Vasaeus would become more highly valued than ever, to bolster not only national or regional pride but orthodox Catholic identity. Many historians in the second half of the century took an interest in the lives and cults of early Spanish saints, but none was more influential in consolidating the legend of first-century Christian origins than Zurita's Castilian counterpart, the royal chronicler Ambrosio de Morales.

5. AMBROSIO DE MORALES

Ambrosio de Morales (1513–91), who became Philip II's royal chronicler for Castile in 1562, shortly before the close of the Council of Trent, was both a well-trained humanist antiquarian and a keen proponent of the Tridentine cult of the saints. Writing in the wake of Trent and personally involved in Philip II's campaign to reinvigorate the cult of the saints in Spain, Morales was even more convinced than his predecessors that the defence of Catholic orthodoxy depended on the preservation of hagiographic traditions.[49] His interest in Roman antiquities had begun during his boyhood in his native

---

[48] Depluvrez, 'Les Retours de Saint Eugène'.

[49] Morales would write a history of the Roman martyrs Justo and Pastor to commemorate their 1568 translation to Alcalá de Henares: *La vida, el martirio, la invencion, las grandezas, y las translaciones de los gloriosos niños mártires San Justo y Pastor* . . . (Alcalá de Henares: Andres de Angulo, 1568). He would later help Philip II to acquire new relics for his collection at El Escorial; see Lazure, 'Possessing the Sacred'. He served from 1567 to 1588 as Philip II's procurator in the

Cordoba, where his own family were prominent antiquarians and collectors, and it would continue at the University of Salamanca and later at Alcalá, where Morales taught rhetoric and mentored a generation of students in the study of Roman antiquities.[50] When the royal chronicler Florián de Ocampo died in 1562, Morales was appointed to continue his ambitious multi-volume official history where Ocampo had left off, in the second century BC. This assignment gave Morales ample opportunity to combine his passion for sacred history with his expertise in Roman history and antiquities. The resulting *Coronica general de España*, published in three parts beginning in 1574, was the most thorough history yet written of Spain's Roman era. It devoted hundreds of pages to the Roman and Visigothic centuries that Jerónimo de Zurita had passed over altogether, and several chapters—much more than any previous chronicle—to the founding of the Spanish Church in the time of the Apostles.[51]

Few sixteenth-century writers were better situated than Morales to appreciate just how tenuous the sources for first-century sacred history were. He knew that there were neither architectural monuments nor archaeological evidence of any Christian presence in first-century Spain, and he knew the limitations of the medieval hagiographic sources. He had studied with the ultra-orthodox but critical-minded Dominican theologian Melchor Cano (1509–60), whose treatise on sources and methods in sacred history had condemned both Vincent of Beauvais's *Speculum historiale* and Jacobus de Voragine's *Legenda aurea* as 'fabulous' collections that provoked 'not only shame but nausea'.[52] Morales avoided invoking either of these authors as authorities. He introduced his own discussion of Spain's Christian origins with a short methodological essay that classified six principal *loci* (sources) for the lives of the saints: notarial and judicial accounts of martyrdoms; saints' lives; liturgical accounts in martyrologies and breviaries; ancient saints' calendars; and oral traditions. He noted that not all of these were equally authoritative and that all had to be weighed carefully.[53] He then presented his account of Christian origins not simply as narrative, as most of his predecessors had done, but as an extensive commentary on the sources and how to interpret them.

Like Beuter, Morales began his account of the first-century Church with James. But instead of recapitulating the stories told in pseudo-Calixtus and

---

cause of Diego de Alcalá, a fifteenth-century Franciscan friar who would become St Didacus in 1588; see Villalón, 'San Diego de Alcalá'; Case, *La historia de San Diego de Alcalá*.

[50] The fullest biography remains Enrique Redel y Aguilar, *Ambrosio de Morales, estudio biográfico* (Cordoba, 1909).

[51] Morales, *La Coronica general de España*. Bks 9 and 10 discuss the first centuries of Spanish Christianity.

[52] Cano, *L'autorità della storia profana*, p. 154. Morales names Cano as his teacher in the *Coronica*, fol. 212^v.

[53] Morales, *Coronica*, fols. 208^{r}ff.

retold so many times since, he compared them with other, newly discovered liturgical sources which he may have been the first Church historian to employ. In 1571, his friend the Inquisitor General Pedro Ponce de León had discovered in Oviedo a manuscript containing works of the ninth-century bishop St Eulogius of Cordoba, which contained evidence for an early cult of Euphrasius (one of the seven apostles) in Andújar.[54] Morales also made use of a 'very ancient book in Gothic hand' from a collegiate library in Alcalá (the tenth-century text now known as the *Pasionario hispánico*), which contained one of the earliest references in Spain to the seven apostles.[55] With such tools at hand, Morales unravelled pseudo-Calixtus's implausible interweaving of the Santiago legend with that of the seven apostles. Recognizing that these 'ancient breviaries' failed to associate James with the *siete varones apostólicos*, Morales reasoned rightly that these must have been two distinct legends in origin. He also showed that the *Codex Calixtinus* could not have been the work of Pope Calixtus II, as traditionally alleged, for that pope never visited Spain while pontiff, and that many of the miracle stories in the book lacked 'verisimilitude'.[56] Here he was invoking one of his teacher Cano's favourite concepts. Morales also pointed out that many of the legends in the *Codex Calixtinus* surrounding the return of James's body to Galicia were either fantastic or anachronistic; for example, James's disciples could not have been imprisoned by a 'king' when Hispania was a Roman province.[57]

Morales also acknowledged that many patristic and other Greek sources failed to mention James's mission to Spain. Beuter had briefly noted this, too, but Morales addressed the problem at much greater length. He cited more than half a dozen distinct scholarly arguments made (by unnamed critics) to challenge the tradition, including the silence of many early sources on James's journey to Spain. Among these silent sources was the New Testament itself, which told only of James's life and death in Judea. Still other difficulties arose from knowledge of later ecclesiastical sources: the story of the translation of James's relics was not related in the records of the early Church councils, either in Galicia or in the metropolitan see of Toledo.[58] This was the same kind of negative evidence that two decades later would lead Roman scholars Roberto Bellarmino and Cesare Baronio to question the tradition of James's Spanish mission. Morales's lengthy discussion of such arguments two decades before Bellarmino and Baronio shows that Spanish scholars were quite aware

---

[54] Morales would publish these works as *Divi Eulogii Cordubensis, martyris, doctoris, et electi archiepiscopi opera* (Alcalá: Juan Iñiguez de Lequerica, 1574).

[55] Morales, *Coronica*, fol. 262[r]; Ángel Fábrega Grau (ed.), *Pasionario hispánico (siglos VII–XI)*, 2 vols. (Madrid and Barcelona: CSIC/Instituto Padre Enrique Florez, 1953–5).

[56] Morales, *Coronica*, fol. 241[r].

[57] Ibid., fol. 234[r].

[58] Ibid., fol. 234[v].

of these scholarly difficulties well before the controversy of the 1590s, even if none had yet committed them to print.

Yet for all his critical erudition, Morales's ultimate aim was to reaffirm, not to undermine, most of the legends of first-century Spanish Christianity that had become commonplace in the national chronicles since the 1530s. After paring away dubious parts of the tradition, Morales vigorously defended both the James legend *and* that of the seven apostles, albeit as two distinct and unrelated historical events. James *had* come to Spain in the first century and he had founded a church in Zaragoza at the Virgin's behest. To those unnamed critics who noted that the translation of James's relics was not mentioned in the earliest Church councils, Morales replied that it was logical for such dangerous enterprises to be carried out in secret in times of religious persecution, and for the relics then to be lost to memory for many centuries. Thus he deftly turned the absence of evidence into a positive argument for authenticity. He also insisted on the historicity of the seven apostles. He disentangled them from Santiago and acknowledged a few anomalies in the original liturgical tradition (such as the implausible assertion that the seven men died in seven different cities—each in his own bishopric—all on the same day); but then he confidently recounted most of the adventures of these first-century missionaries as they had been told in the ninth-century martyrologies, omitting only a few details (such as the fire-breathing dragon) that were 'beyond all verisimilitude'.[59] He supplemented these textual sources with references to local tradition, citing churches from Granada to Galicia (some of which he had visited) where four of the apostles—Torquatus, Caecilius, Indaletius, and Euphrasius—were revered, and shrines where the relics of two of these saints had been preserved since the Middle Ages. All told, for the first century Morales named sixteen saints who could reliably be said to have preached the gospel in the Iberian peninsula, including Pedro of Braga; the Apostle Paul (whose coming was 'a very certain thing'); Paul's disciples Paulus Sergius, Rufus of Tortosa, Facundus, and Primitivus; Eugenius of Toledo; and Hierotheus, who left Spain to become the teacher of Dionysius of Areopagite.

The most valuable historical evidence for Morales was the Church's liturgy itself. Despite the absence of first-century sources and the silence of most patristic and Byzantine authors on James's mission, Morales argued that the hagiographic lessons in the matins readings of the breviaries from 'almost all the churches of Spain' attested that the Santiago tradition had been continuously believed by large communities of faithful Christians.[60] The seven

---

[59] Ibid., fols. 234^r, 261^r–263^r.

[60] Ibid., fol. 230^v. The 'almost' reveals Morales's attempt to minimize the problematic silences in these sources; he knew that neither the *martyrologies* of Ado, Florus, and Lyon nor the *Pasionario hispánico* asserted that James had gone to Spain, but did not wish to highlight this omission.

apostles were attested, in even more unqualified terms, by 'all the ancient breviaries and sanctorals' of Spain.[61] Doubting a liturgical tradition against such evidence, for Morales, was simply impious:

> For good Christians, and those who wish with due simplicity to subject their understanding to devout and pious matters and not to challenge these with excessive stubbornness, the ancient and established tradition shared by the whole church of Spain should serve as sufficient persuasion... That which is received and believed in all of Spain, now becomes so well established that it would not be advisable to insist on the contrary.[62]

'Received and believed' summed up succinctly what Morales considered the foundation of religious knowledge. As the canons of Trent had reasserted against the heretical claims of Protestant reformers, Church tradition was the ultimate source of truth, and this included liturgies, which had the double sanction of clerical approval from above and popular acceptance from below.

Morales also had great respect for popular hagiographic traditions if they seemed consistent with more learned narratives. He had made his own pilgrimage to Santiago de Compostela while writing the *Coronica,* and visited many other Spanish churches where these early missionaries were locally revered. When possible he brought these local oral traditions into his narrative and reported on local relics connected with the legends he was recounting. While acknowledging that not all such traditions were wholly credible, he warned that it was far better to 'praise God for the reverence that people show to the relics of the saints than to condemn them or subject them to dispute'.[63] To document Santiago's burial in Galicia, for example, Morales inserted an illustration of the stone post (now in the church of St James in Padrón, near Compostela) to which locals in the region claimed the Apostle's disciples had tied their boat when they brought James's body ashore (Figure 6.1). This was one of numerous illustrations of Roman inscriptions that adorned the *Coronica.* Morales prided himself on his expertise in deciphering and interpreting such inscriptions, which often shed light on his historical narrative. Often he debunked popular misconceptions about what the origins of these monuments, but he related this particular legend without any overt criticism. He did admit that the inscription (which named a certain Orises, the patron who had it erected) had nothing to do with the events in question, and that the stone was evidently the base of a long-lost statue, but his only further antiquarian commentary was that 'it has beautiful Roman letters, which I have seen, which make one think that it probably is ancient enough to be

---

[61] Morales, *Coronica,* fols. 261^v–262^r.
[62] Ibid., fol. 228^v.   [63] Ibid., fol. 243^v.

El Apoſtol Santiago, ²³³

A en gran veneraciõ: y la viſitá los peregrinos, a la ribera del rio Sar en el Padrõ.
Allitábien en vna igleſia ſe viſita y reuerencia la gran piedra, en que la barca
eſtuuo amarrada. Eſtaua la piedra entonces a la ribera del rio, y como en ella yo
he viſto, tiene letras Romanas muy lindas, de donde ſe puede prouablemente
penſar, que es tan antigua como eſtos tiempos del ſanto Apoſtol. La deuocion
delos peregrinos ha cortado tanto dela piedra, que ya no ſe puedé leer mas que
eſtas letras en ella.

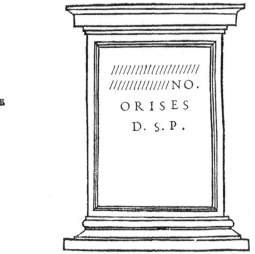

B

C   Parece fue baſa de eſtatua, y vno llamado Oriſes dize la puſo de ſu dinero
faltando el nombre de aquel a quien ſe puſo. Y por ſer eſta gran piedra del ta-
lle delas que en Portugal y en Galizia llaman Padrones, ſe le mudo a la ciudad
de Iria Flauia ſu nõbre antiguo, en eſte que agora tiene: por el inſigne miniſte-
rio, en que aquel ſanto Padron auia ſeruido.

Figure 6.1. Ambrosio de Morales, *Coronica general de España* (Alcalá de Henares: Juan Iñiguez de Lequerica, 1574), fol. 233ʳ. This illustrates the stone monument dating to Roman times that was believed to have marked the spot where Santiago's body was brought ashore for burial in Galicia.

from the time of the holy Apostle', and that the 'devotion of pilgrims' over the centuries had worn off most of the lettering.[64] Morales himself, having been one of these pilgrims, knew how to apply the critical tools of humanist scholarship, but he preferred to apply his erudition to elevating pilgrim traditions rather than to deconstructing them.

---

[64] Ibid., fol. 233ʳ.

6. APOSTOLIC TRADITIONS AFTER MORALES

Morales probably did more than any other writer to solidify the 'Santiago tradition' that by the end of the century came to be almost unanimously accepted as the first chapter in the history of the Spanish Catholic Church. Thus when the scholarly debate about James's coming to Spain erupted into a public controversy shortly after Morales's death in 1591, it was not surprising that the defenders of the Santiago tradition (who evidently far outnumbered the doubters) should turn to Morales as one of their principal authorities. This controversy began in 1593, when Pedro de García de Loaysa Girón, a canon of Toledo, published a collection of documents from Spain's Church councils (*Collectio conciliorum Hispaniae*) which included the speech that the medieval chronicler and archbishop of Toledo, Rodrigo Jiménez de Rada, had allegedly given at the Fourth Lateran Council in 1215, upholding the Eugenius legend and rejecting that of Santiago.[65] In the early 1590s, Cardinal Roberto Bellarmino, working in Rome alongside Cesare Baronio to revise the Roman Breviary under papal auspices, read García de Loaysa's collection and expressed his own doubts about the medieval tradition of James's first-century mission to Spain. These doubts were amplified in the second edition of Baronio's *Annales ecclesiastici* (1602), and in the new Roman breviary of 1602, which incorporated Bellarmino's research and questioned the James-in-Spain tradition in its lesson for James's feast day.[66]

This Italian challenge to the Santiago legend, although it grew out of the scholarship of Spanish authors Jiménez de Rada and García de Loaysa, found very few adherents in Spain. Spanish scholars were particularly sensitive to having their scholarship questioned by Italians, with whom the national rivalry went even further back than the time of Nebrija and Siculus. Thus while the ensuing controversy was carried on largely in the language of historical accuracy and Christian truth, national pride was an important undercurrent in the explosion of polemical books and pamphlets that appeared after 1602 to defend 'the coming of the Apostle'.[67] Francisco de Padilla's *Historia ecclesiastica*, the work that opened this chapter, formed part of this polemical literature. None of these authors was as learned as Morales, with the exception of the Jesuit historian Juan de Mariana (1536–1624). Mariana's *Historia general de España* (1601), which supplanted Morales's *Coronica* as the most widely read history of Spain, was more cautious than Morales in its treatment of the early Church. It presented the story of James's mission as factual truth but reserved judgement

---

[65] Linehan, *History and the Historians*, pp. 329–32.

[66] Ditchfield, *Liturgy, Sanctity and History*, pp. 52ff; Rowe, *Saint and Nation*, ch. 1; Rey Castelao, *La historiografía del Voto de Santiago*, pp. 40ff; Kendrick, *Saint James in Spain*, ch. 3.

[67] These included de Velasco, *Dos discursos*; del Castillo, *Defensa de la venida y predicación de Santiago*; Jesus y Xodar, *Cinco discursos*.

on the legend of the seven apostles.[68] Yet in 1609, after the controversy with Rome had turned the subject into a matter of national honour, Mariana too published a Latin treatise that defended the Santiago legend and that of the seven apostles at great length, naming Beuter and Morales among many modern authorities who helped to substantiate these traditions.[69] The notion of apostolic origins had become an indispensable foundation for Spain's national history, even for a sceptical historian like Mariana.

Meanwhile, far lesser scholars embraced and expanded the legends of the seven apostles in a series of urban histories that were written to popularize and validate their newly revitalized cults. These histories interlaced sacred and profane history in much the way that Beuter, Vasaeus, and Morales had done, but their authors were, almost without exception, even less critical than the earlier chroniclers. Most of them embraced the positive conclusions of Morales's *Coronica* and ignored his scholarly revisionism, enthusiastically recounting the tale of 'James and his seven disciples' as though Morales had never demonstrated that these were two unrelated stories.[70]

By the late sixteenth century, some Spanish Christians' appetite for apostolic origins became so insatiable that they succumbed to the temptation to concoct false sources to bolster and amplify the legends of first-century Spanish Christianity. This served not only to fortify the legends against sceptical challenges but to attach them firmly to particular devotional sites. These early modern falsifications began in the 1580s with the *plomos* (lead books) of Granada, which purported to tell the story of St Secundus (San Segundo), one of the seven apostles, whose relics were now miraculously 'discovered' in the Sacromonte outside Granada. It continued with the false chronicles, or *cronicones*, of the Toledan Jesuit Jerónimo Román de la Higuera (1551–1611), which offered an extensive series of allegedly ancient sources purporting to document the stories of James, the seven apostles, and other early figures of Spanish Christianity. Higuera's false chronicles began to circulate in manuscript form in the 1590s. They were printed in 1619 and widely accepted for more than a century thereafter.[71]

Thus Spanish ecclesiastical history entered a new and unfortunate chapter, in which false sources led even the best scholars astray and induced them

---

[68] The first version, *Historia de rebus Hispaniae libri XX* (Toledo, 1592), was expanded from 20 to 30 books and translated into Castilian as *Historia general de España* (Toledo, 1601), and expanded again in a second Latin edition, *De rebus Hispaniae libri XXX* (Mainz, 1605). On Mariana's own aborted project to write an ecclesiastical history of Spain, see Cirot, *Études sur L'historiographie espagnole*, pp. 72ff.

[69] Mariana, *De adventu Iacobi Apostoli*, p. 18.

[70] Two examples are Cianca, *Historia de . . . S. Segundo*; Pisa, *Descripcion de . . . Toledo*.

[71] García-Arenal and Rodríguez Mediano, *Un Oriente español*; Barrios Aguilera and García-Arenal (eds.), *Los plomos del Sacromonte*; Harris, *From Muslim to Christian Granada*; Caro Baroja, *Las falsificaciones de la historia*; Olds, *The 'False Chronicles'*.

unwittingly to mix fact and fiction. As a result, most of the sacred history written in seventeenth-century Spain about the first centuries is deeply problematic. A minority of early modern scholars, such as Juan Bautista Pérez (*c.*1534–97) and Nicolás Antonio (1617–84), were critical-minded enough to recognize these forgeries for what they were.[72] But Spanish ecclesiastical history as a whole regained its critical edge only in the Enlightenment, with Gregorio de Mayans i Siscar (1699–1781) and the Augustinian Henrique Flórez (1701–73), whose fifty-one-volume *España sagrada* (Madrid, 1747–1886) became (after its posthumous completion) the belated Spanish counterpart to Ferdinando Ughelli's *Italia sacra*.

The Renaissance chroniclers from Siculus to Morales who popularized the legends of the Spanish Church's apostolic origins should not be blamed for the explosion of false history at the end of the sixteenth century. They were not forgers, but well-intentioned humanist scholars working in good faith. Their works not only predated the forged tablets and false chronicles but helped to debunk these forgeries, and subsequently outlived them. This was particularly true of Ambrosio de Morales, whose work was widely respected through the eighteenth century. Juan Bautista Pérez and Nicolás Antonio both drew heavily on Ambrosio de Morales's scholarship in their learned critiques of the false chronicles. Henrique Flórez's *España sagrada* was heavily indebted to Morales's *Coronica,* and the Enlightened Augustinian scholar repaid the debt by writing Morales's biography and publishing some of his manuscripts.[73] Indeed Flórez, like most of his Enlightened contemporaries, followed in Morales's footsteps by continuing to defend the legend of James's mission to Spain, even while rejecting other pious legends and fables.[74] So the chroniclers of the sixteenth century cast a long shadow indeed. Not until the twentieth century would Spanish ecclesiastical history free itself altogether from the myths of first-century apostolic origins that these humanist chroniclers of Renaissance Spain so assiduously constructed and defended.[75]

---

[72] Ehlers, 'Juan Bautista Pérez'; Antonio, *Censura de historias.*

[73] Morales, *Viage de Ambrosio Morales por ordén del Rey Phelipe,* ed. Flórez.

[74] See Antonio Mestre Sanchis, *Ilustración y reforma de la iglesia: pensamiento. político-religioso de Don Gregorio Mayáns y Siscar (1699–1781)* (Valencia: Ayuntamiento de Oliva, 1968), pp. 90ff. The more sceptical Mayans was one of the few dissenters, but he was guarded about his scepticism in print.

[75] The definitive scholarly critique of the Santiago legend was Louis Duchesne, 'Saint Jacques en Galice', *Anales du Midi* 12 (1900), pp. 145–79.

7

Imagining Christian Origins: Catholic Visions of a Holy Past in Central Europe

Howard P. Louthan

The study of Catholic historical writing in Central Europe after the Reformation has until recently been an especially vexing field of inquiry. Research in this area was at best desultory, as scholars more often focused on the contributions of Protestants, positing a historiographical tradition that progressed from the Renaissance through the Enlightenment in the works of Sleidan, Melanchthon, Pufendorf, and Leibniz, and reached its triumphant climax in the nineteenth century at the universities of Göttingen and Berlin. In recent years, however, a more balanced assessment is emerging, as German scholars in particular have begun to consider the rich tradition of Central European Catholic historiography in the sixteenth, seventeenth, and eighteenth centuries.[1] The challenge of validating ecclesiastical tradition in face of the Protestant onslaught was immense and became one of the key issues for Catholic intellectuals active in what was the continent's most confessionally divided region since the late Middle Ages. Though often neglected, their response to the Lutheran and Calvinist offensive was robust. The work of Cesare Baronio for example, was eagerly received and adapted across the region. The *Annales Ecclesiastici* were quickly translated into German and Polish. The German Calvinist scholar Justus Calvinus was allegedly so impressed by the work that he not only converted but returned from a trip to Rome with a new name, Justus Calvinus Baronius.[2]

One of the most important ways that Catholic scholars responded to the Reformation challenge was through the search for Christian origins. As Colin Kidd has noted for the English context, 'Provenance was the keystone of legitimacy, whether Biblical, confessional or institutional.'[3] Through their

---

[1] Benz, *Zwischen Tradition und Kritik, passim*; Sawilla, *Antiquarianismus, passim*.
[2] Benz, *Zwischen Tradition und Kritik*, p. 47.
[3] Colin Kidd, *British Identities before Nationalism* (Cambridge: Cambridge University Press, 1999), p. 287.

efforts to unearth an ancient and distinguished Catholic heritage, ecclesiastical antiquarians across Central Europe were making critical claims of confessional legitimacy. In Paderborn the learned prince-bishop, Ferdinand von Fürstenberg (1626–83), wrote a chronicle that featured Christianity's great victory over the ancient religion of the Saxons when Charlemagne and his allies destroyed the Irminsul, a pagan monument, and replaced it with a magnificently furnished church.[4] In Fulda, Christoph Brower (1559–1617) highlighted the heroic deeds of the 'Apostle of the Germans', St Boniface (*c.*675–754), whose remains were the abbey's most treasured possession. The frontispiece illustration of Brower's *Fuldensium antiquitatum libri III* shows Boniface and the Frankish prince Carloman blessing a Germanic Adam and Eve on whom God's grace is shining.[5] Mainz boasted a still more ancient pedigree. Here Nikolaus Serarius (1555–1609) recounted the debates surrounding the city's Latin name Moguntia. According to one source its name had come from a Trojan soldier who had settled the area. As for its Christian beginnings, he discussed links scholars had drawn to the mysterious Crescens, whom Paul mentioned in 2 Timothy. Indeed, some had even speculated that the Apostle was referring directly to this region in the epistle.[6] Though this search for Christian origins in Central Europe reflected a universal Catholic impulse, it was very much a local enterprise. To appreciate this diversity, we will consider three important case studies where the challenges of the specific context elicited creative responses from scholars who sought to defend the Catholic heritage of their region.

1. COLOGNE—*HISTORIA SACRA* IN A COMMUNAL CONTEXT

In 1518, Erasmus wrote to his friend Elias Marcäus that Cologne ought to be praised as one of the most pious cities in all of Europe. Though Erasmus was writing in his typical tongue-in-cheek fashion, he was correct in identifying the busy metropolis on the Rhine as one of the great repositories of Christian relics from the age of the Apostles to the present.[7] For the devout this was *Sancta Colonia* or *hillige Köln*, holy Cologne, an ancient seat of Christianity that proclaimed its loyalty to the Church in its official seal, *Romae ecclesiae fidelis filia* ('the faithful daughter of the Roman Church'). The Ubii, a Germanic tribe, had founded the city in 38 BC. Its development continued apace

---

[4] Fürstenberg, *Monumenta Paderbornensia*, pp. 112–13.
[5] Brower, *Fuldensium antiquitatum libri III*.
[6] Serarius, *Moguntiacarum rerum ab initio*.
[7] Cited in Schöller, *Kölner Druckgraphik der Gegenreformation*, p. 16.

under the Romans. Agrippina the Younger, who was a native of the city, asked her husband, Emperor Claudius (AD 41–54), to elevate the settlement to the status of *colonia*. In the early fourth century Constantine constructed an important bridge across the Rhine, and a few years later the city had its first bishop, St Maternus (*c*.285–315). It became an archbishopric in 785, with its archbishop eventually becoming one of the imperial electors. Though its busy ecclesiastics transformed the city into a virtual warehouse of relics, there were three sets in particular that made Cologne a major pilgrimage center. The holy remains of the Three Magi, St Gereon and the Theban Legion, and St Ursula and the 11,000 virgins attracted pilgrims from across Europe. Those that came to Cologne found houses of worship in every corner of the city. By 1600 there were, apart from its famous cathedral, nineteen parish churches and nearly forty monasteries and convents. It has been estimated that up to ten per cent of the city's inhabitants were clerics of some sort or other.[8]

Cologne is remembered as the largest imperial free city that successfully resisted the evangelical message during the Reformation. While in retrospect, the city may appear as a stout Catholic bulwark standing firm in hostile Protestant territory, it was far from clear at the time whether Cologne would remain 'a faithful daughter of the Roman Church'. City records indicate that from the 1520s onward an increasing number of religious dissidents openly challenged the Catholic Church. Their numbers swelled in the second half of the century, as Protestant refugees flooded the city from the Low Countries and France. In 1590 a papal nuncio estimated that the city harboured 4,000 Protestants, approximately ten per cent of Cologne's total population.[9] Then there were the city's troublesome archbishops. Hermann von Wied (served 1515–47) had initially promoted an Erasmian agenda of reform, but when he encountered opposition, his evangelical sympathies became even more pronounced. He appointed Martin Bucer (1491–1551) as his court preacher in Bonn and looked to Philipp Melanchthon (1497–1560) for advice. Though von Weid had allies in the provincial diet, within the city proper there was very little support. Civic and ecclesiastical authorities were able to depose him in 1546. A similar scenario played out a few years later with Gebhard Truchsess von Waldburg (served 1577–83). His attempt to introduce the Reformation and secularize the city and surrounding territory was prompted at least in part by his marriage to the Protestant Agnes von Mansfeld-Eisleben. This crisis provoked a six-year war that resulted in a Catholic victory and the installation of a reliable Wittelsbach as archbishop.

A variety of explanations have been proposed to explain why Cologne did not defect to the Protestants. Robert Scribner has highlighted political and economic reasons. The thriving entrepôt on the Rhine had no intention of

---

[8] Schöller, *Kölner Druckgraphik der Gegenreformation*, p. 17.
[9] Heal, *The Cult of the Virgin Mary*, pp. 208–9.

jeopardizing its profitable commercial relations with the Spanish Netherlands and needed imperial political support to maintain its independence, surrounded as it was by opportunistic neighbours envious of its wealth.[10] Opposition to the innovations of the evangelicals came from many different quarters. This was a city with many parishes, each with a distinct and distinguished heritage. Then there were the monastic houses along with other civic institutions such as the cathedral chapter and the university with their own histories, traditions, and memories. Cologne was also the site of Germany's first Jesuit community, although they had limited influence and were but one of many agents of Catholic resistance.[11] During this period it was Catholic culture at the local level—the activities of parishes, confraternities, cloisters, convents, and cathedral—that helped transform Cologne from a 'Christian city' into a 'Catholic metropolis'.[12] This is the context in which we must examine the writing of sacred history in sixteenth and seventeenth-century Cologne.

Cologne had always been an important publishing centre. In 1500 there were twenty printers active in the city.[13] One of the city's early triumphs was the publication of the fifty-seven volumes of the prolific fifteenth-century theologian, Denys the Carthusian. But as the Reformation spread, the character of the city's publishing industry changed, with printers adopting a more strident confessional tone. The publisher, printer, and author, Kaspar von Gennep (d. 1564), was typical in this respect and representative of a militant spirit that made Cologne the most important Catholic publishing centre in Central Europe before the Thirty Years' War.[14] Cologne was at the forefront of the Catholic response to the historical challenge posed by the Protestant historian Johann Sleidan (1506–56) and the Magdeburg Centuriators. The city's energetic Carthusian community played an especially active role. The leading personality here was Laurentius Surius (1522–78) whose *Commentarius brevis* (1566) was an early riposte to Sleidan. As part of this scholarly campaign, Surius also edited the acts of the early Church councils. Surius is best known, however, as a hagiographer. His associates scoured libraries first in the Rhineland and the Low Countries and later in Italy, to collect the saints' lives that appeared in his six-volume *De probatis sanctorum historiis* (1570–7).[15] The diocesan clergy also contributed to this general enterprise. Cornelius Schulting Steinwich (d. 1604) was one of Baronio's

[10] Scribner, 'Why Was there No Reformation in Cologne?', pp. 217–24.
[11] As late as 1589, the city council forbade the distribution of a Jesuit catechism as they feared it could stir popular unrest. Heal, *The Cult of the Virgin Mary*, 215.
[12] Chaix, *De la cité chrétienne à la métropole catholique.*
[13] Schmid, 'Die Stadt und ihre Heiligen', pp. 148–9.
[14] *Allgemeine Deutsche Biographie*, VIII, 793–4; *Neue Deutsche Biographie*, VI, pp. 189–90; Enderle, 'Die Buchdrucker der Reichsstadt Köln', pp. 167–82.
[15] Surius, *De probatis sanctorum historiis*; Benz, *Zwischen Tradition und Kritik*, pp. 50–3.

early German interlocutors. He corresponded regularly with him and adapted the *Annales* to combat the local Calvinist community in Cologne. His most important publication, *Thesaurus antiquitatum ecclesiasticarum* (1601), was a reference handbook drawn from Baronio's work. From the origins of Egyptian monasticism to the early hymns of Bishop Ambrose, from the practice of tonsure to the custom of venerating the Apostles' tombs, Schulting Steinwich produced a practical guide that highlighted the practices of the early Church to help the local clergy respond to Protestant attacks. The search for Christian origins was in full swing during this period. Jacob Middendorp (1537/8–1611) explored the beginnings of monasticism and the anchoritic tradition, an institution that he claimed could be traced back to Seth.[16] For his part, Melchior Hittorp (c.1525–84) investigated early liturgical forms as he sought to recover those offices condemned by the Protestants.[17]

The search for origins, both Roman and Christian, also had a critical local dimension. Important here were the efforts of the well-respected jurist Stephan Broelmann (1551–1622). A member of a prominent patrician family, Broelmann became one of the city's most active antiquarians and collectors of Roman antiquities. With the support of the city council, he embarked on an ambitious four-volume history of Cologne. Though that work remained incomplete in manuscript form, we have some idea of what Broelmann intended through a much shorter but lavishly illustrated text he published in 1608. For that project Broelmann engaged local workshops to execute fourteen magnificent engravings of the city in its early days.[18] Though Broelmann's interests lay primarily in Cologne's Roman past, there was a Christian component to his research that a subsequent generation of ecclesiastical antiquarians developed yet further. Hermann Crombach (1598–1680), a native of Cologne and graduate of the city's new Jesuit school, the Tricoronatum, was typical in this respect. Crombach entered the order in 1617 and distinguished himself through his historical research. The city council commissioned him to edit the manuscripts that Broelmann left in the archives. What pushed him to prominence, though, was his work on the city's ecclesiastical past. Though he published shorter studies on St Ursula and Gerold of Cologne, his most successful publication was a history of the Three Magi whose relics had been brought to the city in the twelfth century.[19]

During this period Cologne's two most important antiquarians were the brothers Johannes and Aegedius Gelenius. The activities of the two, both diocesan priests, were part of a broader programme of Catholic reform that

[16] Middendorp, *Historia monastica*; Middendorp, *Originum anachoreticarum sylva*; on Middendorp, see Fellmann, *Das Gymnaisum Montanum in Köln 1550–1798*, pp. 183–7.
[17] Hittorp, *De divinis Catholicae Ecclesiae officiis ac ministeriis*.
[18] Schöller, 'Arbeitsteilung in der Druckgraphik um 1600', pp. 406–11; on Broelmann, *Allgemeine Deutsche Biographie*, III, pp. 350–1.
[19] Crombach, *Primitiae gentium*.

was accelerating under the Wittelsbach archbishops who had stepped in to restore order after the Cologne War (1583–8).[20] The elder brother Johannes (1585–1631) worked his way up the ecclesiastical ladder first as professor of theology, then member of the cathedral chapter and finally vicar general of the archdiocese. Alongside his administrative duties, he began collecting material concerning Cologne's Christian origins. By 1631 he had compiled five volumes of what became known as the *Farrago diplomatum et notationum pro historia*. On his deathbed he entrusted the undertaking to his brother Aegedius (1595–1656). Aegedius, who had studied in Rome and Perugia before return-ing to Cologne, actually resigned his position as parish priest to continue the project. He expanded the *Farragines* to thirty volumes working, as he claimed, 'day and night' through a wide array of sources.[21] Though the *Farragines* remained in manuscript form, in 1645 he published a weighty one-volume history of the city that drew from much of this material. That work, *De admiranda, sacra, et civili magnitudine Coloniae Claudiae Agrippinensis Au-gustae Ubiorum urbis*, is in many respects the highpoint of ecclesiastical antiquarianism in early modern Cologne.

Gelenius divided the text into four major sections, each focusing on one specific aspect of the city's sacred origins. Part one centres on the actual history of the city. Though he began his narrative with a discussion of the Ubii, early allies of Julius Caesar, he quickly moved into the Christian era. Here he focused directly on the work of the bishops, moving from Maternus to the present day.[22] Though the episcopal administration may have provided the city with critical oversight, Gelenius recognized that the bedrock of this society was the nobility, and it was they who were featured in the book's second section. According to legend, Emperor Trajan (r. 98–117) had sent fifteen senatorial families to help settle Cologne. They converted and became effective missionaries and the city's true Christian founders. Gelenius eulo-gized Cologne's patricians by tracing their genealogies back to these heroic forebears. The real heart of the study is the lengthy third section where Gelenius, in exacting fashion, carefully mapped the city's sacred topography. He surveyed 155 of Cologne's churches, monasteries, hospitals, almshouses, and chapels, placing a special emphasis on the relics of each of these institu-tions. A concluding section is dedicated to the sacred feasts and holidays that the city observed.

In respect to Christian origins, part two of Gelenius's text, his examination of the nobility, merits closer attention. Trajan's connection with Cologne was well known. Here, stationed with his troops, he had been acclaimed Nerva's imperial successor in AD 98. Though this had long been an important source of

---

[20] Franzen, *Der Wiederaufbau*.
[21] *Allgemeine Deutsche Biographie*, VIII, p. 536.
[22] Gelenius, *De admiranda sacra et civili magnitudine*, pp. 36–64.

civic pride, the specific legend concerning the fifteen Roman families had a much later origin, at least in written form. William of Malmesbury (d. 1142) first referenced the story in the *Gesta regum Anglorum*. Chroniclers in Cologne were slow to adopt the account, but eventually included it, with the fullest version appearing in the so-called *Koelhoff'sche Chronik* (1499), one of the earliest printed histories of the city. By the seventeenth century the legend had become muddied and unclear in at least two respects. The original fifteen Roman families sent to Cologne had now multiplied to thirty. Additionally, their origins were no longer exclusively senatorial. According to newer versions, they came from three different classes: knights, senators, and plebs.[23]

Aware of these divergent accounts, Gelenius exploited these differences for maximum effect. He began by highlighting not fifteen or thirty but one hundred families who could trace their origins back to the city's early days. He was careful not to stir up rivalries, claiming that it was impossible to distinguish the specific social class from which these families originally came. It was possible, though, to trace the etymological origins of the city's prominent houses. He gave the Latin equivalents, Superbia and Cervuli, to the Overstolzen and Hirtzlin clans. The Gymenich family, he argued, could find the origins of its name among those of the legionaries. One could also detect the early Christian roots of Cologne's patrician class. Many had worked alongside Bishop Maternus as missionaries. Indeed, their allegiance to the new faith became a literal mark of their identity as a significant number adopted crosses in their family shields. Through heraldry, history, and etymology Gelenius creatively endeavoured to connect so many of Cologne's proud citizens to the city's early Roman and Christian founders.[24]

In Cologne, Catholic antiquarians celebrated a local but multi-polar civic culture. Gelenius highlighted one hundred ancient families and described the city itself as a *sacrarium*, a massive living repository of relics from across the Christian world. Relics were deeply embedded in the city's communal life. The church regularly deployed holy remains such as the head of Pope Sylvester and the staff of St Peter in the frequent processions that wound their way through the narrow streets. Clerics composed a liturgical sequence, 'Gaude felix Agrippina', to praise the city's great patrons, the Three Magi, St Ursula, and St Gereon. But as Gelenius described in such painstaking detail, Cologne's cache of ancient Christian remains was so large that no single institution could possibly monopolize this immense stockpile of sanctity. Distinguished patrician families, members of religious orders, the cathedral chapter, the university, and priests of the city's nineteen parishes all could point to prized relics or age-old traditions that referenced the city's Christian origins. It is important to remember that imperial free cities competed fiercely with each other for

---

[23] Helmrath, 'Sitz und Geschichte', pp. 735–44.
[24] Gelenius, *De admiranda sacra et civili magnitudine*, pp. 113–21, 144–5.

honour and prestige. Cologne's rivalry with Aachen was particularly acute. The city also had difficulties with the archbishopric of Cologne, which was a distinct political entity. Cologne's status as an imperial free city was only confirmed in 1475, and its territory did not extend beyond the city walls. Civic authorities constantly feared annexation. The *Koelhoff'sche Chronik* commemorated the 1265 siege of the city with an illustration of Cologne's saintly patrons rushing to the walls to drive off the army of Archbishop Engelbert. One of the reasons that the Reformation ultimately failed was the very real threat that the archbishop would secularize the territory of the diocese and attempt to take the city with it. In Cologne, then, Catholic antiquarianism reflected the city's proud spirit and independent status as well as its textured religious life.

2. BAVARIA, THE WITTELSBACHS, AND JESUIT ANTIQUARIANISM

For our second area of investigation we turn to the south and east to consider 'greater Bavaria', an area slightly larger than the actual political boundaries of the historical duchy. Here we move from a critical east/west boundary of the Roman world, the Rhine, to an equally important north/south division, the Danube. While in Cologne the antiquarian Stephan Broelmann celebrated his city's connection to the Ubii and the later Caesars, in Augsburg the erudite Marcus Welser (1558–1614) devoted a substantial portion of his own career studying the Roman remains of his native region. Whereas Welser focused primarily on classical origins, his colleague, the Jesuit Matthäus Rader (*c*.1561–1634), devoted substantial attention to Bavaria's Christian beginnings. His most famous effort in this regard was the four-volume *Bavaria sancta* (1615–27). In this wide-ranging work of hagiography, Rader investigated the lives of those early saints who were believed to have brought the Christian message to the area. There was Hermagoras, bishop of Aquileia (now thought to have lived in the third or fourth century but traditionally identified as a companion of St Mark); the enterprising Lucius of Britain, an early missionary who according to legend brought the gospel to both Bavaria and England; and the valiant Afra, martyred in Diocletian's persecutions. Rader's text received significant notice and became an influential model of the *terra sancta* literature.[25]

Although Rader's efforts were in some ways analogous to those of the Gelenii brothers in Cologne, there were significant differences. Rader's work

---

[25] Schmid, 'Die "Bavaria sancta et pia"', pp. 518–20.

was a product of a vibrant late humanist culture that flourished in early seventeenth-century Bavaria. This tradition stretched back to scholars such as Johannes (Turmair) Aventinus (1477–1534) and the Benedictine Wolfgang Seidel (1492–1562). Aventinus's work was particularly significant. His *Bayerische Chronik*, abridged and translated from the original Latin and first published posthumously in 1566, was one of the earliest German-language histories. It set a high critical standard, although confessionally sensitive censors eventually placed it on the *Index of Prohibited Books* for its anticlerical character and perceived Protestant tendencies. There were others, such as the neo-Latin poet and dramatist, Thomas Naogeorg (1508/11–63), and most importantly Marcus Welser. A member of the famous merchant family, Welser had studied in Rome and Venice. He corresponded with Isaac Casaubon, Galileo, and Joseph Scaliger, and back in Augsburg established an important publishing house. While the first book that rolled off the family press was an examination of predestination written by an Orthodox patriarch and dedicated to a Silesian Calvinist, the last, a Marian devotional tract compiled by a Benedictine monk in 1619, reflected an important confessional shift that was transforming the intellectual life of the region.[26]

The critical force behind this humanist movement was the Jesuits, and here we see the first significant contrast with Cologne. Whereas the Society of Jesus was only one of many different Catholic institutions and orders active in the city, in Bavaria and especially at the court in Munich, they played the dominant role. They had come to the region in the middle of the sixteenth century. Duke Wilhelm V of Bavaria (r. 1579–97) made a number of key Jesuit appointments at the university in Ingolstadt to reinvigorate the institution after the death of its influential pro-chancellor Johann Eck in 1543. Alongside Ingolstadt, centres in Dillingen and Munich formed the basis of the Jesuit network in Bavaria. Their college at St Michael's in Munich, consecrated in 1597, became particularly influential, providing the Wittelsbach court with a steady supply of advisors, scholars, and artists. The scientist Christoph Scheiner (1573–1650), the dramatist Jakob Bidermann (1578–1639), the poet Jakob Balde (1604–68), and the political theorist Adam Contzen (1571/3–1635) were all part of this new world of Jesuit learning and helped shaped Bavaria's late humanist culture in a more confessional direction.[27]

At the centre of this network was Matthäus Rader. A native of south Tyrol, he began his studies at Innsbruck and entered the Society of Jesus at twenty. Though Rader is frequently remembered only as a hagiographer, he had considerable expertise in a number of fields. He edited the works of Seneca, Curtius Rufus, and Martial. His edition of Martial circulated widely and even attracted the notice of a critical John Donne, who claimed that the Jesuit's

[26] Evans, 'Rantzau and Welser', p. 262.
[27] Dülmen, 'Die Gesellschaft Jesu und der bayerische Späthumanismus', pp. 358–415.

expurgated version effectively 'gelded' the Latin poet.[28] Rader was an active dramatist, adapting material from the Church Fathers for the stage. He was also an accomplished historian who could read ancient sources critically. In his edition of Martial, he dismissed the Spanish chronicle attributed to Flavius Dexter that detailed Christian origins in first-century Spain as a hodgepodge of legends and fables.[29] He wrote an unpublished history of Bavaria and left behind a massive body of correspondence that reflects interests ranging from the production of paper to the technological achievements of the ancient Egyptians.[30] So considerable was his reputation that in the eighteenth century the Protestant Gottfried Wilhelm Leibniz singled him out as one of the greatest German historians.[31] He came to the attention of the Wittelsbachs during his years teaching rhetoric in Augsburg. Here he became involved in an ambitious architectural project that transformed the city centre.

Plans had long circulated to renovate Augsburg's old gothic *Rathaus*, but in 1615 the city council decided to abandon what was increasingly seen as an impracticable scheme. Instead, the council commissioned the architect Elias Holl to construct an entirely new town hall. Holl's achievement ranks as one of most important Renaissance structures north of the Alps. Apart from its striking façade, the real highlight of the *Rathaus* was the so-called *Goldener Saal*, the massive ceremonial room where princes banqueted, and the Reichstag held its sessions. Rader was the key figure behind the complicated iconographic scheme of the hall, a design that reflected his understanding of the classical and Christian past.[32] The programme actually began outside the building, with a statue of a laurel-wreathed Augustus, under whose rule the city was founded. Busts of the Twelve Caesars flanked the staircase leading up to the *Goldener Saal*. The imperial theme reached its climax within the hall, as a new Christian empire completed and perfected its pagan predecessor. Rader paired eight sets of emperors against each other in a series of facing portraits. Constantine stared out against Augustus, Charlemagne against Alexander the Great. The Christian counterpart to Antoninus Pius was a particularly interesting choice; the cagey Rader decided upon the last Ottonian, Henry II (d. 1024), a Bavarian duke, emperor, and eventually saint, surely an appropriate model for the ambitious Wittelsbachs.

Rader's nod to this influential family highlights another distinctive feature of the search for Christian origins in seventeenth-century Bavaria. To understand this intellectual project aright, we need to look more closely at the

---

[28] Johnson, 'Holy Dynasts', p. 85.

[29] Matthäus Rader, *Analecta, tertiis commentariorum curis, ad Martialem iam editis, addenda* (Cologne: Ioannem Kinckium, 1628), fol. 4ʳ. See Katrina Olds, 'The Ambiguities of the Holy' and Ch. 6 above.

[30] See the two volumes edited by Alois Schmid (1995; 2009).

[31] Schmid, 'Der Briefwechsel des P. Matthäus Rader SJ' (1995), p. 1139.

[32] Walter, *Das Augsburger Rathaus*, pp. 59–72.

Wittelsbachs and a prince whom one scholar has recently called 'Bavaria's great elector'.[33] In 1597, Maximilian I succeeded his father, Wilhelm V, as duke of Bavaria. The energetic twenty-four year old had studied with the Jesuits in Ingolstadt and came to the throne resolved to advance the Catholic cause in Central Europe and determined to elevate his family's status and position within the empire. An able ruler, he helped spread Wittelsbach influence by continuing his father's policy of placing younger sons in strategic bishoprics. After the Cologne War ended in 1588, the Wittelsbachs occupied the see of Cologne for nearly two centuries. Maximilian himself (r. 1597–1651) pursued an aggressive confessional policy as the driving force behind the Catholic League and rival to Emperor Ferdinand II (r. 1619–37) as the Church's greatest champion during the Thirty Years' War (1618–48). Without his timely intervention and military support it is unlikely that the Habsburgs would have regained the Bohemian throne. His most notable achievement was wresting the electoral dignity from his Protestant cousins in the Palatinate and claiming it for the Bavarian house in 1623. Like his predecessors, Maximilian also turned to the resources of representational culture to enhance his family's standing. His grandfather had expanded the Munich Residence with the splendid Antiquarium, a Renaissance hall of antiquities lined with the busts of pagan and Christian emperors. Maximilian continued to renovate the rambling city palace and also began new undertakings to project the glory and dignity of the Wittelsbach dynasty.

The Jesuit Rader was in many ways a perfect match for Maximilian. A professor of rhetoric, he was a versatile scholar whose learning could be adapted just as easily for editing classical texts and compiling saints' lives as for collaborating with artists and architects. He relocated to Munich in 1612 and taught at the Jesuit college until his death. During these early years in Munich, Maximilian commissioned Rader to work with Marcus Welser on a history of the duchy intended to replace Aventinus's chronicle, which was now on the Index.[34] Welser published an introductory volume that traced the region's history up through the eighth century. Rader took sole charge of the undertaking after Welser's death in 1614. Though the assiduous Jesuit completed a three-part manuscript that brought the project up to the seventeenth century, it was never published, for Rader's narrative provoked a significant dispute within the order. Allying himself with his patron, Rader presented a positive portrait of the controversial Wittelsbach emperor, Louis the Bavarian (r. 1328–47), who had been excommunicated in 1324. Rome had never lifted the interdict, and Jesuit leadership greeted Rader's attempt to rehabilitate Maximilian's forebear stonily.

---

[33] Kraus, *Maximilian I: Bayerns grosser Kurfürst.*
[34] Schmid, 'Geschichtsschreibung', p. 331.

Undeterred, the duke sought other ways to repair what he saw as a serious injury to his family's dignity. He engaged painters, poets, and sculptors on a campaign that culminated in a magnificent new bronze tomb for the emperor in the Frauenkirche.[35] At the same time Maximilian took a special interest in Cesare Baronio's grand ecclesiastical history project. In 1617, Baronio's successor, the Polish Dominican Abraham Bzowski, published the fourteenth volume of the *Annales ecclesiastici*. In this examination of the fourteenth century, Bzowski upheld the Church's judgement of the heretic prince and recognized him as neither king nor emperor. In what became a very complicated dispute that eventually drew in Pope Urban VIII, Maximilian did win a concession from the Church; ecclesiastical officials permitted a new edition that portrayed Louis in a more favourable light.[36]

We must view Rader's *Bavaria sancta*, his most celebrated achievement, within this broader cultural context, for aside from its hagiographical content, the project should also be considered as part of the representational culture that Maximilian fostered at his court. The undertaking actually began over a decade earlier, with a splendid series of 142 engravings executed by Raphael Sadeler the Elder based on the designs of court painters Peter Candid and Matthias Kager, two artists with whom Rader collaborated on the Augsburg town hall. Rader composed a short commentary for each of Sadeler's illustrations, with his stylized and florid Latin effectively matching the artist's dramatic engravings. The text of *Bavaria sancta* itself, though, lacks a degree of cohesion. Rader organized his material in chronologically haphazard fashion, and his understanding of sanctity was at least initially problematic. After the publication of volume I, he faced criticism for his lack of precision. Henceforth, he placed each individual in the category of *sancti*, *beati*, or *pii*. Rader, however, was clearly not concerned with technical questions. *Bavaria sancta* had more pedagogical aims. Believers were encouraged to draw inspiration from both picture and text. They were invited to the crypt of a pious hermit to reflect on his ascetic virtues or cheered by the example of heroic martyrs who willingly sacrificed all for their faith.[37] *Bavaria sancta* was most definitely an examination of Christian origins, but the tradition that Rader was investigating was very much a living one. The activities of older saints were mirrored by newer ones. The struggles of Blessed Laurentius of Lorch in the first century, Rader suggested, were not unlike those faced by the Jesuits in the present day. Indeed, later editions of *Bavaria sancta* updated Rader's roster with biographies of Peter Canisius (1521–97), Central Europe's great Jesuit champion, and Catholic heroes from the Thirty Years' War including Maximilian himself.[38]

[35] Glaser (ed.), *Um Glauben und Reich*, II, pp. 218–25.
[36] Kraus, 'Die Annales Ecclesiastici', pp. 253–89.
[37] Rader, *Bavaria sancta*, III, pp. 329–30.
[38] Johnson, 'Holy Dynasts', pp. 95–6.

Such interweaving of ancient and modern sanctity is a common staple of hagiography. What is more distinctive in Rader's work is the political spin that he added to enhance the status of his Wittelsbach patron. One of the first questions that Rader considered was geography. The Bavaria he described corresponded neither to the borders of the seventeenth-century duchy nor the broader Imperial Circle. Rader had a different model in mind. In one of the early illustrations, the archangel Michael holds a map of the territory that included imperial free cities such as Augsburg and Regensburg as well as the Habsburg territory of Tyrol and Upper Austria.[39] Though he claimed that the *Boii* could be traced back to the ancient Galatians of the New Testament era, his work focused on the *terra Bavarica* of the early Middle Ages.[40] Rader's formulation corresponded quite nicely with Maximilian's political aspirations, for the duke had his eye on territory that had once been part of the Bavarian patrimony. Rader devoted significant attention to the ancient diocese of Laureacum near modern-day Linz in Upper Austria. Upper Austria was a particularly sensitive region. Bavarians, in fact, occupied the territory between 1620 and 1628, when they passed it back to the Habsburgs in return for the Rhenish Palatinate.[41] A subtle imperial programme was reflected in Rader's choice of saints and his spiritual annexation of bits and pieces of Habsburg territory. The fifth-century Severinus of Noricum, for example, had had an active ministry around Vienna, but Rader cast him as an 'apostle of Bavaria'. Even further afield was St Quirinus of Sescia, an early fourth-century bishop martyred in what is now Croatia but was then part of the Habsburg conglomerate. Perhaps most galling to his Austrian rivals was Rader's inclusion of St Wolfgang, a tenth-century bishop whose episcopal authority included not only parts of Bavaria but all of Bohemia.[42] The search for Christian origins in Bavaria, then, was not intended merely to promote piety or solidify a Catholic identity, for it had a distinct political agenda as well.

3. BOHEMIA AND THE SEARCH
FOR A CATHOLIC PAST

Our final area of exploration, the Kingdom of Bohemia, differed in two substantial ways from both Bavaria and Cologne. It was well off the Rhine/Danube axis. The Romans had never settled here, and Christianity had arrived significantly later. While Cologne did have a Christian presence by the time of

---

[39] Rader, *Bavaria sancta*, I, p. 9; Johnson, 'Holy Dynasts', pp. 96–7.
[40] Rader, *Bavaria sancta*, I, pp. 11–12.
[41] Heilingsetzer, 'Die Bayern in Oberösterreich (1620–8)', pp. 416–23.
[42] Rader, *Bavaria sancta*, I, pp. 21–4, 26–30, 93–9.

Constantine (indeed, Aegidius Gelenius boasted that a village not far from Cologne was the site of Constantine's famous vision predicting victory over Maxentius and the consequent triumph of Christianity), Bohemian antiquarians could make no comparable claims concerning the antiquity of the faith in their homeland.[43] It was not until the ninth century that Saxon monks had penetrated the region, with Cyril and Methodius coming to Moravia a few years later. The second and more important difference concerns heresy. This was never a serious matter in Bavaria, and while Cologne may have wobbled during the Reformation, ultimately it did not fall. Bohemia was of course markedly different. During the Hussite Revolution (1419–36) the Bohemians had defied the threats of Rome and the armies of the emperor to create a semi-autonomous Church. By the sixteenth century the situation had deteriorated to such an extent that in his debate with Luther, Johann Eck merely had to mention the word 'Bohemia' to conjure the spectre of heresy. Faced with these two substantial handicaps, Bohemia's ecclesiastical antiquarians had to square the proverbial circle in their quest for Christian origins.

The ablest of the Bohemia's antiquarians was the Jesuit Bohuslav Balbín (1621–88). A prolific writer, he left behind a massive literary legacy with texts ranging from an examination of the kingdom's early pilgrimage sites to a defence of the Czech language.[44] Though he wrote on a wide variety of topics, a common theme runs through nearly all his work. At their most basic level Balbín's writings are apologetic, an attempt to rehabilitate his homeland, its people, and their religion. The search for Christian origins was obviously a key component of his programme, and here we see the great creativity of Bohemian antiquarianism: how did one explain that nearly all the great Bohemian families had members who had defected to the Protestant cause? As a genealogist, Balbín responded to this challenge by ignoring the recent past and highlighted the links between the nobility and the kingdom's holy men and women in an era before Jan Hus (c.1370–1415) and the religious wars of the fifteenth century. In one case he connected a family to fourteen saints, ten individuals beatified by the Church, and thirty-eight founders or major patrons of churches and cloisters.[45] As a philologist, Balbín defended Czech from its detractors who saw it as the language of heretics. He pointed to its antiquity and praised its ancient liturgies. Indeed, if one were searching for a language corrupted by heresy, he suggested that one need travel no further than neighbouring Saxony.[46]

---

[43] Gelenius, *De admiranda sacra et civili magnitudine*, pp. 25–6.

[44] The most recent treatment of Balbín is Kučera and Rak, *Bohuslav Balbín*; on Bohemian antiquarianism more generally, see Louthan, *Converting Bohemia*, pp. 115–44.

[45] Louthan, *Converting Bohemia*, p. 70.

[46] Balbín, *Rozprava*, p. 86.

Figure 7.1. Allegory of History. Frontispiece to Bohuslav Balbín, *Epitome historica rerum Bohemicarum* (Prague: Typis Universitatis Carolo-Ferdinandeae, 1677).

Balbín's most important historical work was the *Epitome historica rerum Bohemicarum* (1677), a survey of the Bohemian past from the ninth to seventeenth centuries. The Jesuit offered an important key for understanding the text in the form of an elaborate frontispiece engraving, an allegorical illustration of historical writing (Figure 7.1). The image highlights the destructive power of time, as the past is forgotten through neglect and lethargy, distorted with lies and prejudice, or destroyed by war and violence. The scholar, though, is not bereft of resources. The engraver depicted the historian, lantern in hand, entering the dark grotto of the past to unearth and discover buried fragments of Bohemian antiquity. In figurative language Balbín and the two artists were simply stating that the problematic Hussite interlude was but a brief interruption of a distinguished ecclesiastical heritage. The orientation of the *Epitome* may strike the modern reader as peculiar. The text, in fact, begins with an excursus on the town of Boleslav, which in Balbín's day was a sleepy hamlet outside Prague. Not so in the ninth and tenth centuries when, according to the Jesuit, it was the kingdom's spiritual centre, the 'nourishing source of early Christianity in Bohemia'.[47] From the martyrdom of Duke Wenceslas (*c.*907–29) to the miracles of St Adalbert (*c.*956–97), Boleslav was the site of many critical events of the kingdom's sacred past and home to its most treasured relic, the Madonna of Stará Boleslav. It had been designated as Bohemia's first episcopal see, and perhaps most importantly it was a hub of Christian mission for the Czech lands and beyond.

After this introduction Balbín continued with what was in some respects a more conventional political history of Bohemia, chronicling major events from the ninth-century founder of the Přemyslid dynasty, Duke Bořivoj, to Emperor Ferdinand II in the seventeenth. Balbín approached his subject matter in a somewhat idiosyncratic fashion that accentuated the kingdom's spiritual heritage. While Balbín cursorily reviewed the accomplishments of Otakar II (r. 1253–78) who for a short time made Bohemia the strongest state in central Europe, he devoted substantially more attention to the obscure Boleslav II (r. 972–99), who established the region's first bishopric, and Břetislav I (r. 1034–55) who invaded Poland and returned with the holy remains of St Adalbert. For Balbín the height of Bohemia's glory came in the fourteenth century during the reign of Emperor Charles IV (r. 1355–78) and his ally Arnošt of Pardubice, the first archbishop of Prague. The efforts of these two men transformed the city on the Moldau into the spiritual capital of Central Europe. Both emperor and archbishop were watchful guardians of orthodoxy. When heresy did arrive with the Flagellants in 1347, Balbín was quick to point to its origins, the German lands, and the fact that it was effectively suppressed.[48]

The final two books of the *Epitome*, nearly a quarter of its entire length, deal most directly with sacred history. Book Six focuses more closely on Boleslav, celebrating its antiquity and unbroken commitment to the Church. Book Seven is a history of its famous relic, a simple metal relief of the Virgin and child. Though relatively modest in shape and size, no other relic in the kingdom could be connected to so many holy men and women, and for Balbín this was its most compelling feature, as it offered an alternative history to the

---

[47] Balbín, *Epitome*, p. 1.   [48] Ibid., p. 360.

narrative of dissent. According to one legend, it came originally from Byzantium; the missionary brothers Cyril and Methodius had brought it with them to Bohemia in the ninth century where it was passed down and connected with the first Christian princes of the region, Duke Bořivoj and his wife Ludmila. It later passed through the hands of Wenceslas and his faithful servant, the Blessed Podiven, who had hidden it to protect it from the duke's pagan enemies. It was miraculously recovered in the twelfth century, held in high esteem by Charles IV and Arnošt, and then survived Hussite marauders. During the Thirty Years' War it was captured twice by Protestant armies, and its recovery was an important part of the peace negotiations. It was triumphantly reinstalled in the town's basilica in 1650, a living embodiment of Bohemia's embattled but ultimately triumphant Catholic community.

Balbín's most ambitious project, an enterprise he worked on his entire career, was the *Miscellanea historica regni Bohemiae*. Though he never completed what he intended to be a thirty-volume overview of Bohemian culture and history, Balbín did publish portions of the massive undertaking including his answer to Matthäus Rader, the *Bohemia sancta* (1682). Despite their best efforts to remember a vibrant ecclesiastical culture that had existed before Hus, the antiquarians still confronted a significant problem, for there was a basic fact they could not alter. From the death of Hus (1415) to the Battle of White Mountain (1620), Bohemia had been a land of heretics. The surest antidote to heresy was sanctity, but in the fifteenth and sixteenth centuries many of the region's saints occupied a place on the margins of Church and society. In response to this problem, antiquarians produced a steady stream of literature that promoted these neglected cults. Balbín's *Bohemia sancta* was the most important and extensive of these texts. In encyclopedic fashion, he highlighted the lives of more than 200 holy men and women who had been active in the Czech lands. More important than actual numbers, however, is the type of saint or holy person Balbín featured. Here he cleverly turned the tables on the critics and transformed Bohemia from a nation of heretics into a kingdom of martyrs. Following a pattern established by Rader, Balbín divided Part I of the text into three sections. The first covers those either canonized or beatified by the Church, while the second focuses on individuals who, though not officially recognized by Rome, were venerated locally. Martyrs comprise a substantial group in both. Indeed, more than a quarter of the figures in the first section are martyrs. In the third division, however, Balbín broke with Rader and constructed a category larger than the first two combined and devoted exclusively to martyrs. Working chronologically, the Jesuit compiled a fascinating list that included not only individuals but monastic communities and even entire towns. On the honour roll are priests executed by Wenceslas's pagan mother, Drahomíra, the victims of sinister Jewish plots, and of course the many believers killed during the Hussite wars. Using a rather liberal accounting method, Balbín also included individuals who passed through

Bohemia but were martyred elsewhere, such as the English Jesuit Edmund Campion (d. 1581) and the Scottish Jesuit John Ogilvie (d. 1615).

Balbín's most effective work as hagiographer yielded the ultimate reward: the canonization of his subject. In the 1670s, the Jesuit set to work on a biography of John Nepomuk (d. 1393), a fourteenth-century priest who for his refusal to give up the secrets of the confessional was thrown in the Moldau by the henchmen of Wenceslas IV. The Bollandists eventually published Balbín's biography in 1680, and this became an important source in the campaign to canonize Nepomuk, which culminated in 1729 when the confessor became only one of two martyrs raised to sainthood between 1523 and 1767.[49] The case of Balbín and Nepomuk is particularly intriguing as it highlights the inventive dimension of the quest for origins. One scholar has recently noted that the sources Balbín acknowledged having used in his biography are conveniently missing.[50] Although Balbín's claim may be true, a suggestive pattern emerges when we compare the Nepomuk text with Balbín's efforts to promote the case of another late medieval holy man.

The fourteenth-century Moravian priest Jan Milíč of Kroměříž (d. 1374) gave up a promising career in the Church for a life of poverty and preaching. He was a popular figure in Prague, especially with the poor. He established a religious community whose members included repentant prostitutes.[51] His activities, apocalyptic rhetoric, and fiery temperament, however, earned him a number of powerful enemies, and he was compelled to journey to Avignon where he was tried before the pope. He died before he could return to Prague. Balbín's role in this story begins with an account in the *Epitome*; he claims that while travelling in southern Bohemia he discovered a manuscript biography of Milíč. He published it a few years later in *Bohemia sancta*. Like the Nepomuk biography, no one has been able to discover the original source from which Balbín purportedly compiled the new seventeenth-century edition. It seems likely, in fact, that the Jesuit fabricated this life of Milíč. Scholars have demonstrated that significant portions of the text were lifted directly from a variety of sources including William of St Thierry's life of Bernard of Clairvaux, the homilies of Gregory the Great, and the chronicle of Cosmas of Prague (d. 1125).[52]

What is the significance, then, of this creative pastiche that Balbín fashioned? This affair tells us something very important concerning the search for Christian origins in seventeenth-century Bohemia. First, Milíč in many early modern circles was seen as a forerunner of Hus and thus of the Reformation. He had harsh words for the papacy and elicited fulsome praise from Flacius

---

[49] Burke, 'How to Be a Counter-Reformation Saint', p. 51.
[50] Vlnas, *Jan Nepomucký*, p. 86.
[51] Mengel, 'From Venice to Jerusalem', pp. 407–42.
[52] Mengel, 'A Monk, a Preacher, and a Jesuit', pp. 33–55.

Illyricus. Balbín, however, was able to shape the story in a slightly different fashion. It seems likely that he massaged its ending by adding a portion that described Milíč's exoneration before the papal court, a disputed issue to this day. In an even bolder move, and as part of the campaign to canonize the popular preacher, he included or more likely contrived a remark by Cardinal Grimoard, the brother of Pope Urban V (1362–70). After reading a letter by the recently deceased Milíč, the cardinal, who had actively promoted the cult of the his late brother Urban, allegedly exclaimed, 'Even though my brother, Pope Urban, is becoming famous for his miracles, I believe that this Milíč should be canonized before him.'[53] This story may best capture the tremendous resourcefulness and creativity of Bohemian antiquarianism. The Milíč example is only one of many where Balbín and his colleagues were able to take elements of a heterodox past, recast them in orthodox fashion, and incorporate them into a new narrative of a *Bohemia sacra*.

4. CONCLUSIONS

What broader conclusions can we reach from these case studies concerning the nature of *historia sacra* and the search for Christian origins in Central Europe after the Reformation? Most obviously, Catholics responded vigorously to the Protestant historical challenge. This brief and limited overview can hardly do justice to such an immense body of literature. The writers examined here constitute the first chapter of an enterprise that would continue for more than two centuries; from David Aichler in the late sixteenth century to Johann Anton Zunggo in the early eighteenth, Central Europe was awash with historical studies validating and vindicating the region's Catholic heritage.[54] But this confessional agenda was only part of what motivated Catholic historiography in Central Europe. Though in a broad sense Catholic antiquarians were responding to Protestant interpretations of the past, with scholars such as Laurentius Surius and Jacob Gretser (1562–1625) addressing a pan-European audience with their work, a top-down model that considers such literary activity merely as part of a confessionalization process bolstering a common Catholic identity is limited. Central Europe was a vast continent unto itself. The Holy Roman Empire alone comprised more than 1,000 territorial units. The Jesuits of the Austrian province spoke German, Czech, Hungarian, Slovenian, Croatian, and Italian. To understand this Catholic scholarship

---

[53] Cited ibid., p. 46.
[54] David Aichler, *Chronicon andecense* (Munich: Adam Berg, 1595); Johann Anton Zunggo, *Historiae generalis et specialis de ordine canonicorum regularium S. Augustini duobus tomis comprehensae prodromus* (Munich: Joannes Gastl, 1749).

properly, historians of Central Europe especially in the Anglophone world must begin by acknowledging the social, cultural, and political diversity of this wide territory. The case studies examined here suggest that the writing of *historia sacra* is best examined from the bottom up. As the contrasting settings of Cologne, Bavaria, and Bohemia illustrate, the search for Christian origins was most frequently an enterprise rooted in local concerns and challenges.

8

Elizabethan Histories of English Christian Origins

Rosamund Oates

The origins of English Christianity suddenly became a matter of pressing urgency in the 1520s, when Pope Clement VII refused to grant Henry VIII a divorce from his first wife, Catherine of Aragon. While Cardinal Thomas Wolsey sought a diplomatic solution for Henry's 'Great Matter', the king employed a team of scholars to build a legal case for the divorce. Led by Bishop Edward Foxe (*c.*1496–1538), these scholars rifled through the annals of English history to prove that Henry, not the pope, was in fact the rightful head of the English Church. They eventually found a powerful historical precedent in the writings of Geoffrey of Monmouth, a twelfth-century chronicler whose taste ran to the fantastical. Monmouth had credited King Lucius, a second-century British king, with converting his nation to Christianity. Monmouth recorded that Lucius had written to Pope Eleutherius seeking admission into the Roman Church and asking for two missionaries to convert the Britons. Pope Eleutherius's letter in reply was included in Monmouth's history, and became a crucial piece of evidence for Foxe and his team of scholars. Eleutherius accepted King Lucius into the Church but—and here Foxe's team hit the jackpot—the pope told Lucius that he had no need of Roman law because the king was *already* 'God's Vicar in his Kingdom'. This letter proving the ancient independence of the English Church was worth its weight in gold. Edward Foxe included Eleutherius's letter in his dossier of documents proving the legitimacy of Henry VIII's rejection of papal power, the *Collectanea satis copiosa*. In 1533, when the English Parliament passed the Act in Restraint of Appeals, ending papal authority in England, Eleutherius's letter to Lucius raised its head again. The preamble to the Act opened by declaring the antiquity of the English Church. It asserted that 'by divers sundry old authentic histories and chronicles' it was shown that 'the English Church...hath been always thought, and is also at this hour, sufficient and meet of itself, without the intermeddling of any exterior person or persons'.[1] Over the following decades, as the Tudor Reformations followed a tortuous path, histories of English Christianity would play an increasingly important role in arguments about the jurisdiction and the liturgy of the English Church.

The origins of Christianity and accounts of the early Church in England came to be the mainstay of two elements of the Elizabethan Reformation—so closely entwined that they were usually inseparable. From Henry VIII (r. 1509–47) onwards, apologists looked to the past to defend the legitimacy of royal government—or in the case of his Catholic daughter Mary I (r. 1553–8) —the legitimacy of papal rule. And Evangelicals had another reason to look to the past: the concept of returning the Church to its primitive state was a central part of the reforming programme across Europe. The diversity of ecclesiastical histories produced during Elizabeth's reign (1558–1603) reflects the different confessional positions that emerged during this period. Ecclesiastical histories could be powerful fodder for apologetics, but history-writing was more than a polemical exercise.[2] Authors read their sources through confessional lenses, and in turn their historical knowledge shaped perceptions of the contemporary Church, explaining in part why ecclesiastical history became so important in intra- and interconfessional debates.

Matthew Parker (1504–75), Elizabeth's first archbishop of Canterbury, was particularly fascinated by the Anglo-Saxon Church, using it to prove that the Elizabethan Church in many ways represented a return to ancient practices. However, there were Protestants—called the 'godly' by themselves and 'Puritans' by their critics—who criticized the Elizabethan Church as only halfly reformed. They rejected the conformist argument that English Christianity had, historically, always been unique and instead sought to bring the Elizabethan Church into line with its Calvinist contemporaries on the Continent. As hopes of reforming the Elizabethan Church faded, 'godly' authors increasingly sought comfort in histories of the 'True Church' that emphasized its universal, rather than its national, manifestation. Catholics, too, found solace and polemical material in ecclesiastical histories. Successive Catholic authors wrote accounts of the past proving that it was the Roman Catholic—not the Elizabethan— Church that could lay claim to antiquity. They also presented their own vision of an English Church that balanced papal claims with a celebration of native Catholicism.

---

[1] See 24 Henry VIII, c.12. 'An Act That appeals in such cases have been used to be pursued to the see of Rome shall not be from henceforth had nor used but within this realm' (1533); G. R. Elton (ed.), *The Tudor Constitution* (Cambridge, 1965), pp. 344–9. For a discussion of the Lucius myth, see Heal, 'What Can King Lucius Do for You?'; Bernard, *The King's Reformation*, pp. 26–50; MacCulloch, *Thomas Cranmer*, pp. 52–9.

[2] For a counter-argument, see Polman, *L'élément historique*, recently reassessed by Backus, *Historical Method*, esp. ch. 6.

F. J. Levy and A. B. Ferguson have shown how the Reformation debates of the sixteenth century encouraged a scholarly approach to history that could be described as proto-modern. Influenced by humanist historians—for example Lorenzo Valla's influential work proving the Donation of Constantine to be a fake—English writers employed a range of scholarly tools, including a critical approach to primary sources, a sense of anachronism, and a clear search for cause in their histories.[3] By the Elizabethan period, ecclesiastical history writing was flourishing across Europe and with it new thoughts on the *ars historica*. On the Continent, Matthias Flacius Illyricus (1520–75) was working with a team of Protestant historians, the 'Magdeburg Centuriators', to produce the *Ecclesiastical History* (1559–74). Widely known as the *Magdeburg Centuries*, this monumental history used a wide range of primary texts to prove the historical decline of the Catholic Church.[4] When John Foxe (1517–87) published the first edition of his history of the English Church, the *Acts and Monuments*, in 1563, he also included vast amounts of primary material printed with careful glosses. Nor were Protestants the only ones to look to source material to clinch an argument. Cardinal Cesare Baronio made extensive use of primary material in his *Annales ecclesiastici* (1588–1607) to refute the *Magdeburg Centuries*, while English Catholics sought to prove the antiquity of their faith with an English edition of Bede's *Historia ecclesiastica gentis Anglorum* (*The History of the Church of England*) (1565). But while Elizabethan histories of the Church often bore the mark of humanist tools of critical analysis, sometimes *historia sacra*—in all its forms—required a different approach. Authors of ecclesiastical histories were aware that their work was a spiritual, as well as an intellectual, endeavour. To write the history of the post-apostolic Church was to discern God's will for humankind: to continue where the Bible had ended. Writing in the preface to the *Acts and Monuments*, John Foxe argued that his history was like 'Christes gospell' and hoped his work would help readers to 'both knowe God in his workes and to work the thynge that is godly'.[5]

1. EVANGELICALS AND THE PRIMITIVE CHURCH

The Evangelical Reformation in England was, as elsewhere in Europe, an extended conversation with the past, as reformers sought to return to primitive

---

[3] On Valla, see above, Ch. 1. See also Levy, *Tudor Historical Thought*; Ferguson, *Clio Unbound*; Woolf, *Social Circulation of the Past*; and Grafton, *What Was History?*.

[4] See above, Ch. 2.

[5] Foxe, *Acts and Monuments* (1570), preface, sig. *2ᵛ. Hereafter *A&M*, followed by edition in parentheses.

Christianity. Historical analysis was, therefore, a central part of the evolution of English Protestantism. While Edward Foxe was searching the annals of history for evidence of Henry VIII's claim to be head of the English Church, William Tyndale read his histories for evidence of doctrinal corruption in the medieval Church. In 1528, Tyndale made a case for Evangelical reform based on his sense of the Church's historical decline, arguing that AD 700—when a rapid increase in papal power could be seen—marked the end of the primitive Church. Later, in the mid 1540s, John Bale used the apocalyptic vision of the Book of Revelation to frame his account of a Church in decline since the apostolic age.[6] The primitive Church became the ideal to which every reformer aspired. In 1549, when Archbishop Thomas Cranmer made a tentative attack on transubstantiation in the first Edwardian prayer book, he argued that his changes were 'approved by ye consent of the most auncient doctrine of the Churche'. Later, when Cranmer sought to reform English canon law—unchanged since the days of papal supremacy—he argued that 'proof from antiquity' would be his guide.[7]

Seeking to restore the primitive Church raised the questions of exactly when that Church had existed, when had it been corrupted, and by whom. English authors writing in the context of Henry VIII's anti-papalism thought they knew the answer, pointing the finger of blame at papal imperialism. Edward Foxe published some of the findings of the *Collectanea* as a tract entitled *De vera differentia regiae* (1538), in which he argued that the ancient rights of English kings had prevented the corruption of native Christianity until the pope had begun to interfere in the English Church. In 1536, Robert Barnes— later burned by Henry VIII for denying transubstantiation—traced the decline of the Church's purity through a history of the papacy, blaming an increase in papal power for doctrinal corruption.[8] The apocalyptic vision of the Book of Revelation provided reformers with further support for their model of papal corruption. Archbishop Thomas Cranmer argued that the primitive Church had ended in AD 600, using the model of history outlined by St John in Revelation. John Bale followed suit, arguing that AD 666 marked the end of primitive Christianity. Twenty years later, Bale's friend John Foxe copied this model in the *Acts and Monuments*. Foxe divided the history of the Church into five periods of roughly three hundred years each: AD 600, Foxe argued, was the start of the 'declinynge time of the Church' before the final descent when Satan arrived at the turn of the millennium.[9] AD 600 was a date with particular significance for

---

[6] Tyndale, *Obedience of the Christen Man* (1528); Bale, *Image of Bothe Churches* (n.d. [1545?]).

[7] Cranmer, *Defence of . . . the Sacrament* (1550); MacCulloch, *Cranmer*, pp. 499–504.

[8] Barnes, *Vitae Romanorum pontificarum*; Foxe, *De vera differentia regiae* (1538). For the influence of Henrician reformers on the development of history writing, see Levy, *Tudor Historical Thought*, ch. 2; and Ferguson, *Clio Unbound*, ch. 5.

[9] Foxe, *A&M* (1570), sig. e1ʳ; Ferguson, *Clio Unbound*, p. 181; Levy, *Tudor Historical Thought*, pp. 89–91.

English reformers, marking the beginning of papal interference in the domestic Church. The end of the sixth century coincided with the pontificate of Gregory I (590–604). His enforcement of clerical celibacy and his involvement in secular affairs had already made him the *bête noir* of reformers, but, most significantly, it was Gregory I who had encouraged Augustine's mission to England in 597. And Augustine's mission had, inescapably, established papal authority over the native Church. By Elizabeth's reign, then, reformers had established a model of Church history which was inspired by the Bible and justified by English history. It was also, in its outlook, a peculiarly insular account of Christianity, providing a historical perspective which shaped later histories of the English Church.

2. THE ORIGINS OF CHRISTIANITY AND THE ELIZABETHAN CHURCH

Henry VIII's divorce team had demonstrated how politically useful ecclesiastical history could be, and when Elizabeth I succeeded her Catholic half-sister, Mary I, in 1558, the origins of English Christianity once more rose to the top of the political agenda. Protestants sought to downplay the significance of Augustine's mission at the end of the sixth century—described in the popular *Historia ecclesiastica* of Bede—by arguing instead that that English Christianity predated the arrival of Augustine. By Elizabeth's reign, Protestants claimed that there had actually been three conversions of the British Isles (or at least those parts now governed by the Tudors): one apostolic, one Celtic, and (last of all) one Roman. John Foxe repeated long-held beliefs found in authors as diverse as Origen, Tertullian, and the sixth-century chronicler, Gildas, when he reported that Joseph of Arimathea (or possibly Simon Zelotes) led the first conversion of England. This established the English Church as one of the apostolic Churches, with an antiquity to rival her European counterparts.[10]

If the Arimathean conversion ensured that England could claim to have one of the oldest Churches in the Christian world, the story of King Lucius prompted reformers to claim that England had also had the first godly magistrate. Lucius's request for Christian missionaries was thought to have prompted the second conversion. Archbishop Parker oversaw the production of a new edition of the English Bible, first printed in 1568. In his preface to the 'Bishops' Bible'—as it became known—Parker included Pope Eleutherius's letter to King Lucius. Parker, like his Henrician counterparts, used Lucius to

---

[10] Foxe. *A&M* (1570) sigs. g3^v, n1^r–n2^r.

prove the antiquity of royal supremacy, and he carefully glossed the account of Eleutherius's involvement in order to diminish the role of the pope in the second conversion. Parker made it clear that King Lucius was *already* 'in great love with the true faith' when he wrote to the pope. Furthermore, Parker argued that the papal missionaries sent by Eleutherius to convert the Britons were actually native Britons who happened to find themselves in Rome *after* converting to Christianity.[11] By this point, Parker had ensured that no credit whatsoever could be laid at Pope Eleutherius's door for the second conversion.

This meant that the mission of Augustine, or Austen as he was known in England, was denied its earlier significance of introducing Christianity to the British Isles. In this view, Augustine, sent to Britain at the behest of Pope Gregory I, brought papal influence to bear over an already flourishing English Church. In his history, Foxe entitled his account of Augustine's arrival in *c*.597 as 'Britayne Conquered'. And when Parliament debated the restoration of a Protestant Church in 1559, Elizabeth I defended her role as head of the English Church by arguing that Joseph of Arimathea, not Augustine, was responsible for introducing Christianity to the British Isles. However, as the reign progressed, both Protestant and Catholic authors returned to the Anglo-Saxon Church to prove the antiquity of their brand of Christianity.[12]

3. PRIMITIVE CHRISTIANITY AND POLEMICAL DEBATE

The tone for Protestant–Catholic polemic was set by John Jewel, Bishop of Salisbury, in 1559. In a well-publicized sermon in London, Jewel launched an attack on Catholic critics that elevated *historia sacra* to a crucial role in confessional conflict. Responding to the Catholic taunt, 'where was your Church before Luther?' Jewel argued that it was the Protestant, not the Catholic, Church that could lay claim to antiquity. Jewel challenged opponents of the Elizabethan Church to prove the antiquity of fifteen Catholic practices (a number he would later raise to twenty-seven) from 'oute of the examples of the primitiue Church, out of the auncient fathers [or] out of the olde Councels'. Following in the footsteps of Cranmer and Bale, he used the year 600 to mark the end of the primitive Church.[13] The argument that it was the Reformed Church that could claim historical continuity continued to be a mainstay of apologetics throughout Elizabeth's reign. Preaching in his

---

[11] Parker (ed.), *The Holie Bible*, sig. *2ᵛ.
[12] Foxe, *A&M* (1570), sig. n8ʳ.
[13] Jewel, *An apologie*, sigs. L1ᵛ–L2ʳ.

archdiocese of York, Archbishop Edwin Sandys told his congregation that Catholics should 'remember their religion is as newe as false, six hundred years after Christ unknowne'.[14] When the Puritan Meredith Hanmer translated an edition of Eusebius's *Ecclesiastical Histories*, he added material to bring it up to AD 600 and encouraged his readers to note the 'difference that is in these our dayes between the Churche and the Apostolike times'.[15]

Jewel's sermon prompted an outpouring of ecclesiastical histories from Protestant and Catholic alike. Of these, perhaps the best known and most influential was John Foxe's history of English Christianity, the *Acts and Monuments*, popularly known as the 'Book of Martyrs' because of its graphic account of native martyrdoms up to the end of Mary I's reign. Encouraged by William Cecil, Elizabeth I's chief minister, Foxe published what would be the first edition of the *Acts and Monuments* in 1563, starting in the year 1000, when 'Sathan broke loose.' Foxe had worked with Matthias Flacius Illyricus on the Continent, was imbued with the spirit of controversialist Protestant history writing, and portrayed the history of English Christianity as part of a universal—and European—history.[16] Jewel's 'Challenge' and the Catholic response, however encouraged Foxe to focus on the primitive Church in England, and the second edition of the *Acts and Monuments* (1570) started by proving that 'Britons' had been converted by Joseph of Arimathea. The polemical value of his history was instantly clear: the Privy Council ordered that a chained copy should be placed in every cathedral and deanery, and tried to extend this injunction to all parish churches.[17] Foxe continued working on his history after 1570, producing two expanded editions in 1576 and 1583. With the last edition running to almost 2,200 pages, the *Acts and Monuments* was beyond most people's means. So, in 1589 the Protestant physician and cryptopgrapher, Timothy Bright, produced an abridged version under the aegis of Archbishop Whitgift. 'There is not a booke, under the scriptures', Bright claimed, 'more necessarie for a Christian to be conversant in.'[18]

History was not the exclusive preserve of Elizabethan Protestants. Spurred into action by Jewel's challenge and the first edition of Foxe's *Acts and Monuments*, Elizabethan Catholics turned their attention to the history of the Church. In 1565, the first English translation of Bede's *Historia*

---

[14] Sandys, *Sermons*, sig. D4^{r-v}.

[15] Eusebius, *Ecclesiastical Histories*, tr. and ed. Hanmer, sig. *5^r.

[16] Foxe, *A&M* (1563), sigs. C1^r-D1^r. Foxe, *A&M* (1570), bk 1, sig. e1^r. For Cecil's financial support, see Evenden and Freeman, 'Print, Profit and Propaganda', pp. 1288-307.

[17] For discussions of Foxe's work as an historian, see the introductory essays accompanying John Foxe, the *Unabridged Acts and Monuments Online* (HRI Online publications, Sheffield, 2011), <http://www.johnfoxe.org>, in particular Collinson, 'John Foxe as Historian'; Freeman, 'John Foxe: A Biography'; and Greengrass and Freeman, 'The Acts and Monuments and Protestant Continental Martyrologies'. See also Evenden, *Patents, Pictures and Patronage*, pp. 120-1; Elizabeth Evenden and Thomas Freeman, *Religion and the Book in Early Modern England* (Cambridge: Cambridge University Press, 2011).

[18] Foxe, *An Abridgement*, ed. Bright, sig. ¶7^v.

ecclesiastica was published as *The History of the Church of England* by Thomas
Stapleton, a Catholic priest then in exile in Louvain. Stapleton would later
publish a detailed response to Jewel's 'Challenge Sermon', demonstrating the
antiquity of Catholicism, but in the meantime, he attached to Bede's *Historia* a
list of 'more than forty differences between the primitive Church' of Bede and
the Elizabethan Church.[19] In response to Jewel's vision of a Church in decline
since 600, Stapleton reclaimed Augustine and the Anglo-Saxon Church for the
Catholic cause. Countering Protestant claims of corruption, Stapleton argued
that Bede's history 'proved that the faith of us Englishmen all these six
hundred yeares could not possibly be a corrupted faith . . . but is a true and
right Christianite no lesse then the first vi c. [= 600] yeares'.[20]

Stapleton's reading of Bede showed the difficult line that Catholics found
themselves treading between the universal claims of the papacy and an Anglo-
centric view of history. Promoting a papal Church, imbued with the spirit of
the Counter-Reformation, was sometimes difficult to reconcile with an attach-
ment to the native Church. Catholics, as well as Protestants, it seemed, were
attracted to an account of English history which emphasized the country's
special place in God's plans. When Cardinal Reginald Pole (Archbishop of
Canterbury from 1556 to 1558) effected the reconciliation with Rome under
Mary I, he spoke to Parliament about England's importance within universal
Catholic Church history, describing it as the 'first of all islands [that] received
the light of Christ's religion'.[21] Later, in Elizabeth's reign, Nicholas Sanders
and Robert Persons would both celebrate the antiquity of the English Church
by endorsing the notion that there had been three conversions of the Britons.
In his *Treatise of Three Conversions*, published in 1603, Persons argued,
however, that the first conversion was led by St Peter himself.[22] At a stroke,
he turned the English Church into one that was not just ancient, but above all,
papal, in origin.

Stapleton's translation of Bede began with a description of the state of the
British Isles in the late sixth century on Augustine's arrival and included the
story of King Lucius and his appeal to Pope Eleutherius. However, where
Thomas Cromwell and Matthew Parker had seen evidence of the Church's
ancient independence, Stapleton made it clear that Pope Eleutherius was
responsible for introducing Christianity, 'sound and undefiled', into a pagan
land.[23] The Church established by Lucius been wiped out during the Diocletian persecutions, and there was no continuity between the Lucian and
Augustinian Churches. Instead, Stapleton was at pains to stress that Augustine

---

[19] Bede, *History*, sigs. *3ᵛ, Δ3ʳ–8ᵛ. Stapleton, *Returne of Untruths*.

[20] Bede, *History*, sig. *3ᵛ.

[21] David Starkey, *Elizabeth: Apprenticeship* (London: Chatto and Windus, 2000), pp. 72–3; Highley, *Catholics Writing the Nation*, pp. 18–19.

[22] Sanders, *De origine*; Persons, *Treatise*, I (1603).

[23] Bede, *History*, sig. D4ʳ.

was the 'first bishop of the Englishmen' and that he also created a 'new Church of the English people'.[24] That Church was, of course, a papal Church. In his 1556 *Treatise of the Pretended Divorce of Henry VIII*, the Catholic cleric and historian, Nicholas Harpsfield, followed a similar line, arguing that the pope was responsible for the successive introductions of Christianity to England: 'as well in the time of the Brittaines and King Lucius by Pope Eleutherius, as afterwardes in the time of the Saxons by St Gregory'.[25]

Stapleton's *History of the English People* was enormously influential. It was a powerful response to Protestant attempts to downplay the role of Augustine in their history and encouraged Matthew Parker and his associates in their work on the Anglo-Saxon Church. Nor was Stapleton a lone voice. The *History*, which was reprinted several times, reflected awareness among English Catholics at home and abroad of the polemical and spiritual value of ecclesiastical history. At the end of the century, the Catholic author and exile Richard Verstegan (1548–1636?), asked his fellow exile in Antwerp, William Reynolds, to write an English history of the Church that would answer Foxe's *Acts and Monuments*. Reynolds was too ill to undertake the task, but he told Verstegan what such a history should contain. Reynolds envisioned a two-volume work, with volume one running 'from the first Christianity of our nation unto the revolt of King Henry the Eight'. Stapleton's version of Bede's history should, he argued, be reprinted in full for this volume, alongside Nicholas Harpsfield's manuscript '*Historia anglicana ecclesiae*'.[26] William Allen, who founded the English College at Rome in 1579 for English Catholic exiles, thought that his students should read Stapleton's *History* in preparation for their missionary work in England. Later, several men entering the College would claim that Stapleton's version of Bede had converted them to Catholicism. Stapleton, however, was more circumspect about the value of history alone. He had accompanied his text with notes on doctrine and, as Felicity Heal has shown, the *History* was frequently printed together with Stapleton's theological tract, *A Fortresse of Faith*.[27]

The notion that the Augustine mission was 'the coming in of Christen Fathe in to oure countre' was a powerful story for Catholic authors throughout the period.[28] It stressed the ancient roots of papal authority in England and reclaimed Augustine from Protestant authors who either dismissed the Anglo-Saxon Church as corrupt on one hand, or celebrated it as proto-reformed on the other. In the seventeenth century this story would be supplemented with ethnic arguments for the antiquity of English Catholicism. In

---

[24] Bede, *History*, sigs. K8ᵛ–L1ʳ.

[25] Pocock (ed.), *A Treatise . . . by Harpsfield*, pp. 261–2.

[26] Verstegan to Persons, Antwerp, 30 April 1593, in Petti (ed.), *Letters*, pp. 134 and 138.

[27] Bede, *History*, sigs. Δ3v–Δ8r; Stapleton, *Fortresse*; Highley, *Catholics Writing the Nation*, pp. 84–5; Heal, 'Appropriating History', pp. 116–19.

[28] Bede, *History*, sig. A3ʳ.

1605, Catholic exile Richard Verstegan (alias Richard Rowlands) published an influential account of the English Church and people, *Restitution of Decayed Intelligence*, in which he argued that the English were actually descended from the Anglo-Saxons (not the Britons who populated many foundation myths). They were in turn from Germany and could therefore trace their origins back to the tower of Babel.[29] This English analogue to Annius of Viterbo's fanciful history of the Etruscans privileged the English people above many of their European (and Scottish) cousins; Verstegan's work also firmly located the roots of Christianity in the Anglo-Saxon Church described by Bede. Verstegan published his history soon after the succession in 1603 of James VI of Scotland to the English throne as James I of England. This might seem an odd time to challenge 'British' mythology, but the roots of this project seem to have lain in 1560s Oxford, where Verstegan was a student during Parker's investigation into the Anglo-Saxon Church.[30] The *Restitution of Decayed Intelligence* blended an account of the English Catholic Church as part of the Roman Church with a celebration of the unique nature of the English—much like Stapleton had done forty years previously.

4. EUROPEAN CONNECTIONS AND ENGLISH HISTORIES

Verstegan was at the heart of the English Catholic exile community, working as a publisher, intelligence agent, and author for the English Catholic mission and for Philip II of Spain. In the previous decades, his work—including wall maps outlining the historical development of heresies and the *Theatrum crudelitatum haereticorum nostri temporis* (*Theatre of Cruelties of our Times*)—reflected the tensions of the Counter-Reformation. The *Theatrum crudelitatum*, a response to Foxe's 'Book of Martyrs', recounted martyrdoms at the hands of French, Dutch, and English Calvinists, and popularized the plight of English Catholics, while supporting Philip II's militant Catholic agenda. First printed in 1587, it was reissued in 1588 to coincide with Philip's launching of the Spanish Armada against England, and again in 1604 during Anglo-Spanish peace negotiations. In 1588, a French version of the *Theatrum crudelitatem* was produced—*Theatre des cruatez*—tailored to meet the polemical needs of the Catholic League in

---

[29] Verstegan, *Restitution of Decayed Intelligence*; Arblaster, *Antwerp and the World*, pp. 85–93.

[30] Parry, *Trophies of Time*, ch. 2. For the influence of Annius of Viterbo (Giovanni Nanni), see Grafton, *What Was History?* pp. 95–105. For Verstegan's implicit criticism of James VI/I's 'British' project, see Highley, *Catholics Writing the Nation*, pp. 101–13.

France.[31] The production of Catholic history was inextricably bound up in the political agenda of the exile community. Richard Verstegan was involved in historical enterprises from Robert Persons's *Treatise of Three Conversions* to plans for a general history of the English Church. He was also involved in the production of more overtly provocative texts, including *A Conference about the Next Succession to the Crowne of Ingland* (1595). Published under the pseudonym 'R. Doleman', *A Conference* used legal and historical evidence to argue for an elected monarch and included a list of potential Catholic heirs to the throne, including the *infanta* of Spain and the sons of the Duke of Parma.[32]

English Catholic historians were aware that they were part of a European-wide endeavour. In 1566, the prominent Marian cleric Nicholas Harpsfield produced *Dialogi sex* (under the pseudonym Alan Cope), in which he attacked the historical methodology of Continental Protestant historians Johann Sleidan, Jean Crespin, and the Magdeburg Centuriators, before moving on to criticize their English counterparts Jewel, Bale, and Foxe. The publication of the first volume of Cesare Baronio's *Annales* in 1588 inspired Persons and Verstegan to produce their own histories of England.[33] However, few of those histories were aimed at a specifically English audience. Richard White, an exile in Louvain, who dedicated part of his multi-volume history of the British Isles from Brutus onwards, the *Historiarum Britanniae libri* (1597–1607), to Baronio, published in Latin for a Continental audience. The antiquarian Richard Stanihurst, in exile in Antwerp, produced histories of the Irish that emphasized their unwavering loyalty to the Catholic Church, for example in his portrayal of St Patrick.[34] Another Louvain exile, Nicholas Sanders (*c.*1530–81), wrote an account of the break with Rome, *De origine ac progressu schismatis anglicani*, which was published after his death to galvanize support abroad for English Catholics. *De origine* was reprinted several times, but only in Spanish and French. This reflected, of course, the exiles' search for support, which was more likely to be inspired by details of recent persecution than by accounts of the primitive Church. When Reynolds outlined his plans for an English ecclesiastical history, he imagined that the second volume of the history—dealing with the period from Henry's divorce onwards—would be far longer than the first. He suggested using Sander's *De origine* and Harpsfield's account

---

[31] Verstegan was receiving a pension from Philip II at this stage, and the *Theatrum* was published by Christopher Plantin, Philip II's typographer Royal. Arblaster, *Antwerp and the World*, pp. 40–3; Verstegan, *Theatrum crudelitatem* (1587) [repr. 1588, 1592, 1604]; Verstegan, *Theatre des cruautez* (1588) [repr. and rev. 1607]. Another French edition, differing from that of the pro-League version, was also published in Antwerp in 1588, with (confusingly) the same title.

[32] Petti (ed.), *Letters*, p.134; Doleman, *A Conference*; Arblaster, *Antwerp and the World*, pp. 61–2.

[33] Arblaster, *Antwerp and the World*, pp. 86–7. On Baronio's work, see above, Ch. 3.

[34] Stanihurst, *Rebus in Hibernia*; Stanihurst, *Vita Sancti Patricii*.

of the divorce to show, as Verstegan reported, the 'troobles that have been caused by schisme and heresy'.[35]

Protestants and Catholics alike found themselves balancing an appeal to the European-wide historical debates about the true Church with a particular focus on the English Church. Elizabethan Protestant authors, many of whom had been in exile under Mary I, were influenced by the methodology and intellectual vision of their European counterparts. John Foxe knew the Lutheran historian Johann Sleidan, and while in exile had worked alongside Heinrich Pantaleon (1522–95) and Matthias Flacius Illyricus, who spearheaded the *Magdeburg Centuries*.[36] Back in England, while writing the *Acts and Monuments*, Foxe continued to consult with European colleagues, in particular Sleidan and Ludwig Rabus (1523–92). He lifted material and historical details from the martyrologies of Crespin and Pantaleon.[37] Archbishop Matthew Parker had not been in exile under Mary I, but he too felt the influence of the Centuriators. In 1560, a letter from Magdeburg arrived requesting information from Parker on the history of the English Church, in particular details of reformed beliefs in the medieval Church, early scriptural translations, and evidence of papal corruption.[38] This spurred Parker to hunt down ancient manuscripts, many from the monasteries that had been dissolved during the reign of Henry VIII in the 1530s, for his own history of the English Church. In contrast to the Centuriators, however, his focus was specifically on the national, rather than the international, Church.

5. ARCHBISHOP PARKER AND THE ANGLO-SAXON CHURCH

Matthew Parker's secretary, John Joscelyn (1529–1603), recorded the Archbishop's 'diligent search for such writings of historye and other monuments of antiquity as might reveale unto us what hath bene the state of the Church in England from tyme to tyme'.[39] Parker found the most valuable evidence in the history of the Anglo-Saxon Church. While reformers held up the first six centuries of the Church as the ideal, Parker believed that the Church of Anglo-Saxon times (i.e. from the seventh century until the Norman Conquest of 1066) offered powerful evidence to counter Catholic jeers about Protestant

---

[35] Petti (ed.), *Letters*, pp. 134 and 138; Highley, 'Nicholas Sander's *Schismatis Anglicani*', pp. 147–67; Parry, *Trophies of Time*, pp. 52–3.

[36] Backus, *Historical Method*, pp. 358–70.

[37] Greengrass and Freeman, 'Protestant Continental Martyrologies'.

[38] Graham, 'Matthew Parker's Manuscripts', p. 324.

[39] Joscelyn, 'Preface' in Aelfric, *A Testimonie*, sig. A3ʳ.

innovation. Parker and his team of scholars scoured their manuscripts for evidence of current reformed practices in this earlier period. The sermons of Aelfric (*c.*955– *c.*1020), an Anglo-Saxon abbot of Eynsham, produced the most powerful polemical material. Parker and Joscelyn discovered that Aelfric had suggested that the bread and wine became Christ's body in the spiritual sense only, denying Catholic claims for the antiquity of the doctrine of transubstantiation.[40] Parker had Aelfric's sermons published immediately, along with other Anglo-Saxon manuscripts which proved the antiquity of reformed practices: that clerics had married, and that both the Scripture and services had been in the vernacular in the early medieval Church. The English edition of Aelfric's sermon was followed by translations of these texts, including Asser's *De Aelfredi regis res gestae* and an edition of the Anglo-Saxon gospels.[41]

While Parker's interest in the Anglo-Saxon Church apparently contradicted the standard Protestant narrative of medieval corruption, he was able to find enough material from these centuries to prove the historical continuity of the English Church with the ancient one, and to answer both Catholic accusations of innovation and Puritan demands for further reform. His account of the Church was a history of an institution, measured through its ceremonial life. By stressing the ancient traditions of an English Church which had always differed from her European counterparts, Parker's work shored up the conformist position that all English Protestants should be content to follow the national Church in 'things indifferent'. Like John Jewel, Matthew Parker did not appeal to universal Evangelical principles to defend the Anglican Church—shared with reformers across Europe—but to an institutional continuity between the primitive and Elizabethan Churches. Parker echoed his Henrician predecessors by emphasizing both the historical independence and self-sufficiency of the English Church, and of course the ancient legitimacy of royal government within in. In his preface to the Bishops' Bible, Parker dwelt on the use of the vernacular in the Anglo-Saxon Church, assuring his readers that the Church was returning 'to that devine nature wherein once we were made'.[42]

Matthew Parker's celebration of the Anglo-Saxon Church was an attempt to undermine Catholic efforts to claim Augustine as their own. However, Parker's interest in Anglo-Saxon Christianity was at odds with the historical arguments of other reformers who insisted that the post-Augustinian Church was in many ways corrupt. It was those around Parker, rather than the

---

[40] Joscelyn, 'Preface' in Aelfric, *A Testimonie*, sig. A3ʳ; Robinson, 'Matthew Parker and the Reforming of History', pp. 1061–83; Graham, 'Matthew Parker's Manuscripts', pp. 322–44.

[41] Asser, *Aelfredi regis res gestae* (London, 1574); John Foxe (ed.), *The Gospels of the Fower Euangelistes*.

[42] Parker (ed.), *The Holie Bible*, sig. *2ʳ.

archbishop himself, who articulated any unease that Parker may have felt about the Anglo-Saxon Church. For example, John Foxe worked with Parker on the publication of the Anglo-Saxon Gospels; but when he reprinted Anglo-Saxon documents in the *Acts and Monuments*, Foxe edited them to remove some of the more offensive elements for a reformed sensibility.[43] John Joscelyn, one of Parker's Anglo-Saxon specialists, was even less circumspect. In the preface to Aelfric's sermons, printed in 1566, he noted that the Anglo-Saxon Church was 'in divers pointes of religion so full of blindness and ignorance, [and] full of childish servitude to ceremonies'. Joscelyn also attached a theological health warning to Aletric's sermon, cautioning that 'in this sermon, here published, some thynges be spoken not consonant to sounde doctrine'.[44]

Despite the anxieties that many Protestants evinced about the medieval Church after AD 600, Parker continued to direct a busy publishing schedule of primary material intended to prove beyond doubt that the Elizabethan Settlement was a return to the status quo, not an innovation. As well as Anglo-Saxon texts, Parker oversaw the publication of medieval chronicles proving the historical continuity of the Church, including works by Matthew Paris (*c.*1200–59), Thomas Walsingham (d. *c.*1422) and the (so-called) Matthew of Westminster.[45] He also produced his own historical account of the Church, drawn from his large manuscript collection, which traced the Church from the time of Joseph of Arimathea and outlined the careers of successive archbishops.[46] Parker's histories reflected his vision of a national Church defined by a ceremonial and institutional life, a vision which underpinned his drive to secure conformity to the Elizabethan Church. Those who resisted the drive for conformity—the godly clerics who criticized the Catholic remnants in the Elizabethan Church—developed their own vision of the historical Church. In contrast to Parker's model of the national Church, this Puritan model of the Church increasingly focused on the community of believers that existed beyond the limits of an established Church.

6. JOHN FOXE AND THE 'TRUE CHURCH'

If Matthew Parker's interests lay in the historical institution of the Church of England, John Foxe chose instead to write a history of 'Christes True Church'

---

[43] Robinson, 'Foxe and the Anglo Saxons', pp. 54–72.

[44] Aelfric, *A Testimonie*, sigs. K3^{r-v}; Robinson, 'Matthew Parker and the Reforming of History', pp. 1078–80.

[45] Paris, *Elegans, illustris et facilis rerum*; Matthew of Westminster [*pseud*], *Flores historiarum*; Walsingham, *Historia brevis*; Paris, *Historia maior*; Walsingham, *Ypodigma Neustriae* (1574).

[46] Parker, *De antiquitate*.

as a body of believers united by their relationship with God rather than by a ceremonial life. Of course, this was a good model for any Protestant history: as *sola fides* had replaced sacramental observance as the path to heaven, it was logical that *historia ecclesiastica* should focus less on ceremonies and more on believers. However, as Elizabeth's reign progressed, and Puritans became more frustrated with the lack of reform, focusing on the community of believers also allowed Foxe to circumvent some of the limitations of the English Church. The *Acts and Monuments*, first published in 1563 and further revised in 1570, 1576, and 1583, reflected the evolution of English Puritanism throughout Elizabeth I's reign.[47]

In 1563, when the first edition of the *Acts and Monuments* was published, those disappointments were in the future, and godly clerics celebrated Elizabeth I's succession as a manifestation of divine providence. While in exile from the Marian persecutions, Foxe had written histories of the 'True Church' and its martyrs, and so, when he wrote the preface of the 1563 *Acts and Monuments*, he cast himself in the great tradition of Church history writing represented by Eusebius's *Ecclesiastical History*.[48] Eusebius was an important influence for reforming clerics: the Magdeburg Centuriators modelled their work on Eusebius' history, while the Flemish Calvinist author Andreas Hyperius (1511–64) prescribed Eusebius as a key text for young scholars of Scripture[49] Foxe not only employed Eusebius' methodology—and frequently his sources too—but also laid claim to the great narrative vision of Eusebius's work. Foxe had spent his exile from Mary's reign in Frankfurt, Basel, and Strasbourg, working with other Protestant historians. He saw himself as experiencing an age of persecution just like the one Eusebius had lived through. And, as Eusebius had seen Constantine's reign as bringing the age of Christian persecution to an end, Foxe thought Elizabeth's reign achieved the same for her Protestant subjects. In his 1563 preface, Foxe echoed Eusebius's claims, portraying Elizabeth I as the Emperor Constantine: it seemed clear that England enjoyed a special place in God's apocalyptic plan. 'Let Constantine be never so great', Foxe told the queen, 'in many things equal, in this superior, for that Constantius only being a helper unto the persecuted, your highness hath dispatched that persecution from other, under which ye were entangled yourself.'[50] Constantine was recast as being half-English, and the emperor

---

[47] On Foxe's project in general, see Evenden and Freeman, *Religion and the Book in Early Modern England: The Making of John Foxe's 'Book of Martyrs'*.

[48] Foxe, *Commentarii rerum in ecclesia gestarum* (Strasbourg, 1554). Later revised and published with additional material, Foxe, *Rerum in ecclesia gestarum* (Basel, 1559). For Foxe's work in exile, see Freeman, 'John Foxe: A Biography'.

[49] Grafton, *What Was History?*, pp.107–12. On Eusebius, see Grafton and Williams, *Christianity and the Transformation of the Book*; Hyperius; *Methodi theologicae libri tres* (Basel, 1563), preface.

[50] Foxe, *A&M* (1563), preface, quotation on sig. B2ʳ. On Foxe's use of Eusebius, see Pucci, 'Reforming Roman Emperors' and Collinson, 'John Foxe as an Historian'.

became a popular model for godly clerics celebrating Elizabeth's rule. On the anniversary of Elizabeth I's accession to the throne, Archbishop Edwin Sandys compared her succession to that of the Emperor Constantine, and likened himself to Eusebius. Another preacher, Thomas Holland, suggested that to commemorate Elizabeth's succession was to celebrate 'such a day as Eusebius hath spoken of'.[51]

However, while Foxe's first edition of the *Acts and Monuments* celebrated the special place of England in eschatological history, by the time his second edition appeared in 1570 the hopes of Puritan reformers had been crushed. It was clear that the Elizabethan Church would not meet the reforming aspirations of a large section of its clergy, never mind occupy a special place in apocalyptic history. As the hopes of 1563 faded, the Eusebian model of Constantine was no longer relevant: the preface to the 1570 edition saw no mention of the Roman emperor. Thomas Betteridge has argued that the second and subsequent editions of the *Acts and Monuments* reflected Foxe's disappointment with the Elizabethan Reformation, seen in an increasing focus on the universal history of Christianity rather than on its English manifestation.[52] By 1570, Foxe depicted the English as one godly nation among many: the story of English Christianity, its recent persecution, and subsequent restoration reflected an oft-repeated cycle of sacred history, experienced by godly nations from the Israelites onwards.

This changing emphasis is seen in the cuts and additions Foxe made to his accounts of recent history. The long account of the Westminster conference of 1559, for example, which created the framework for the Elizabethan Church, was cut from the 1570 edition. In contrast, Foxe's account of the death of Mary's chancellor, Bishop Stephen Gardiner, identified as chief persecutor of the Marian Protestants, was recast as parallel to the story of Heliodorus, struck down in the Temple in Jerusalem.[53] As Foxe no longer celebrated the Elizabethan Church as the fulfilment of God's will, he focused less and less on the institutional history of English Christianity. Instead, his interest lay with Christ's true Church, a Church that Foxe—like many Elizabethan Puritans—increasingly saw as being distinct from the established Church in England.

---

[51] Holland, *Sermon*, sig. K2^r; Sandys, *Sermons*, p. 45.

[52] Betteridge, 'From Prophetic to Apocalyptic', pp. 210–32. Loades has argued that England had a 'special place' in eschatological history for Foxe; see Loades, 'John Foxe and the Editors', in Loades (ed.) *John Foxe and the English Reformation*, pp. 1–11.

[53] Compare the account of Gardiner's death in the 1563 edition Foxe, *A&M* (1563) sigs. NNNN8^{r-v}, and Foxe, *A&M* (1570), sigs. BBBBB1^v–BBBBB2^v. For the Westminster conference, see Foxe, *A&M* (1563), sigs. OOOO1^r–OOOO8^v. Details of the conference were once more included in the 1583 edition, Foxe, *A&M* (1583), sigs. CCCCC5^r–DDDDD2^r.

7. *HISTORIA ECCLESIASTICA* AND SPIRITUAL GROWTH

Foxe's historical vision, like that of many 'godly' contemporaries, was shaped by his own experience of persecution and exile. Whereas Foxe thought in 1563 that England had a special place in God's apocalyptic plan, after a decade of failure by Puritan reformers, Foxe saw the English Church as one godly church among many: no longer did he see it as the fulfilment of God's will. In 1570, Foxe described the 'True Church' as being 'universall and sparsedly through all countrie[s] dilated'. That Church was more difficult to discern, and Foxe followed John Bale's model writing a history of a true and false Church. In the *Acts and Monuments*, Foxe identified the 'true Church of Christ' at the various moments when it 'stode in open defence of the truth against the disordered Church of Rome'. This implied a history of martyrs.[54] In his last work before he died, *Eicasmi*, published by his son, Samuel Foxe, John Foxe was even more explicit about the limitations of writing 'national' ecclesiastical history. The *Eicasmi* explored the apocalyptic visions of the Bible, which Foxe believed to be a mystical outline of ecclesiastical history. For Foxe, the succession of the Church was to be found in 'faith and doctrine', not in a particular location. Foxe promised his readers that 'the reign of Christ and his divine promise is not confined to Rome, nor England, nor France'.[55]

Identifying the true Church, which was represented in Foxe's *Acts and Monuments* by the martyrs who died to defend its doctrines, could bring better knowledge of Christ's rule. Foxe's history writing was, therefore, clearly a spiritual activity. Foxe equated ecclesiastical history with the Bible, arguing that the English had been 'longe ledde in ignouraunce and wrapt in blindness for lacke specially of God's word and partly also for wanting the light of history'.[56] And, unlike Matthew Parker, Foxe knew 'the goods and ornaments of the Church chiefly to consist not in the Donatives and patrimonies, but in the bloud, actes and lyfes of the martyrs'.[57] Helped by colleagues and friends, Foxe included letters, eyewitness accounts, and other sources relating to martyrdoms, giving particular attention to the deaths of the recent Marian martyrs. These were the 'monuments' of the title, and were intended to be a spiritual aid as well as a form of memorialization.

In 1577, Meredith Hanmer hoped that readers of his translation of Eusebius's history and the accounts of early martyrdoms would 'experience a lively beholding of Christ'; for him, ecclesiastical histories were 'bookes of divinitie to edifie the soule and instructe the inwarde man'.[58] The martyrs in Foxe's

---

[54] Foxe, *A&M* (1570), sigs. ☞ 3^{r-v}, a1^v.
[55] Foxe, *Eicasmi*, p.12.
[56] Foxe, *A&M* (1576), sig. ¶1^v.
[57] Foxe, *A&M* (1563), sig. B2^v.
[58] Eusebius, *Ecclesiastical Histories*, sig. *2^v.

history and in Hanmer's version of Eusebius fulfilled many of the same functions as medieval saints' *vitae* had, offering instruction and stimulating piety. In the second edition of the *Acts and Monuments*, published in 1570, Foxe no longer portrayed himself as Eusebius to Elizabeth's Constantine. Instead, he looked to the Bible for inspiration, portraying himself as King Solomon of the Old Testament. Foxe declared that his work compiling his history and collating primary sources was akin to Solomon's work building the Temple. He hoped that his readers, like visitors to Solomon's Temple, would 'receive some spirituall fruit to their soules'.[59] The spiritual purpose of the work was explicit; the *Acts and Monuments* were not only a repository of divine truth, but also a means of spiritual growth. Although Foxe and Hanmer were more explicit than most historians about their hopes that their work would increase the community of the godly, at some level all ecclesiastical history was designed to increase or strengthen confessional identities.

8. SOURCES AND THE ECCLESIASTICAL HISTORIAN

Primary sources were promoted as repositories of divine truth, and played an increasingly important role in polemical and confessional debate. On the Continent Flacius Illyricus and Baronio were defending their respective Churches by reproducing large amounts of primary material. As mentioned above, Nicholas Harpsfield's 1566 *Dialogi sex* (published under the name Alan Cope) attacked other Protestant histories by highlighting flaws in other writers' historical method and their use of sources. His attack on Foxe's account of Oldcastle's rebellion was so persuasive that Foxe dedicated thirty-four pages in the second edition of the *Acts and Monuments* to answering Harpsfield's criticisms. Having learned his lesson once, Foxe's response drew heavily on extensive research he was forced to do on parliamentary rolls.[60] Sources, however, produced different answers depending on how they were read, and sometimes the source alone could not secure the argument. In another work, Harpsfield compared Protestant historians to the Trojan historian who, 'contrary to the writing of all other and contrary to the belief of the whole world, writeth that the Trojans overcame the Grecians and not the Grecians the Trojans'. The English Jesuit Edmund Campion was similarly scathing, arguing that Protestant historians consistently failed to produce convincing sources: 'no wonder', he mocked,

---

[59] Foxe, *A&M* (1570), preface.
[60] Foxe, *A&M* (1570), sigs. Nn1ᵛ–Pp2ᵛ. See e.g. Foxe's use of parliamentary papers to argue whether Oldcastle was a martyr or a traitor, sig. Pp1ʳ; Freeman, 'Nicholas Harpsfield', ODNB.

'that they be constrained to vaunt of their Church (if anie Church they will challenge) as lying in perpetuall obscuritie'.[61]

The influence of humanist historiography was certainly felt in England, and by writers of ecclesiastical histories. As more primary sources were marshalled to defend an argument, the interpretation of sources became increasingly open to debate. Proving mastery of these primary texts through the philological tools necessary to analyse and edit sources implied intellectual authority. Catholics and Protestants rushed to present their own versions of primary texts. Thomas Stapleton's translation of Bede's history was, in part, a response to an edition of Bede recently produced by 'the protestants themselves of Basill'.[62] Similarly, Matthew Parker oversaw a new translation of the sixth-century chronicler Gildas to replace the edition of his works published by the Catholic humanist, Polydore Vergil.[63] Editions of primary texts were increasingly hedged about with scholarly apparatus meant to prove their intellectual credentials. When Parker's secretary, John Joscelyn, published a translation of Aelfric's sermons, it was accompanied by tools showing his scholarly brilliance. In a flourish that paid homage to his humanist forebears, Joscelyn included the Lord's Prayer, Creed, and Ten Commandments in the 'Saxon tongue' interlined with English, and printed 'the Saxon characters, or letters, that be most straunge'. Furthermore, he included a list of thirteen bishops and the two archbishops willing to testify that Aelfric's sermons had been translated and 'truelye put forth in print without the adding, or withdrawing of any one thing'.[64] It is unlikely that so many of Elizabeth's bishops were able to read the Anglo-Saxon original. However, the stamp of authentication reflected the extent to which historical sources—and their veracity—were becoming increasingly important in polemical conflicts.

Sometimes, however, the spiritual purpose of ecclesiastical history made those newly fashionable tools of critical analysis irrelevant. Ecclesiastical history required methods of historical analysis that sometimes fell short of Levy's model of academic rigour. Truth was an elastic concept. Sources could be faked: Lorenzo Valla's work on the Donation of Constantine had proved that. But Foxe, no fan of the papacy, had argued that the Donation, though false, might illustrate a greater truth about papal power.[65] And when Foxe extended his history back to the earliest Church, he relied heavily on Eusebius for accounts of the first Christian martyrs. Of these, the second-century martyr St Polycarp was a favourite among Catholics and Protestants alike.

---

[61] Harpsfield, *Treatise*, p. 16; Campion, *Campian Englished*, pp. 66–7.

[62] Bede, *History*, sig. A2ᵛ. The Basel edition was published two years earlier by John Herwagen, a printer with reformist sympathies. However, Herwagen dedicated this edition to the Catholic Bishop of Speyer—perhaps an example of the dedication of Basel printers to maximizing sales: Bede, *Opera Bedae*, 4 vols. (Basel, 1563)

[63] Gildas, *De excidio et conquestu Britanniae*.

[64] Aelfric, *A Testimonie*, sigs. K4ʳ–L6ᵛ.

[65] Foxe, *A&M* (1563), sig. B1ᵛ.

John Jewel argued that Polycarp's death was evidence of the original purity of the Christian Church, and Foxe included a lengthy account of his martyrdom in the *Acts and Monuments*.[66] Drawing on Eusebius, Foxe recounted that at Polycarp's death a heavenly voice was heard instructing the saint 'to be of good cheare Polycarpus and playe the man'. Foxe later recycled this piece of evidence, inserting the heavenly injunction 'to playe the man' into his account of the deaths of the Marian martyrs, Latimer and Ridley.[67] Reusing this material might seem odd, particularly bearing in mind the number of eye-witnesses to Latimer and Ridley's deaths who were still alive. However, Eusebius's story was of eternal (and therefore transhistorical) significance and offered a template of martyrdom in which the deaths of Latimer and Ridley could be fashioned as authentic martyrs. Just as significantly, of course, the death of Polycarp was in its essentials no different from that of the Marian martyrs—both were evidence of faithful obedience to God's will, unchanging across time and space.

Similarly, when Elizabethan Protestants explained the historical context of the Church's recent past, they turned to the Bible rather than to Matthew Parker's carefully crafted accounts of the Anglo-Saxon Church. In the first decade of Elizabeth's reign, a practice started up of commemorating her accession to the throne and, with it, the establishment of a Protestant regime. The 'Queen's Day' or 'Crownation Day', as it became known, was marked by sermons, church services, and celebrations. An official service was printed in 1576, followed a few years later by a collection of 'godly exercises' to be used on the 'Queen's Day'.[68] It was a moment to explore the historical significance, and the eschatological role, of the Elizabethan Church. But in the sermons that survive, preachers and authors spoke not of King Lucius, but of King Josiah and King David. It was the Old Testament and the experience of Israel that provided the historical context for thousands of parishioners when they were asked to think about the origins of the English Church. Archbishop Edwin Sandys told a congregation that Elizabeth's succession 'brought us out of Egypt, the house of Roman servitude'. And just as Foxe had used the story of Polycarp to fashion his account of Latimer and Ridley's deaths, why should Old Testament history not be a powerful source of historical information? As the Elizabethan Bishop of Durham, Tobie Matthew, argued: 'He that triumphed in Israel is not altered'.[69]

---

[66] Jewel, *Apologie*, sig. F2ʳ.

[67] Foxe, *A&M* (1570), sig. E6ᵛ; King, 'Fact and Fiction', pp. 20–3.

[68] 'A form of prayer with thanksgiving, to be used every year, the 17th November', in W. Keatinge Clay (ed.), *Liturgical Services*, pp. 548–61; Bunny, *Certaine Prayers*.

[69] Bodleian Library, Oxford, Ms. Top Oxon E 5, p. 214; Colfe, *A Sermon Preached on the Queenes Day*, sigs. C3ᵛ–C4ʳ; Sandys, *Sermons*, p. 45. See also John King, *Lectures upon Ionas Delivered at York in the Yeare of our Lorde 1595* (London, 1611), p. 706; and Thomas Holland, *A Sermon Preached at Paul's in London the 17 of November Ann. Dom. 1599* (Oxford, 1601).

Ecclesiastical history was a form of sacred history: like biblical history it provided evidence of God's will for humankind, if read properly. While ecclesiastical historians employed humanist tools of analysis, these were often subordinated to the larger purpose of illuminating God's will. Despite the work of Foxe and Parker in promoting a historical defence of the English Church, perhaps it is not surprising that in the parishes the historical analysis which mattered was to be found in the Book of Revelation, while historical examples came from the Chronicles of the Old Testament. The Bible presented a universal reading of the past whose relevance to the present was immediate and indisputable. While Stapleton, Verstegan, Foxe, and Parker wrote about the national past of the Church, in the parishes it was the local experience of the universal that mattered. Conflicting histories of English Christianity played an important part in the polemical conflicts of the sixteenth century and informed the confessional positions that emerged within both Catholic and Protestant communities. However, in the parishes of Elizabethan England, the Bible—and its eschatological framework—continued to shape historical debates about the Church's past, present, and future.

9

Reconstructing Irish Catholic History
after the Reformation

Salvador Ryan

1. INTRODUCTION

Ecclesiastical history, especially concerning Christian origins, pervaded the ecclesiological controversies of Reformation and post-Reformation Europe. The different interpretations that competing religious groups gave to the early Christian period, whose rightful heirs they claimed to be, fuelled the need to reconstruct a convincing narrative of the Christian past that could robustly withstand the most rigorous of Renaissance humanist critiques. Late sixteenth- and seventeenth-century Irish Catholic writing represents a particular manifestation of this phenomenon. As crypto-Catholicism in Ireland evolved into full-blown Catholic recusancy, the question of constructing an Irish Catholic identity and of sorting out its relationship with the Protestant English monarchy became more acute. With the arrival of a wave of new, mostly Protestant, English settlers to Ireland beginning in the 1550s and climaxing during Oliver Cromwell's Protectorate a century later, the new common ground found between the native Irish and their Anglo-Norman (now regarded as 'Old English') Catholic counterparts would need historical legitimization. These 'New English' were regarded with some disdain by the Old English, who considered them 'upstarts' lacking a nuanced understanding of Irish governance—something that could only be acquired after centuries of controlling municipal and local government, which the Old English had largely done since the twelfth century.

The Old English community was the most important constituency to win over for the successful implementation of the Reformation in Ireland; if it was not willing to come on board, the project would founder. And the results were not encouraging. It is a curious fact that by the 1570s Old English impropriators of former monastic lands in Ireland were using the profits acquired from the monasteries' dissolution to support Irish Catholic 'massing priests', an increasing number of whom were now being educated on the Continent.[1] In the wake of the papal bull *Regnans in excelsis* (1570), which excommunicated Queen Elizabeth, the loyalty of these Catholics to their monarch was put to the test. The uprising of Old English leaders exemplified in the Desmond rebellion in 1579, and the Baltinglass and Nugent risings of 1580 and 1581, which used Counter-Reformation and even crusading rhetoric under a papal banner, sowed seeds of doubt in the minds of the English administration. The conclusion was drawn that all Catholics were potential traitors. This, in turn, led to a brutal suppression of revolts through the 1580s and 1590s, the hardening of Old English Catholic resistance, and the creation of Catholic martyrs.

As a result, the English government increasingly turned to the New English community to fill administrative positions in Ireland, further alienating the Old English community and helping to fuel the notion that they were being excluded from the corridors of power. This came to a head in the Dublin Parliament, which opened on 18 May 1613. A majority of New English members were returned from newly created pocket boroughs which King James I's Attorney-General, Sir John Davies (1569–1626), termed 'perpetual seminaries of Protestant burgesses'.[2] The Old English community would struggle to reconcile its deepening commitment to the Catholic Counter-Reformation with its loyalty to the monarchy. By the reign of King James I (r. 1603–25), the monarchy had come to regard the Old English as damaged goods, or at most 'half subjects'.[3]

The Irish Catholic community was, however, divided over the question of whether to resist the Protestant monarchy. By 1600 Pope Clement VIII (pope 1592–1605) had declared the English war against the Catholic religion to be unjust, and the indulgence that he issued for those engaged in Catholic resistance rendered the struggle against the English just as spiritually meritorious as that against the Turks.[4] The Waterford-born Old English scholar, Peter Lombard (c.1555–1625), completed his *De regno Hiberniae sanctorum insula commentarius* in Rome in 1600 and dedicated it to the pope. Its aim was to justify the stance of Hugh O'Neill (c.1550–1616), earl of Tyrone and protagonist of the Nine Years' War, and to win Pope Clement VIII's support for a crusade.[5] The pope would appoint Lombard as archbishop of Armagh in the following year. By the 1610s, figures such as Philip O'Sullivan Beare, Donal Cam O'Sullivan, and the Irish Franciscan, Florence Conry, the latter based at St Anthony's College, Louvain, sought a new military intervention in Ireland

---

[1] Lennon, *The Lords of Dublin*, pp. 144–50.
[2] Hazard, *Faith and Patronage*, p. 100.
[3] O'Connor, 'Custom, Authority and Tolerance', p. 134.
[4] Morgan, 'Making Ireland Spanish', p. 88.
[5] Lennon, 'Political Thought', p. 184.

by King Philip III of Spain (r. 1598–1621).[6] Spanish theologians at the universities of Salamanca and Valladolid debated the question of whether Hugh O'Neill's war against the Protestant English was just, and answered in the affirmative in 1603, declaring furthermore that Irish Catholic loyalists who supported the monarchy had no 'surreption' or exemption from the pope, and that no Catholic was justified in abetting an unjust war.[7] At the Dublin Parliament of 1613, many Catholic members voted for O'Neill's attainder, and Florence Conry argued that all those who had refused to support O'Neill in his fight against heresy were complicit in accepting the attainder and that God would duly retaliate against Ireland, for civil obedience should only be shown towards a just Catholic ruler.[8] But some Catholics disagreed. David Rothe, one-time secretary of Peter Lombard and vicar-general of Armagh from 1609, rejected Lombard's espousal of military intervention, arguing that Catholics in the Dublin Parliament who refrained from resorting to arms were like Esther in the Old Testament, who prayed and did penance. When Catholic members of the Dublin parliament appealed to foreign powers, their pleas were for solidarity in prayer and fasting, not for military intervention.[9]

The division among Catholics regarding the monarchy was also replicated in religious communities, but here the tendency to profess respect for the monarchy was even more pronounced. In 1618, Conry's Franciscan confrere, Hugh McCaughwell (Aodh Mac Aingil), dedicated his treatise on the sacrament of penance, *Scáthán Shacramuinte na hAithridhe*, to King James I, referring to him as 'ar ríogh' (our king), 'ar rí uasal óirdheirc' ('our noble illustrious king') and claiming that he was writing this work 'for the people who are under the majesty of the king'.[10] By the 1620s, Irish Catholic writers were seeking a new kind of history that would unite native Irish and Old English Catholics under one banner, emphasizing their common faith, Ireland as their homeland and (by this time) Charles I (r. 1625–49) as their true king. The title of 'Éireannach' or 'Irish person' was now conceived to include those who were Catholic and Irish-born, of Gaelic Irish and Anglo-Norman (Old English) stock alike. The work of reconstructing Irish history (and particularly Irish religious history) would involve an emphasis on continuity and the assertion of a brand of Catholic confidence that could be shared across these two groups and proven with reference to ancient sources.[11]

In the late sixteenth and seventeenth centuries, Irish Catholic writers sought to address two fundamental questions in particular. The first concerned Irish

---

[6] Morgan, 'Making Ireland Spanish', p. 87.
[7] Morgan, '"Un pueblo unido . . ."'.
[8] Hazard, *Faith and Patronage*, p. 101.
[9] O'Connor, 'Custom, Authority and Tolerance', pp. 142–3.
[10] Mac Aingil, *Scáthán Shacramuinte*, pp. 4, 166–7.
[11] See Cunningham, 'The Culture and Ideology of Irish Franciscan Historians'.

Catholic origins: how should one characterize the early Irish Church founded by Patrick? Was it, as some reformers such as James Ussher (1581–1656), Protestant bishop of Meath and later archbishop of Armagh, seemed to emphasize, proto-Protestant in character? What were its connections with Rome and the authority of the Roman pontiff? A particular difficulty for Irish Catholics who wanted to insist on the purity of the medieval Irish Church stemmed from the papal bull *Laudabiliter* of 1155. Issued by Adrian IV (pope 1154–9), the only English pope, this bull (whose authenticity would later be disputed) granted King Henry II of England (r. 1154–89) the lordship of Ireland, thus legitimating Henry's conquest of Ireland in 1169–71 as necessary to reform the Irish Church. The Anglo-Norman monk Giraldus Cambrensis (also known as Gerald of Wales, *c*.1146–*c*.1223) had given credence to this claim, suggesting in his writings that the twelfth-century Irish Church was in grave need of reform. For seventeenth-century Irish Catholic historians, the alleged papal sponsorship of the twelfth-century Anglo-Norman conquest was a particularly difficult issue to navigate. How might an increasingly assertive Irish Catholic community question the legitimacy of a papal bull?

A second, and related, question facing Irish Catholic writers concerned the place in Irish history of the Old English Catholics who had arrived in the wake of Henry II's conquest. Now that Irish Catholics were moving to forge a new common Catholic identity that included the native Irish and Old English over and against the Protestant newcomers, it might seem that to question the legitimacy of *Laudabiliter* and, in turn, the Anglo-Norman conquest itself, would not only offend the papacy but also undermine the Old English community's legitimacy and unnecessarily perpetuate division among Catholics rather than unite them. Thus these writers had to address the history of the Old English in Ireland, and most crucially the events surrounding their arrival as Anglo-Normans.

In sum, then, two key questions required urgent attention: (1) What are the origins of the Catholic Church in Ireland? (2) Who are the Irish Catholics? Within such a cultural context, 'hagiography, catechetics, and history blended together so that none developed in isolation from the others'.[12] In this period, therefore, it is very difficult to delineate clearly what should be regarded as national history, political history, and, indeed, what might be termed 'sacred history'. However, one thing is clear: these works, which aimed to forge an Irish Catholic identity that would transcend old ethnic divisions, aspired to the highest standards of late Renaissance humanist scholarship. They achieved this goal with varying degrees of success. This kind of scholarship was now being taught in the slowly evolving Irish grammar school system, exemplified in famous schools such as those of Peter White in Kilkenny and Richard

---

[12] Ibid., p. 15.

Creagh in Limerick, both established in the 1550s.[13] The seeds of Renaissance humanist learning sown in such schools would be brought to fruition in the confessional controversy which produced so many works of political, national, and sacred history from Irish writers during this period. It would grow to maturity in Irish Continental colleges such as those at Paris, Salamanca, Douai, and Louvain, in which so many Irish scholars received their professional training.

2. IRISH CATHOLIC ORIGINS

The task of rebutting the claims of that *bête noire* of Irish national historiography, the twelfth-century clergyman Giraldus Cambrensis, occupied a number of Irish writers from the early seventeenth century onwards, and thus provides a useful starting point for examining their methods and conclusions. One Old English scholar who might be regarded as a sixteenth-century embodiment of many of Cambrensis's views on Ireland is the Dublin-born Richard Stanihurst (1547–1618). While at Oxford during the 1560s, Stanihurst became a protégé of the English Jesuit Edmund Campion, and it was while visiting the Stanihursts' house in Dublin in 1570 that Campion would compile his *Two bokes of the Histories of Ireland*; this in turn greatly influenced Stanihurst's 'Description of Ireland', which he contributed to the *Chronicles* of Holinshed.[14] After Campion's execution in London in 1581, Stanihurst also fled to the Continent, where he would publish his *De rebus in Hibernia gestis* at Antwerp in 1584. This was essentially a Ciceronian rewriting and updating of Cambrensis's *Topographia hibernica* and *Expugnatio hibernica*. Cambrensis's manuscripts had been only recently rediscovered, and in this period his work was to exercise an influence perhaps far greater than that wielded during his own day, as it came to be seen as one of the leading writings on medieval Ireland.[15] Thus for many writers, both native Irish and Gaelicized Old English, Stanihurst came to be regarded as Giraldus Cambrensis reincarnate, and his critics would vehemently refute what they saw as the Cambrensian attempt to sully Ireland's reputation for scholarship and sanctity.

One of these critics, the Irish scholar Stephen White (1574–1646), born in Clonmel, County Tipperary, became in 1596 the first student of the Irish College in Salamanca to enter the Society of Jesus. As a Jesuit he wrote two works refuting the claims of Cambrensis and Stanihurst. The first of these, the

---

[13] Lennon, 'Pedagogy and Reform', p. 46. White's school produced such notable graduates as Richard Stanihurst and Peter Lombard.

[14] Barry, 'Derrike and Stanihurst: A Dialogue', p. 36.

[15] Harris, 'A Case Study in Rhetorical Composition', p. 126.

Apologia pro Hibernia in the 1610, was a direct answer to the English antiquarian William Camden's publication of Cambrensis's works in 1602. The second, the *Apologia pro innocentibus Ibernis*, was written in *c.*1630s in response to Stanihurst's *De rebus in Hibernia gestis.*[16] White's dismantling of Cambrensis's arguments embodies what Peter Burke identifies as one of the hallmarks of Renaissance historical scholarship: a keen 'awareness of evidence'.[17] White states in his later *Apologia* that he would like the reader to assent neither to Cambrensis's pronouncements nor to White's own counter-statements, but rather to find answers 'in my proofs (when you find them full and sound) and in the evidence of your own eyes'.[18] White demonstrates a certain suspicion of rhetoric, claiming that Cambrensis distorted evidence to suit his patrons and that his style lacked reliable argument, preferring rhetorical colour. Therefore, White attempts to convince the reader by exposing the glaring contradictions in Cambrensis's account, an argumentative style found in the well-known ancient rhetorical handbook, *Rhetorica ad Herennium.*[19] However, White's approach is less convincing when he suggests that Cambrensis's loose morals may have affected his accuracy as an historian.[20]

To counter Stanihurst's assertion that the medieval Irish Church was insufficiently Christian, White listed at length the names of Irish saints and martyrs who lived during this period. Likewise, he countered the claim that the native Irish are culturally and racially distinct from the Old English by producing long lists of instances of intermarriage between the two groups. White also questioned the authenticity of the papal bull *Laudabiliter*, stating the lack of contemporary evidence for its existence, highlighting instances of manuscript corruption and contending that it was not consistent with contemporary papal policy.[21] Although he was in fact mistaken on the question of the bull's authenticity, the manner in which White approached the question does suggest an awareness of humanist critical principles.

The Old English priest Geoffrey Keating (*c.*1570–*c.*1644), also from Tipperary, sought similarly to refute the account of Cambrensis and Richard Stanihurst, along with those of a host of other pro-English writers, including Edmund Spenser, Meredith Hanmer, William Camden, John Barclay, Fynes Moryson, Sir John Davies, and Edmund Campion. He saw all these scholars as denigrating Ireland's culture and heritage. Keating wished to replicate for Ireland what the humanist Hector Boece (*c.*1465–1536) had done for Scotland in his *Scotorum historiae*. In his *Foras Feasa ar Éirinn* ('*Compendium of Knowledge on Ireland*'), written in the early 1630s, Keating belittled Cambrensis as little more than a muckraker, by adapting a metaphor of the late twelfth-century English Cistercian, Odo de Ceritona, for corrupt clergy:

---

[16] Ibid., pp. 127–9.   [17] Burke, *The Renaissance Sense of the Past*, p. 1.
[18] Harris, 'A Case Study', p. 129.   [19] Ibid., pp. 131–3.
[20] Ibid., pp. 132.   [21] Ibid., p. 142.

for it is the fashion of the beetle, when it lifts its head in the summertime, to go about fluttering and not to stoop towards any delicate flower that may be in the field, or any blossom in the garden, though they be all roses and lilies, but it keeps bustling about until it meets with dung of horse or cow, and proceeds to roll itself therein.[22]

Keating's account serves as what Brendan Bradshaw calls a 'national narrative in a modern idiom', offering an origin legend for a newly emerging Irish nation with a newly forged Catholic identity.[23] He divides his history of Ireland into three epochs: the first from the earliest period to the conversion of Ireland to Christianity; the second constituting the golden age of saints and scholars, and the third from the arrival of the Anglo-Normans after 1169. Keating espouses the methods of humanist historiography by citing primary sources at length throughout the work. He retrieves from the earliest mythological material relating to Ireland the hallmarks of an early modern sovereign kingdom, including a monarchy (the high king), militia (the legendary *Fianna* warriors), a written law code (the Brehon Law), and a parliament (the *Aonach Tailteann*). The subsequent era of saints and scholars he portrays as being thoroughly Catholic in the best Tridentine sense: the structure of the early Church was diocesan and centred on Rome.[24] Keating thus sought to bolster many of the features of medieval Irish Catholicism which were under attack by Protestant reformers.

Keating's appeal to authorities did not always work particularly well, however. In one instance he makes an embarrassing error when attempting to demonstrate the Patrician identity of St Patrick's Purgatory (Lough Derg) in County Donegal, a famous Irish pilgrimage site which drew visitors from all over Europe in the Middle Ages. Tradition held that the site dated back to St Patrick himself and offered a way into the underworld. Meredith Hanmer (1543–1604), prebendary of Christ Church, Dublin, had attempted to debunk this idea by arguing that the Patrick associated with the Purgatory was an abbot who lived around 850. Keating challenged Hanmer's argument:

There is no truth in what he [Hanmer] says on the subject, as may be proved from St. Caesarius who lived about six hundred years after Christ, and, consequently, two centuries and a half before that second Patrick lived in this country. This holy writer says in the thirty-eighth chapter of his twelfth book entitled *Liber Dialogorum*: '*Let whomsoever has any doubt of Purgatory go to Scotia and enter the Purgatory of St Patrick and thenceforth he will no longer question the pains of Purgatory.*' From this quotation it is evident that St. Patrick's Purgatory was not

---

[22] Cunningham, *The World of Geoffrey Keating*, p. 115; Ó Dúshláine, 'Medium and Message', p. 79.

[23] Bradshaw, 'Reading Seathrún Céitinn's *Foras Feasa ar Éirinn*', p. 9.

[24] Ibid., pp. 9–10.

originally discovered or invented by the Patrick of whom Hanmer speaks, but that it was instituted by St. Patrick the Apostle.[25]

Unfortunately for Keating, his critique of Hanmer was based on a dating error. He had managed to confuse Caesarius of Arles (*c.*470–543) with the much later Caesarius of Heisterbach (*c.*1180–1240) from whose work *Dialogus magnus visionum atque miraculorum* (1481) the quotation derives. James Ussher in his *Discourse of the Religion Anciently Professed by the Irish and Brittish* (1631) referred to the same passage of Heisterbach, correctly calling Caesarius 'a Germane monke of the Cistercian order'.[26]

Despite this *faux pas*, Keating consistently presents himself in *Foras Feasa* as a rigorous humanist, using the principle of source criticism as a stick to beat English writers on Ireland with whom he disagrees; Fynes Moryson and others, he argues, break the rules of historical writing set forth by the Italian historian Polydore Vergil (1470–1555), principally through their ignorance of the primary sources. These writers on Ireland thus cannot support their claims with authority, for they are 'blind ignorant of the language of the country', and without knowledge of the sources, they fall into mere storytelling. In contrast, Keating argues, 'I saw and understand the primary sources of the tradition, whereas they did not; and even if they had seen them, they would not have understood them.'[27]

Irish Catholic writers sought to defend the medieval Irish Church not only from the Catholic critiques of Cambrensis and his latter-day admirer Stanihurst, but also from the sharper critiques of Protestant authors who used the argument of the Irish Church's medieval decadence as a premise for defending the Reformation. According to the Irish Jesuit Henry Fitzsimon (*c.*1566–1643), in his *A Catholicke Confutation of M. John Riders Clayme of Antiquitie* (Douai, 1608), John Rider, Protestant Dean of St Patrick's Cathedral, had asserted that the difference between the belief of the early Church and its medieval counterpart was 'as great, as betwixt protestancye and papistrie; because the first Catholicks, by his saying, had beene protestants'.[28] This vision of a pristine ancient Catholic Church, corrupted in the *medium aevum* and direly in need of a Reformation that would restore it to its original purity, was characteristic of Protestant historical thinking across Europe.[29] In the Irish context, such provocative statements would goad Irish Catholic writers of the seventeenth century into an increasingly confessional mode, as they sought to demonstrate that the Irish Church had never been corrupted, and that the seventeenth-century Catholic Church was its rightful heir.

---

[25] Keating, *Foras Feasa*, pp. xliii–xlv.
[26] Ussher, *Discourse*, ch. 3, p. 21.
[27] Ó Buachalla, p. 78 (translation mine).
[28] Cited in Ford, *James Ussher*, p. 13.
[29] See above, Ch. 2.

The definitive Irish response to Cambrensis's critique of the medieval Irish Church was undoubtedly that of the Galway priest John Lynch (*c.*1599–1677), in his *Cambrensis eversus* (*Cambrensis Overthrown*), published in Saint Malo in 1662.[30] Lynch had already worked on a Latin translation of Geoffrey Keating's *Foras Feasa ar Éirinn* to help make Keating's work known to readers on the Continent. He had also included large translated extracts of *Foras Feasa* in his own work.[31] Lynch dedicated *Cambrensis eversus* to the restored English monarch, Charles II (r. 1660–85), whom he hoped would be more sympathetic than the earlier Stuarts to the plight of Ireland's Catholics. In making the case for the toleration of Catholicism, Lynch likened the plight of Irish Catholics to that of fourth-century Christians under Julian the Apostate: Protestant authorities 'consign all our youth to the darkness of ignorance; for as [Julian] closed all the schools against the Christians they adopt similar measures against the education of our children'.[32] Most important of all, however, is Lynch's argument for the antiquity and continuity of the Irish Catholic faith: 'Is it a crime to profess that religion which securely appeals to antiquity for its truth, to long ages of existence for its permanence, and to its wide diffusion for its strength? . . . Tertullian also says "whatever is prior in time is truth; what is later is adulterated".'[33] Lynch insists that Catholics profess belief in the same articles of faith 'which the Magdeburg historians themselves admit were known and professed in ages immediately subsequent to the days of the apostles . . .'.[34] Such a rhetorical appeal to the sources and authorities of one's opposition was a common device in seventeenth-century Irish Catholic polemic; Geoffrey Keating, for instance, drew historical evidence from Richard Stanihurst and Sir John Davies when it suited his argument.[35]

The central aim of Lynch's *Cambrensis eversus* is to expose the fallacious nature of Cambrensis's material. Lynch situates this critical project within the larger context of Renaissance critical scholarship. For example, he draws attention to another notable instance in which a fable circulated among the vulgar for many centuries and was debunked by Renaissance erudition: the case of the legendary Pope Joan, 'which for 600 years had an undisputed hold on the minds of men until it was at length refuted by the most eminent writers—Cardinals Baronio and Bellarmino, Robert Parsons the Jesuit, Florimond Raimond, and David Blondel, a man of varied erudition, as far as heresy allows him'.[36] Lynch cites this cast of sixteenth-century scholars, four Catholics and one Protestant, to emphasize the necessity of bringing the most

---

[30] On Lynch, see d'Ambrières and Ó Cíosáin, 'John Lynch of Galway'.
[31] Ibid., p. 55.
[32] Lynch, *Cambrensis eversus*, I, p. 21.
[33] Lynch, *Cambrensis eversus*, I, p. 71.
[34] Ibid.
[35] Cunningham, *The World of Geoffrey Keating*, pp. 98–9.
[36] Lynch, *Cambrensis eversus*, p. 99.

rigorous standards of Renaissance scholarship to bear on one's subject (though just as Stephen White believed Cambrensis's loose morals to have had an adverse effect on his historical accuracy, so too Lynch understands the 'heresy' of the Huguenot Blondel to have had a debilitating effect on his scholarship).

Lynch's invocation of Cesare Baronio (1538–1607) is far less surprising than that of the Huguenot Blondel, as Baronio was now widely recognized as the modern Roman Catholic historian *par excellence.*[37] A fascinating earlier example of Irish deferral to the 'eminent' Baronio has been unearthed by Bernadette Cunningham in her study of on the *Annals of the Kingdom of Ireland* (more commonly known as *Annals of the Four Masters*), a secular work of chronology compiled in the 1630s to complement the Irish hagiographical project begun at Louvain. Two autograph manuscripts of the *Four Masters* diverge on whether St Patrick was sent to Ireland in the year 431 or 432. A correction is made, and the latter is substituted for the former in what becomes a reworked entry (and the entry noting the commission of Patrick's precursor, Palladius, is likewise moved back a year, from 430 to 431) on the authority of Cardinal Baronio's *Annales ecclesiastici*, for he had written that Pope Celestine sent Palladius to Ireland in 431. Thus where the native sources on which the *Four Masters* met the new standards of Baronian scholarship, the former gave way.[38]

To refute Cambrensis's claim that the Irish were ignorant of the most rudimentary elements of their faith, the *Cambrensis eversus* assembles copious historical evidence of medieval Irish piety, learning, and devotion to the papacy. One testament to the strength of Irish Christian learning is that the Irish were well known as missionaries to England: was it not 'absurd to suppose that men highly eminent for sanctity and learning would go forth to propagate the religion of Christ through most of the regions of Europe and leave the inhabitants of their own island without the bread of salvation?'[39] Further affirmation of Ireland's impeccably orthodox credentials is that Ireland alone among all Catholic kingdoms never incurred excommunication or papal interdict.[40] Loyalty to the pope was one of the hallmarks of Irish Catholicism, Lynch argued, and no other principle attracted more persecution for its adherents.[41] This devotion to the pope can be traced to the most ancient

---

[37] See above, Ch. 3.
[38] Cunningham, *The Annals of the Four Masters*, pp. 164–5.
[39] Lynch, *Cambrensis eversus*, II, p. 289.
[40] Ibid., p. 581.
[41] Ibid., p. 609–13; Salvador Ryan, '"Holding Up a Lamp to the Sun"'.

times, Lynch continues, quoting the assertion of Peter Lombard (d. 1160) that the Irish deferred to the apostolic see both in ecclesiastical and in temporal matters. Lynch also cites Polydore Vergil to the effect that the Irish subjected themselves and all their dominions to the authority of the apostolic see from the earliest days of Irish Christianity.[42] He notes that Keating dates this acknowledgement of papal temporal authority to a later period—the eleventh century—when the son of High King Brian Boru (d. 1014), Donough O'Brien, went on pilgrimage to Rome and surrendered the supreme dominion of Ireland into the hands of the pope.[43] Lynch does not, however, accept these historical accounts of Irish subordination to the pope in their entirety. While Lombard, Polydore, and Keating all asserted that the Irish deferred to the pope in temporal as well as spiritual matters, Lynch takes a more limited view. He doubts the accuracy of Polydore and Keating's accounts of the Irish surrender of temporal authority to the pope; in his view, the Irish Church surrendered religious but not temporal authority to Rome.[44]

As further support for the papal link with Ireland, Lynch cites André du Saussay (1589–1675)—bishop of Toul, theologian, and publisher of the *Martyrologium gallicanum* (Paris, 1637)—to the effect that St Mansuetus, an Irishman, went to Rome in AD 66 and was baptized by St Peter, prince of the Apostles.[45] Lynch continues at length in this vein, drawing further connections between the early Irish Church and the See of Peter until he admits, 'If I allowed myself to detail at length the intercourse of the Irish with Rome in former ages my page would swell to unreasonable limits and exhaust my power of language.'[46]

Positing decadence in the medieval Irish Church, as Cambrensis had done, was not the only way that earlier writers had undermined the image of Irish–Roman unity. The English Protestant Thomas Ryves, a former judge of faculties in the prerogative court of Ireland, had argued in his *Regiminis anglicani in Hibernia defensio adversus analecten libri tres* (*A defence of English rule in Ireland…*) (London, 1624) that before the arrival of King Henry II in Ireland, the Irish had followed the customs of the Greek and not the Latin Church. Ryves' allegation, based on the words of St Bernard, ran as follows:

> Before St. Celsus, predecessor of St. Malachy, there were eight married men bishops in the see of Ardmacha [Armagh] according to the custom of the Greeks (bless the mark!) whose bishops and priests were married.[47]

Ryves had also argued that fasting practices in Ireland, particularly the custom of fasting on Wednesday, were of Greek origin. Lynch countered Ryves's claim

---

[42] Lynch, *Cambrensis eversus*, II, p. 621.   [43] Ibid., p. 623.
[44] Ibid., p. 623.   [45] Ibid., pp. 623–5.
[46] Ibid., p. 635.   [47] Ibid., pp. 635–7.

by citing an observation of St Augustine that this was a custom among the Romans (who fasted for three days—Wednesday, Friday, and Saturday).[48]

Another historical claim Lynch felt called to refute was that the *Scotti* 'believing in Christ' to whom Pope Celestine had sent Patrick were Scots rather than Irish. This argument had been employed by a number of seventeenth-century Scottish 'saint-stealers', as they came to be regarded among the Irish. To counter the claim, Lynch piled authority upon authority to prove that the *Scotti* had not emigrated to *Albania* at this early stage. These authorities included Bede, Paul the Deacon, Cambrensis, Henry of Huntingdon, Polydore Vergil, Tommaso Bozio, and Joseph Scaliger.[49]

Most surprising of all, perhaps, Lynch underscored Ireland's ancient loyalty to the Roman Church by claiming that the Gospel had first been preached in Ireland by no less than one of the twelve Apostles. *Cambrensis eversus* cites Joseph Pellicer (1602–79), chronicler to King Philip IV of Spain, who in the course of expounding on the legend that St James the Apostle had preached the Gospel in Spain, had also claimed that there were 'many authorities and facts proving that James had also preached in Ireland'.[50] Here Lynch also quotes the work of his fellow countryman, the historian Philip O'Sullivan Beare (c.1590–1660), whose *Tenebriomastix* ('A Scourge for the Trickster'), written in the early 1630s, details how St James, on his return from Spain, had preached in Ireland, accompanied by his father Aristobolus or Zebedee, who stayed on after him as Ireland's first bishop. Only then had James passed over to Britain.[51] Lynch thus established an impeccable Roman and even apostolic pedigree for the Irish Church. Indeed, these early successes actually helped to explain the scarcity of recorded contacts between Rome and Ireland in the twelfth century, for such was the reliability of the Irish that 'when the popes beheld the Irish Church radiant with such surpassing splendour they relaxed for a considerable amount of time their ancient solicitude for the Irish, sending neither legates nor letters, lest they might be said to be holding up a lamp to the sun'.[52] This glory was almost extinguished by the arrival of the Vikings, after which, Lynch explained, the popes needed to renew their pastoral care of Ireland; hence the sending of papal legates such as Gilbert of Limerick, who presided over the Synod of Rathbreasail in 1111.[53]

Later seventeenth-century Irish Catholic writers repeatedly reasserted Ireland's traditional loyalty to Rome. David Rothe, in his *Analecta* of 1616, made the point that for the Irish 'hartie obedience to the apostolicall seate' had been 'sucked from the breath of the Romish fathers' through the mediacy of

---

[48] Ibid., p. 639.   [49] Ibid., pp. 655–7.
[50] Ibid., p. 663. On the legend of James in Spain, see above, Ch. 6.
[51] Lynch, *Cambrensis Eversus*, vol. II, p. 663.
[52] Ibid., p. 725.   [53] Ibid., p. 729.

Patrick.[54] In a move characteristic of this genre of writing, Rothe employs the testimony of a hostile witness to strengthen this point: he cites Lord Deputy Chichester's remarks that the very soil of Ireland seemed to be infected with the 'manure' of the Catholic faith, for settlers in Ireland seemed to convert as if the very clay were Catholic.[55] Therefore, Rothe argues, all efforts to uproot the Catholic faith will ultimately founder, for just as Tertullian had noted during the persecution of the early Church, the 'Catholique communion' became stronger through its suffering.[56]

Similar arguments were made by Philip O'Sullivan Beare in his *Historiae catholicae Iberniae compendium*, which was printed at Lisbon in 1621 and became the first published history of Catholic Ireland. O'Sullivan Beare wrote for a Spanish audience and dedicated the work to King Philip IV (r. 1621–65), underscoring Spain's value for Irish Catholics both as a political ally against an oppressive English monarchy and as a historical model of a Church with allegedly ancient ties to Rome. For O'Sullivan Beare, Ireland's loyalty to the papacy throughout its history was further proof that the papal bull *Laudabiliter* lacked authenticity, for how could the pope ever countenance denying 'their inheritance to these Christian men, who never deviated from the Church even by a nail's breadth?'[57] He contrasted the Catholic record of the Irish with that of their English counterparts, who already had a record of heresy: from the first arrival of Christianity in Britain in AD 156, the English Church had suffered from bouts of Pelagianism, Arianism, and relapses into paganism.[58] The later history of the English Church was no better, he continued, with Henry II murdering Thomas Becket, Henry VIII murdering Thomas More, a brief respite under Queen Mary, and then the return of England 'to its old vomit' under Queen Elizabeth.[59]

O'Sullivan Beare also makes every effort to identify Ireland's early history with that of Catholic Spain.[60] He emphasizes the 'Milesian myth' which details how the Irish race is descended from four sons of King Milesius of Spain, who came to Ireland in 1342 BC, and how since that date Ireland has been ruled by no less than 181 kings of Milesian lineage. In one notable episode from the distant past, a mythical king of Munster is restored to his kingship by 3,000 Spaniards after he flees to Spain and marries the king's

---

[54] Lennon, 'Political Thought', p. 199.

[55] O'Connor, 'Custom, Authority and Tolerance', p. 138.

[56] Lennon, 'Political Thought', p. 195.

[57] Morgan, 'Making Ireland Spanish', p. 90. For the late medieval Irish historical tradition, see Cunningham, *The Annals of the Four Masters*, ch. 3, pp. 41–73.

[58] Cunningham, *The Annals of the Four Masters*, ch. 3, pp. 92–3.

[59] Ibid., pp. 93.

[60] O'Sullivan Beare's historiography has also been compared with that of the Florentine humanist Francesco Guicciardini, whose *Historia d'Italia* influenced the Spanish historian Antonio Herrera y Tordesillas; see Carroll, 'Irish and Spanish Cultural and Political Relations', p. 135.

daughter. Like Lynch, O'Sullivan Beare also makes reference to Ireland's supposed link with St James the Apostle. Modern scholars have noted that throughout this period Ireland is spelt as *Ibernia* rather than *Hibernia* in an effort to create the optical illusion that the name is somehow cognate with *Iberia*.[61]

The acknowledgement of the role of outside intervention in restoring the golden age of Irish Christianity would be a consistent theme in many of the subsequent Irish Catholic histories written in the seventeenth century. The Irish Franciscan John Colgan (*c.*1600–*c.*1657) made this claim in the preface to his 1645 *Acta sanctorum Hiberniae* (discussed below). The coming of Patrick from outside had produced the first golden age of the Irish Church, which would later be shattered by the Vikings; revitalization then came through St Malachy and his ties with Bernard of Clairvaux, a renewal which would later be undone by King Henry VIII. From where, then, would the next eagerly awaited rejuvenation of the Irish Church now come? The implication was that regeneration would come, once again, from outside.[62]

Yet if the modern Irish Church needed outside help, this would merely represent a temporary inversion of Ireland's customary relationship to the rest of Catholic Europe; for historically, Irish Catholic authors were eager to point out, the Irish Church had been a net exporter of orthodox Catholicism, through its abundant saints. Indeed, one of the most effective ways for Irish Catholic writers to counter Protestant efforts to claim the early Irish Church as their spiritual patrimony was to present details of the lives of early Irish saints. Thomas Messingham (*c.*1575–1638?), a Douai-educated priest of the diocese of Meath, in his collection of Irish saints' lives entitled *Florilegium insulae sanctorum*, published at Paris in 1624, argued that the best way to refute heresy was to present the lives of the saints to the public 'and allow them to speak for themselves'.[63] The message was expected to be crystal clear; by reading the lives of the early saints one would discern a direct line of continuity between their beliefs and practices and those of the seventeenth-century Church. In Messingham's own words, 'We believe what our Fathers and Patrons believed, the testimony of Patrick, Columba and Brigid; what they taught we teach too, what they preached, we now preach.'[64]

The saints, therefore, would play a crucial part in seventeenth-century Irish Catholic polemics. The story of the Irish hagiographical renaissance of the seventeenth century is long and complex and has been well treated elsewhere.[65] Irish writers of both Old English and native Irish stock were

---

[61] Cunningham, *The Annals of the Four Masters*, ch. 3, pp. 96–7.
[62] Colgan, *Acta sanctorum*, quoted in Gillespie, 'The Irish Franciscans', p. 62.
[63] O'Connor, 'Towards the Invention of the Irish Catholic *Natio*', p. 168.
[64] Ibid., p.169.
[65] See Ryan, 'Steadfast Saints or Malleable Models?'; also Harris, 'Exiles and Saints in Baroque Europe'.

particularly proud of Ireland's saints and were eager to showcase their exemplary lives before a European audience, and at the same time to display their own humanist credentials. Geoffrey Keating, while praising both the Irish people in general and their saints in particular in the preface to *Foras Feasa*, states in so many words that Ireland is renowned across Europe as the continent's greatest exporter of saints:

> If, then, a true account were to be given of the natives of Ireland, they would be found as praiseworthy as any people in Europe, in these three qualities, namely in valour, in learning and in a steady adherence to the Catholic faith. I shall not here boast of the great number of our Irish saints because every European author confesses that Ireland produced more saints than any other country in Europe. It is also acknowledged that the empire of learning prevailed so widely in Ireland that swarms of learned men were sent forth therefrom to France, Italy, Germany, Flanders, England and Scotland, as is clearly shown in the preface of the book, written in English, which contains the lives of Saints Patrick, Columb-kille and Bridget . . . [66]

These lives, however, where possible, would now need to be solidly traceable to reputable sources.

The Irish Franciscan John Colgan was largely responsible for the mammoth project of compiling dossiers of all the available material on the lives of Irish saints in the 1640s, resulting in major works such as *Acta sanctorum Hiberniae* (1645) and *Triadis thaumaturgae* ('The Acts of a Wonder-working Triad') (1647). He made sure to attribute the contents of the lives comprehensively to particular authors or Lives. In the preface to *Triadis Thaumaturgae*, which recounted the lives of Saints Patrick, Brigid, and Columba, he explained that the virtues of these wonderful saints, often ridiculed by heretics, required a proper presentation of their documentation and sources.[67] Colgan's work has been said to exhibit a Renaissance humanist mindset, especially in the area of heuristics, and in the author's enthusiasm for the humanist rallying cry, '*ad fontes*'.[68] Thomas Messingham and other Catholic hagiographers believed that if the sources were examined thoroughly, it would become evident that the early Irish saints were the polar opposites of the Protestants who were attempting to appropriate them for their own purposes. In this spirit, the Franciscan Robert Rochford in his 1625 work, *The life of the glorious bishop S. Patricke apostle and primate togeather with the lives of the holy virgin Bridgit and of the glorious abbot S. Columbe patrons of Ireland*, presented Patrick's life as a model of Catholic orthodoxy:

---

[66] This refers, presumably, to the Franciscan, Robert Rochford's work on Patrick, Bridget and Columcille, published at St Omer in 1625.

[67] Robert Rochford, *The life . . . of S. Patricke . . .* , p. ix; quoted in Ryan, 'Steadfast Saints', pp. 261–2.

[68] MacCraith, 'Gaelic Ireland and the Renaissance', p. 79.

He liued an hundred and two and twenty yeares, most part of which tyme he spent in reclayming the Irish from idolatry to the agnition of one true God: during the course of so many yeares so fruitfully spent among us, his pen neuer deliuered, his tongue neuer uttered, nor himself neuer practised indeed any thing that might haue the least colour of fauoring or establishing that Religion, which the preachers of the fift[h] Ghospel proudly vaunt, and vainely boast, to be the doctrine and faith of the Primitiue Church . . . We offer here S. Patricke's Life . . . let them search it & point vs out what they shall find in it to countenance their cause, or to aduance their religion . . . [69]

Irish writers who aspired to the rigorous critical scholarship of the Renaissance were not always consistent in how they applied the standards that they set for themselves. John Colgan's method when dealing with saints' lives was to edit the best text rather than produce a critical text, and his reverence for the lives of holy men could disarm his critical faculties on occasion.[70] In 1640, Stephen White would write to Colgan to remind him to remain vigilant about dubious material, for 'the lives of SS Ailbe, Declan, and Gerald of Mayo, who are mentioned in the catalogue you sent me, are swarming (if the Lives you have are the same as those I have read here) with improbable fables'[71] Geoffrey Keating could be selective in his view of what constituted reputable and spurious material. For instance, he criticizes Edmund Campion for his inclusion of a tale relating how Saints Patrick and Peter became involved in a dispute over the destination of an Irish galloglass, or mercenary, who teetered at the brink of the heavenly gates. When Patrick attempts to overrule Peter's rejection of the Irishman, the chief Apostle is forced to crack open Patrick's skull with his set of keys. Keating castigates Campion for including such a 'stupid fable' in his work.[72] However, in another part of *Foras Feasa* Keating relates that in the year 527 'the head fell off a cripple at the fair, or assembly, of Tailti, because he had sworn falsely by the hand of St. Kieran. Some say that he lived amongst the monks for the space of five years without a head',[73] without further comment.

3. CREATING IRISH CATHOLICS IN THE SEVENTEENTH CENTURY

One of the most sensitive areas where the humanist technique of historical textual criticism could be applied to the cause of defending the Irish Catholic

[69] Ryan, 'Steadfast Saints', pp. 261–2.

[70] MacCraith, 'Gaelic Ireland and the Renaissance', p. 79.

[71] Richard Sharpe, *Medieval Irish Saints' Lives: An Introduction to Vitae Sanctorum Hiberniae* (Oxford: Clarendon Press, 1991), p. 60.

[72] Keating, *Foras Feasa*, p. li.

[73] Ibid., p. 429.

Church concerned *Laudabiliter*, the papal bull of 1155 issued by Pope Adrian IV which granted the lordship of Ireland to Henry II of England so that he might reform both Ireland's religion and its morals.[74] By the seventeenth century, Giraldus Cambrensis's *Expugnatio hibernica* (*c.*1188) contained the only record of this papal document. This gave seventeenth-century Irish Catholic writers several options for challenging it, although they would have to do so cautiously in order to prevent a clash with Rome. It might be argued, for one, that the bull was legitimate but that the Irish had been misrepresented to the papacy or, alternatively, that the papal document was a forgery of Cambrensis's concoction. As we saw above, the Jesuit Stephen White took the bolder, second option, denouncing *Laudabiliter* as a forgery. To reinforce the point that there was no need for such a bull, White cited a work of Icelandic Protestant scholar Arngrímur Jónson (1568–1648) entitled *Crymogaea sive rerum islandicarum* (Hamburg, 1609), which told of a hibernicized Viking called Ornulfus who established a church dedicated to Columcille (Columba) in pagan Iceland. In White's view, this demonstrated that the medieval Irish Church had not only survived the Viking invasions intact, but was confident enough to be missionary in outlook, and thus could not possibly have been in the appalling state that the bull *Laudabiliter* alleged.[75]

The Old English historian Geoffrey Keating's response was somewhat more conservative. In *Foras Feasa*, he declined to declare *Laudabiliter* a forgery, but like White he used various arguments to defend the Irish against the charge of irreligion brought against them by Pope Adrian IV's bull. The principal arguments used by Keating are as follows: (1) In the period before the Norman invasion many of the chief nobles of Ireland routinely chose to end their days in penance and prayer in the most important churches (here read also monasteries) of Ireland and Europe.[76] (2) Irish noblemen built a large number of monasteries immediately prior to the Anglo-Norman invasion (including notable Cistercian foundations).[77] (3) Church councils were held in Ireland in the period immediately prior to the Norman invasion. This third argument of Keating's is somewhat risky, for elsewhere he admits that such early councils could be evidence of disciplinary or doctrinal issues within the Irish Church. Thus he takes pains here to explain that the Synod of Kells of 1152 'was the council convened for the purpose of presenting the four *pallia*, that is, for instituting four archbishops over Ireland, and also for condemning simony and usury; for enforcing the payment of tithes, and for putting down robbery, and violence, and lust, and bad morals, and every other evil thenceforth'.[78]

However, the problem remained: how might Keating explain the papal bull and the subsequent Anglo-Norman settlement in a manner that would stress a

[74] Morgan, 'The Island Defenders'.   [75] Ibid.
[76] Keating, *Foras Feasa*, p. 639.
[77] Ibid., p. 640.   [78] Ibid., p. 641.

degree of continuity from ancient Ireland and yet still embrace the 'Old English' as members of a kingdom which would henceforth be 'the common patrimony of the natives who established it and its twelfth-century conquerors'?[79] Keating achieved this by arguing that the papal bull was the result of a constitutional adjustment initiated by Irish ruling elites to resolve a series of power struggles after the death of High King Brian Boru in 1014. In 1092, Keating explained, the disputed high king, Donough O'Brien, with the agreement of the nobility, had entrusted sovereign authority to Pope Urban II (pope 1188–99). The *translatio imperii* had thus been in train long before the bull *Laudabiliter* of 1155, and the native ruling elite, in conjunction with the ecclesiastics, were its prime instigators. Keating also drew attention to the obligation that this bull placed on Henry II of England to 'maintain and protect the privileges and liberties (*tearmain*) of the country', guaranteeing the status of the island as a kingdom.[80]

Keating also took pains to refute the claim by Cambrensis and others that in ancient times the kings of Ireland had rendered fealty to the English monarch. In *Foras Feasa*, he drew on the testimonies of English antiquarians such as John Speed (1552–1629) and William Camden (1551–1623) to support his own contention that ancient Ireland had never been subjected to foreign jurisdiction.[81] Likewise, he challenged the claim of Meredith Hanmer and others that the archbishop of Canterbury had had jurisdiction over Irish clergy from the time of Augustine of Canterbury (d. 604) onwards. Keating cited the authority of James Ussher in support of this point:

> It is nowhere found that the prelates of Canterbury had ever claimed any authority over any portion of the clergy of Ireland except during the prelacies of the Archbishops Lanfranc, Ranulph, and Anselm; and even then it was only over a few of the Irish clergy that they held supremacy . . . This fact is clearly proved in the work of Doctor Usher.[82]

Although Keating's *Foras Feasa* gives a relatively short account of the Anglo-Norman conquest, it is perhaps the most crucial section in the entire work. As a descendant of the Anglo-Normans, Keating needed to accord them a share in a common history of the Irish. *Foras Feasa* expanded the traditional image of Irish identity represented in the eleventh-century *Lebar Gabála Érenn* (literally, *Book of the Taking of Ireland*) by including the Anglo-Normans in the story, albeit as latecomers. It was very clear, however, that the New English settlers of the sixteenth century were excluded, and by several centuries; Keating drew a clear distinction between the twelfth-century Anglo-Norman conquest and the more recent Elizabethan conquests. This distinction was not shared by all Irish chroniclers; Philip O'Sullivan Beare described both

---

[79] Bradshaw, 'Geoffrey Keating', p. 174.   [80] Ibid., pp. 175–6.
[81] Ibid., pp. 171–2.   [82] Keating, *Foras Feasa*, p. 598.

conquests as destructive and unjust.[83] Keating does not admire the twelfth-century Anglo-Norman invaders per se; indeed he presents them more as ruthless *conquistadores* than as Christian crusaders; he names five in particular—Richard Strongbow, Robert FitzStephen, Hugo de Lacy, John de Courcy, and William FitzAldelm—who committed acts of bloodshed and reckless violence. Those who perpetrated such atrocities did not prosper, and many met horrific ends. On William FitzAldelm, for instance, Keating reports that:

> God sent down a foul and incurable disease upon this man, as a punishment for his evil deeds, and . . . he finally suffered a loathsome death in consequence thereof. He received neither penance nor extreme unction, nor was his body laid in any consecrated ground, but he was buried on a desolate farm.[84]

However, Keating goes on to redeem his twelfth-century forbears through a providential reading of history—essentially the notion that 'God writes straight with crooked lines.' While the first wave of Anglo-Normans was duly punished, he reports, the second wave behaved differently, prospered, and 'conferred many benefits upon Ireland, inasmuch as they built churches and monasteries, and performed many good works besides. Therefore in reward thereof has God granted them the blessing of a numerous progeny.'[85] While this was a skilful way of rehabilitating the Old English within Irish Catholic history, Keating's account of the variant fortunes of the early Anglo-Normans also conveyed a warning for the 1630s: that 'those who collaborated with unacceptable New English activities were contravening the moral order'[86] and would come to a similarly nasty end.

4. CONCLUSIONS

Late sixteenth and seventeenth-century Ireland participated fully in the renewal of ecclesiastical history that was a feature of Reformation and Counter-Reformation Europe as a whole. However, in the case of Ireland, there was far more at stake than debating whether Protestantism represented continuity with or schism from the traditions of the early Church (although this question did, of course, play a prominent role in the polemics of the period). At a time when new Protestant settlers were arriving and new displacements of Catholics were occurring, there was the issue of identity to sort out—who might properly be considered to be Irish and, conversely (and perhaps more importantly) who

---

[83] Carroll, 'Irish and Spanish Cultural and Political Relations', p. 235.
[84] Keating, *Foras Feasa*, p. 646.
[85] Ibid., p. 651.
[86] Cunningham, *The World of Geoffrey Keating*, p. 121.

might not. This matter was, of course, not merely a question of ethnicity, but also of religion. The forging of a new Irish Catholic identity, which embraced the descendants of the Anglo-Norman settlers of the twelfth century, would necessitate a historical narrative that could clearly establish these ethno-religious boundaries. In charting their way through a changing political and cultural landscape, Irish Catholic writers, both at home and on the Continent, would attempt to bring to bear on their polemical works the standards of Renaissance humanist scholarship. In some cases they did so with more success than others; however, whatever their achievements in this regard, none of these writers remained in doubt as to the new standards of scholarship that were coming to be universally expected if one was to make an impression on the emerging European republic of letters.

Part III

Uses of Sacred History
in the Early Modern Catholic World

10

The Lives of the Saints in the French Renaissance *c*.1500–*c*.1650[*]

Jean-Marie Le Gall

The European Renaissance witnessed not only the rediscovery of Antiquity and of its great men and literature, but also a revitalization of less ancient literary forms under the influence of humanism and the humanist passion for returning *ad fontes* (to the sources). This included a hagiographic renaissance in the various medieval genres devoted to writing about the lives of saints. In Italy, poets like Baptista Spagnoli of Mantua (1448–1516) used the renewed power of poetry to glorify the saints through *laudationes* or hymns. Biographers such as Giovanni Garzoni (1419–1505) rewrote the lives of the *Golden Legend* to conform to the standards of humanist eloquence.[1] Some authors pursued more philological and historical directions by collecting, editing, and translating new collections of ancient saints' lives, such as Bonino Mombrizio's *Sanctuarium* (Milan, 1480), Georg Witzel's *Hagiologium seu de sanctis ecclesiae* (Mainz, 1541), and Luigi Lippomano's *Catalogus sanctorum* (Venice, 1551). By the last quarter of the sixteenth century, these interests were widely diffused across Europe. The main centres for European hagiography were Cologne, Antwerp, and Rome. In Cologne, the Carthusian friar Lorenz Sauer (Laurentius Surius) built on Lippomano's work, arranged it according to the liturgical calendar, and published the results (*De probatis sanctorum historiis*) between 1570 and 1578. In Rome, Cesare Baronio and his assistants corrected the Roman martyrology and wrote their massive *Annales* of the Church. The Jesuit Héribert Rosweyde (1569–1629) would print the *Fasti sanctorum* (Antwerp, 1607), thus launching the enterprise of the *Acta sanctorum*, which the Jesuit Jean Bolland (1596–1665) and his disciples would continue down to modern times.[2]

---

[*] Translated by Katherine Van Liere.
[1] See Frazier, *Possible Lives*, chs. 3 and 4.
[2] See above, Chs. 3 (on Baronio) and 4 (on other Catholic hagiographic enterprises from Baronio to the Bollandists); on the latter, see also Godding et al., *Bollandistes saints et légendes*.

As Simon Ditchfield has shown above (Ch. 4), these scholarly enterprises involved exhaustive individual and collective efforts to gather sources, and extensive learned correspondence and travel. Such large-scale collaborative efforts, which gave the renaissance of European hagiography some of its most characteristic features, enabled not only the publication of new collections of saints' lives such as those just mentioned, but also the first printed editions of much older martyrologies such as the ninth-century 'Little Roman Martyrology' (or *Vetus romanum*) published by Rosweyde in 1613.

It may appear at first that there were no French protagonists in this hagiographic renaissance, but Renaissance France was in fact fertile soil for writing about the lives of the saints. In the seventeenth century, the Maurists, Bollandists, and other leading Catholic scholars recognized France as one of the nations whose scholars had mastered both sacred and profane history as well as the history of positive theology.[3] When Lodovico Antonio Muratori (1672–1750), the great Italian scholar of Enlightened Catholic reform (*'riformismo illuminato'*), published his *Della regolata devozione dei cristiani* in 1747, he cited the seventeenth-century French Jesuits Théophyle Raynaud (1583–1663), Jean-Baptiste Thiers (1636–1790), and Adrien Baillet (1649–1706) as foundational to his own work. He could easily have named even more French scholars, for the reign of Louis XIV (1643–1715) was the golden age of French Catholic scholarship.

The French Catholic scholars of the Baroque era were deeply indebted to their Renaissance predecessors. Sixteenth-century French Catholics took great interest in the lives of the saints, and French Renaissance scholars treated these lives in a rich variety of literary genres. Indeed, a survey of French Renaissance hagiography affords a valuable way to approach Renaissance hagiography at large, for most of the major intellectual and religious movements of the early modern period were manifested in Western Europe's largest Catholic kingdom, including humanism, scholasticism, and Protestantism. The varied forms of Renaissance hagiographic writing that flourished in early modern France responded, as they did elsewhere in Europe, to a range of cultural appetites for the sacred. But hagiography also faced certain challenges in this period, some inspired by religious developments and some resulting from new intellectual currents. By the seventeenth century, some traditional forms of hagiographic writing were in decline, and some long-cherished saints' legends had been called into question. Indeed, critical scholarship of the seventeenth century is sometimes accused of 'disenchanting' the cult of saints. One must not, however, exaggerate the extent of this disenchantment, for the critical scholarship of the early modern period remained deeply religious in character.

---

[3] Quantin, *Le catholicisme classique.*

1. LITERARY GEOGRAPHY OF THE LIVES
OF THE SAINTS

Saints' lives were often presented in the form of small volumes dedicated to a single saint. Between the birth of printing in France and 1550, seventy-five saints' lives were printed in French, treating sixty-five saints.[4] After Paris, the principal centres of publication were Lyon and Rouen. Such editions catered to a popular appetite for devout and edifying literature. These individual lives formed a Renaissance legendary that was heavily indebted to medieval hagiographic collections. The most important of these collections, Jacobus de Voragine's *Golden Legend*, a thirteenth-century hagiographic encyclopaedia, has deeply influenced writing about the saints down to modern times. Since 1476 it has been reprinted in eighty-eight Latin editions and eighteen French editions. It joined a wider Renaissance body of cheap popular literature that was exemplified by such works as Noël du Faïl's *Propos rustiques* (Lyon, 1547), a collection of rustic folktales. A later medieval catalogue of saints' lives composed by Pietro de' Natali (Petrus de Natalibus, d. *c*.1400) was printed in Latin at Strasbourg in 1513 and at Lyon in 1542, and a French translation was printed at Paris in 1524.

The hagiographic renaissance that occurred across Europe in the fifteenth and sixteenth centuries was by no means ignored in France. The translation of such work into French stimulated a renewal of native French hagiographical writing. The Fontevrist monk Gabriel Dupuyherbault (*c*.1490–1566) produced his own translation of Luigi Lippomano's saints' lives, revised from a Gallican perspective, at Rome (1558–60), which Parisian printer Michel de Roigny published in 1577 under the title *Histoire, vie et légendes de saints*. Jacques Tigeon produced another French translation of Lippomano in 1607.[5] In 1608, Jacques Gaulthier translated the Spanish Jesuit Pedro de Ribadeneyra's *Flos sanctorum*, which the Sorbonnist André Duval supplemented with the lives of forty more French saints.[6] These anthologies, or *florilegia*, which essentially replaced the popular medieval *Golden Legend*, served as the most common vehicles for the lives of the saints until the nineteenth century.

As in the Middle Ages, saints' lives and sermons continued to influence one another. At the beginning of the sixteenth century there appeared various collections of *sermones de sanctis*. This genre was inherited from medieval authors and compilers such as Anthony of Padua and Jacobus de Voragine. Their Renaissance authors included Nicolas Denysse (1507), Olivier Maillard (1507, 1513), Jean Raulin (1524, 1530, and 1611), Guillaume Pépin (1536),

---

[4] Bledniak, 'L'hagiographie: Œuvres imprimée en français 1476–1550'.
[5] On Lippomano, see Gajano (ed.), *Raccolte di vite di santi del XIII al XVIII secolo*.
[6] This was reprinted at Paris in 1609, 1618, 1632, and 1664. Another translation appeared at Lyon in 1649, with a table for preachers.

and François Le Picart (1566) all of whose sermons were published after their death.[7] The great preachers of the Wars of Religion, like Simon Vigor, Jean Boucher, René Benoist, François Feuardent, Jacques Le Bossu, and Gilbert Génébrard, seem to have abandoned this genre, but in the seventeenth century it regained popularity.[8] Martial du Mans's *Almanach spirituel* (1647) shows that sermons on the saints were still frequently delivered from Paris pulpits, although the publication of sermons in this period declined. The second half of the seventeenth century saw something of a publishing revival, as the sermons of such preachers as Jacques Biroat (d. 1666) and Antoine Castillon (1599–1671) were posthumously printed in 1676. Sermons not only waxed and waned in frequency; they also evolved in style over the course of the French Renaissance. Early sixteenth-century sermons still largely followed medieval forms, with their scholastic subdivisions. Later Renaissance writers introduced the classical model of panegyric, which presented specific virtues that could be associated with the lives of particular saints.[9]

Sermons on the saints were not just preached to live audiences; they were also preserved in the Church's written liturgy. In the sixteenth century, many French dioceses produced published martyrologies, collections of the lives of martyrs. The collections often interpolated and embellished their medieval sources. The creativity of some of these sixteenth-century martyrologies was brought to light in the seventeenth century, when several controversies erupted about the historical authenticity of saints' legends that had flourished in the Middle Ages and Renaissance, the most notable case being that of St Denis the Areopagite.[10]

In the sixteenth century, the main field of scholarly reform was the Roman martyrology, whose revision was undertaken under papal auspices first by Pietro Galesini and then by Cesare Baronio. Some French scholars, most notably the Jesuit Jacques Sirmond (1559–1651), contributed to this project, and the revised Roman Martyrology, which was first published in Rome in 1583, also saw publication in France beginning in 1584.[11] This Roman project stimulated further researches into various French diocesan martyrologies, and inspired a Gallican project, André Du Saussay's *Martyrologium gallicanum*

---

[7] Taylor, *Heresy and Orthodoxy in Sixteenth Century Paris*.

[8] Martin, *Livre, pouvoirs et société à Paris au XVIIe siècle*, II, p. 788.

[9] Truchet, *Bossuet panégyriste*.

[10] Le Gall, *Le Mythe de saint Denis*, pp. 275–84. 'Saint Denis' was understood to combine three identities that later scholars disentangled into three distinct figures: Dionysius the Areopagite (a convert of St Paul mentioned in the Acts of the Apostles 17:34); Pseudo-Dionysius, the author of the mystical *Corpus Areopagiticum*; and Denis the first bishop of Paris and patron saint of France, whose relics were venerated at the Abbey of Saint Denis.

[11] Further French editions (in Latin) of the *Martyrologium romanum* were published in 1607 and 1625, and a French translation was published in 1676.

(1637).[12] Scholars in France and beyond would judge this work rather severely, but it was approved by the censor Jean de Launoy, the same famous scholar who learnedly dismantled the St Denis legend.[13]

In the seventeenth century, the enterprise of revising the martyrology became one aspect of a European-wide movement to compose catalogues of saints who were associated not with any one religious order but with particular territories, whether by birth, residence, preaching, death, or the presence of their relics. These catalogues served not so much to construct a sacred Europe as to highlight the sacred histories of political and national entities by localizing and appropriating the universal.[14] This movement seems to have begun in the Low Countries with Johannes Molanus's *Natales sanctorum belgiis* (1595), which was expanded in 1625 by Arnold de Raisse. In Bavaria, the Jesuit Matthias Rader published *Bavaria sacra* between 1615 and 1628.[15] In Italy, the Tuscan Camaldolese Abbot Silvano Razzi began editing a *Vite de' santi e beati Toscane* in 1593. Giovanni Arca did the same for Sardinia in 1591. The Servite monk Filippo Ferrari's *Catalogus sanctorum* (1613) was followed by Ferdinando Ughelli's *Italia sacra* (9 vols., 1644–62).[16] These publications treating the saints of the whole peninsula complemented regional collections, like those of Ludivico Jacobelli for Umbria, and Ottavio Gaetani's research on the saints of Sicily (begun in 1617 and published posthumously in 1657).[17] All these large collections rested on the backs of local researches.

The enterprise of recording the lives of the bishops of a particular diocese, or *chronologia praesulum*, embodied a Europe-wide Counter-Reformation impulse to establish the antiquity of Catholic dioceses. Against Protestants, Catholic scholars, such as Antoine de Mouchy, alias Démocharès (1494–1574), reasserted the continuity of the Church with apostolic times by identifying the earliest possible diocesan founders.[18] In 1573, the reformist Catholic cardinal and bishop of Milan Carlo Borromeo (1538–84) urged European bishops to preserve the memory of their predecessors. The enterprise accelerated towards the end of the sixteenth century and reached its peak between 1600 and 1650, with seventy more works appearing; it then declined considerably over the

---

[12] Du Saussay's *Martyrologium gallicanum*, which borrowed heavily from Vincent Barralis's lives of the saints of Lérins and from Dom Marrier's work on Cluny, restored many French saints whom the Roman martyrology had omitted.

[13] On Launoy, see Grès-Gayer, 'L'Aristarque de son siècle'; Le Gall, *Le Mythe de saint Denis*, chs. 7 and 8.

[14] Le Gall, 'Denis, George, Jacques, Antoine, André, Patrick et les autres'.

[15] See above, Ch. 7.

[16] On Skarga, Ferrario, and Rader, see Boesch Gajano et al. (eds.), *Europa sacra: Raccolte agiografiche e identità politiche*. For Ughelli, see Hay, 'Scholars and Ecclesiastical History'; Ditchfield, *Liturgy, Sanctity and History*, ch. 12.

[17] Cabibbo, *Il paradiso del magnifico regno*.

[18] Lemaitre, 'Le Culte épiscopal et la résistance au protestantisme au XVIe siècle'.

next century, and disappeared almost completely after 1750.[19] These works, produced primarily by canons, jurists, and the clergy, aspired to assemble a complete list of all French bishops, with special attention given to saints and *beati*, and sometimes including dioceses outside France as well. The most important of these collections was the *Gallia christiana*, different versions of which were published by Jean Chenu (1621), Claude Robert (1626), and the two Sainte-Marthe brothers (1656).[20] Containing only brief lives, they were concerned mainly with compiling accurate names and dates.

Hagiography was essential not only for liturgy and episcopal identity, but also for patristics, as some saints were also authors and thus religious authorities in their own right. It became common in the Renaissance to preface editions of patristic works with short biographies of the authors. Erasmus went a step further and published separate lives of some of the Church Fathers, including Jerome and Origen.[21] In 1512, Jacques Merlin published an edition of Origen's works together with a life and an appended Apologia that defended the orthodoxy of this controversial Greek theologian. Some lives published in the Renaissance were older compositions, like the early medieval life of St John Damascene, attributed to John the Patriarch of Jerusalem, that Jacques de Billy appended to his edition of Damascene's works.[22] Hagiography was particularly valuable for saints whose authorship of important works was contested, as in the case of Dionysius the Areopagite; his biography served to authorize his corpus of writings. In his 1498 edition of Dionysius's works, Jacques Lefèvre d'Etaples included a letter by the translator Ambrogio Traversari confirming Dionysius's authorship and identifying him as a disciple of St Paul. This was intended to refute doubts that had been raised about Dionysius's authorship in the Middle Ages and recently revived by Lorenzo Valla. As the polemic over this saintly author's life grew more intense, translators prefaced his works with steadily more hagiographic material, in either Latin or French.

At first, the principal aim of the Catholic editors of patristic works was to publish elegant Catholic translations that would correct the supposed errors of Erasmus and compete with Protestant editions.[23] The first such *patrologia* published in Paris in 1575, that of Margerin de la Bigne, took more pains to identify the authors' works and to affirm their orthodoxy than to relate their lives in detail, in a manner similar to Trithemius's *Scriptoribus ecclesiasticis* (1494) or Sixtus of Siena's *Bibliotheca sacra* (1566). La Bigne was certainly inspired by Surius's great catalogue of saints, but he imitated the German scholar's collecting spirit more than his scholarly precision; La

---

[19] Of the twelve known episcopal lists compiled in sixteenth-century France, nine were produced after 1550; see Le Gall, 'Catalogues et séries de vies d'évêques'.

[20] Poncet, 'La *Gallia christiana* des frères Sainte-Marthe'.

[21] Godin, *Erasme lecteur d'Origène*; Rice, *Saint Jerome in the Renaissance*.

[22] Backus, *La Patristique et les guerres de religion en France*, p. 120.

[23] Backus, *La Patristique et les guerres de religion*, p. 131.

Bigne's Roman critics reproached him for having applied the title '*sanctus*' too liberally.[24] But as Renaissance scholarship became increasingly critical over the course of the sixteenth and seventeenth centuries, anonymous or uncertain authors enjoyed less and less authority, and reliable knowledge of the author's life became correspondingly more important.[25] In this climate, the editions of the Church Fathers which issued from Port-Royal Abbey in the 1640s also stimulated new writing about their lives. The authority of a text required a credible biography. To this end Antoine Le Maistre wrote a life of St Bernard in 1648, and Godefroy Hermant (1617–90) produced biographies of Ambrose, Athanasius, and Chrysostom.[26] Works that could not be reliably attributed now lost authority; the editions of St Denis's works, for example, ceased after 1650, once the author's identity had become decisively challenged. The new label 'pseudo-Dionysius' suggested a figure of doubtful authority, an unknown old writer without a life.

Theatre served as another way to record the lives of the saints. Verse plays on the lives of the saints remained popular in the sixteenth century, despite some attempts to prohibit them. The Parlement of Paris banned the performance of mystery plays in 1548, but the practice continued in the provinces, despite periodic prohibitions like those issued in Brittany beginning in 1565.[27] Of the five medieval mystery plays that were reprinted after 1550, three concern early saints: Mary Magdalene, Margaret, and Barbara. Protestants by this time were beginning to substitute biblical tragedies for medieval mystery plays, and Catholic dramatists were reluctant to abandon the field of sacred drama to their confessional rivals. After the humanists, the Jesuits advocated a new scholastic theatre in their schools. The theatre offered an excellent venue for dramatizing the heroism of the saints, especially the martyrs.

By the early seventeenth century, in France as well as in Italy, there was increasing demand for theatrical works to be used in the public celebration of saints' feasts, and many medieval mystery plays were reworked and repub-lished.[28] In France, John Spencer Street's inventory for the dramatic representations of sacred themes identified 190 for the century from 1550 to 1650, a figure that will undoubtedly be revised upwards in due course.[29] For example, I have located a play on the life of the sixth-century abbot St Bertin that was performed at the Jesuit College of Saint Omer on 13 September 1621.[30] André

---

[24] Petitmengin, 'Deux bibliothèques de la Contre Réforme'.

[25] Jehasse, *La Renaissance de la critique*.

[26] Quantin, *Le Catholicisme classique*, pp. 206–48.

[27] Gwennolé Le Menn, *Histoire du théâtre populaire breton XVe–XIXe siècles* (Saint Brieuc: Institut Culturel de Bretagne, 1983), pp. 37–8.

[28] For Italy, see Cioni, *Bibliografia delle sacre rappresentazioni*.

[29] Street, *French Sacred Drama*, pp. 249–97.

[30] *St Bertin, parfait religieux... représenté en la grand court du susdict monastère par la jeunesse du collège de la compagnie de Jésus à Saint Omer*, Bibliothèque Nationale de France (Paris), res. M-YF-24.

Stegmann has discovered fourteen plays put on by the Jesuits at La Flèche, whose Jesuit authors included Denis Pétau, the great chronologer.[31] Of the fourteen La Flèche dramas, six dealt with saints, among whom Eustasius, Hermenegilde and Adrian (alias St Genest or Genesius) were familiar figures in sacred drama. Of the 190 productions of sacred drama listed by Street 109 were devoted to saints.

In addition to the scholastic and popular representation of saints' lives, a new theatrical genre emerged, performed by professional theatre troupes, which Georges Couton has called the 'comedy of devotion'. This was influenced by Rome, especially Cardinal Rospigliosi, the future Pope Clement IX, and by Spain.[32] It became fashionable in high society between the 1630s and 1650s, when the Parisian theatre companies the Théâtre du Marais, the Hôtel de Bourgogne, and the Théâtre Illustré were active. The most famous example of this rather short-lived genre was Pierre Corneille's *Polyeucte* (1643). Compelled to observe the Aristotelian rule of unity of time, place, and action, these plays were not true life stories. Playwrights generally focused on the climactic episode of martyrdom, and did not feel obliged to follow the scholarly accounts rigorously, but often wove in intrigue-laced secondary plots that had no historical basis. Thus in his preface to *Polyeucte*, Corneille gave a summary of the martyrdom of this little-known third-century Roman saint, based on Simeon Metaphrastes and Laurentius Surius. Acknowledging that poetry required 'the ingenious interweaving of fiction and truth', he then enumerated the parts of the play that had sprung from his own imagination.

After 1660, French sacred theatre was struggling to find an appreciative audience in the capital. Parisian literary critics judged the saints' lives inappropriate material for the theatre, while learned clerics came to see theatre as wholly incompatible with the demands of scholarly accuracy. Adapting the lives of the saints to the stage also posed a moral problem. Professional actors, after all, were not known for their upstanding moral lives. Not all of them emulated the dramatic conversion of St Genesius, the patron saint of actors. The poet and exegete Antoine Godeau, bishop of Grasse and Vence, protested that 'To improve their behaviour and regulate their devotion, Christians have the church, not the theatre.'[33]

Still, sacred theatre did not disappear entirely. It continued to thrive in the provinces, as attested by a performance of the life of St Honoratus in Lérins in 1668,[34] and the survival of five different versions of a life of St Regina (Ste Reine) written between 1661 and 1687 by a monk, a canon, a libertine adventurer, and

---

[31] André Stegmann, 'Le théâtre jésuite à La Flèche. Analyse et mise en perspective', *Revue d'histoire du théâtre*, 43 (1991), pp. 95–106.

[32] Fumaroli, 'Théâtre humaniste et Contre Réforme à Rome 1597–1642'.

[33] De Reyff, *L'Eglise et le théâtre*, p. 62.

[34] *Histoire de l'Abbaye de Lérins*, p. 324.

a mathematics professor.[35] In eighteenth-century Brittany, authorities conti-nued to denounce these 'grotesque and licentious spectacles', and to warn of the dangers that they would lead the faithful to deride religion, showing that they still enjoyed healthy popularity. But by that time fewer works were written, and fewer still were printed.[36]

This brief overview has made clear that French hagiographic writing flour-ished in numerous literary contexts between 1500 and 1650. It now remains to consider more the cultural and intellectual factors that nourished it, on the one hand, and challenged it, on the other.

2. STIMULI AND CHALLENGES TO HAGIOGRAPHY

Hagiographic writing in Renaissance France served essentially the same pur-poses as in other parts of Europe. Ancient saints inspired the greatest interest, for their relics and their history tied them closely to particular communities. The saints of the earliest times (*priora tempora*)—apostles, martyrs, and confessors—appeared in the historical records of the nation and of provinces, episcopal dioceses, and towns. St Dionysius, an apostle of Paul, was believed to be the apostle of Gaul, and his disciples to have laid the foundations of the French Church. St Martial, the apostle of Limousin, was likewise credited with numerous episcopal foundations. Cathedral and monastery chapters proudly enumerated the saintly bishops, cardinals, and popes who had established their churches and whom the churches in turn had sent forth into the world. The saints were the central protagonists in these tales of the apostolic origins of the Gallican Church, but catalogues of bishops (whether saintly or not) were also crucial for urban history. The place of a bishop's seat was often taken to be identical with the diocese as a whole, and the close relationship between civil and religious history meant that bishops' lives constituted a central part of urban and provincial histories. The martyrdom, antiquity, and fame of a saint rendered him worthy of exaltation and brought glory to his territory. Pro-vinces often rendered this exaltation through provincial hagiographies, which mingled accounts of the saints' lives and deeds with praise for their lineage and places of residence. Examples include *La Vie gestes et mort et miracles des saints de Bretagne* of Albertus Magnus, published in Nantes in 1637, and the *Vie des saints d'Auvergne et du Velay* published in 1652 by Jacques Branche.[37]

At the local level, civic festivals were often organized around these founder saints, and hagiographies were produced and performed as an integral part of

---

[35] Boutry and Julia (eds.), *Reine au Mont Auxois*, pp. 217–42.
[36] Le Braz, *Le Théâtre celtique*, pp. 494–500.
[37] Brémond, *Histoire littéraire du sentiment religieux*, I, pp. 230–52.

the celebrations. Works like the life of St Tropez performed in 1604 and 1608 in the town of the same name, and that of St Rémy performed in Saint Rémy of Savoy in 1605, typify this kind of writing. The life of St Geneviève printed in Paris likewise served the procession of this patron saint's relics, a civic ritual which peaked during the Renaissance.[38] Publishing the lives of ancient patron saints was also a way to defend local interests and privileges. The life of St Romain published at Rouen in 1492 and 1498, for example, reaffirmed that St Ouen (Romain's successor as bishop of Rouen) had obtained from the cathedral chapter the right to free a prisoner on Ascension Day, in commemoration of St Romain's saving the town from a dragon, just when Charles VIII was calling that traditional privilege into question.

Monastic houses also produced writings on saints who had honored their communities. The reform of Saint-Martin des Champs of Paris in the early sixteenth century was accompanied by the publication of a life of St Paxent, whose relics belonged to the monastery and whose monks had recently renewed his shrine.[39] At the Abbey of Lérins, on the island of Saint-Honorat, successive reforms stimulated a renewal of interest in several of the islands' early saints. In 1613, the monk Vincent Barralis published a *Chronologis sanctorum et aliorum illustrium virorum . . . sacrae insulae Lerinensis* which incorporated numerous earlier biographes of saints associated with the island. This practice of publishing the lives of saintly founders nourished the spiritual life of their successors, who often adopted the same monastic names as their illustrious predecessors.[40]

Rivalries among competing shrines over a saint's memory, often in hopes capturing the associated pilgrimage, were an important stimulus to hagiography. The relics of martyr Saint Regina, for example, had long been venerated at the Abbey of Flavigny. But the building of a chapel in 1498 over a therapeutic thermal spring not connected with the abbey inspired Jehan Piquelin to write a life of St Regina which made opportune mention of this miraculous fountain. In 1644, when a community of Cordeliers monks was installed near the fountain, relics of St Regina were brought from Germany to mark the occasion. This unleashed a pamphlet war between the Cordeliers and the Benedictines of Flavigny.[41]

Naturally, this passion for the ancient saints as bearers of personal and corporate identity did not encourage a spirit of critical hagiography. The past, rather, provided roots and legitimacy for noble houses and noble families. In this spirit the Montmorency invented a highly implausible genealogy in the

---

[38] Sluhovsky, *Patroness of Paris*.
[39] Le Gall, *Les Moines au temps des réformes*, p. 379.
[40] *Histoire de l'Abbaye de Lérins*, p. 401.
[41] Boutry and Julia (eds.), *Reine au Mont Auxois*, pp. 217–42.

sixteenth century that traced their lineage back to the first notable convert of St Denis.[42]

This keen interest in the saints of antiquity was all the more remarkable given that, by comparison, French Catholics in the Renaissance appeared relatively uninterested in the saints and religious reformers of more recent times. The French Renaissance Church did not create new religious orders on nearly the same scale as Italy or Spain. The life of Joan of Valois (Jeanne de France), who founded the Order of the Annunciation shortly before her death in 1505, was written by her confessor Gabriel Maria, but never published. The important monastic reform movements of the early sixteenth century rarely resulted in biographies of the reformers, even though their relics sometimes were credited with miracles. It was not until the second half of the sixteenth century that the lives of Marguerite of Lorraine (1463–1521) and Philippa of Guelders, the duchess of Lorraine (1467–1547) were published.[43]

The waning interest in modern saints was due in part to the political climate of the later sixteenth century. The Wars of Religion (1562–98) between French Calvinists and Catholics created divisions among the Catholics themselves, fostering an environment of distrust which did not favour the writing of hagiographic lives of the protagonists of reform. Jean de la Barrière, for example, founder of the Feuillants, was denied hagiographic treatment because of his excessive proximity to Henri III (1574–89) and his subsequent loss of authority in his congregation when the extremist Catholic League came to power in 1588.[44] Although Protestant martyrs constituted a focus for commemorative literature among Huguenots,[45] equivalent writing by Catholics was scarce before the end of political conflict. It was only in 1625 that, in order to remedy the gap, Hilarion de Coste published his *Histoire catholique où sont descrites les vies, faicts et actions héroïques des hommes et dames illustres qui par leur piété ou sainteté de vie se sont rendus recommandables dans les XVIe et XVIIe siècles*, a work he dedicated the king. For the most part, the 'century of saints' was more inclined to promote the saintly renown ('*fama sanctitatis*') of seventeenth-century founders of religious congregations. But most of these individuals would only be canonized in the nineteenth or twentieth centuries. Of the 346 French saints who lived between 1546 and 1783, only seven were canonized before 1789. The volume of publications of lives of the saints declined towards the end of the seventeenth century, according to Eric Suire, because of a decline in the marketability of such works, and for other reasons including opposition to Quietism, conflicts

---

[42] Le Gall, 'Vieux saints et grande noblesse'.
[43] Le Gall, *Les Moines au temps des réformes*, pp. 494–9.
[44] Pierre, *La Bure et le sceptre*.
[45] El Kenz, *Les Bûchers du roi*.

between Jesuits and Jansenists, and the advent of critical rationality (to which we shall return shortly).[46]

This relative paucity in the canonization of French saints in the early modern period up to 1700 still left room, however, for the celebration of older saints' lives. Indeed, there had never been competition between new and old saints. Early modern religious reformers often encouraged the veneration of early saints. César de Bus (1544–1607) venerated St Veran, the sixth-century bishop of Cavaillon; Nicolas Roland (1642–78) and Jean-Baptiste de La Salle (1651–1719), both originally from Reims, honoured St Rémy, and the Jesuit missionary Julien Maunoir (1606–83) encouraged the veneration of the old Breton saints as part of his campaign to evangelize that province.[47]

If recent saints did not overshadow those of Antiquity, neither did they displace those of the Middle Ages. In France, the Middle Ages were often coterminous with the formation of religious orders: the roots of the Chartreux, Cluniacs, and Cistercians all lay in that period. The Cluniac Dom Martin Marrier (1572–1644) assembled the lives of the great medieval saints of his order and published his *Bibliotheca Cluniacensis* in 1614. From the beginning of the seventeenth century, as a result of the ascent to the throne of the Bourbon dynasty and the promotion of the feast of St Louis (d. 1270) as a public holiday through the kingdom in 1618, the life of the saint-king was the subject of numerous works. But the medieval saints were less prominent than the ancient ones in the overall hagiographical production in France.

France, then, had many of the same reasons as the rest of Europe for participating in the hagiographic renaissance, because the saints of antiquity were an integral part of a corporate Catholic identity that still flourished in the sixteenth century. They reinforced the identities of religious, civic, and provincial communities. To this extent France followed the same pattern, broadly speaking, as Italy, Spain, or the Low Countries. Nonetheless, despite these common patterns, French culture did pose certain challenges that made the landscape of hagiography more complex and more troubled than some of its European counterparts.

The first of these challenges was the hostility of French academia to humanist scholarship. Monastic reform and Renaissance humanism both reached the University of Paris shortly after 1480 and the end of the Hundred Years' War, but the two movements did not become immediate allies. French monastic reform, like its Spanish and Italian counterparts, passed through an immature phase that led its proponents to reject the liberal arts altogether as pagan and immoral. But the reform of the religious orders occurred later in France than in Spain or Italy. The French reformers saw Christianity as

---

[46] Suire, *La Sainteté française de la Réforme catholique.*
[47] Suire, *La Sainteté française de la Réforme catholique*, pp. 141–2.

incompatible with the spirit of Cicero.[48] Such attitudes did not encourage the application of Ciceronian Latin, or humanist philological and chronological skills, to the study and writing of the saints' lives. France monasticism had no counterparts to the humanist hagiographers of *quattrocento* Italy like Giovanni Garzoni, who wrote the lives of Dominican saints and trained contemporary Dominican reformers, including Girolamo Savonarola, in the art of public speaking.[49] The animating spirit of French monastic reform, Jean Standonck (1454–1504), became, instead (along with the College of Montaigu and the library of St Victor) the object of François Rabelais' famous ridicule as a peddler of pedantic nonsense.

The rift between monks and humanists was further accentuated by the strong influence of the mendicant orders in the theology faculties, which was much greater in France than in Italy or Spain. Early sixteenth-century France, and Paris especially, remained, as in the Middle Ages, the homeland of scholastic theology, largely indifferent to history and philology. The Paris theology faculty regarded humanism with suspicion, particularly after the 'Reuchlin affair' of the 1510s, which bitterly divided humanist and scholastic theologians over the question of how much freedom Christian scholars should have to pursue Hebrew studies. When the Reformation began a few years later, conservative theologians saw it as the daughter of humanism, reinforcing their misgivings about the dangers of humanistic studies.[50] The Paris theology faculty thus gained the reputation among humanists of being a refuge for narrow-minded and pedantic 'obscure men'. The Paris theologian and Fontevrist monk Gabriel Dupuyherbault (immortalized by Rabelais as 'the crazed Putherbeus'), would become a staunch enemy of Erasmus.[51] Erasmus himself became the bogeyman of French monks in general, although he counted some monks among his friends and praised the merits of the Carthusian life. In short, there can be no doubt that sixteenth-century French monasticism did not serve to renovate hagiography. The disdain of French humanists for the cloister inevitably extended to the cult of the saints, since convents and monasteries often housed the relics of the saints and closely guarded their distinct liturgies.

Moreover, the evangelical and reformed currents that developed in France after 1517 were often closely tied to humanism. The *Bibliens* and other supporters of the 'true Gospel' offered a radical critique of the cult of the saints which naturally undermined the enterprise of writing their lives, as did Erasmus's *philosophia Christi* and the christocentrism of Jacques Lefèvre

---

[48] Le Gall, 'Les Moines et les universités'.

[49] Frazier, *Possible Lives*; Kristeller, 'The Contribution of the Religious Orders'. On the links between studies and monasticism, see *Los monjes y los estudios* (Poblet, 1961); Renaudet, *Préréforme et humanisme*.

[50] Farge, *Orthodoxy and Reform in Early Reformation France*.

[51] Droz, 'Frère Gabriel Dupuyherbault l'agresseur de François Rabelais'.

d'Etaples (1455–1537) and his followers.[52] In 1518, Lefèvre developed a critical hagiography that challenged traditional medieval exegesis by distinguishing three separate Marys, on the basis of ancient tradition: Mary the sister of Martha; Mary Magdalene; and the sinful woman who anointed Jesus's feet (Luke 7:36–50).[53] His student Josse Clichtove (1472–1543) sharpened these exegetical principles by elaborating a critical method in which truth depended on the testimony of witnesses closest in time to the events described. Liturgy thus became a source to be historicized, which implied a sharp departure from the medieval tradition of *lex orandi, lex credendi* ('the law of prayer is the law of belief'). The doctrines of Lefèvre were condemned by the theology faculty of Paris and would become, in due course, a current that fed into both Catholic and Protestant confessions.

As the Reformation spread across France, it posed a radical challenge to the cult of the saints and its traditional expressions in liturgy, pilgrimage, and iconography. The Protestant attack generally focused on the question of relics, under the influence of John Calvin's famous *Treatise on Relics* (1543). There was inevitably a close connection between hagiography and the discovery ('invention'), translation, and veneration of relics. Calvin's brilliant polemical work threw into doubt the authenticity of all relics, thus undermining many local cults. Although he focused on the alleged relics of Christ, the Virgin, and the Apostles, Calvin also gave particular attention to the relics and sanctuaries in France.[54] This negative publicity dissuaded French religious houses from publicizing their collections.[55] It also undermined hagiography, for it seemed problematic to write the life story of a saint whose body (or certain parts thereof) was claimed to rest in two different places at once. Critical hagiography, in turn, raised further doubts about the authenticity of such relics. If Mary Magdalene's visit to Provence was really a foolish fable, as Calvin alleged, then whose remains were pilgrims actually venerating at the church of Saint-Maximin-la-Sainte-Baume? Calvin's ecclesiology, written from a universal Christian viewpoint, also implicitly challenged the traditional Catholic ecclesiology, in which the saints, while they participated in the universal Church, embodied a 'corporative Catholicism' or a 'national Catholicism'.[56]

In this evangelical and reformed context, interest in hagiography declined.[57] In the years 1521–5, more books by Erasmus were published in Paris than

---

[52] E.g. see the condemnation of Pierre Caroli, for forgetting the cult of saints in his preaching; Veissière, *L'Évêque Guillaume Briçonnet*, p. 300.

[53] Massaut, *Critique et tradition à la veille de la Réforme en France*; Porter (ed.), *Jacques Lefèvre d'Etaples and the Three Maries Debates*.

[54] Fabre and Wilmart, 'Le Traité des reliques de Calvin', p. 35.

[55] Le Gall, *Le Mythe de saint Denis*, p. 348.

[56] Tallon, *Conscience nationale et sentiment religieux*, pp. 60–1.

[57] In Paris, the number of publications dealing with the saints declined from nineteen in the interval 1501–7 to ten in the comparable interval 1531–7. As a percentage of total publishing, the decline was even greater, from 1.8% (1501–7) to 1.0% (1521–5) to 0.46% (1531–7).

saints' lives. The Calvinist iconoclasm of Huguenots was as much a continuation of this earlier disaffection with the saints as it was an abrupt break with Catholic tradition.[58] When Huguenots attacked and removed relics from French churches, as they did at Notre-Dame de Cléry in 1562 and in both the municipal and abbey churches of St Denis in Paris in 1567, they were not only uprooting what they saw as the signs of idolatry but also aiming to 'disenchant' the nation as a whole.

By its very excesses, however, Calvinist iconoclasm also laid the groundwork for a Catholic response, which would be presented a holy counter-attack. New discoveries of relics served to revive the camp of the saints. In 1577, ten years after the Huguenots sacked the churches of St Denis, the original tomb of St Denis was discovered in one of them. Towards the end of the Wars of Religion, the translation of relics across France multiplied, and in 1625 a miraculous statue of St Anne was discovered at Auray. Especially after the 1620s, the lives of the saints took on a new importance. The resurgence in hagiography lasted until the 1690s, culminating in the decade of the 1640s during the regency of Anne of Austria, a great lover of relics and of devotion to the saints.

But Anne of Austria's passion for sanctity came late in the French Renaissance, and represented a change for the French monarchy. During the sixteenth century, French sovereigns were lukewarm in their embrace of the cults of the saints. The dynasty of Valois-Angoulême, which ruled from 1515 to 1589, hardly collected relics at all, unlike their ancestor Louis XI (d. 1483), or the many contemporary sovereigns who amassed great relics collections (e.g. Galeazzo Maria Sforza in Pavia, Frederick III of Saxony in Wittenberg, and Philip II of Spain in his palace at El Escorial). Although they did commission diplomats and scholars to make copies of ancient works and to acquire paintings, sculptures, and manuscripts, no French king ever patronized hagiographic research projects like that of Ambrosio de Morales in northern Spain in the 1570s[59] or Ottavio Gaetani in Sicily in 1595, both commissioned by Philip II.[60] The royal collection of relics at Sainte-Chapelle and the 'Treasure of Saint-Denis' remained as they were; their royal owners did not seek to expand them with new elements.[61] At the same time, they were willing to export relics from the kingdom for diplomatic purposes, like the body of St Eugenius, an alleged disciple of St Denis, which was removed from St Denis by royal command and handed over to Philip II when the monarch met with Catherine de Medici in 1565 at the Conference of Bayonne. It was subsequently translated to Toledo, Spain's archiepiscopal see, with great pomp and solemnity.[62]

---

[58] Christin, *Une Révolution symbolique*.
[59] Edouard, 'Enquête hagiographique et mythification historique'.
[60] Cabibbo, *Il paradiso del magnifico regno*, pp. 29–30.
[61] On the treasure of St Denis, see Le Gall, *Le Mythe de saint Denis*, pp. 359–71.
[62] Le Gall, *Le Mythe de saint Denis*, pp. 136–8; Depluvez, 'Le Retour de saint Eugène et de sainte Léocade à Tolède', pp. 113–32. See also above, pp. 126ff.

Royal pilgrimages in this period were directed mainly towards the Marian shrines at Chartres, Liesse, Le Puy, and Notre-Dame de Cléry.[63] Louis XIII in 1638 placed the kingdom under the Virgin's protection. This in itself was not unusual; other European monarchs also honoured the Virgin, and the Spanish monarchs' defence of the doctrine of the Immaculate Conception is well known. But in Spain the patronage of the Virgin did not diminish that of other saints, as seen, for example, in the controversy that arose over the co-patronage of Castile between supporters of St James and supporters of St Teresa of Avila (canonized in 1622).[64] French kings never actually questioned the cult of the saints. Pontus de Tyard (d. 1605), a humanist poet and bishop close to Henri III, even wrote homilies to defend it.[65] But the monarchs' favourite scholars did not write hagiography; they preferred classical biography. Henri III supported the religious orders, immersing himself in penance and even living as a monk on occasion, but the orders he patronized, the Minim Friars, the Feuillants, and the Jeronymites, were all more ascetic than scholarly.

The exaltation of Mary by France's Renaissance kings tended to overshadow the major national saints, St Michael and St Denis. The prestige of the chivalric order of St Michael founded by Louis XI in 1469 declined sharply in the sixteenth century. Henri III founded a competing order of chivalry in 1578, but under the patronage of the Holy Spirit rather than any saint. The monarchy continued to honour St Denis himself until 1571, but subsequently abandoned his cult. St Denis's cult was exploited by the rival Catholic League, which adopted St Denis as a sort of Catholic ruler when the Calvinist Henri IV ascended the throne in 1589. This king's own conversion to Catholicism four years later in the abbey of St Denis reconciled the dynasty with the apostle only temporarily, for the new Bourbon dynasty that Henri IV established reserved most of its tribute for a medieval dynastic saint, St Louis, as noted above.

3. HAGIOGRAPHIC CONTROVERSIES

This royal indifference to the cult of the saints created a freer environment for critical scholarship to flourish. A hagiography less concerned with miracles appeared, principally in the work of learned magistrates, but also from Jesuit historians like Jean Papire Masson (1544–1611). One of the principal subjects of this new critical hagiography was St Denis himself. The identity of St Denis

[63] Brian, 'Le roi pèlerin'; Maes, *Le Roi, la vierge, et la nation*.

[64] Rowe, 'St. Teresa and Olivares'.

[65] Fragonard, 'Didactique et polémique: le culte des saints', pp. 301–16.

of Paris with Dionysius the Areopagite had already been doubted by Peter Abelard in the twelfth century, but these scholarly doubts had not disturbed the medieval cult of St Denis. Renaissance humanist scholars, beginning in the fifteenth century with Lorenzo Valla (1406–57), had revived this challenge in a more systematic way. In the late sixteenth century, a large cast of Catholic historians called into doubt the legend of Dionysius the Areopagite's coming to Gaul. The historians Antoine du Verdier (d. 1600), Claude Fauchet (d. 1601), Etienne Pasquier (d. 1615), and Antoine Loisel (d. 1617) all pointed out the contradictions and chronological incoherencies of the traditional hagiographies and foundation stories.

These incidental challenges to the legend of St Denis, made within French national histories, did not inspire a general revision of French hagiography, nor did they provoke great controversy in the sixteenth century.[66] Alain Tallon has suggested that these authors restrained from forceful revisionism because did not want to 'disenchant' the national story.[67] These prudent magistrates were anxious not to stoke the fires of antagonism during the Wars of Religion. Many belonged to the moderate party of the *politiques*, who, although mainly Catholic, did not wish to antagonize more hard-line Catholics by appearing to cede ground to the Protestants. Nor were they particularly sympathetic to the outlook of the reformers of the Council of Trent, which was prone to make articles of religious faith out of historical facts. They were interested in profane and civil history primarily as a source of possible remedies for the religious conflict.[68] Trained in the humanist tradition, they respected disciplinary boundaries and thus did not consider their chronological remarks threatening to theology. When scholarly controversies did erupt in the 1640s over the lives of French saints, they did not pit clerics against laymen, but rather one group of clerics against another. Paradoxically, the ensuing battles over the proper relationship between hagiography and criticism were waged largely within the field of positive theology.

Jean de Launoy (1603–78), a doctor of theology at the Sorbonne and friend of the Jesuit Jacques Sirmond, became the central figure in these disputes when he published his dissertations on St Bruno, Mary Magdalene, St Julian du Mans, and St Denis in the 1640s. He argued that Hilduin, a ninth-century abbot of St Denis and St Denis's biographer, had deliberately conflated three figures—the disciple of St Paul; the author of the mystical corpus; and the first bishop of Paris, who had in fact lived in the mid third century—in order to bring glory to his monastery. Launoy had a reputation for being hyper-critical and seeing forgeries under every bed, which earned him the sobriquet 'dénicheur de saint' ('saint-remover'). His mindset was more destructive than

---

[66] Le Gall, *Le Mythe de saint Denis*, pp. 235–6.
[67] Tallon, *Conscience nationale et sentiment religieux au XVIe siècle*.
[68] Huppert, *The Idea of Perfect History*.

constructive; he reduced historiography to historical biography, deconstructed existing traditions in the name of chronological accuracy, and questioned miracles that were not attested by contemporary witnesses, but he did not aim at a thorough renovation of hagiography. For all his efforts, Launoy was reviled as a bad Christian, a libertine who needlessly disturbed the piety of the faithful, and even a bad Frenchman.

By the seventeenth century the crown had grown quite indifferent to the fate of St Denis, and thus gave Launoy free reign in this controversy. Mary Magdalene, however, was a much more sensitive case. The people of Provence were scandalized by Launoy's calling into question the legend that Mary Magdalene had evangelized their province. On 3 March 1644, the theologians of the University of Aix-en-Provence declared Launoy's work 'contrary to our histories and to the truth of traditions' and condemned him for subverting 'the common sense of the universal Church', for 'undermining the testimonies of popes, kings, and rulers', and for disturbing the peace of the whole Church and the Gallican Church in particular. The sentence issued by the Parlement of Aix two weeks later declared that Launoy's book 'leaned towards heresy', offended common beliefs, attacked devotion, and diminished faith. Parlement prohibited the sale of the book, ordered bookshops to be inspected, and decreed that violators would pay a fine that would be remitted to the church of Saint-Maximin-la-Sainte-Baume in Provence, the shrine that housed the Magdalene's relics. Work was prohibited on the feast day of Sainte-Madeleine.[69] The Parlement's threats seem to have worked, for the lawyer-historian Nicolas Chorier from Vienne, who had written a work denying Mary Magdalene's coming to Provence, refused to publish it despite Launoy's friendly encouragement.[70]

These learned revisions of saintly legends were not motivated by religious scepticism. Although Launoy's work initiated a polemic about the date of Gaul's Christianization, he shared the desire of his predecessor Jacques Lefèvre d'Etaples to reconcile piety and truth. Lefèvre d'Etaples, in his 1518 critique of the Magdalene tradition, had maintained that by distinguishing three separate Marys he was restoring biblical truth and thus supporting piety. What was pious, after all, about confusing the sister of Martha with the sinful woman of Luke 7 and with Mary Magdalene, from whom Christ cast out seven demons? King Francis I had found nothing wrong with Lefèvre's arguments, although scholastic theologians and some humanists, including John Fisher, had attacked Lefèvre. Sirmond and Launoy defended their revision of St Denis in similar fashion, insisting that by unmasking Denis of Paris as a distinct figure who had

---

[69] Etienne-Michel Faillon, Monuments inédits sur l'apostolat de Sainte Marie Madeleine en Provence, II (Paris: Jacques-Paul Migne, 1848–65), pp. 1479–82.

[70] F. Crozet (ed.), *Mémoires de Nicolas Chorier de Vienne sur sa vie et ses affaires* (Grenoble: Prudhomme, 1868), p. 41.

been falsely concealed behind Dionysius the Areopagite, they were enabling the apostle of Paris to be venerated in his own right. Launoy wished to be seen not as a destroyer or debunker of saints but as a disentangler of genuine saints' legends. He even dedicated a *vita* to the Areopagite to show that he meant him no dishonour by restoring the other Denis to his rightful place in the Paris episcopacy. As a result of Sirmond and Launoy's revisions, the Parisian martyrology was now revised in accordance with the earliest usages, re-establishing two dates to honour the two Denises: 3 October and 9 October. In the wake of these reforms, other falsely conflated saints, including Trophimus of Arles, Eugenius of Toledo, and Paul of Narbonne, were likewise disentangled and given their due recognition as distinct holy personages.

Although Lefèvre in the early sixteenth century and Launoy in the mid-seventeenth were united by a common desire to reconcile truth with religion, we can discern a certain change in critical attitude over this long interval. Lefèvre, writing before the Reformation and not dealing with the question of when or how Gaul was evangelized, wanted above all to make piety better informed. Within this framework, however, some factual error was permissible; Lefèvre believed that 'honour with some error does no more harm than honour that is free of error'.[71] The more intransigent Launoy was determined to expunge all misconceptions from the legends of the saints, especially those founded on vain ideas of apostolic origins. He therefore tended to revise the age of Christian origins forward from the first century to a later era, for the existing legends offered too many first-century founding saints whose martyrdom could not be confirmed. For Launoy, Antiquity was too bloody to be godly. Christian antiquity had become a matter of accurate chronology and was less swathed in the marvellous halo that had still surrounded it in Lefèvre's day. From Launoy's vantage point, once one could correctly reconcile the competing origins stories and establish the identity of the true founders of the Gallican Church in their rightful historical context, then post-dating the evangelization of Gaul should be no cause for great alarm; on the contrary, religion should take comfort from knowing that it possessed the truth, on historical as well as theological points, against the libertines and the Protestants.

While it is sometimes alleged that all of this criticism undermined or 'disenchanted' the cult of the saints and undermined the genre of historiography in general, in fact the opposite is true. The more doubts critics raised about the traditional legends of the saints, the more they inspired their adversaries to publish a hagiography intended to strengthen belief and mobilize the *consensus fidelium*. Thus, far from inhibiting the production of hagiography, the polemics of the sixteenth and seventeenth centuries actually

---

[71] Massaut, *Critique et tradition*, p. 70.

revived it.[72] The cult of St Denis, as we have seen, experienced a renewal in the seventeenth century. The Dominicans who guarded the Magdalene's relics at Saint-Maximin published several lives of Mary Magdalen in the later seventeenth century. The polemics also helped to convince Catholics that it was more important than ever to find other ways of establishing religious truth than by appealing to history. Thus, the later seventeenth century saw a revival of rituals, devotional activity and pilgrimages around saints, promoting them through a pious hagiography with its mixture of saintly life, descriptions of relics, *lieux de memoire* (sites of memory), fountains, sanctuaries, and prayers and hymns.

We must firmly reject, then, any suggestion that the hagiographic controversies of the French Renaissance brought about the 'disenchantment' of the cult of the saints or undermined hagiography. French Renaissance scholars may indeed have pulled some of their punches and avoided more strident criticism in order to avoid playing into the hands of the Protestants.[73] But Renaissance criticism did no damage to hagiography per se. On the contrary, the rise of critical polemics was a stimulus to writing about the saints, and Catholic scholars, even the more strident ones like Launoy, should not be branded as being cynical or disaffected towards the saints in general. Whether there was indeed a 'disenchantment' of the saints in the culture at large is still a matter for debate. If there was, it probably had other causes altogether. Jean Delumeau may be correct, for example, to suggest that a lessened sense of insecurity gave people fewer reasons to seek divine assistance.[74]

We must reject the verdict of nineteenth-century Catholic historiography that Renaissance historical criticism had a damaging effect on Christian piety. Writers of the nineteenth century greatly overstated the incompatibility of reason and faith. In their reactionary fear of the Renaissance and all that it had allegedly ushered in—Gallicanism, Jansenism, the Age of Reason, and the French Revolution—Catholic historians of the nineteenth century sought to return to what they considered historical essentials, including the coming of Dionysius the Areopagite and Mary Magdalene to first-century Gaul. But this was an exaggerated reaction, which underestimated the sophistication of French Catholic scholarship between the Renaissance and the Enlightenment. The seventeenth-century hagiographers and historians of Port-Royal Abbey, and the scholars who drew inspiration from them, took up the mantle of Sirmond and Launoy, and sought to reconcile edifying tales with historical accuracy. Thus the saints' lives written by Thomas du Fossé, Louis-Sébastien Le Nain de Tillemont, and Adrien Baillet in the second half of the seventeenth century were both edifying and historically illuminating. After

---

[72] On controversies revived during the Wars of Religion, see Dompnier, *Le Venin de l'hérésie*.
[73] This was clearly the case e.g. in the controversy over the *Corpus Dionysiacum*.
[74] Delumeau, *Sin and Fear, passim*.

Launoy, the origins of France's bishoprics were less often anchored in the earliest decades of Christian antiquity, and their founders were less likely to be identified as foreigners to Gaul, for the idea of *translatio* had given way to that of an autochthonous Gallican Church. Some names disappeared altogether from the episcopal lists. But the episcopal lists furnished by the *Gallia christiana* in the early eighteenth century are richer in names and more chronologically compact, reinforcing the impression of uninterrupted apostolic continuity. By this time, continuity had come to matter more than antiquity itself; the truth about a church's origins had become more important than the prestige of antiquity. After more than a century of critical historiography, the saints who had founded France's bishoprics appeared less Roman or Greek, and rather more Celtic and indigenous.

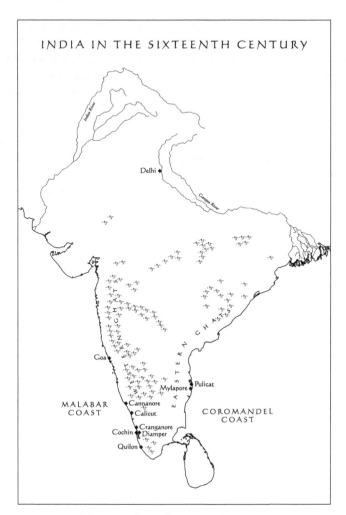

Map 2. India in the sixteenth century

11

Doubting Thomas: The Apostle and the Portuguese Empire in Early Modern Asia

Liam Matthew Brockey

In the late spring of 1521, a band of Portuguese adventurers beat through seven leagues of brush on the Coromandel Coast of south-eastern India in search of holy relics. They were following a trail blazed by one of their company, Diogo Fernandes, who had first come this way with a group of Armenian Christians four years earlier. When word of this initial reconnaissance had made its way back to Lisbon, King Manuel I (r. 1495–1521) had promptly issued orders for another expedition to be mounted from Cochin (now Kochi).[1] Thus in 1521, roughly a dozen Portuguese set out under the command of Captain Pero Lopes de Sampayo to visit the reputed resting place of the Apostle Thomas. According to Gaspar Correia (1495–1561), the author of *Lendas da Índia* and a member of this party, the group travelled 'as on pilgrimage, ... singing and rejoicing, with much to eat and drink'. But once they beheld their destination, the men were touched with 'a devout sadness', ceasing their revelry and falling into silent prayer. With 'arms and legs going weak and trembling', they knelt before the crumbling edifice that they believed held the Apostle's tomb to offer their confessions to the priest who was with them, and then heard Mass. After surveying the surrounding ruins of what had once been a great city, long since consumed by the jungle, the party entered the structure to begin their task of discovering the saint's relics and renovating the church. At the captain's command, workmen selected a spot in the crossing and began to dig.[2]

The first excavations undertaken in the *Santa Casa*, or Holy House, revealed that the structure was solidly built on stone foundations which had weathered the storms of time far better than others in the area. More impressive was the

---

[1] The initial report can be found in Manuel Gomes, 'Carta que foy feita na India na casa do apostolo São Thomé', July 1517, in da Silva Rego (ed.), *Documentação*, I, pp. 296–9.

[2] Correia, *Lendas da Índia*, II, bk 2, pp. 725–6.

fact that the massive wooden beams, 'all made from one trunk' according to Correia, had survived the millennium and a half since the Apostle had installed them. Correia observed that the wood 'was the colour of dried dates, neither pierced with holes nor eaten by bugs, but very sound'. Although its appearance was decrepit, the structure of the Holy House was mostly firm, including the brick dome over the chapel. The Portuguese therefore only made minor changes to make the building a proper sanctuary, cleaning the altars and adding a sacristy.[3]

While examining the foundations of the Holy House, the workmen uncovered a brick tomb. Correia reported that inside it lay the bones of a king whom the Apostle had converted. Local informants identified this ruler as 'Tanimudolyar, which in their tongue means Thomas servant of God', and deciphered the inscription on a stone slab found underneath the bones. Here it was decreed that a tenth of the value of the ruined city's commerce, 'whether by sea and by land', revert to the sanctuary 'as long as the sun and moon shall last'. Correia also described the other monuments that demonstrated the hoary antiquity of the site, and specifically its Christian origins: Three carved crosses adorned the chapel walls, similar to the crosses and peacock motifs incised on the roof beams. And while they did not unearth the body of the Apostle during this visit, the Portuguese pilgrims did leave with a tangible memory of the saint. Correia claimed to have seen part of a stone bearing Thomas's foot and knee prints, and in particular one showing the marks of 'the big toe and the two toes next to it'. These impressions had hung in the chapel for centuries, Correia noted, before being 'broken and removed as relics' by his companions.[4]

The ruins of Mylapore, known to the Portuguese as São Tomé de Meliapor and now a suburb of Madras (Chennai), seem an unlikely destination for early modern pilgrims. Yet the identification of the site with Doubting Thomas was confirmed not only by medieval hagiography in Europe but also by long-standing traditions in India. Nevertheless, attempts to reconcile the two narratives about Thomas in the sixteenth century gave rise to uncertainty, since the contours of European and Asian stories were not identical. It was perhaps only appropriate that the Apostle who questioned the first reports of the resurrection should spark questions about his own acts and the site of his burial. In the early modern period, European explorers, chroniclers, and ecclesiastical historians sought to learn how the Apostle's remains had come to rest in this far corner of India while doubting if they should believe the lore that South Asians (Christians and non-Christians alike) preserved about Thomas. The Europeans' initial queries gave rise to others. What had the

---

[3] Ibid., p. 726.

[4] Ibid., pp. 724 and 726. The Holy House is described in Zupanov, *Missionary Tropics*, pp. 87–110, esp. 94–100.

Apostle done there fifteen hundred years before the arrival of the Portuguese? Were there any other traces of his presence in Asia, apart from the relics in Mylapore? Or were the Christian communities that had been found on the Malabar Coast of western India (modern Kerala), the so-called Thomas Christians, Thomas's spiritual progeny? Finally, did the arrival in India of the Portuguese, a Christian nation with imperial designs, somehow fulfil a divine plan for the resumption of the spread of Christianity in Asia?

This chapter will examine some of the responses to these questions given by sixteenth and early seventeenth-century Portuguese authors. In their writings, the figure of Thomas sits at the intersection of religion and empire, and between Christian antiquity and the first missionary projects of the modern age. For many of the Portuguese traders, sailors, soldiers, and priests who disembarked in India in the wake of Vasco da Gama's 1498 voyage, the Apostle's presence in the East was divine sanction for their imperial ambitions. Yet little was known about him in the West beyond his famous encounter with the risen Christ and a few details drawn from the writings of the early Church Fathers. The contours of his life, works, and legacy that were not found in these sources would therefore have to be discovered in Asia and reimported to Europe. In sum, a new version of the Apostle's life would emerge, one which blended a Western narrative with elements provided by the excavations carried out in Mylapore, and by the discoveries of missionary scholars who examined evidence from non-European traditions. This melding of European and Asian information was no easy task, and the scholars who attempted it did not resolve all the conflicting claims of the variant traditions.

For some of the Portuguese who sailed to the East, the route to the Indies was not simply a search for riches and imperium; it was an expedition into Christian antiquity. Like the excavation of Roman catacombs or the textual criticism of medieval hagiography, the discovery of Indian Christians opened a window onto the primitive Church and its divergent legacies. The presence of the Thomas Christians offered European scholars an opportunity to gauge the accuracy of the writings of the patristic period about the diffusion of the faith in the ancient world, and to contemplate the mechanisms that had permitted its preservation over the course of the centuries. But not all perspectives are happy ones, and the realities of the Christian presence in maritime Asia *c*.1500 did not cause universal jubilation among the Portuguese clergy. Once they had ascertained where the trail of the Apostle Thomas came to an end and identified the surviving traces of Christian antiquity, they questioned whether these relics could serve as the basis for the new church they intended to erect. Ultimately, Roman Catholic missionaries would respond in the negative. They would opt to recast the history of Thomas in India as a preface to their own missionary endeavours, situating his legacy in the distant past rather than infusing it with new life. At a practical level, their emphasis shifted from recovering a lost Asian Church to remaking Asian Christendom in their own image. From the Portuguese point of view, this too was an apostolic effort, but it was met with indifference or rejection by many of the Thomas Christians who were its primary targets. Apparently the deep foundations of Christianity that had been laid by Thomas were not appropriate for supporting a Portuguese edifice.

***

The first expeditions to the Holy House of St Thomas were important moments in the Portuguese perception of the apostolic legacy in maritime Asia. The two visits in 1517 and 1521 confirmed the principal points of the Thomas legend that the Portuguese had brought with them from Europe. Medieval traditions had sketched the contours of the Apostle's life after the first Pentecost, and generally agreed that he had travelled to and was martyred in India. Brief references to Thomas's journey east to India (or Parthia, in some texts) can be found in writings of Church Fathers such as Origen, Eusebius, Ambrose, and Jerome, statements confirmed and embellished by later medieval authors such as Gregory of Tours and Isidore of Seville. The passages in *Glory of the Martyrs* by Gregory of Tours (538–94) are perhaps the most elaborate ones from the Late Antique period, stating a 'spectacularly large and carefully decorated and constructed' church and monastery existed at the spot of Thomas's martyrdom. In this sacred edifice, the Frankish bishop continued, a miracle ensured that a candle burned day and night, without need of oil: 'The lamp continues to burn because of the power of the Apostle that is unfamiliar to men but is nevertheless associated with divine power.'[5]

Eager to underscore the validity of this information about such a remote place, Gregory told his readers that he had been informed by a man named Theodorus, 'who had visited the spot'. This claim set the bar for information about Mylapore somewhat higher for later authors: the most widely circulated accounts of Thomas's shrine from the Middle Ages gained authority by virtue of their descriptions of pilgrimages to western India. The most famous pilgrim to the shrine was Marco Polo (c.1254–1324), the Venetian merchant who served at the court of Khubilai Khan, and who sailed from southern China back to Europe across maritime Asia in the last decade of the thirteenth century. The different manuscript versions of the account of Polo's travels contain information about the shrine of St Thomas in *Maabar*, a province of southern India, in 'a certain little town having no great population'. The remains of the saint lay in that place, revered by Christians and

---

[5] Gregory of Tours, *Glory of the Martyrs*, p. 51.

Muslims alike, Polo reported, and pilgrims bear away with them a reddish earth known to cure fevers.[6]

Another text from the mid-fourteenth century, the *Livre des merveilles du monde*, also insisted that Thomas's shrine was in India. This book, likely written by an Englishman named John Mandeville (d. *c.*1372) who based his text on his experiences in the Levant and the accounts of others who had travelled farther East, asserted that the saint's body had been taken to Edessa in northern Mesopotamia (modern southern Turkey)—as was claimed in Gregory of Tours's *Glory of the Martyrs* and Jacobus de Voragine's *Legenda aurea* (composed *c.*1260)—but that it had been returned to the city of Calamie in the kingdom of Mabar.[7] There, the relics were housed in a sanctuary which was 'great and fair', and filled with towering statues the size of two men.[8] And in the early fifteenth century, another authoritative account of the shrine came from Nicolò Conti (*c.*1385–1469), also a Venetian merchant who had travelled widely in Asia, who recalled that the saint's remains were found 'honourably buried in a very large and beautiful church'.[9]

Educated readers in late medieval Europe, then, knew that Thomas's relics were supposed to be in a church somewhere in India, most likely in its southern reaches. But the ships that plied the Indies route in the early sixteenth century carried few such men to Asia. The adventurers, priests, and crown servants who sought to locate Thomas's shrine had to have been spurred on by accounts that were accessible to a wide readership at beginning of the sixteenth century. The immediate prod for their efforts came from a new edition of Marco Polo's text printed at Lisbon in 1502 by Valentim Fernandes (*c.*1460–1519), a German printing pioneer in Portugal and a retainer at the royal court. Fernandes prefaced his Portuguese translation of the Italian (not French) versions of Polo with the passage from Luke's Gospel, *vidimus mirabilia hodie*, invoking the recent discovery of the 'marvels of the lands and new peoples and their things'.[10] He asserted that his text was destined to inform 'those who now go to the Indies', and so included the more recent account by Nicolò Conti as well. So Fernandes's readers, ready to embark for India from Lisbon, were given the information deemed most accurate in 1502 about Thomas's tomb, as well as about the Christians 'found in the other

---

[6] Polo, *The Travels of Marco Polo*, II, pp. 353–4. Compare to *Il Milione*, pp. 265–7 and *La Description du monde*, pp. 264–6. For further on Polo, see Larner, *Marco Polo and the Discovery of the World*, pp. 31–45.

[7] Although the authorship of this book has been debated for over a century, recent scholarship has offered a firm attribution to an English Mandeville living in Liège in the mid fourteenth century. See Mandeville, *Le Livre des merveilles du monde*, pp. 7–14. The reference to Edessa can be found in Gregory of Tours, *Glory of the Martyrs*, p. 51; and Voragine, *The Golden Legend*, I, p. 35.

[8] Mandeville, *Mandeville's Travels*, pp. 127–8.

[9] Conti, 'The Travels of Nicolò Conti, in the East', independent pagination, p. 7.

[10] 'We have seen wonderful things today', Luke 5:26.

world, who with such joy ask to know of our lands, as we seek to know of theirs'.[11]

These communities of co-religionists were crucial intermediaries for the Portuguese, not only because they appeared as natural allies in a land filled with non-Christians, but also because they were seen to preserve traditions from the early Church. They were the so-called Thomas Christians, Syrian Rite communities which dated at least to late antiquity. Conti's report had noted that they could be found 'scattered over all India, in like manner as are the Jews among us'.[12] Thankfully for the Portuguese, their greatest concentrations could be found in precisely the areas reconnoitred on the first Portuguese voyages to India—that is, along the Malabar Coast.[13] As the Portuguese presence began to grow at commercial entrepôts such as Calicut (Kozhikode) and Cochin (Kochi), interactions with these indigenous Christians became more frequent. Of course, the fact that the Thomas Christians were key intermediaries for the Portuguese in the pepper trade gave them a doubly strong force of attraction. In the estimation of one European observer at Cochin in 1529, the members of this community held 'all of the pepper in their hands'.[14] Yet these Christians told stories to inquiring Europeans about St Thomas that were different from what the Westerners expected to hear. Thus began a process of reconciliation between European and Indian traditions that would last for over a century, and which would involve incipient forms of anthropology, archeology, ethnography, and hagiography.

***

Portuguese inquiries about the Thomas legend began with questions about the saint's life and the circumstances of his death. Some of the first European accounts of Thomas from the modern period appear in the writings of contemporary chroniclers such as Gaspar Correia or Duarte Barbosa (d. *c*.1546). Barbosa, who travelled to India perhaps as early as 1500, acquired a knowledge of Malayalam that eventually earned him the post of crown factor (the royal trading representative) at Cannanore (Kannur) and later that of chief secretary in Cochin. His *Book of What He Saw and Heard in the Orient* (composed *c*.1515) offers one of the first accounts of Thomas's evangelization of the region, which he claimed 'the local Christians affirm can be found

---

[11] Fernandes, *Marco Paulo*, preface and colophon.

[12] Major (ed.), *India in the Fifteenth Century*, p. 7.

[13] Further on the Christian communities in Southern India is found in Frykenberg, *Christianity in India*, pp. 91–141; Bayly, *Saints, Goddesses and Kings*, pp. 241–452; and Brown, *The Indian Christians of St. Thomas*.

[14] João Carcere to King João III, Cochin, 2 January 1529, in Silva Rego (ed.), *Documentação*, II (1947–58), p. 175.

written in their books, which they conserve with great veneration'.[15] It is likely that they were referring to apocryphal texts such as the *Acts of Thomas*, a Syriac text that modern scholarship has dated to the early third century.[16] These Christians informed Barbosa about some of the most durable aspects of the local Thomas tradition: that the Apostle had been a great builder of churches and had built one using a massive piece of wood that he had pulled from the sea; that he had performed a miracle of turning sand into rice or coins which he used to pay the workers who helped him; that Thomas was martyred by a hunter who shot him after mistaking him for a peacock; and that when he was buried, the Apostle's right arm refused to be interred, stretching up until a Chinese pilgrim attempted to sever it with a sword to take as a relic, which caused it instead to disappear into the earth.[17] Distant echoes of these traditions can be found in European versions of the Thomas legend, and in particular the story that the Apostle had been renowned for his skill at architecture and had gone to India at the behest of a king who wanted someone who could erect a building in Roman fashion.[18]

While the mere presence of substantial Christian communities living along the Malabar Coast in the vicinity of the Portuguese settlements at Cochin and Quilon (Kollam) was taken as an undeniable testament to the Apostle's passage to India, the Europeans still hungered for further evidence. The 1517 expedition, mounted from the trading outpost of Pulicat on the eastern Indian coast, provided the first tangible proof of the Thomas Christians' assertions. The 1521 expedition, and the subsequent excavation of Thomas's tomb in 1524, confirmed further elements of their story, as did the discovery, in 1546, of a carved stone cross on a nearby hill. Once again, Gaspar Correia was a privileged informant about this last event, since he was present during the second expedition and followed the subsequent explorations of ancient Mylapore with great interest.[19] He had observed earlier that the wooden beams of the Holy House appeared to have been made of a single tree. This fact corresponded to the episode in the legend when Thomas offered to pull a massive tree from the ocean as a display of the power of the Christian God. Mocked by the local king who had attempted to draw the trunk ashore with hundreds of men and elephants, Thomas agreed to heft the wood if the

---

[15] Barbosa, *Livro em que dá relação do que viu e ouviu no Oriente*, p. 170. A brief biography of Barbosa is Rubiés, *Travel and Ethnology in the Renaissance*, pp. 204–6.

[16] Klijn (ed. and tr.), *The Acts of Thomas*, p. 15.

[17] Barbosa, *Livro em que dá relação do que viu e ouviu no Oriente*, pp. 170–2 and 185–6. Mandeville told another story about Thomas's arm, wherein the relic was used in the city of Edessa for judging court cases. When posed questions of guilt or innocence on slips of paper, the arm would discard the slip with the unjust or false part. See Mandeville, *Mandeville's Travels*, p. 127.

[18] See e.g. the account of St Thomas in the *Legenda aurea* in Voragine, *The Golden Legend*, I, pp. 29–35.

[19] Correia, *Lendas da Índia*, I, bk 1, pp. 419–25; II, bk 2, pp. 722–6; and III, bk 1, pp. 419–25.

king would grant him land to build a church.[20] Once this feat was accomplished, the king lived up to his end of the bargain and was even converted (and buried in the Holy House alongside the Apostle in the tomb discovered during the first excavations). The church at Mylapore, concluded the early Portuguese visitors to the site, was the same edifice and therefore the same wood. When the nave of the sanctuary was rebuilt in 1524, the wood was gathered in a small shed and 'taken away in pieces as relics' by those who visited the shrine.[21]

It was during these rebuilding efforts in 1524 that the Portuguese decided to excavate the Apostle's tomb. After uncovering successive layers of brickwork sunk deep into the floor of the church, the workmen at the site finally pierced the chamber where they expected to find human remains. More than just bones, they uncovered a jar filled with sand and a metal spear point with some of its wooden shaft still attached. According to Correia, the bones were 'so worn that they broke as soon as they were moved,' and so were gingerly placed into a silk bag by Álvaro Penteado, the priest who oversaw the work.[22] Here again, the findings appeared to confirm elements of the Indian legends. The jar, it seemed, was the same one that Thomas had used to dole out rice or coins to the men who worked on his church. According to the tradition, it was filled with sand that was transformed when the Apostle reached inside. And the spear point was clearly the instrument that had been used to kill him. Whether he had attracted the ire of the local Brahmans and received the fatal blow from an assassin or had been mistaken for a peacock by a hunter while deep in prayer in the forest, the Portuguese commentators were unsure. Both versions of the story can be found in the early chronicles, but all confirm Thomas's death by a blow from a spear—a detail also mentioned in the *Legenda aurea*, where it is attributed to Isidore of Seville.[23] All of the relics collected at the site were gathered by Penteado, writes Correia, and hidden from sight somewhere inside this primitive church in a location only known to the shrine's caretaker. In other words, what was once unearthed was reburied, so that greedy pilgrims would not make off with all of the relics.[24]

After this initial burst of interest in the Holy House in the early 1520s, almost a decade passed before royal initiative spurred fresh investigations of the Apostle's presence in India. By special request from Lisbon, Captain Ambrósio do Rego was sent to Coromandel in 1531 at the head of a small

---

[20] The story of the trunk is in Barbosa, *Livro em que dá relação*, pp. 170–1, although Barbosa asserts that the church was one located on a spit of land near Kollam, not the church at Mylapore; another version of the story is in Correia, *Lendas da Índia*, III, bk 1, p. 420.

[21] Correia, *Lendas da Índia*, II, bk 2, p. 789.

[22] Ibid., p.788.

[23] Voragine, *The Golden Legend*, I, p. 35.

[24] Correia, *Lendas da Índia*, II, bk 2, p. 789.

fleet with orders to inquire among all possible informants about the antiquity of the sanctuary. Rego's deputies sought out 'the oldest men that he could find, Moors and Heathens, locals and foreigners, who were asked under oath, according to their customs', to confirm the Thomas traditions. In Correia's words, 'they all attested one substance, as if they were all speaking from one mouth', namely that 'one thousand four hundred and some odd years ago, a holy man had lived there' in the structure, and that he had performed miracles.[25] In light of such common accord, the Portuguese desire to settle at Mylapore grew stronger, and subsequent discoveries in the vicinity only served to confirm the conviction that they were on holy ground.[26]

One further discovery related to the Apostle Thomas was made near the site of the Holy House in the first half of the sixteenth century. During the construction of the new Portuguese town of São Tomé in the 1540s, workers found a stone slab with a bas-relief cross and an indecipherable inscription. This find was more miraculous than the others, since it was not only an iconographic testimony to an ancient Christian presence but it also continued to work wonders. According to Correia, 'on one part of the cross there were some drops that the workmen tried very hard to remove by scraping the stone, which indeed turned white, but after a short while the stains returned'.[27] No one present at the time of the discovery was able to make sense of the writing, copies of which were forwarded to Portugal, but no further illuminations were forthcoming from Continental scholars in the early modern period.[28] In 1548 the slab was taken in procession to the *Santa Casa*, and rumours began to spread about the curious indelible stains. One Portuguese scholar writing of the feats of his compatriots in maritime Asia reported that the local Christians had divergent views on the subject: 'Some say that the blessed Apostle suffered on this stone, while he was there praying; others say that it was one of his disciples.'[29] Local memory of Thomas's presence finally led the Portuguese to a small grotto situated between the Holy House and the hill where the stone was found. This cave, it was held, was where the Apostle would retire to pray, and where he had miraculously caused a spring to burst forth after piercing the stone with his staff.[30]

***

The discovery of these proofs of Thomas's presence in India was heralded by mid sixteenth-century Portuguese authors as divine sanction for their imperial

---

[25] Ibid., III, bk 1, pp. 419–20.
[26] The Portuguese colony at Mylapore is discussed in Subrahmanyam, 'Profit at the Apostle's Feet'.
[27] Correia, *Lendas da Índia*, III, bk 1, p. 421.
[28] A discussion of this inscription is in Zupanov, *Missionary Tropics*, pp. 103–4.
[29] Barros, *Da Ásia*, I, bk 2, pp. 303–4.
[30] Correia, *Lendas da Índia*, III, bk 1, pp. 421–2.

project. The dramatic discoveries at Mylapore not only fulfilled the pious dreams of King Manuel, they also served as foundations for what would be, it was assumed, the rapid spread of the faith around the newly explored globe. Of course, witnesses such as Gaspar Correia, who was a pioneering adventurer with no pretence to erudition, did not make this conceptual link in their writings. The task of describing the noble feats of the early Portuguese in India in a prophetic and apostolic register fell to the second generation chroniclers such as João de Barros (1496–1570). Unlike his predecessors, Barros was a secular scholar trained in humanist methods whose task was to write the official history of the Portuguese feats in Asia. He was the first to offer a new version of the Thomas legend based on knowledge derived from Indian sources and present it to a wide reading public in Europe as part of his *Décadas da Ásia*, published at Lisbon between 1552 and 1563. As crown factor of the *Casa da Índia* in Lisbon, Barros held an administrative post which offered him unrivalled access to the information that reached the metropole from the colonies.[31] In his history, Barros brought together European and Indian traditions about Thomas and Mylapore, precisely because they seemed to conform readily to the religious dimensions of the Portuguese imperial project in Asia.

In the most direct passage linking the presence of the Apostle to the advent of the Portuguese in India, Barros included a prophecy issued by Thomas at the moment when he drew the massive tree trunk from the ocean. After he recounted the story, the chronicler noted that 'one thousand five hundred and some odd years ago' the city was situated twelve leagues inland. The saint's feat was therefore doubly miraculous: in addition to pulling the wood out of the sea, he had carried it across the stretch of land that had, in the meantime, been consumed by the waters. 'And as the local people affirm,' Barros continued, 'the Saint himself prophesied that it would be thus; saying that at the time when the sea arrived at the city a white people from the West, who believed in the Lord that he proclaimed, would come to those parts and settle in them.'[32] These 'white people from the West' were a clear foreshadowing of the Portuguese arrival, and further divine approval for them to rebuild the city of Mylapore which had lain in ruins since shortly after the Apostle's martyrdom.

A diligent scholar, João de Barros made clear the sources that he had employed in his history, even if he did not challenge their veracity. His yardstick for gauging the usefulness of a source appears to have been geographic proximity: Asians (and those who had lived in Asia) knew best about Asian matters. With regard to the accounts of the excavations at Mylapore and the Thomas legends derived from indigenous informants, he mentioned the inquiries commissioned by Governor Nuno da Cunha in 1531 as well as the

---

[31] A biography of Barros is in Boxer, 'Three Historians of Portuguese Asia'.
[32] Barros, *Da Ásia*, III, bk 1, p. 107.

news of the cross unearthed in 1546. Two years later, Barros noted, a three-page sketch of that monument was sent to him in Lisbon.[33] Another piece of information that he received was even more revealing, given his interest in how the Apostle came to be India in the first place. This was the testimony, also collected on Cunha's orders, from an 'Armenian bishop' who claimed to have lived in India for twenty years. This priest referred to his Church's writings to explain how three Apostles, Thomas, Bartholomew, and Judas Thaddeus, had travelled together after the crucifixion as far as Babylon (Baghdad) and then parted ways. Thomas, this priest claimed, embarked at Basra for India, stopping along the way at the island of Socotra and also making a side trip to China 'where he converted many people and made temples to honour Christ'.[34]

Barros gained further insights into the history of the primitive Church in India from a Thomas Christian who had travelled to Lisbon to study Latin and theology. The chronicler claims to have conversed with him many times, learning about the two disciples of Thomas who were buried in Cranganore and Quilon, and about the tenuous bonds between the local Christians and their 'Armenian bishops'. (These bishops were not 'Armenian' as he claimed, but rather West Asian clerics from the region of Mosul in northern Iraq who were affiliated with the Nestorian primates who used the title 'Catholicos of Babylon'.[35]) According to this informant, many of the Thomas Christians remained unbaptized since their bishops demanded payment for the sacrament (at least until just before the arrival of the Portuguese). But the most original story that Barros got from his Malabari acquaintance concerned the church of the Apostle's disciple at Quilon, where there was to be found 'the tomb of the Sibyl called Indica, and this church was one of her oratories'. When the Sybil had prophesied the birth of Christ to the nearby kingdoms, a Ceylonese king called Pirimal had sailed to the Arabian coast to join the other two kings 'who went to adore the Lord at Bethlehem, and he was the third'. In obedience to the Sibyl's wishes, the king had returned to India with a portrait of Mary, 'which was placed inside her tomb'.[36]

In the course of his investigations of Thomas's legacy, Barros naturally asked his Indian interlocutors about the communities of Thomas Christians in western India. He was especially keen to resolve one crucial issue for his readers: why had they migrated from the region of Mylapore all the way to the other (western) side of the subcontinent? Chroniclers before him had suggested that the communities in the area of Quilon were originally founded by the Apostle but had continued for generations, in Duarte Barbosa's words,

---

[33] Ibid., I, bk 2, p. 305.
[34] Ibid., III, bk 2, pp. 232–3.
[35] Bayly, *Saints, Goddesses and Kings*, pp. 254–7.
[36] Barros, *Da Ásia*, III, bk 2, pp. 235–7.

'without doctrine, nor priests to baptize them, for much time without anything more than the name of Christians'.[37] In his discussion of the ruins of Myla-pore, Gaspar Correia added that there had been 'so much war between Christians and heathens, that the city and all of the land was destroyed'.[38] João de Barros took the story one step further, asserting that the Christian refugees who had abandoned Coromandel had travelled west and sought refuge among their co-religionists in Malabar. Many of Thomas's followers, he explained, took up residence in the area of Cochin, especially in the area of Diamper (Udayamperoor) and Cranganore (Kodungallur).[39]

✳✳✳

For all of his celebration of the traces of Christianity in India, João de Barros was a secular chronicler, not a Church historian in the mold of many others described in this volume. The aspects of the Thomas legend that he included in the *Décadas* served the purposes of his primarily political and geographic work, demonstrating the apostolic pedigree of the Portuguese enterprise with reference to both European and Asian sources. Barros, and his predecessors Barbosa and Correia, had few scruples about relying on Indian information, since it seemed to confirm the notion of divine sanction for their empire. The educated churchmen who arrived in India in the second half of the sixteenth century would have more problems believing what non-Westerners (and laymen) said about ecclesiastical matters, and especially about the primitive Church. Men with different goals and intellectual pedigrees, these missionaries brought different scholarly criteria to their task of understanding Thomas and his legacy in Asia. They re-examined both the relics and the local traditions that had been accepted seemingly without question by an earlier generation of chroniclers. It is ironic that the greatest beneficiaries of the Thomas tradition, the Jesuits, would be among the first to question the authenticity of the findings at Mylapore. After all, members of the Society of Jesus would be the first Europeans elevated to the status of archbishops of the Thomas Christian churches in western India, and the Jesuits would be given responsibility for protecting the Apostle's shrines in eastern India. Yet there are hints of trepidation in early Jesuit accounts of Mylapore—they seem to have wanted to see before they believed.

Before the Jesuits took up residence in eastern India in the 1560s, their attitude towards the Mylapore traditions was marked by scepticism. Perhaps in order to distinguish their voices from those of indigenous informants, phrases such as 'so they claim' or 'as they say' appear frequently with regard to the Thomas legends. For example, when Luís Fróis (1532–97) described the

---

[37] Barbosa, *Livro em que dá relação do que viu e ouviu no Oriente*, p. 172.
[38] Correia, *Lendas da Índia*, III, bk 1, p. 422.
[39] Barros, *Da Ásia*, III, bk 2, p. 234.

temporary seizure of the relics in Mylapore by Rama Raja, ruler of the Vijayanagara Empire, in 1559, he recounted how that prince marched 'with more than seventy thousand men and a great number of elephants on the city in Coromandel where lies, according to what they say, the body of the glorious Apostle Saint Thomas'.[40] Yet other Jesuits did not seem so sceptical of the claims of their local informants. Unlike Fróis who lived in Goa, the Jesuit missionaries who resided in Mylapore do not appear to have doubted that the Apostle had preached in the region 'and consecrated it with his blood', thereby making it a worthy site for their own apostolic activities.[41] According to Melchior Nunes Barreto (1520–71), a Jesuit who visited the site in 1566, the people of Mylapore were certain that Thomas had built the church where his tomb was located. This fact, Barreto wrote, 'is something very certain and believed by the Christians as well as by the heathens'. In similar fashion, the Little Mount where the bloody cross was found in 1546, was 'by the common opinion of the people, both Christians and heathens' the place where the Apostle used to pray and where his martyrdom occurred.[42]

Such stories were perhaps appropriate for local people to believe, but were they fit for Jesuits to accept? To be sure, the Jesuits were highly educated men who were being asked to accept what Nestorians, Hindus, and Muslims told them about a disciple of Christ. While the feats of Thomas in India seemed certain, they still harboured doubts about the relics at Mylapore. Yes, bones had been discovered in tombs in the Holy House, but were they really those of Thomas? For the Jesuits and other early modern scholars, some traditions commanded greater respect than others—especially those from the waning years of Antiquity. Writings from the late fourth and early fifth century such as the travels of the pilgrim Egeria, Rufinus's translation of Eusebius, and the sermons of John Chrysostom asserted that Thomas's body was buried in Edessa.[43] Evidence from later authors made it doubly difficult to reconcile what they heard in Mylapore with what they had read in Europe. For instance, Gregory of Tours had stated that the Apostle's body had been taken to Edessa, and this assertion had been repeated in the *Legenda aurea*. Based on these authorities, Continental scholars such as the Spaniard Antonio de Torquemada (c.1507–69) could argue that the Portuguese were mistaken. In his *Jardín de Flores Curiosas*, first printed in Salamanca in 1570 (and translated

---

[40] Luís Fróis to João de Moura, Goa, 16 November 1559, in Wicki, *Documenta indica*, IV, pp. 363–71, 368. On Rama Raja's aborted theft of the relics, see Zupanov, *Missionary Tropics*, p. 104.

[41] Francisco Perez to Francisco de Borja, São Tomé de Meliapor, 20 November 1571 in Wicki, *Documenta indica*, VIII, pp. 426–8, 427.

[42] Melchior Nunes Barreto to Francisco de Borja, Cochin, 20 January 1567, in Wicki, *Documenta indica*, VII, pp. 199–200.

[43] Most, *Doubting Thomas*, pp. 218–19. On the cult of Thomas in Edessa, see Segel, *Edessa, the Blessed City*, pp. 174–6.

into English as *The Spanish Mandeville* in 1600), he explicitly contrasted the knowledge derived from India with that of 'the Church'. While he could have mentioned any of a number of Western sources, Torquemada cited Isidore of Seville as the basis for claiming that Thomas's body was in Edessa. 'And this', he wrote, 'is what we should principally believe.'[44]

But the Jesuits in India were aware of the Edessa story and confronted their local informants with its inconvenient truths. Melchior Nunes Barreto seems to have been the first to pose this question to the Thomas Christians during his stay at Mylapore in the late summer of 1566. The answer he received, however, only served to muddy the waters further:

> Although it is said that the body of St. Thomas was transferred from India to Edessa, a city in Armenia, the local people say that it is true that people came long ago from Armenia to ask for the body of the Apostle, but that they were given the body of a disciple of Saint Thomas, who was also called Thomas, instead, and tricked the ambassadors owing to the devotion and veneration in which they hold the holy Apostle in the city.[45]

So questions about the authenticity of the relics remained unresolved in the minds of the sixteenth-century missionaries who worked in Malabar and Coromandel, and there were no obvious means left to settle them. Erring on the side of belief, the Jesuits confided in the evident piety of those who came to Mylapore, leaving the debate over Thomas to be resolved by Church historians elsewhere.

***

By the beginning of the seventeenth century, at the time when the general European impulse to produce local and national Church histories was nearing its height, Portuguese authors began to produce the first ecclesiastical histories of the missions under the patronage of their king. The reports of priests who had served in India were now transformed into chronicles by ecclesiastical historians similar to those treated elsewhere in this volume. These new histories did not put an end to the doubts of priests who visited Mylapore—since it was impossible to reconcile the contradictions between European accounts and the evidence discovered in India, not to mention the unreliability of Asian sources—but rather shifted the thrust of the story of Thomas and the Thomas Christians so as to make it form part of a modern Church history. Men such as the Jesuit João de Lucena and the Augustinian Frei António de Gouvea reconciled medieval traditions with modern discoveries, and con-structed a new record of the Christian past, present, and future in Asia. They synthesized the accounts of the discovery of the Holy House and the

---

[44] Torquemada, *Jardín de Flores Curiosas*, p. 240.
[45] Barreto to Borja, Cochin, 20 January 1567, in Wicki, *Documenta indica*, VII, p. 200.

Thomas relics, critiqued inherited traditions about their origins and importance, and situated the revised version of the story within the framework of the Portuguese expansion in Asia and the missionary efforts of their religious orders. This new history, its proponents made clear, would be the foundation stone for the reunification of the Asian Christians with the Roman Church, under the patronage of the Portuguese crown. The story of Thomas in India and the Christians who bore his name would therefore become a prelude to the larger story of the march of the faith around the globe under the Portuguese standard.

The obvious place for recasting the Thomas legend, at least for the Jesuits, was in the first vita of one of their own founder-saints, Francis Xavier (1506–52), the first Jesuit to visit India. João de Lucena (1549–1600), the Portuguese confrère charged with the task of producing the first biography of the Apostle of the Orient, dedicated a significant section of his *História da vida do padre Francisco de Xavier* (first edition Lisbon, 1600) to the earlier Apostle of the East. Xavier, Lucena relates, was a fervent devotee of Thomas and carried with him, in a pendant, a bone fragment he had acquired in Mylapore wrapped in slivers of paper which bore the signature of Ignatius Loyola and a copy of the vows made by the first Jesuits in 1534.[46] The invocation of Xavier's personal devotion provides Lucena with the pretext for surveying the Thomas legend and laying to rest the doubts that had emerged about the relics. He describes the discovery of the Holy House and the bloody cross, and summarizes local traditions in a chapter entitled 'Some Arguments about the Truth of this Story and the Tradition of the Indians'.[47] Lucena's argument for the authenticity of the discoveries at Mylapore rests on the common consent (among Indians and Portuguese) about their antiquity and the willingness of pious Christians to preserve relics in the face of peril, as recorded by such redoubtable commentators as Augustine, Gregory of Tours, and Bede. He then turns to the textual relics found at the site, both the inscribed cross and the plaque found in the Holy House stipulating the annual tribute paid by the local kings to the shrine.[48]

João de Lucena then confronts the doubts about Thomas head on. 'There is no reason', he writes, 'to avoid confronting the primary doubt that occurs to many about this matter': there were two distinct European traditions that situated the Apostle's relics far from India. The first was the Edessa tradition, and the other concerned Ortona, on the eastern coast of Italy. This second tradition claimed Thomas's relics had been brought there from the Aegean island of Chios by the Venetians in the thirteenth century. While the traditions of Nestorian Christians might be dismissed as corruptions that necessarily accompany heresy, those of Italians had to be handled more carefully in

---

[46] Lucena, *História da vida do padre Francisco de Xavier*, p. 158.
[47] Ibid., pp. 165–8.   [48] Ibid., pp. 169–73.

hagiographic texts aimed at European audiences. Lucena recognized that Thomas enjoyed the veneration of 'the whole of the Province of Apulia in Italy, and even Rome'.[49] But the weight of tradition and evidence was far greater, Lucena judged, for India than for either Edessa or Ortona. What those cities had were empty monuments or other relics of the saint's presence, the smallest of which, Lucena argued, were sufficient to summon all of a saint's virtues and holy power to a given altar, church, or city. Where there could be no doubt was that some part of the Apostle's body was still at Mylapore, even if it was simply the blood that had soaked into the ground at the spot of his martyrdom. Moreover, Lucena concluded, if generations of eastern bishops had visited the shrine before the arrival of the Portuguese, 'there is no reason to deny that most of him is there, since for so many years there have been so many worthy testimonies to his presence'.[50] For Lucena, these debates were distractions from his main point: that the Thomas tradition offered an apostolic pedigree for the work of his confrere, Francis Xavier.

The other major question raised by Portuguese Church historians about the Thomas legend concerned the origins of the Thomas Christians. The first major history of this community written by a European author was António de Gouvea's *Jornada do arcebispo de Goa Dom Frey Aleixo de Menezes primaz da India oriental* (first edition Coimbra, 1606). The book's full title reveals more of its content: 'Journey of the Archbishop of Goa, Dom Frey Aleixo de Menezes, Primate of East India, Religious of the Order of St. Augustine, when he went to the Mountains of Malabar & the places where the ancient Christians of St. Thomas reside, & brought them away from many errors & heresies in which they were mired, & reduced them to our Holy Catholic Faith, & obedience to the Holy Roman Church, from which they had been separated for more than a thousand years'. The author, Gouvea (1575–1628), also an Augustinian friar and prior of his order's convent in Goa who was later elevated to the dignity of bishop of Cyrene, produced this account of his confrere's 1599 visitation of the Thomas Christians in the district of Quilon. The triumphal events related in this lengthy account tell of how Aleixo de Menezes won the recognition of (and jurisdiction over) the indigenous Church after its last Middle Eastern bishop died. The *Jornada* contains the fullest account of the unofficial 'Synod of Diamper' between the archbishop of Goa and the Indian prelates, as well as a lengthy description of the origins, customs, and errors of the Thomas Christians.

As should be expected, Gouvea begins his book by recapitulating the various episodes of the Thomas legend. Here, as in Lucena's life of Xavier, they serve as a prelude to the heroic deeds of the Portuguese Church in Asia. Gouvea mentions the presence of the Apostle in Socotra, in Quilon, in

[49] Ibid., p. 173.
[50] Lucena, *História da vida do padre Francisco de Xavier*, p. 176.

Mylapore, and even in China (as mentioned in the medieval office prayed on the Feast of St Thomas). He also recounts some of the stories of Thomas's relations with local kings and the eventual relocation of the Mylapore Christians to western India, though he is curiously silent on the construction of the Holy House. To be sure, discussion of the shrines on the Coromandel Coast (which were not under the control of Augustinians) were not particularly germane to Gouvea's narrative. The episodes concerning Thomas's relics are treated as pious curiosities, and serve primarily to preface Gouvea's detailed treatment of the development of the Thomas Christian community after its migration to the *Serra*, or mountains, of Malabar. His account offers some of the first substantial references to the figure of Mar Thoma, otherwise known as Thomas of Cana, a merchant of Middle Eastern origin who was said to have re-established the links between the local Christians and the Eastern Churches in the fourth century.[51] In addition to securing a host of privileges for the Christian community from the local rulers, Thomas of Cana also succeeded in attracting the first bishops from 'Babylonia' (Baghdad) to the Quilon area.

According to Gouvea, it was at that moment that the problems began for the Thomas Christians, since the link to the Eastern Churches provided a conduit for the Nestorian heresy to infect them. In Gouvea's view, the Christians situated to the east of Edessa—that is, those churches that followed the Syrian rites, such as the Armenian and Persian Churches—'were aflame with the fires of that damned sect, with the disciples of Nestorius introducing the false doctrine to the uncultivated and unversed people of these provinces'. Since Babylon was also touched by these heresies, he continues, 'the poison spread to the churches that she furnished with priests and prelates'. In an effort to be precise about the distinctions among the schismatic Eastern Christians, Gouvea notes that previous chroniclers (naming João de Barros) were incorrect in linking these doctrinal errors to those of the Ethiopians, since the Africans derived their teachings from Dioscorus of Alexandria and Eutyches, not Nestorius.[52]

António de Gouvea's story does not end with despair at the contagion of heresy, but rather with the triumph of orthodoxy. His version of orthodoxy was nevertheless radically different from what had previously been deemed sound doctrine by the Thomas Christians, and so began the process of transforming these indigenous Christians into Roman Catholics, just as religious reformers had done in recent memory in Europe itself. From Gouvea's point of view, the firm hand of a talented shepherd such as Aleixo de Menezes was needed for resolving doubts, reorganizing Christian practice, and retraining the local clergy. Menezes was therefore a distant imitator of his

---

[51] Further on Mar Thoma and his successors in Bayly, *Saints, Goddesses and Kings*, pp. 268–72.
[52] Gouvea, *Iornada do Arcebispo de Goa*, fols. 5ᵛ–6ʳ.

contemporary, the reforming archbishop of Milan, Carlo Borromeo. His efforts would reshape the ancient practices of the Thomas Christians, bringing them into line, as much as colonial authorities could, with his vision of proper Catholic practice. Yet Menezes and his European (at first Jesuit, and later Carmelite) successors who held positions of authority over these ancient Christian communities pushed their reforms with an excess of zeal, creating a split in the second half of the seventeenth century between those under Portuguese ecclesiastical jurisdiction and those obedient to a new line of Near Eastern bishops.[53] Both communities continue to exist today, forming parts of the complex, ancient web of religious cultures of India.

***

It is fitting that the figure of Thomas led early modern explorers, chroniclers, and missionaries to confront doubt. Drawing on European traditions, they sought the ancient remnants of the primitive Church in the new worlds that had only recently been discovered. But what they found at the end of the earth was ambiguous: they found Thomas, but they did not recognize him at first, and they found Christians, but they were not the same as they had expected. Seeing with pious eyes, the earliest Portuguese observers insisted that they beheld a vision of the apostolic age. Indeed, they understood the presence of Thomas in India as a prophecy of their own arrival and the deeds they intended to accomplish there for God and king. But the churchmen who arrived at the Apostle's shrine in later decades did not see enjoy the same clear vision. They had come from Europe possessing knowledge of the story of Thomas that had a thousand-year pedigree, a tradition formed by some of the most venerable Christian authors. Yet in India they found shrines, relics, and traditions about the Apostle which were defended by local Christians and non-Christians alike. Unable to resolve the discrepancies between these two traditions, they attempted to paper them over. Histories written at the turn of the seventeenth century which discussed Thomas and the indigenous Christians of India offered piety as proof, sidestepping debates over the authenticity of relics.

In the end, the Jesuits and other early modern Portuguese clergy would believe what their Asian informants told them about Thomas, but they did so by making his trail coterminous with their own missionary path. That is, they would put aside the doubts about Thomas in their histories by casting him firmly back into the age of the primitive Church, where his efforts were seen as a hazy foreshadowing of their own apostolic endeavours. Thomas had gone to India, they were sure, but others had gone there too, and had corrupted his work. For the Portuguese, the Thomas Christians were a portrait of historical

---

[53]   The fractious relationship between the two branches of Thomas Christians are discussed in Bayly, *Saints, Goddesses and Kings*, pp. 272–320.

corruption, revealing the long-term effects of religious indiscipline and schism. Both the Mylapore bones and the Thomas Christians were relics most valuable as a testament to the pious memory of the Apostle, rather than foundations upon which the Portuguese might build a new Catholic Church in Asia.

12

Cultural History in the Catacombs: Early Christian Art and Macarius's *Hagioglypta**

Irina Oryshkevich

In the age of the Reformation, the origins of Christian figurative art were a source of great contention. While Protestants categorically denied that the Church had commissioned or used images for devotional purposes in the earliest, purest stages of its existence, Catholics claimed the opposite, namely, that the Church had sanctioned and incorporated them into liturgy from the very outset. And while Protestants blamed the rise of such material aids to devotion on the Church's relapse into pagan practice and Jewish ritualism, Catholics insisted that Christian images had come into being independently of outside forces and, more importantly, through God's direct sanction. Finally, while Protestants appealed to the First (or to them Second) Commandment to uphold their claim, Catholics countered by denying the relevance of Mosaic Law to the New Testament, a position they bolstered with the authority of tradition, patristic texts, and physical evidence.[1]

The need to defend the early origins of various Catholic cults and rituals led, in fact, to a kind of artistic palaeo-Christian revival in Rome and other papal strongholds in the late sixteenth century.[2] The ideological agenda behind the

---

* My thanks extend to Simon Ditchfield and all the participants at the 'Christian Origins' conference held at Calvin College in October 2008; to Ioannis Mylonopoulos, who read the initial draft of this essay; and to David Freedberg, who first drew *Hagioglypta* to my attention and lent me his copy of the book before it was easily obtainable in the United States.

[1] Literature on the debate of images in the sixteenth century is extensive. Seminal still are Campenhausen, 'Die Bilderfrage in der Reformation', and Jedin, 'Entstehung und Tragweite des Trienter Dekrets'. On the Catholic stance, see Hecht, *Katholische Bildertheologie*, and Scavizzi, *The Controversy on Images from Calvin to Baronius*. On modern debates over the origins of Christian images, see Finney, *The Invisible God*, and bibliography.

[2] On this phenomenon, see, among others, Buser, 'Jerome Nadal and Early Jesuit Art in Rome'; Herz, 'Cardinal Cesare Baronio's Restoration of SS. Nereo ed Achilleo and S. Cesareo de Appia'; and Zuccari, 'La politica culturale dell'Oratorio romano'.

movement betrayed itself in the excitement roused by the discovery of a catacomb in 1578.[3] The revelation of this cemetery on the via Salaria was hailed as providential, above all because it contained murals of sacred subjects that offered incontestable proof of the antiquity of the Christian cult of images. Nonetheless, and rather surprisingly, the images unearthed were given no role to play in the ongoing debate over the origins of devotional art. Although the *Avviso* that publicized the event described several of the site's wall paintings, these and similar ones discovered elsewhere stirred but little interest among Catholic polemicists until over sixty years later, when Giovanni Severano appended a chapter on catacomb imagery to Antonio Bosio's posthumously published *Roma sotterranea* (1632–4).[4] Gabriele Paleotti, for example, did not note their existence despite upholding the antiquity of Christian art in his *Discorso intorno alle imagini sacre e profane* (1582). Cesare Baronio, in the first volume of his *Annales ecclesiastici* (1588), referred to the image of the Good Shepherd only in a general sense in the eighteen colophons he allocated to the origins of devotional images and ecclesiastical architecture.[5] Among artists, too, neither the murals nor the reliefs of the cemeteries generated anywhere near the excitement of the discovery of the richly decorated *Domus Aurea* in the late fifteenth century.[6] The images seem to have piqued the interest only of antiquarians, most notably Philip van Winghe (1560–92), Alfonso Chacón (1540–99), Pompeo Ugonio (d. 1614), the young Antonio Bosio (*c.*1576–1629), and the various obscure draftsmen whom they hired.[7] Nor were the images generally recognized as art. Indeed, the degree of damage inflicted on them by relic hunters, whose activity was authorized by the Roman Church, reveals that they were regarded as expendable.[8]

Admittedly, no one claimed that catacomb paintings marked the origins of Christian image-making. This 'prize' had traditionally been awarded to a very

---

[3] Sauerland, '*De coemeterio Priscillae Romae invento in canicularibus anno 1578*'.

[4] Bosio, *Roma sotterranea*. Severano notes in his introduction to the chapter that he added it as a supplement to Bosio's illustrations since it was necessary to explain why early Christians made these images; p. 593.

[5] Baronio, *Annales ecclesiastici*, I, pp. 450–9 (image of Good Shepherd noted on p. 456). For more on Baronio and the *Annales*, see above, Ch. 3. Federico Borromeo does refer to a few specific catacomb images in *De pictura sacra* (1624) but apparently derived his information from notes and drawings compiled by Alfonso Chacón. He allegedly planned to write a separate treatise on early Christian art, but never got around to it; *Sacred Painting*, I, pp. 2–6, 67–71; II, pp. 2–3, 7, 99–101. On the cardinal's interest in early Christian art, see Agosti, *Collezionismo e archeologia cristiana nel seicento*.

[6] There is no evidence—in the form of graffiti or sketches—that local Italian artists besides those hired by antiquarians went to the catacombs to look at art. On artists' reaction to the *Domus Aurea*, see Dacos, *La découverte de la Domus Aurea*.

[7] On antiquarian interest in the catacombs and relevant bibliography, see Herklotz, 'Historia Sacra und mittelalterliche Kunst', pp. 21–74.

[8] On the destruction of the cemeteries by relic hunters, see Signorotto, 'Cercatori di reliquie'; and Ghilardi, 'D'all'*inventio* del corpo santo alla costruzione della reliquia'.

different category of works: miraculously generated icons whose origins were recounted in well-established legends.[9] Catholic apologists invariably insisted that the earliest Christian image had been created by Christ after he projected his likeness onto a blank canvas at the behest of King Agbar of Edessa. Next in order of importance were the images of Christ represented on the '*sudarium*' (the so-called *Veronica*), the Shroud of Turin, the 'Lateran Saviour' icon, the wooden crucifix in Lucca known as the *volto santo*, and the myriad Marian icons produced by the evangelist Luke with angelic assistance.

Many of these images still drew hordes of pilgrims in the sixteenth century. The Edessan icon (known also as the Mandylion), for example, was venerated in the Roman Church of San Silvestro in Capite, the *Veronica* at St Peter's, and the various Virgins attributed to the brush of St Luke in Rome's foremost Marian churches. Most, however, were hidden behind locked doors and displayed only on special occasions, or else lay barely visible beneath the armour of precious adornments. Authors who used such works to prove God's sanction of images did little to demystify the public by illustrating or describing their physical features. Instead they dwelt on their status as *acheiropoieta* (icons not made by hand, i.e. of divine provenance), on the documents and legends that sustained their authenticity, or on their unmitigated power to perform miracles. The scant attention paid to the formal qualities of these ancient images is all the more striking in a period that laid increasing emphasis on artistic style and the divine nature of creative genius. One cannot but suspect that the reluctance of Catholic authors to discuss the physical traits of such *acheiropoieta* owed something to their crude manufacture and unappealing (at least from a Renaissance perspective) formal features, which to anyone with even a slight awareness of historical style must have looked suspiciously medieval. Indeed eyes accustomed to the perspectival settings, idealized proportions, and technical virtuosity of *cinquecento* art, would certainly have required a transformatory lens to detect God's hand in the crude likenesses conveyed by these effigies.

On some level Catholic apologists realized that any discussion of style could jeopardize public credence in the supernatural provenance of these objects, since style or *maniera* was a historical phenomenon, as Giorgio Vasari had argued—a product of an individual's training, familiarity with earlier art, aptitude, and temperament.[10] By sidestepping the issue of style and fixating instead on the miraculous creation and properties of *acheiropoieta*, Catholic authorities presented the origins of Christian art as a supernatural phenomenon

---

[9] On the following images in the writings of the Catholic reformers, see Hecht, *Katholische Bildertheologie*, pp. 124–37.

[10] Vasari assigned distinct artistic styles to different historical epochs. See especially his prefaces to the three parts of the 1568 edition of *The Lives of the Artists*, pp. 25–47, 83–93, and 249–54.

with no roots in either the Old Testament or pagan antiquity. Arriving on earth fully fashioned or through the intervention of Christ, angels, or some other divinely appointed agent, *acheiropoieta* transcended history as well as comparison with images crafted by human hands. Classified as relics rather than devotional icons, they did not invite any discussion of style since their importance lay in their miraculous properties rather than in their formal features. More importantly, their supernatural provenance rendered them invulnerable to Protestant claims that the cult of images was a holdover from or relapse into pagan or Old Testament idolatry. By the same token, *acheiropoieta* absolved Catholics of breaking the First Commandment, since they made God rather than mortals responsible for circumscribing His form.

In the Counter Reformation, Catholic didactic tracts on sacred art generally fell into one of two categories: those defending the use of devotional images and those demanding reform in the arts. Specimens of the first type, which began appearing in the 1520s in the wake of Protestant iconoclasm, relied principally on textual sources and *acheiropoieta* to prove the use of images in biblical and early Christian times. While some of these, such as Iohannes Cochlaeus's *Quaestiones duae, quarum altera est, de imaginibus in ecclesia retinendis altera de adoratione altaris sacrificio* (1546), Konrad Bruin's *De imaginibus* (1548), Nicholas Harpsfield, *Dialogi sex contra summi pontificatus, monasticae vitae sanctorum, sacrarum imaginum oppugnatores* (1566), or Simon Maiolus's *Pro defensione sacrarum imaginum adversus iconomachos libri seu centuriae sexdecim* (1585),[11] were strictly polemical and directed ostensibly at Protestants or sceptical Catholics, others were embedded in broader historical studies of the early Church, such as Cesare Baronio's *Annales ecclesiastici* (1588–1607), and Antonio Bosio's *Roma sotterranea* (1632–4).[12] Treatises in the second, reform-oriented category, such as Andrea Gilio's *Dialogo nel quale si ragiona degli errori e degli abusi de' pittori circa l'istorie* (1564), Johannes Molanus's *De historia SS. imaginum et picturarum, pro vero earum usu contra abusus* (1568), Carlo Borromeo's *Instructiones fabricae et supellectilis ecclesiasticae* (1577), Gabriele Paleotti's *Discorso intorno alle imagini sacre e profane* (1584), and Federico Borromeo's *De pictura sacra* (1624), emerged after the Council of Trent in order to flesh out the general and somewhat vague directives in the decree on images drafted at the Council's final session in 1563. With the notable exception of the Flemish Molanus (a.k.a. Jan Vermeulen), most authors of these treatises were Italian. Aiming their texts at ecclesiastical supervisors, artists, and potential

---

[11] On these treatises, see n. 1 above.

[12] Baronio discusses the validity of sacred images in various sections of the *Annales ecclesiastici*, most forcefully in vol. I (anno 57), pp. 456ff and vol. IV (anno 324), pp. 67ff. The long-winded defence of images in bk IV of Bosio's *Roma sotterranea* was written entirely by Giovanni Severano, an Oratorian priest who prepared Bosio's incomplete treatise for publication after his death; *Roma sotterranea*, pp. 599–604.

patrons of the arts, they aimed chiefly to strip images of erotic and obscene elements, simplify iconography, ensure easy readability, curtail artistic license, and push art back to some tenuously defined 'primitive' state.[13] Despite the difference in their respective agendas, both categories of tracts—polemical and reform-oriented—sanctioned devotional images, granted them miraculous powers, championed their function as books of the illiterate, and backed their arguments with the same type of evidence—legends, tradition, and *acheiropoieta*.

But not all Catholic observers accepted these premises. Lost amid this ideologically driven discourse lies Jean l'Heureux's *Hagioglypta sive picturae et sculpturae sacrae antiquores praesertim quae Romae reperiuntur*, a long and erudite essay on the origins of Christian art in ancient Rome. A minor cleric from Gravelines, L'Heureux—better known by his nickname Macarius (1551–1617)—was chiefly interested in letters, Greek, classical, and patristic.[14] *Hagioglypta*, his sole foray into art criticism, conceived during his twenty-year residence in Rome (1580–c.1600) is a testament to his friendly relations with many of the city's foremost antiquarians—Chacón, van Winghe, Bosio, Fulvio Orsini (1529–1600), Lelio Pasqualini (d. 1611), Angelo Beneventano (d. 1597)—whose assistance and opinions he warmly recollects throughout its pages. The work also exemplifies Macarius's unique synthesis of Renaissance theories on the emotive power and intellectual potential of the visual arts—as outlined by writers like Leon Battista Alberti (1404–72), Giorgio Vasari (1511–74), Giovanni Paolo Lomazzo (1538–1600)—and the Catholic reformers' interest in the physical remains of Christian antiquity, which had been ignored if not maligned by humanists and artists who had written on the visual arts.[15]

For reasons that remain unclear, Macarius did not publish *Hagioglypta* despite receiving ecclesiastical permission to do so from the Inquisitor of St-Omer in 1605. After his death the manuscript found its way to Jean Bolland, the great Flemish hagiographer, who annotated it with his own hand. Through him it entered the Bollandist Library, then a private collection, where it was discovered by the Jesuit scholar Raffaele Garrucci, who published it with minor revisions and brief commentary in 1856. The original manuscript has since vanished, a victim perhaps of one of the world wars.

---

[13] For a summary of these treatises and a general discussion of the reform of the arts after the Council of Trent, see Prodi, 'Ricerche sulla teoria delle arti figurative'; Scavizzi, 'La teologia cattolica e le immagini'; and Beltramme, 'Le teoriche dell'Academia di San Luca'.

[14] What little is known about Macarius's life and the history of the *Hagioglypta* manuscript is summarized by Raphael Garrucci in his preface to L'Heureux, *Hagioglypta*, pp. v–xii; and Le Glay, 'Notice sur un traité inédit d'iconographie chrétienne intitulé: *Hagioglypta*'.

[15] The literature on Renaissance theories of the arts is much too vast to summarize here; see the useful introduction in Blunt, *Artistic Theory, 1450–1600*. For Alberti's discussion of the importance and power of painting, see *On Painting*, especially bk II. Vasari celebrates the importance of all three visual arts (painting, sculpture, architecture) throughout his *Lives of the Artists*, but especially in the introduction to his corpus. Lomazzo raised art to a metaphysical level in *Trattato dell'arte de la pittura*, published in 1584.

Virtually unknown outside a small circle of highly specialized historians, *Hagioglypta* has never been reprinted, translated into a living language, or subjected to intense or systematic analysis.[16] On the rare occasions that scholars recall its existence, they tend to assume that it is yet another Catholic treatise defending the cult of images against iconoclasts.[17]

Although Macarius's book *is* a defence of images of sorts, it bears little if any resemblance to other Counter-Reformation treatises of this ilk. It is neither an apology for the cult of images nor a manual on how to restore Christian art to its 'primitive' innocence by ridding it of excessive sophistication and artistic licence. It does not denounce iconoclasm or reiterate the time-worn legends about *acheiropoieta*, or even uphold their indubitable antiquity. More astonishingly, it does not reaffirm the commonplace defining pictures as the books of the illiterate.[18] Indeed *Hagioglypta* aims to prove the opposite, that is, that any true understanding of the complexity and depth of early Christian art requires profound erudition.

On its most basic level, *Hagioglypta* reveals an earnest attempt to deal with the origins and early evolution of Christian imagery in a comprehensive and scholarly manner. Noting that many have already written on the paintings and sculptures of recent ages, Macarius promises instead to treat the neglected category of ancient Christian art.[19] By framing his objective in this manner, he places his book among the critical and historical studies of Renaissance art, such as Giorgio Vasari's *Lives of the Artists* (1550 and 1568) and Antonio Possevino's *Tractatio de poesi & pictura ethnica, humana, & fabulosa* (1594), rather than among the various Catholic defences of images or the attempts to reform them. Furthermore, unlike representatives of both these more polemical camps, who tended to treat all Christian art produced before the early modern period as a stylistically undifferentiated mass, Macarius distinguishes works produced in the first few centuries of Christianity's existence from those of the later middle ages.

Hagioglypta consists of a preface and two books: the first on images in early Christian basilicas and cemeteries, the second on the more general significance of their iconography.[20] Accordingly, the text proceeds from the particular to the general. The transition is not always smooth, however, since in many

---

[16] The sole modern study of the text—enlightening though essentially descriptive—is Herklotz, 'Die *Hagioglypta* des Jean L'Heureux'.

[17] See e.g. Ferretto, *Note storico-bibliografiche di archeologia cristiana*, p. 125. This assumption is also made by Garrucci, who introduces the book as a vindication of the cult of images; 'Praefatio editoris' in L'Heureux, *Hagioglypta*, pp. xi–xii.

[18] A topos that dates back at least to Gregory I's letter of 599 to Bishop Serenus of Marseilles; Chazelle, 'Pictures, Books, and the Illiterate'.

[19] *Hagioglypta*, p. 210.

[20] Garrucci changed the format of the original by eliminating a long digression on fish and vine motifs in images of Jonah in bk I (p. 74), and appending it as an *excursus*; *Hagioglypta*, pp. 211–22.

instances Macarius confesses his inability to unravel a motif's arcane meaning and leaves it open to further investigation by better-qualified scholars, thus further underscoring the depth and complexity of these deceptively simple images.[21]

Macarius opens his treatise with Horace's oft-cited phrase from the *Ars poetica*, '*ut pictura poesis . . .*' ('As in painting, so in poetry; some works are more compelling when viewed from up close, others when perceived from afar').[22] Macarius uses the passage not only in the typical humanist sense—to draw a parallel between the visual and literary arts—but also to argue that the value of both media is relative and contingent on the perspective of the audience. He goes on to state that, to the same degree that the painting and sculpture of his time surpass those of the early Christians in terms of elegance, so theirs far surpassed those of the sixteenth century in terms of iconographic complexity. Without berating either, he nonetheless demonstrates that form is but one criterion of artistic quality. He thus distances himself not only from those classical enthusiasts who dismiss palaeo-Christian art as inept or crude, but also from Catholic polemicists who, despite their professed interest in it, can appreciate it solely as a historical witness to Rome's primacy and the unchanging traditions of the Catholic Church.[23]

Committed to this *via media* view throughout his book, Macarius makes no attempt to apologize for the lack of 'elegance' in ancient Christian art. Unlike his contemporary Giulio Mancini (1558–1630), who includes a brief, but generally unpolemical section on catacomb paintings in his *Considerazioni sulla pittura* (1619), he does not claim that the murals in the catacombs are crude because Christians were too poor to hire better artists, or because they were compelled to work quickly and furtively during persecutions.[24] Nor does he, like Cesare Baronio, rationalize the art's 'low quality' by arguing that all the best ancient artists had converted to Christianity and had thus been martyred by the early fourth century, leaving no one behind to perpetuate their craft.[25] Alternatively, Macarius does not repeat the theory—so popular among other sixteenth-century artists and art theorists—that blamed palaeo-Christian artists' break with the classical canon on the fall of Rome or the puritanical zeal of early prelates.[26] In fact, apart from his contention that the works of his

---

[21] *Hagioglypta*, p. 6.

[22] *Hagioglypta*, p. 1. Cf. Horace, *Ars poetica*, ll. 361–5. On the various interpretations of this passage, see Lee, '*Ut pictura poesis*'; and Trimpi, 'The Meaning of Horace's *Ut pictura poesis*'.

[23] Hecht, *Katholische Bildertheologie*, pp. 338–47. The practical application of this view is analysed by Alessandro Borgomainerio in the case of the restoration of a famous early Christian monument, the Lateran Baptistery in 'Domenico Castelli, Gian Lorenzo Bernini and the *Symmetry* of the Lateran Baptistery', forthcoming.

[24] Mancini, *Considerazioni sulla pittura*, I, pp. 48–9.

[25] Baronio, *Annales ecclesiastici*, III, anno 303, CXV–CXVI, pp. 365–6.

[26] As did Ghiberti, *Lorenzo Ghibertis Denkwürdigkeiten*, p. 35; and Vasari, *The Lives of the Artists*, pp. 36–7.

day are more elegant while those of the ancient Church more profound, Macarius passes few value judgements on either. Rather than criticize early Christian artists for their failure to adhere to classical standards, he presents their deviation as a product of conscious will—a desire to give visual definition to a new culture emerging from an older one on the brink of obsolescence. At the same time, his choice of introductory quotes, as well as his frequent references to and citations from a host of Greek and Roman literary figures, reveal the ease with which he applies classical principles, examples, and anecdotes to his analysis of Christian culture. Thus when describing the concept of salvation through self-annihilation, for instance, he draws an analogy between Christians martyrs and Cleombrotus Ambraciotus, who hastened his end after reading Plato on the immortality of the soul.[27] The parallel is all the more astounding coming from cleric at a time when theologians on both sides of the confessional divide were anxiously distinguishing genuine martyrdom from self-aggrandizing suicide.[28]

Throughout *Hagioglypta*, Macarius presents Christian art as either an extension of or a response to pagan art. Thus after bemoaning the lack of appreciation for palaeo-Christian art among modern Romans in his *praefatio*, he opens Chapter I not with the legendary Christian *acheiropoieta* (which he barely mentions) but with a discussion of the structure, layout, and decoration of the earliest Christian basilicas, and their derivation from the pagan ones described by Vitruvius.[29] He conjectures, for example, that the apse of a church developed from the judge's tribunal in the older building type, and that the customary image of Christ at its centre—dressed in Roman garb and displaying the gestures of the classical orator—supplanted that of the presiding judge. He also points out that a figure of authority represented in the apse of any basilica, Christian or otherwise, was meant to induce trepidation and awe. From the outset, Macarius makes it clear that Christian art was the product of mortal beings, who appropriated from earlier forms and symbols whatever best met their needs. In this respect the Flemish antiquarian differed both from Catholic apologists who minimize the role of pagan influence on Christian culture and from the many humanist authors, who attributed the 'decline' of palaeo-Christian art to ignorance or a rejection of classical norms.

---

[27] *Hagioglypta*, p. 197. The story of Cleombrotus, alternately called Theombratus of Ambracia, is related by Augustine, *De civitate dei*, I, 22, who presumably learned it from Cicero, *Tusculanae disputationes*, I, 34 and 84.

[28] Much ink was spilled over the definition of martyrdom on both sides of the confessional divide; see e.g. Cope [Nicholas Harpsfield], *Dialogi sex contra . . . sacrarum imaginum oppugnatores* as well as the Protestant martyrologies compiled by Jean Crespin, John Foxe, and Ludwig Rabus. On this theme, see the classic study by Gregory, *Salvation at Stake*, as well as the comments above, in Chs. 3 and 4.

[29] *Hagioglypta*, pp. 7–9.

Throughout the book, Macarius juxtaposes Christian images and symbols with pagan and Jewish ones, tracing their origins with the help of long passages from Greek, Roman, and patristic sources. He claims, for instance, that the figure of Christ in depictions of the *Raising of Lazarus* harks back to images of Asklepios, the ancient god of healing, while the rod that He uses to effect the miracle is a reference to the wand used by Mercury to drive away death and disease rather than those used by Aaron and Moses to denote leadership.[30] He likewise points out that the *aedicula* that is not mentioned in the Gospels but invariably encloses Lazarus in early Christian representations of his resurrection alludes to the mausolea of wealthy Jews, but is simultaneously a prefiguration of the Holy Sepulchre, since Christ, like Lazarus, was buried according to Jewish custom. By carefully weighing meanings against each other, and selecting those that work best with the Christian subject in a particular context, Macarius demonstrates the complexity and potential polyvalence of symbols, and thus subtly undermines the idea that pictures are books of the illiterate—that is, simplifications of theological texts or mere illustrations of biblical or hagiographical narratives.

Macarius neither apologizes for the Christians' appropriation of pagan and Jewish symbols, nor appeals to the Church Fathers to justify the practice. Instead, he presents the phenomenon as a process of cultural evolution; the Christians adopted the visual vocabulary of pagans and Jews because they lived in their midst. He acknowledges, of course, that the symbols assumed different nuances once they were embedded into Christian contexts, so that a phoenix minted on the coin of the Empress Faustina, for example, referred to eternity, while one painted in a catacomb alluded specifically to rebirth.[31]

By drawing multiple parallels between Christian and pagan images, and demonstrating how the former evolved from the latter, Macarius risked confirming the Protestant allegation that the cult of images had been born of heathen idolatry. As a professing Catholic, he could not regard the use of art in religious praxis as a sign of spiritual corruption. Yet he did not explicitly defend the Tridentine Church's use of images; instead, he opted to heighten public awareness of these ancient monuments, to make people 'occasionally recognize as sacred what they had formerly believed to be profane'.[32] Ironically, he seems to have been more exasperated by modern Romans' lack of appreciation for Christian antiquities than by Protestant iconophobia, to which, in fact, he never alludes.[33]

Also intriguing is Macarius's insistence that early Christian symbols could vary according to setting. He points out, for instance, that in a cemetery an image of a peacock atop an orb signifies resurrection, while in the apse of a

---

[30] Ibid., pp. 79–89.   [31] Ibid., pp. 205–6.   [32] Ibid., p. 5.
[33] He reveals his frustration especially when describing the poor state of the mosaics in S. Maria Maggiore; ibid., p. 153.

church it alludes to the efficacy of baptism, or alternatively to the conception of Christ, since peacocks reproduce without sex.[34] He notes too that the iconography of sarcophagi differs from that of church interiors since artists had more freedom to invent when working for private patrons than when creating programmes for public houses of worship.[35]

To Macarius, however, not only the meanings of images are relative, but so is their function, which is site-specific. As he reaches the end of his discussion on basilicas and cemeteries, he concludes that the function of an image in an apse is to inspire veneration; in a nave, to relate the stories of the Scriptures; and in a cemetery, to express Christian hope in resurrection.[36] In other words, careful interpretation of any visual motif demands consideration of both its physical context and purpose.

Yet even with all this information at hand, Macarius does not feel fully confident in his interpretations, which he often leaves open. The provisional tone of his analyses contrasts sharply with the more dogmatic approach of Catholic authors, such as Molanus, Paleotti, and Severano, whose definitive readings of Christian imagery seem to betray their fear of initiating a scholarly debate on a subject so sensitive to the papacy.

Hagioglypta also demonstrates Macarius's awareness of stylistic and iconographic evolution. The author notes, for example, that initially Christians did not represent the crucified Christ, but only the bare cross.[37] While Antonio Bosio was later to use the unique *Crucifixion* in the Christian cemetery of Priscilla on the via Salaria (one of Rome's oldest) as proof that the motif had existed in pre-Constantinian times, Macarius uses the same image to make the reverse argument, namely, that the image may have been executed much later than the other murals in the area since the catacomb continued to be frequented until Lombard times.[38] Similarly, he points out that the oldest representations of saints and Christ in the catacombs do not show them with haloes, and that this attribute—which originated in representations of Caesar—only appears in apse mosaics made after the Edict of Milan of 313.[39]

Further evidence of Macarius's historical consciousness appears in his desire to avoid anachronism. When discussing the early Christian significance of doves, for example, he refers to those depicted in the apse of the church of San Clemente, but admits that these cannot illuminate their meaning in antiquity since the mosaic is not that old.[40] He is equally quick to note differences between iconographical programs in Rome and elsewhere, claiming, for instance, that the apse in the basilica of Nola described by Paulinus in

---

[34] Ibid., pp. 105–6.   [35] Ibid., pp. 19–20.   [36] Ibid., p. 197.
[37] Ibid., pp. 30–1.   [38] Ibid., p. 31; Bosio, *Roma Sotteranea*, p. 581.
[39] *Hagioglypta*, p. 24.   [40] Ibid., pp. 29–30.

the fourth century contained images of doves, the Trinity, and goats—subjects that were seldom depicted in the churches of the capital.[41]

Although Macarius does not discuss later medieval Christian imagery, he does compare iconographic conventions of antiquity to those of his own day. For instance, he points out that early Christians represented Noah's Ark very differently, as a sort of box,[42] and that saints in the past were not rendered recognizable by their attributes, but by inscription or characteristic garb.[43] He also observes that for a long time Christ was represented on the cross fully dressed, and was stripped down to his loincloth in gradual stages.[44] He infers too that images of the Virgin and Child were relatively late developments and that earlier on Mary had always been depicted alone and dressed in blue, but a common, natural shade of the colour rather than one manufactured from costly pigments.[45] In making this claim he (perhaps inadvertently) questions the antiquity and thereby the authenticity of the various Madonnas attributed to Luke, which were naturally dated to apostolic times.[46] Among other discrepancies, he also mentions the early aversion to representing God the Father in human form, and asserts that when it was necessary to include Him in Old Testament scenes such as the Creation, Christians customarily portrayed Him in the guise of His Son.[47]

In similar fashion, Macarius explains that when rendering a narrative early Christians tended to depict important characters, such as Christ, larger, and lesser ones, such as the freshly resurrected Lazarus, on a miniature scale in order to demonstrate that like children, the latter were helpless and in need of assistance.[48] Similarly he justifies the recurrent representations of protagonists in narrative scenes as a device that helps viewers follow the thread of a story.[49]

Although he alerts the reader to disparities between ancient and modern modes of representation, Macarius does not voice his moral indignation at the stylistic or iconographical innovations of more recent artists. To the same degree that he refrains from scoffing at the early Christians' ignorance of perspective and classical proportions, he desists from censuring his contemporaries for representing Christ nearly nude on the cross or Mary in sumptuous dress. Unlike Paleotti, Molanus, or Borromeo, for instance, he does not urge painters to revert to a more chaste and 'primitive' style, or prelates to exercise stricter control over artistic licence. Quite the contrary, he seems to reconcile himself with the inevitability of change.

In this respect, Macarius's view of history differs greatly from that of Cardinal Cesare Baronio, who, in the introduction to his monumental *Annales*

---

[41] Ibid., pp. 47–8.   [42] Ibid., p. 70.   [43] Ibid., pp. 27–9.

[44] Ibid., pp. 9–10.   [45] Ibid., pp. 35–6.

[46] Macarius does note that Luke painted images of Christ, but does not mention the typical Virgin and Christ child icons that are historically associated with the Evangelist; ibid., p. 12.

[47] Ibid., pp. 48–9.   [48] Ibid., pp. 11, 87–90.

[49] Ibid., pp. 73–4.

ecclesiastici, the official Catholic history of Christianity, claimed that the Church had undergone no changes since its foundation. Indeed Baronio strategically inserted a discussion of the origins of Christian images in the *Annales* in the year AD 57, implying thereby that they coincided with Peter's arrival in Rome.[50] In doing so he implicitly refuted the Protestant contention that images were introduced in the Middle Ages by a Church already in decline. Macarius however, approaches the matter from a drastically different angle, since he not only views the Christian use of images as an appropriation and continuation of pre-Christian practice, but also goes to a great deal of trouble to demonstrate the degree to which Christian iconography and artistic style *have* changed since apostolic times. Whereas Baronio's Church is immutable, rigid, and frozen in time—an artificial and defensive construct designed to counter Protestant accusations of corruption—Macarius's is a flexible and malleable institution that adapts to the needs and situation of a given era.

Remarkable too is Macarius's treatment of the catacombs. Writing at a moment when the ancient cemeteries were being reconfigured in pictures and descriptions as vast and secret subterranean cities—labyrinthine networks housing thousands if not millions of persecuted Christians[51]—the Flemish cleric remained remarkably untouched by the martyromania sweeping Counter-Reformation Rome.

For one, he treats the catacombs exclusively as cemeteries excavated outside the city's walls in compliance with the Roman prohibition against intramural burial, and omits any mention of their supposed function as clandestine meeting-places for Christians.[52] Although he likens the catacombs to cities, he does so only with respect to their size, noting that the larger ones take six to seven hours to cross. He also points out that they lie along the same major arteries into Rome as do thousands of pagan mausolea and crematoria. This observation too suggests that he placed little credence in the story of the secrecy of the crypts, since it hints at the absurdity of the belief that the persecuted sect would have engaged in the large-scale construction of a temporary home beneath such heavily traversed thoroughfares. Although he acknowledges that some martyrs were buried in the catacombs, he never insists—as did most Romans of his time—that the vast majority of the graves were excavated for saints.[53] Similarly, he makes no attempt to identify the

---

[50] Baronio, *Annales ecclesiastici*, I, anno 57, cxxx, p. 462.

[51] On the literary and visual reconfiguration of catacombs as cities, see Panciroli, *I tesori nascosti nell'alma città di Roma*, pp. 72–88; Baronio, *Annales ecclesiastici*, II, pp. 117–18; Oryshkevich, 'Roma sotterranea and the biogenesis of New Jerusalem'; as well as the plates and especially the frontispiece of Bosio's *Roma sotterranea*.

[52] *Hagioglypta*, pp. 59–64.

[53] The idea that the cemeteries were full of martyrs dates to the middle ages, and was confirmed in an inscription over the entrance to the catacomb of San Sebastiano, which noted that 174,000 martyrs and 46 popes had been laid to rest in that cemetery alone; Bosio, *Roma*

graves of martyrs on the basis of the various symbols (palms, crowns, anchors, hearts, instruments of martyrdom, crosses) incised on them, and ignores the popular theory that the glass phials frequently cemented in lime around *loculi* contain the blood of martyrs.[54] Macarius admits in passing that certain people in Rome 'claim to have seen' mysterious ciphers of the kind described by the fourth-century poet Prudentius, who believed them to be cryptic indicators of mass graves of anonymous martyrs. He neither denies nor espouses this belief, however, but points out that the *loculi* in the catacombs are extremely shallow, and thus designed to hold only one body, or at most—and only in rare cases— two or three.[55] He also refers to an urn that he saw in a certain cemetery to state that contrary to common belief, early Christians were occasionally cremated.[56] Finally, unlike Severano and Girolamo Bruni, a cleric who was to compose a long essay on catacombs in 1614, Macarius does not spend pages insisting that heretics, schismatics, and pagans were never interred in the crypts.[57] To him the problem was clearly irresolvable, or at least irrelevant to the subject at hand.

Macarius may have obtained some information on the cemeteries from Onofrio Panvinio, who in 1568 had written a treatise on early Christian burial rites that included a chapter on the catacombs of Rome.[58] What distinguishes Macarius's essay, however, is the precedence he grants to empirical observa- tion. While Panvinio derives nearly all his information on the cemeteries from textual sources—including the *Liber pontificalis* and the various editions of the *Mirabilia urbis Romae*, Macarius substantiates all his claims with specific paintings, inscriptions, and artefacts, and often poses new questions based on his observations. Moreover, unlike Panvinio, who assume that the niches (*arcosolia*) in the *cubicula* were used as altars at ceremonies or for Mass during persecutions,[59] Macarius discusses them solely as grave markers.

While Macarius devotes much effort to describing and analysing the works of art in the cemeteries, he does not use them to defend or discuss the antiquity of the cult of images. In fact, not once does he suggest that the images were venerated or employed as devotional aids. Instead he posits that they were made as tributes to the dead as well as expressions of faith in corporeal resurrection. Furthermore, unlike Severano and Borromeo, who read references

---

sotterranea, p. 178. Girolamo Bruni calculated, *c.*1614, that 64,000,000 martyrs in toto had been buried in the catacombs of Rome: *De coemeteriis* (Vat. Lat. 9498, fols. 1–23), pp. 70–2.

[54] For a comprehensive history of this theory, see Meyer, 'The Phial of Blood Controversy'.

[55] *Hagioglypta*, p. 64.

[56] Ibid., p. 156.

[57] See Bosio, *Roma sotterranea*, bk IV, cap. I, 593–600; and Bruni, *De coemeteriis*, caps. I, and XI.

[58] Panvinio, *De ritu sepeliendi mortuos*, cap. XII, n.p.

[59] Ibid., cap. XI, n.p.

to Christian persecutions into many of the biblical motifs depicted in the crypts, Macarius grants these same images positive and universal meanings. Thus, for example, while Severano insists that *Daniel in the Lion's Den*, the *Three Young Men in the Fiery Furnace*, and the *Afflictions of Job* allude to the physical torments suffered by Christians during persecutions, Macarius interprets such images as episodes of spiritual salvation.[60]

Macarius also discusses renderings of biblical subjects in considerable depth. He scrutinizes details of dress, discrepancies between images and the Scriptures, the relationship between Christian and pagan iconography, and degrees of artistic licence. He observes, for example, that Daniel is depicted between two lions even though the Bible mentions seven, and that he is shown naked to reveal his vulnerability despite the general Christian aversion to nudity.[61] When analysing the *Three Young Men in the Fiery Furnace*, Macarius considers the ethnic origins and details of their costume, which he compares to those of Parthian slaves on Roman reliefs.[62]

Macarius also devotes thirteen pages to the pagan Orpheus, the discovery of whose images in the catacombs caused some consternation among Catholic authorities.[63] Although Borromeo and Severano do refer to depictions of the mythological character in the cemeteries, they do so apologetically and tersely, merely noting that when set among animals Orpheus represents Christ bringing harmony to the world.[64] Macarius, in contrast, not only discusses the rich symbolism (verbal and visual) associated with the Greek bard, but also uses the subject as an excuse to digress on conflicting views of the Golden Age among the Church Fathers. In doing so, he undermines the pristine image of an absolutely concordant primitive Church.

Macarius likewise discerns the rarity of certain iconographical motifs in the catacombs. He notes, for example, that the Holy Virgin is seldom portrayed, and argues that when a female orant appears in the centre of a sarcophagus it is probably not Mary but the occupant of the tomb.[65] He also points out that most orants in the catacombs are female and conjectures that they refer to the blessed matrons who donated land for Christian burial and whose names came to identify many of the cemeteries. Although he interprets their open-armed gesture as one of prayer, he proposes that they are extolling God rather than interceding for mankind.[66]

---

[60] Bosio, *Roma sotterranea*, bk IV, esp. pp. 606, 614, 616, *passim*; Borromeo, *Sacred Painting*, II, 2. 3–4, 99–101.

[61] *Hagioglypta*, p. 75.

[62] Ibid., pp. 76–7.

[63] Ibid., pp. 176–88.

[64] Borromeo, *Sacred Painting*, II, 2. 4, 69; Bosio, *Roma sotterranea*, pp. 627–9. See also Mancini, *Considerazioni*, I, pp. 49–51.

[65] Ibid., p. 170.

[66] Ibid., pp. 169–70.

Unusual too is Macarius's excursus on a fantastical creature—half fish, half bull—which he calls the '*Tauropiscis*'.[67] He infers that this binary being signifies the dual nature of Christ—mortal and divine—and tentatively dates its origins to the papacy of Celestine I (422–32), under whom the doctrine of Christ's nature was established at the Council of Ephesus. His discussion of the motif is all the more remarkable in view of Borromeo's and Bellarmino's condemnation of three-headed images of the Trinity, which, they claim, are unnatural and monstrous and too much like Janus, the double-faced deity of ancient Rome.[68]

Throughout *Hagioglypta*, Macarius draws equally on Graeco-Roman and patristic sources. In this respect he again differs sharply from Severano, who barely refers to pagan authorities in his chapter on catacomb imagery in *Roma sotterranea*. Although the Oratorian attributes this lacuna to the pressures of time, he justifies it by adding that the writings of the Fathers are far more relevant than pagan letters to a work dealing with sacred and ecclesiastic matters.[69] Sound as Severano's reasoning may appear, a closer reading of his text reveals that most of the 'patristic' sources that he uses to decode the symbols in the cemeteries postdate these works by decades if not centuries.

Macarius, however, seeks in pagan letters and objects not only parallels to Christian themes but also discrepancies that help clarify meanings embedded in all ancient sepulchral imagery. In his long excursus on gentile sarcophagi, for example, he maintains that the Romans revived the long-abandoned practice of inhumation in response to Christianity. Although he acknowledges that certain pagans, like Socrates and Cicero, did place some faith in an afterlife, he insists that the majority of them believed that death was followed by eternal nothingness. All the same, and despite their ignorance of the true God, they, like Christians, were intent on preserving human remains, and carved beautiful sarcophagi with images that either commemorated the deceased or reminded viewers that they should enjoy life while they could. Macarius provides many concrete examples of such works, using them as testimony that the chief difference between ancient Christians and pagans lay in their attitude to death. He thus leaves the reader with the impression that pagans were ignorant rather than wicked. Indeed, by juxtaposing gentile and Christian tomb decoration, Macarius implies a dynamic dialogue between the two camps rather than complete and unconditional rejection of either by its opponent. As he demonstrates time and time again, both drew from the same

---

[67] Ibid., pp. 191–2.
[68] Borromeo, *Sacred Painting* II.1, 26–7; de Laurentiis, 'Immagini ed arte in Bellarmino', pp. 599–600. In 1628, Urban VIII banned all triple-headed representations of the Trinity; Coulton, *Art and the Reformation*, p. 380.
[69] Bosio, *Roma sotterranea*, p. 656.

pool of symbols and artistic devices in order to define and defend their position.

In the end, however, what is most extraordinary about *Hagioglypta* is the respect, even awe, with which Macarius acknowledges the power of early Christian art. As he admits in his preface, he cannot pretend to comprehend in full the profundity of such abstruse images. He urges the reader to examine them side by side with the sacred and profane texts of the ancients, since the two modes of expression work reciprocally, and what might be passed over in silence in the one often manifests itself clearly in the other.[70] By placing images and text on an equal footing and respecting the complexity of both, Macarius rejects Gregory the Great's dismissal of images as the books of the illiterate, for if—as he insists—their enigmatic meaning can be grasped only through huge intellectual effort and broad erudition, then pictures are anything but didactic tools for the uneducated. What also comes to the fore in his discussion is the conviction that the beauty of figurative art lies not in its verisimilitude or refinement but in its depth, raw power, and ability to capture a glimmer of a God shrouded in awesome mystery.

Interesting too is Macarius's silence on the intercessory function of images. When claiming that apse mosaics were designed to inspire veneration, he specifies that their function was to impress and humble the beholder rather than to relay his or her prayers to heaven. Rather than circumscribe God in order to facilitate prayer, these images were meant to heighten the viewer's awareness of God's complexity and his or her incapacity to comprehend His full majesty.

In Macarius's view, therefore, images, do not simplify the message of the Word as interpreted by the Church Fathers, but are the products of autonomous exegesis. Text and image work symbiotically in his mind when he asks: 'Why, if we admire the writings of the Church Fathers, do we not esteem their paintings, which express the same things in paint that texts do in line and letters and which flow from the same fount of wisdom and devotion?' His rhetorical question threatens the traditional supremacy of letters over the so-called imitative arts, since if, as he insists, images and the writings of the Church Fathers flow from the same fount, then images are not the handmaidens of theology, but theology herself.

Macarius was thus proposing something quite audacious at a time when high-ranking prelates were anxious to regain control over artistic invention and make it subservient to the literal meaning of canonical texts. For he was arguing that just as theologians had the right to grapple with and interpret the Word, so too did artists. Bolder still is his celebration of works by unknown masters whose style must have appeared awkward and childish to modern

---

[70] *Hagioglypta*, p. 5.

audiences weaned on the paintings of Renaissance and Mannerist masters. In fact, it was precisely in this period and despite the revival of an allegedly early Christian style,[71] that so many 'primitive' mosaics, frescoes, and churches in Rome (including, of course, St Peter's) were destroyed or modified, often beyond recognition. The possibility of making Romans more appreciative of the integral value of ancient Christian art diminished with each additional act of demolition or renovation. Perhaps it was the realization of the futility of the endeavour that discouraged the Flemish scholar from setting his manuscript in print.

Although Macarius's ideas on palaeo-Christian art and its functions deviate from sixteenth-century Catholic norms, his essay ultimately offers a defence of sacred images that is more cogent and compelling than those expounded by any of his contemporaries, for he places the visual arts on a par with literature and grants to both the right to engage in sophisticated interpretation.

It is easy to dismiss *Hagioglypta* as an anomaly of its period, a work well ahead of its time. Since it was never published, it is difficult to assess its contribution to the budding discipline of Christian archaeology, the origins of which scholars like to date to the 1578 discovery of the catacomb on via Salaria. Given Macarius's scholarly connections, however, as well as his twenty-year residence in Rome and his appointment as apostolic penitentiary by Gregory XIII, it seems reasonable to assume that his analyses did not emerge from a vacuum but evolved from discussions with antiquarians, historians, and erudite friends. If this more plausible scenario is accepted, then *Hagioglypta* becomes less of an anomaly and more of a tool for investigating how scholars outside the circle of Catholic polemicists perceived the origins of Christian art.

---

[71] Many early Christian basilicas in Rome were restored between 1550 and 1650, including S. Sabina, SS. Nereo e Achilleo, I Quattro Coronati, S. Sebastiano in Pallara, S. Stefano Rotondo, S. Susanna, S. Crisogono, SS. Cosma e Damiano, S. Cecilia, and above all, St. Peter's. In each case, the building was heavily modified and much of its earlier adornments and furnishings discarded. Although scholars often view such campaigns as evidence of a palaeo-Christian revival, few have attempted to analyse the understanding of 'early Christian' style in art and architecture among late Renaissance artists or patrons. See, among others, Herz, 'Cardinal Cesare Baronio's Restoration'; Brummer, 'Cesare Baronio and the Convent of Gregory the Great'; and Kämpf, 'Framing Cecilia's Sacred Body'.

13

Scholarly Pilgrims: Antiquarian Visions of the Holy Land

Adam G. Beaver

1. THE FIFTH GOSPEL?

In 1860, Ernest Renan (1823–92)—already, in his thirties, a superstar among Western Orientalists, an expert on the cutting edge of nineteenth-century Semitic philology, and the youngest member of the great Académie des Inscriptions et Belles-Lettres[1]—departed Paris bound for Lebanon, where he was to oversee a French expedition dedicated to the excavation of Phoenician antiquities. Over the course of a year, Renan would apply his considerable scholarly talents to the dig, ultimately producing a celebrated report 884 pages in length and graced with dozens of maps and plates illustrating the French team's discoveries. It was not, however, Phoenician potsherds that most impressed Renan. Rather, it was his first encounter with the Christian Holy Land. Within months of his arrival in the East, Renan later confessed, he began to steal away to the Galilean countryside. There, in the course of his wanderings (and in spite of his avowed hostility to organized religion), he visited nearly all of the places associated with the life of Christ. 'I have traversed, in all directions, the country of the Gospels', he reported; 'scarcely any important locality of the history of Jesus has escaped me'. As he did so, he found himself marvelling that in Palestine, although he had always considered the Bible a work of fiction,

> All this [biblical] history, which at a distance seems to float in the clouds of an unreal world, . . . took a form, a solidity which astonished me. The striking agreement of the texts with the places, the marvelous harmony of the Gospel ideal with the country which served it as a framework, were like a revelation to

---

[1] For Renan's life, see Charles Chauvin, *Renan: 1823–1892* (Paris: Desclée de Brouwer, 2000). The Phoenician mission is discussed on pp. 40–3.

me. I had before my eyes a fifth Gospel, torn, but still legible, and henceforward, through the recitals of Matthew and Mark, in place of an abstract being, whose existence might have been doubted, I saw living and moving an admirable human figure.[2]

To put it another way, it occurred to Renan that there might actually be sound archeological and geographical evidence corroborating the biography of Christ—enough, even, to be able to write a 'scientific' history of the Gospels on good antiquarian principles. And so, during the course of a holiday spent in a Maronite cabin in Ghazir, Renan collated this 'fifth Gospel' with the textual evidence for Jesus' life in the New Testament and wrote his seminal *Vie de Jésus* (1863), an instant bestseller in spite of Renan's radical argument that Jesus was no more than an exceptionally charismatic human being.

One might consider Renan's quest to recover the ancient biblical landscape a liminal moment in the long history of scholarly encounters with the Holy Land. On the one hand, its imperialist, Orientalist context and secularist conclusions render it quintessentially modern.[3] Contemporary biblical critics regard the *Vie de Jésus* as a pioneering departure from the pious and gullible descriptions of the Holy Land which they imagine earlier Christian scholars to have produced. This celebration of Renan's innovativeness rests upon the assumption that it was only in the nineteenth century, with the advent of the Higher Criticism, that biblical critics—trained to staff Western empires, and organized into new learned societies like the Palestine Exploration Fund (est. 1865)—recognized the importance of historicizing the Holy Land and began to study its historical geography and antiquities.[4] Yet this assumption is only partly correct. While its Orientalist frame may have been new, Renan's scholarly method—which presumed that the places and artefacts observable in the modern Levant had changed so little in the intervening centuries that simple eyewitness examination would reveal their one-to-one correspondence with the biblical text—was fundamentally old. Indeed, ancient and medieval exegetes running all the way back to Eusebius of Caesarea (*c.*265–339/40), the first Church historian, routinely cited the utility of eyewitness knowledge of the Levant and invoked geographical knowledge gleaned from contemporary travel in their pursuit of the *sensus literalis* of Scripture.[5]

Renan's closest scholarly ancestors, though, are the sacred antiquarians— they would have preferred the term '*critici sacri*'—of the High and Late Renaissance. Forgotten already by the age of Renan, these sixteenth- and

---

[2] Renan, *Life of Jesus*, p. 61.

[3] For the marriage of Western imperialism and modern Orientalist scholarship, see Saïd, *Orientalism*, as well as the revisions and critiques of Irwin, *Dangerous Knowledge*, and Marchand, *German Orientalism*, esp. ch. 1.

[4] See Moxnes, 'Construction of Galilee'; Ben-Arieh, 'Nineteenth-Century Historical Geographies'; Saïd, *Orientalism*.

[5] Smalley, *Study of the Bible*.

seventeenth-century scholars were the first to fuse the new technologies of Renaissance historical scholarship, from printing to epigraphy, to the more traditional approach to the land and material culture of the Near East inherited from over a millennium of Christian pilgrimage to the Levant. In the process, they created a massive literature on the geography and civilizations of the Bible, constructing a vision of the Holy Land defined simultaneously by its scholarly rigour and its devotional fervour. To a significant extent, it is this Renaissance vision that remains with us today, for Renan and his modern descendants—however unconsciously—adopted many of the goals and assumptions of the early modern literature even as they refined its textual and archaeological methods.[6]

In an effort to explore the complex relationship between religious devotion and critical research within the larger field of *historia sacra*, this chapter aims to understand the symbiosis of antiquarian innovation and pious tradition that characterized Renaissance reconstructions of the Holy Land. To do so, it is necessary not only to sketch the outlines of early modern scholarship on the Holy Land, but also to draw a pointed comparison between the secular antiquarianism usually associated with the Renaissance and the less empirical, more devotional preoccupations characteristic of those scholars who focused on the biblical Near East. What such comparisons ultimately reveal is that the Renaissance's Holy Land was neither entirely 'medieval' nor entirely 'modern', neither credulous nor critical in any meaningful sense of those terms. Indeed, such distinctions hardly made sense to the *critici sacri* of the age: not because they could not yet understand them, but rather, because they did not accept them.

2. RENAISSANCE VISIONS OF THE HOLY LAND

The antiquarians' interest in the Holy Land—an interest which becomes recognizable sometime around 1500—was born largely of an exegetical imperative.[7] That is to say, it was fostered by a growing sense among humanist commentators that their biblical scholarship would benefit from the incorporation of information derived from the burgeoning disciplines of archaeology, epigraphy, numismatics, and historical geography made popular in the fifteenth century by 'secular' antiquarians like Poggio Bracciolini, Flavio

---

[6] See e.g. Nina Burleigh, *Unholy Business: A True Tale of Faith, Greed and Forgery in the Holy Land* (New York, NY: Smithsonian Books/Collins, 2008).

[7] On Renaissance exegesis, see Hall, 'Biblical Scholarship'; Bentley, *Humanists and Holy Writ*; Laplanche, *L'écriture*; Laplanche, *Bible, sciences et pouvoirs*; Shuger, *Renaissance Bible*; Hamilton, 'Humanists and the Bible'; Saebø, *Hebrew Bible/Old Testament*; Griffiths (ed.), *Bible in the Renaissance*.

Biondo, and Pomponio Leto.[8] One of the earliest humanists to advocate for historiated exegesis was Erasmus, who urged his fellow exegetes to cultivate a thorough understanding of the Holy Land and its ancient civilizations in his 1518 *Ratio seu methodus compendio perveniendi ad veram theologiam*:

> Once we learn from cosmographers about the [biblical] regions, we can follow the shifting scenes of the story in our minds, as if we were being carried along with it, as if we were witnessing the events and not reading about them. This is not unpleasant; moreover, what you read in such a way will stick much faster in your mind. . . . And when we have learned from historical books about the peoples among whom the events happened, or whom the Apostles were addressing—not only where they lived, but also their origin, customs, institutions, religion, and character—a marvelous amount of light and, as it were, life will be added to our reading.[9]

In spite of this paean to cosmography, Erasmus's biblical scholarship—like that of nearly all of his contemporaries—remained, for the time being, almost exclusively philological. By the middle of the sixteenth century, however, it was possible to find scattered among the universities and royal courts of Europe the beginnings of a *respublica sacrarum litterarum* (a republic of sacred letters), whose members were interested in using the study of historical geography and Near Eastern antiquities to read the Bible as a historical record of the civilizations of ancient Israel, similar to (if not quite the same as) the histories of ancient Greece and Rome.[10] Both Michael Servetus (Miguel Servet, 1511–53) and Sebastian Münster (1488–1552), for example, included 'Tabulae Terrae Sanctae' in their editions of Ptolemy's *Geography* published (respectively) at Lyon in 1535 and Basel in 1552.[11]

These early sparks of antiquarian interest in the Holy Land finally ignited in the final few decades of the century. From the 1570s forward, as Jonathan Sheehan has observed, biblical criticism 'exploded off the page and included not just words but also a panorama of natural, historical, political, and anthropological details'.[12] Historians typically point to three factors as instrumental in the sudden turn from pure philology to a more capacious Orientalism. The first

---

[8] The historiography of Renaissance antiquarianism is large and ever-expanding. See, among others, Momigliano, 'Ancient History', Weiss, *Renaissance Discovery*; Woolf, 'Varieties of Antiquarianism', in *The Social Circulation of the Past* (Oxford: Oxford University Press, 2003), pp. 141–82; Stenhouse, *Reading Inscriptions*.

[9] Erasmus, *Ratio*, 5:66–7, quoted in Kristine L. Haugen, 'A French Jesuit's Lectures on Vergil, 1582–1583: Jacques Sirmond between Literature, History, and Myth', *Sixteenth Century Journal* 30 (1999), pp. 967–85, here at p. 979 n. 38.

[10] Cf. Burke, *Renaissance Sense*, p. 61; Miller, '"Antiquarianization"', p. 464. I borrow the term *respublica sacrarum litterarum* from Shuger, *Renaissance Bible*.

[11] Shalev, 'Sacred Geography', p. 67 n. 53. See also Delano-Smith and Ingram, *Maps in Bibles*; Walter Goffart, *Historical Atlases: The First Three Hundred Years, 1570–1870* (Chicago: University of Chicago Press, 2003), pp. 34–5.

[12] Sheehan, 'Philology to Fossils', p. 48.

was the expansion of Christian Hebraism. What was once a small, even suspect, area of learning *c.*1500 had become by the end of the century a standard feature of the learned exegete's toolkit, and the humanists' increased access to Hebrew literature (modern as well as ancient) was crucial to their reconstruction of the material and cultural worlds of the biblical Levant.[13] The second factor in the explosion of antiquarian exegesis was the simple expansion of European scholars' encounters with physical remains of the Near East. While purely scholarly travellers like the great Cyriac of Ancona (1391–1452?) were rare, merchants, diplomatic travellers, and pilgrims sated the prodigious curiosity of the Republic of Letters with an ever-increasing stream of dispatches.[14] The third factor, though it is more difficult to quantify, was confessional conflict. Particularly among the Protestant scholars of Northern Europe, the fact that rival Churches so frequently proclaimed the superior accuracy of their literal interpretations of the Bible only raised the stakes of historiated criticism.[15]

The first two of these factors are clearly visible in Benito Arias Montano's 1572 apparatus to the Antwerp Polyglot Bible, which Peter Miller has called an 'intellectual revolution' marking the late Renaissance 'eruption of antiquarian work on the ancient Near Eastern context of the Hebrew Bible'.[16] Spain's leading biblical scholar, Arias Montano (1527–98) was a master of Near Eastern languages, and used his knowledge of Hebrew to read Jewish commentaries and—sometimes on their authority—make complicated etymological claims about the locations of biblical places long since lost to geographers. At the same time, though he never travelled to the East himself, he cultivated throughout his life a number of other scholars who had.[17] His most vivid secondhand encounter with the Holy Land was certainly that facilitated by his childhhod tutor Iago Vázquez Matamoros, who had made the arduous trek to Palestine in his middle age. Upon his return, Vázquez narrated his adventures to the wide-eyed Arias Montano, and master and student pored over the notes and diagrams that Vázquez had composed on the ground in the Levant. So detailed were these accounts and maps, the manuscripts of which Arias Montano kept, that he claimed to be able to imagine himself walking through the Holy Land.[18] The value of knowledge like Vázquez's was not lost on Arias

---

[13] For a vivid example, see Grafton and Weinberg, '*I Have Always Loved*'. More generally, see Friedman, *Most Ancient Testimony*; Burnett, *Christian Hebraism*; Grell and Laplanche (eds.), *République des lettres*.

[14] Hamilton, van den Boogert, and Westerweel (eds.), *Republic of Letters*.

[15] See particularly Laplanche, *L'écriture, le sacré et l'histoire*; Marchand, *German Orientalism in the Age of Empire*, pp. 30–1.

[16] Arias Montano's apparatus was subsequently published separately as *Antiqvitatvm Ivdaicarvm libri IX* (Leiden: Plantin, 1593). I will cite from the modern edition: Arias Montano, *Prefacios*. The quotation is from Miller, *Peiresc's Europe*, p. 80.

[17] For Arias Montano's life, see Rekers, *Benito Arias Montano*.

[18] For Vázquez Matamoros's 'learned pilgrimage' to the Holy Land, see Arias Montano, *Prefacios*, pp. 228–30.

Montano. 'All histories', Arias Montano admonished the reader of his 1572 Polyglot apparatus, 'show openly how necessary it is to have knowledge of the places which appear in various passages in Sacred Scripture. If one were to narrate warlike deeds without taking note of their places, or read histories without knowledge of the topography', he continued, 'everything would seem so confused and mixed-up as to appear dark and difficult.'[19]

By century's end, distinguished students of the ancient Levant like Carlo Sigonio (*c.*1524–84), Cornelius Beltramus (fl. 1574), Cesare Baronio (1538–1607), Joseph Scaliger (1540–1609), Justus Lipsius (1547–1606), and Isaac Casaubon (1559–1614) took for granted Erasmus's thesis that a deeper understanding of the landscape in which biblical events occurred, and biblical authors wrote, would lead naturally to a truer understanding of the meaning of Scripture. This passion for reconstructing the geography, architecture, flora and fauna, and customs of the ancient Holy Land and its inhabitants became even more pronounced in the seventeenth century, the golden age of early modern biblical criticism, in the works of Hugo Grotius (1583–1645), John Selden (1584–1644), Petrus Cunaeus (Peter van der Kun, 1586–1638), Richard Simon (1638–1712), and the dozens of other scholars anthologized in the famous *Critici sacri* published at London in 1660—Drusius, Zegerus, Gualtperius, Cappel, Vatabulus et al.[20] Many of these scholars, as Debora Shuger has lamented, have been forgotten; those that remain tend to be remembered for their tedium.[21] Yet George Eliot did the original Casaubon a great injustice in borrowing his name for *Middlemarch's* insufferable pedant. Though the questions which animated and infuriated the *critici sacri* may now seem less urgent, it is hard to deny that the best of the polyglot antiquarianism which they provoked is remarkably creative, inspired, and interdisciplinary.

3. THE PARADOX OF SACRED ANTIQUARIANISM

Whether pioneering or pedantic, these late Renaissance reconstructions of the ancient Levant made ample use of all of the customary tools of the antiquarian trade, and it is tempting to describe them solely as the fruit of humanist exegetes' efforts to import methods developed by classical antiquarians into their biblical scholarship. Like Poggio in Rome, biblical critics measured the Holy Land—its topography, its architectural ruins, and its relics—and weighed its coinage, citing the declaration, found in the apocryphal book of Wisdom,

---

[19] Arias Montano, *Prefacios*, p. 190. Cf. Shalev, 'Sacred Geography', p. 69.

[20] Shuger, *Renaissance Bible*; Rosenblatt, *Renaissance England's Chief Rabbi*. Ugolini, *Thesaurus* compiles a great many of these scholars' works.

[21] Shuger, *Renaissance Bible*, p. 11.

that God had created the universe 'according to "measure and number and weight"'.[22] They also mapped and engraved the East, so much so that it became a commonplace among humanist churchmen that the meticulous study of scaled maps and printed views of the Holy Land's topography and architectural ruins was crucial preparation for any aspiring exegete.[23] All things considered, it is difficult to contest Miller's claim that early modern antiquarians 'were . . . responsible for the first generation of serious scholarship about the ancient and modern Near East', that they single-handedly 'created oriental studies', and that, as such, biblical antiquarians deserve to be celebrated as 'heroes of intellectual inquiry in the same praiseworthy way as Galileo. For they provided the tools with which the properly educated could acquire knowledge of the ancient Near East and thus see clearly and truly the rise of Christianity, like the birth of new stars in the sky.'[24]

There is, however, at least one glaring obstacle to seeing humanist reconstructions of the Holy Land as a characteristically Renaissance project born of the same impulses which drove classical antiquarians into the Graeco-Roman past. As Arnaldo Momigliano's intellectual descendants have shown, classical antiquarians—who, Anthony Grafton suggests, introduced 'systematic field archaeology' into the study of the Roman past—typically defined themselves against pilgrims, whom they excoriated in their treatises for their sloppy misidentifications of historic sites and their willingness to accept absurd myths about Roman history plainly contradicted by the material evidence.[25] Humanists like Poggio despised medieval pilgrimage guides like the *Mirabilia urbis Romae* for creating the myths and misattributions attached to ancient ruins, myths that they felt called to banish. No longer would pilgrims be allowed to mistake the Quirinal's ancient statues of the Dioscuri for 'horse tamers'; no longer would they identify the Colosseum as a temple of the sun; no longer could they get away with mistaking the Lateran's equestrian statue of Marcus Aurelius for Constantine.[26] On reflection, the antiquarians' antipathy towards pilgrims' way of seeing the world makes perfect sense. Pilgrims are, after all, supposed to suppress their historicist instincts: pilgrimage is about creating subjective immanence, not distance. Historicism, scepticism, and objectivity, ostensibly the antiquarian's best friends, are the pilgrim's worst enemies.[27]

Among those antiquarians who concerned themselves with the Holy Land, however, such unqualified antipathy or critical distance was nearly impossible

[22] The reference is from Wisdom 11:21 ('omnia mensura et numero et pondere disposuisti'), and was a favourite of sacred antiquarians; see Rowland, *Culture*.

[23] Fiorani, 'Post-Tridentine geographia sacra', pp. 124–48.

[24] Miller, '"Antiquarianization"', p. 482; cf. Marchand, *German Orientalism*.

[25] Grafton, 'Ancient City', p. 38.

[26] Ibid., p. 38; Stinger, *Renaissance in Rome*, pp. 24, 34–7, 67; Miglio et al., *Antiquaria a Roma*.

[27] See, among many others, Cohen, 'Pilgrimage and Tourism'; Turner, *Image and Pilgrimage*.

to maintain. While one of the defining features of Roman antiquarianism was its explicit hostility to medieval pilgrims' way of seeing the landscape, in the case of the Holy Land, the antiquarian project was inextricably enmeshed with the anachronistic, eyewitness observations of pilgrims from the very start.

There are at least two reasons for this symbiosis. The first of these was entirely pragmatic: in the sixteenth century, pilgrimage was practically the only source of Europeans' information about the people and places of the Holy Land. As previously noted, to be a good antiquarian, one had to learn as much as possible about the land under study—not only where everything was and how everything looked, but also how many people lived there and the nature of their customs. For armchair antiquarians interested in the Christian Levant, this meant reading detailed descriptions of the Holy Land and studying reliable views and maps of it—the only examples of which were to be found in illustrated pilgrim narratives like the famous one written by Bernard von Breydenbach and illustrated by Erhard Reuwich, published in multiple Latin, German, French, and Spanish editions between 1484 and 1498.[28] For more intrepid souls, nothing could take the place of actually making the journey to Palestine in person, and many antiquarians—including, for example, Arias Montano's aforementioned tutor—did just that so as to be able to measure, sketch, and study its monuments for themselves.[29] Because European Christians were only permitted to travel in the company of the Franciscans of the *Custodia Terrae Sanctae*, whose job it was to take ordinary pilgrims on carefully orchestrated tours of conventional devotional sites, antiquarians, too, found themselves at the mercy of their Franciscan guides' interpretations of the landscape. Along the way, they also collected 'long-lived traditions preserved by marginal groups like the Samaritans', which they might consider just as reliable as historical texts.[30] Given this reality, the discovery of Peter Miller, Paula Findlen, and others that many antiquarians (and naturalists) referred to themselves as 'scholarly pilgrims' does not seem particularly surprising.[31]

Such practical considerations aside, the Franciscans and their tour groups point to the second (and more clearly problematic) reason for Holy Land antiquarianism's co-dependency with the contemporary culture of pilgrimage. To put it plainly, the Holy Land itself was the invention of the pilgrims and

---

[28] Von Breydenbach's pilgrimage account was first published in German and Latin at Mainz and Magdeburg in 1486. It was then published in French and Dutch translations in 1488, and in Spanish translation in 1498. There were multiple sixteenth- and seventeenth-century editions, perhaps the most interesting of which is Richard Brathwait's 1652 translation, which deliberately posed as an antiquarian commentary: von Breybenbach, *Itinerarium*.

[29] See above, n. 18.

[30] Miller, '"Antiquarianization"', p. 464.

[31] Ibid., p. 464; Findlen, *Possessing Nature*, pp. 160–3. See also Elsner and Rubiés, 'Introduction', p. 46.

their Franciscan guides. As the antiquarians knew, even the most educated traveller would find it virtually impossible to locate a single remnant of the Promised Land of the Bible in the Palestine of the Mamluks and Ottomans. Astute readers of Josephus, they knew that Titus and Vespasian had razed Jerusalem to the ground and expelled its residents in AD 70, leaving behind nary a trace of the city that formed the backdrop to the Hebrew Bible and the crucifixion. Moreover, when Emperor Hadrian finally rebuilt Jerusalem (as Aelia Capitolina) in AD 138, in the wake of the Bar Khokba rebellion, he did so demonstrably to the west of the city's original site. As the French sociologist Maurice Halbwachs argued in his brilliant 1941 book on the *Topographie légendaire des évangiles en Terre Sainte*, this meant that Constantine's well-known Christian 'restoration' of the Holy City in the fourth century was nothing more than a fantasy—the emperor had not 'rediscovered' Calvary or the Holy Sepulchre, but rather had superimposed imaginary localizations upon Hadrian's Aelia Capitolina, while the true Jerusalem of Christ lay undiscovered at the edge of town.[32] The Holy Places known to sixteenth-century travellers, then, were by and large untrustworthy fourth- and twelfth-century localizations, the fruits of Constantine's and the Crusaders' efforts to recreate the Holy Land according to contemporary tastes. Unlike Rome, where antiquarians could replace pilgrim legends with reliable Roman testimony, the Holy Land offered no such core of truth. Strip away the legends surrounding Pilate's praetorium or the Cave of the Nativity, and there would be nothing left at all. To paraphrase Leonard Barkan, who has written of Roman antiquarians that they were writing the 'history of the idea of a city that used to be', in the Holy Land the antiquarian was challenged to write the history of the idea of a place that, in some sense, never was.[33]

Renaissance antiquarians responded in different ways to this challenge. Some of them reacted as we might expect: fretting over what they saw as a compromising entanglement with the culture of pilgrimage, they came fundamentally to distrust the Holy Land. Thus one occasionally finds Renaissance antiquarians daring to question or even to reject the most hallowed traditions surrounding Palestine. Erasmus, at the same time as he exhorted his fellow exegetes with great sanguinity to study the topography of the Holy Land, was nevertheless among the clutch of humanists who dismissed pilgrim testimony out of hand. In his 1522 colloquy entitled *De visendo loca sacra*, Erasmus equated the putative Holy Places of Jerusalem with a pack of falsehoods. Early in the colloquy, when Arnoldus asks, 'Is there anything worth seeing [in Jerusalem]?' Cornelius responds, 'To be frank with you, almost nothing. Some monuments of antiquity are pointed out, all of which I thought faked

---

[32] Halbwachs, *Topographie légendaire*. See also MacCormack, 'Loca sancta'; Bowman, 'Pilgrim Narratives'.

[33] Barkan, *Unearthing the Past*, p. 20.

and contrived for the purpose of enticing naïve and credulous folk. What's more, *I don't think it's known for certain where ancient Jerusalem was.*[34] Most immediately, of course, Erasmus' assertion that the authentic Holy City had been lost to the vicissitudes of time was meant to rebound with discredit upon the city's Franciscan tour guides, whom Erasmus wished to paint as guilty of fakery and deception designed to exploit the faithful's 'credulity'. More broadly, however, the critique could apply just as trenchantly to the careless antiquarian pilgrim deluded into thinking that it was possible to obtain a true picture of biblical topography by visiting modern Palestine.

Some later antiquarians raised the same doubts in more scholarly genres. When Servet published his 'Tabula Terrae Sanctae' in his edition of Ptolemy's *Geography*, for example, he added a gloss arguing that the Promised Land could not possibly have been as fertile as it was always said to be.[35] Later in the sixteenth century, the Franciscans of the *Custodia Terrae Sanctae* (the province of the Order charged with maintaining the holy places and shepherding European pilgrims in the Levant) found themselves on the defensive against a group of sceptical antiquarians who, having read up on their late Roman history, sided with Erasmus to reject Constantine's siting of the Holy Sepulchre.[36] Here the debate was ignited by the Dutch priest Christiaan van Adrichem (1533–85), author of two influential studies of ancient Jerusalem.[37] Adrichomius, as he was widely known, had never travelled to the Holy Land in person; rather, his treatise was a thoroughly armchair production based on a handful of early sixteenth-century pilgrimage accounts written by fellow Dutchmen like Pieter Calentijn and Jan Pascha.[38] The derivative nature of his knowledge did not, however, dissuade van Adrichem from making a series of confident assertions about the conventional localizations of the Holy Places. Most vexing for him, it seems, was the fact that Calvary was said to be outside of the city walls in the Bible, but within the city limits according to the accounts written by modern pilgrims. Perhaps the city walls had moved; but perhaps things were not so simple. What if Calvary itself had been misidentified?

Unlike Erasmus or Adrichomius, however, the vast majority of antiquarians evinced no such concern about their near-total dependence upon not only the anachronistic reconnaissance, but even the judgements, of pilgrims and their

---

[34] Erasmus, *Rash Vows*, in *Colloquies*, I, pp. 35–43; quote at p. 37 (emphasis mine).

[35] See above, n. 11. Sebastian Münster raised similar doubts in the 'Appendix geographica' of his own edition of Ptolemy.

[36] For an overview of this heated sixteenth-century controversy, see the editors' introduction to Amico da Gallipoli, *Plans of the Sacred Edifices*, pp. 4–8. It is worth noting that the Franciscans themselves had long been willing to admit doubt on this issue: see Aveiro, *Itinerario*, fols. 50–2.

[37] Van Adrichem, *Ierusalem* [3rd edn: *Urbis Hierosolymae*]; van Adrichem, *Theatrum Terrae Sanctae*.

[38] Van Adrichem, *Urbis Hierosolymae*, pp. 63–4, 96.

Franciscan hosts. In fact, many of them embraced these. Accounting for this unexpected methodological commitment on the antiquarians' part is the key not only to understanding something important about the unique place of the Holy Land in Christian scholarship, but also to obtaining a more nuanced understanding of the relationship between Renaissance *historia sacra* and the canons of modern historical scholarship.

To a significant degree, the antiquarians' cosy embrace of accumulated pilgrim tradition about the Holy Land can be attributed to the active participation of Franciscan scholars in the *respublica sacrarum litterarum* in the late sixteenth and early seventeenth centuries, which deserves mention in its own right as an important subculture within early modern *historia sacra*. Franciscan scholars like Boniface of Ragusa (a.k.a, Bonifazio Drakolica, d. 1582) and Francesco Quaresmio (1583–1656) joined the debates provoked by scholars like Adrichomius, defending the traditional localizations of the Holy Places in prose (at the same time as they urged European princes to do so with the sword, by retaking the mantle of Crusade).[39] The Franciscan *érudit* Bernardino Amico da Gallipoli, who spent perhaps as much as a decade in the Near East in the 1590s, challenged van Adrichem in the *Trattato delle piante & imagini de sacri edificii di Terra Santa* which he published at Rome shortly after returning home to Europe.[40] He clearly resented his Dutch antagonist's armchair incursion into the study of biblical topography, just as he must have been offended by van Adrichem's implicit accusation that his fellow Franciscans were guilty of guiding pilgrims to sham Holy Places. Amico's determination to marshal his research against these critiques is apparent in the chapter of his *Trattato* dedicated to a 'Discussion on the Design of the Ancient Said City [i.e. Jerusalem] at the Time of Christ'. Referencing a map purporting to show Jerusalem 'at the time of Christ . . . showing by the numbers all the places of the Passion and Death of Our Lord, and the known sites that are within and without the city', Amico criticized academics who raised questions about such matters as the true location of Calvary:

> I shall force myself to remove that bad opinion of some [i.e. van Adrichem] who wish with poor reason to state that this [i.e. Jerusalem] is not the [biblical] City, but that it has been transferred and that Holy Mount Calvary is found inside it, as is seen in the previous plan . . . The author who advances this query affirms that such say so because they have never seen these countries, nor this City; and I add that in fact they have seen it, but not having wished to employ the necessary diligence, they left confused, and later said that only which pleased them.[41]

---

[39] Drakolica, *Liber*; Quaresmio, *Elucidatio*.

[40] Amico da Gallipoli, *Trattato delle piante & imagini de sacri edificii di Terra Santa* (Rome: Typographia Linguarum Externarum, 1609). I cite from a modern translation: Amico da Gallipoli, *Plans*.

[41] Amico da Gallipoli, *Plans*, pp. 132–3.

After boasting that 'I have seen [Jerusalem] and read many books, modern and ancient, and in particular *The Wars of the Jews* by the celebrated author Josephus, on whom I rely', Amico adduced several proofs from Josephus, scriptural passages, and eyewitness testimony about the disposition of contemporary Jerusalem in order to reassure the reader that:

> the site of this Holy City is that which it has always has been and will be, because positively it is surrounded by mountains and valleys . . . And these valleys are not known to all, save by reflection, because some of them are covered with houses; but if one wishes to exercise himself and investigate things, he will find, if not all, at least a part.[42]

Yet while Franciscans like Amico may have been among the most ardent partisans of blurring the boundaries between pilgrimage and antiquarian method, the friars were hardly the only scholars to do so. Indeed, sacred antiquarians of all sorts were content to incorporate pilgrimage accounts— particularly early ones—into their sources.[43] Perhaps even more strikingly, when it came time to publish the conclusions of their researches, the antiquarians typically did so in formats that would have been familiar to pilgrims—one might even say, in formats indistinguishable from contemporary pilgrimage accounts. Antiquarian publishers were not above simply reusing existing, often deeply mythologized, pilgrim maps and city views to illustrate supposedly carefully ascertained antiquarian points. Perhaps the most obvious case is that of Benito Arias Montano's map of Jerusalem from the Antwerp Polyglot: the map is nearly identical to Pieter Lacksteyn's engraved view of Jerusalem, printed in Antwerp five years before Arias Montano published his treatise in the seventh volume of Philip II's *Biblia Regia* in the same city.[44]

While it is always possible that such direct borrowings reflect the budgets of antiquarian publishers, there is something more to it than that; even the most lavishly illustrated antiquarian treatises on the Holy Land—like the 1609 printing of Amico's *Trattato*, which was furnished with dozens of original, customized illustrations of Palestinian ruins—clearly took both their artistic language and their very purpose from contemporary pilgrimage literature. These books, as other scholars have noted, were designed to be usable not only for scholarly researches, but also as devotional aids with which their readers

---

[42] Ibid., p. 137.

[43] At the court of Philip II, which Guy Lazure has recently described as a virtual 'institute' for the study of biblical antiquities, Arias Montano and Juan Bautista Villalpando relied almost exclusively upon travel accounts, including the twelfth-century account of the Iberian Jew Benjamin of Tudela, for the physical descriptions and measurements which they used to reconstruct the Temple of Solomon. See Prado and Villalpando, *In Ezechiel explanationes*; and Lazure, 'Possessing the Sacred'.

[44] For a discussion of the reuse of pilgrimage images, see Meliom, 'Ad ductum itineris'; Sylvaine Hänsel, *Der spanische Humanist Benito Arias Montano (1527–1598) und die Kunst* (Münster: Aschendorffsche Verlagsbuchhandlung, 1991).

might go on a 'virtual' or 'mental' pilgrimage.[45] Virtual pilgrimages, born in the monastic milieu of thirteenth-century Northern Europe, remained as popular as ever among the laity in the sixteenth and seventeenth centuries; and the Holy Land's antiquarian students, in spite of their aspirations to scholarly rigour, continued to believe in the salutary nature of such imaginative journeys. Though it might seem to fall outside of a purely scholarly agenda, facilitating such mental pilgrimages thus became one of the most important ancillary goals of antiquarian publishing. By the middle of the century, *devotees* of mental pilgrimage, once dependent upon the amateur sketches and rough woodcuts typical of pilgrimage guides, could also turn to antiquarian texts boasting more refined and realistic illustrations to fire their imaginations.[46] Arias Montano and Amico fully expected readers of their learned texts to press their faces to Amico's maps and views of Jerusalem, looking down upon the city from the engraver's vantage point and tracing a route through its streets with their eyes, recreating the experience of visiting the Holy Land without leaving the *studiolo*.[47]

These borrowings of content, genre, and even scholarly priorities suggest that the majority of early modern scholars focused on the biblical Levant wished not only to countenance the subjective impressions of pilgrimage as one among many ways of knowing the Holy Land. They also wished actively to promote it as the most effective means to obtain a truer knowledge of the Holy Land—that is, of the Holy Land conceived of as the *theatrum salvationis*, the site of the salvation of the human race, the one historical place not subject to the writing of purely human history. This was a knowledge that could, as Erasmus hinted in the very first quotation in this chapter, transform the heart as well as the mind. The relationship between these two ways of knowing is perhaps one of the most interesting tensions intrinsic to the entire programme of *historia sacra*.

4. *HISTORIA SACRA* AND PILGRIMAGE BEFORE THE RENAISSANCE

Antiquarians were not, after all, the first Christians to engage in the minute study of the biblical landscape. Across the Middle Ages, pilgrims like the

---

[45] The notion of 'virtual pilgrimage' can be traced back at least as far as the fourteenth century; it appears in both Petrarch and the Dominican Heinrich Suso. For a history of virtual pilgrimage, see Kathryn Rudy, 'Northern European Visual Responses to Holy Land Pilgrimage, 1453–1550', PhD dissertation (Columbia University, 2001).

[46] Meliom, 'Ad ductum itineris'.

[47] See Shalev, 'Sacred Geography', p. 69; Ramiro Flórez, 'El arte en Arias Montano: didáctica y piedad ilustrada', in Francisco Javier Campos y Fernández de Sevilla (ed.), *Religiosidad Popular en España*, 2 vols., II (El Escorial: Ediciones Escurialenses, 1997), pp. 51–80.

eighth-century Frankish bishop Arculf or the fifteenth-century Englishman John Poloner carried home exacting architectural measurements taken *in situ* at the Holy Places.[48] Nor were Renaissance scholars the first to attempt to reconcile that landscape with the biblical text, as attested by the long chain of medieval exegetes interested in the *sensus literalis* of Scripture.[49] As Beryl Smalley has shown, such 'antiquarianizing' exegesis was (not surprisingly) associated with the Franciscan Order and its scholarly friars like Nicholas of Lyra (c.1270–1349). Lyra illustrated his glosses with maps and sketches of biblical architecture in the belief that their sacred measures and divine proportions concealed new layers of understanding to the text.[50]

One could go back still further, to St Jerome (c.341–420), the humanists' favourite Church Father.[51] From his own experience as a Roman transplant in Palestine, Jerome knew that influential contemporaries like Gregory of Nyssa (c.335–94) were more likely to denounce Palestine as a wicked and worthless land 'because it had drunk in the blood of the Lord', and to dismiss the study of the Holy Places as 'Judaizing',[52] than to follow his lead in taking up residence in Bethlehem. Jerome, however, was not one to be dissuaded, and he recognized that he would need to generate a compelling counter-argument to Gregory if he was to persuade acolytes to join him *in situ* in the Levant.

To make that argument, Jerome turned to the same Graeco-Roman tradition of learned travel that Amaldo Momigliano identified as the source of inspiration to the Renaissance's secular antiquarians.[53] An active participant in the culture of the late imperial Mediterranean, Jerome surely knew the character of Demetrius of Tarsus in Plutarch's first-century dialogue *On the Decline of the Oracles*, who was said to have travelled on imperial orders as far as Britain 'for the purposes of investigation and sightseeing'.[54] He may also have known Pausanias' second-century *Description of Greece*, perhaps the most comprehensive example of antique 'scholarly pilgrimage'.[55] In fact, these classical models of learned travel had already begun to colour the

---

[48] Leyerle, 'Landscape as Cartography'. For pilgrims' interest in measuring the Holy Places, see H. F. M. Prescott, *Jerusalem Journey: Pilgrimage to the Holy Land in the Fifteenth Century* (London: Eyre & Spottiswoode, 1954), p. 213.

[49] On medieval interest in the literal sense of Scripture, see Smalley, *Study of the Bible*.

[50] On Lyra's exegesis, see the essays in Philip D. W. Krey and Lesley Smith (eds.), *Nicholas of Lyra: The Senses of Scripture* (Leiden: Brill, 2000).

[51] Momigliano, 'Ancient History'; Rice, *Saint Jerome*.

[52] The quote is from Jerome, Ep. 46, in *Patrologia Latina*, XXII: *Sancti Eusebii Hieronymi Stridonensis Presbyteri Epistolae . . .*, cols. 483–92, here at col. 489. On early Christian opposition to the veneration of the Holy Land, see Bitton-Ashkelony, *Encountering the Sacred*; Walker, *Holy City*.

[53] See Adams and Roy (eds.), *Travel, Geography and Culture*; Alcock, *Graecia Capta*.

[54] For Demetrius, see Plutarch, *Plutarch's Moralia*, tr. Babbitt, V, pp. 402–4. For other Roman travellers in Plutarch, see *Plutarch's Moralia*, V, pp. 260, 276, 292.

[55] Hunt, 'Were there Christian Pilgrims?', p. 37. On Pausanias, see Alcock, Cherry, and Elsner (eds.), *Pausanias*.

Christian exegetical tradition by the third century, if not earlier. Eusebius of Caesarea's *Historia ecclesiastica*, for example, offers a description of two early 'sacred antiquarians': Bishop Melito of Sardis, who travelled to the East to learn definitive information about setting of the Old Testament, and the Anatolian bishop Alexander, who in his old age 'journeyed from Cappadocia, his original see, to Jerusalem, in order to worship there and to examine the historic sites'.[56]

It was Jerome's genius to see that this pagan tradition could be domesticated and brought within Christian exegetical practice as a means of justifying Christian pilgrimage to the East. Soon after arriving in Bethlehem, Jerome began to argue persuasively that no exegete could understand the historical narrative encapsulated within the Bible without first familiarizing himself with the historical sites of Old- and New-Testament Judea. In the preface to his Latin translation of the Septuagint's version of the Book of Chronicles (*Paralipomenon*), written in 387, Jerome argued that:

> In the same way that one understands better the Greek historians when one has seen Athens with his own eyes, and the third book of the Aeneid when one has journeyed from Troy to Sicily and from Sicily to the mouth of the Tiber, so one understands better the Holy Scriptures when one has seen Judea with one's own eyes and contemplated the ruins of its ancient cities.[57]

Thus it was every serious Christian's duty to experience, or at least to study, the topography of Palestine, God's classroom. In an effort to encourage such studies, Jerome translated Eusebius's Greek *Onomasticon* (*c.*330), a rough sort of biblical atlas, into Latin as the *De situ et nominibus locorum Hebraeorum* in *c.*390.[58]

For Jerome, then, the pilgrim's devotion and the scholar's curiosity were complementary activities, inextricably linked. To understand the Bible, one had to see the Holy Land; but to see the Holy Land properly, one had to know the Bible. Whether inspired by Jerome or by the more proximate example of Lyra, the antiquarian commentaries of the Renaissance accepted this perspective. It is, therefore, difficult to see them as fundamentally new. Though Peter Miller has argued that early modern antiquarians 'were . . . responsible for the first generation of serious scholarship about the ancient and modern Near East', that they single-handedly 'created oriental studies', and that they were 'heroes of intellectual inquiry', the claim that Renaissance scholars somehow 'invented' the systematic archaeology of the Holy Land is not tenable. This is not to say that Renaissance scholarship had no impact; quite to the contrary,

---

[56] Hunt, 'Were there Christian Pilgrims?', pp. 26, 38–9. Origen, too, Hunt believes, shared 'the biblical scholar's interest in the topography of the contemporary Holy Land' (p. 35).

[57] Jerome, *Praefatio in librum Paralipomenon*.

[58] Eusebius, *Onomasticon*. See also Wilkinson, 'L'apport de Saint Jérôme'.

the new research and print technologies mastered by the antiquarians presented Europeans with a much richer picture of biblical antiquity than they had ever known. But it was a picture which deliberately blurred the boundaries between past and present. The Holy Land, which had always been a pilgrim's world, remained a pilgrim's world—even when it was 'rediscovered' by the Higher Criticism in the nineteenth century.

5. THE WANING OF *HISTORIA SACRA*

This return to the nineteenth century and the Higher Criticism prompts a final question: namely, what happened to the *critici sacri* in the intervening centuries such that Renan could believe that he was the first to discover an unknown 'fifth gospel' in Galilee?[59] Why are modern biblical critics dismissive, or even ignorant, of the Casaubons who came before?

This is not an easy question to answer, and a definitive response is beyond the scope of this chapter. In some sense, the most obvious explanation—that the fictional pedantry of Eliot's Casaubon was not far from the mark—may be the most tempting. That is to say, perhaps early modern biblical scholars wrote themselves into irrelevance. Indeed, by the late seventeenth century, the project of reconstructing the ancient Near Eastern context of the Bible—its *naturalia*, in particular—had acquired a momentum and a passion for minutiae which the modern reader struggles to comprehend. It is not hard to imagine why the Enlightenment had little use for Johann Heinrich Alsted (1588–1638), for example; among his many *desiderata* was a 'special physics [or science] of the nature of terrestrial beasts, collected from Scripture', which he pre-emptively dubbed *theriologia sacra*. The specialized treatises on biblical flora and fauna which answered his call, like Wolfgang Franz's *Historia animialium sacra* (1613), Samuel Bochart's *Hierozoicon, sive, bipertitum opus de animalibus sacrae scripturae* (1663), and Johann Ursin's *Continuatio historiae plantarum biblicae* (1665), are unlikely to find many modern enthusiasts.[60] Yet it may well be that it was precisely the success and appeal of projects like Alsted's '*theriologia sacra*'—or the similar search for a pious, biblically based 'Mosaic physics'[61]—that explain the demise of early modern antiquarian scholarship on the Holy Land. In some sense, reconstructing the ancient Near Eastern world of the Bible took on a life of its own that inverted

---

[59] Sheehan, *Enlightenment Bible*.

[60] The French Protestant Bochart (1599–1667) is perhaps better known for the two volumes of his *Geographia sacra*. The quotation is from Alsted's *Triumphus bibliorum*, p. 92, quoted in Sheehan, 'Philology to Fossils', p. 45.

[61] Blair, 'Mosaic Physics'.

the original project of sacred antiquarianism. What began *c.*1500 as an effort to use material culture to illuminate the biblical text had become instead, by *c.*1650, a project of studying the biblical text to illuminate the material world of the eastern Mediterranean in antiquity.

In that sense, the intellectual pursuits of the *critici sacri*, if not *modern*, may at least be called *modernizing*. That is to say, the scholarly techniques and publications which Renaissance antiquarians brought to bear on the ancient Levant may have laid the foundations of a host of modern, even secular, disciplines in spite of their ostensibly conventional goals. Recent works on the early modern origins of fields as diverse as modern republicanism and comparative religion have made much the same argument about the unintended consequences of Renaissance scholars' rediscovery of the biblical Near East.[62] The recovery of the ancient 'Hebrew republic', for example, is now thought to be at least as responsible as secularization for the rise of an ideal of religious toleration. Some such arguments may outlast others; but whatever their particular strengths and vulnerabilities, they should not obscure the original harmony of scholarly innovation and pious curiosity at the heart of the antiquarians' laborious efforts not only to reconstruct the Holy Land, but to place its image before their readers' eyes in unprecedented detail.

---

[62] Nelson, *The Hebrew Republic*; Stroumsa, *A New Science*.

Bibliography

Primary Sources

Acta sanctorum quotquot toto orbe coluntur, vel a Catholicis Scriptoribus celebrantur, quae ex Latinis et Graecis, aliarumque gentium antiquis monumentis collegit, digessit, notis illustravit Ioannes Bollandus Societatis Iesu theologus, ed. Jean Bolland and Godfried Henschen, I (Antwerp: Johannes Meursius, 1643).

Adrichem, Christiaan van, *Ierusalem, sicut Christi tempore floruit, et suburbanorum, insigniorumque historiarum eius brevis descriptio . . .* (Cologne: n.p., 1584).

—— *Urbis Hierosolymae quemadmodum ea Christi tempore floruit, et suburbanorum eius brevis descriptio* (Cologne: Birckmann, 1588).

—— *Theatrum Terrae Sanctae et biblicarum historiarum* (Cologne: Birckmann, 1590).

Aelfric, Abbot of Eynsham, *A Testimonie of Antiquitie Shewing the Auncient Fayth in the Church of England*, ed. J. Joscelyn and M. Parker (London: John Day, 1566).

Alberti, Leon Battista, *L'Architettura*, ed. and tr. Giovanni Orlandi, 2 vols. (Milan: Polifilo, 1966).

—— *On the Art of Building in Ten Books*, tr. Joseph Rykwert, Neil Leach, and Robert Tavernor (Cambridge, Mass.: MIT Press, 1988).

—— *On Painting* [*De pictura*], tr. Cecil Grayson (London: Penguin Books, 2004).

Alcocer, Pedro, *Hystoria, o descripcion de la imperial cibdad de Toledo* (Toledo: Juan Ferrer, 1554). (Facsimile: Madrid: Instituto Provincial de Investigación y Estudios Toledanos, 1973.)

Allacci, Leone, *De ecclesiae occidentalis atque orientalis perpetua consensione, libri tres* (Cologne: J. Kolcovius, 1648).

Alsted, Johann Heinrich, *Triumphus bibliorum sacrorum seu encyclopaedia biblica* (Frankfurt: B. Schmidt, 1625).

Amico da Gallipoli, Bernardino, *Plans of the Sacred Edifices of the Holy Land*, tr. Theophilus Bellorini and Eugene Hoade; ed. Bellarmino Bagatti (Jerusalem: Franciscan Press, 1953). (English translation of *Trattato delle piante & imagini de sacri edificii di Terra Santa* (orig. pub. Rome: n.p., 1609).)

Antonio, Nicolás, *Censura de historias fabulosas* (Valencia: Antonio Bordazar de Artazu, 1742).

Arcudius, Petrus, *De concordia ecclesiae occidentalis et orientalis in septem sacramentorum administratione* (Paris: S. Cramoisy, 1626).

Arias Montano, Benito, (ed.), *Biblia sacra, hebraice, chaldaice, graece et latine, Philippi II regis catholici pietate et studio ad sacrosanctae ecclesiae usum*, 8 vols. (Antwerp: C. Plantin, 1569–73).

—— *Prefacios de Benito Arias Montano a la Biblia regia de Felipe II*, ed. and tr. María Asunción Sánchez Manzano (León: Universidad de León, 2006).

Arnpeck, Veit, 'Bayerische Chronik' in Georg Leidinger (ed.), *Veit Arnpeck: Sämtliche Chroniken* (Munich: M. Rieger, 1915), pp. 445–705.

Arnpeck, Veit, 'Chronica Baioariorum', in Georg Leidinger (ed.), *Veit Arnpeck: Sämtliche Chroniken* (Munich: M. Rieger, 1915), pp. 1–444.

—— 'Chronicon Austriacum', in Georg Leidinger (ed.), *Veit Arnpeck: Sämtliche Chroniken* (Munich: M. Rieger, 1915), pp. 707–845.

—— 'Liber de gestis episcoporum Frisingensium', in Georg Leidinger (ed.), *Veit Arnpeck: Sämtliche Chroniken* (Munich: M. Rieger, 1915), pp. 847–914.

Asser, *Aelfredi regis res gestae* (London: John Day, 1574).

Aveiro, Pantaleão de, *Itinerário da Terra Sancta, e suas particularidades* (Lisbon: Simão Lopez, 1593).

Aventinus, Johannes, *Annales ducum Boiariae*, ed. Sigmund Riezler, 2 vols. (Munich: Christian Kaiser, 1882, 1884).

—— *Bayerische Chronik*, ed. Matthias von Lexer, 2 vols. (Munich: Christian Kaiser, 1883, 1886).

Bacon, Francis, *Works*, ed. James Spedding, Robert Leslie Ellis, and Douglas Denon Heath, 14 vols. (Cambridge, Mass.: Riverside Press, 1863).

—— *The Advancement of Learning and New Atlantis*, ed. Arthur Johnston (Oxford: Clarendon Press, 1974).

Baillie, Robert, *Operis historici et chronologici libri duo in quibus historia sacra et profana compendiose deducitur ex ipsis fontibus a creatione mundi ad Constantinum Magnum* (Amsterdam: Johan Janssonius, 1663).

Balbín, Bohuslav *Epitome historica rerum Bohemicarum* (Prague: Typis Universitatis Carolo-Ferdinandeae, 1677).

—— *Miscellanea historica regni Bohemiae Decadis I. liber IV. Hagiographicus: seu Bohemia sancta, continens sanctos et beatos Bohemiae, Moraviae, Silesiae, Lusatiae* (Prague: Georg Czernoch, 1682).

—— *Vita B. Joannis Nepomuceni martyris* (Augsburg: J. J. Lotterus, 1725).

—— *Dissertatio apologetica pro lingua Slavonica, praecipue Bohemica* (Prague: Felicianus Mangold, & Filius, 1775).

—— *Rozprava na obrana jazyka slovanského, zvláště pak českého* (Prague: E. Tonner, 1869).

Bale, John, *The Image of Bothe Churches, after revelacyon of saynt Iohan the evangelist* (Antwerp: n.p., n.d. [1545?]).

Barbosa, Duarte, *Livro em que dá relação do que viu e ouviu no Oriente*, ed. Augusto Reis Machado (Lisbon: Agência Geral das Colónias, 1946).

Barnes, Robert, *Vitae Romanorum pontificum: quos Papas vocamus, diligenter & fideliter collectae . . .* (Wittenberg: Joseph Clug, 1536).

Baronio, Cesare, *Vita Sancti Ambrosii Mediolanensis* in *Operum Sancti Ambrosij Mediolanensis episcopi*, VI: *Sancti Ambrosii . . . operibus adiunctus . . .* (Rome: Typografia Vaticana, 1587), pp. 1–46.

—— *Annales ecclesiastici*, III (Rome: Tornieri, 1592).

—— *Vita S. Gregorii Nazianzeni* in *Acta sanctorum, Maii II* (Antwerp: Michael Cnobarus, 1680), pp. 373–429.

—— *Annales ecclesiastici . . . una cum critica historico-chronologica P. Antonii Pagii*, 19 vols. (Lucca: Venturini, 1738–46).

—— *Annalium ecclesiasticorum Caesaris Baronii . . . Apparatus, in quo praeter ea, quae Baronius et Pagius annalibus praemiserunt, alia plura continentur . . .* (Lucca: Venturini, 1740).

Barros, João de, *Da Ásia*, 24 vols. (Lisbon: Regia Officina Typografica, 1777–88).

Basnage, Jacques, sieur de Beauval, *The History of the Jews, from Jesus Christ to the Present Time: Containing their Antiquities, their Religion, their Rites* (London: Beaver and Lintot, 1708).

Beauvais, Vincent de, *Bibliotheca mundi seu speculi maioris*, IV: *Speculum historiale* (Douai: Baltazar Bellerus, 1624). (Facsimile: Graz: Akademische Druk—u. Verlaganstalt, 1965.)

Bede, *Opera Bedae*, 4 vols. (Basel: John Herwagen, 1563).

—— *The History of the Church of England. Compiled by Venerable Bede, Englishman*, ed. and tr. Thomas Stapleton (Antwerp: John Laet, 1565).

Beuter, Pere Antoni, *Cróniques de València: primera part de la història de València . . .* (València: Joan Mei, 1538); *Segunda parte de la corónica general . . .* (València: Pedro Patricio Mey, 1604), ed. and intro. Vincent Josep Escartí (Valencia: Consell Valencià de Cultura, 1995). (A facsimile edition combining the first edition of part I, in Valencian, with the second edition of part II, in Castilian.)

—— *Primera parte de la coronica general de toda España, y especialmente del reyno de Valencia* (Valencia: Pedro Patricio Mey, 1604). (The first Castilian edition of part I.)

Bèze, Théodore de, *Icones, id est verae imagines virorum doctrina simul et pietate illustrium* (Geneva: I. Laonius, 1580).

Bochart, Samuel, *Geographia sacra seu Phaleg et Canaan* (Caen: Petrus Cardonellus, 1646).

Borromeo, Federico, *Sacred Painting* [*De pictura sacra*], tr. Kenneth S. Rothwell, Jr (Cambridge, Mass.: Harvard University Press, 2010).

Bosio, Antonio, *Roma sotterranea* (Rome: Guglielmo Facciotti, [1632] 1635).

A Briefe Cronicle Contayning the Accompte of the Raygnes of all Kynges of the Realme, anonymous (London: Thomas Marshe, 1561).

Broelmann, Stephan, *Epideigma, sive specimen historiae vet. omnis et purae, florentis atq. amplae civitatis Ubiorum . . .* (Cologne: Grevenbruch, 1608).

Brower, Christoph, *Fuldensium antiquitatum libri III* (Antwerp: C. Plantin, 1612).

Bruin, Conrad, *De imaginibus liber D. Conradi Bruni iureconsulti, cancellarii Landeshutensis, in Bavaria catholica, Germaniae provincia, adversus iconoclastas*, in *Opera tria nunc primum aedita* (Mainz: Francisci Behem, 1548).

Bruni, Girolamo, *De coemeteriis* in Giovanni Battista de Rossi, *Sulla questione del vaso di sangue*, ed. Antonio Ferrua (Rome: Pontificio istituto di archeologia cristiana, 1944).

Bullinger, Heinrich, *De origine erroris in negocio Eucharistiae ac Missae* (Basel: Wolffius, 1528).

—— *De origine erroris, in diuorum ac simulachrorum cultu* (Basel: Wolffius, 1529).

—— *De origine erroris libri duo Heinrychi Bullingeri: In priore agitur de Dei veri iusta invocatione & cultu vero, . . . In posteriore disseritur de institutione & vi sacrae coenae domini, & de origine ac progressu Missae papisticae . . .* (Zurich: Froschauer, 1539).

—— *Heinrich Bullingers Reformationsgeschichte*, ed. J. J. Hottinger and H. H. Vögeli, 3 vols. (Frauenfeld: C. Beyel, 1838–40).

Bunny, Edmund, *Certaine Prayers and other godly exercises, for the seventeenth of November: wherein we solemnize the blessed reigne of our gracious Soveraigne, Lady Elizabeth* (London: Christopher Barker, 1585).

Camões, Luís Vaz de, *Os Lusíadas* (Lisbon: Antonio Gonçalves, 1572).

—— *The Lusíads*, tr. Landeg White (Oxford: Oxford University Press, 1997).

Campi, Pietro Maria, *Dell' historia ecclesiastica di Piacenza*, 3 vols. (Piacenza: G. Bazachi, 1651–62).

Campion, Edmund, *Campian Englished, or a Translation of the Ten reasons in which Edmund Campian (of the Societie of Iesus) Priest, Insisted in his Challenge, to the Vniuersities of Oxford and Cambridge* (n.p. [Rouen?], 1632).

Cano, Melchor, *L'autorità della storia profana (De humanae historiae auctoritate)*, ed. and tr. Albano Biondi, Pubblicazioni dell'istituto di scienze politiche dell'Università di Torino, XXVIII (Torino: Edizioni Giappichelli, 1973).

[Carion, Johannes], *Chronica, durch Magistrum Johan Carion, vleissig zusamen gezogen, meniglich nützlich zu lesen* (Wittenberg: Rhaw, 1531).

—— *Chronicon Carionis expositum et auctum multis et veteribus et recentibus historiis . . . ab exordio mundi usque ad Carolum Quintum imperatorem, a Philippo Melanthone et Casparo Peucero: Adjecta est narratio historica de electione et coronatione Caroli V imperatoris . . .* (Wittenberg: J. Crato, 1572).

Casaubon, Isaac, *De rebus sacris et ecclesiasticis exercitationes XVI. Ad Cardinalis Baronii Prolegomena in Annales, & primam eorum partem, de Domini Nostri Iesu Christi natiuitate, vita, passione, assumtione* (London: Norton, 1614).

—— *Ephemerides*, ed. John Russell, 2 vols. (Oxford: Clarendon Press, 1850).

Castillo, Diego del, *Defensa de la venida y predicación de Santiago en España* (Zaragoza: Lorenzo de Robles, 1608).

Celtis, Conrad (ed.), *Opera Hrosvite, illustris virginis et monialis germane, gente Saxonico orte* (Nuremberg: Sodalitas Celtica, 1501).

—— *Norimberga* (Nuremberg: Johannes Koberg, 1518).

—— *Der Briefwechsel des Konrad Celtis*, ed. Hans Rupprich, Veröffentlichungen der Kommission zur Erforschung der Geschichte der Reformation und Gegenreformation: Humanistenbriefe, III (Munich: C. H. Beck, 1934).

—— *'Quattuor libri amorum secundum quattuor latera Germaniae'; 'Germania generalis': Accendunt carmina aliorum ad libros amorum pertinentia*, ed. Felicitas Pindter, Bibliotheca scriptorum Medii Recentisque Aevorum, Saecula XV–XVI (Leipzig: B.G. Teubner, 1934).

—— *Panegyris ad duces Bavariae*, ed. and tr. Joachim Gruber (Wiesbaden: Harrassowitz, 2003). (Gratia: Bamberger Schriften zur Renaissanceforschung, 41.)

Chacón, Alfonso, *Historia ceu verissima a calumniis multorum vindicata, quae refert Traiani animam precibus divi Gregorii pontificis romani a tartareis cruciatibus ereptam* (Rome: Zanetti & Tosi, 1576).

Chytraeus, David, *De lectione historiarum recte instituenda* (Strasbourg: Mylius, 1563).

—— *Chronologia historiae Herodoti et Thucydidis: recognita, et additis ecclesiae Christi ac imperii romani rebus praecipuis, ab initio mundi, usque ad nostram aetatem contexta* (Rostock: Jacobus Lucius, 1573).

Cianca, Antonio de, *Historia de la vida, invencion, milagros, y translacion de S. Segundo, primero obispo de Auila . . .* (Madrid: Luis Sanchez, 1595). (Facsimile: Ávila: Ediciones de la Obra Cultural de la Caja de Ahorros, 1993.)

Clay, W. Keatinge (ed.), *Liturgical Services: Liturgies and Occasional Forms of Prayer Set Forth in the Reign of Queen Elizabeth* (Cambridge: Cambridge University Press, 1847).

Cochlaeus, Iohannis, *Necessaria et catholica consyderatio super Lutheri articulis, quos velit concilio generali proponi* (Ingolstadt: Alexander Weissenhorn, 1546).

Colfe, Isaac, *A Sermon Preached on the Queenes Day* (London: John Wolfe, 1588).

Concilium tridentinum. Actorum, diarorum, epistolarum, tractatuum nova collectio, 13 vols. in 19 parts. (Fribourg im Breisgau: Societas Görresiana, 1901–2001).

Contelori, Felice, *Concordiae inter Alexandrum III S. P. et Fridaricum I imperatorem Venetiis confirmatae narratio* (Paris: Dionysius de la Noüe, 1632).

—— *Tractatus et praxis de canonizatione sanctorum* (Lyon: L. Durand, 1634).

Conti, Nicolò, 'The Travels of Nicolò Conti, in the East', with independent pagination in *India in the Fifteenth Century*, ed. R.H. Major (London: Hakluyt Society, 1857), pp. 1–39.

Conversio Bagoariorum et Carantanorum, ed. Fritz Losek, in *Monumenta Germaniae Historica: Texten und Studien*, XV (Hannover, 1997), pp. 90–135.

Cope, Alan, see Nicholas Harpsfield.

Correia, Gaspar, *Lendas da Índia*, ed. Rodrigo José de Lima Felner, 3 vols. in 6 bks. (Lisbon: Academia Real das Sciencias, 1858–63).

Cranmer, Thomas, *A Defence of the True and Catholike Doctrine of the Sacrament* (London: Reginald Wolfe, 1550).

Crombach, Hermann, *Vita et martyrium S. Ursulae et sociarum undecim millium virginum etc.* (Cologne: Hermann Mylius, 1647).

—— *Primitiae gentium: seu historia SS. Trium Regum Magorum evangelicorum . . . (* Cologne: Ioannes Kinchius, 1654).

Doleman, Robert [pseud.], *A Conference about the next succession to the crowne of Ingland . . . Where unto is also added a new & perfect arbor or genealogie of the discents of all the kinges and princes of Ingland* (n.p., 1594).

Drakolica, Bonifazio, *Liber de perenni cultu Terrae Sanctae et de fructuosa ejus peregrinatione* (Venice: Guerraea, 1573).

Erasmus, Desiderius, *Ratio seu methodus compendio perveniendi ad veram theologiam* in *Opera omnia*, 9 vols., V (Basel: Froben, 1540–2), pp. 63–116.

—— *Ausgewählte Werke*, ed. Hajo Holborn with Annemarie Holborn (Munich: Beck, 1933).

—— *Praise of Folly* in A. H. T. Levi (ed.) *Collected Works of Erasmus*, XXVII: *Literary and Educational Writings* 5 (Toronto: University of Toronto Press 1986).

—— *Colloquies* in Craig R. Thompson (ed. and tr.), *Collected Works of Erasmus*, XXXIX–XL (Toronto: University of Toronto Press, 1997).

Escavias, Pedro, *Repertorio de principes de España y obra poética del alcaide Pedro de Escavias*, ed. Michel García (Jaén: Instituto de Estudios Giennenses del C.S.I.C., 1972).

Eusebius of Caesarea, *The Auncient Ecclesiastical Histories of the First Six Hundred Yeares after Christ*, ed. and tr. Meredith Hanmer (London: Thomas Vautrollier, 1577).

—— (Eusebius Pamphilius), *Church History*, tr. Arthur C. McGiffert and Ernest C. Richardson, in Philip Schaff and Henry Wace (eds.), *A Select Library of Nicene and Post-Nicene Fathers of the Christian Church*, 2nd ser. (New York: Christian Literature Publishing, 1890). Available online at Christian Classics Ethereal Library: <http://www.ccel.org/ccel/schaff/npnf201.toc.html>.

—— *The History of the Church from Christ to Constantine*, tr. G. A. Williamson; rev. and ed. Andrew Louth (London and New York: Penguin, 1989).

—— *Onomasticon: The Place Names of Divine Scripture, including the Latin Edition of Jerome*, ed. and tr. R. Steven Notley and Ze'ev Safrai (Leiden: Brill, 2005).

Fagius, Paulus, *Precationes hebraicae* (Isny: Fagius, 1542).

Fernandes, Valentim (tr.) *O livro de Marco Paulo* [Lisbon, 1502], ed. Francisco Maria Esteves Pereira (Lisbon: Biblioteca Nacional Lisboa, 1922).

Flacius Illyricus, Matthias, *Historia certaminum inter romanos episcopos & sextam carthaginensem synodum* (Basel: Johannes Oporinus, 1554).

—— *Catalogus testium veritatis: qui ante nostram aetatem reclamarunt papae* (Basel: Joannes Oporinus, 1556). (Later editions: ed. S. Goulart, 2 vols. (Lyon: A. Candidus, 1597); (Geneva: Jacobus Stoer & Jacobus Chouët, 1608).)

—— et al., *Ecclesiastica historia, integram ecclesiae Christi ideam, quantum ad locum, propagationem, persecutionem, tranquillitatem, doctrinam, haereses, ceremonias, gubernationem, schismata, synodos, personas, miracula, martyria, religiones extra ecclesiam, & statum imperij politicum attinet, secundum singulas centurias, perspicuo ordine complectens*, 13 vols. (Basel: Johannes Oporinus, 1559–74).

—— *Historiae ecclesiasticae*, ed. Ludovicus Lucius, 3 vols. (Basel: typis Ludovici Regis, 1624).

Flinsbachius, Cunmannus [Chunemann Flinsbach], *Confirmatio chronologiae atque locorum difficilium, qui in tota computatione occurrunt, expositio, unà cum coniecturis extremi iudicij* (Strasbourg: Wendelin Rihel, 1552).

Foxe, Edward, *De vera differentia regiae potestatis et ecclesiasticae* (London: Thomas Berthelet, 1538).

Foxe, John, *Commentarii rerum in ecclesia gestarum* (Strasbourg: Wendelin Rihel, 1554).

—— *Rerum in ecclesia gestarum* (Basel: Nikolas Brylinger and Johannes Oporinus, 1559).

—— *The Unabridged Acts and Monuments Online* (Humanities Research Institute Online Publications, Sheffield, 2011): <http://www.johnfoxe.org> (Contains full text of 1563, 1570, and 1588 editions.)

—— *Actes and Monuments of these Latter and Perillous Dayes Touching Matters of the Church* (London: John Day, 1563).

—— *Actes and Monumentes of Thynges Passed in Euery Kynges Tyme in this Realme, especially in the Church of England* (London: John Day, 1570).

Foxe, John, *Actes [and] Monumentes of Thinges Passed in Euery Kinges Time, in this Realme, especially in the Churche of England . . . newly recognised and inlarged by the author I. Foxe* (London: John Day, 1576).

—— *Actes and Monuments of Matters Most Speciall and Memorable, Happenyng in the Church with an Vniuersall History of the Same* (London: John Day, 1583).

—— *Eicasmi seu meditationes in sacram Apocalypsin, authore Io Foxe,* ed. Samuel Foxe and Abraham Fleming (London: Thomas Dawson, 1587).

—— *An Abridgement of the Booke of Acts and Monuments of the Church,* ed. and abr. Timothy Bright (London: John Windet, 1589).

Foxe, John (ed.), *The Gospels of the Fower Euangelistes* (London: John Day, 1571).

Franzius, Wolfgang, *Animalium historia sacra in qua plerorumque animalium praeci-pue proprietates in gratiam studiosorum theologiae a ministrorum verbi ad usum eikondogikon breviter accommodatur* (Wittenberg: Zacharias Schurer and Johannes Gormann, 1612).

Füetrer, Ulrich, *Bayerische Chronik,* ed. Reinhold Spiller, Quellen und Erörterungen zur bayerischen und deutschen Geschichte (Munich: M. Rieger, 1909).

—— *Das Buch der Abenteuer,* ed. Bernd Bastert and Heinz Thoelen, 2 vols. (Göppingen: Kümmerle, 1997).

Fürstenberg, Ferdinand von, *Monumenta Paderbornensia ex historia romana, francica, saxonica eruta* (Amsterdam: Elzevir, 1672).

Gallonio, Antonio, *Trattato de gli istrumenti di martirio, e delle varie maniere di martoriare usate da gentili contro christiani* (Roma: Ascanio and Girolamo Donangeli, 1591)

Garin, Eugenio (ed.), *Prosatori latini del quattrocento,* (Milan: R. Ricciardi, 1952).

Gelenius, Aegedius, *De admiranda sacra et civili magnitudine Coloniae Claudiae Agrippinensis Augustae Ubiorum urbis* (Cologne: Kalcovius, 1645).

Ghiberti, Lorenzo, *Lorenzo Ghibertis Denkwürdigkeiten [I commentarii],* ed. J. von Schlosser (Berlin: Julius Bard, 1912).

Gildas, *De excidio et conquestu Britanniae,* ed. John Joscelyn (London: John Day, 1567).

Gilio, Giovanni Andrea, *Dialogo nel quale si ragiona degli errori e degli abusi de' pittori circa l'istorie,* in *Trattati d'arte del cinquecento fra manierismo e controriforma,* II, ed. Paola Barocchi (Bari: G. Laterza, 1961).

Gouvea, António de, *Iornada do arcebispo de Goa Dom Frey Aleixo de Menezes Primaz da India oriental* (Coimbra: Diogo Gomez Loureiro, 1606).

Gregory of Tours, *Glory of the Martyrs,* ed. and tr. Raymond Van Dam (Liverpool: Liverpool University Press, 1988).

Grynaeus, Johann Jakob (ed.), *Monumenta s. patrum orthodoxographa,* 3 vols. (Basel: Petri, 1569).

Harpsfield, Nicholas [Alan Cope], *Dialogi sex contra summi pontificatus, monasticae vitae, sanctorum, sacrarum imaginum oppugnatores, et pseudo-martyres. Nunc primum . . . ab Alano Copo anglo editi* (Antwerp: C. Plantin, 1566).

Harpsfield, Nicholas, *Historia anglicana ecclesiastica a primis gentis susceptae fidei incunabilis ad nostra fere tempora deducta . . . adjecta brevi narratione de divortio Henrici VIII regis ab uxore Catharina, et ab ecclesia catholica romana discessione, scripta ab E. Campiano,* ed. Richard Gibbons (Douai: Marcus Wyon, 1622).

Harpsfield, Nicholas, *A Treatise on the Pretended Divorce between Henry VIII and Catharine of Aragon by Nicholas Harpsfield*, ed. Nicholas Pocock, Camden Soc., new ser., 21 (London: Camden Society, 1878).

Historia de la corona de Aragón (la más antigua de que se tiene noticia) conocida generalmente con el nombre de crónica de San Juan de la Peña, ed. Diputación Provincial de Zaragoza (Zaragoza: Imprenta del Hospicio, 1876).

Hittorp, Melchior, *De divinis catholicae ecclesiae officiis ac ministeriis* (Cologne: Gerwinus Calenius & haeredes Iohannis Quentel, 1568).

Holland, Thomas, *A Sermon Preached at Paul's in London the 17 of November Ann. Dom. 1599* (Oxford: Joseph Barnes, 1601).

Holstenius [Holste], Lucas, *Passio sanctarum martyrum Perpetuae et Felicitatis. Prodit nunc primum e. ms. codice sacri casinensis monasterij. Opera et studio Lucae Holstenij Vaticanae Basil. canon. et bibliothecae praefecti. Notis eius posthumis adiunctis* (Rome: I. Dragondelli, 1663).

Hyperius, Andreas, *Methodi theologiae . . . libri tres* (Basel: Johannes Oporinus, 1567).

Jerome, 'Epistola XLVI', *Patrologia latina*, ed. J. P. Migne, XX (Paris: Migne, 1854), pp. 490–1.

—— *Praefatio in librum paralipomenon de graeco emmendato*, in *Biblia sacra iuxta latinam vulgatam versionem ad codicum fidem . . .*, VII: *Liber verborum dierum* (Rome: Typis Polyglottis Vaticanis, 1948), pp. 7–10.

Jesus y Xodar, Francisco, *Cinco discursos con que se confirma la antigua tradicion que el Apostol Santiago vino y predicó en España* (Madrid: Imprenta Real, 1612).

Jewel, John, *An Apologie, or Aunswer in Defence of the Church of England* (London: Reginald Wolf, 1562).

Keating, Geoffrey, *Foras Feasa ar Érinn: The History of Ireland from the Earliest Period to the English Invasion*, tr. and annotated John O'Mahony (New York: James B. Kirker, 1866; repr. Ann Arbor, Mich.: Michigan Historical Reprint ser., 2005).

Kelley, Donald (ed.), *Versions of History from Antiquity to the Enlightenment* (New Haven, Conn.: Yale University Press, 1991).

Kessler, Johannes, *Johannes Kesslers Sabbata mit kleineren Schriften und Briefen*, ed. Der Historische Vereins des Kantons St Gallen (St. Gallen: Fehr'sche Buchhandlung, 1902).

L'Heureux, Jean [Macarius], *Hagioglypta, sive picturae et sculpturae sacrae antiquiores praesertim quae Romae reperiuntur* (Paris: J. A. Toulouse, 1856).

Ligorio, Pirro, *Pirro Ligorio's Roman Antiquities: The Drawings in MS XIII. B 7 in the National Library of Naples*, ed. Erna Mandowsky and Charles Mitchell (London, Warburg Institute, 1963).

Lomazzo, Giovanni Paolo, *Trattato dell'arte de la pittura* (Milan: Paolo Gottardo Pontio, 1584).

Lucena, João de, *História da vida do padre Francisco de Xavier* (Lisbon: Pedro Crasbeeck, 1600).

Luther, Martin, *Decem praecepta wittenbergensi predicata populo. Per p. Martinum Luther Augustinianum* (Wittenberg: Johann Rhau-Grunenberg, 1518).

—— *Luther's Works*, ed. Jaroslav Pelikan and H. T. Lehmann, 55 vols. (St. Louis, Mo. and Philadelphia, Pa.: Concordia Publishing House and Fortress Press, 1955–86).

Lynch, John, *Cambrensis eversus*, ed. and tr. Matthew Kelly, 3 vols. (Dublin: The Celtic Society, 1848–51).

Mabillon, Jean, *Brèves réflexions sur quelques règles de l'histoire*, ed. Blandine Barret-Kriegel (Paris: P.O.L., 1990).

Mac Aingil, Aodh. *Scáthán Shacramuinte na haithridhe*, ed. Cainneach Ó Maonaigh (Dublin: Dublin Institute for Advanced Studies, 1952).

Macarius, see L'Heureux, Jean.

Maiolus, Simon, *Pro defensione sacrarum imaginum adversus iconomachos libri seu centuriae sexdecim* (Rome: Populi Romani, 1585).

Major, Georgius, *Vitae Patrum, in usum ministrorum verbi, quo ad eius fieri potuit repurgatae* (Wittenberg: Petrus Seitz, 1544).

—— *De origine et autoritate verbi Dei, & quae pontificum, patrum & conciliorum sit autoritas, admonitio... Additus est catalogus doctorum ecclesiae Dei...* (Wittenberg: Johannes Lufft, 1550).

Mancini, Giulio, *Considerazioni sulla pittura*, ed. Luigi Salerno (Rome: Accademia nazionale dei Lincei, 1957).

Mandeville, Jean de [John], *Le Livre des merveilles du monde*, ed. Christiane Deluz (Paris: CNRS Editions, 2000).

Mandeville, John, *Mandeville's Travels*, ed. M. C. Seymour (Oxford: Oxford University Press, 1967).

Mariana, Juan, S.J., *Historia ecclesiastica de todos los santos de España* (Cuenca: Pedro del Valle, 1596).

—— *De adventu Iacobi apostoli maioris in Hispaniam* (Cologne: Hieratus, 1609).

—— *Historia general de España* (Madrid: Gaspar y Roig, 1855).

Marineus Siculus, Lucius, *Cronica d'Aragon*, tr. Juan de Molina (Valencia: Joan Joffré, 1524). (Facsimile: Barcelona, Ediciones El Albir, 1974.)

—— *De las cosas memorables de España* (Alcalá de Henares: Juan de Brocar, 1539).

—— *De rebus Hispaniae libri XXII*, in *Hispaniae illustratae... scriptores varii*, ed. Andreas Schottus, I (Frankfurt: Claudius Marnius & haeredes, 1603), pp. 291–517.

Marrier, Martin, and André du Chesne, *Bibliotheca Clvniacensis: in qua ss. patrum abb. Clun. vitae, miracula, scripta, statuta, priuilegia chronologiaeque duplex...* (Paris: Robert Fovet, 1614).

Martyrologium romanum ad novam kalendarii rationem, et ecclesiasticae historiae veritatem restitutum, Gregorii XIII Pont. Max. iussu editum. Accesserunt Notationes atque Tractatio de Martyrologio romano, auctore Caesare Baronio sorano Congregationis Oratorii presbytero (Rome: Basa, 1586).

Martyrologium romanum ad novam kalendarii rationem & ecclesiasticae historiae veritatem restitutum (Cologne: Ioannes Gymnicus, 1610).

Matthew of Westminster [pseud.], *Flores historiarum per Matthaeum Westmonasteriensem collecti; praecipuè de rebus Britannicis ab exordio mundi vsque ad annum Domini 1307*, ed. Matthew Parker (London: Thomas Marshe, 1570).

Melanchthon, Phillipp, *Historiae de Saracenorum sive Turcarum origine* (Basel: Johannes Oporinus, 1543).

—— *Melanchthons Briefwechsel: Kritische und kommentierte Gesamtausgabe*, ed. H. Scheible (Stuttgart-Bad Cannstatt: Frommann-Holzboog, 1977–).

Middendorp, Jacob, *Historia monastica quae religiosae et solitariae vitae originem, progressionis, incrementa, & naturam, ex scriptura sacra, ex pontificio & caesareo iure, ex antiquissimis historiis, ex veterum patrum, atque iurisconsultorum scriptis demonstrat* (Cologne: Gosuinus Cholinus, 1603).

—— *Originum anachoreticarum sylva* (Cologne: Petrus Cholinus: 1615).

Mikropresbutikon: Veterum quorundam brevium theologorum, sive episcoporum sive presbyterorum, aut sacri ordinis aliorum qui aut tempore apostolorum, aut non multò post vixerunt, elenchus (Basel: Petri, 1550).

Molanus, Ioannis, *De historia ss imaginum et picturarum, pro vero earum usu contra abusus* (London: Laurentii Durand, 1619).

—— Traité des saintes images, 2 vols. (Paris: Éditions du Cerf, 1996).

Montaigne, Michel de, *Travel Journal*, tr. Donald Frame (San Francisco: North Point, 1983).

—— *Journal de voyage*, ed. François Rigolot (Paris: Presses universitaires de France, 1992).

Morales, Ambrosio de, *La coronica general de España* (Alcalá de Henares: Juan Iñiguez de Lequerica, 1574).

—— *Viage de Ambrosio Morales por ordén del Rey Phelipe II a los reynos de León, Galicia, y principado de Asturias*, ed. (with a biographical introduction) Henrique Flórez (Madrid: Antonio Marín, 1765).

Muzio, Girolamo, *Della historia sacra del Mutio Iustinopolitano, libro primo . . . ; libro secondo; dottrine di scrittori . . . ; e decreti di dieci santi pontefici* (Venice: Gio Andrea Valvassori, 1570).

Nebrija, Antonio de, *Obras históricas de Nebrija: estudio filológico*, ed. Gregorio Hinojo Andrés. (Salamanca: Universidad de Salamanca, 1991).

—— *Aurelii Prudentii Clementis V.C.: libelli cum commento Antoni Nebrissensis*, ed. Felipe González Vega (Salamanca: Universidad de Salamanca, 2002).

Osiander, Lucas [the Elder], *Epitomes historiae ecclesiasticae, centuriae I.–XVI.*, 10 vols. (Tübingen: Georgius Gruppenbachius, 1592–1604).

Padilla, Francisco, *Historia ecclesiastica de España*, 2 vols. (Málaga: Claudio Bolán, 1605).

Paleotti, Gabrielle, *Discorso intorno alle imagini sacre e profane*, in *Trattai d'arte del cinquecento fra manierismo e controriforma*, ed. Paola Barocchi, II (Bari: G. Laterza, 1961).

Panciroli, Ottavio, *I tesori nascosti nell'alma città di Roma* (Rome: Luigi Zannetti, 1600).

Pantaleon, Heinricus, *Chronographia ecclesiae Christi: in qua dilucide patrum et doctorum praecipuorum ordo, cum omnium haeresum origine, & multiplici innouatione ceremoniarum, decretorum, & rituum in ecclesia, per imperatores, principes, concilia, aut pontifices Romanos, à Christi natiuitate ad praesentem hunc 1568 annum usque ostenditur . . .* (Basel: Haeredes Nicolai Brylingeri, 1568).

Panvinio, Onofrio, *De ritu sepeliendi mortuos apud veteres Christianos et eorundem coemeterijs liber* (Cologne: Maternus Cholinus, 1568).

—— *De rebus antiquis memorabilibus et praestantia basilicae Sancti Petri apostolorum principis libri septem*. As printed in A. Mai (ed.), *Spicilegium romanum*, IX (Rome: Collegii Urbani, 1843), pp. 194–382.

Pappus, Johannes, *Historiae ecclesiasticae de conversionibus gentium, persecutionibus ecclesiae, haeresibus et conciliis oecumenicis epitome* (Strasbourg: Jobin, 1584).

—— and Eusebius Bohemus, *Epitome historiae ecclesiasticae Novi Testamenti . . . Omnia etiam ad haec nostra usque tempora . . . continuata* (Wittenberg: Bergerus, 1626).

—— and Heinrich Kipping, *Epitome historiae ecclesiasticae . . . Recognovit . . . M. Henricus Kipping* (Frankfurt: Bergerus, 1661–2).

Paris, Matthew, *Elegans, illustris et facilis rerum, praesertim britannicarum, ad* A.D. *1307 narratio*, ed. Matthew Parker (London: Richard Jugge, 1567).

—— *Matthaei Paris, monachi albanensis Angli, historia maior à Guilielmo Conquaestore, ad vltimum annum Henrici terti*, ed. Matthew Parker (London: Reginald Wolfe, 1571).

Parker, Matthew, (ed.), *The Holie Bible* (London: Richard Jugge, 1568).

—— *De antiquitate britannicae ecclesiae & priuilegiis ecclesiae cantuariensis cum archiepiscopis eiusdem 70* (London: John Day, 1572).

Parsons [Persons], Robert, *De persecutione anglicana libellus* (Rome: Francesco Zanetti, 1582).

—— *A Treatise of Three Conversions of England from Paganisme to Christian Religion*, 3 vols. (n.p. [St.Omer], 1603–4).

Paula and Eustochium, Sts, *The Letter of Paula and Eustochium to Marcella about the Holy Places (365* A.D.*)*, tr. Aubrey Stewart (London: Palestine Pilgrims' Text Society, 1896).

Persons, Robert, see Robert Parsons.

Pétau [Petavius], Denis, *Rationarium temporum in partes duas, libros tredecim distributum. In quis aetatum omnium sacra profanaque historia chronologicus probationibus monita summatim traditur* (Paris: S. & G. Cramoisy, 1633).

Pexenfelder, Michael, *Florus biblicus, sive narrationes ex historia sacra testamenti veteris selectae et doctrina moralis illustratae* (Straubing: Joannis Chrysostomi Haan, 1672).

Pezel, Christoph, *Mellificium historicum integrum*, ed. Johannes Lampadius (Marburg: Paulus Egenolphus, 1617).

Piccolomini, Aeneas Silvius, *Orationes politicae et ecclesiasticae*, ed. Joannes Dominicus Mansi, 3 vols. (Lucca: Ph. M. Benedini, 1755–59).

—— *Pii II Commentarii rerum memorabilium que temporibus suis contigerunt*, ed. Adrian van Heck, 2 vols., Studi e testi, CCCXII and CCCXIII (Vatican City: Biblioteca Apostolica Vaticana, 1984).

—— *Descripción de Asia*, tr. Francisco Socas (Madrid: Alianza, 1992).

—— *De Europa*, ed. Adrian van Heck, Studi e testi, CCCXCVIII (Vatican City: Biblioteca Apostolica Vaticana, 2001).

—— *Commentaries*, bks I–IV, 2 vols., tr. Margaret Meserve, I Tatti Renaissance Library (Cambridge, Mass.: Harvard University Press, 2004–7).

—— *Historia bohemica*, ed. Karl Gutschmidt et al., 3 vols., Bausteine zur slavischen Philologie und Kulturgeschichte, neue Folge: Editionen (Cologne: Böhlau, 2005).

—— *Germania*, ed. Maria Giovanna Fadiga, Edizione nazionale dei testi della storiografia umanistica (Florence: SISMEL, 2009).

—— *Historia Austrialis*, ed. Martin Wagendorfer and Julia Knödler, 2 vols., Monumenta Germaniae Historica: Scriptores Rerum Germanicarum, nova ser., XXIV (Hannover: Hahnsche Buchhandlung, 2009).

Pirri, Rocco, *Notitiae siciliensium ecclesiarum* (Palermo: Giovanni Battista Maringo, 1630).

Pisa, Francisco de, *Descripcion de la imperial ciudad de Toledo, y historia de sus antiguedades, y grandezas, y cosas memorables que en ella han acontecido . . . Primera parte, repartida en cinco libros con la historia de Santa Leocadia* (Toledo: Pedro Rodriguez, 1605). (Facsimile: Madrid: Villena Artes Gráficas, 1974.)

Pius II, see Piccolomini, Aeneas Silvius

Platina, Bartolomeo, *Historia de vitis pontificum romanorum a D. N. Iesu Christo usque ad Paulum Papam II. Longe quam antea emendatior, cui Onuphrii Panvinii . . . opera, reliquorum quoque pontificum vitae usque ad Pium IIII pontificem maximum adiunctae sunt. Et totum opus variis annotationibus illustratum* (Venice: Tramezino, 1562).

Plutarch, *Plutarch's Moralia*, tr. Frank Cole Babbitt, 16 vols., Loeb Classical Library (Cambridge, Mass.: Harvard University Press, 1969–2004).

Polo, Marco, *La Description du monde: Texte intégrale en français moderne avec introduction et notes*, ed. Louis Hambis (Paris: Librarie C. Klincksieck, 1955).

—— *Il Milione: Introduzione, edizione del testo toscano ("Ottimo") note illustrative, esegetiche, linguistiche repertori onomastici e lessicali*, ed. Ruggero M. Ruggieri (Florence: Leo S. Olschki, 1986).

—— *The Travels of Marco Polo: The Complete Yule-Cordier Edition*, ed. and tr. Henry Yule and Henri Cordier, 2 vols. (London: John Murray, 1903 and 1920; repr. Mineola, New York: Dover Press, 1993).

Possevino, Antonio, *Tractatio de poesi & pictura ethnica, humana, & fabulosa collata cum vera, honesta, & sacra* (Lyon: Ioannis Pillehotte, 1594).

Prado, Jerónimo, and Juan Bautista Villalpando, *In Ezechiel explanationes et apparatus urbis, ac templi hierosolymitani*, 3 vols. (Rome: Aloysius Zanetti, 1596–1605).

Quaresmio, Franceso, *Elucidatio terrae sanctae*, ed. Sabino de Sandoli (Jerusalem: Franciscan Printing Press, 1989).

Rader, Matthäus, *Bavaria sancta*, 3 vols. (Munich: Anna Bergia vidua, 1615–27).

—— *P. Matthäus Rader, 1595–1612*, ed. Helmut Zäh and Silvia Strodel. Bayerische Gelehrtenkorrespondenz (Munich: C. H. Beck, 1995).

—— *Die Korrespondenz mit Marcus Welser 1597–1614*, ed. Alois Schmid, Bayerische Gelehrtenkorrespondenz (Munich: C. H. Beck, 2009).

Ratti, Achille [Pius XI] (ed.), *Acta ecclesiae mediolanensis*, II (Milan: Typographia Pontificia Sancti Iosephi, 1890).

Renan, Ernest, *The Life of Jesus*, ed. John Haynes Holmes (New York, NY: Modern Library, 1927).

Rhenanus, Beatus, *Briefwechsel*, ed. Adalbert Horawitz and Karl Hartfelder (Leipzig: B. G. Teubner, 1886).

Ribadeneyra, Pedro, S. J., *Flos sanctorum o libro de las vidas de los santos* (Madrid: Imprenta Real, 1675).

Ross, James Bruce and Mary Martin McLaughlin (eds.), *The Portable Renaissance Reader* (New York: Viking, 1968).

Sainte-Marthe, Denis de, *Gallia christiana in provincias ecclesiasticas distributa*, I (Paris: ex typographia Regia, 1715).

Sanders, Nicholas, *De origine ac progressu schismatis anglicani libri trei*, ed. Edward Rishton (Cologne, n.p. [actually Rheims: Jean Foigny], 1585).

—— *Nicolai Sanderi de origine ac progressu schismatis anglicani libri tres . . . Aucti per Edouardum Rishtonum . . . nunc iterum locupletius & castigatius editi*, ed. Edward Rishton and Robert Persons (Rome: Bartholomaeo Bonfadino, 1586).

—— *Les Trois Liures de Nicholas Sander, touchant l'origine et progres du schisme d'Angleterre* (Ausbourg: Hans Mark, 1587).

—— *Warhaffte Engellaendische Histori in wellicher was sich, besonder in Religionssachen, von LX Jaren* (Salzburg: Kürner, 1594).

Sandys, Edwin, *Sermons Made by the Most Reuerende Father in God, Edwin, Archbishop of Yorke* (London: Henrie Midleton, 1585).

Santo Stefano, Geronimo di, 'Account of the Journey of Hieronimo di Santo Stefano', with independent pagination, in *India in the Fifteenth Century*, ed. R.H. Major (London: Hakluyt Society, 1857), pp. 3–10.

Sarpi, Paolo [Paolo Soave], *Istoria del Concilio Tridentino* (London: G. Billio, 1619).

Schaff, Philip and Henry Wace (eds.), *A Select Library of Nicene and Post-Nicene Fathers of the Christian Church*, 2nd ser., 14 vols. (New York: Christian Literature Company, 1890–1900). (Christian Classics Ethereal Library: <http://www.ccel.org/ccel/schaff?show=worksBy>.)

Schedel, Hartmann, *Liber chronicarum* (Nuremberg: Anton Koberger, 1493).

Schottus, Franciscus, Italy in its Original Glory, Ruine and Revival. Being an exact survey of the whole geography and history of that famous country . . . and whatever is remarkable in Rome (the mistress of the world), tr. Edmund Warcup (London: S. Griffin, 1660). (English translation of *Itinerarium Italiae*, first published 1600.)

Schulting Steinwich, Cornelius, *Thesaurus antiquitatum ecclesiasticarum, ex septem prioribus tomis Annalium ecclesiasticorum cardinalis Caesaris Baronii ab incunabulis nascentis ecclesiae usque ad aetatem Gregorii Magni collectus. Adjunctis singularibus scholijs aduersus Centurias Magdeburgensium et Caluinistas* (Cologne: Stephan Hemmerden, 1601).

Serarius, Nikolaus, *Moguntiacarum rerum ab initio vsque ad reuerendissimum et illustrissimum hodiernum archiepiscopum, ac electorum, Dominum D. Ioannem Schwichardum, libri quinque* (Mainz: Balthasarus Lippius, 1604).

Siculus, Lucius Marineus, see Marineus Siculus, Lucius.

Silva Rego, António da (ed.), *Documentação para a história das missões do padroado Português do oriente*, 12 vols. (Lisbon: Agência Geral das Colónias, 1947–58).

Sleidanus, Johannes, *De statu religionis et reipublicae, Carolo Quinto Caesare, commentarii* (Strasbourg: Wendelin Rihel, 1555).

—— *De quatuor summis imperiis, babylonico, persico, graeco, & romano, Libri tres* (Paris: Conradus Badius, 1559).

—— *The General History of the Reformation of the Church, from the Errors and Corruptions of the Church of Rome: begun in Germany by Martin Luther: with the progress thereof in all parts of Christendom, from the year 1517, to the year 1556*, tr. Edmund Bohun (London: Jones, Swall, and Bonwicke, 1689).

Spanheimius, Fridericus, *Introductio ad chronologiam et historiam sacram ac praecipue Christianam, ad tempora proxima Reformationi* (Leiden: Daniel à Gaesbeeck, 1683).

Stanihurst, Richard, *De rebus in Hibernia gestis, libri quattor* (Antwerp: C. Plantin, 1584).

Stanihurst, Richard, *De vita sancti patricii, Hiberniae apostolici, libri II* (Antwerp: C. Plantin, 1587).

Stapleton, Thomas, *A Fortresse of the Faith First Planted amonge Vs Englishmen, and Continued Hitherto in the Vniuersall Church of Christ. The faith of which time protestants call, papistry* (Antwerp: John Laet 1565).

—— *Returne of Untruths* (Antwerp: John Latius (John Laet), 1566).

Stumpf, Johann, and Joachim Vadian, *Gemeiner loblicher Eydgnoschafft Stetten, Landen vnd Völckeren Chronick* (Zürich: Froschauer, 1547-8).

Surius, Laurentius, *Commentarius brevis rerum in orbe gestarum* (Cologne: haeredes Iohannis Quentel & Gervinus Calenius, 1566).

—— *De probatis sanctorum historiis . . .* (Cologne: Gervinus Calenius, 1576).

Tafur, Pero, *Pero Tafur: Travels and Adventures, 1435-1439*, ed. and tr. Malcolm Letts (London: George Routledge and Sons, 1926).

Torelli, Luigi, *Ristretto delle vite de gli uomini e delle donne illustri in santità dell'ordine agostiniano . . . e diviso in sei centurie* (Bologna, G. Monti, 1647).

—— *Secoli agostiniani*, 3 vols. (Bologna: G. Monti, 1659-86).

Torquemada, Antonio de, *Jardín de flores curiosas*, ed. Giovanni Allegra (Madrid: Editorial Castalia, 1982s).

Truxillo, Thomas de, O.P., *Thesaurus concionatorum* (Paris: Nicolas Nivelle, 1585).

Tyndale, William, *The Obedience of a Christen Man* (Antwerp: Merten de Keyser, 1528).

Ugolini, Blasius, *Thesaurus antiquitatum sacrarum*, 35 vols. (Venice: J. G. Hertz, 1744-67).

Ussher, James, *A Discourse of the Religion Anciently Professed by the Irish and British* (London: Printed by R. Y. for the partners of the Irish Stocke, 1631).

Vadian, Joachim, *Epitome trium terrae partium, Asiae, Africae et Europae compendiarium locorum descriptionem continens, praecipue autem quorum in Actis Lucas, passim autem Evangelistae et Apostoli meminere . . .* (Zürich: Froschauer, 1534).

—— *Deutsche historische Schriften: Joachim v. Watt (Vadian)*, ed. Ernst Götzinger, 3 vols. (St Gallen: Zollikofer'schen Buchdruckerei, 1875-97).

Valera, Mosén Diego de, *Crónica abreviada de España*, ed. Cristina Moya García (Madrid: Fundación Universitaria Española, 2009).

Valla, Lorenzo, *Antidotum in Poggium, opera* (Basel: Henric Petri, 1540).

—— *Le postille all'"Institutio Oratoria' di Quintiliano*, ed. Lucia Cesarini Martinell and Alessandro Perosa (Padua: Antenore, 1996).

—— *On the Donation of Constantine*, tr. Glenn W. Bowersock, I Tatti Renaissance Library (Cambridge, Mass.: Harvard University Press, 2007).

Vasaeus, Johannes, *Chronici rerum memorabilium Hispaniae tomus prior* (Salamanca: Juan de Junta, 1552).

Vasari, Giorgio, *The Lives of the Artists* [1568], tr. George Bull (Harmondsworth: Penguin, 1987).

Velasco, Juan de, *Dos discursos en que se defiende la venida y predicación del apóstol Santiago en España* (Valladolid: Luys Sanchez, 1605).

Vergil, Polydore, *Anglicae historiae libri vigintisex* (Basel: Michael Isingrin, 1546).

Verstegan, Richard, *Theatrum crudelitatum haereticorum nostri temporis* (Antwerp: Adrian Huberti, 1587).

—— *A Restitution of Decayed Intelligence: In Antiquities. Concerning the Most Noble and Renovvmed English Nation* (Antwerp: Robert Bruney, 1605).

—— *Theatre des cruautez des hereticques de nostre temps par Richard Versteganus* (revised edn, Antwerp: Adrien Hubert 1607).

—— *The Letters and Despatches of Richard Verstegan (c.1550–1640)*, ed. Anthony G. Petti (London: Catholic Record Society, 52, 1959).

Villegas, Alonso, *Flos sanctorum quarta y ultima parte* (Barcelona: Pau Mal, 1594).

von Breydenbach, Bernhard, *Itinerarium totius sacrae scripturae. A description of the land of Canaan; with other provinces, tovvns & places mentioned in the Old & New Testaments . . .*, tr. Richard Brathwait (London: Printed by S.I. and are to be sold by Abel Roper . . . , 1652).

Voragine, Jacobus de, *The Golden Legend: Readings on the Saints*, tr. William Granger Ryan, 2 vols. (Princeton: Princeton University Press, 1993).

Walsingham, Thomas, *Historia brevis* (London: Henry Binneman, 1574).

—— *Ypodigma Neustriae vel Normanniae* (London: John Day, 1574).

Weigel, Helmut and Henny Grüneisen (eds.), *Deutsche Reichstagsakten unter Kaiser Friedrich III* (Göttingen: Vandenhoeck und Ruprecht, 1969).

Welser, Marcus, *Marci Velseri . . . opera historica et philologica, sacra et profana* (Nuremberg: Typis ac sumtibus W. Mauritii, & filiorum J. Andreae, 1682).

White, Richard, *Historiarum Britanniae libri XI*, 11 vols. (Douai: Carolus Boscardus; Arras: Gullielmus Riverius, 1597–1607).

Wimpfeling, Jakob, *Epithoma Germanorum et suorum opera contextum* (Strasbourg: Johannes Prüs, 1505).

Zurita, Jerónimo. *Anales de la corona de Aragón*, ed. Angel Canellas López (Zaragoza: Institución 'Fernando el Católico' (C.S.I.C.), 1998).

Secondary Sources

Abray, Lorna Jane, *The People's Reformation: Magistrates, Clergy and Commons in Strasbourg, 1500–1598* (Oxford: Blackwell, 1985).

Adams, Colin and Jim Roy (eds.), *Travel, Geography and Culture in Ancient Greece, Egypt and the Near East* (Oxford: Oxbow Books, 2007).

Agosti, Barbara, *Collezionismo e archeologia cristiana nel seicento: Federico Borromeo e il medioevo artistico tra Roma e Milano* (Milan: Jaca Book, 1996).

Alcock, Susan E., *Graecia Capta: The Landscapes of Roman Greece* (Cambridge: Cambridge University Press, 1993).

——, John F. Cherry, and Jaś Elsner (eds.), *Pausanias: Travel and Memory in Roman Greece* (Oxford: Oxford University Press, 2001).

Allison, Antony F. and David M. Rogers, *The Contemporary Printed Literature of the English Counter-Reformation between 1558 and 1640*, 2 vols. (Aldershot: Scholar Press, 1989–94).

Almond, Philip C. *Adam and Eve in Seventeenth-Century Thought* (Cambridge: Cambridge University Press, 1999).

Arblaster, Paul, *Antwerp and the World: Richard Verstegan and the International Culture of Catholic Reformation* (Leuven: Leuven University Press, 2004).

Aubertin, Bernard-Nicolas (ed.), *Histoire de l'Abbaye de Lérins* (Bellefontaine: Abbaye de Bellefontaine, 2005).

Backus, Irena, *La Patristique et les guerres de religion en France. Etude de l'activité littéraire de Jacques de Billy* (Paris: Institut des études augustiniennes, 1993).

—— *Historical Method and Confessional Identity in the Era of the Reformation (1378–1615)* (Leiden: Brill, 2003).

Backus, Irena and Benoît Gain, 'Le Cardinale Guglielmo Sirleto (1514–85), sa bibliothèque et ses traductions de Saint Basile', *Mélanges de l'Ecole Française de Rome: Moyen-Age, Temps modernes*, 98(2) (1986), pp. 889–955.

Barkan, Leonard, *Unearthing the Past: Archaeology and Aesthetics in the Making of Renaissance Culture* (New Haven, Conn.: Yale University Press, 1999).

Barret-Kriegel, Blandine, *Jean Mabillon* (Paris: Presses Universitaires de France, 1988).

Barrios Aguilera, Manuel, and Mercedes García-Arenal (eds.), *Los plomos del sacromonte: invención y tesoro* (Valencia: Universitat de València, 2006).

Barry, John, 'Derrike and Stanihurst: A Dialogue' in Jason Harris and Keith Sidwell (eds.), *Making Ireland Roman: Irish Neo-Latin Writers and the Republic of Letters* (Cork: Cork University Press, 2009), pp. 36–47.

Bauer, Stefan, *The Censorship and Fortuna of Platina's Lives of the Popes in the Sixteenth Century* (Turnhout: Brepols, 2006).

Bautz, Friedrich Wilhelm and Traugott Bautz (eds.), *Biographisch-bibliographisches Kirchenlexikon* (Hamm [Westfalen]: Bautz, 1970–).

Bayley, Susan, *Saints, Goddesses and Kings: Muslims and Christians in South Indian Society, 1700–1900* (Cambridge: Cambridge University Press, 1989).

Beltramme, Marcello, 'Le teoriche dell'Academia di San Luca nella politica artistica di Clemente VIII (1592–1602)', *Storia dell'arte*, 69 (1990), pp. 201–33.

Ben-Arieh, Yehoshua, 'Nineteenth-Century Historical Geographies of the Holy Land', *Journal of Historical Geography*, 15 (1989), pp. 69–79.

Benedetti, Marina, 'Cesare Baronio e gli eretici: le fonti della controversia' in Giuseppe. A. Guazzelli et al. (eds.), *Cesare Baronio tra santità e scrittura storica*.

Bentley, Jerry H., *Humanists and Holy Writ: New Testament Scholarship in the Renaissance* (Princeton, NJ: Princeton University Press, 1983).

Benz, Stefan, *Zwischen Tradition und Kritik: katholische Geschichtsschreibung im barocken Heiligen Römischen Reich* (Husum: Matthiesen, 2003).

Bernard, George W., *The King's Reformation: Henry VIII and the Remaking of the English Church* (New Haven, Conn.: Yale University Press, 2005).

Betteridge, Thomas, 'From Prophetic to Apocalyptic: John Foxe and the Writing of History' in David Loades (ed.), *John Foxe and the English Reformation* (Aldershot: Scholar Press, 1997), pp. 210–32.

—— *Tudor Histories of the English Reformations, 1530–1583* (Aldershot: Ashgate, 1999).

Bitton-Ashkelony, Brouria, *Encountering the Sacred: The Debate on Christian Pilgrimage in Late Antiquity* (Berkeley, Calif.: University of California Press, 2005).

Bizzocchi, Roberto, *Genealogie incredibili: scritti di storia nell'Europa moderna*, 2nd edn (Bologna: Il mulino, 2009).

Blair, Ann M., 'Mosaic Physics and the Search for a Pious Natural Philosophy in the Late Renaissance', *Isis*, 91 (2000), pp. 32–58.

—— *Too Much To Know: Managing Scholarly Information Before the Modern Age* (New Haven, Conn.: Yale University Press, 2010).

Bledniak, Sonia, 'L'hagiographie imprimée: Œuvres en français 1476–1550' in Guy Philippart (ed.), *Histoire internationale de la littérature hagiographique latine et vernaculaire en Occident* (Turnhout: Brepols, 1994).

Blunt, Anthony, *Artistic Theory in Italy, 1450–1600* (Oxford: Clarendon Press, 1962).

Boesch Gajano, Sofia (ed.), *Raccolte di vite di santi del XIII al XVIII secolo: strutture, messaggi, fruizioni* (Fasano di Brindisi: Schena Editore, 1990).

—— and Raimondo Michetti (eds.), *Europa sacra: raccolte agiografiche e identità politiche in Europa fra medioevo ed età moderna* (Rome: Carocci, 2002).

Bonorand, Conradin, *Vadians Weg vom Humanismus zur Reformation und seine Vorträge über die Apostelgeschichte (1523)* (St Gallen: Verlag der Fehr'schen Buchhandlung, 1962).

Bossy, John, *The English Catholic Community 1570–1850* (London: Darton, Longman and Todd, 1975/New York: Oxford University Press, 1976).

Boutcher, Warren, '"Le moyen de voir ce Senecque escrit à la main": Montaigne's *Journal de Voyage* and the Politics of *Science* and *Faveur* in the Vatican Library' in John O'Brien (ed.), *(Ré)interprétations: Études sur le seizième siècle*, Michigan Romance Studies 15 (1995), pp. 177–214.

Boutry, Philippe, and Dominique Julia (eds.), *Reine au Mont Auxois. Le culte et le pèlerinage de sainte Reine des origines à nos jours* (Paris-Dijon: Éditions du Cerf, 1997).

Bowersock, G. W., 'Peter and Constantine' in W. Tronzo (ed.), *St. Peter's in the Vatican* (Cambridge: Cambridge University Press, 2005), pp. 5–15.

Bowman, Glenn, 'Pilgrim Narratives of Jerusalem and the Holy Land: A Study in Ideological Distortion' in Alan Morinis (ed.), *Sacred Journeys: The Anthropology of Pilgrimage* (Westport, Conn.: Greenwood Press, 1992), pp. 149–68.

Boxer, Charles, 'Three Historians of Portuguese Asia: João de Barros, Diogo do Couto, and António Bocarro' in Diogo Ramada Curto (ed.), *Opera minora*, 3 vols., II (Lisbon: Fundação Oriente, 2002), pp. 13–38.

Bradshaw, Brendan, 'Geoffrey Keating: Apologist of Irish Ireland' in Brendan Bradshaw, Andrew Hadfield, and Willy Maley (eds.), *Representing Ireland: Literature and the Origins of Conflict, 1534–1660* (Cambridge: Cambridge University Press, 1993), pp. 166–90.

—— 'Reading Seathrún Céitinn's *Foras Feasa ar Éirinn*' in Pádraig Ó Riain (ed.), *Geoffrey Keating's Foras Feasa ar Éirinn: Reassessments* (London: Irish Texts Society, 2008), pp. 1–18.

Brémond, Henri, *Histoire littéraire du sentiment religieux en France* (Grenoble: Jérôme Millon, 2006).

Brendle, Franz et al. (eds.), *Deutsche Landesgeschichtsschreibung im Zeichen des Humanismus*, Contubernium: Tübinger Beiträge zur Universitäts- und Wissenschaftsgeschichte XLVI (Stuttgart: Steiner, 2001).

Brian, Isabelle, 'Le roi pèlerin. Pèlerinages royaux dans la France moderne' in Philippe Boutry, Pierre Antoine Fabre, and Dominique Julia (eds.), *Rendre ses vœux: les identités pèlerines dans l'Europe moderne (XVIe–XVIIIe siècle)* (Paris: EHESS, 2000), pp. 363–79.

Brown, Leslie, *The Indian Christians of St. Thomas: An Account of the Ancient Syrian Church of Malabar* (Cambridge: Cambridge University Press, 1956).

Brown, Peter, *The Cult of the Saints: Its Rise and Function in Latin Christianity* (Chicago: University of Chicago Press, 1981).

Brummer, Hans Henrik, 'Cesare Baronio and the Convent of Gregory the Great', *Konsthistorisk Tidskrift*, 43 (1974), pp. 101–20.

Burke, Peter, 'How to Become a Counter-Reformation Saint' in Kaspar von Greyerz (ed.), *Religion and Society in Early Modern Europe, 1500–1800* (London: German Historical Institute, 1984), pp. 45–55.

—— *The Renaissance Sense of the Past* (New York: St Martin's Press, 1970).

Burnett, Stephen G., *From Christian Hebraism to Jewish Studies: Johannes Buxtorf (1564–1629) and Hebrew Learning in the Seventeenth Century* (Leiden: Brill, 1996).

Buser, Thomas, 'Jerome Nadal and Early Jesuit Art in Rome', *Art Bulletin*, 58 (1976), pp. 424–33.

Cabibbo, Sara, *Il paradiso del magnifico regno: agiografia, santi e culti nella Sicilia spagnola* (Rome: Viella, 1996).

Calenzio, Generoso, *La vita e gli scritti del cardinale Cesare Baronio* (Rome: Tipografia vaticana, 1907).

Cameron, Euan, *The European Reformation* (Oxford: Clarendon Press; New York: Oxford University Press, 1991).

—— 'One Reformation or Many: Protestant Identities in the Later Reformation in Germany' in Ole Peter Grell and Bob Scribner (eds.), *Tolerance and Intolerance in the European Reformation* (Cambridge: Cambridge University Press, 1996), pp. 108–27.

—— *Enchanted Europe: Superstition, Reason, and Religion 1250–1750* (Oxford and New York: Oxford University Press, 2010).

Campenhausen, Hans Freiherr von, 'Die Bilderfrage in der Reformation', *Zeitschrift für Kirchengeschichte*, 68 (1957), pp. 96–128.

Camporeale, Salvatore, 'Lorenzo Valla's Oratio on the Pseudo-Donation of Constantine: Dissent and Innovation in Early Renaissance Humanism', *Journal of the History of Ideas*, 57 (1996), pp. 9–26.

Caro Baroja, Julio, *Las falsificaciones de la historia (en relación con la de España)* (Barcelona: Seix Barral, 1992).

Carroll, Clare, 'Irish and Spanish Cultural and Political Relations in the Work of O'Sullivan Beare' in Hiram Morgan (ed.), *Political Ideology in Ireland, 1541–1641* (Dublin: Four Courts Press, 1999), pp. 229–53.

Case, Thomas E., *La historia de San Diego de Alcalá: su vida, su canonización y su legado/The Story of San Diego de Alcalá: His Life, his Canonization and his Legacy* (bilingual edn) (Alcalá de Henares: Universidad de Alcalá, 1998).

Cattaneo, Enrico, 'La singolare fortuna degli "Acta ecclesiae Mediolanensis"', *Scuola cattolica*, 111 (1983), pp. 191–217.

Celenza, Christopher, *Renaissance Humanism and the Papal Curia: Lapo da Castiglionchio the Younger's De curiae commodis* (Ann Arbor, Mich.: University of Michigan Press, 1999).

Chadwick, Owen, *Catholicism and History: The Opening of the Vatican Archives* (Cambridge: Cambridge University Press, 1978).

Chaix, Gerald, 'De la cité chrétienne à la métropole catholique. Cologne et le processus confessionnel', PhD dissertation (University of Strasbourg, 1994).

Chastel, André, *The Sack of Rome, 1527*, tr. Beth Archer (Princeton, NJ: Princeton University Press, 1983).

Chazelle, Celia M., 'Pictures, Books, and the Illiterate: Pope Gregory I's Letters to Serenus of Marseilles', *Word and Image*, 6 (1990), pp. 138–53.

Christin, Olivier, *Une Révolution symbolique: l'iconoclasme huguenot et la reconstruction catholique* (Paris: Minuit, 1991).

Cioni, Alfredo, *Bibliografia delle sacre rappresentazioni* (Florence: Sansoni Antiquario, 1961).

Cirot, Georges, *Études sur l'historiographie espagnole: Mariana historien* (Paris: Feret et fils, 1905).

Cistellini, Antonio, *San Filippo Neri. L'Oratorio e la Congregazione oratoriana. Storia e spiritualità*, 3 vols. (Brescia: Morcelliana, 1989).

Cochrane, Eric W., *Historians and Historiography in the Italian Renaissance* (Chicago: University of Chicago Press, 1981).

Cohen, Erik, 'Pilgrimage and Tourism: Convergence and Divergence' in Alan Morinis (ed.), *Sacred Journeys: The Anthropology of Pilgrimage* (Westport, Conn.: Greenwood Press, 1992), pp. 47–60.

Collins, David J., *Reforming Saints: Saints' Lives and Their Authors in Germany, 1470–1530*, Oxford Studies in Historical Theology (Oxford: Oxford University Press, 2008).

Collinson, Patrick, 'John Foxe as Historian' in John Foxe, *The Unabridged Acts and Monuments Online*.

Coulton, G. G., *Art and the Reformation* (Cambridge: Cambridge University Press, 1953).

Cressy, David, *Bonfires and Bells: National Memory and the Protestant Calendar in Elizabethan and Stuart England* (London: Weidenfield and Nicholson, 1989).

Cunnally, John, *Images of the Illustrious: The Numismatic Presence in the Renaissance* (Princeton, NJ: Princeton University Press, 1999).

Cunningham, Bernadette, The Culture and Ideology of Irish Franciscan Historians at Louvain, 1607–1650' in Ciarán Brady (ed.), *Ideology and the Historians: Historical Studies XVII* (Dublin: Lilliput Press, 1991), pp. 11–30.

——*The World of Geoffrey Keating: History, Myth and Religion in Seventeenth-Century Ireland* (Dublin: Four Courts Press, 2000).

—— *The Annals of the Four Masters: Irish History, Kingship and Society in the Early Seventeenth Century* (Dublin: Four Courts Press, 2010).

Curran, Brian and Anthony Grafton, 'A Fifteenth-Century Site Report on the Vatican Obelisk', *Journal of the Warburg and Courtauld Institutes*, 58 (1995), pp. 234–48.

Dacos, Nicole, *La Découverte de la Domus Aurea et la formation des grotesques a la Renaissance* (London: Warburg Institute, 1969).

D'Ambrières, René and Éamon Ó Cíosáin, 'John Lynch of Galway (*c*.1599–1677): His Career, Exile and Writing', *Journal of the Galway Archaeological and Historical Society*, 55 (2003), pp. 50–63.

D'Amico, John F., *Theory and Practice in Renaissance Textual Criticism: Beatus Rhenanus between Conjecture and History* (Berkeley, Calif.: University of California Press, 1988).

—— 'Ulrich von Hutten and Beatus Rhenanus as Medieval Historians and Religious Propagandists in the Early Reformation' in D'Amico, *Roman and German Humanism, 1450–1550*, ed. Paul F. Grendler (Aldershot: Variorum, 1993), pp. 11–33.

Davies, P. R., 'Daniel Chapter Two', *Journal of Theological Studies*, n.s.: 27 (1976), pp. 392–401.

Davies, W. D., *The Gospel and the Land: Early Christianity and Jewish Territorial Doctrine* (Berkeley, Calif.: University of California Press, 1974).

de Gaiffier, Baudouin, 'Hagiographie et critique: quelques aspects de l'oeuvre des Bollandistes au XVIIe siècle' in de Gaiffier, *Études critiques d'hagiographie et d'iconologie* (Brussels: Société des Bollandistes, 1967), pp. 289–310.

de Laurentiis, Valeria, 'Immagini ed arte in Bellarmino' in Romeo de Maio et al. (eds.), *Bellarmino e la Controriforma* (Sora: Centro di studi sorani 'Vincenzo Patriarca', 1990), pp. 599–600.

de Maio, Romeo et al. (eds.), *Baronio storico e la Controriforma. Atti del convegno internazionale di studi, Sora, 6–10 ottobre 1979* (Sora: Centro di Studi Sorani 'Vincenzo Patriarca', 1982).

—— (eds.), *Baronio e l'arte. Atti del convegno internazionale di studi, Sora, 10–13 ottobre 1984* (Sora: Centro di Studi Sorani 'Vincenzo Patriarca', 1985).

Delano-Smith, Catherine and Elizabeth M. Ingram, *Maps in Bibles, 1500–1600: An Illustrated Catalogue* (Geneva: Droz, 1991).

Delph, Ronald, 'Valla Grammaticus, Agostino Steuco, and the Donation of Constantine', *Journal of the History of Ideas*, 57 (1996), pp. 55–77.

Delumeau, Jean, *Sin and Fear: The Emergence of a Western Guilt Culture, 13th–18th Centuries* (New York: St Martin's Press, 1990).

Denzler, Georg, *Kardinal Guglielmo Sirleto (1514–1585), Leben und Werk; ein Beitrag zur nachtridentinischen Reform* (Munich: M. Hueber, 1964).

Depluvrez, Jean Marc, 'Les retours de Saint Eugène et Sainte Léocadie a Tolède en 1565 et 1587' in Bernard Dompnier and Geneviève Demerson (eds.), *Les Signes de Dieu aux XVIe et XVIIe siècles* (Clermont Ferrand: Faculté des Lettres de Clermont-Ferrand, 1993), pp. 113–32.

Ditchfield, Simon, *Liturgy, Sanctity, and History in Tridentine Italy: Pietro Maria Campi and the Preservation of the Particular* (Cambridge: Cambridge University Press, 1995).

—— 'Sanctity in Early Modern History', *Journal of Ecclesiastical History*, 47(1) (1996), pp. 98–112.

—— 'Erudizione ecclesiastica e particolarismi tra tardo medioevo e prima età moderna' in Sergio Gensini (ed.), *Vita religiosa e identità politiche: universalità e particolarismi nell'Europa del tardo medioevo* (San Miniato: Fondazione Centro di studi sulla civiltà dell tardo medioevo, 1998), pp. 465–80.

——'"Historia magistra sanctitatis"? The Relationship between Historiography and Hagiography in Italy after the Council of Trent (ca.1564–1742)', *Studies in Medieval and Renaissance History*, 3rd ser., III (2006), pp. 159–84.

—— 'Baronio storico nel suo tempo' in Giuseppe A. Guazzelli et al. (ed.), *Cesare Baronio tra santità e scrittura storica* (Rome: Viella forthcoming).

Dompnier, Bernard, *Le Venin de l'hérésie: image du protestantisme et combat catholique au XVIIe siècle* (Paris: Le Centurion, 1985).

Dost, Timothy P., *Renaissance Humanism in Support of the Gospel in Luther's Early Correspondence: Taking All Things Captive* (Aldershot: Ashgate, 2001).

Droz, Eugénie, 'Frère Gabriel DuPuyherbault l'agresseur de François Rabelais', *Studi francesi*, 30 (1966), pp. 401–27.

Dülmen, Richard von, 'Die Gesellschaft Jesu und der bayerische Späthumanismus', *Zeitschrift für bayerische Landesgeschichte*, 37 (1974), pp. 358–415.

Eco, Umberto, *La vertigine della lista* (Milano: Bompiani, 2009). (English translation: *The Infinity of Lists* (London: Quercus, 2009).)

Eden, Kathy, *Hermeneutics and the Rhetorical Tradition: Chapters in the Ancient Legacy and its Humanist Reception* (New Haven, Conn.: Yale University Press, 1997).

Edouard, Sylvène, 'Enquête hagiographique et mythification historique. Le "saint voyage" d'Ambrosio de Morales (1572)' in Jean Croizat-Viallet and Marc Vitse (eds.), *El tiempo de los santos: hagiografía en el Siglo de Oro*, Mélanges de la Casa de Velázquez, 33/2 (Madrid: Casa de Velazquez, 2003), pp. 33–60.

Ehlers, Benjamin, 'Juan Bautista Pérez and the *Plomos de Granada*: Spanish humanism in the late sixteenth century', *Al-Qantara*, 24(2) (2003), pp. 427–48.

El Kenz, David, *Les Bûchers du roi: la culture protestante des martyrs (1523–1572)* (Seyssel: Champ Vallon, 1997).

Elsner, Jaś and Joan-Pau Rubiés (eds.), 'Introduction' in *Voyages and Visions: Towards a Cultural History of Travel* (London: Reaktion Books, 1999), pp. 1–56.

Elukin, Jonathan, 'Jacques Basnage and the History of the Jews: Anti-Catholic Polemic and Historical Allegory in the Republic of Letters', *Journal of the History of Ideas*, 53 (1992), pp. 603–30.

Enderle, Wilfried, 'Die Buchdrucker der Reichsstadt Köln und die katholische Publizistik zwischen 1555 und 1648' in Georg Mölich and Gerd Schwerhoff (eds.), *Köln als Kommunikationszentrum* (Cologne: DuMont, 1999), pp. 167–82.

Erbe, Michael, *François Bauduin (1520–1573): Biographie eines Humanisten* (Gütersloh: Gütersloher Verlagshaus Mohn, 1978).

Escartí, Vicent Josep, 'Narrar la historia remota de un país: Beuter y la *Història de València* (1538)', *Espéculo, Revista de estudios literarios* (revista digital de la Universidad Complutense de Madrid), no. 44 (<http://www.ucm.es/info/especulo/numero44/beuterva.html>).

Evans, R. J. W., 'Rantzau and Welser: Aspects of Later German Humanism', *History of European Ideas*, 5 (1984), pp. 257–72.

Evenden, Elizabeth, *Patents, Pictures and Patronage: John Day and the Tudor Book Trade* (Aldershot: Ashgate, 2008).

—— and Thomas Freeman, 'Print, Profit and Propaganda: The Elizabethan Privy Council and the 1570 Edition of Foxe's "Book of Martyrs"', *English Historical Review*, 119 (2004), pp. 1288–307.

—— —— *Religion and the Book in Early Modern England: The Making of John Foxe's 'Book of Martyrs'* (Cambridge: Cambridge University Press, 2011).

Fabre, Pierre Antoine, and Mickaïl Wilmart, 'Le Traité des reliques de Calvin (1543)' in Philippe Boutry, Pierre Antoine Fabre and Dominique Julia (eds.), *Reliques modernes: cultes et usages chrétiens des corps saints des réformes aux révolutions*, I (Paris: EHESS, 2009), pp. 29–68.

Farge, James K, *Orthodoxy and Reform in Early Reformation France: The Faculty of Theology of Paris, 1500–1543* (Leiden: Brill, 1985).

Fellmann, Dorothea, *Das Gymnaisum Montanum in Köln 1550–1798* (Cologne: Böhlau, 1999).

Ferguson, Arthur B., *Clio Unbound: Perceptions of the Social and Cultural Past in Renaissance England* (Durham, NC: Duke University Press, 1979).

Ferrary, Jean-Louis, *Onofrio Panvinio et les antiquités romaines* (Rome: École française de Rome, 1996).

Ferretto, Giuseppe, *Note storico-bibliografiche di archeologia cristiana* (Vatican City: Tip. Poliglotta Vaticana, 1942).

Filippini, Orietta, *Memoria della chiesa, memoria dello stato. Carlo Cartari (1614–1697) e l'archivio di Castel Sant'Angelo* (Bologna: Il Mulino, 2010).

Findlen, Paula, *Possessing Nature: Museums, Collecting, and Scientific Culture in Early Modern Italy* (Berkeley, Calif.: University of California Press, 1994).

Finney, Paul Corby, *The Invisible God: The Earliest Christians on Art* (New York: Oxford University Press, 1994).

Finocchiaro, Giuseppe, *Cesare Baronio e la tipografia dell'Oratorio. Impresa e ideologia* (Florence: Leo S. Olschki, 2005).

—— (ed.), *I libri di Cesare Baronio in Vallicelliana* (Rome: Biblioteca Vallicelliana, 2008).

Fiorani, Francesca, 'Post-Tridentine Geographia Sacra: The Galleria Della Carte Geografiche in the Vatican Palace', *Imago Mundi*, 48 (1996), pp. 124–48.

Firpo, Massimo (ed.), *'Nunc alia tempora, alii mores': storici e storia in età postridentina* (Florence: Leo S. Olschki, 2005).

Ford, Alan, *James Ussher: Theology, History and Politics in Early Modern Ireland and England* (Oxford: Oxford University Press, 2007).

Fragonard, Marie-Madeleine, 'Didactique et polémique: le culte des saints' in Sylviane Bokdam and Jean Cénard (eds.), *Pontus de Tyard, poète, philosophe, théologien* (Paris: Honoré Champion, 2003), pp. 301–16.

Frajese, Vittorio, *Filippo Neri*, in *Dizionario biografico degli Italiani*, 47 (Rome: Istituto dell'Enciclopedia italiana, 1997), pp. 741–50.

Franzen, August, *Der Wiederaufbau des kirchlichen Lebens im Erzbistum Köln unter Ferdinand von Bayern Erzbischof von Köln* (Münster: Aschendorff, 1941).

Frazier, Alison Knowles, *Possible Lives: Authors and Saints in Renaissance Italy* (New York: Columbia University Press, 2005).

Freeman, Thomas, 'John Foxe: A Biography' in John Foxe, *The Unabridged Acts and Monuments Online*.

Friedman, Jerome, *The Most Ancient Testimony: Sixteenth-Century Christian-Hebraica in the Age of Renaissance Nostalgia* (Athens, Ohio: Ohio University Press, 1983).

Frykenberg, Robert Eric, *Christianity in India: From Beginnings to the Present* (Oxford: Oxford University Press, 2008).

Fubini, Riccardo, 'Humanism and Truth: Valla Writes against the Donation of Constantine', *Journal of the History of Ideas*, 57 (1996), pp. 79–86.

—— 'Baronio e la tradizione umanistica. Note su di un libro recente', *Cristianesimo nella storia*, 20 (1999), pp. 147–59.

Fuchs, Thomas, *Geschichtsbewußtsein und Geschichtsschreibung zwischen Reformation und Aufklärung: Städtechroniken, Kirchenbücher und historische Befragungen in Hessen, 1500 bis 1800* (Marburg: Hessisches Landesamt für geschichtliche Landeskunde, 2006).

Fueter, Eduard, *Geschichte der neueren Historiographie* (Munich and Berlin: R. Oldenbourg, 1911).

Fumaroli, Marc, 'Théâtre humaniste et Contre Réforme à Rome 1597–1642', *Bulletin de l'association Guillaume Budé*, 33 (1974), pp. 397–412.

García-Arenal, Mercedes and Fernando Rodríguez Mediano, *Un Oriente español: los moriscos y el Sacromonte en tiempos de Contrarreforma* (Madrid: Marcial Pons, 2010).

Gaston, Robert, ed., *Pirro Ligorio, Artist and Antiquarian* (Florence: Silvana, 1988).

Ghilardi, Massimiliano, 'Dall'*inventio* del corpo santo alla costruzione della reliquia: Giovanni Toccafondi, pittore romano', *Studi romani*, 53 (2005), pp. 94–121.

Gillespie, Raymond, 'The Irish Franciscans, 1600–1700' in Edel Bhreathnach, Joseph MacMahon, and John McCafferty (eds.), *The Irish Franciscans, 1534–1990* (Dublin: Four Courts Press, 2009), pp. 45–76.

Ginzburg, Carlo, *History, Rhetoric, and Proof* (Hanover, NH: University Press of New England, 1999).

Glaser, Hubert (ed.), *Um Glauben und Reich, Kurfürst Maximilian I*, 2 vols. (Munich: Hirmer, 1980).

Godding, Robert et al., *Bollandistes. Saints et légendes. Quatre siècles de recherche* (Brussels: Société des Bollandistes, 2007).

—— et al., *De Rosweyde aux Acta sanctorum: la recherche hagiographique à travers quatre siècles* (Brussels: Société des Bollandistes, 2009).

Godin, André, *Erasme lecteur d'Origène* (Geneva: Droz, 1982).

Gordon, Bruce, *The Swiss Reformation* (Manchester and New York: Manchester University Press, 2002).

—— and Emidio Campi (eds.), *Architect of Reformation: An Introduction to Heinrich Bullinger, 1504–1575* (Grand Rapids, Mich.: Baker Academic, 2004).

Grafton, Anthony, *Joseph Scaliger*, 2 vols. (Oxford: Clarendon Press, 1983–93).

—— *Forgers and Critics: Creativity and Duplicity in Renaissance Scholarship* (Princeton: Princeton University Press, 1990).

—— *Defenders of the Text: The Traditions of Scholarship in an Age of Science, 1450–1800* (Cambridge, Mass.: Harvard University Press, 1991).

—— *The Footnote: A Curious History* (Cambridge, Mass.: Harvard University Press, 1997).

—— *Leon Battista Alberti* (New York: Hill & Wang, 2000).

—— 'The Ancient City Restored: Archaeology, Ecclesiastical History, and Egyptology' in *Bring Out Your Dead: The Past as Revelation* (Cambridge, Mass.: Harvard University Press, 2001), pp. 31–61.

Grafton, Anthony, *What Was History? The Art of History in Early Modern Europe* (Cambridge: Cambridge University Press, 2007).

—— and Joanna Weinberg, *'I Have Always Loved the Holy Tongue': Isaac Casaubon, the Jews, and a Forgotten Chapter in Renaissance Scholarship* (Cambridge, Mass.: Belknap Press, 2011).

—— and Megan Williams, *Christianity and the Transformation of the Book: Eusebius and the Library at Caesarea* (Cambridge, Mass.: Belknap Press, 2006).

Graham, Timothy, and Andrew Watson, *The Recovery of the Past in Early Elizabethan England: Documents by John Bale and John Joscelyn from the Circle of Matthew Parker* (Cambridge: Cambridge Bibliographical Society, 1998).

—— Elisabeth S. Leedham-Green, and Teresa Webber (eds.), 'Matthew Parker's Manuscripts: An Elizabethan Library and Its Use' in *The Cambridge History of Libraries in Britain and Ireland*, I: *To 1640* (Cambridge: Cambridge University Press, 2006), pp. 322–44.

Greengrass, Mark and Thomas S. Freeman, 'The Acts and Monuments and the Protestant Continental Martyrologies' in John Foxe, *The Unabridged Acts and Monuments Online*.

Gregory, Brad S., *Salvation at Stake: Christian Martyrdom in Early Modern Europe* (Cambridge, Mass.: Harvard University Press, 1999).

Grell, Chantal, and François Laplanche (eds.), *La République des lettres et l'histoire du judaïsme antique XVIe–XVIIIe siècles: colloque tenu en Sorbonne en mai 1990* (Paris: Presses de l'Université de Paris-Sorbonne, 1992).

Grès-Gayer, Jacques, 'L'Aristarque de son siècle: le docteur Jean de Launoy 1601–1678' in Jean-Louis Quantin and Jean-Claude Waquet (eds.), *Papes, princes et savants: mélanges à la mémoire de Bruno Neveu* (Geneva: Droz, 2007), pp. 269–85.

Griffiths, Richard (ed.), *The Bible in the Renaissance: Essays on Biblical Commentary and Translation in the Fifteenth and Sixteenth Centuries* (Aldershot: Ashgate, 2001).

Guazzelli, Giuseppe A., 'Riferimenti archeologici nell'opera di Cesare Baronio' (Pontificio Istituto di Archeologia Cristiana, 1999–2000). Unpublished MA thesis anno accadamico.

—— 'Cesare Baronio e il *Martyrologium romanum*: problemi interpretativi e linee evolutive di un rapporto diacronico' in Massimo Firpo (ed.), *Nunc alia tempora, alii mores*, pp. 47–89.

—— 'L'immagine del *Christianus Orbis* nelle prime edizioni del *Martyrologium romanum*', *Sanctorum*, 5 (2008), pp. 261–84.

—— 'La documentazione numismatica negli *Annales ecclesiastici* di Cesare Baronio' in Luigi Gulia (ed.), *Baronio e le sue fonti*, pp. 489–548.

—— 'Gregorio Magno nell'erudizione ecclesiastica della seconda metà del XVI secolo' in Claudio Leonardi (ed.), *Gregorio Magno e le origini dell'Europa* (forthcoming).

—— 'Cesare Baronio attraverso il *Martyrologium romanum*' in Giuseppe A. Guazzelli et al. (eds.), *Cesare Baronio tra santità e scrittura storica*.

——, Raimondo Michetti, and Francesco Scorza Barcellona (eds.), *Cesare Baronio tra santità e scrittura storica* (Rome: Viella, forthcoming).

Gulia, Luigi (ed.), *Baronio e le sue fonti: atti del convegno internazionale di studi, Sora, 10–13 ottobre 2007* (Sora: Centro di Studi Sorani 'Vincenzo Patriarca', 2009).

Haberkern, Phillip, '"After Me There Will Come Braver Men": Jan Hus and Reformation Polemics in the 1530s', *German History*, 27(2) (2009), pp. 177–95.

Habicht, Christian, *Pausanias' Guide to Ancient Greece*, Sather Classical Lectures, 50 (Berkeley, Calif.: University of California Press, 1985).

Halbwachs, Maurice, *La topographie légendaire des évangiles en terre sainte. Étude de mémoire collective* (Paris: Presses Universitaires de France, 1941).

Hall, Basil, 'Biblical Scholarship: Editions and Commentaries' in S. L. Greenslade (ed.), *Cambridge History of the Bible*, III: *The West from the Reformation to the Present Day* (Cambridge: Cambridge University Press, 1963), pp. 38–93.

Hamilton, Alastair, 'Humanists and the Bible' in Jill Kraye (ed.), *The Cambridge Companion to Renaissance Humanism* (Cambridge: Cambridge University Press, 1996), pp. 100–17.

—— Maurits H. van den Boogert, and Bart Westerweel (eds.), *The Republic of Letters and the Levant* (Leiden: Brill, 2005).

Hankins, James, 'Introduction' in Leonardo Bruni, *History of the Florentine People*, I: *Books I–IV* (Cambridge, Mass.: I Tatti Renaissance Library, Harvard University Press, 2001).

Harris, A. Katie, *From Muslim to Christian Granada: Inventing a City's Past in Early Modern Spain* (Baltimore: Johns Hopkins University Press, 2007).

Harris, Jason, 'A Case Study in Rhetorical Composition: Stephen White's Two *Apologiae* for Ireland' in Jason Harris and Keith Sidwell (eds.), *Making Ireland Roman: Irish Neo-Latin Writers and the Republic of Letters* (Cork: Cork University Press, 2009), pp. 126–53.

—— 'Exiles and Saints in Baroque Europe: George Conn and the Scotic Debate' in Thomas O'Connor and Mary Ann Lyons (eds.), *The Ulster Earls and Baroque Europe: Refashioning Catholic Identities, 1600–1800* (Dublin: Four Courts Press, 2010), pp. 306–26.

—— and Keith Sidwell (eds.), *Making Ireland Roman: Irish Neo-Latin Writers and the Republic of Letters* (Cork: Cork University Press, 2009).

Hartmann, Martina, *Humanismus und Kirchenkritik: Matthias Flacius Illyricus als Erforscher des Mittelalters* (Stuttgart: Thorbecke, 2001).

Hay, Denys, 'Scholars and Ecclesiastical History in the Early Modern Period: The Influence of Ferdinando Ughelli' in Phyllis Mack and Margaret C. Jacob (ed.), *Politics and Culture in Early Modern Europe: Essays in Honour of H. G. Koenigsberger* (Cambridge: Cambridge University Press, 1987), pp. 215–29.

Haye, Thomas, 'Der Catalogus testium veritatis des Matthias Flacius Illyricus—Eine Einführung in die Literatur des Mittelalters', *Archiv für Reformationsgeschichte*, 83 (1992), pp. 31–47.

Hazard, Benjamin, *Faith and Patronage: The Political Career of Flaithrí Ó Maolchonaire c.1560–1629* (Dublin: Irish Academic Press, 2010).

Heal, Bridget, *The Cult of the Virgin Mary in Early Modern Germany* (Cambridge: Cambridge University Press, 2007).

Heal, Felicity, 'What Can King Lucius Do for You? The Reformation and the Early British Church', *English Historical Review*, 120(487) (2005), pp. 593–614.

Heal, Felicity, 'Appropriating History: Catholic and Protestant Polemics and the National Past' in Pauline Kewes (ed.), *The Uses of History in Early Modern England* (San Marino, Calif.: Huntington Library, 2006), pp. 105–28.

Hecht, Christian, *Katholische Bildertheologie im Zeitalter von Gegenreformation und Barock. Studien zu Traktaten von Johannes Molanus, Gabriele Paleotti und anderen Autoren* (Berlin: Mann, 1995).

Heide, Albert, van der, *Hebraica veritas: Christopher Plantin and the Christian Hebraists* (Antwerp: Plantin-Moretus Museum/Printroom, 2008).

Heilingsetzer, Georg, 'Die Bayern in Oberösterreich (1620–1628)' in Hubert Glaser (ed.), *Um Glauben und Reich, Kurfürst Maximilian I*, I (Munich: Hirmer, 1980), pp. 416–23.

Helgerson, Richard, *Forms of Nationhood: The Elizabethan Writing of England* (Chicago: Chicago University Press, 1992).

Helmrath, Johannes, 'Sitz und Geschichte. Köln im Rangstreit mit Aachen auf den Reichstagen des 15. Jahrhunderts' in Hanna Vollrath and Stefan Weinfurter (eds.), *Köln: Stadt und Bistum in Kirche und Reich des Mittelalters: Festschrift für Odilo Engels zum 65. Geburtstag* (Cologne: Böhlau, 1993), pp. 719–60.

—— 'Probleme und Formen nationaler und regionaler Historiographie des deutschen und Europäischen Humanismus um 1500' in Matthias Werner (ed.), *Spätmittelalterliches Landesbewusstsein in Deutschland* (Ostfildern: Thorbecke, 2005), pp. 333–92.

—— 'Bildfunktionen der antiken Kaisermünze in der Renaissance oder Die Entstehung der Numismatik aus der Faszination der Serie' in Kathrin Schade, Detlef Rößler, and Alfred Schäfer (eds.), *Zentren und Wirkungsräume der Antikerezeption. Zur Bedeutung von Raum und Kommunikation für die neuzeitliche Transformation der griechisch-römischen Antike* (Münster: Scriptorium, 2007), pp. 77–97.

—— Ulrich Muhlack, and Gerrit Walther (eds.), *Diffusion des Humanismus: Studien zur nationalen Geschichtsschreibung europäischer Humanisten* (Göttingen: Wallstein Verlag, 2002).

Herklotz, Ingo, '*Historia sacra* und mittelalterliche Kunst während der zweiten Hälfte des 16. Jahrhunderts in Rom' in Romeo de Maio et al. (eds.), *Baronio e l'arte*, pp. 21–74.

—— 'Die *Hagioglypta* des Jean L'Heureux. Ein vergessener Beitrag zur Historisierung der Kunstbetrachtung um 1600' in Eliana Carrara and Silvia Ginzburg (ed.), *Testi, immagini e filologia nel XVI secolo* (Pisa: Edizioni della Normale, 2007), pp. 471–504.

—— *Die Academia Basiliana: Griechische Philologie, Kirchengeschichte und Unionsbemühungen im Rom der Barberini* (Rome: Herder, 2008).

—— 'Basilica e edificio a pianta centrale: continuità ed esclusione nella storiografia architettonica all'epoca del Baronio' in Luigi Gulia (ed.), *Baronio e le sue fonti*, pp. 549–78.

Herz, Alexandra, 'Cardinal Cesare Baronio's Restoration of SS. Nereo ed Achilleo and S. Cesareo de Appia', *Art Bulletin*, 70 (1988), pp. 590–620.

Highley, Christopher, '"A Pestilent and Seditious Book": Nicholas Sander's *Schismatis Anglicani* and Catholic Histories of the Reformation' in Pauline Kewes (ed.), *The Uses of History in Early Modern England* (San Marino, Calif.: Huntington Library, 2006), pp. 147–67.

—— *Catholics Writing the Nation in Early Modern Britain and Ireland* (Oxford: Oxford University Press, 2008).

—— and John King, *John Foxe and His World* (Aldershot: Ashgate, 2002).

Hunt, E. D., *Holy Land Pilgrimage in the Later Roman Empire, AD 312–460* (Oxford: Clarendon Press, 1982).

—— 'Were There Christian Pilgrims before Constantine?' in Jennie Stopford (ed.), *Pilgrimage Explored* (Suffolk: York Medieval Press, 1999), pp. 25–40.

Huppert, George, *The Idea of Perfect History: Historical Erudition and Historical Philosophy in Renaissance France* (Urbana and Chicago: University of Illinois Press, 1970).

Hurel, Daniel-Odon (ed.), *Érudition et commerce épistolaire: Jean Mabillon et la tradition monastique* (Paris: Vrin, 2003).

Huskinson, J. M., 'The Crucifixion of St. Peter: A Fifteenth-Century Topographical Problem', *Journal of the Warburg and Courtauld Institutes*, 32 (1969), pp. 135–61.

Incisa della Rocchetta, Giovanni, Nello Vian, and Carlo Gasbarri (eds.), *Il primo processo per San Filippo Neri. Nel codice Vaticano Latino 3798 e in altri esemplari dell'archivio dell'Oratorio di Roma*, 4 vols. (Vatican City: Biblioteca apostolica Vaticana, 1957–63).

Irwin, Robert, *Dangerous Knowledge: Orientalism and its Discontents* (London: Allen Lane, 2006; Woodstock, NY: Overlook Press, 2008).

Jacks, Philip J., 'Baronius and the Antiquities of Rome' in Romeo de Maio et al. (eds.), *Baronio e l'arte*, pp. 75–96.

Jacobs, Andrew, *Remains of the Jews: The Holy Land and Christian Empire in Late Antiquity* (Stanford: Stanford University Press, 2004).

Jardine, Lisa, *Erasmus, Man of Letters: The Construction of Charisma in Print* (Princeton, NJ: Princeton University Press, 1993).

Jedin, Hubert, 'Entstehung und Tragweite des Trienter Dekrets über die Bilderverehrung', *Tübinger Theologische Quartalschrift*, 116 (1935), pp. 143–88.

—— *Kardinal Caesar Baronius. Der Anfang der katholischen Kirchengeschichtsschreibung im 16. Jahrhundert* (Münster: Aschendorff, 1978).

Jehasse, Jean, *La Renaissance de la critique: l'essor de l'humanisme érudit 1560–1614* (Paris: Honoré Champion, 2002).

Jenkins, Gary W., *John Jewel and the English National Church: The Dilemmas of an Erastian Reformer* (Aldershot: Ashgate, 2006).

Johnson, Trevor, 'Holy Fabrications: The Catacomb Saints and the Counter-Reformation in Bavaria', *Journal of Ecclesiastical History*, 47 (1996), pp. 274–97.

—— 'Holy Dynasts and Sacred Soil: Politics and Sanctity in Matthaeus Rader's *Bavaria Sancta* (1615–1628)' in Sofia Boesch Gajano and Raimondo Michetti (eds.), *Europa sacra*, pp. 83–100.

Jones, Norman, 'Matthew Parker, John Bale, and the Magdeburg Centuriators', *Sixteenth Century Journal*, 12 (1981), pp. 35–49.

Jones, Pamela, *Federico Borromeo and the Ambrosiana: Art and Patronage in Seventeenth-Century Milan* (Cambridge: Cambridge University Press, 1993).

Kagan, Richard, *Clio and the Crown: The Politics of History in Medieval and Early Modern Spain* (Baltimore: John Hopkins University Press, 2009).

Kämpf, Tobias, 'Framing Cecilia's Sacred Body: Paolo Camillo Sfondrato and the Language of Revelation', *Sculpture Journal*, 6 (2001), pp. 10–20.

Kelley, Donald R., 'Johann Sleidan and the Origins of History as a Profession', *Journal of Modern History*, 52 (1980), pp. 573–98.

—— *Faces of History: Historical Inquiry from Herodotus to Herder* (New Haven, Conn.: Yale University Press, 1998).

Kendrick, Thomas D., *Saint James in Spain* (London: Methuen and Co., 1960).

Kess, Alexandra, *Johann Sleidan and the Protestant Vision of History* (Aldershot: Ashgate, 2008).

King, John, 'Fact and Fiction in Foxe's *Book of Martyrs*' in David Loades (ed.), *John Foxe and the English Reformation* (Aldershot: Scholar Press 1997), pp. 12–35.

Kintzinger, Marion, *Chronos und Historia. Studien zur Titelblattikonographie historiographischer Werke vom 16. bis zum 18. Jahrhundert* (Wiesbaden: Harrassowitz, 1995).

Klijn, A. F. J. (ed. and tr.), *The Acts of Thomas: Introduction, Text, and Commentary* (Leiden: Brill, 2003).

Knowles, David, *Great Historical Enterprises: Problems in Monastic History* (London: Nelson, 1963).

Kraus, Andreas, 'Die Annales Ecclesiastici des Abraham Bzovius und Maximilian I. von Bayern' in Erwin Iserloh and Konrad Repgen (eds.), *Reformata Reformanda: Festgabe für Hubert Jedin*, II (Münster: Aschendorff, 1965), pp. 253–89.

—— *Maximlian I: Bayerns grosser Kurfürst* (Graz: Styria Verlag, 1990).

—— 'Bayerns Frühzeit im Spiegel der Geschichtsschreibung von Aventin bis Westenrieder' in Lothar Kolmer and Peter Segl (ed.), *Regensburg, Bayern und Europa* (Regensburg: Universitätsverlag, 1995), pp. 435–52.

Krebs, Christopher B., *Negotiatio Germaniae: Tacitus' Germania und Enea Silvio Piccolomini, Giannantonio Campano, Conrad Celtis und Heinrich Bebel*, ed. Albrecht Dihle et al., Hypomnemata 158: Untersuchungen zur Antike und zu ihrem Nachleben (Göttingen: Vandenhoeck & Ruprecht, 2005).

Kristeller, Paul Oskar, 'The Contribution of the Religious Orders to Renaissance Thought and Learning', *American Benedictine Review*, 21 (1970), pp. 1–55, repr. in Edward P. Mahoney (ed.), *Medieval Aspects of Renaissance Learning: Three Essays by Paul Oskar Kristeller* (Durham, NC: Duke University Press, 1974).

Kučera, Jan and Jiří Rak, *Bohuslav Balbín a jeho místo v české kultuře* (Prague: Vyšehrad, 1983).

Kusukawa, Sachiko, *The Transformation of Natural Philosophy: The Case of Philip Melanchthon* (Cambridge; New York: Cambridge University Press, 1995).

Laplanche, François, *L'Écriture, le sacré et l'histoire: érudits et politiques protestants devant la bible en France au XVIIe siècle* (Amsterdam/Maarssen: APA-Holland University Press, 1986).

—— *Bible, sciences et pouvoirs au XVIIe siècle* (Naples: Bibliopolis, 1997).

Larner, John, *Marco Polo and the Discovery of the World* (New Haven, Conn.: Yale University Press, 1999).

Lazure, Guy, 'Possessing the Sacred: Monarchy and Identity in Philip II's Relic Collection at the Escorial', *Renaissance Quarterly*, 60 (2007), pp. 58–93.

Le Braz, Anatole, *Le Théâtre celtique* (Paris: Calmann-Lévy, 1905; repr. Geneva: Editions Slatkine, 1981).

Le Gall, Jean-Marie, *Les Moines au temps des réformes: France (1480–1560)* (Seyssel: Champ Vallon, 2002).

—— 'Les Moines et les universités au temps de la renaissance' in Michel Bideaux and Marie-Madeleine Fragonard (eds.), *Les Échanges entre les universités européennes à la renaissance*, Travaux d'Humanisme et Renaissance (Geneva: Droz, 2003), pp. 69–72.

—— 'Vieux saints et grande noblesse: Saint Denis, les Montmorency et les Guise', Revue d'histoire moderne et contemporaine, 50 (2003), pp. 7–33.

—— 'Denis, George, Jacques, Antoine, André, Patrick et les autres: identité nationale et culte des saints XVe–XVIIIe siècle' in Gilbert Buti and Anne Carol (eds.), *Comportements, croyances et mémoires: Europe méridionale, XVe–XXe siècles: Etudes offertes à Régis Bertrand* (Aix: Université de Provence, 2007), pp. 147–69.

—— *Le Mythe de Saint Denis entre renaissance et révolution* (Seyssel: Champ Vallon, 2007).

—— 'Catalogues et séries de vies d'évêques dans la France moderne. Lutte contre l'hérésie ou illustration de la patrie?' in François Bougard and Michel Sot (eds.), *Liber, gesta, histoire. Ecrire l'histoire des évêques etdes pape*s (Turnhout: Brepols, 2009), pp. 375–95.

Le Glay, A., 'Notice sur un traité inédit d'iconographie chrétienne intitulé: *Hagioglypta*' in *Mémoires de la Société Nationale des sciences, de l'agriculture et des arts de Lille* (1851), pp. 376–84.

Lee, Rensselaer, '*Ut pictura poesis*: The Humanistic Theory of Painting', *Art Bulletin*, 22 (1940), pp. 197–269.

Legaspi, Michael, *The Death of Scripture and the Rise of Biblical Studies* (Oxford: Oxford University Press, 2010).

Lemaitre, Nicole, 'Le Culte épiscopal et la résistance au protestantisme au XVIe siècle' in Gérald Chaix (ed.), *Le Diocèse: espace, représentations, pouvoirs (France XVe–XXe siècles)* (Paris: Éditions du Cerf, 2002), pp. 307–27.

Lennon, Colm, *The Lords of Dublin in the Age of the Reformation* (Dublin: Irish Academic Press, 1989).

—— 'Political Thought of Irish Counter-Reformation Churchmen: The Testimony of the "Analecta" of Bishop David Rothe' in Hiram Morgan (ed.), *Political Ideology in Ireland, 1541–1641* (Dublin: Four Courts Press, 1999), pp. 181–202.

—— 'Pedagogy and Reform: The Influence of Peter White on Irish Scholarship in the Renaissance' in Thomas Herron and Michael Potterton (eds.), *Ireland in the Renaissance, c.1540–1660* (Dublin: Four Courts Press, 2007), pp. 43–51.

Léonard, Émile G, *A History of Protestantism*, ed. H. H. Rowley, tr. Joyce M. H. Reid, 2 vols. (London: Nelson, 1965–7).

Levine, Joseph, 'Reginald Pecock and Lorenzo Valla on the Donation of Constantine', *Studies in the Renaissance*, 20 (1973), pp. 118–43.

—— *Humanism and History* (Ithaca: Cornell University Press, 1987).

—— *The Autonomy of History: Truth and Method from Erasmus to Gibbon* (Chicago: University of Chicago Press, 1999).

Levy, Fred Jacob, *Tudor Historical Thought* (San Marino, Calif.: Huntington Library, 1967; repr. Toronto: University of Toronto, 2004).

Leyerle, Blake, 'Landscape as Cartography in Early Christian Pilgrimage Narratives', *Journal of the American Academy of Religion*, 64 (1996), pp. 119–38.

Lifshitz, Felice, 'Beyond Positivism and Genre: "Hagiographical" Texts as Historical Narrative', *Viator*, 25 (1994), pp. 95–113.

Loades, David (ed.), *John Foxe and the English Reformation* (Aldershot: Scholar Press, 1997).

—— (ed.), *John Foxe: An Historical Perspective* (Aldershot: Scholar Press, 1999).

Los monjes y los estudios, IV semana de estudios monásticos, Poblet, 1961 (Poblet: Abadía de Poblet, 1963).

Louthan, Howard, *Converting Bohemia: Force and Persuasion in the Catholic Reformation* (Cambridge: Cambridge University Press, 2009).

Lutz, Georg, 'Marx Fugger (1529–1597) und die *Annales Ecclesiastici* des Baronius. Eine Verdeutschung aus dem Augsburg der Gegenreformation' in Romeo de Maio et al. (eds.), *Baronio storico e la controriforma*, pp. 421–545.

Lyon, Gregory, 'Baudouin, Flacius, and the Plan for the Magdeburg Centuries', *Journal of the History of Ideas*, 64 (2003), pp. 253–72.

McCahill, Elizabeth, 'Humanism in the Theater of Lies: Classical Scholarship in the Early Quattrocento Curia', PhD dissertation (Princeton University, 2005).

MacCormack, Sabine, 'Loca sancta: The Organization of Sacred Topography in Late Antiquity' in Robert Ousterhout (ed.), *The Blessings of Pilgrimage* (Urbana/Chicago, Ill.: University of Illinois Press, 1990), pp. 7–40.

MacCraith, Mícheál, 'Gaelic Ireland and the Renaissance' in Glanmor Williams and Robert Owen Jones (eds.), *The Celts and the Renaissance: Tradition and Innovation. Proceedings of the Eighth International Congress of Celtic Studies* (Cardiff: University of Wales Press, 1990), pp. 57–90.

MacCulloch, Diarmaid, *Thomas Cranmer: A Life* (New Haven, Conn.: Yale University Press, 1996).

McGrath, Alister, *The Intellectual Origins of the European Reformation* (Oxford and New York: Blackwell, 1987).

Machielson, Jan, 'How (Not) to Get Published: The Plantin Press in the 1590s', *Dutch Crossing*, 34(2) (2010), pp. 99–114.

McKisack, May, *Medieval History in the Tudor Age* (Oxford, Clarendon Press, 1971).

Maes, Bruno, *Le Roi, la vierge, et la nation: pèlerinages et identité nationale entre guerre de cent ans et révolution* (Paris: Publisud, 2003).

Marchand, Suzanne L., *German Orientalism in the Age of Empire: Religion, Race, and Scholarship* (Washington, DC: German Historical Institute/Cambridge: Cambridge University Press, 2009).

Martin, Henri Jean, *Livre, pouvoirs et société à Paris au XVIIe siècle, 1598–1701*, 3rd edn (Geneva: Droz, 1999).

Massaut, Jean-Pierre, *Critique et tradition à la veille de la Réforme en France* (Paris: J. Vrin, 1974).

Mauro, Thomas, 'Praeceptor Austriae: Aeneas Sylvius Piccolomini (Pius II) and the Transalpine Diffusion of Italian Humanism before Erasmus', PhD dissertation (University of Chicago, 2003).

Mazza, Mario, 'La metodologia storica nella *Praefatio* degli *Annales ecclesastici*' in Giuseppe A. Guazzelli et al. (eds.), *Cesare Baronio tra santità e scrittura storica*.

Meder, Joseph, *Dürer-Katalog: Ein Handbuch über Albrecht Dürers Stiche, Radierungen, Holzschnitte, deren Zustände, Ausgaben und Wasserzeichen* (Wien: Gilhofer und Rauschburg, 1932).

Melion, Walter, 'Ad ductum itineris et dispositionem mansionum ostendendam: Meditation, Vocation, and Sacred History in Abraham Ortelius's *Parergon*', *Journal of the Walters Art Gallery*, 57 (1999), pp. 49–72.

Menéndez y Pelayo, Marcelino, *Historia de los héterodoxos españoles* (Madrid: Librería Católica de San José 1880–82).

Mengel, David, 'From Venice to Jerusalem and Beyond: Milíč of Kroměříž and the Topography of Prostitution in Fourteenth-century Prague', *Speculum*, 79 (2004), pp. 407–42.

—— 'A Monk, a Preacher, and a Jesuit: Making the Life of Milíč' in Z. David and D. Holeton (eds.), *The Bohemian Reformation and Religious Practice*, V (Prague: Academy of Sciences, 2004), pp. 33–55.

Meserve, Margaret, 'From Samarkand to Scythia: Reinventions of Asia in Renaissance Geography and Political Thought' in Zweder von Martels and Arjo Vanderjagt (eds.), *Pius II, 'el più expeditivo pontifice'* (Leiden: Brill, 2003), pp. 13–40.

Meyer, Wendel W., 'The Phial of Blood Controversy and the Decline of the Liberal Catholic Movement', *Journal of Ecclesiastical History*, 46 (1995), pp. 75–94.

Miglio, Massimo et al., *Antiquaria a Roma: intorno a Pomponio Leto e Paolo II* (Rome: Roma nel Rinascimento, 2003).

Miller, Peter N., *Peiresc's Europe: Learning and Virtue in the Seventeenth Century* (New Haven, Conn.: Yale University Press, 2000).

—— 'The "Antiquarianization" of Biblical Scholarship and the London Polyglot Bible (1653–57)', *Journal of the History of Ideas*, 62 (2001), pp. 463–82.

Momigliano, Arnaldo, 'Ancient History and the Antiquarian', *Journal of the Warburg and Courtauld Institutes*, 13 (1950), pp. 285–315.

—— 'Pagan and Christian Historiography in the Fourth Century A.D.' in Arnaldo Momigliano (ed.), *The Conflict Between Paganism and Christianity in the Fourth Century* (Oxford: Clarendon Press, 1963), pp. 79–99.

Montecalvo, Rolando, 'Between Empire and Papacy: Aeneas Silvius and German Regional Historiography', PhD dissertation (University of California, 2000).

—— 'The New *Landesgeschichte*: Aeneas Silvius on Austria and Bohemia' in Zweder von Martels and Arjo Vanderjagt (eds.), *Pius II, 'el più expeditivo pontifice'* (Leiden: Brill, 2003), pp. 55–86.

Morgan, Hiram, (ed.) *Political Ideology in Ireland, 1541–1641* (Dublin: Four Courts Press, 1999).

—— 'The Island Defenders: Humanist Patriots in Early Modern Iceland and Ireland', Online paper, Centre for Neo-Latin Studies (University College Cork. 2001): <http://www.ucc.ie/acad/CNLS/lectures/Morgan_iceland.html>.

—— '"Un pueblo unido...": The Politics of Philip O'Sullivan Beare', in Enrique García Hernán, Miguel Ángel de Bunes, Óscar Recio Morales and Bernardo J. García García (eds.), *Irlanda y la monarquía hispánica: Kinsale 1601–2001: guerra, política, exilio y religión* (Madrid: CSIC, 2002), pp. 265–82.

Most, Glenn W., *Doubting Thomas* (Cambridge, Mass.: Harvard University Press, 2005).

Moxnes, Halvor, 'The Construction of Galilee as a Place for the Historical Jesus', *Biblical Theology Bulletin*, 31 (2001), pp. 26–37, 64–77.

Muhlack, Ulrich, 'Beatus Rhenanus (1485–1547): Vom Humanismus zur Philologie' in Paul Gerhard Schmidt (ed.), *Humanismus im deutschen Südwesten* (Stuttgart: Jan Thorbecke, 2000), pp. 195–220.

—— 'Die humanistische Historiographie: Umfang, Bedeutung, Probleme' in Franz Brendle et al. (ed.), *Deutsche Landesgeschichtsschreibung* (Stuttgart: Steiner, 2001), pp. 3–18.

—— 'Humanistische Historiographie' in Johannes Helmrath et al. (ed.), *Diffusion des Humanismus* (Göttingen: Wallstein Verlag, 2002), pp. 30–4.

Müller, Markus, *Die spätmittelalterliche Bistumsgeschichtsschreibung: Überlieferung und Entwicklung* (Cologne: Böhlau, 1998).

—— 'Die humanistische Bistumsgeschichtsschreibung' in Franz Brendle et al. (ed.), *Deutsche Landesgeschichtsschreibung* (Stuttgart: Steiner, 2001), pp. 167–87.

Nelles, Paul, 'The Public Library and Late Humanist Scholarship in Early Modern Europe: Antiquarianism and Encyclopaedism', PhD dissertation (The Johns Hopkins University, 1994).

—— 'The Uses of Orthodoxy and Jacobean Erudition: Thomas James and the Bodleian Library', *History of Universities*, 22 (2007), pp. 21–70.

Nelson, Eric, *The Hebrew Republic: Jewish Sources and the Transformation of European Political Thought* (Cambridge, Mass.: Harvard University Press, 2010).

Ó Buachalla, Breandán, 'Annála Ríoghachta Éireann agus Foras Feasa ar Éireann: an comhthéacs comhaimseartha', *Studia hibernica*, 22–3 (1982–3), pp. 59–105.

O'Connor, Thomas, 'Towards the Invention of the Irish Catholic *Natio*: Thomas Messingham's *Florilegium* (1624)', *Archivium Hibernicum*, 64(2) (1999), pp. 155–77.

—— 'Custom, Authority and Tolerance in Irish Political Thought: David Rothe's *Analecta Sacra et Mira* (1616)', *Irish Theological Quarterly*, 65(2) (2000), pp. 133–56.

Ó Dúshláine, Tadhg, 'Medium and Message: The Rhetoric of *Foras Feasa ar Éirinn*' in Pádraig Ó Riain (ed.), *Geoffrey Keating's Foras Feasa ar Éirinn: Reassessments* (London: Irish Texts Society, 2008), pp. 68–89.

Ojetti, Ugo, *Cose viste, 1921–43* (Florence: Sansoni, 1960).

Olds, Katrina, 'The "False Chronicles" in Early Modern Spain: Forgery, Tradition, and the Invention of Texts and Relics, *c.*1595–*c.*1670', PhD dissertation (Princeton University, 2009).

—— 'The Ambiguities of the Holy: Authenticating Relics in Seventeenth-century Spain', *Renaissance Quarterly* (forthcoming 2012).

Ó Riain, Pádraig, 'Irish Hagiography of the Late Sixteenth and Early Seventeenth Centuries' in Sofia Boesch Gajano and Raimondo Michetti (eds.), *Europa sacra: raccolte agiografiche e identità politiche*, pp. 45–55.

Oryshkevich, Irina, '*Roma sotterranea* and the biogenesis of New Jerusalem', *Res: Anthropology and Esthetics*, 55/56 (2009), pp. 174–81.

Ostrow, Steven F., 'The *Confessio* in Post-Tridentine Rome' in Patrizia Tosini (ed.), *Arte e committenza*, pp. 19–32.

Pabel, Hilmar, *Herculean Labours: Erasmus and the Editing of St. Jerome's Letters in the Renaissance* (Leiden: Brill, 2008).

—— and Mark Vessey (eds.), *Holy Scripture Speaks: The Production and Reception of Erasmus' Paraphrases on the New Testament* (Toronto: University of Toronto Press, 2002).

Parish, Helen L., *Monks, Miracles and Magic: Reformation Representations of the Medieval Church* (Abingdon: Routledge, 2005).

Parlato, Enrico, 'Enrico Caetani a S. Pudenziana: antichità cristiane, magnificenza decorativa e prestigio del casato nella Roma di fine cinquecento' in Patrizia Tosini (ed.), *Arte e commitenza*, pp. 143–64.

Parry, Graham, *The Trophies of Time: English Antiquarians of the Seventeenth Century* (Oxford: Oxford University Press, 1995).

Pastor, Ludwig, *The History of the Popes, from the Close of the Middle Ages*, tr. Frederick Ignatius Antrobus, 5th edn, 40 vols. (London: Routledge, 1950).

Patze, Hans (ed.), *Geschichtsschreibung und Geschichtsbewußtsein im späten Mittelalter*, Vorträge und Forschungen, XXXI (Sigmaringen: Thorbecke, 1987).

Pelc, Milan, *Illustrium Imagines: Das Porträtbuch der Renaissance* (Leiden: Brill, 2002).

Petimengin, Pierre, 'Deux bibliothèques de la Contre Réforme: la panoplie du père Torres et la Bibliotheca veterum patrum' in A. C. Dionisotti, Anthony Grafton, and Jill Kraye (eds.), *The Uses of Greek and Latin, Historical Essays* (London: Warburg Institute, 1988), pp. 136–53.

Piacentini, Paola, *La biblioteca di Marcello II Cervini. Una ricostruzione dalle carte di Jeanne Bignami Odier. I libri a stampa* (Vatican City: Biblioteca Apostolica Vaticana, 2001).

Pierre, Benoist, *La Bure et le sceptre. La congrégation des feuillants dans l'affirmation des états et des pouvoirs princiers (vers 1560 – vers 1660)* (Paris: Publication de la Sorbonne, 2006).

Pincherle, Alberto, 'Baronio, Cesare' in *Dizionario biografico degli Italiani*, VI (Rome: Istituto della Enciclopedia italiana, 1964), pp. 470–8.

Pohlig, Matthias, *Zwischen Gelehrsamkeit und konfessioneller Identitätsstiftung: Lutherische Kirchen- und Universalgeschichtsschreibung 1546–1617* (Tübingen: Mohr Siebeck, 2007).

Pokorná, Zuzana and Martin Svatoš (eds.), *Bohuslav Balbín und die Kultur seiner Zeit in Böhmen* (Cologne: Böhlau, 1993).

Polman, Pontien, *L'Élément historique dans la controverse religieuse du XVIe siècle* (Gembloux: J. Duculot, 1932).

Pomian, Krzysztof, 'De la lettre au périodique: la circulation des information dans la milieux des historiens aux XVIIe siècle', *Organon*, 10 (1974), pp. 25–43.

Poncet, Olivier, 'La *Gallia christiana* des frères Sainte-Marthe: une entreprise gallicane?', *Revue de l'histoire des religions*, 226(3) (2009), pp. 375–95.

Porter, Sheila M. (ed. and tr.), *Jacques Lefèvre d'Etaples and the Three Maries Debates*, Travaux d'Humanisme et Renaissance (Geneva: Droz, 2009).

Prinz, Friedrich, 'Zeitkritik im Spiegel der Historie: Wie der deutsche Humanist Aventinus Investiturstreit und Völkerwanderung beurteilte', *Damals*, 20 (1988), pp. 533–44.

Prodi, Paolo, 'Ricerche sulla teoria delle arti figurative nella riforma cattolica', *Archivio italiano per la storia della pietà*, 4 (1965), pp. 123–212.

Prodi, Paolo, 'La spiritualità di san Filippo Neri e l'Oratorio' in Franco Bolgiani et al. (eds.), *Oratorio e laboratorio: l'intuizione di san Filippo Neri e la figura di Sebastiano Valfré* (Bologna: Il Mulino, 2008), pp. 13–35.

Pucci, Michael S., 'Reforming Roman Emperors: John Foxe's Characterisation of Constantine in the *Acts and Monuments*' in David Loades (ed.), *John Foxe: An Historical Perspective* (Aldershot: Ashgate, 1999), pp. 29–51.

Pullapilly, Cyriac K., *Caesar Baronius: Counter-Reformation Historian* (Notre Dame, Ind. and London: University of Notre Dame Press, 1975).

Quantin, Jean-Louis, *Le Catholicisme classique et les pères de l'église, un retour aux sources* (Paris: Institut d'Études Augustiniennes, 1999).

Quaranta, Chiara, *Marcello II Cervini (1501–55). Riforma della chiesa, concilio, inquisizione* (Bologna: Il Mulino, 2010).

Rekers, Bernard, *Benito Arias Montano (1527–1598)* (London/Leiden: Warburg Institute and Brill, 1972).

Renaudet, Augustin, *Préréforme et humanisme à Paris pendant les premières guerres d'Italie (1494–1517)*, 2nd edn (Paris: Librairie d'Argences, 1953; repr. Geneva: Slatkine Reprints, 1981).

Rey Castelao, Ofelia, *La historiografía del voto de Santiago: recopilación de una polémica histórica* (Santiago de Compostela: Universidad de Santiago de Compostela, 1985).

Reyff, Simone de, *L'Église et le théâtre. L'exemple de la France au XVIIe siècle* (Paris: Éditions du Cerf, 1998).

Rice, Eugene F., Jr, *Saint Jerome in the Renaissance* (Baltimore: The Johns Hopkins University Press, 1985).

Rietbergen, Peter J., 'Lucas Holstenius (1596–1661): Seventeenth-century Scholar, Librarian and Book-collector. A Preliminary Note', *Quaerendo*, 17 (1987), pp. 205–31.

Rivera Recio, Juan Francisco, *San Eugenio de Toledo y su culto* (Toledo: Diputación Provincial, 1963).

Robinson, Benedict Scott, '"Darke Speech": Matthew Parker and the Reforming of History', *Sixteenth Century Journal*, 29(4) (1998), pp. 1061–83.

—— 'Foxe and the Anglo Saxons' in Christopher Highley and John King (eds.), *John Foxe and His World* (Aldershot: Ashgate, 2002), pp. 54–72.

Rosenblatt, Jason P., *Renaissance England's Chief Rabbi: John Selden* (Oxford: Oxford University Press, 2006).

Rowe, Erin Kathleen, *Saint and Nation: Santiago, Teresa of Avila, and Plural Identities in Early Modern Spain* (University Park, Pa.: Penn State Press, 2011).

—— 'St. Teresa and Olivares: Patron Sainthood, Royal Favorites, and the Politics of Plurality in Seventeenth-century Spain', *Sixteenth Century Journal*, 37 (2006), pp. 721–37.

Rowland, Ingrid D., *The Culture of the High Renaissance: Ancients and Moderns in Sixteenth-century Rome* (Cambridge: Cambridge University Press, 1998).

—— *The Scarith of Scornello: A Tale of Renaissance Forgery* (Chicago: University of Chicago Press, 2004).

Rubiés, Joan-Pau, *Travel and Ethnology in the Renaissance: South India through European Eyes, 1250–1625* (Cambridge: Cambridge University Press, 2000).

Rummel, Erika, *Erasmus' 'Annotations' on the New Testament: From Philologist to Theologian* (Toronto: University of Toronto Press, 1986).

—— 'Marineo Siculo: A Protagonist of Humanism in Spain', *Renaissance Quarterly*, 50 (1997), pp. 701–22.

—— *The Case Against Johannes Reuchlin: Religious and Social Controversy in Sixteenth-century Germany* (Toronto: University of Toronto Press, 2002).

Rupp, Gordon, *Frontiers of Reformation* (London: Epworth, 1969).

Rupprich, Hans (ed.), *Der Briefwechsel des Konrad Celtis*, Veröffentlichungen der Kommission zur Erforschung der Geschichte der Reformation und Gegenreformation. Humanistenbriefe, III (Munich: C. H. Beck, 1934).

Ryan, Salvador, 'Steadfast Saints or Malleable Models? Seventeenth-century Irish Hagiography Revisited', *Catholic Historical Review*, 91(2) (2005), pp. 251–78.

—— '"Holding up a Lamp to the Sun": Hiberno-Papal Relations and the Construction of Irish Orthodoxy in John Lynch's *Cambrensis Eversus* (1662)', in Peter Clarke and Charlotte Methuen (eds.), *The Church on its Past: Studies in Church History* 49 (Woodbridge: Boydell Press, forthcoming 2013).

Saebø, Magne, *Hebrew Bible/Old Testament: The History of its Interpretation*, 2 vols. (Göttingen: Vandenhoeck & Ruprecht, 1996).

Saïd, Edward, *Orientalism* (London: Routledge, 1978).

Sallmann, Jean-Michel, *Naples et ses saints à l'âge baroque: 1540–1750* (Paris: Presses universitaires de France, 1994).

Sauerland, H. V., '*De coemeterio Priscillae Romae invento in canicularibus anno 1578*', *Römische Quartalschrift für Christliche Alterthumskunde*, 2 (1888), pp. 210–16.

Sawilla, Jan Marco, *Antiquarianismus, Hagiographie und Historie im 17. Jahrhundert: zum Werk der Bollandisten: ein wissenschaftshistorischer Versuch* (Tübingen: Niemeyer, 2009).

Scavizzi, Giuseppe, 'La teologia cattolica e le immagini durante il XVI secolo', *Storia dell'arte*, 20–2 (1974), pp. 171–211.

—— *The Controversy on Images from Calvin to Baronius*, Toronto Studies in Religion, XIV (New York: Peter Lang, 1992).

Scherer, Emil Clemens, *Geschichte und Kirchengeschichte an den deutschen Universitäten: ihre Anfänge im Zeitalter des Humanismus und ihre Ausbildung zu selbständigen Disziplinen* (Freiburg im Breisgau: Herder, 1927).

Schmid, Alois, 'Die historische Methode des Johannes Aventinus', *Blätter für deutsche Landesgeschichte*, 113 (1977), pp. 338–95.

—— 'Geschichtsschreibung am Hofe Kurfürst Maximilians I. von Bayern' in Hubert Glaser (ed.), *Um Glauben und Reich: Kurfürst Maximilian I*, I (Munich: Hirmer, 1980), pp. 330–40.

—— 'Der Briefwechsel des P. Matthaus Rader SJ: eine neue Quelle zur Kulturgeschichte Bayerns im 17. Jahrhundert', *Zeitschrift für bayerische Landesgeschichte*, 60 (1997), pp. 1109–40.

—— 'Die "Bavaria sancta et pia" des P. Matthäus Rader, S.J.' in Chantal Grell, Werner Paravicini, and Jürgen Voss (eds.), *Les Princes et l'histoire du XIVe au XVIIIe siècle* (Bonn: Bouvier, 1998), pp. 499–522.

Schmid, Alois, 'Die Kleinen Annalen des Johannes Aventinus aus dem Jahre 1511' in Franz Brendle et al. (eds.), *Deutsche Landesgeschichtsschreibung* (Stuttgart: Steiner, 2001), pp. 69–96.

Schmid, Wolfgang, 'Die Stadt und ihre Heiligen. Die "Sancta Treviris" und die "Sancta Colonia" am Ende des Mittelalters', *Kurtrierisches Jahrbuch*, 48 (2008), pp. 123–54.

Schmidt-Biggemann, Wilhelm, *Topica universalis: Eine Modellgeschichte humanistischer und barocker Wissenschaft* (Hamburg: Meiner, 1983).

Schöller, Bernadette, 'Arbeitsteilung in der Druckgraphik um 1600. Die *Epideigma* des Stephan Broelmann', *Zeitschrift für Kunstgeschichte*, 54 (1991), pp. 406–11.

—— *Kölner Druckgraphik der Gegenreformation* (Cologne: Kölnisches Stadtmuseum, 1992).

Schürer, Emil, *The History of the Jewish People in the Age of Jesus Christ (175 B.C.–A.D. 135)*, tr. T.A. Burkill et al.; rev. and ed. Géza Vermès and Fergus Millar, 3 vols. (Edinburgh: Clark, 1973–87).

Schwaiger, Georg (ed.), *Historische Kritik in der Theologie: Beiträge zu ihrer Geschichte* (Göttingen: Vandenhoeck & Ruprecht, 1980).

Schwartz, Eduard, 'Über Kirchengeschichte' in *Gesammelte Schriften*, I (Berlin, de Gruyter, 1938–63), pp. 110–30.

Scribner, Robert, 'Why Was There No Reformation in Cologne?', *Bulletin of the Institute of Historical Research*, 49 (1976), pp. 217–24.

Seeberg, Erich, *Gottfried Arnold, die Wissenschaft und die Mystik seiner Zeit: Studien zur Historiographie und zur Mystik* (Meerane: Herzog, 1923; repr. Darmstadt, Wissenschaftliche Buchgesellschaft, 1964).

Segel, J. B., *Edessa, the Blessed City* (Oxford: Oxford University Press, 1970; repr. Piscataway: Gorgias Press, 2005).

Seifert, Arno, *Der Rückzug der biblischen Prophetie von der neueren Geschichte: Studien zur Geschichte der Reichstheologie des frühneuzeitlichen deutschen Protestantismus* (Cologne: Böhlau, 1990).

Serrai, Alfredo, *La biblioteca di Lucas Holstenius* (Udine: Forum, 2000).

—— *La Biblioteca altempsiana ovvero le raccolte librarie di Marco Sittico III e del nipote Giovanni Angeli Altemps* (Rome: Bulzoni, 2008).

Shalev, Zur, 'Sacred Geography, Antiquarianism, and Visual Erudition: Benito Arias Montano and the Maps of the Antwerp Polyglot Bible', *Imago Mundi*, 55 (2003), pp. 56–80.

Sharpe, Kevin, *Reading Revolutions: The Politics of Reading in Early Modern England* (New Haven, Conn.: Yale University Press, 2000).

Sheehan, Jonathan, 'From Philology to Fossils: The Biblical Encyclopedia in Early Modern Europe', *Journal of the History of Ideas*, 64 (2003), pp. 41–60.

—— *The Enlightenment Bible: Translation, Scholarship, Culture* (Princeton, NJ: Princeton University Press, 2005).

Sherman, William, *Used Books: Marking Readers in Renaissance England* (Philadelphia: University of Pennsylvania Press, 2008).

Shuger, Debora Kuller, *The Renaissance Bible: Scholarship, Sacrifice, and Subjectivity* (Berkeley, Calif.: University of California Press, 1987).

Signori, Gabriela (ed.), *Heiliges Westfalen*, Religion in der Geschichte (Bielefeld: Verlag für Regionalgeschichte, 2003).

—— 'Patriotische heilige?' in Dieter R. Bauer et al. (eds.), *Patriotische Heilige* (Stuttgart: Franz Steiner, 2007), pp. 11–31.

Signorotto, Gianvittorio, 'Cercatori di reliquie', *Rivista di storia e letteratura religiosa*, 21 (1985), pp. 383–41.

Sluhovsky, Moshe, *Patroness of Paris: Rituals of Devotion in Early Modern France* (Leiden: Brill, 1998).

Smalley, Beryl, *The Study of the Bible in the Middle Ages* (Notre Dame, Ind.: Notre Dame University Press, 1964).

Smith O'Neill, Maryvelma, 'The Patronage of Cardinal Cesare Baronio at San Gregorio Magno. Renovation and Innovation' in Romeo de Mario et al. (eds.), *Baronio e L'arte*, pp. 135–71.

Sotomayor, Manuel et al., *Historia de la Iglesia en España*, I: *La Iglesia en la España romana y visigoda*, ed. Ricardo García Villoslada (Madrid: Biblioteca de Autores Cristianos, 1979).

Southern, Richard, 'Presidential Address: Aspects of the European Tradition of Historical Writing: 4. The Sense of the Past', *Transactions of the Royal Historical Society*, 5th ser., 23 (1973), pp. 243–63.

Spera, Lucrezia, 'Il recupero dei monumenti per la restituzione del cristianesimo antico nell'opera di Cesare Baronio' in Patrizia Tosini (ed.), *Arte e committenza*, pp. 69–86.

—— 'Cesare Baronio, "peritissimus antiquitatis", e le origini dell'archeologia cristiana' in Giuseppe A. Guazzelli et al. (eds.), *Cesare Baronio tra santità e scrittura storica*.

Spitz, Lewis William, *Luther and German Humanism* (Aldershot: Variorum, 1996).

Stadtwald, Kurt, 'Conrad Celtis, Erasmus of Rotterdam and Ulrich von Hutten' in *Roman Popes and German Patriots: Antipapalism in the Politics of the German Humanist Movement from Gregor Heimburg to Martin Luther* (Geneva: Droz, 1996), pp. 70–103.

Stenhouse, William, *Reading Inscriptions and Writing Ancient History: Historical Scholarship in the Late Renaissance* (London: Institute of Classical Studies, 2005).

Stephens, Walter, 'When Pope Noah ruled the Etruscans: Annius of Viterbo and his Forged "Antiquities"', *Modern Language Notes*, 119(1) (Italian Issue Supplement) (2004), pp. S201–S223.

Stieglecker, Roland, *Die Renaissance eines Heiligen: Sebastian Brant und Onuphrius eremita*, ed. Dieter Wuttke, Gratia: Bamberger Schriften zur Renaissanceforschung, XXXVII (Wiesbaden: Harrassowitz Verlag, 2001).

Stinger, Charles L., *The Renaissance in Rome* (Bloomington, Ind.: Indiana University Press, 1998).

Strauss, Gerald, 'Germania illustrata: Topographical-Historical Descriptions of Germany in the Sixteenth Century', PhD dissertation (Columbia University, 1957).

—— *Sixteenth-Century Germany: Its Topography and Topographers* (Madison, Wis.: University of Wisconsin Press, 1959).

—— *Historian in an Age of Crisis: The Life and Work of Johannes Aventinus, 1477–1534* (Cambridge, Mass.: Harvard University Press, 1963).

Street, John S., *French Sacred Drama from Bèze to Corneille: Dramatic Forms and their Purposes in the Early Modern Theatre* (Cambridge: Cambridge University Press, 1983).

Stroumsa, Guy G., *A New Science: The Discovery of Religion in the Age of Reason* (Cambridge, Mass.: Harvard University Press, 2010).

Subrahmanyam, Sanjay, 'Profit at the Apostle's Feet: The Portuguese Settlement at Mylapur in the Sixteenth Century' in *Improvising Empire: Portuguese Trade and Settlement in the Bay of Bengal, 1500–1700* (Delhi and New York: Oxford University Press, 1990), pp. 47–67.

Suire, Eric, *La Sainteté Française de la Réforme catholique (XVIe–XVIIIe siècle) d'après les textes hagiographiques et les procès de canonisation* (Bordeaux: Presses Universitaires de Bourdeaux, 2001).

Summit, Jennifer, *Memory's Library: Medieval Books in Early Modern England* (Chicago: University of Chicago Press, 2008).

Tallon, Allain, *Le Concile de Trente* (Paris: Éditions du Cerf, 2000).

—— *Conscience nationale et sentiment religieux en France au XVIe siècle* (Paris, Presse Universitaire de France, 2002).

Tate, Robert Brian, 'The Rewriting of the Historical Past: *Hispania et Europa*' in Alan Deyermond (ed.), *Historical Literature in Medieval Iberia* (London: Queen Mary and Westfield College, 1996), pp. 67–84.

Taylor, Larissa, *Heresy and Orthodoxy in Sixteenth-century Paris: François Le Picart and the Beginning of the Catholic Reformation* (Leiden: Brill, 1999).

Tite, Colin, *The Manuscript Library of Sir Robert Cotton* (London: British Library, 1994).

—— *The Early Records of Sir Robert Cotton's Library: Formation, Cataloguing, Use* (London: British Library, 2003).

Tosini, Patrizia (ed.), *Arte e commitenza nel Lazio nell'età di Cesare Baronio: atti del convegno internazionale di studi, Frosinone, Sora, 16–18 maggio 2007* (Rome: Gangemi, 2009).

Trimpi, Wesley, 'The Meaning of Horace's *Ut pictura poesis*', *Journal of the Warburg and Courtauld Institutes*, 36 (1973), pp. 1–34.

Truchet, Jacques, *Bossuet panégyriste* (Paris: Éditions du Cerf, 1962).

Turco, Maria Grazia, *Il titulus dei Santi Nereo ed Achilleo emblema della riforma cattolica* (Rome: Librerie Dedalo, 1997).

—— 'Cesare Baronio e i dettani tridentini nelle sistemazioni presbiteriali romane' in Patrizia Tosini (ed.), *Arte e committenza*, pp. 87–107.

Turner, Victor and Edith Turner, *Image and Pilgrimage in Christian Culture: Anthropological Perspectives* (New York, NY: Columbia University Press, 1978).

Van Liere, Katherine Elliot, 'The Moorslayer and the Missionary: James the Apostle in Spanish Historiography from Isidore of Seville to Ambrosio de Morales', *Viator*, 37 (2006), pp. 519–43.

—— '"Shared Studies Foster Friendship": Humanism and history in Spain' in John Jeffries Martin (ed.), *The Renaissance World* (New York and London: Routledge, 2007), pp. 242–61.

Veissière, Michel, *L'Évêque Guillaume Briçonnet (1470–1534): contribution* à la connaissance de la Réforme catholique à la veille du Concile de Trente (Provins: Société d'histoire et d'archéologie, 1986).

Vessey, Mark, 'Erasmus' Jerome: The Publishing of a Christian Author', *Erasmus of Rotterdam Society Yearbook* 14 (1994), pp. 62–99.

Villalon, Andrew, 'San Diego de Alcalá and the Politics of Saint-making in Counter-Reformation Europe', *Catholic Historical Review*, 83 (1997), pp. 691–715.

Vlnas, Vít, *Jan Nepomucký: Česká legenda* (Prague: Mladá fronta, 1993).

Völkel, Markus, *Römische Kardinalshaushalte des 17. Jahrhunderts: Borghese—Barberini—Chigi* (Tübingen: Max Niemeyer Verlag, 1993).

—— 'Theologische Heilanstalt und Erfahrungswissen: David Chytraeus' Auslegung der Universalhistorie zwischen Prophetie und Modernisierung (Universitätsbibliothek Rostock, Mss. hist. 5)' in Karl-Heinz Glaser und Steffen Stuth (eds.), *David Chytraeus (1530–1600): Norddeutscher Humanismus in Europa. Beiträge zum Wirken des Kraichgauer Gelehrten* (Ubstadt-Weiher: Verlag Regionalkultur, 2000), pp. 121–37.

—— 'Das Verhältnis von *religio, patriae, confessio*, und *eruditio* bei Marx Welser' in Herbert Jaumann (ed.), *Die europäische Gelehrtenrepublik im Zeitalter des Konfessionalismus* (Wiesbaden: Harrassowitz, 2001), pp. 127–40.

Vogelstein, Ingeborg Berlin, *Johann Sleidan's Commentaries: Vantage Point of a Second Generation Lutheran* (Lanham and New York: University Press of America, 1986).

Voigt, Georg, *Enea Silvio de Piccolomini, als Papst Pius der Zweite und sein Zeitalter*, 3 vols. (Berlin: Georg Reimer, 1856–1863).

Vollmann, Benedikt Konrad, 'Aeneas Silvius Piccolomini as a Historiographer: *Asia*' in Zweder von Martels and Arjo Vanderjagt (eds.), *Pius II, 'el più expeditivo pontifice'* (Leiden: Brill, 2003), pp. 41–54.

Wagendorfer, Martin, 'Eneas Silvius Piccolomini und die Wiener Universität: Ein Beitrag zum Frühhumanismus in Österreich' in Franz Fuchs (ed.), *Enea Silvio Piccolomni nördlich der Alpen* (Wiesbaden: Harrassowitz, 2007), pp. 21–52.

Walker, P. W. L., *Holy City, Holy Places? Christian Attitudes to Jerusalem and the Holy Land in the Fourth Century* (Oxford: Clarendon Press, 1990).

Walter, Renate von, *Das Augsburger Rathaus* (Augsburg: Mühlberger, 1972).

Weinberg, Joanna, 'A Hebraic Approach to the New Testament' in Christopher Ligota and Jean-Louis Quantin (eds.), *History of Scholarship: A Selection of Papers from the Seminar on the History of Scholarship Held Annually at the Warburg Institute* (Oxford: Oxford University Press, 2006), pp. 238–47.

Weiss, Roberto, *The Renaissance Discovery of Classical Antiquity*, 2nd edn (Oxford: Blackwell, 1988).

Werminghoff, Albert (ed.), *Conrad Celtis und sein Buch über Nürnberg* (Freiburg: Boltze, 1921).

Werner, Matthias (ed.), *Spätmittelalterliches Landesbewusstsein in Deutschland*, Vorträge und Forschungen (Ostfildern: Thorbecke, 2005).

Whatley, E. Gordon, 'The Uses of Hagiography: The Legend of Pope Gregory and the Emperor Trajan in the Middle Ages', *Viator*, 15 (1984), pp. 25–63.

Wicki, Josef (ed.), *Documenta Indica*, 18 vols. (Rome: Institutum Historicum Societatis Iesu, 1948–88).

Wilkinson, John, 'L'apport de Saint Jérôme à la topographie de la Terre Sainte', *Revue Biblique*, 81 (1974), pp. 245–57.

Wojtyska, H. D., 'L'influsso in Polonia e in Lituania' in *San Carlo e il suo tempo*, 2 vols., II (Rome: Edizione di storia e letteratura, 1986), pp. 527–49.

Woolf, Daniel R., *Reading History in Early Modern England* (Cambridge: Cambridge University Press, 2000).

Woolf, Daniel R., *The Social Circulation of the Past: English Historical Culture 1500–1730* (Oxford: Oxford University Press, 2003).

Zarri, Gabriella, *Le Sante Vive: cultura e religiosità femminile nella prima età moderna* (Torino: Rosenberg & Sellier, 1990).

Zedelmaier, Helmut, *Der Anfang der Geschichte: Studien zur Ursprungsdebatte im 18. Jahrhundert*, Studien zum achtzehnten Jahrhundert (Hamburg: Felix Meiner, 2003).

Zen, Stefano, *Baronio storico: controriforma e crisi del metodo umanistico* (Naples: Vivarium, 1994).

—— 'Cesare Baronio sulla Donazione di Costantino tra critica storica e autocensura' in *Censura, riscrittura, restauro* (Annali della Scuola Normale Superiore di Pisa, Classe di Lettere e Filosofia, serie 5 [2010]), pp. 179–219.

Zuccari, Alessandro, 'La politica culturale dell'Oratorio romano nelle imprese artistiche promosse da Cesare Baronio', *Storia dell'arte*, 42 (1981), pp. 171–93.

—— 'La politica culturale dell'Oratorio romano nella seconda metà del cinquecento', *Storia dell'arte*, 42 (1981), pp. 77–112.

—— 'Restauro e filologia baroniani' in Romeo de Maio et al. (eds.), *Baronio e l'arte*, pp. 489–510.

Zupanov, Ines, *Missionary Tropics: The Catholic Frontier in India (16th and 17th Centuries)* (Ann Arbor, Mich.: University of Michigan Press, 2005).

Index

Abdias, bishop of Babylon 6
Abelard, Peter 225
Abgar, king of Edessa 1
Academia Basiliana (Rome) 19, 83
Académie des Inscriptions et
    Belles-Lettres 267
acheiropoieta 252–5, 257
Acta ecclesiae mediolanensis 87–8
Acta sanctorum 8, 20, 74, 79–80, 84,
    93–5, 162
Acta sanctorum Hiberniae 94, 199–200
Acts of the Apostles (New Testament
    Book) 58
Acts of Thomas 237
Adalbert, St 160
Adrian IV, pope (1154–9) 189, 202
Adrian, St, *see* Genesius, St
Adrichem, Christiaan van 276–7
Aelfric of Eynsham 177–8, 183
Afra, St 37, 114 n.50, 152
Agatha, St 37
Agustín, Antonio 135
Aichler, David 163
Ailbe, St 201
Aix-en-Provence, University of 226
Alberti, Leon Battista 12, 254
Albertus Magnus 109, 217
Albrecht IV, duke of Bavaria
    (r.1465–1508) 112
Alcalá de Henares, University of 137–8
Alexander the Great 154
Alexander Severus, Roman emperor
    (r.222–35) 3
Alexander, St, bishop of Cappadocia and
    Jerusalem (d.251) 281
Alexander III, pope (1159–81) 90
Alfonso I of Naples (r.1442–58) 10
Allacci, Leone 83
Allen, William 173
Almería (Urci) 130
Alsted, Johann Heinrich 282
Altemps, Giovanni Angelo 76–7
Altemps Library (Rome) 76–81
Altötting, *see* Bavaria
Ambrose, St, bishop of Milan (d.397) 26,
    57 n.11, 149, 215, 234
Ambrosian Library, *see* Biblioteca
    Ambrosiana

Amico da Gallipoli, Bernardino, O.F.M. 276
    n.36, 277–9
    *Trattato delle piante & imagini de sacri
    edificii di Terra Santa* 277
Anabaptists 5, 34, 41
Anchorites, *see also* hermits 35, 149
Andújar 138
Angeli, Paolo de 83–4
Anglo-Saxon Church 21, 166, 170, 172–4,
    176–8, 183–4
Anne of Austria (regent of France
    1643–51) 223
Anne, St 223
Annius of Viterbo, *Antiquities* 174
Anthony of Padua, St 211
Antichrist 24, 38, 47, 50–1
Antioch (diocese) 58–60
antiquarianism 4–5, 12, 17, 20, 65, 69, 136–7,
    140, 146, 149–52, 158, 161, 163, 175, 191,
    203, 251, 254, 257, 266–83
Antoninus of Florence, O.P., St, bishop of
    Florence (d.1446–59) 114
Antoninus Pius, Roman emperor
    (r.138–61) 76, 154
Antonio, Nicolás 144
Antony of Egypt, St 34, 50
Antwerp 3, 20–1, 77–8, 95, 173, 175, 190,
    209, 271, 278
Aphra, St *see* Afra
Apocalypse 31
apocalypticism ix, 27, 31, 40, 45, 50–1, 116,
    120, 162, 168, 179–81
Apostles (biblical) ix–x, 15, 22, 36–7, 50,
    57–60, 62, 124–6, 132, 137, 146, 149,
    194, 196–7, 217, 222, 241, 270
apostolic origins 32, 58–9, 61–2, 75, 86, 121,
    123, 135, 144, 169, 197, 213, 217, 227,
    229, 234, 240, 242, 246, 260–1
Apostles of Spain, seven, *see* Seven apostles
Aragon 128–32, 135, 168
Aramaic 4, 22, 24
Arca, Giovanni 213
archaeology 13, 24, 92, 137, 266, 269, 273, 281
Arianism 61, 67, 127, 198
Arias Montano, Benito 22, 271–2, 274,
    278–9
Armagh (archdiocese) 187–9, 196
Armenia 244

Armenian Christians, *see also* Thomas
  Christians 34, 231, 241, 247
Arnold, Gottfried 8, 18–9, 24
Arnošt of Pardubice 160
Arnpeck, Veit 104, 111, 113–15, 117–18
  Bayerische Chronik 115ff
Ars historica 167
Ars poetica 256
art, Christian, *see* iconography
Asia, maritime 233–4, 239
Asia, South 232
Asklepios(Asclepius), god of healing 258
Assyria 5, 42
Athanasius, bishop of Alexandria (d.373) 215
Augsburg 45, 111, 116, 152–4, 156–7
  Rathaus 154
Augustine, St, archbishop of Canterbury
  (d.604) 169–70, 172–3, 177, 203
Augustine, St, bishop of Hippo (d.430) 26,
  34, 36, 38, 64, 84, 89, 144. 197, 245,
  257 n.27
Augustinians 6, 77, 81, 244, 246–7
Aurelian, Roman emperor (r.270–5)
  64 n.34
Austria 105, 108, 113, 115, 163
  Upper Austria 157
Aventinus, Johannes (Turmair) 104, 111–2,
  115–9, 153, 155
  Annales ducum Baioariae 115ff
  Bayerische Chronik 115, 153

Babylon 6, 22, 42, 241, 247
Backus, Irena 72–3
Bacon, Sir Francis 25–6
Baghdad 241, 247
Baillet, Adrien, S.J. 210, 228
Baillie, Robert 74
Balbín, Bohuslav, S.J. 158–63
  *Epitome historica rerum
    Bohemicarum* 159–60, 162
  Miscellanea historica regni Bohemiae 161
Balde, Jakob, S.J. 153
Bale, John 168, 170, 175, 181
Barbara, St 215
Barberini, Francesco 81, 83
Barbarossa, Frederick, *see* Frederick
  Barbarossa
Barbosa, Duarte 236–8, 241–2
Barclay, John 191
Barkan, Leonard 275
Barnes, Robert 47, 168
Baronio, Cesare 6, 19, 21, 23–4, 49, 52–71,
  73–4, 77–9, 82–3, 86, 91–2, 95–6, 121–3,
  138, 142, 145, 148–9, 156, 167, 175,
  182, 194–5, 209, 212, 251, 253, 256,
  260–1, 272

Annales ecclesiastici 6–7, 19, 21, 49, 53–8,
  61–2, 64–6, 68, 71, 73, 77–8, 80, 83, 90–1,
  121–2, 142, 145, 149, 156, 167, 175, 195,
  209, 251, 253, 260–1
Barralis, Vincent 218
Barreto, Melchior Nunes, S.J. 243–4
Barrière, Jean de la 219
Barros, João de 240–2, 247
Basel 6–7, 13, 53, 104, 110, 179, 183, 214, 270
Basil of Caesarea, St (d.379) 35
Basilian Academy, *see* Academia Basiliana
Basnage de Beauval, Jacques 8, 24
Baudouin, François 14, 23
Bavaria 103–4, 111–18, 108, 152–8,
  164, 213
  Altötting in 114
  Christian origins of 113
  humanist movement in 153
Bayle, Pierre 8
Bayonne, Conference of (1565) 223
Beauvais, Vincent of, O.P. 82, 114 n.49, 126,
  132, 137
Becilli, Cesare 73–4, 91
Becket, Thomas, archbishop of Canterbury
  (d.1170) 198
Bede of Jarrow (Venerable Bede) 9, 18, 24. 75,
  121–2, 169, 174, 183, 197, 245
  Historia ecclesiastica gentis Anglorum 75.
  167, 171–3
Beleth, John 132
Bellarmino, Roberto 122, 138, 142, 194, 264
Beltramus, Cornelius 272
Benedict XIV, pope (1740–58) 74
Benedictines, *see also* Maurists 20, 33–4,
  153, 218
Beneventano, Angelo 254
Benoist, René 212
Bentley, Richard 20
Benz, Stefan 8
Bernaerts, Jean 14
Bernard of Clairvaux, St 47, 162, 196,
  199, 215
Betteridge, Thomas 180
Beuter, Pere Antoni, *Coronica general de toda
  España* 123, 132–4, 138, 143
Beza, Theodore 37
Biblical scholarship v, 3–4, 14–5, 22–5, 28,
  3–5, 41–3, 47, 52, 74–6, 113–4, 117,
  169, 181–5, 263, 267–283
  New Testament, *see also* Acts, Galatians,
    Timothy, Revelation 4, 14, 20, 22, 58,
    138, 157, 250, 268, 281
  Old Testament, *see also* Daniel, Ezekiel
    4, 21, 24–5, 38, 43, 182, 184–5, 188,
    253, 260, 281
Bibliens 221

Biblioteca Ambrosiana (Milan) 19
Bidermann, Jakob 153
Billy, Jacques de 214
Biondo, Flavio 13, 30, 30, 39, 51, 77, 101, 117. 270
Biroat, Jacques 212
Bishops' Bible 169, 177
Blandina, St 9
Blondel, David 194–5
Bochart, Samuel 282
Bodin, Jean 5, 14
Bodleian Library, *see* Oxford
Boece, Hector 191
Bohemia 10, 38, 105, 155, 157–64
Bohemus, Eusebius 49
Boleslav (Bohemian town) 160
Boleslav II, duke of Bohemia (r.972–99) 160
Bolland, Jean, S.J. 20, 79, 93–4, 209, 254
Bollandists, *see also Acta Sanctorum* 79, 93–5, 162, 210
Bologna, University of 84, 128
Bomberg, Daniel 22
Bonfant, Dionigio 82–3
Boni, Giacomo 92
Boniface III, pope (607) 39
Boniface IV, pope (608–15) 69
Boniface of Ragusa, O.F.M. 277
Boniface VIII, pope (1294–1303) 30
Boniface, St 115, 146
Book of Martyrs, see Foxe, John
book production 16, 20–2, 77–8, 84, 87, 148, 211, 235, 269, 278
Bordeaux 3
Bořivoj I, duke of Bohemia (r. *c.*870–89) 160–1
Borromeo, Carlo, St, archbishop of Milan (1564–84) 87–8, 96, 213, 248, 253, 260, 262–4
Borromeo, Federico 19, 251 n.5
Bosio, Antonio 82, 84, 251, 253–4, 259
Boucher, Jean 212
Bourbon dynasty 220, 224
Bozio, Tomasso 197
Bracciolini, Poggio 8–9, 11, 106 n.16, 269
Bradshaw, Brendan 192
Břetislav I, duke of Bohemia (r.1034–55) 160
breviaries 3, 125 n.10, 137–40
Breviarium romanum (Roman Breviary) 55, 57, 61–2, 73, 96, 142
Breydenbach, Bernard von 274
Brian Boru, high king of Ireland (r.1002–14) 196, 203
Bright, Timothy 171
Brigid, St 199–200
Broelmann, Stephan 149, 152
Brower, Christoph, S.J. 82, 146
Bruin, Konrad 253

Bruni, Girolamo 262
Bruni, Leonardo 5, 8, 30
Bruno, St 225
Bucer, Martin 147
Budé, Guillaume 4
Bulenger, Jules-César, S.J. 7
Bullinger, Heinrich 28, 32, 36–9, 46
Burckhardt, Jacob vi
Burke, Peter vi–vii
Bus, César de 220
Byzantinium 43, 139, 161
Bzowski, Abraham, O.P. 83, 156

Caesar Augustus, emperor of Rome (r.27BC –14AD) 129, 154
Caesar, Julius, dictator of Rome (r.49–44 BC) 106, n.16, 117, 132, 150, 259
Caesarea 18–20, 37, 58–9
Caesarius of Heisterbach 193
Caesarius of Arles, St 192–3
Calamie (India) 235
Calentijn, Pieter 276
Calicut (Calcutta/ Kozhikode) 236
Calixtus II, pope (1119–24), *see* pseudo-Calixtus
Calvin, John, *Treatise on Relics* 222
Calvinists, *see also* Huguenots, Puritans 3–4, 7, 14, 23–4, 48–9, 145, 149, 153, 166, 174, 179, 219, 222–4, 253
Cambrensis, Giraldus 189–91, 193–7, 202–3
Cambridge University Press 20
Camden, William 4, 191, 203
Campion, Edmund, S.J. 75 n.9, 162, 182, 190–1, 201
Candid, Peter 156
Canini, Angelo 22
Canisius, Peter, S.J. 156
Cannanore 236
Cano, Melchor, O.P. 137–8
canon law 11, 330, 39, 52, 135, 168
canonization 53, 79, 90–1, 94 n.58, 135, 161–3, 219–20, 224
Canterbury (archdiocese) 16, 203
Caracciolo, Eugenio 83
Carion, Johannes 42
Carmelites 46 n.102, 248
Carolingians 39, 63
Carthusians 94, 148, 209, 221
Casaubon, Isaac 7, 17, 23–4, 83, 153, 272, 282
Castile 129–32, 135–6, 224
Castillon, Antoine 212
Catacombs, *see* Rome, monuments
Catherine of Aragon, queen of England (d.1536) 165
Catholic League (France) 174, 219, 224
Cecil, William 171

Celestine I, pope (422–32) 195, 197, 264
celibacy 22, 43, 61, 76, 169
Celsus, St 196
Celtis, Conrad 33, 101–4, 106–10, 112, 115
    Amores 108–9
    De situ, moribus et institutis Norimbergae libellus 107
    Panegyris ad duces Bavaria 108
cemeteries. early Christian, *see also* Rome 255, 258–9
censorship, *see also Index of Prohibited Books* 153, 213
Cervini, Marcello 81
Chacón, Alfonso, O.P. 65, 82, 91, 251
Charlemagne, Holy Roman Emperor (r.800–14) 46, 110, 117, 146, 154
Charles I, king of England (r.1625–49) 188
Charles II, king of England (r.1660–85) 194
Charles IV, Holy Roman Emperor (r.1355–78) 160–1
Charles V, king of Spain (r.1516–56) 130
Charles VIII, king of France (r.1483–98) 218
Charles IX, king of France (r.1560–74) 136
Chartres 224
Chartreux 220
Chennai, *see* Madras
Chenu, Jean 214
chronologia praesulum 213
chronology and periodization of church history 5, 29, 31–3, 42–51, 58–69, 74–5, 122, 195, 216
Chrysostom, St John 215, 243
Church Fathers, *see* Patristic writings
Church, early or "primitive" 27–51, 52–71, 167–72, 233, 238, 241–2, 248, 263
Chytraeus, David 14, 42
Cistercians 83, 85, 191, 193, 202, 220
Claudius, Roman emperor (r.41–54) 147
Clement VII, pope (1523–34) 90, 165
Clement VIII (Ippolito Aldobrandini), pope (1592–1605) 91, 187
Clement IX, pope (1667–9) 216
Clichtoveus, Jodocus 115, 222
Cluniac order 213 n.12, 220
Cochin (Kochi) 231, 236–7
Codex Calixtinus, see pseudo-Calixtus 125, 129–31, 138
Colgan, John, O.F.M. 82, 94, 199–201
Collegio Romano (Rome) 74
Cologne 94, 146–53, 155, 157–8, 164, 209, 233
Cologne War (1583–8) 150, 155
Colonna, Ascanio 77
Columba, St 199–200, 202
Columcille, St, *see* St Columba
comedies, *see* theatre

confession (sacrament) 39, 50, 162, 217, 231
Conry, Florence, O.F.M. 187–8
Constantine, Roman emperor (r.306–37),
    see also Donation of Constantine 6–7, 10–11, 43, 37, 64, 67–9, 74–5, 89, 147, 154, 158, 179–80, 182, 273, 275–6
Contelori, Felice 90
Conti, Nicolò 235
Contzen, Adam, S.J. 153
Cope, Alan (pseudonym), *see* Harpsfield, Nicholas
Corbinian, St 114 n.50, 115, 118 n.67
Cordeliers monks 218
Corneille, Pierre 216
Coromandel Coast 231, 242–4, 247
Correia, Gaspar 231–32, 236–40, 242
Cosmas of Prague 162
Coste, Hilarion de 219
Cotton, Robert 17
Councils of the Church 47, 49, 138–9, 142, 148, 170, 202
    Council of Basel 104
    Council of Constance 10
    Council of Ephesus 264
    Council, Fourth Lateran 127, 142
    Councils of Toledo 127 n.17, 135
    Council of Trent (and Tridentine liturgical reform) 54–7, 60–1, 72–3, 81, 83, 87–8, 96–7, 124, 135–6, 140, 205, 225, 253–4
Cranganore 241
Cranmer, Thomas, archbishop of Canterbury (1533–56) 168, 170
Creagh, Richard 189–90
Creation 29, 42–3, 74, 77, 107, 114, 117, 119, 260
Crescens 146
Cristina, queen of Sweden (r.1632–54) 81
critici sacri 268–9, 272, 282–3
Crombach, Hermann 149
Cromwell, Oliver 186
Cromwell, Thomas 172
cult of images, *see* iconography
cult of the saints, *see* saints
Cunaeus, Petrus 272
Curia, papal (Roman Curia) 10, 54, 57, 105
Cusa, Nicholas of 10–11
Cuspinianus, Johannes 115
Cyprian, St, bishop of Carthage (248–258) 36, 38, 60
Cyriac of Ancona 5, 271
Cyril and Methodius, Sts 112, 158, 161

Damascene, John, St, *see* John Damascene
Daniel (Old Testament book) 5, 38, 42, 45, 263

Danube river 67
Davies, John 187, 191, 194
Day, John 16, 21
de Thou, Jacques-Auguste, *see* Thou
Declan, St 201
Decretals, False 50
Decretum 11
Delumeau, Jean 228
Demetrius of Tarsus 280
Denis of Paris, St 83, 126–7, 131, 133, 136,
212–5, 217, 219, 222–8
Denys the Carthusian 148
Denysse, Nicolas 211
Dexter, Flavius 154
Didacus of Alcalá, St (San Diego) 80, 137 n.49
Dillingen 153
Diocletian, Roman emperor (r.284–305) 70,
152, 172
Dionysius the Areopagite, St, *see also* Denis,
St, and Pseudo-Dionysius 83, 114 n.50,
126, 131, 133, 139, 212, 214, 217, 225,
227–8
Dionysius of Halicarnassus 19
Dioscorus of Alexandria 247
Ditchfield, Simon 62, 210
Dominicans 3, 65, 82–3, 137, 156, 221, 228,
279 n.45
Domitian, Roman emperor (r.81–96) 133
Donation of Constantine 10–12, 19, 50, 67,
167, 183
Donatists 34, 61
Donne, John 153
Douai, English College 190, 199
Drahomíra 161
Drakolica, Bonifazio, *see* Boniface of Ragusa
du Faïl, Noël, *see* Faïl
du Saussay, André, *see* Saussay
Dublin 187–192
Dugdale, William 83, 84
Dupuyherbault, Gabriel (*c.*1490–1566) 211, 221
Duval, André 211

Eck, Johann 153, 158
Edessa 11, 235, 237, 243–7, 252
Egeria 243
Eleutherius, pope (*c.*174–89) 165, 169–70,
172–3
Elizabeth I, queen of England (r.1558–1603)
16–17, 75, 165, 169, 172, 179–80, 182–4,
187, 198
Elizabethan Church 165–73, 176–84, 187, 203
Endtime *see* Apocalype, Parousia
England 16, 20, 49, 75, 84, 86, 152, 165–85,
189, 195, 198, 200, 202
conversion of 16, 169–70, 172–3, 175, 177
Enlightenment v, 36, 51, 95, 144–5, 228, 282

Erasmus, Desiderius 14–15, 28, 111, 115 n.60,
131, 146, 214, 221–2, 270, 272, 275–6,
279
Escavias, Pedro de 128
Eucharist 4, 34, 36–9, 43, 45–6, 50, 61, 76,
231, 262
Eugenius IV, pope (1431–47) 13
Eugenius, St, bishop of Toledo (first
century) 126–8, 131, 133, 136, 139, 142,
223, 227
Euphrasius, St 125, 138–9
Eusebius of Caesarea 4, 9, 11, 17–25, 31,
37–8, 43, 45–6, 58, 67, 75, 77, 82, 96,
121–2, 132, 171, 179–84, 234, 243,
268, 281
Eustasius, St 216
Eutyches 247
Evagrius 'Scholasticus' 77
Ezekiel (Old Testament book) 45

Faber Stapulensis, Jacobus, *see* Lefèvre
d'Etaples, Jacques
Facundus, St 139
Fagius, Paulus 22
Faïl, Noël du 211
Fathers of the Church, *see* Church Fathers and
patristics
Fauchet, Claude 225
Felicitas, St 76, 84
Ferdinand II, Holy Roman Emperor
(r.1619–37) 155, 160
Ferdinand II, king of Aragon
(r.1479–1516) 129–30
Ferguson, A.B. 167
Fernandes, Diogo 231
Fernandes, Valentim 235
Ferrari, Filippo 213
Feuardent, François 212
Feuillants 219, 224
Fiamma, Gabriele 80
Filarete (Antonio di Pietro Averlino) 13
Findlen, Paula 274
Firminius of Pamplona, St 133
Fisher, John 226
FitzAldelm, William 204
Fitzsimon, Henry, S.J. 193
FitzStephen, Robert 204
Flacius Illyricus, Matthias, *see also Magdeburg
Centuries* 6–7, 15–16, 19, 23, 25–6, 45,
48, 50–1, 73, 75, 162, 167, 171, 176, 182
Flagellants, 160
Flórez, Henrique, *España sagrada* 144
Foras Feasa 191, 193–4, 200–3
Fossé, Thomas du 228
Four Empires, *see* Daniel
Foxe, Edward 165, 168

Foxe, John 21, 75, 167–71, 175–6, 178–85, 257 n.28
  Acts and Monuments 21, 45, 49, 75, 167–8, 171, 173–4, 178–82, 184
  Eicasmi 181
Foxe, Samuel 181
France 3, 76, 136, 147, 174–5, 200, 209–29
  Wars of Religion 3, 212, 219, 223, 225
Francis I, king of France (r.1515–47) 226
Francis Xavier, S.J., St 80, 245–6
Franciscans 46 n.102, 94, 137 n.49, 187–8, 199–200, 274–8, 280
  Custodia Terrae Sanctae 274, 276
Frankfurt 105, 146, 179
Franks 43–4, 110, 117, 234, 280
Franz, Wolfgang 282
Frazier, Alison vi
Frederick III, Elector of Saxony (r.1486–1525) 223, 108 n.26, 223
Frederick III, Holy Roman Emperor (r.1440–93) 104
Frederick Barbarossa, Holy Roman Emperor (r.1155–90) 90
Freising (diocese) 113–14, 118
Fróis, Luís (1532–97) 242–3
Fueter, Eduard 35
Füetrer, Ulrich 104, 111–13
  Bavarian Chronicle 112ff
  Buch der Abenteuer 112ff
Fulda 146
Fürstenberg, Ferdinand von (1623–83) 146

Gaelic 188
Gaetani, Ottavio 213, 223
Galatians (New Testament) 157
Galesini, Pietro 80, 212
Galicia (Spanish province) 124, 138–41
Galilee 267, 282
Galilei, Galileo 153, 273
Gallonio, Antonio 80
Gama, Vasco da 233
García de Loaysa Girón, Pedro (1534–99) 142
Gardiner, Stephen 180
Garzoni, Giovanni 209, 221
Garruci, Raffaele, S.J. 254
Gaul (Roman province) 217, 225–9
Gaulthier, Jacques 211
Gelenius, Aegedius 149–51, 158
Gelenius, Johannes 149–50
Génébrard, Gilbert 212
Genesius, St 216
Geneviève, St 218
Gennep, Kaspar von 148
Geoffrey of Monmouth 165
geography 20, 29 n.8, 33, 69, 77, 81, 91, 94 n.58, 131, 157, 242, 268–70, 272–3, 276

George, St 12
Gerald of Mayo, St 201
Gerald of Wales, *see* Cambrensis, Giraldus
Gereon, St and the Theban Legion 147, 151
Germania illustrata project 101–4, 107–8, 110–11, 117
Germany 40–51, 92, 101–20, 145–64, 174, 200, 218
Gerold of Cologne 149
Gnesio-Lutherans 42 n.86, 45–6, 48, 51
Godeau, Antoine 216
Göttingen 24, 145
Gog and Magog 45
Golden Legend (Legenda aurea), see Voragine
Gordon, Bruce 37
Gouvea, António de 244, 246–7
Grafton, Anthony 273
Granada, Sacromonte 143
Greece, ancient 42, 270
Greek language & literature 4–5, 9, 12, 14, 19, 54, 67, 79, 81, 83, 93–4, 254, 257–8, 263, 281
Greek College (Rome) 83
Greek Orthdox Church 19, 43, 83
Gregory I (the Great), pope (590–604) 3, 37, 50, 58, 63–5, 69, 162, 169–70, 265
Gregory VII (Hildebrandt), pope (1073–85) 117
Gregory XIII (Ugo Boncompagni), pope (1572–85) 52, 54–5, 57 n.11, 266
Gregory of Nazianzus, archbishop of Constantinople (d.390) 57 n.11
Gregory of Nyssa, St 35, 110, 173, 280
Gretser, Jacob 163
Grimoard, Angelic de 163
Grotius, Hugo 272
Grynaeus, Jakob 14

Hadrian, Roman emperor (r.117–138) 64 n.34, 69, 275
Haggadah 24
hagiography vi, 10, 20, 56–7, 62, 64, 70, 76–84, 91–6, 102, 148, 152–7, 161–2, 189, 232–3, 246, 258
  Bollandist 82, 93–5, 162, 254
  French 209–29
  Greek 94
  Irish 82, 189, 195, 199–201
  liturgy 57, 62, 96
  medieval 82, 96, 126, 129, 232–3
  provincial 83, 103, 112, 114
  Spanish 122, 126–9, 132, 135–40
Halbwachs, Maurice 275
Hanmer, Meredith 171, 181–2, 191–3, 203
Harpsfield, Nicholas 75, 82, 173, 175, 182, 253
  Dialogi Sex 75 n.9, 175, 182, 253

Heal, Felicity 173
Hebraism, Christian 21–4, 271
Hebrew 4, 21–2, 24, 42, 101, 221, 271, 275, 283
Henri III, king of France (r.1573–75) 219, 224
Henri IV, king of France (r.1589–1610) 224
Henrique of Portugal, cardinal-prince, archbishop of Braga, and king of Portugal (r.1578–80) 134
Henry II, Holy Roman Emperor (r.1002–24) 154
Henry IV, Holy Roman Emperor (r.1084–1105) 117
Henry II, king of England (r.1154–89) 189, 196, 198, 202–3
Henry VIII, king of England (r.1509–47) 75 n.82, 165–6, 168–9, 173, 175–6, 198–9
Henry of Huntingdon 197
Henschen, Godfried 79, 93–5
Hermagoras of Aquileia, St 152
Hermant, Godefroy 215
Hermenegilde, St 216
hermits 6, 34, 50, 102 n.4, 125, 156
Herrwick, Johann 46 n.102
Hierotheus 139
Hilduin, abbot 225
Hiltenius of Eisenach 46
História da vida do padre Francisco de Xavier 245
Historia de la Corona de Aragon (anon.) 128
'historia sacra' (literary genre discussed) 29, 72–97, 163–4, 167, 170, 269, 277, 279
Hittorp, Melchior 149
Hohenhems, Marcus Sittich 77
Holinshed, Raphael, *Chronicles* 190
Holl, Elias 154
Holste, Lukas (Lucas Holstenius) 81–4
Holy House of St Thomas (*Santa Casa*) 231–2, 234, 237–9, 243–5, 247
Holy Land, *see* Palestine
Holy Roman Empire 101, 111, 119, 163
Holy Sepulchre 258, 275–6
Honoratus, St 216
Horace 256
Hottinger, Johann 49
Hrotsvitha of Gandersheim 108
Huguenots 195, 219, 223
humanists and humanism 4–5, 12–14, 19–20, 22, 27–36, 38–41, 43, 46–8, 51, 64, 67, 101–8, 110–15, 117–20, 123–4, 126, 128–9, 131–2, 134–6, 141, 144, 153, 167, 183, 185–6, 189–93, 198, 200–01, 205, 209, 215–6, 220–1, 224–6, 240, 254, 256–7, 269–73, 275, 280
Hundred Years' War 220
Hus, Jan 38, 46, 158, 162

Hussite Wars 158, 160–2
Hyperius, Andreas 179

Iceland 202
iconoclasm 223, 253, 255
iconography and religious images 36–7, 50, 61, 66–8, 154, 222, 239, 250–66
iconophobia 258
idols, *see* images
images, religious, *see* iconography
Indaletius, St 125 n.10, 130, 139
Index of Prohibited Books 57, 82, 153
India 21, 230–49
   mission of St Thomas to 125, 231–49
Ingolstadt, University of 101, 106, 115, 153, 155
Innocent III, pope (1198–1216) 30
Inquisition
   German 22
   Low Countries 254
   Roman 96
   Spanish 22
Interdict, papal 155, 195
Investiture Controversy 34, 45, 117–18
Ireland 186–205
Irish Catholic historiography 82, 94, 175, 186–205
Isabel, queen of Castile (r.1474–1504) 129
Isidore, St, archbishop of Seville (d.636) 127, 234, 238, 244
Islam 43, 105, 235, 243

Jacobelli, Ludovico 213
Jacobus de Voragine, *see* Voragine
James I, king of England (r.1603–25) 174, 187–8
James the Greater (apostle), St 83, 121–2, 124–9, 131–4, 136–40, 142–4, 197, 199, 224
James, Thomas (d. 1629) 19
Jansenists 220, 228
Jeanne de France, *see* Joan of Valois
Jedin, Hubert 53–4
Jerome of Prague (d.1416) 9–10, 46
Jerome, St 15, 38, 58, 214, 280–1
Jeronymites 224
Jerusalem 59, 107, 125–6, 132–3, 180, 214, 275–9
Jesuits 7, 20, 24, 74, 79, 82, 93–4, 142–3, 148–9, 152–3, 155–6, 158–63, 182, 190, 193–4, 202, 209–13, 215–16, 220, 224–5, 242–5, 248, 254
Jesus 16, 22–5, 36–7, 222, 267–8
Jewel, John, bishop of Salisbury (1566–71) 7, 170–2, 175, 177, 183
Jewish culture 21–5, 250, 258

Jewish studies, *see* Hebraism, Christian
Jiménez de Rada, Rodrigo, archbishop of
    Toledo (1209–47) 127, 142
Joan (legendary pope) 14, 48, 82, 194
Joan of Valois 219
John (apostle), St 125
John Chrysostom, St 215, 243
John Damascene, St (John of Damascus) 214
John, Patriarch of Jerusalem 214
Jónson, Arngrímur 202
Joscelyn, John 17, 176–8, 183
Joseph of Arimathea 16, 169–71, 178
Josephus 23, 42, 275, 278
Judea 138, 281
Judex, Matthaeus 48
Julian the Apostate, Roman emperor
    (r.355–63) 68, 194
Julius II, pope (1503–13) 13
justification, *see* salvation
Justus, Calvinus 145

Kager, Matthias 156
Kabbalah 24
Kannur, *see* Cannanore
Keating, Geoffrey 191–4, 196, 200–04
Kerala (Malabar) 233
Kessler, Johannes 32–3, 38–9, 40, 46 n.102, 51
Kidd, Colin 145
Kieran, St 201
Kilkenny 189
Kipping, Heinrich 49
Kollam, *see* Quilon
Kun, Peter van der, *see* Cunaeus, Petrus

La Flèche, Jesuit College 216
La Salle, Jean-Baptiste de 220
Lacksteyn, Pieter 278
Lambertini, Prospero, *see also* Benedict XIV,
    pope 91
Last Judgement, *see* Apocalypse
Lateran basilica 6, 12
Lateran Council, Fourth (1215), *see* Council,
    Forth Lateran
Latimer, Hugh 184
Latin/Latinity 3–4, 6, 9, 10, 11, 14–15, 30,
    33–4, 37, 42, 50, 81, 93, 101, 108, 113–15,
    117, 129–30, 134, 143, 146, 151, 153–4,
    156, 175, 194, 196, 211–12, 214, 221, 241,
    274, 281
Laudabiliter, papal bull (1155) 189, 191, 198,
    202–03
Launoy, Jean de 213, 225–9
Laureacum 157
Laurentius of Lorch 156
laus Hispaniae (literary eulogy of Spain)
    130–1

Lawrence, St 112, 127
Le Bossu, Jacques 212
Le Maistre, Antoine 215
Le Picart, François 212
Lefèvre d'Etaples, Jacques 214, 221–2,
    226–7
Legenda aurea (Golden Legend), see Voragine
Leibniz, Gottfried Wilhelm 154
Lendas da Índia 231
Leo XIII, pope (1878–1903) 89
Levant 235, 268–74, 276, 279–80, 283
Levy, F.J. 167, 183
Liber pontificalis 67, 82, 262
Liber sancti Iacobi, see pseudo-Calixtus
libraries 3–4, 6, 17, 19, 54, 57, 73, 77,
    79–83, 85, 88–9, 94 n.58, 95 n.63,
    138, 221, 254
Lifshitz, Felice 92
Limerick 190, 197
Linz 157
Lippomano, Luigi 70, 122, 209, 211
Lipsius, Justus 272
Lisbon 198, 231, 235, 238, 240–1, 245
liturgical books 54, 57, 70, 135
liturgical calendar 93, 209
liturgical sources 125, 137–8, 149
liturgies 3, 7, 16, 25, 36, 55–7, 61–3, 70, 86, 96,
    118, 125–6, 129, 133–6, 139–40, 151, 158,
    212, 214, 221–2, 250
    academic chair of, 74
    Greek rite 83
    of the English church 166
    of the Swiss Reformation 32
    reform of 54–5
Livre des Merveilles du Monde 235
Livy (Titus Livius) 132
Loisel, Antoine 225
Lombard, Peter (d.1160) 196
Lombard, Peter (c.1555–1625) 187–8,
    190 n.13
Lough Derg, *see* St Patrick's Purgatory
Louis, St (Louis IX of France (r.1226–70))
    220, 224
Louis the Pious, Frankish king (r.814–40) 46
Louis IV, the Bavarian, Holy Roman Emperor
    (r.1328–47) 155–6
Louis IX, king of France, *see* Louis, St
Louis XI, king of France (r.1461–83) 223–4
Louis XIII, king of France (r.1610–43) 224
Louis XIV, king of France (r.1643–1715) 210
Louvain 172, 175, 195
    University of 187, 190, 195
Lucas, bishop of Tuy (d.1249) 127
Lucena, João de, S.J. 244–6
Lucius of Britain, St 152, 165, 166 n.1,
    169–70, 172–73, 184

Luke, St 6, 58, 222, 235, 252, 260
Luther, Martin 28–9, 39–41, 45–8, 50, 111, 158, 170
Lutherans 4–8, 14, 22–3, 27–30, 39–42, 45, 48–51, 81, 85–6, 103 n.7, 111 n.32, 116 n.60, 145, 176
Lynch, John 194–7, 199
Lyon 87 n.32, 211, 270
Lyon, breviary of 125 n.10, 139 n.60
Lyra, Nicholas of, O.F.M. 280–1

Mabillon, Jean 8
McCaughwell, Hugh, O.F.M. 188
Macedonians 42
Madras 232
Magdeburg 16, 49, 176, 194, 274 n.28
Magdeburg Centuries 6–7, 14, 16, 23–4, 26, 48–9, 50, 53, 57–9, 73, 75, 148, 167, 175–6, 179
Magi 147, 149, 151
Mailapur, *see* Mylapore
Maillard, Olivier 211
Mainz 105, 146, 209, 274 n.28
Maiolus, Simon 253
Malabar Coast 233, 236ff
Malachy, St 196, 199
Mancini, Giulio 256
Mandeville, John (Jean de Mandeville) 235, 237 n.17
Manuel I, king of Portugal (r.1495–1521) 231, 240
Mans, Julian du, St 225
Mans, Martial du 212
Mansfeld-Eisleben, Agnes von 147
Mansuetus, St 196
Maozim 45
Mar Thoma, *see* Thomas of Cana
Marcäus, Elias 146
Marcellus II, pope (1555), *see* Cervini, Marcello
Marcus Aurelius, Roman emperor (r.161–77) 70, 76, 273
Margaret, St 215
Margarit i Pau, Joan 128–9, 134
Marguerite of Lorraine (1463–1521) 219
Maria, Gabriel 219
Marian martyrs 181, 184
Mariana, Juan de, S.J. 142–3
Marieta, Juan de 122
Marineus Siculus, Lucius 123, 129–34, 136, 142, 144
   Crónica de Aragon 130
   De rebus Hispaniæ memorabilibus 127, 130–2, 143 n.68
Marnix, Philippe de 51
Marrier, Martin 213 n.12, 220

Martial (poet, d.104) 153–4
Martial, St 217
Martial du Mans 212
martyrs 9–10, 15, 18, 37–8, 49, 55–7, 62–4, 69, 79, 82, 84, 86, 121, 123, 127, 131, 133–4, 156, 161–2, 179, 181, 183–4, 187, 191, 212, 215, 217–19, 257, 261–2
Martyrologium benedictinum 83
Martyrologium gallicanum 196, 212–3
Martyrologium romanum 55–8, 62, 64–5, 69–70, 80, 82, 86, 94 n.58, 96, 209–10, 212 n.11
martyrologies 7, 55, 79, 93, 95, 125–6, 137, 139, 176, 210, 212–13, 227
Mary I, queen of England (r.1553–58) 16, 21, 166, 169, 171–2, 176, 179–80, 198
Mary Magdalene, St 37, 215, 222, 225–6, 228
Mary, sister of Martha 222, 226
Mary, St (the Virgin) 69, 93, 131–3, 139, 160, 222, 224, 241, 260, 263
Mass, *see* Eucharist
Masson, Jean Papire, S.J. 224
Maternus, St 147, 150–1
"Matthew of Westminster" (pseud.), *Flores historiarum* 178
Matthew, Tobie 184
Maunoir, Julien, S.J. 220
Maurists (Benedictines of St Maur) 20, 74, 210
Maurolico, Francesco 80
Maxentius, Roman emperor (r.306–12) 67, 158
Maximilian I, duke/elector of Bavaria (r.1597–1651) 155–7
Maximilian I, Holy Roman Emperor (r.1493–1519) 33
Mayans i Siscar, Gregorio de 144
Meath 189, 199
Medici, Catherine de, queen and regent of France (d.1589) 223
Ménard, Nicolas-Hugues 83
Melanchthon, Philipp 14, 41ff, 111, 145, 147
   Followers (Philippists) 48–51
Melito, St, bishop of Sardis (d. c.180) 281
mendicants 221
Menezes, Aleixo de 246–8
Merlin, Jacques 214
Merovingians 39
Messingham, Thomas 199–200
Metaphrastes, Simeon 216
Michael, St 69, 153, 157, 224
Michaelis, Johann David 25
Middendorp, Jacob 149
Mikropresbutikon 7
Milan 19, 86–7
   Edict of Milan 259

Milesius, king of Spain (legendary) 198
Milíč, Jan of Kroměříž 162–3
Miller, Peter 271, 273–4, 281
Minim Friars 224
Mirabilia urbis Romae 262, 273
miracles 5, 48, 50, 58, 76, 117 n.65, 125–6,
    131, 160, 163, 217, 219, 224, 226,
    239, 252
missionaries 52, 104, 112–13, 115, 117–18,
    122, 125, 134, 136, 139–40, 150–2, 161,
    165, 169–70, 173, 195, 202, 220, 233–4,
    242–5, 248
Molanus, Johannes 83, 94 n.58, 213, 23,
    259–60
Moldau 160, 162
Mombrizio, Bonino 209
Momigliano, Arnaldo 17, 273, 280
monasteries (as sources and subjects for
    historical research) 62–3, 82, 84, 112ff,
    130, 150, 176, 187, 218, 221, 234
monasteries, dissolution of (English) 186–7
monastic chronicles 82, 86, 114, 116, 130
monastic reform (as influence on historical
    writing) 219–21
monasticism (as subject of historical
    analysis) 34 ff, 39, 44, 46–7, 149,
    161, 221
Montaigne, Michel de 3–4
Montecassino, monastery of 84
Montfaucon, Bernard de 8
Montmorency, house of 218
Monumenta Germaniae Historica 92, 101
Monumenta S. patrum orthodoxographa 7
Morales, Ambrosio de, *Coronica General de
    España* 123, 136–44, 223
More, Thomas 198
Moryson, Fynes 191, 193
Mouchy, Antoine de 213
Muhammad 24, 43
Munich 153, 155
Münster 198
Münster, Sebastian 270, 276 n.35
Müntzer, Thomas 41
Muratori, Lodovico Antonio 92, 210
Muslims, *see* Islam
Muzio, Girolamo 75–6
Mylapore 232–4, 237–47, 249
    Little Mount 243

Naogeorg, Thomas 153
Natalibus, Petrus de 79, 211
Near East, *see* Levant
Nebrija, Antonio de 128–30, 134–5, 142
Nelles, Paul 20 n.66, 89
Nepomuk, St John 162
Neri, St Filippo, *see* Philip Neri, St

Nero, Roman emperor (r.54–68) 133
Nerva, Roman emperor (r.96–8) 150
Nestorians 243
Nestorius 247
'New English' in Ireland 186–7, 203–4
Nicholas V, pope (1447–55) 12
Nicholas, St, bishop of Myra (4th cent.) 37
Nuremberg 107

O'Brien, Donough 196, 203
O'Neill, Hugh 187–8
O'Sullivan Beare, Philip 187–8, 198–9, 203
O'Sullivan, Donal Cam 187
Ocampo, Florián de 137
Ogilvie, John, S.J. 162
Ojetti, Ugo 92
'Old English' settlers in Ireland, *see*
    Anglo-Norman settlers
Oporinus, Johannes 16
Order of the Annunciation 219
Order of St Michael 224
Orientalism 270
Origen 169, 214, 234, 281 n.56
Orsini, Fulvio 254
Ortona 245–6
Osiander, Lucas, the Elder 23, 49–51
Otakar II, king of Bohemia (r.1253–78)
Otto, bishop of Freising (d.1158) 117
Ottomans, *see* Turks
Ouen, St 218
Oxford University 174, 190
    Bodleian Library 17, 19

Paderborn 146
Padilla, Francisco, *Historia ecclesiastica de
    España* 121–3, 127, 142
Padrón (Spain), Church of Saint James 140
paganism 24, 36–7, 64, 68–9, 104, 113, 129,
    132, 146, 154–5, 161, 172, 198, 202, 220,
    250, 253, 257–8, 261–4, 281
Paleotti, Gabriele 251
Palestine, 20, 59, 125, 267–83
Palladius, St, Irish bishop (5th cent.) 195
panegyric 102, 108, 115, 212
Pantaleon, Heinrich 176
Panvinio, Onofrio 6, 58, 64, 70, 77, 82, 89,
    123, 262
Papacy 4, 10–12, 30, 38–9, 44–5, 47–8, 58, 61,
    70–1, 74, 95, 116 n.60, 162, 168, 172, 183,
    189, 195, 198, 202, 259, 264
Papebroch, Daniel 94–5
Pappus, Johann 49
Paris 126–7, 131, 136, 196, 199, 211–12,
    214–6, 218, 222–7, 267
    University of (Sorbonne) 22, 110, 115, 190,
    211, 220–2, 225

Parker, Matthew, archbishop of Canterbury
  (1559–75) 16–7, 19–21, 166, 169–70,
  172–4, 176–8, 181, 183–5
Parlement of Aix-en-Provence 226
Parlement of Paris 215
Parliament
  English 165, 170, 172, 182
  Dublin 187–8, 192
Parousia (second coming) 107, 114
Parsons, Robert, S.J. 80, 194
Parthia 234, 263
Pascha, Jan 276
Pasionario hispánico 138
Pasqualini, Lelio 254
Pasquier, Etienne 225
Patrick, St 175, 189, 192–3, 195, 197–201
patria 103, 119, 132
Patristic writings 7, 15, 19, 34–7, 43, 57,
    81–2, 127, 134, 138–9, 154, 170, 197,
    214–5, 233–4, 250, 254, 258,
    263–5, 280
Paul (apostle), St 14, 33, 62, 70, 124–8,
    132–4, 139, 146, 171, 212 n.10, 214,
    217, 225
Paul II, pope (1464–71) 13
Paul V, pope (1605–21) 88
Paul of Narbonne, St, *see also* Sergius
    Paulus 133, 227
Paul the Deacon 113, 197
Paul the Hermit, St 34
Paula, St 15
Paulinus of Nola 259
Paulus Fagius 22
Pausanias (geographer) 280
Paxent, St 218
peacocks 232, 237–8, 258–9
Pelagianism 39, 198
Pellicer, Joseph 197
Penteado, Álvaro 238
Pépin, Guillaume 211
Pérez, Juan Bautista 144
periodization, *see* chronology
Perpetua, St 84
Persia 5, 42, 47
Persons, Robert, *see* Parsons, Robert,
Pétau, Denis, S.J. 74, 216
Peter of Braga, St, bishop of Braga
    (legendary) 124 n.5, 134, 139
Peter (apostle), St 7, 13, 33–4, 58–60,
    62, 69–70, 89, 91, 102, 125–6, 132–3,
    151, 172, 196, 201, 225, 252,
    261, 266
Peucer, Caspar 42, 44–6, 51
Pezel, Christoph 44
Pfeiffer, Heinrich 41
Pharisees 23, 29

Philip II, king of Spain (r.1556–98) 68, 79,
    135–6, 174, 175 n.31, 223, 278
Philip III, king of Spain (r.1598–1621) 188
Philip IV, king of Spain (r.1621–65) 197–8
Philip Neri, St 52–4, 57, 62, 80
Philippa of Guelders, duchess of Lorraine
    (d. 1547) 219
Philippists, *see* Melanchthon
Philo of Alexandria 22
philology 11, 221, 267, 270
Piccolomini, Aeneo Silvio (Pope Pius II
    1458–64) 104–6, 110, 114, 119
  Europa 105, 114
  Historia austrialis 105
  Historia bohemica 105, 114
pilgrimage 11, 114, 124–5, 140–1, 147, 158,
    192, 196, 218, 222, 224, 228, 231–8, 252,
    267–83
Pincherle, Alberto 52 n.1, 54 n.6
Piquelin, Jehan 218
Pirimal, king of Ceylon (legendary) 241
Pius II, pope (1458–64) 13, 31
Pius IV, pope (1559–65) 77, 88
Pius V, pope (1566–72) 55, 88, 96–7
Plantin, Christopher 3, 21, 78, 175 n.31
Platina (Bartolomeo Sacchi) 6, 13, 36, 58,
    77, 82, 91
Plato 109, 257
Pliny the Elder 69, 132
Plutarch 280
Poggio Bracciolini, Gian Francesco, *see*
    Bracciolini
Pohlig, Matthias 7–8, 86
Pole, Reginald 172
Politiques (French party) 225
Polman, Pontien 72, 103 n.7
Polo, Marco 234–5
Poloner, John 280
Polycarp, St, bishop of Smyrna (d.155) 183–4
Polyglot Bible (Antwerp) 3, 22, 271–2
Pomponio Leto, Giulio 77, 270
Ponce de León, Pedro 138
Port-Royal Abbey 215, 228
Portugal 134, 231–49
Possevino, Antonio 255
Prague 10, 46, 160, 162
Praxedes, St (Santa Prassede) 76
Přemyslid dynasty 160
Prideaux, Matthias vii
Primitivus, St 139
printers, printing, *see* book production
prophecy 42, 45, 240, 248
Protestant historiography 6–7, viii–xiii, 15–7,
    23–5, 27–51, 73–5, 145, 163, 165–71,
    176–85, 189, 193–6, 202, 215, 219, 222,
    250, 253

Prudentius, Aurelius 262
Pseudo-Calixtus, *Codex Calixtinus* 125–6,
 129–132, 134, 137–8
Pseudo-Dionysius, *see also* Dionysius the
 Aeropagite and Denis, St 212 n.10, 215
Ptolemies 42
Ptolemy (90–168) 69, 77, 109, 270, 276
Purgatory 34, 39, 192
Puritans 166, 177–81
Puyherbault, Gabriel de, *see* Dupuyherbault

Quaresmio, Franceso, O.F.M. 277
Quietism 219
Quilon 237, 241–2, 246–7
Quintilian 12
Quirinus of Sescia, St 157

Rabus, Ludwig 176, 257 n.28
Rader, Matthäus, S.J. 152–7, 161, 213
 Bavaria sancta 156ff
Raimond, Florimond 194
Raimundus (Raymond), archbishop of Toledo
 (1125–52) 126, 131
Rainaldi, Oderico 83
Raisse, Arnold de 213
Rama Raja 243
Raulin, Jean 211
Raynaud, Théophyle, S.J. 210
Razzi, Silvano 213
Reccared, king of Spain (r.586–601) 127
Regensburg 105, 114 n.49, 157
Regina, St, *see* Reine, St
Rego, Ambrósio do 238–9
Reims 220
 Synod of (1148) 126
Reine, St 216
relics 57, 61, 88, 96, 124, 130, 135–6,
 138–40, 143, 149–51, 160, 212–13,
 217–19, 221–3, 226, 228, 231–3, 235,
 237–8, 242–9, 253, 272
 collections of 132, 136 n.49, 146–7,
 151, 223
 fake 11, 222
 liturgical use of 63
 translation of 125, 135–6, 223
Rémy, St 218, 220
Renan, Ernest 267–9, 282
 Vie de Jésus 268
Republic of Letters 95, 115, 205, 270–1
Resende, Andrés de 134
Reuchlin, Johannes 22
Reuwich, Erhard 274
Revelation (New Testament book) 168
Reynolds, William 173, 175
Rhenanus, Beatus 104, 108–10, 115, 117
 Rerum germanicarum libri tres 110–11

rhetoric 9, 12, 28–31, 34, 38, 45, 65, 134, 137,
 154–5, 162, 191
Rhine river 146–7, 152, 157
Ribadeneyra, Pedro de, S.J. 122, 211
Rider, John 193
Ridley, Nicholas 184
Río, Martin del 83
Robert, Claude 214
Rochford, Robert, O.F.M. 200
Roigny, Michel de 211
Roland, Nicolas 220
Romain, St 218
Román de la Higuera, Jerónimo, S.J. 143
Roman emperors, *see also* individual
 emperors 17, 64–5, 132, 154–5, 180
Roman Empire 10, 28, 59, 63, 69, 110,
 111, 132
Roman history 6, 42, 63, 67, 106, 133,
 137, 273
Roman Martyrology, see *Martyrologium
 romanum*
Roman Republic 117
Romano, Giulio 13, 70 n.59
Rome 3–6, 12, 15–6, 19, 21, 23, 33, 42–3,
 52–3, 57–62, 69–70, 73–4, 76, 79, 81–4,
 88, 90, 94, 96, 106–7, 115, 119, 121–3,
 125–7, 132–4, 142, 145, 150, 153, 157–8,
 161, 170, 172–3, 175, 181, 187, 192, 196,
 197, 198, 202, 209, 211, 212, 216, 233,
 246, 250, 252, 254, 256, 259, 261–2, 264,
 266, 270, 272–3, 275, 277
Rome, monuments and churches
 catacombs 62, 82, 233, 250–66
 cemeteries 69, 251, 261–4
 Diocletian's baths (Santa Maria degli
  Angeli) 70
 Domus Aurea 251
 Hadrian's mausoleum (Castel
  S. Angelo) 69
 Marcus Aurelius's column 70
 Mamertine prisons 69
 Pantheon 12, 69
 San Cesareo de Appia 63
 San Gregorio al Celio 63
 Sancta Maria ad Martyres 69
 Santa Maria sopra Minerva 133 n.35
 Santa Pudenziana 63
 Santi Nereo ed Achilleo 63, 266 n.71
 St Peter's basilica (Vatican basilica) 6–7,
  12–13, 82, 89, 252, 266
 Trajan's column 70
 Vatican Obelisk 12
 See also Altemps Library, Basilian
  Academy, Collegio Romano, Greek
  College, Vallicelliana Library
Rospigliosi, Giulio *see* Clement IX

Rostock 14, 42
Rosweyde, Héribert, S.J. 20, 79, 82, 93–4, 209–10
Rothe, David 188, 197–8
Rowlands, Richard, *see* Verstegan, Richard
Rufinus of Aquileia 9, 243
Rufus of Tortosa, St 124 n.5, 133, 139
Rupert, St 112–15, 117–18
Ryves, Thomas 196

Sacchi, Bartolomeo, *see* Platina
sacraments 30, 41, 44, 50, 61, 110, 118, 179, 188, 241
'sacred history', *see historica sacra*
Sadeler, Raphael the Elder 156
St-Gallen 32–3, 38
St Omer, Jesuit College 215
St Patrick's Purgatory 192
St Peter's basilica (Vatican basilica), *see* Rome, monuments and churches
Sainte-Marthe brothers 83, 214
saints, cult of 36–7, 39, 50, 61–2, 76, 112, 124, 131, 135–6, 138, 147–8, 163, 210, 221–2, 224–5, 227–8, 243, 251, 253, 255, 258, 262
saints' lives, *see* hagiography
Salamanca 128–19, 134, 137, 188, 190, 243
    University of 129, 137, 138
salvation 13, 29–31, 38, 47, 102, 114, 195, 257, 263, 279
Sampayo, Pero Lopes de 231
San Juan de la Peña (Aragon), monastery of 128, 130
Sancho I, king of Aragon (r.1063–94) 130
Sanders, Nicholas 172, 175
Sandys, Edwin 171, 180, 184
Santiago, *see* James the Greater (apostle), Saint
Santiago de Compostela 124–5, 128, 131, 133, 140
São Tomé de Meliapor 231–2, 239, 243
sarcophagi 259, 263–4
Sarpi, Paolo 97
Sauer, Lorenz, *see* Surius, Laurentius
Saussay, André du 196, 212–3
Savonarola, Girolamo, O.P. 221
Scaliger, Joseph 22, 82, 94, 153, 197, 272
Schedel, Hartmann 107, 114, 119
Scheiner, Christoph, S.J. 153
scholasticism 3, 28–9, 32, 209, 228, 134, 210, 212, 215–16, 221, 226
Schulting Steinwich, Cornelius 148–9
Scots 74, 114 n.49, 162, 174, 191–2, 197, 200
Scribner, Robert 147
Scripture, *see* Bible
Sebald, St 107–8
Second coming, *see* Parousia

Secundus of Avila, St 136, 143
Seidel, Wolfgang 153
Selden, John 272
Seleucid empire 42
Seneca 153
Serarius, Nikolaus 146
Sergius Paulus, St, *see also* Paul of Narbonne, St 133, 139
Seripando, Girolamo 81
sermons 13, 53, 62, 96, 170–2, 177–8, 180, 183–4, 211–12, 243
Servetus, Michael (Miguel Servet) 270, 276
Seven Apostles (*siete varones apostólicos*) of Spain 125–7, 129–31, 134, 136, 138–40, 143
Severano, Giovanni 251, 253, 259, 262–4
Severinus of Noricum 157
Sforza, Galeazzo Maria 223
Sheehan, Jonathan 270, 282
Shuger, Debora 272
Sibyl Indica 241
Siculus, *see* Marineus Siculus, Lucius
Sigonio, Carlo 272
Simon, Richard 272
Sirleto, Guglielmo 54–5, 77, 80–1
Sirmond, Jacques, S.J. 212, 225–8
Sixtus I, pope (*c*.117–26) 76
Sixtus V (Felice Peretti), pope (1585–90) 57 n.11, 70
Sixtus of Siena 82, 214
Sixtus of Tannberg, bishop of Freising (d.1495) 114
Sleidan, Johann 40–1, 145, 148, 176
Smalley, Beryl 280
Society of Jesus, *see* Jesuits
Socrates (philosopher, d.399 BC) 264
Socrates 'Scholasticus' (*c*.380–450) 9, 77
Sollier, Jean-Baptiste du 95
Sophronius (d.638) 132
Sorbonne, *see* Paris, University of
Southern, Richard 86
Sozomenus (d. *c*.450) 9, 77
Spagnoli of Mantua, Baptista 209
Spain 79, 121–44, 154, 174–5, 188, 197–8, 216, 219–21, 223–4, 271
Spanheim, Friedrich 29
Spanish Netherlands 93, 148
Speculum Historiale, see Beauvais, Vincent
Speed, John 203
Spenser, Edmund 191
Stabius, Johannes 115
Standonck, Jean 221
Stanihurst, Richard 175, 190–1, 193–4
Stapleton, Thomas 75, 172–4, 183, 185
statues 3, 37, 50, 70, 140, 154, 223, 235, 273
    cultic use 50, 235

statues (*cont.*)
  miraculous 223
Stegmann, André 216
Stephen, St 132
Steuco, Agostino 19
Strabo 77, 106 n.16
Strasbourg 41, 49, 179, 212
Street, John Spencer 215–6
Stumpf, Johann 33
Suetonius, *Lives of the Caesars* 65
Suire, Eric 219
Sulpicius Severus 77
Surius, Laurentius 80, 94, 122, 148, 163, 209,
  214, 216, 251
  Commentarius brevis 148
  De probatis Sanctorum historiis 94,
    148, 209
Swiss Confederation 33
Swiss Reformation 27–29, 32, 35, 38, 40
Sylvester II, pope (999–1003) 11, 13, 48, 151
Syriac 4, 237
Syrian Rite, *see also* Thomas Christians 82,
  236, 247

Tacitus, *Germania* 106, 113
Tallon, Alain 61, 222, 225
Tauler, Johannes 46
Tertullian 28 n.3, 84, 132, 169,
  194, 198
theatre, sacred 153–4, 215–16
Theodo V, duke of Bavaria (r.680(?)-716) 113
Theodoret, bishop of Cyrrhus (d. c.460) 77
Theodorus, bishop of Zaragoza
  (legendary) 133
Teresa of Avila, St 224
Thiers, Jean-Baptiste, S.J. 210
Thirty Years' War 148, 155–6, 161
Thomas (apostle), St, legend of mission to
  India 125, 231–49
Thomas Aquinas, O.P., St 3
Thomas Christians (*see also* Syrian Rite and
  Armenian Christians) 231–49
Thomas of Cana 247
Thou, Jacques-Auguste de 4
Thucydides 42–3
Tiberius, Roman emperor (r.14–37) 114
Tigeon, Jacques 211
Timothy (New Testament) 146
Tillemont, Louis-Sébastien Le Nain de 228
Tipperary 190–1
Toledo 126–8, 131, 133, 135–6, 138–9, 142–3,
  223, 227
Torelli, Luigi 84–5
Torquemada, Antonio de 243–3
Torsellino, Orazio, S.J. 80
torture 9, 79

Trajan, Roman emperor (r.98–117) 64–5, 67,
  70, 150
translatio imperii 203
Traversari, Ambrogio 214
Trent, Council of, *see* Councils
Trithemius, Johannes 214
Trojans 42 n.84, 146, 182
Tropez, St 218
Trophimus of Arles, St 227
Truxillo, Thomas de 122
Turkey 235
Turks 5, 15, 45, 105, 118–9, 187, 275
Turmair, Johann Georg, *see* Aventinus,
  Johannes
Tyard, Pontus de 224
Tyndale, William 168
Tyrol 153, 157

Ubii 146, 150, 152
Ughelli, Ferdinando 74, 83–5, 88, 144, 213
Ugonio, Pompeo 251
Urban I, pope (222–30) 76
Urban II, pope (1188–99) 203
Urban VIII, pope (1623–44) 90, 156,
  264 n.68
Urbino, duchy of 90
Ursin (Ursinus), Johann Heinrich 282
Ursula, St 147, 149, 151
Ussher, James, bishop of Meath (d.1656) 189,
  193, 203
Usuard (d. c.875) 55, 80, 125 n.10

Vadian, Joachim 32–6, 38–40, 46
Valencia 132
Valier, Agostino 83
Valera, Diego de 128
Valla, Lorenzo 5, 10–12, 19, 50, 167, 183,
  214, 225
Valladolid 188
Vallicelliana library (Rome) 73ff
Valois-Angoulême dynasty 223
Vasaeus, Johannes, *Chronici rerum
  memorabilium Hispaniae* 123, 134,
  136, 143
Vasari, Giorgio 252, 254–5
Vaseo, Juan, *see* Vasaeus, Johannes
Vatican archive 85, 88–90
Vatican library 3–4, 6, 19, 54, 57, 81, 85, 88–9
Vázquez Matamoros, Iago 271
Vegio, Maffeo 13
Venice 58, 90, 97, 153, 209
Veran, St, bishop of Cavaillon (d. c.590) 220
Verdier, Antoine du 225
Vergil, Polydore 4, 183, 193, 196–7
Veronica (sudarium of St Veronica) 252
Verstegan, Richard 173–6, 185

Vesta, (goddess) 37
Vienna 104, 115, 157
  University of 33, 105 n.9
Vienne 226
Vigor, Simon 212
Vijayanagara Empire 243
Vikings 197, 199, 202
Villegas, Alonso de 122
Vincent of Beauvais, *see* Beauvais
Vitruvius 257
Vltava, *see* Moldau
Voltaire v–vi
Voragine, Jacobus de, O.P., *Golden Legend*
  82, 93, 96, 126, 137, 211, 235

Wadding, Luke, O.F.M. 94
Waldburg, Gebhard Truchsess von,
  archbishop of Cologne (1577–83) 147
Walsingham, Thomas 178
Watt, Joachim von, *see* Vadian, Joachim
Welser, Marcus 152–3, 155
Wenceslas IV, king of Bohemia
  (r.1378–1419) 162
Wenceslas I, duke of Bohemia
  (r. *c*.907–29) 160–1
Wessel of Groningen (Wessel Gansfort) 46
Westminster, conference of (1559) 180
Wheare, Degory 14
White, Peter 189

White, Richard 175
White, Stephen, S.J. 190–1, 195, 201–2
Whitgift, John, archbishop of Canterbury
  (1583–1604) 171
Wied, Hermann von, archbishop-elector
  of Cologne (1515–47) 147, 150
Wigand, Johannes 48
Wilhelm V, duke of Bavaria (r.1579–97)
  153, 155
William of Malmesbury 18, 151, 169
William of St Thierry 162
Wimpfeling, Jacob, *Germania* 110
Winghe, Philip van 251, 254
Wittelsbach family 112, 115, 118, 147, 150,
  153–5, 157
Wittenberg 40–1, 44, 223
Witzel, Georg 209

Xavier, Francis, *see* Francis Xavier, St

Zaragoza, Church of La Virgen del Pilar
  131, 133, 139
Zelotes, Simon 169
Zunggo, Johann Anton 163
Zürich 32–3, 36, 41, 49
Zurita, Jerónimo de, *Anales de la corona de
  Aragón* 135–7
Zwingli, Huldrych 28–9, 33
Zwinglians 27, 40